Remembering Clarence Byrd and Ida Chen

Pearson Canada grieves the loss of both Clarence Byrd and Ida Chen, the beloved authors of **Canadian Tax Principles**. For more than 35 years, Clarence and Ida have been extensively involved in Canadian accounting education. Their book, **Canadian Tax Principles**, has been used by thousands of instructors and students and continues to be read and relied upon by learners across the country.

Our thoughts are with their family, friends, and the education community who worked with them and knew them personally.

Husband and wife, Clarence Byrd and Ida Chen, authors of Canadian Tax Principles, *passed away on May 30, 2020, and November 6, 2019, respectively. Their impact on accounting education will not be forgotten.*

In Memoriam of Ida Chen

On November 6, 2019, Ida Chen, my wife of 43 years, died from cancer.

In our years together, Ida and I authored some 150 books on financial accounting and tax.

These books were used by tens of thousands of students, as well as by many accounting professionals.

Canadian Tax Principles has been, by far, our most successful effort. Through more than 25 annual editions, we piloted this publication from a niche product that we self-published to its position today as the most widely adopted text in Canadian university and college tax courses. We had an ongoing discussion about responsibility for this success. Ida believed that it was based on the quality of my writing, while I was equally convinced that its success resulted from her editing work on my often rough first drafts. The truth is that this publication would have had no success without the synergy resulting from our unusually complementary contributions.

While Ida's efforts were essential to the success of our publications, her contributions to our life together were even more important to me. We were best friends from the beginning of our marriage and, during the last 15 years, after my teaching was restricted to online efforts, we spent pretty much 24/7 together. We skied, hiked, climbed, and biked all over North America. We shared great food and, over the years, had several beautiful homes. Both the success of our books and the joy we found in our life together were beyond our wildest dreams.

We have lived the greatest love story that I have ever witnessed. I miss her terribly.

Clarence Byrd
May 6, 2020

In Memoriam of Clarence Byrd

I was first introduced to Clarence indirectly while working towards a Bachelor of Commerce degree in Montreal in the early eighties. I was taking an intermediate level accounting course with emphasis upon the *CICA Handbook,* consolidation accounting, and other topics that created a sense of dread in most accounting students. Unfortunately, the required textbook was not helpful in clarifying these difficult abstract concepts. The professor, recognizing the difficulty, recommended a two volume textbook written by Clarence Byrd and Ida Chen on accounting principles and concepts. I immediately purchased the books and was sold. The concepts were clearly explained in easy-to-read language, dissecting the words of the *CICA Handbook* to carefully explain step by step (with plenty of examples) these abstract concepts. Clarence and Ida had taken a complex topic and broken it down in such a way to make it easy to understand—the mark of true educators.

Flash forward 15 plus years to the late nineties and our paths would cross once again in a much more direct way. At the time I worked for the training organization of the CRA, teaching and writing courses, and became an income tax rulings officer in Ottawa shortly thereafter. I regularly read tax textbooks and other tax literature and came across a relatively new publication, *Canadian Tax Principles,* written by Clarence Byrd and Ida Chen. I read through the textbook and reached out, making recommendations as to improvements. It was a bit of a bold move, but it was well received by Clarence who reciprocated by personally reaching out to me. Clarence realized that my background with the CRA could only improve the textbook and our collaboration, which would last for more than 20 years, had begun. Ida once described our complementary skills as producing one of the finest writing teams she had ever seen. What made it all work was that Clarence, Ida, and myself were dedicated to effective quality tax education.

Over the years my wife, Michelle, and I learned firsthand that Clarence and Ida loved to entertain, and we were invited to their amazing homes in both Ottawa and Chelsea with the occasional outing to restaurants in Ottawa and Gatineau. We had become friends. Clarence would cook, Ida would make certain that everything was perfect, and the evening would finish with a song or two as Clarence, a gifted concert pianist, would tickle the keys on his Viennese-made Bosendorfer Concert Grand 290 piano with Ida accompanying him on occasion on an electric keyboard. They were good, memorable times.

My role with Clarence and Ida was as a consultant, advisor, technical reviewer, and sometimes co-author, writing a handful of chapters and some problem material. It was not unusual for me to speak to Clarence two or three times a day, particularly during annual federal budgets or unexpected changes to the income tax laws such as the Accelerated Investment Incentive property rules, trust reporting, income splitting, etc. Our collaboration led to constant discussions on what to add, what not to add, and how to go about introducing new topics in the most effective manner.

In September 2019 my wife and I visited Maui for a couple of weeks. Before leaving, Ida sent me this email…

> We hope you and Michelle find Hawaii great, but not so great you want to move there. We really need you on the CTP project. Safe travels, Ida.

Ida was the glue that kept it all together. She was a dynamo, a gifted organizer and administrator who could have easily fit into the fabric of the largest companies in the world. We knew that Ida had been struggling with cancer for a few years and beaten the odds more than a few times, but her passing in November of 2019 was an incredibly difficult time for my wife and I and everyone who knew her (https://ohfoundation.ca/be-inspired/symptoms-strike-and-reveal-shocking-brain-cancer-diagnosis/).

Through it all, Clarence, always a rock, began to show the signs of stress and his own medical situation worsened. Our collaboration accelerated as he was dedicated to completing what would be his final edition of *Canadian Tax Principles*. This publication held a special place in his heart. Clarence and Ida had created the textbook together from scratch and they took exceptional pride in each and every annual release.

In the final weeks before Clarence passed on Saturday, May 30, 2020, he worked furiously with a dedication to complete all the necessary steps possible to ready the textbook for publication. Our telephone conversations increased substantially during this time as our collaborative efforts took on a new urgency, purpose, and meaning. Clarence took comfort in knowing that I would pick up the reins to ensure the continuity of the successful text that both he and Ida had created together.

I look back on my relationship with these two remarkable individuals with happiness that our paths crossed for a common purpose and dedication to ideals of education. Along the way on this journey my wife and I had the opportunity to enjoy their company and friendship. We think of them every day and will miss them tremendously.

Gary Donell
June 9, 2020

CLARENCE BYRD
Clarence Byrd Inc.

IDA CHEN
Clarence Byrd Inc.

With contributions by
GARY DONELL

Byrd & Chen's
Canadian
Tax
Principles

2020–2021 EDITION

Volume II

Pearson

Please contact https://support.pearson.com/getsupport/s/contactsupport with any queries on this content.

Pearson Canada Inc., 26 Prince Andrew Place, North York, Ontario M3C 2H4.

ISBN 978-0-13-674526-6

1 2020

CONTENTS

The textbook is published in two Volumes:	**Volume I** = Chapters 1 to 10 **Volume II** = Chapters 11 to 21

CHAPTER 11

Taxable Income And Tax Payable For Individuals Revisited

CHAPTER 12

Taxable Income And Tax Payable For Corporations

Chapter 12 - Continued

CHAPTER 13

Taxation Of Corporate Investment Income

CHAPTER 14

Other Issues In Corporate Taxation

CHAPTER 15

Corporate Taxation And Management Decisions

CHAPTER 20

International Issues In Taxation

CHAPTER 21

GST/HST

Chapter 21 - Continued

Study Guide

Your two volume textbook is accompanied by a separate Study Guide that is available in print and online.

The chapters of this Study Guide correspond to the chapters of *Byrd & Chen's Canadian Tax Principles*.

Each of these Study Guide chapters contains the following:

- Detailed guidance on how to work through the text and problems in the chapter.
- Detailed solutions to the Exercises and Self Study Problems in the textbook for the chapter.
- A list of learning objectives for the material in the chapter.

In addition, the Study Guide contains:

- Two sample personal tax returns and two Self Study Tax Software Problems in Chapters 4 and 11.
- A sample corporate tax return in Chapter 13.
- An extensive Glossary.

PREFACE

Complete Preface In Volume I

The complete preface to this three volume set of *Byrd & Chen's Canadian Tax Principles* can be found in Volume I.

Online Student Supplements

MyLab Accounting

MyLab Accounting for *Canadian Tax Principles* contains a great deal of additional material that will provide significant assistance to users of this text. Instructions on how to access MyLab can be found on the access card provided with this package. The URL for MyLab is:

http://www.pearsonmylabandmastering.com

The various items available on MyLab include:

- Pearson eText
- NEW Data Analytics Project
- Self Study Problems
- Supplementary Self Study Problems and Solutions
- Practice Examinations and Solutions
- PowerPoint Presentations
- Tax returns for examples and Self Study tax return problems
- Corrections to the textbook and Study Guide. Please check periodically to help avoid frustration
- 2020 tax rates, credits, and common CCA classes
- Access to EY's Canada's Federal Income Tax Collection (FITAC)
- Access to Intuit Canada's ProFile tax return preparation software
- Glossary Flashcards

2020 Rates, Credits, And Other Data

For your convenience, this information, as well as the Chapter 5
Appendix of common CCA rates, is available **online** as a .PDF file.

Information Applicable To Individuals

Federal Tax Rates For Individuals

Taxable Income In Excess Of	Federal Tax	Marginal Rate On Excess
$ -0-	$ -0-	15.0%
48,535	7,280	20.5%
97,069	17,230	26.0%
150,473	31,115	29.0%
214,368	49,645	33.0%

Federal Tax Credits For Individuals – Personal Tax Credits (ITA 118)

Reference

118(1.1) **Basic Personal Amount (BPA)**   There are three alternatives dependent upon Net Income. (1) For individuals with Net Income of $150,473 or less the BPA is $13,229, (2) for individuals with Net Income of $214,368 or higher the BPA is $12,298, and (3) for individuals with Net Income between $150,474 and $214,367 the BPA is calculated as $13,229 – [$931][(Net Income – $150,473) ÷ $63,895]

118(1)(a) **Married Persons**   15% the of **BPA** for the individual

118(1)(a) **Spousal**   15% of the **BPA** for the individual and:

if the spouse of the married individual is dependent because of a mental or physical infirmity, there is an additional amount of $2,273 added to the **BPA**. The total of these two amounts ($15,502) is reduced by the income of the individual's spouse.

118(1)(b) **Eligible Dependant**   15% of **BPA** for the individual and:

if the dependent person is dependent because of a mental or physical infirmity, there is an additional amount of $2,273 added to the **BPA**. The total of these two amounts ($15,502) is reduced by the income of the dependent person.

118(1)(b.1) **Canada Caregiver For Child Under 18**   15% of $2,273 ($341).

118(1)(c) **Single Persons**   15% of the **BPA**.

118(1)(d) **Canada Caregiver**   15% of $7,276 ($1,091), reduced by 15% of the dependant's income in excess of $17,085.

118(2) **Age**   15% of $7,637 ($1,146). The base for this credit is reduced by the lesser of $7,637 and 15% of the individual's net income in excess of $38,508. Not available when income is more than $89,421. If the individual cannot use this credit, it can be transferred to a spouse or common-law partner.

118(3) **Pension**   15% of up to $2,000 of eligible pension income for a maximum credit of $300 [(15%) ($2,000)]. If the individual cannot use this credit, it can be transferred to a spouse or common-law partner.

118(10) **Canada Employment Credit**   15% of up to $1,245. This produces a maximum credit of $187.

Other Common Federal Personal Credits (Various ITA)

118.01   **Adoption Expenses Credit**   15% of eligible expenses (reduced by any reimbursements) up to a maximum of $16,563 per adoption. This results in a maximum credit of $2,484.

118.02   **Digital News Subscriptions**   15% of the lesser of $500 and the cost of qualifying subscription expenses.

118.041   **Home Accessibility Credit**   15% of lesser of $10,000 and the amount of qualifying expenditures for the year.

118.05   **First Time Home Buyer's Credit**   15% of $5,000 ($750) of the cost of an eligible home.

118.06   **Volunteer Firefighters Credit**   15% of $3,000 ($450) for qualifying volunteers.

118.07   **Volunteer Search And Rescue Workers Credit**   15% of $3,000 ($450) for qualifying volunteers.

118.1   **Charitable Donations - Regular**   The general limit on amounts for this credit is 75% of Net Income. There is an addition to this general limit equal to 25% of any taxable capital gains and 25% of any recapture of CCA resulting from a gift of capital property. In addition, the income inclusion on capital gains arising from a gift of some publicly traded shares is reduced from one-half to nil. For individuals, the credit is equal to:

$$[(15\%)(A)] + [(33\%)(B)] + [(29\%)(C)] \text{ where:}$$

A = The first $200 of eligible gifts.
B = The lesser of:
  - Total gifts, less $200; and
  - Taxable Income, less $214,368.
C = The excess, if any, by which the individual's total gifts exceed the sum of $200 plus the amount determined in B.

118.2   **Medical Expenses**   The medical expense tax credit is determined by the following formula:

$$[15\%] [(B - C) + D], \text{ where:}$$

B   is the total of an individual's medical expenses for him- or herself, his or her spouse or common-law partner, and any of his or her children who have not reached 18 years of age at the end of the year.

C   is the lesser of 3% of the individual's Net Income For Tax Purposes and $2,397 (2020 figure).

D   is the total of all amounts each of which is, in respect of a dependant of the individual (other than a child of the individual who has not attained the age of 18 years before the end of the taxation year), an amount determined by the formula:

$$E - F, \text{ where:}$$

E   is the total of the dependant's medical expenses

F   is the lesser of 3% of the dependant's Net Income For Tax Purposes and $2,397 (2020 figure).

118.3   **Disability - All Ages**   15% of $8,576 ($1,286). If not used by the disabled individual, it can be transferred to a person claiming that individual as a dependant.

118.3   **Disability Supplement - Under 18 And Qualifies For The Disability Tax Credit**   15% of $5,003 ($750), reduced by the total of amounts paid for attendant care or supervision in excess of $2,930 that are deducted as child care costs, deducted as a disability support amount, or claimed as a medical expense in calculating the medical expense tax credit.

Education Related Credits

118.5   • **Tuition Fees, Which Includes Examination And Ancillary Fees**
- 15% of qualifying tuition fees
- 15% of examination fees for both post-secondary examinations and examinations required in a professional program
- 15% of ancillary fees that are imposed by a post-secondary educational institution on all of their full or part time students. Up to $250 in such ancillary fees can be claimed even if not required of all students.

118.62   • **Interest On Student Loans**
15% of interest paid on qualifying student loans.

118.9   • **Transfer Of Tuition Credit**
If the individual cannot use the credit, is not claimed as a dependant by his or her spouse, and does not transfer the unused credit to a spouse or common-law partner, then a parent or grandparent of the individual can claim up to $750 [(15%)($5,000)] of any unused tuition credit. The amount that can be transferred is reduced by the amount of the credit claimed by the student for the year.

118.7   **Employment Insurance**   15% of amounts paid by employees up to the maximum Employment Insurance premium of $856 (1.58% of $54,200). This produces a maximum tax credit of $128 [(15%)($856)].

118.7   **Canada Pension Plan**   15% of 4.95 percent of contributions. The maximum credit base for all individuals is $2,732 [(4.95%)($58,700 - $3,500)]. This produces a maximum tax credit of $410 [(15%)($2,732)].

122.51   **Refundable Medical Expense Supplement**   The individual claiming this amount must be over 17 and have earned income of at least $3,714. The amount is equal to the lesser of $1,272 and 25/15 of the medical expense tax credit. The refundable amount is then reduced by 5% of family Net Income in excess of $28,164. Not available when family income is more than $53,604.

122.9   **Refundable Teacher And Early Childhood Educator School Supply Tax Credit**   A maximum of 15% of up to $1,000 ($150) of eligible expenditures that are made by eligible educators.

122.91   **Canada Training Credit**   The lesser of training amount limit and 50% of eligible training costs incurred in the previous year.

127(3)   **Political Donations**   Three-quarters of the first $400, one-half of the next $350, one-third of the next $525, to a maximum credit of $650 on donations of $1,275.

127.4   **Labour Sponsored Venture Capital Corporations (LSVCC) Credit**   The federal credit is equal to 15 percent of acquisitions of provincially registered LSVCCs.

ITA 82 and ITA 121   **Dividend Tax Credit**

- **Eligible Dividends**   These dividends are grossed up by 38%. The federal dividend tax credit is equal to 6/11 of the gross up. The credit can also be calculated as 15.02% of the grossed up dividends, or 20.7272% of the actual dividends received.

- **Non-Eligible Dividends**   These dividends are grossed up by 15%. The federal dividend tax credit is equal to 9/13 of the gross up. The credit can also be calculated as 9.0301% of the grossed up dividends, or 10.3846% of the actual dividends received.

Other Data For Individuals

ITA 82   **Dividend Gross Up**

> **Eligible Dividends**   For these dividends, the gross up is 38% of dividends received.

> **Non-Eligible Dividends**   For these dividends, the gross up is 15% of dividends received.

Chapter 4   **OAS Clawback Limits**   The tax (clawback) on Old Age Security (OAS) benefits is based on the lesser of 100% of OAS benefits received, and 15% of the amount by which "threshold income" (Net Income For Tax Purposes, calculated without the OAS clawback) exceeds $79,054.

Chapter 4   **EI Clawback Limits**   The tax (clawback) on Employment Insurance (EI) benefits under the *Employment Insurance Act* is based on the lesser of 30% of the EI benefits received, and 30% of the amount by which "threshold income" exceeds $67,750 (1.25 times the maximum insurable earnings of $54,200). For this purpose, "threshold income" is Net Income For Tax Purposes, calculated without the OAS or EI clawbacks.

Chapter 9   **Child Care Expenses**   The least of three amounts:

1.   The amount actually paid for child care services. If the child is at a camp or boarding school, this amount is limited to a weekly amount $275 (any age if eligible for disability tax credit), $200 (under 7 year of age), or $125 (age 7 through 16 or over 16 with a mental or physical impairment).

2.   The sum of the **Annual Child Care Expense Amounts** for the taxpayer's eligible children. The per child amounts are $11,000 (any age if eligible for disability tax credit), $8,000 (under 7 year of age), or $5,000 (age 7 through 16 or over 16 with a mental or physical impairment).

3.   2/3 of the taxpayer's **Earned Income** (for child care expenses purposes).

Chapter 10   **RRSP Deduction Room**   For 2020, the addition to RRSP deduction room is equal to:

- the lesser of $27,230 and 18% of 2019 Earned Income,
- reduced by the 2019 Pension Adjustment and any 2020 Past Service Pension Adjustment,
- and increased by any 2020 Pension Adjustment Reversal.

Chapter 11   **Lifetime Capital Gains Deduction**   For 2020, the deduction limit for dispositions of shares of qualified small business corporations is $883,384. There is an additional amount for farm or fishing properties of $116,616, providing a total of $1,000,000 for such properties.

> **Provincial Tax Rates And Provincial Credits For Individuals**   Provincial taxes are based on Taxable Income, with most provinces adopting multiple rates. The number of brackets range from three to five. Provincial tax credits are generally based on the minimum provincial rate applied to a credit base that is similar to that used for federal credits. In addition to regular rates, two provinces, Ontario and Prince Edward Island, use surtaxes.

Information Applicable To Individuals And Corporations

ITR 4301   **Prescribed Rate**   The following figures show the base rate that would be used in calculations such as imputed interest on loans. It also shows the rates applicable on amounts owing to and from the CRA. For recent quarters, the interest rates were as follows:

Year	Quarter	Base Rate	Owing From*	Owing To
2017	All	1%	3%	5%
2019	I	1%	3%	5%
2019	II to IV	2%	4%	6%
2020	**I, II**	**2%**	**4%**	**6%**

*The rate on refunds to corporations is limited to the base rate, without the additional 2%.

Automobile Deduction Limits

- CCA is limited to the first $30,000 of the automobiles cost, plus applicable GST/HST/ PST (not including amounts that will be refunded through input tax credits).
- Interest on financing of automobiles is limited to $10 per day.
- Deductible leasing costs are limited to $800 per month (other constraints apply).
- Operating cost benefit = $0.28 per kilometre.
- Deductible rates = $0.58 for first 5,000 kilometres, $0.52 for additional kilometres.

CCA Rates   See Appendix to Chapter 5.

Quick Method Rates (GST Only)

	Percentage On GST Included Sales	
	First $30,000	On Excess
Retailers And Wholesalers	0.8%	1.8%
Service Providers And Manufacturers	2.6%	3.6%

Note   Different rates apply in the provinces that have adopted an HST system.

Information Applicable To Corporations

Federal Corporate Tax Rates   are as follows (federal tax abatement removed):

General Business (Before General Rate Reduction)	28%
General Business (After General Rate Reduction Of 13%)	15%
Income Eligible For M&P Deduction	15%
Income Eligible For Small Business Deduction	9%
Part IV Refundable Tax	38-1/3%
Part I Refundable Tax On Investment Income Of CCPC (ART)	10-2/3%

Reference 89(1)

General Rate Income Pool   A CCPC's General Rate Income Pool (GRIP) is defined as follows:

- The GRIP balance at the end of the preceding year; plus
- 72% of the CCPC's Taxable Income after it has been reduced by amounts eligible for the small business deduction and aggregate investment income; plus
- 100% of eligible dividends received during the year; plus
- adjustments related to amalgamations and wind-ups; less
- eligible dividends paid during the preceding year.

125(1)

Small Business Deduction   is equal to 19% of the least of:

A. Net Canadian active business income.

B. Taxable Income, less:

1. 100/28 times the ITA 126(1) credit for taxes paid on foreign non-business income, calculated without consideration of the additional refundable tax under ITA 123.3 or the general rate reduction under ITA 123.4; and

2. 4 times the ITA 126(2) credit for taxes paid on foreign business income, calculated without consideration of the general rate reduction under ITA 123.4.

C. The annual business limit of $500,000, less any portion allocated to associated corporations, less the grinds for large corporations and passive income.

123.3

Additional Refundable Tax On Investment Income (ART)   is equal to 10-2/3% of the lesser of:

- the corporation's "aggregate investment income" for the year [as defined in ITA 129(4)]; and
- the amount, if any, by which the corporation's Taxable Income for the year exceeds the amount that is eligible for the small business deduction.

123.4(2)   **General Rate Reduction**   is equal to 13% of Full Rate Taxable Income. This is Taxable Income reduced by income eligible for the small business deduction, income eligible for the M&P deduction, and the corporation's "aggregate investment income" for the year.

125.1   **Manufacturing And Processing Deduction**   is equal to 13% of the lesser of:

A.   Manufacturing and processing profits, less amounts eligible for the small business deduction; and

B.   Taxable Income, less the sum of:

   1.   the amount eligible for the small business deduction;
   2.   4 times the foreign tax credit for business income calculated without consideration of the ITA 123.4 general rate reduction; and
   3.   "aggregate investment income" (of CCPCs) as defined in ITA 129(4).

126(1)   **Foreign Tax Credits For Corporations**   The Foreign Non-Business Income Tax Credit is the lesser of:

- The tax paid to the foreign government (for corporations, there is no 15% limit on the foreign non-business taxes paid); and

- An amount determined by the following formula:

$$\left[\frac{\text{Foreign Non} - \text{Business Income}}{\text{Adjusted Division B Income}} \right] [\text{Tax Otherwise Payable}]$$

126(2)   The Foreign Business Income Tax Credit is equal to the least of:

- The tax paid to the foreign government;

- An amount determined by the following formula:

$$\left[\frac{\text{Foreign Business Income}}{\text{Adjusted Division B Income}} \right] [\text{Tax Otherwise Payable}] \text{ ; and}$$

- Tax Otherwise Payable for the year, less any foreign tax credit taken on non-business income under ITA 126(1).

129(4)   **Refundable Portion Of Part I Tax Payable**   is defined as the least of three items:

   1.   the amount determined by the formula

   A - B, where

   A   is 30-2/3% of the corporation's aggregate investment income for the year, and

   B   is the amount, if any, by which the foreign non-business income tax credit exceeds 8% of its foreign investment income for the year.

   2.   30-2/3% of the amount, if any, by which the corporation's taxable income for the year exceeds the total of:

   - the amount eligible for the small business deduction;
   - 100 ÷ 38-2/3 of the tax credit for foreign non-business income; and
   - 4 times the tax credit for foreign business income.

   3.   the corporation's tax for the year payable under Part I.

129(4)   **Aggregate Investment Income**   is the sum of:

- net taxable capital gains for the year, reduced by any net capital loss carry overs deducted during the year; and

- income from property including interest, rents, and royalties, but excluding dividends that are deductible in computing Taxable Income. Since foreign dividends are generally not deductible, they would be included in aggregate investment income.

129(4)   **ELIGIBLE 2019 Refundable Dividend Tax On Hand**   (RDTOH) is defined as follows:

Beginning Balance   The balance in the Eligible RDTOH at the end of the preceding taxation year.

Additions

- Part IV taxes paid on eligible dividends from non-connected taxable Canadian corporations. These are commonly referred to as portfolio dividends.
- Part IV taxes paid on eligible dividends from connected corporations to the extent that such dividends included a refund from the paying corporation's Eligible RDTOH.

Deduction   Deducted from this total would be any dividend refund claimed from the Eligible RDTOH account in the previous taxation year.

NON-ELIGIBLE 2019 Refundable Dividend Tax On Hand   (RDTOH) is defined as follows:

Beginning Balance   The balance in the Non-Eligible RDTOH at the end of the preceding taxation year.

Additions   There are three items that are added to the Non-Eligible RDTOH beginning balance:

- All of the Part I refundable tax for the year.
- Part IV taxes paid on non-eligible dividends from connected corporations to the extent that such dividends included a refund from the paying corporation's Non-Eligible RDTOH.
- Part IV taxes paid on non-eligible dividends from non-connected taxable Canadian corporations.

Deduction   Deducted from this total would be any dividend refund claimed from the Non-Eligible RDTOH account in the previous taxation year. For 2019, this deduction is reflected in the transitional RDTOH and will not be deducted again.

186(1)   **Part IV Tax**   is assessed at a rate of 38-1/3% of portfolio dividends, plus dividends received from a connected company that gave rise to a dividend refund for the connected company as a result of the payment.

Tax Related Web Sites

GOVERNMENT

Canada Revenue Agency   www.canada.ca/en/revenue-agency
Department of Finance Canada   www.canada.ca/en/department-finance.html

CPA FIRMS

BDO   www.bdo.ca/en-ca/services/tax/domestic-tax-services/overview/
Deloitte.   www2.deloitte.com/ca/en/pages/tax/topics/tax.html
Ernst & Young   www.ey.com/CA/en/Services/Tax
KPMG   www.kpmg.com/ca/en/services/tax
PricewaterhouseCoopers   www.pwc.com/ca/en/tax/publications.html

OTHER

CPA Canada   www.CPAcanada.ca
Canadian Tax Foundation   www.ctf.ca
ProFile Tax Suite   www.profile.intuit.ca

CHAPTER 11

Taxable Income And Tax Payable For Individuals Revisited

Introduction

The Problem

11-1. The subjects of Taxable Income for individuals and Tax Payable for individuals were introduced in Chapter 4. This earlier Chapter provided a general overview of how we arrive at the Taxable Income figure and, in addition, covered in detail the majority of credits that can be applied in the determination of Tax Payable. We chose to cover this material in Chapter 4 in order to enhance your understanding of some of the material dealing with specific types of income in Chapters 5 through 9.

11-2. The problem with this early coverage of these subjects is that there are some concepts and procedures involved in determining Taxable Income and Tax Payable for individuals that cannot be explained without some understanding of the additional components of Net Income For Tax Purposes that are covered in subsequent chapters.

11-3. For example, it is not possible to meaningfully discuss the deduction of loss carry overs in calculating Taxable Income without knowledge of the difference between net capital and non-capital losses, a subject that is not covered until Chapter 8. A similar problem arises in dealing with the transfer of dividend tax credits to a spouse. This idea is not comprehensible to an individual who does not have an understanding of the dividend gross up and tax credit procedures, which are not introduced until Chapter 7.

Our Solution

11-4. Our solution to this problem is this second chapter on Taxable Income and Tax Payable for individuals. At this point, we have provided comprehensive coverage of all of the components of Net Income For Tax Purposes. Chapter 3 dealt with employment income, Chapters 5 and 6 dealt with CCA and business income, Chapter 7 provided coverage of property income, and Chapter 8 dealt with taxable capital gains and allowable capital losses. This coverage of income components concluded with Chapter 9's coverage of miscellaneous sources of and deductions from Net Income For Tax Purposes.

11-5. With this background, we can now finish our coverage of Taxable Income and Tax Payable for individuals. With respect to Taxable Income, we will provide complete coverage of both loss carry overs and the lifetime capital gains deduction. We will also be able to deal with the additional credits required in the determination of Tax Payable, as well as the procedures associated with the determination of alternative minimum tax.

Taxable Income Overview

11-6.   As was discussed in Chapter 4, Taxable Income is calculated by deducting certain specified items from Net Income For Tax Purposes. These deductions, which are found in Division C of the *Income Tax Act*, are as follows:

ITA 110(1)(d), (d.01), and (d.1) - Employee Stock Options   Our basic coverage of stock options and stock option deductions was included in Chapter 3. Adding to this coverage in this Chapter 11, we deal with some special rules that are associated with gifts of shares that have been acquired through the exercise of stock options.

ITA 110(1)(f) - Deductions For Payments   This deduction is designed to ensure that certain amounts are not subject to tax. Included here are such amounts as social assistance received, workers' compensation received (covered in Chapter 4), and amounts exempted from Canadian tax by tax treaty (covered in Chapter 20). Also included here are deductions for employment income received from certain prescribed international organizations and employment income earned by a member of the Canadian Forces serving in certain prescribed missions.

ITA 110.2 - Lump Sum Payments   This Section provides a deduction for certain lump sum payments (e.g., an amount received as a court-ordered termination benefit and included in employment income). It provides the basis for taxing this amount as though it was received over several periods (a.k.a. income averaging). Limited coverage of this provision can be found in the next section of this Chapter.

ITA 110.6 - Lifetime Capital Gains Deduction   The provisions related to this deduction are very complex and require a fairly complete understanding of capital gains. As a consequence, it was not covered in Chapter 4 and will be given coverage in this Chapter.

ITA 110.7 - Residing In Prescribed Zone (Northern Residents Deductions)   These deductions, which are limited to individuals living in prescribed regions of northern Canada, were covered in Chapter 4.

ITA 111 - Losses Deductible   This is a group of deductions that is available for carrying over various types of losses from preceding or subsequent taxation years. The application of these provisions can be complex and requires a fairly complete understanding of business income, property income, and capital gains. As a consequence, this group of deductions was not covered in Chapter 4 and will be covered in detail in this Chapter.

11-7.   The material in this Chapter will complete our coverage of Taxable Income for individuals. Of the Taxable Income deductions available to individuals, only amounts exempted by treaty under ITA 110(1)(f) and loss carry overs under ITA 111 are available to corporations. There are, however, additional deductions available to corporate taxpayers for charitable contributions and dividends received from other taxable Canadian corporations. These additional deductions are covered in Chapter 12.

Lump Sum Payments

The Problem

11-8.   Individuals sometimes receive lump sum payments that relate to services provided in one or more previous years. An example of this would be an employment termination payment that included amounts that related to service provided in previous years.

11-9.   There is an advantage in such situations in that there has been some deferral of the tax on these amounts. However, because of the presence of progressive rates in the Canadian tax system, the tax liability on such lump sum payments may be higher than would have been the case had the payments been received and taxed over multiple years. This would be a particularly severe problem in situations where a very large taxable amount is involved. Because of this problem, there is tax relief available for certain lump sum payments.

Qualifying Amounts

11-10.   The relief can be applied to payments that are referred to as "qualifying amounts". These are given a technical definition in ITA 110.2(1). In the Explanatory Notes that accompany the legislation, the following more general description is found:

> A **qualifying amount** is the principal portion (e.g., not including interest) of certain amounts included in income. Those amounts are: spousal or child support amounts, superannuation or pension benefits otherwise payable on a periodic basis, employment insurance benefits and benefits paid under wage loss replacement plans. Also included is the income received from an office or employment (or because of a termination of an office or employment) under the terms of a court order or judgment, an arbitration award or in settlement of a lawsuit.

Relief Mechanism

11-11.   ITA 110.2(2) provides a deduction for the "specified portion" of a "qualifying amount" that was received by an individual during a particular taxation year. The "specified portion" is the fraction of the qualifying amount that relates to an "eligible taxation year". An "eligible taxation year" is any prior year after 1977 in which the individual was a resident of Canada throughout the year and during which the individual did not become bankrupt. No deduction is available if the qualifying amount is less than \$3,000. In somewhat simplified terms, this means that an individual can remove the types of payments described as qualifying amounts from the current year's income, to the extent that they relate to prior years.

11-12.   ITA 120.31 describes an alternative tax that will be payable on the amounts that are deducted under ITA 110.2(2). This tax is the total of the additional taxes that would have been triggered for each relevant preceding year if the portion of the qualifying amount that relates to that preceding year was added to the individual's Taxable Income for that year. In addition to the tax for those years, a notional amount of interest is added to reflect the fact that the tax was not paid in the relevant years. This interest is accrued from May 1 of the year following the relevant preceding year through the end of the year prior to the receipt of the lump sum payment.

11-13.   The goal of these procedures is to spread the lump sum payment over earlier years, thereby eliminating the influence of progressive rates on the total tax bill. For example, if a 2020 court settlement reflected a wage adjustment for the years 2015 through 2019, the recipient would pay the amount of taxes that would have been paid if he or she had received the amounts in those earlier years, reduced by the amount of taxes that were paid in those years. In many cases this will provide significant tax relief. However, there may be some situations in which, because of differing marginal tax rates in the years under consideration, using this approach could result in higher taxes because of the addition of the notional amount of interest. In such cases, the taxpayer would not make the deduction under ITA 110.2(2).

Treatment Of Losses

Carry Over Provisions

General Rules

11-14.   In earlier Chapters there have been references to a taxpayer's ability to carry back or carry forward losses. Before covering the carry over rules related to specific types of losses, we will consider the general procedures associated with these carry overs.

11-15.   If a taxpayer experiences a loss in the current year with respect to a particular type of income, it must be used, to the extent possible, to offset other types of income in the current year.

The taxpayer does not have any real discretion in this matter. If he or she is in a position to apply a loss to other types of income that are available in the loss year and he or she chooses not to do so, the loss cannot be carried over to either earlier or later years.

11-16.   However, there are situations in which one or more losses cannot be used during the current year. There are two basic reasons why this may be the case:

- The taxpayer may not have sufficient other sources of income to absorb the loss (e.g., a business loss that is greater than all other current sources of income).

- The taxpayer may not have sufficient income of the right type to absorb the loss (e.g., an allowable capital loss that is greater than current taxable capital gains).

11-17.   If either of these situations arises in the current year, the taxpayer can either carry the loss back to apply against Taxable Income in previous years or, alternatively, carry the loss forward to apply against Taxable Income in future years. Unlike the situation with current year losses, provided that the use is within the specified carry back and carry forward periods, the decision as to when a loss carry over should be used is at the discretion of the taxpayer.

Carry Backs

11-18.   With one exception, all types of current year losses can be applied against income in the three preceding taxation years. The one exception is limited partnership losses, which cannot be carried back (see Chapter 18). When the loss is applied, the carry back will result in a refund of some or all of the taxes that were paid in the carry back year.

11-19.   Note that, with several types of losses, the carry back amount can only be applied against income of the same type. More specifically:

- Net capital losses can only be applied against net taxable capital gains realized in the carry back year.

- Net listed personal property losses (see Chapter 8) can only be applied against listed personal property gains realized in the carry back year.

- Restricted farm losses (see Chapter 6) can only be applied against farm income realized in the carry back year.

Carry Forwards

11-20.   In general, because of the certainty of a refund, taxpayers will want to carry losses back if there is sufficient income of the appropriate type in any of the three preceding years. While variations in applicable tax rates for the relevant years might generate a situation where a taxpayer might wish to risk carrying an amount forward on the possibility that it would eliminate income that is being taxed at a higher rate in the carry forward period, this is unlikely to be a common choice.

11-21.   Any amount of current year loss that is not carried back will become a loss carry forward. Unlike the situation with carry backs, there is some variation in the carry forward period for different types of losses. The current rules are as follows:

Non-Capital Losses And Farm Losses   For non-capital and farm losses, the carry forward period is 20 years. Non-capital and regular farm losses can be applied against any type of income in the carry forward year. If the farm loss is restricted, it can only be applied against farm income in the carry forward year.

Net Capital Losses   Net capital losses can be carried forward indefinitely, limited only by the life of the taxpayer. However, they can only be applied against taxable capital gains that arise in the carry forward year. As will be discussed later in this Chapter, there is an exception for deceased taxpayers who can generally deduct any unused net capital losses against any type of income in the year immediately preceding death and in the year of death. Note that, as this term is used in the *Income Tax Act*, net capital loss refers to the excess of the allowable (one-half) portion of capital losses over the taxable (one-half) portion of capital gains.

Net Listed Personal Property Losses   Listed personal property losses can be carried forward for seven years. As noted previously, they can only be deducted against net listed personal property gains that arise in the carry forward year.

Segregation By Type

11-22.   We have noted that, with both loss carry backs and loss carry forwards, some types of losses can only be applied against income of the same type. Because of this requirement, loss carry forward balances must be segregated by type. More specifically, the separate balances that must be tracked are:

- Non-Capital Losses [employment losses, business losses, property losses, and business investment losses (defined in Paragraph 11-55)]
- Net Capital Losses
- Regular Farm Losses
- Restricted Farm Losses

Applying The Deduction

11-23.   With the exception of listed personal property losses (see coverage beginning in Paragraph 11-31), loss carry overs are deducted from Net Income For Tax Purposes in the determination of Taxable Income.

11-24.   In the case of a carry back, there is a reduction of both Taxable Income and Tax Payable in the carry back year. Provided the taxes for that year have been paid, the result will be a refund. As you would expect, the refund will be based on the tax rates applicable to the carry back year.

11-25.   With respect to carry forwards, they serve to reduce Taxable Income and Tax Payable in the carry forward year. As was the case with carry backs, the loss carry forward benefit will accrue at the tax rates applicable to the carry forward year.

Loss Carry Overs And Tax Credits

11-26.   You will recall from Chapter 4 that most of the credits against Tax Payable that are available to individuals are not refundable. Further, most of them cannot be carried over to be used in subsequent taxation years. This means that, in the absence of sufficient Tax Payable to absorb these credits, they will be permanently lost.

11-27.   These facts relate to loss carry overs in that, given that many tax credits have no value in the absence of a Tax Payable amount, it is generally not advisable to use loss carry overs to reduce Taxable Income to nil in the carry over year.

EXAMPLE   In 2019, Jan Teason had employment income of $25,000 and a net rental loss of $55,000. She had no reported income in the three preceding years. In 2020, she has no employment income and net rental income of $25,000. Ms. Teason's only 2020 tax credit is the basic personal credit of $1,984 [(15%)($13,229)].

ANALYSIS   In 2019, Ms. Teason had Net Income For Tax Purposes of nil and, at the end of the year, non-capital loss carry forward of $30,000. Note that she did not have the option of reducing the amount of the 2019 rental loss in order to use her personal tax credit for that year.

If she wished to do so, Ms. Teason could reduce her 2020 Taxable Income to nil by applying $25,000 of the 2019 non-capital loss carry forward. However, if she limits her carry forward deduction to $11,771 ($25,000 - $13,229), her Taxable Income will be reduced to $13,229. The tax on this would be $1,984 [(15%)($13,229)], an amount that would be eliminated by her basic personal credit. This approach leaves an unused carry forward balance of $16,771 ($30,000 - $13,229).

11-28.   What this example illustrates is that, in practical situations, loss carry overs should not be used to reduce Taxable Income to nil. In the real world, tax preparation software should automatically limit loss carry overs to prevent this from happening. However, trying to build this consideration into the examples and problems included in this text can have the effect of significantly complicating material that is already very difficult to understand. As a result, in some problems we ask that you ignore this issue.

11-29.   While this approach is not consistent with real world tax planning considerations, we feel that it can be justified in terms of aiding your understanding of this difficult material on loss carry overs.

Personal Use Property Losses

11-30.   You will recall that personal use property is defined as "property owned by the taxpayer that is used primarily for the personal use or enjoyment of the taxpayer, or for the personal use or enjoyment of one or more individuals related to the taxpayer". As covered in Chapter 8, taxable capital gains on personal use property, determined on the assumption that both the proceeds of disposition and the adjusted cost base are at least $1,000, are included in the calculation of Net Income For Tax Purposes. However, unless the personal use property qualifies as "listed personal property" as described in the following material, losses on personal use property are never deductible.

Listed Personal Property Losses

General Rules

11-31.   Listed personal property is a designation that has been given to five specific categories of personal use property. As listed in ITA 54, these categories are:

- a print, etching, drawing, painting, sculpture, or other similar work of art;
- jewelry;
- a rare folio, rare manuscript, or rare book;
- a stamp; or
- a coin.

11-32.   As was the case with personal use property, taxable capital gains on listed personal property are included in Net Income For Tax Purposes, and are also calculated on the assumption that both the proceeds of disposition and the adjusted cost base are at least $1,000 (as noted in Chapter 8, this rule may not be applicable when a charitable donation is involved).

11-33.   The difference with these categories of personal use property is that allowable capital losses on listed personal property can be deducted. However, they can only be deducted against taxable capital gains on listed personal property. They cannot be used to reduce taxes on any other type of income, including taxable capital gains on property that is not listed personal property.

Carry Over Provisions

11-34.   If a loss on listed personal property cannot be used in the current year, it can be carried back three years or forward for seven years. In the carry over year, the loss can only be used to the extent that there are gains on listed personal property in that year.

11-35.   Unlike other loss carry overs, listed personal property losses are not deducted from Net Income For Tax Purposes in the calculation of Taxable Income. Under ITA 41(2), the net gain on listed personal property is defined as the gains for the current year, reduced by the carry over amounts from the seven preceding years, or the three subsequent years. If this amount is positive, it is added in the calculation of Net Income For Tax Purposes under ITA 3(b). While the process is somewhat different, the final result is the same reduction in Taxable Income that would result from the carry over of some other type of loss.

Exercise Eleven - 1

Subject: Listed Personal Property Losses

During 2019, Mr. Ronald Smothers was unemployed and had no income of any kind. In order to survive, he sold a painting on December 1, 2019, for $89,000. This painting had been left to Mr. Smothers by his mother and, at the time of her death, it had a fair market value of $100,000. During 2020, Mr. Smothers finds a job and has employment income of $62,000. In addition, during June he sells a second painting for $5,000. He had purchased this painting several years ago for $1,000. Determine Mr. Smothers' minimum Net Income For Tax Purposes and Taxable Income for 2020. Indicate the amount and type of any losses available for carry forward at the end of the year. Assume the December 1, 2019, sale had been of publicly traded shares instead of a painting. How would this change your solution?

SOLUTION available in print and online Study Guide.

Non-Capital Losses

General Rules

11-36.   In terms of a simple dictionary meaning, the term non-capital would mean any loss other than a loss on the disposition of a capital asset. In fact, in many situations, this non-technical approach would provide the correct result. However, ITA 111(8) contains a very technical definition that must be used in more complex situations in order to ensure that we arrive at the appropriate answer. In simplified form, this definition is as follows:

ITA 111(8)   The non-capital loss of a taxpayer for a taxation year means the amount determined by the formula:

$$A - D, \text{ where}$$

A   is the amount determined by the formula:

$$E - F, \text{ where}$$

E   is the total of all amounts each of which is the taxpayer's loss for the year from an office, employment, business, or property (including farm losses), the taxpayer's allowable Business Investment Loss for the year, and net capital loss carry overs deducted in the calculation of Taxable Income for the year (this net capital loss amount cannot exceed the taxable capital gains for the year).

F   is the amount of income determined under ITA 3(c). [Sum of ITA 3(a) non-capital positive sources and ITA 3(b) net taxable capital gains, less Division B, Subdivision e deductions.]

D   is the taxpayer's farm loss for the year (amount included in E).

11-37.   Note that this definition excludes both current year capital losses and farm losses. These two types of losses are subject to different rules and, as a consequence, their balances must be tracked separately. The inclusion of net capital losses in this definition will be explained in our later discussion of net capital losses.

11-38.   As can be seen in the definition, non-capital losses can result from the calculation of income from employment, income from a business, or income from property. However, given the limited number of deductions from employment income, it is very unlikely that an individual will experience an employment loss. Normally, non-capital losses would result from the operation of a business or the ownership of property. For example, a non-capital loss on a rental property could occur when expenses, other than CCA, associated with the property exceed the rental revenues.

Exercise Eleven - 2

Subject: Non-Capital Losses

During 2020, Janice McMann has net employment income of $35,000, as well as a taxable capital gain of $13,000. In addition, she has a business loss of $58,000 and a farm loss of $2,200. Determine her 2020 non-capital loss.

SOLUTION available in print and online Study Guide.

Carry Over Provisions

11-39.   Non-capital losses are defined in ITA 111(8) in such a fashion that a carry over is only available after the current year's income is reduced to nil. Stated alternatively, a carry over is only possible after all current year losses, other than current year capital losses, have been deducted. If losses remain and are available for carry over, they can be applied, at the taxpayer's discretion, to any of the eligible carry over years. However, ITA 111(3) indicates that a non-capital loss carry over for a particular year cannot be used until the available non-capital loss carry overs from all preceding years have been exhausted.

11-40.   As we have noted, such losses may be carried back three years and applied against any type of income in those years. If there is not sufficient income in those years to absorb the full amount of these non-capital losses, any remaining balance can be carried forward for a period of 20 years. Whether the amounts are carried back or forward, they will be deducted under ITA 111(1)(a) in the computation of Taxable Income.

Net Capital Losses

General Rules

11-41.   The term "net capital loss" is defined in ITA 111(8) as the excess of allowable capital losses over taxable capital gains for the current taxation year. Note carefully that, as the term is used in the *Act*, "net capital loss" refers to the deductible portion of capital losses, not to the 100 percent amounts. When these annual amounts are carried forward, the resulting balance is normally referred to as the "net capital loss balance".

Carry Over Provisions

11-42.   While a net capital loss for the current year cannot be deducted in the calculation of the current year's Net Income For Tax Purposes, this amount is available for carry over to other years. Such losses may be carried back three years and forward to any subsequent year.

11-43.   When they are carried forward or back, they will be deducted under ITA 111(1)(b) in the calculation of Taxable Income. However, ITA 111(1.1) restricts the deduction of such carry over amounts to the amount included in Net Income For Tax Purposes under ITA 3(b) (net taxable capital gains). Expressed in less technical terms, you can only deduct a net capital loss carry over to the extent that you have net taxable capital gains in the carry over year.

11-44.   You will recall from Chapter 8 that the inclusion rate for capital gains has varied over the years. Further, the relevant legislation is such that, when net capital losses are carried over they must be deducted at the rate that is applicable to the carry over year. However, the inclusion rate for capital gains has been one-half since 2000. Given this, our only coverage of situations involving different inclusion rates for capital gains will be in our discussion of net capital losses that are present when a taxpayer dies.

Conversion Of A Net Capital Loss Carry Over
To A Non-Capital Loss Carry Over

11-45.   A problem can arise when a taxpayer has a net capital loss carry over, taxable capital gains in the current year, and a current year business or property loss that is large enough to reduce his or her Net Income For Tax Purposes to nil. As a net capital loss carry over can only be deducted to the extent of current year net taxable capital gains, the taxpayer usually prefers to use such carry overs whenever current year taxable capital gains are available. A simple example will illustrate this problem.

> **EXAMPLE**   For 2020, Mr. Waring has property income of $25,000, taxable capital gains of $45,000 [(1/2)($90,000)], and a business loss of $150,000. He also has a net capital loss carry forward from 2019 of $60,000 [(1/2)($120,000)]. He does not anticipate having any further taxable capital gains in the foreseeable future.

11-46.   The usual ITA 3 calculation of Net Income For Tax Purposes would be as follows:

ITA 3(a) Non-Capital Positive Sources	$ 25,000
ITA 3(b) Net Taxable Capital Gains	45,000
ITA 3(c) Sum Of ITA 3(a) And 3(b)	$ 70,000
ITA 3(d) Business Loss	(150,000)
Net Income For Tax Purposes	Nil

11-47.   The business loss reduced Net Income For Tax Purposes to nil, and this is a problem for Mr. Waring in that he does not anticipate having further taxable capital gains in the near future. Given this, it would appear that he has lost the ability to use this year's net taxable capital gains to absorb the 2019 net capital loss carry forward.

11-48.   Fortunately, this is not the case. You will recall that, in the definition of non-capital loss in Paragraph 11-36, the taxpayer can add to the E component of the definition any net capital loss carry overs deducted in the current year. This means that, if we assume that Mr. Waring chooses to deduct the maximum amount of his net capital loss carry forward in 2020, the non-capital loss carry over for 2020 would be as follows:

Business Loss For Year	$ 150,000
Net Capital Loss Carry Forward Deducted	
(Limited To Taxable Capital Gains)	45,000
Total For Amount E	$ 195,000
Amount F = Income Under ITA 3(c) ($25,000 + $45,000)	(70,000)
Non-Capital Loss Available For Carry Over	$ 125,000

11-49.   There are two points that should be made with respect to this analysis:

- The amount of the net capital loss carry forward deducted is limited to the $45,000 in net taxable capital gains that were realized during the year. As a result, he has utilized $45,000 of the $60,000 net capital loss carry forward from 2019.

- The deduction of the net capital loss carry over is discretionary. That is, the taxpayer can deduct any amount between $1 and the maximum value of $45,000. In the solution presented, he has deducted the maximum amount, which results in a non-capital loss carry over of $125,000 and leaves a net capital loss carry forward of $15,000 ($60,000 - $45,000). An alternative would have been to deduct none of the net capital loss carry forward, leaving a net capital loss carry forward of $60,000. Under this scenario, the non-capital loss for the year would be calculated as follows:

Business Loss For Year (Amount E)	$150,000
Amount F = Income Under ITA 3(c) ($25,000 + $45,000)	(70,000)
Non-Capital Loss Available For Carry Over	$ 80,000

As this calculation illustrates, the combined non-capital and net capital loss total will be the same in these situations, without regard to what amount of the net capital loss is used. If $45,000 of the net capital loss is used, the total loss remaining is $140,000 ($15,000 + $125,000). If none is used, the total is still $140,000 ($60,000 + $80,000). In simple economic terms, this procedure allows the taxpayer to convert a net capital loss balance with restricted deductibility into a non-capital loss balance that can be deducted against any type of income.

Exercise Eleven - 3

Subject: Net Capital Loss Carry Overs

During 2019, Ms. Laura Macky had an allowable capital loss of $15,000. Prior to 2020, she had no taxable capital gains and, as a consequence, she has not been able to deduct this loss. In 2020, her income consists of a taxable capital gain of $40,000 [(1/2)($80,000)] and a net rental loss of $30,000. She does not anticipate any future capital gains. Determine Ms. Macky's minimum 2020 Net Income For Tax Purposes and minimum 2020 Taxable Income, as well as the amount and type of any losses available for carry over at the end of the year. Ignore the effects of her tax credits.

SOLUTION available in print and online Study Guide.

Net Capital Losses At Death

11-50.   One of the difficulties with net capital loss carry overs is that they can normally only be deducted against taxable capital gains. As there is no time limit on the carry forward of such undeducted losses, an individual can die with a substantial balance of these amounts on hand. Capital losses may also arise in the year of death, either through a disposition prior to death or through a deemed disposition at death.

11-51.   ITA 111(2) contains a special provision with respect to both net capital losses from years prior to death and to allowable capital losses arising in the year of death. Essentially, this provision allows these accumulated losses to be applied against any type of income in the year of death or the immediately preceding year.

11-52.   An example will illustrate these provisions:

> **EXAMPLE**   Ms. Vincent dies in December 2020. She has a net capital loss carry forward of $35,300 [(1/2)($70,600)]. Her final return has a Net Income For Tax Purposes of $40,000, which includes a taxable capital gain of $4,500 [(1/2)($9,000)]. The only tax credit on her final return is her BPA.

> **ANALYSIS**   If Ms. Vincent was alive at the end of the year, her 2020 taxable capital gain would limit the use of her net capital loss carry forward in 2020 to the taxable capital gain of $4,500. This would result in a Taxable Income of $35,500 ($40,000 - $4,500).

> However, this limitation does not apply in the year of death, allowing her to apply her net capital loss to any type of income. As explained in Paragraph 11-27, she should limit her loss deduction to an amount that would reduce her Taxable Income to the BPA. For 2020, this amount would be $13,229, requiring that she use $26,771 ($40,000 - $13,229) of her net capital loss.

> This would leave a net capital loss of $8,529 ($35,300 - $26,771), which could be carried back and applied against any type of income in 2019.

11-53.   Capital losses realized by the estate on dispositions of an individual's property in the first taxation year after his or her death can be carried back and applied against any type of income in the final return of the deceased. Note, however, that these losses cannot be carried back to the tax return for the year preceding death.

11-54.   The inclusion rate has been at one-half since 2000. As a result, calculations where an inclusion rate that is not one-half is relevant are increasingly rare. However, we would note the following points:

- If there are taxable capital gains in the year of death, the net capital loss must first be applied at the inclusion rate for the current year to the extent of those gains. If a net capital loss balance remains, ITA 111(2) allows it to be applied against other types of income, using the inclusion rate that prevailed in the year in which the net capital loss was realized.

- The ability to use this provision is reduced by the previous deduction of amounts under the lifetime capital gains provision (see discussion later in this Chapter). This reduction reflects the actual amount of the lifetime capital gains deduction made, without regard to the capital gains inclusion rate that was applicable at the time.

Exercise Eleven - 4

Subject: Net Capital Losses At Death

Mr. Derek Barnes dies during 2020. He has a net capital loss carry forward of $20,000 [(1/2)($40,000)] at the time of his death. His final return has a Net Income For Tax Purposes of $23,800, which includes a taxable capital gain of $9,200 [(1/2)($18,400)]. The only tax credit on his final return is his basic personal tax credit. Describe the optimal tax treatment of Derek's net capital loss carry forward.

SOLUTION available in print and online Study Guide.

Allowable Business Investment Losses

Defined

11-55.   A Business Investment Loss (BIL), as defined in ITA 39(1)(c), is a special type of capital loss resulting from the disposition of shares or debt of a "small business corporation." In addition to losses on arm's length sales, Business Investment Losses can be incurred when there is a deemed disposition for nil proceeds. This could occur for shares of a small business corporation due to bankruptcy or insolvency, or if the debt is considered uncollectible.

11-56.   A small business corporation is defined in ITA 248(1) as a Canadian controlled private corporation (CCPC) of which "all or substantially all" of the fair market value of its assets are used in an active business carried on "primarily" in Canada. In tax work, the term "substantially all" generally means 90 percent or more, while "primarily" is generally interpreted to mean more than 50 percent.

11-57.   In making this determination, shares or debt of a connected small business corporation would count toward the required 90 percent. A corporation is connected if the potential small business corporation either controls it or owns more than 10 percent of its voting shares and shares that represent more than 10 percent of the fair market value of all of the corporation's outstanding shares. As you would expect, an Allowable Business Investment Loss (ABIL) is the deductible one-half of a BIL.

Special Treatment

11-58.   In general, allowable capital losses can only be deducted against taxable capital gains. However, ABILs are given special treatment in that the taxpayer is permitted to deduct these amounts from any source of income.

EXAMPLE An individual with net employment income of $50,000 has an ABIL of $10,500 [(1/2)($21,000)].

ANALYSIS This individual would be able to deduct the $10,500 ABIL against the employment income, resulting in a Net Income For Tax Purposes of $39,500. If this had been an ordinary allowable capital loss, the taxpayer's Net Income For Tax Purposes would be $50,000 and the unapplied allowable capital loss would become a net capital loss for the year, which would be available for carry over to other years.

11-59. If there is sufficient income, the ABIL must be deducted in the year in which it is realized. However, if other sources of income are not sufficient for deducting all or part of an ABIL under ITA 3(d) in the current year, it becomes a part of the non-capital loss carry over balance. This permits this special type of allowable capital loss to be deducted against any type of income when they are carried back or carried forward.

11-60. If the ABIL has not been applied during the 10 years subsequent to its occurrence, it reverts to its original status as an allowable capital loss and becomes a component of the net capital loss carry forward balance. While this restricts the types of income that the loss can be applied against, it gives the loss an unlimited carry forward period.

Effect Of The ITA 110.6 Lifetime Capital Gains Deduction

11-61. As we shall see in our discussion of the ITA 110.6 lifetime capital gains deduction beginning in Paragraph 11-68, the realization of a Business Investment Loss reduces the taxpayer's ability to take advantage of this deduction. Of note here, however, is the fact that under ITA 39(9), Business Investment Losses are disallowed by the use of the ITA 110.6 lifetime capital gains deduction. What this means is, to the extent that the individual has made a deduction under ITA 110.6, an equivalent portion of the Business Investment Loss will be disallowed (i.e., converted to an ordinary capital loss).

EXAMPLE Mr. Mercer had a taxable capital gain in 2013 of $8,000 [(1/2)($16,000)] and deducted this amount under the provisions of the ITA 110.6 lifetime capital gains deduction. In July 2020, he has a $60,000 loss on the sale of shares of a small business corporation. Mr. Mercer has no capital gains or losses in any other year.

ANALYSIS If Mr. Mercer had made no use of ITA 110.6, he would have an Allowable Business Investment Loss of $30,000 [(1/2)($60,000)] in 2020. However, since he has made a deduction under ITA 110.6, the Business Investment Loss would be reduced as follows:

Actual Loss On Disposition	$60,000
Disallowed By Lifetime Capital Gains Deduction Use	(16,000)
Business Investment Loss	$44,000
Inclusion Rate	1/2
Allowable Business Investment Loss (ABIL)	$22,000

11-62. As we have noted, the disallowed $16,000 does not disappear. It becomes an ordinary capital loss, subject to the usual restriction that it can only be deducted against capital gains. The remaining $22,000 ABIL can be deducted in 2020 against any source of income. If it is not deducted in that year or carried back, it becomes part of the non-capital loss carry forward for 10 (not 20) years. If it is still not used after 10 years, in year 11 it becomes part of the net capital loss carry forward.

Exercise Eleven - 5

Subject: Business Investment Losses

During 2019, Mr. Lawrence Latvik used his lifetime capital gains deduction to eliminate a taxable capital gain of $13,000 [(1/2)($26,000)]. During 2020, he has capital gains on publicly traded securities of $18,000 and a loss of $50,000 on the disposition of shares of a small business corporation. His employment income for 2020 is over $200,000. Determine the amount of the Allowable Business Investment Loss that can be deducted in 2020, as well as the amount and type of any losses available for carry over at the end of the year.

SOLUTION available in print and online Study Guide.

We suggest you work Self Study Problem Eleven-1 at this point.

Farm Losses

Regular Farm Losses

11-63.   For full time farmers, farm losses are not restricted. They are treated in the same manner as non-capital losses in that they can be carried back three years and forward for 20 years. Unlike restricted farm losses (see the following Paragraph), when they are deducted on a carry over basis, regular farm losses can be applied against any type of income.

Restricted Farm Losses

11-64.   As noted in Chapter 6, if a farm operation does not have a reasonable expectation of profit (the so-called hobby farm), none of the losses associated with the operation will be deductible. However, even if there is a reasonable expectation of profit, farm losses may be restricted. More specifically, under ITA 31, farm losses are restricted if:

> ... a farmer's chief source of income for a taxation year is neither farming nor a combination of farming and some other source of income that **is a subordinate source of income** for the taxpayer ...

11-65.   In effect, if farming is only a secondary source of income, farm losses will be restricted, even if the farming operation has a reasonable expectation of a profit. The restriction limits losses that can be deducted against other sources of income to the first $2,500 of such losses, plus one-half of the next $30,000, for a maximum deduction of $17,500 [$2,500 + (1/2) ($32,500 maximum - $2,500)] on farm losses of $32,500 or greater. Any amount of the farm loss that is not deductible in the current year is commonly referred to as a "restricted farm loss".

11-66.   Restricted farm losses can be carried over to other years. Such losses can be carried back three years and forward for a maximum of 20 years. In carry over periods, restricted farm losses can only be deducted to the extent that income from farming has been included in Net Income For Tax Purposes. For example, if a restricted farm loss carry forward of $15,000 was available at the beginning of 2020 and 2020 farming income totaled $12,000, only $12,000 of the carry forward could be deducted in calculating 2020 Taxable Income. The remaining $3,000 of the restricted loss could not be deducted, even if the taxpayer had large amounts of other types of income available.

11-67.   If land used in a farming business is disposed of before the taxpayer has an opportunity to fully utilize restricted farm losses carried forward, a part of the undeducted losses can be used to increase the adjusted cost base of the property. This would have the effect of reducing any capital gains arising on the disposition of the property. This treatment is only possible to the extent that the loss was created by property taxes or interest payments on the farm property.

Exercise Eleven - 6

Subject: Farm Losses

Ms. Elena Bodkin has a full time appointment as a professor at a Canadian university. As she has considerable free time, she is developing an organic vegetable farm. In 2019, the first year of operation, she had a loss of $36,000 and deducted the maximum allowable amount. In 2020, in addition to her employment income of $85,000, her farming operation showed a profit of $3,500. Determine Ms. Bodkin's minimum 2020 Net Income For Tax Purposes and Taxable Income, as well as the amount and type of any losses available for carry forward at the end of the year.

SOLUTION available in print and online Study Guide.

We suggest you work Self Study Problem Eleven-2 at this point.

Lifetime Capital Gains Deduction

Background

The Original Legislation

11-68.   The lifetime capital gains legislation was first introduced in 1985 and, in its original form, it allowed every individual resident in Canada to enjoy up to $100,000 in tax free capital gains during the course of their lifetime. This privilege was available without regard to the type of property on which the gain accrued. A resident Canadian could acquire a major tax benefit through the process of owning and disposing of a Florida condominium. This original legislation was modified in 1988, providing an enhanced $500,000 deduction for shares in qualified small business corporations and for qualified farm properties.

Limiting Its Scope

11-69.   Without reviewing the long history of this legislation, changes to the original legislation have limited the use of this valuable deduction to dispositions involving qualified farm properties, qualified fishing properties, and shares of qualified small business corporations. These changes left in place a number of issues related to determining the adjusted cost base of assets that had previously qualified for the deduction. However, at this time, these issues are no longer of sufficient importance to warrant coverage in a general text such as this.

Current And Future Limits

11-70.   As of 2020, the deduction limit for dispositions of shares of qualified small business corporations is $883,384. This is an indexed figure that was established at $800,000 in 2014 and is indexed each year for inflation. The available deduction for qualified farm property and qualified fishing property was increased to $1,000,000 for dispositions after April 20, 2015. The $1,000,000 limit will remain unchanged until the indexed limit for qualified small business shares exceeds $1,000,000. At that time the same indexed figure will apply to all types of qualified property. For 2020, the extra amount for farm or fishing properties is $116,616 ($1,000,000 - $883,384).

11-71.   You should note that the limits are cumulative for all three types of qualified property. That is, you do not get $883,384 for qualified small business shares and an additional $1,000,000 for qualified farm and fishing property. Given that we have two different limits, there is a problem in applying a cumulative limit. The solution is that gains on all three types of qualified property are accumulated until they reach the indexed figure ($883,384 for 2020). To go beyond this to the $1,000,000 limit, only gains on dispositions of farm or fishing property are eligible, even if gains on these types of property are included in the first $883,384.

> **EXAMPLE**   In 2019, Mary Geary has a $500,000 gain on a qualified farm property and a $300,000 gain on shares of a qualified small business corporation. In October 2020, Mary has a $75,000 gain on a qualified farm property and a $100,000 gain on shares of a qualified small business corporation.

> **ANALYSIS**   In 2019, both gains, a total of $800,000, would qualify for the lifetime capital gains deduction. In 2020, only $83,384 of the gain on the qualified small business shares could be eliminated through the use of the lifetime capital gains deduction. The remaining $16,616 ($100,000 - $83,384) would not be eligible as it exceeds the indexed limit for qualified small business shares. However, the $75,000 gain on the qualified farm property could be eliminated with the lifetime capital gains deduction, bringing the total claimed to $958,384 ($800,000 + $83,384 + $75,000).

Qualified Property

Types Of Property

11-72.   The ITA 110.6 lifetime capital gains deduction is available on a disposition of shares of a qualified small business corporation and interests in qualified farm and fishing properties. As it is the most common application of this provision, we will focus our attention on shares of qualified small business corporations. With respect to the other two types of qualified property, they can be generally described as follows:

Qualified Farm or Fishing Property   Qualified farm property and qualified fishing property are defined in ITA 110.6(1). They include real property and Class 14.1 assets used in Canada for farming or fishing by a taxpayer, the taxpayer's spouse, or their children. The definition also includes a share of a family farm or fishing corporation and an interest in a family farm or fishing partnership. To qualify, during the 24 months preceding the disposition, the property must not be owned by anyone other than the selling taxpayer, his or her spouse or common-law partner, his or her children, or his or her parents.

Small Business Corporations

11-73.   As noted in our discussion of Business Investment Losses in Paragraph 11-55, ITA 248(1) defines a small business corporation as a Canadian controlled private corporation (CCPC) of which all, or substantially all (90 percent or more), of the fair market value of its assets are used in an active business carried on primarily (more than 50 percent) in Canada. In order to be a qualified small business corporation for the purposes of the lifetime capital gains deduction, the corporation is only required to satisfy this definition of a small business corporation at the point in time at which the shares are sold.

11-74.   In many cases this is not a difficult criterion to satisfy. If, at a particular point in time, less than 90 percent of the fair market value of the corporation's assets are involved in producing active business income, it is often a simple matter to sell some of the non-qualifying assets and distribute the proceeds to the shareholders. This process, commonly referred to as "the purification of a small business corporation", can normally be carried out in a short period of time, thereby satisfying the small business corporation criteria prior to the disposition of the shares.

Qualified Small Business Corporations

11-75.   Not all small business corporations are qualified small business corporations. To achieve this stature, ITA 110.6(1) requires that two other conditions be met. In somewhat simplified terms, they are:

- the shares must not be owned by anyone other than the taxpayer or a related person for at least 24 months preceding the disposition; and

- throughout this 24 month period, more than 50 percent of the fair market value of the corporation's assets must be used in an active business carried on primarily in Canada.

11-76.   There are additional rules that are applicable when intercorporate investments are involved in the preceding determinations. More specifically, additional requirements apply when the condition that 50 percent of the assets must be used in active business for a 24 month period can only be met by adding in the shares of another small business corporation. These special rules go beyond the scope of this text and, as a result, will not be covered here.

11-77.   As compared to meeting the small business corporation criteria, a failure to meet these additional qualifying criteria is more difficult to correct. As they involve measurements made over a period of time, a failure to satisfy them can only be corrected by the passage of time.

Determining The Deductible Amount

General Rules

11-78.   The determination of the amount of the lifetime capital gains deduction that can be deducted in a year involves calculations that can be complex. In general terms, the available deduction is the least of the following three items:

- Capital Gains Deduction Available
- Annual Gains Limit
- Cumulative Gains Limit

11-79.   These items will be explained in detail in the following material.

Capital Gains Deduction Available

11-80.   The "capital gains deduction available" is the lifetime maximum for the capital gains deduction, less any amounts that have been used up in preceding years. As discussed and illustrated with an example in Paragraph 11-71, there are two limits:

- For shares of qualified small business corporations, the limit for 2020 is $441,692 [(1/2) ($883,384)].

- For qualified farm and fishing properties the limit is $500,000 [(1/2)($1,000,000)].

11-81.   A problem can arise in determining the amounts used up in years prior to 2000. Clearly, it would not be appropriate to subtract a $12,000 deduction made in 1990 which represented the taxable three-quarters of a $16,000 capital gain, from the 2019 limit of $441,692, which is based on one-half of the limit. However, as noted in Paragraph 11-44, the inclusion rate has been at one-half since 2000. Given this, we will not complicate our lifetime capital gains deduction calculations with this issue as it is now much less common.

Annual Gains Limit

11-82.   The annual gains limit is defined in ITA 110.6(1) as follows:

Annual Gains Limit of an individual for a taxation year means the amount determined by the formula

$$A - B\text{, where}$$

A is equal to the lesser of:

- net taxable capital gains for the current year on all capital asset dispositions [ITA 3(b)]; and
- net taxable capital gains for the current year on dispositions of qualified farm property, qualified fishing property, and qualified small business corporation shares.

B is equal to the total of:

- the amount, if any, by which net capital loss carry overs deducted for the year under ITA 111(1)(b) exceeds the excess of net taxable capital gains for the year [ITA 3(b)] over the amount determined in Part A of this formula; and
- Allowable Business Investment Losses realized during the current year.

11-83.   The annual gains limit formula is made complex by the possibility of having a capital gain on an asset that is not eligible for the deduction in the same year that there is a capital gain on a qualified property. In a year in which there is a capital gain on a qualified property and no other capital gains, the formula can be stated more simply as follows:

Annual gains limit is equal to the taxable capital gains on qualified property, less:

- Allowable capital losses realized.
- Net capital loss carry overs deducted.
- Allowable Business Investment Losses realized.

11-84.   We will make use of this abbreviated formula when the only capital gains during the year are those on qualified property.

11-85.   Additional points here are as follows:

- With respect to the Allowable Business Investment Losses realized, the full amount is subtracted in the preceding formula, without regard to whether they have been deducted in the calculation of Net Income For Tax Purposes. Also keep in mind that the amount of Allowable Business Investment Losses realized is based only on those amounts that have not been disallowed by the previous use of the lifetime capital gains deduction.

- As a further point here, the deduction of net capital loss carry forwards is discretionary. This means that, in cases where there is the possibility of using either the lifetime capital gains deduction or a net capital loss carry forward, the individual must choose between the two alternatives. This is inherent in the annual gains limit formula which, in most situations, will reduce the limit on a dollar for dollar basis for net capital loss carry overs deducted.

While this choice between the two alternatives may have no influence on the current year's Taxable Income, we would suggest a preference for making maximum use of the lifetime capital gains deduction. There is no time limit on using the net capital loss carry forward and, more importantly, it can be used when any type of taxable capital gain is realized. In contrast, the lifetime capital gains deduction can only be used for particular types of capital gains.

Exercise Eleven - 7

Subject: Annual Gains Limit

On January 1, 2020, your client, Miss Jana Slovena, has a net capital loss carry forward from 2018 of $45,000. During 2020, Miss Slovena has the following:

- taxable capital gains on sales of real estate in the amount of $114,000
- allowable capital losses of $82,000
- a taxable capital gain of $42,000 on sales of shares in a qualified small business corporation
- an Allowable Business Investment Loss of $3,000 on sales of shares of a small business corporation that does not qualify for the lifetime capital gains deduction

As she does not expect to have additional capital gains in the near future, Miss Slovena has asked you to deduct the full $45,000 of the 2018 net capital loss during 2020. Determine her annual gains limit for 2020 using this approach. What advice would you give Ms. Slovena regarding her net capital loss?

SOLUTION available in print and online Study Guide.

Cumulative Net Investment Loss (CNIL)

11-86.   Many individuals who have high income invest in products that are, in general, referred to as tax shelters. Such products include limited partnerships, certain types of investments in resource properties and, in some situations, real estate. These investments, while producing positive overall results for investors, also generate significant tax savings. Hence the name tax shelter. The government concluded that it was inequitable for individuals to simultaneously deduct such investment losses while sheltering capital gains through the use of the lifetime capital gains deduction. As a result, the legislation restricts the use of the lifetime capital gains deduction by an individual's Cumulative Net Investment Losses (CNIL).

11-87.   CNIL is defined as the amount by which the aggregate of investment expenses for the current year and prior years ending after 1987 exceeds the aggregate of investment income for that period. That is, the CNIL consists of post-1987 investment expenses minus investment income. You should note that, in this context, both investment income and investment expense are defined in the *Income Tax Act*. As a consequence, they have a meaning that can be different from the meaning associated with the everyday use of these terms.

11-88.   As will be explained in the following material, individuals who have a CNIL will have their ability to use the lifetime capital gains deduction reduced. As a result, if qualified capital gains are anticipated, it is advantageous to minimize any CNIL. Some examples of ways in which the impact of the CNIL can be reduced are as follows:

- Realizing capital gains on qualified assets early, if Cumulative Net Investment Losses are anticipated in future years.

- Delaying the disposition of qualified assets with accrued capital gains until the CNIL has been eliminated or reduced as much as possible.

- For owner/managers, having their corporation pay dividends or interest on shareholder loan accounts, rather than salaries, to increase investment income.

Cumulative Gains Limit

11-89.   In somewhat simplified form, the cumulative gains limit can be defined as follows:

The sum of all annual gains limits for the current and previous years, unadjusted for changes in the capital gains inclusion rate. This total is reduced by:

- The sum of all amounts deducted under the lifetime capital gains deduction provision in computing the individual's taxable incomes for preceding taxation years (unadjusted for changes in the capital gains inclusion rate); and
- the individual's CNIL at the end of the year.

11-90.   In the absence of a CNIL balance, this formula would simply be the sum of all annual gains limits, reduced by all of the lifetime capital gains deductions made in previous years. As individuals will normally deduct the full amount of their annual gains limit, this balance will usually be equal to the annual gains limit for the current year. This result can be altered by an individual's failure to deduct the full amount of the annual gains limit in some previous year, either as a tax planning choice or as the result of a CNIL balance.

11-91.   The following is a simple example of cumulative gains limit calculations.

EXAMPLE   In 2020, Ms. Nolan has $5,600 of deductible interest on loans for investment purposes and $2,600 of net rental income. She has had no investment income or investment expenses in years prior to 2020, so her Cumulative Net Investment Loss (CNIL) is $3,000 ($5,600 - $2,600). During August 2020, she has a $60,000 taxable capital gain on the sale of shares in a qualified small corporation. Ms. Nolan has no other capital gains or losses in 2020.

ANALYSIS   As she has made no previous use of her lifetime capital gains deduction, her unused lifetime limit for qualified small business shares is $441,692. While her annual gains limit would be $60,000, the amount of the taxable capital gain, her ability to use the lifetime capital gains deduction would be reduced by her CNIL as her cumulative gains limit is only $57,000 ($60,000 - $3,000).

Comprehensive Example

11-92.   The example that follows illustrates the basic rules involved in the application of the lifetime capital gains deduction.

EXAMPLE   Dwight Treadway's 2020 Net Income For Tax Purposes is as follows:

Employment Income	$ 60,000
Taxable Capital Gain On The Sale Of	
Shares In A Qualified Small Business Corporation	200,000
Net Income For Tax Purposes	$260,000

In 2014, Mr. Treadway realized a $20,000 taxable capital gain [(1/2)($40,000)] from the sale of shares in a qualified small business corporation and used his lifetime capital gains deduction to claim a deduction for this amount. In 2013, Mr. Treadway realized an allowable capital loss of $9,000 [(1/2)($18,000)]. He was not able to use the loss in that year, or any other year, and he intends to deduct it as a net capital loss carry forward in 2020. Other than the 2014 taxable capital gain of $20,000 and the 2013 allowable capital loss of $9,000, Mr. Treadway had no capital gains, capital losses, loss carry overs, or Business Investment Losses from 2013 through 2020. He has no CNIL balance in 2020.

ANALYSIS   For 2020, the maximum deduction under ITA 110.6 would be the least of the following amounts:

- **Capital Gains Deduction Available = $421,692**   ($441,692 - $20,000).

- **Annual Gains Limit = $191,000**   As Mr. Treadway has had no capital gains on non-qualified property in 2020, we can use the simplified version of this calculation. (See Paragraph 11-83.) This would result in an annual gains limit of $191,000, the $200,000 taxable capital gain for the year, less the 2014 net capital loss carry forward of $9,000 deducted under ITA 111(1)(b).

- **Cumulative Gains Limit = $191,000**   As the annual gains limit for 2014 would be equal to the $20,000 taxable capital gain on qualifying property, the sum of the annual gains limits would be $211,000 ($20,000 + $191,000). Subtracting from this the $20,000 lifetime capital gains deduction for 2014 leaves the cumulative gains limit of $191,000.

11-93.   Given these calculations, the maximum deduction for 2020 would be $191,000, the amount of both the annual gains limit and the cumulative gains limit. The full $200,000 gain on the shares could have been deducted if Mr. Treadway had not chosen to deduct the net capital loss carry forward. The deduction of this amount reduced both the annual gains limit and the cumulative gains limit by $9,000. It would be advisable for Mr. Treadway not to deduct any of the net capital loss carry forward. If he did this, his annual gains limit would increase to $200,000. Although he would have used $9,000 more of his lifetime capital gains deduction, his tax liability for 2020 would not change and he would still have a net capital loss carry forward of $9,000 that could be applied against any type of capital gain for an unlimited period of time.

Exercise Eleven - 8

Subject: Lifetime Capital Gains Deduction (ITA 110.6 Deduction)

Mr. Edwin Loussier had a 2013 taxable capital gain on shares of a qualified small business corporation of $5,000 [(1/2)($10,000)] and a 2015 taxable capital gain on shares of a qualified small business corporation of $13,000 [(1/2)($26,000)]. He used his ITA 110.6 lifetime capital gains deduction to eliminate both of these gains. He has no other capital gains, capital losses, or Business Investment Losses in the period 2013 through 2018. In December 2019, he has a $63,000 capital loss which, because he has no capital gains in that year, he cannot deduct. In 2020, he has a $510,000 capital gain on the sale of shares of a qualified small business corporation. In addition, he deducts the $63,000 capital loss from 2019. Mr. Loussier does not have a CNIL balance. Determine Mr. Loussier's maximum lifetime capital gains deduction for 2020. Provide all of the calculations required to determine the maximum ITA 110.6 deduction.

SOLUTION available in print and online Study Guide.

We suggest you work Self Study Problem Eleven-3 at this point.

Ordering Of Deductions And Losses

Significance Of Ordering

11-94.   If an individual has sufficient income to absorb all of the losses and deductions that are available in the calculation of Taxable Income, the question of ordering is not important. The real significance of provisions covering the ordering of losses and other deductions is in the determination of the amounts and types of items that can be carried over to previous or subsequent years.

11-95.   For example, assume that a taxpayer has taxable capital gains of $25,000, a business loss of $25,000, and allowable capital losses of $25,000. No matter how these items are ordered, the Net Income For Tax Purposes will be nil. However, it does make a difference whether the loss carry over is for the business loss or for the net capital losses. A net capital loss carry forward can only be deducted to the extent of taxable capital gains in the carry forward period. On the other hand, the non-capital losses can only be used for a limited period of time (20 years) while, by contrast, the net capital losses can be carried forward indefinitely. Note, however, with a time limit of 20 years, having a limited carry forward period of this length is not likely to be a significant factor in most situations.

Ordering In Computing Net Income For Tax Purposes

11-96.   The basic rules for the computation of Net Income For Tax Purposes under Division B are found in ITA 3. In computing Net Income For Tax Purposes, ITA 3 indicates that we begin by adding together positive amounts of income from non-capital sources, plus net taxable capital gains. Net taxable capital gains are defined as the amount, if any, by which the current year's taxable capital gains exceed the current year's allowable capital losses. This, in effect, requires that capital losses, to the extent there are capital gains during the year, be deducted prior to the deduction of any other type of loss.

11-97.   The various deductions available under Subdivision e (RRSP deductions, spousal support paid, child care costs, moving expenses, etc.) are subtracted from this total. If a positive balance remains, the final step in computing Net Income For Tax Purposes is to subtract any employment, business, or property losses, as well as Allowable Business Investment Losses. If this process does not seem familiar to you, you might want to review the material on ITA 3 that is contained in Chapter 1.

Ordering In Computing Taxable Income

11-98.   The ordering rules in ITA 3 are applicable to all taxpayers - individuals, corporation and trusts. Further, they are not discretionary. Items that occur during a given taxation year, must be added or deducted in that year. In contrast, the ordering rule in ITA 111.1 only applies to individuals. Under this rule, the order in which Division C items must be deducted is as follows:

- Various deductions provided by ITA 110 (e.g., stock options)
- Retroactive lump sum payments under ITA 110.2
- Loss carry overs under ITA 111 (non-capital, net capital, and farm)
- Lifetime capital gains deduction under ITA 110.6
- Northern residents deductions under ITA 110.7

11-99.   Within ITA 111 (loss carry overs), available amounts can be deducted in any order the taxpayer wishes. The only constraint is the ITA 111(3)(b) requirement that, within a particular type of loss (e.g., non-capital losses), the oldest losses have to be deducted first.

11-100.   When several different types of loss carry overs are available, decisions in this area can be difficult. On the one hand, certain types of carry overs have a limited period of availability (i.e., non-capital losses and farm losses can be carried forward for 20 years). In contrast, net capital losses have no time limit, but can only be deducted to the extent of taxable capital gains that have been realized in the year. Restricted farm loss carry overs and carry overs of losses on listed personal property have more onerous limitations. These losses are restricted with respect to both time and type of income (e.g., restricted farm loss carry forwards are available for 20 years and can only be deducted to the extent of farm income earned in the year).

11-101.   Decisions in this area will involve a careful weighing of which type of loss carry over is most likely to have continued usefulness in future years. For example, if a non-capital loss carry forward is 19 years old and the business is expecting no Taxable Income in the following year, then use of this carry forward would appear to be a prudent course of action. An additional constraint is that the deduction of loss carry overs should leave sufficient Taxable Income that Tax Payable does not become less than the amount of available tax credits. As discussed in Paragraph 11-26 through 11-29, tax credits that are not used during the current taxation year are, in general, permanently lost.

Example

11-102.   The following is an example of the ordering rules used in computing Taxable Income for individuals:

> **EXAMPLE**   At the beginning of 2020, Miss Farnum had the following loss carry forwards available:
>
> | | |
> |---|---|
> | Non-Capital Losses | $40,000 |
> | Net Capital Losses [(1/2)($20,000)] | 10,000 |
> | Restricted Farm Losses | 5,000 |
>
> For 2020, she can claim only the basic personal amount of $13,229. Also during 2020, she has no available Subdivision e deductions. For this year, she had the following income amounts as calculated under Division B rules:
>
> | | |
> |---|---|
> | Employment Income | $15,000 |
> | Property Income (Interest) | 4,000 |
> | Farm Income | 2,000 |
> | Income From Sole Proprietorship | 15,000 |
> | Capital Gains | 12,000 |
>
> **ANALYSIS**   Miss Farnum's 2020 Net Income For Tax Purposes and Taxable Income would be calculated as follows:
>
> | | | |
> |---|---|---|
> | Income Under ITA 3(a): | | |
> | Employment Income | $15,000 | |
> | Property Income | 4,000 | |
> | Farming Income | 2,000 | |
> | Business Income (Proprietorship) | 15,000 | $36,000 |
> | Income Under ITA 3(b): | | |
> | Taxable Capital Gains [(1/2)($12,000)] | | 6,000 |
> | **Net Income For Tax Purposes** | | **$42,000** |
> | Restricted Farm Loss Carry Forward (Limited to farming income) | | (2,000) |
> | Net Capital Loss Carry Forward (Limited to taxable capital gains) | | (6,000) |
> | Subtotal | | $34,000 |
> | Non-Capital Loss Carry Forward ($34,000 - $13,229) | | (20,771) |
> | **Taxable Income = Basic Personal Amount** | | **$13,229** |
>
> **Loss Carry Forwards**
>
> | | |
> |---|---|
> | • Restricted farm loss carry forward ($5,000 - $2,000) | $ 3,000 |
> | • Net capital loss carry forward ($10,000 - $6,000) | 4,000 |
> | • Non-capital loss carry forward ($40,000 - $20,771) | 19,229 |

11-103. Note that, in this example, the amount of net capital and restricted farm losses deducted was limited by the amount of the taxable capital gains and farm income. The non-capital loss deducted was limited to the amount that would reduce her Taxable Income to her basic personal amount of $13,229. Since her Tax Payable will be nil at this point, there is no reason to deduct any further amount of the non-capital loss available.

Exercise Eleven - 9

Subject: Ordering Of Losses

At the beginning of 2020, Alan Barter had the following loss carry forwards available:

Restricted Farm Losses	$ 8,000
Non-Capital Losses	36,000
Net Capital Losses [(1/2)($40,000)]	20,000

During 2020, he had the following amounts of income:

Taxable Capital Gains	$ 9,000
Business Income	12,000
Employment Income	56,000
Farm Income	3,500

Determine Alan's Net Income For Tax Purposes, as well as his minimum Taxable Income for 2020. Indicate the amount and type of any losses available for carry forward at the end of the year.

SOLUTION available in print and online Study Guide.

Tax Payable Overview

General

11-104. Chapter 4 provided detailed coverage of the application of federal tax rates to Taxable Income in order to provide an initial figure for an individual's Tax Payable. In addition, coverage of most of the tax credits available to individuals was provided. The coverage of tax credits was extended in Chapter 7 with coverage of the dividend tax credit, as well as the credit for taxes withheld on foreign source income.

11-105. None of this material will be repeated in this Chapter. However, as many of the Self Study and Assignment Problems that accompany this Chapter are comprehensive in nature and will require you to apply tax calculations and credits, you might wish to review the material in Chapters 4 and 7 before working the problems in this Chapter.

11-106. As was the case with the material on Taxable Income, there are issues involved with the determination of Tax Payable for individuals that could not be dealt with in Chapter 4 because of the need to understand income concepts not presented until subsequent chapters. As a result, additional coverage of Tax Payable is included in this Chapter. Specifically, the following concepts and procedures are discussed in this material:

Tax On Split Income (TOSI) This is a special tax, assessed at the maximum federal rate of 33 percent on certain types of income received from a related source.

Transfer Of Dividends To A Spouse Or Common-Law Partner The calculations related to this tax credit require an understanding of the dividend gross up and tax credit procedures, which were not introduced until Chapter 7.

Charitable Donations The basic calculation of this tax credit was presented in Chapter 4. However, it was not possible to deal with gifts of capital property until the material in Chapters 5 through 8 on business income, property income, and capital gains had been covered.

Foreign Tax Credits   These credits were introduced in Chapter 7. However, the full determination of the eligible amounts requires the additional material on Taxable Income that is included in this Chapter.

11-107.   Now that we have covered the material in Chapters 5 to 10, we are in a position to complete our coverage of the determination of Tax Payable for individuals.

Basic Federal Tax Payable

11-108.   Basic federal Tax Payable is a figure from which some, but not all tax credits have been deducted. At one time, this was an important figure in that it was the base that the provinces and territories used in calculating their respective provincial Tax Payable. Since the provinces now base provincial taxes on Taxable Income, the basic federal tax figure is no longer of general importance.

11-109.   This concept does have some limited use in specialized situations and, because of this, you will see references to this figure in the T1 tax return. The most important of these is that it is used to calculate the additional federal Tax Payable that must be paid by individuals who are deemed Canadian residents but do not reside in a province (e.g., members of the Canadian Armed Forces stationed outside of Canada). However, other than indicating that this concept exists, we will give basic federal Tax Payable no further consideration.

Tax On Split Income (TOSI)

A Note Of Caution

11-110.   The 2000 introduction of the TOSI had a very dramatic impact on tax planning involving related minors. Perhaps even more dramatic was the impact of the 2018 expansion of this tax to include related adults. Because of this impact, the related legislation needed to be very complex in order to prevent the creation of various arrangements which would avoid this extremely onerous tax.

11-111.   Unfortunately, the complexity of the legislation was accompanied by an unusual lack of clarity in the meaning of some of its provisions. This has resulted in a situation where dealing with the TOSI has become one of the more difficult areas of tax practice.

11-112.   The goal of the material that follows is to provide students and general practitioners with an overview of this material and its application in relatively simple situations. It does not contain sufficient depth or detail to be used by an individual who has to deal with TOSI issues as part of their tax practice.

Background

The Problem

11-113.   As discussed in Chapter 1, income splitting is one of the most powerful weapons in the tax planner's arsenal. If an individual with large amounts of income in the top 33 percent federal tax bracket can find a way to channel parts of this income to related parties with either no income or income that leaves them in a lower tax bracket, the tax savings can be significant. Further, in many situations the savings can be repeated year after year.

11-114.   As we have seen in earlier chapters, some amount of income splitting is available to all taxpayers without the use of complicated tax structures. The use of spousal RRSPs and the ability to split certain types of pension income are examples of provisions that allow some amount of income splitting. The government appears to be comfortable with these arrangements based on the fact that they are generally available to all Canadian taxpayers that have a spouse or common-law partner.

11-115.   What did make the government uncomfortable was the ability of wealthy individuals to use more complex tax structures to transfer large amounts of their income to related parties, typically their spouse or their children.

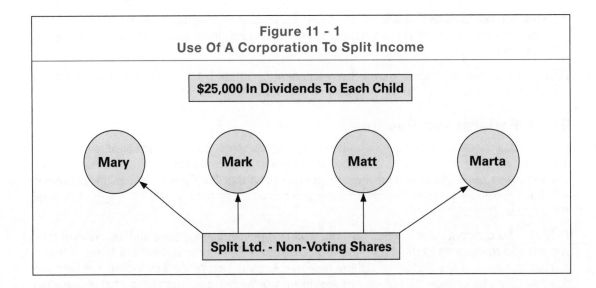

Figure 11 - 1
Use Of A Corporation To Split Income

$25,000 In Dividends To Each Child

Mary   Mark   Matt   Marta

Split Ltd. - Non-Voting Shares

EXAMPLE Melissa Hanson is a very successful individual with annual Net Income For Tax Purposes that regularly places her well into the maximum tax bracket. She owns all of the voting shares in a Canadian controlled private corporation, Split Ltd. Her four children (Mary, Mark, Matt, and Marta) hold all of the Split Ltd. non-voting shares. They had acquired the shares with their own funds.

None of the children have any income of their own, other than dividends received from Split Ltd. During the current year, the corporation pays dividends of $25,000 per year to each child. This situation is illustrated in Figure 11-1.

11-116.   Prior to the 2000 introduction of the TOSI, the amount of dividends received by each child could have been received tax free. (The amount of tax free dividends that can be received by an individual with no other source of income is explained in Chapter 15.) In contrast, if she had received the same amount of dividends, Melissa would have been taxed on such dividends at a rate of around 45 percent, depending on the province. This arrangement for allocating Split Ltd. income to her children would provide an annual savings of around $45,000 [($100,000)(45% - Nil)].

The Basic TOSI Model

11-117.   While we will define these terms more completely in the material that follows, the TOSI rules are applicable to Split Income. This type of income can occur when Specified Individuals (Melissa's children in our example) receive income from a business that is a Related Business (Split Ltd.) with respect to a Specified Individual because of the involvement of the Source Individual (Melissa) in that business. You should note that there are many exceptions to the applicability of these provisions and when they occur, even in situations such as in our example, the term Split Income is not applicable.

11-118.   For amounts of income that are identified as Split Income, the rules are very harsh. Such amounts are subject to the maximum federal tax rate of 33 percent. When this is combined with maximum provincial rates, the result is that such income is taxed at rates as high as 54 percent, the actual rate depending on the province.

11-119.   This provision effectively converted such situations as that illustrated in Figure 11-1 from an effective income splitting arrangement to an arrangement that had no tax benefits. Melissa's children will pay the same taxes on the dividends they received as Melissa would have paid had she received the dividends.

The 2018 TOSI Changes

11-120.   The original version of the TOSI, which became effective in 2000, applied only to related persons who were under the age of 18 at the end of the taxation year, were resident in Canada, and who had a parent who was resident in Canada. Because of this, it was sometimes referred to as the "kiddie tax".

11-121.   Further, the definition of Split Income in the 2000 legislation only included dividends from private companies, shareholder benefits on loans received from a private company, or, in some cases, income from a partnership or trust if the income is derived from the provision of property or services to a business.

11-122.   There is little question that the 2000 introduction of the TOSI served to curtail income splitting with related minors. However, it was also clear that similar income splitting benefits were being achieved both with other types of income and with related individuals 18 years of age and over. Of particular concern was the use by a parent of various income splitting arrangements to finance the post-secondary education for their children. This specific concern is reflected in the 2018 TOSI legislation, which singles out individuals in the 18 to 24 age group for less favourable treatment than is afforded to older related persons.

11-123.   Reflecting these concerns, the TOSI legislation that became effective in 2018 expands coverage of this tax in two ways:

Types Of Income   As noted, the original TOSI legislation generally limited its coverage to private company dividends, shareholder benefits, and some types of partnership and trust income. Under the current legislation, its coverage has been expanded to include interest received on debt issued by a private corporation, as well as some capital gains on the disposition of private company shares.

Types Of Individuals   The applicability of the TOSI has been expanded to include all Canadian residents, without regard to age.

11-124.   The current TOSI provisions came into effect on January 1, 2018. Complete coverage of these provisions could occupy an entire Chapter in this text, a result which would not be appropriate in a general text such as this. Our coverage will be limited to fairly basic situations and will not deal with the many complications that are found in the complete legislative provisions. While this will provide both students and professionals with a basic understanding of these provisions, this presentation will not provide a satisfactory reference for individuals dealing with complex, real-world cases.

Determining Applicability

Relevant Individuals

11-125.   Determining the applicability of the TOSI involves identifying two classifications of individuals. These classifications are defined in ITA 120.4(1) and can be described as follows:

A Specified Individual   is an individual who is resident in Canada at the end of the year. A further condition for an individual who has not attained the age of 17 before the start of the year is that they must have a parent resident in Canada at any time during the year.

While any Canadian resident could be a Specified Individual, in applying the TOSI, such individuals will generally be a low income individual related to a Source Individual in a high tax bracket.

A Source Individual   is any individual who, at any time during the year, is resident in Canada and related to the Specified Individual.

In applying the TOSI, Source Individuals will generally be high tax bracket individuals who are attempting to split income with related low tax bracket individuals.

11-126.   You will notice the extreme breadth of these definitions. Every Canadian resident is a potential Specified Individual. In turn, this means that any person related to that individual could be a Source Individual. Most typical situations would involve a Source Individual operating a private company, with his or her spouse and/or children being identified as Specified Individuals. However, there are a great many potential relationships that could be viewed as a Specified Individual who is related to a Source Individual.

Related Business

11-127. In somewhat simplified terms, a business is a related business to a Specified Individual if the income received by that individual is from a business where:

- in the case of a proprietorship, partnership, or corporation, a Source Individual with respect to the Specified Individual is actively and regularly engaged in the business; or

- a Source Individual with respect to that Specified Individual has an ownership interest. In the case of a corporation, this definition would apply when the Source Individual owns 10 percent or more of the fair market value of all issued and outstanding shares of the corporation. For a partnership, any ownership interest would meet this criterion.

11-128. This is, in fact, a very confusing concept. For purposes of the TOSI, the term Related Business refers to a relationship between the business and the Specified Individual that results from the ownership of, or the involvement in that business by, the Source Individual. This is confusing terminology in that, in many cases, the business and the Source Individual would also be considered related because of other provisions in the *Income Tax Act* (e.g., under ITA 251(2)(b), a corporation is related to a person who controls it). This is not the meaning of "related" that is relevant under the TOSI legislation.

11-129. As an additional point here, we would note that, while the share ownership criteria is easy to apply, the concept of "actively engaged in the business" is not clearly defined and likely to be the source of disputes with taxpayers.

Split Income

11-130. The actual ITA 120.4(1) definition of Split Income is lengthy and complex. However, for purposes of our coverage, the following items may be classified as Split Income if they are received by a Specified Individual, either directly or indirectly:

- Dividends from a private company that is a Related Business.

- Shareholder benefits or loans from a Related Business.

- Interest from a Related Business.

- Distributions from a proprietorship, or partnership if they are a Related Business.

- Capital gains on the disposition of private company shares if it is a Related Business.

- Distributions from trusts where the source of the income is a Related Business.

11-131. You should note that employment income is not on this list. Employment income is specifically excluded from Split Income, even in situations where it is received from a Related Business.

Excluded Amounts

General Approach

11-132. The items listed in Paragraph 11-130 are potential Split Income amounts. However, there are a number of Excluded Amounts and if the item is eligible for one of these exclusions, it is not considered Split Income and will not be subject to the TOSI. Only items that remain after Excluded Amounts are identified will be subject to this tax.

11-133. As with the other amounts we have described, Excluded Amounts are defined under ITA 120.4(1). The analysis of the various Excluded Amounts is complicated by the fact that some of the defined amounts are only available to individuals in certain age groups. Based on this, we have organized our description of the various Excluded Amounts by age group. Note, however, the available amounts overlap these age groups (e.g., an Excluded Amount that is available to individuals over 18 is also available to the 18 to 24 age group).

Excluded Amounts Available To Individuals Under 25

11-134. The only Excluded Amount that is available to all individuals under 25 is income or taxable capital gains from a property that is acquired as the result of:

- the death of a parent; or

- the death of any person, provided the individual is either:

  - enrolled as a full time student at a post-secondary educational institution; or
  - eligible for the disability tax credit.

Excluded Amounts For Individuals Age 18 And Over

11-135. One of the most important of the Excluded Amounts involves the concept of an Excluded Business. This concept can be described as follows:

EXCLUDED BUSINESS (Taxpayers Age 18 And Over)   Amounts received from an Excluded Business are not considered Split Income and are not subject to the TOSI. An Excluded Business is one in which the taxpayer is actively engaged on a regular, continuous, and substantial basis. This active engagement must be in the current taxation year or in at least five prior taxation years. Note, however, the years do not have to be current or consecutive. That is, any five years of active engagement will satisfy this condition.

To simplify the application of this rule, the CRA guidance on the TOSI has provided what is referred to as a "bright line" test. This test requires that the taxpayer work in the business an average of at least 20 hours per week during the time the business is in operation. Note that, if the business is seasonal (e.g., a landscaping business), the 20 hours per week requirement is only required for the portion of the year during which the business operates.

The CRA materials also note that a failure to meet this bright line test does not necessarily prevent the taxpayer from using the Excluded Business exception. Whether or not an individual is actively engaged will depend on the facts and circumstances in individual cases.

Excluded Amounts For Individuals Age 25 And Over

11-136.   There are two types of Excluded Amounts that are generally available to taxpayers age 25 and over. The first, Excluded Shares, can be described as follows:

EXCLUDED SHARES   Amounts received from Excluded Shares are not considered Split Income and are not subject to the TOSI. For shares to be classified as Excluded Shares, the taxpayer must own, in terms of both fair market value and voting rights, at least 10 percent of the outstanding shares of the corporation. In addition, the corporation must meet the following conditions:

- It must not be a professional corporation. ITA 248(1) defines a professional corporation as a corporation that carries on the professional practice of an accountant, dentist, lawyer, medical doctor, veterinarian, or chiropractor. Corporations carrying on the practice of other professionals, for example architects, do not fall within this definition.
- Less than 90 percent of its income in the previous year is from the provision of services.
- Less than 10 percent of its income in the previous year was from a related business.

11-137.   The second type of Excluded Amount can be described as follows:

REASONABLENESS TEST   If the income received by the individual represents a reasonable return, taking into consideration labour contributions, the assumption of business risk, as well as capital contributions, it will not be Split Income and will not be subject to the TOSI.

Excluded Amounts For Individuals Age 18 to 24

11-138.   The TOSI legislation indicates two Excluded Amounts for this group of individuals.

SAFE HARBOUR CAPITAL RETURN   For the income of these individuals to be excluded from the TOSI, it must represent a Safe Harbour Capital Return. This is based on the lowest prescribed rate applied to the capital contributions made by the individual.

REASONABLENESS TEST (Taxpayers Age 18 To 24)   This second reasonableness test is based on a return on contributed capital only, with no consideration of other contributions made to the business by the Specified Individual. This is a much more restrictive test than the one that is available to individuals age 25 and over.

11-139.   It is unlikely that this reasonableness test will be widely available to Specified Individuals. It would be unusual for an individual in this age bracket to have been able to accumulate a large amount of capital to contribute to a business. However, when this does occur, it prevents income from the business being classified as Split Income.

Excluded Amounts Available To Individuals Of Any Age

11-140.   The following amounts are Excluded Amounts for an individual of any age, including under 18:

Capital Gains On Qualified Property   Split Income does not include capital gains on qualified property that is eligible for the lifetime capital gains deduction. This is true even if the lifetime capital gains deduction is not claimed.

Property Acquired Through Marriage Breakdown   Split Income does not include amounts that a Specified Individual receives from a property that is acquired as a result of a marriage breakdown agreement. This only applies to property received under a written agreement. Further, it does not apply to property that the Specified Individual owned prior to the marriage breakdown.

Property Acquired As The Result Of The Death Of A Parent Or Other Individual
Split Income does not include income resulting from property received as the result of the death of a parent or other individual.

Spouse Is 65 Or Older   For a number of years, legislation has allowed spouses and common-law partners to split pension income (see coverage in Chapter 9). An additional exception has been added to the TOSI legislation to allow a similar result for amounts that might be considered Split Income.

Specifically, Split Income does not include income received by a spouse of any age if that income would not have been Split Income if it had been received by their spouse who is 65 years of age or older.

11-141.   In many cases, the process of determining whether there are Excluded Amounts will be very complex. When this is combined with the procedures needed to identify related Source Individuals and potential Split Income amounts, most individuals who use their businesses to Split Income will require professional advice.

11-142.   That being said, the importance of making good decisions in this area is crucial. As will be demonstrated in the next section, the TOSI is a very costly tax. It can turn what was intended to be a source of tax reduction through income splitting into a situation that actually has a tax cost to the taxpayer.

Calculation Of The Tax

The Tax Credit Problem

11-143.   When a Specified Individual has received Split Income, their Tax Payable is made up of two components. The first component is based on a calculation that, under ITA 20(1)(ww), removes the Specified Individual's Split Income from the total. This can create a problem in determining tax credits that are income tested.

EXAMPLE   Josh Browning has Taxable Income of $250,000, while his spouse Maria has Taxable Income of $15,000, all of which is Split Income. When the deduction is made under ITA 20(1)(ww), the remaining balance of Maria's Income will be nil.

ANALYSIS   The problem with this result is that if the nil amount was used for calculating income tested tax credits, the subtraction of the Split Income would result in the creation of a spousal tax credit for Josh of $1,810 [(15%)($13,229 - nil)]. In contrast, if there had been no Split Income subtraction, Maria's income would exceed the 2019 base for the spousal tax credit of $13,229, resulting in no spousal tax credit for Josh.

The government did not believe that this was an appropriate result and added ITA 118(4)(a.2). This provision indicates that for purposes of determining personal tax credits, the Net Income figure that would be used would be before the ITA 20(1)(ww) deduction. This means that Josh's spousal tax credit would be nil ($13,229 - $15,000).

Two Components

11-144.   With the ITA 20(1)(ww) subtraction, the taxpayer's income is made up of two components:

Split Income Component   This component will be subject to a federal flat rate of 33 percent. The only credits against the resulting Tax Payable will be dividend tax credits, foreign tax credits that relate to the amounts included in Split Income, and the disability tax credit.

Regular Income Component   This component will be subject to the regular graduated rates and will be eligible for the usual tax credits, subject to the ITA 118(4)(a.2) provision (see ANALYSIS in Paragraph 11-143).

11-145.   A simple example will serve to illustrate these calculations.

EXAMPLE   Helen, who is 25 years old, receives non-eligible dividends of $20,000 from a private company controlled by her father. In addition, she has interest income of $5,500 from a savings account funded by an inheritance. Her only tax credits are the basic personal credit and the dividend tax credit. She is not eligible for any exclusion from the application of the TOSI.

ANALYSIS   The initial calculation involves determining the tax on total income, reduced by amounts that fall within the definition of Split Income (the non-eligible dividends). All of the usual tax credits can be claimed in this calculation.

Taxable Non-Eligible Dividends [(115%)($20,000)]	$23,000
Interest Income	5,500
Deduction For Split Income - Non-Eligible Dividends	(23,000)
Net Income For Tax Purposes = Taxable Income	$ 5,500
Tax Rate	15%
Tax Payable Before Credits	$ 825
Basic Personal Credit [(15%)($13,229)]	(1,984)
Federal Tax Payable On Regular Income	Nil

The TOSI Payable would be calculated as follows:

Split Income - Taxable Non-Eligible Dividends	$23,000
Tax Rate	33%
Tax Payable Before Dividend Tax Credit	$ 7,590
Dividend Tax Credit [(9/13)(15%)($20,000)]	(2,077)
TOSI Payable	$ 5,513

With the regular component being nil, the total Tax Payable will be $5,513, the amount based on the Split Income sources.

11-146. In some circumstances, Source Individuals may be liable for payment of the TOSI if the Specified Individual fails to make the required payment.

Evaluation

11-147. Both the original kiddie tax legislation, as well as the expansion of the TOSI coverage to adult taxpayers, were met with howls of protest from many in the tax community. In our view, these changes represented appropriate modifications. The type of income splitting that is being attacked in these provisions is, in general, only available to higher income Canadians. It would be difficult to describe our tax system as fair if such arrangements were allowed to continue.

Exercise Eleven - 10

Subject: Tax On Split Income

During 2020, Norton James, who is 16 years old, receives non-eligible dividends of $15,000 from a private corporation controlled by his mother. He also has income of $15,200 from contracts to create computer games. As he has used the income that he has earned from these contracts in previous years to invest in the stock market, he has eligible dividends from publicly traded companies of $8,600. Assume his only tax credits are his basic personal credit and dividend tax credits on the shares that he owns. Determine Norton's federal Tax Payable for 2020.

SOLUTION available in print and online Study Guide.

We suggest you work Self Study Problem Eleven-4 at this point.

Tax Credits Revisited

Transfer Of Dividends To A Spouse Or Common-Law Partner

11-148. There may be situations in which a taxpayer's spousal credit has been reduced or eliminated by dividends received by that spouse. The ITA 82(3) election permits a transfer of all of the dividends from the spouse or common-law partner's income to that of the taxpayer, if it creates or increases the spousal credit. Consider the following example:

EXAMPLE Mrs. Barba's total income consisted of $12,000 in eligible dividends received from taxable Canadian corporations. Mrs. Barba's basic personal tax credit, along with part of the dividend tax credit, eliminate all taxation on the grossed up amount of $16,560 [(138%)($12,000)]. However, because she has this income receipt, Mr. Barba is not able to claim a spousal tax credit.

ANALYSIS In this situation, the transfer of dividends under ITA 82(3) would eliminate all of Mrs. Barba's income, and Mr. Barba would be able to claim the full spousal credit of $1,984. Mr. Barba would then be taxed on the $16,560 of grossed up dividends. He would, however, be eligible for the dividend tax credit associated with these dividends. Whether this is a good alternative or not depends on Mr. Barba's marginal tax rate, as can be seen in the following calculations:

Mr. Barba's Tax Bracket	15%	33%
Increase In Taxable Income	$16,560	$16,560
Tax On $16,560	$ 2,484	$ 5,465
Increase In Spousal Credit	(1,984)	(1,984)
Dividend Tax Credit [(6/11)(38%)($12,000)]	(2,487)	(2,487)
Increase (Decrease) In Tax Payable	($ 1,987)	$ 994

As can be seen in the table, if Mr. Barba is in the 15 percent tax bracket, his federal tax would be decreased by $1,987. Alternatively, if he is in the 33 percent bracket, the transfer would not be desirable as his federal tax would be increased by $994.

Exercise Eleven - 11

Subject: Transfer Of Dividends To A Spouse

Mr. Albert Ho is 38 years old and has over $250,000 in 2020 Taxable Income. His wife's only 2020 source of income is $8,500 in eligible dividends received from taxable Canadian corporations. In terms of federal Tax Payable, would Mr. Ho benefit from the use of the ITA 82(3) election to include the eligible dividends received by his spouse in his Net Income For Tax Purposes? Justify your conclusion.

SOLUTION available in print and online Study Guide.

We suggest you work Self Study Problems Eleven-5 and 6 at this point.

Charitable Donations Credit Revisited
Introduction

11-149.   A basic treatment of this credit was provided in Chapter 4. In that Chapter, we noted that, for individuals, the first $200 of donations was eligible for a tax credit of 15 percent. The rate applicable to additional amounts was either 29 percent or 33 percent depending on the Taxable Income of the donor. In general, the base for calculating this credit was limited to 75 percent of the taxpayer's Net Income For Tax Purposes.

11-150.   In Chapter 4, we dealt only with simple situations involving gifts of cash. Coverage of more complex issues involving gifts of various types of capital property was deferred and is included in this Chapter 11.

11-151.   As many of you are aware, in recent years, a number of gift giving programs have been developed that appear to provide the taxpayer with benefits that exceed his or her cost and, in some cases, the value of the gift to the recipient charity.

11-152.   A classic example of this was the so-called art flips. Such arrangements might involve a taxpayer buying a large block of paintings directly from the inventories of the artist. The cost of the block was essentially a wholesale value and was significantly lower than the sum of the retail prices of the individual paintings. The paintings would then be appraised on the basis of individual retail values, followed by a gift of the art works to a registered charity. The taxpayer would then claim a tax credit based on the significantly higher appraised value, often resulting in a tax credit that was worth more than the original cost of the paintings.

11-153.   Because of problems such as this, ITA 248(30) through ITA 248(41) were added to the *Income Tax Act*. These subsections are intended to curtail the ability of taxpayers to use schemes that abuse the intent of the basic charitable donations legislation.

Donations Classified

11-154.   ITA 118.1 defines four types of charitable donations:

1. **Total Charitable Gifts** is defined to include all eligible amounts donated by an individual to a registered charity, a registered Canadian amateur athletic association, a Canadian municipality, the United Nations or an agency thereof, a university outside of Canada that normally enrolls Canadian students, and a charitable organization outside of Canada to which Her Majesty in right of Canada has made a gift in the year or in the immediately preceding year.

2. **Total Crown Gifts** is defined as the aggregate of eligible amounts donated to Her Majesty in right of Canada or a province.

3. **Total Cultural Gifts** is defined as the aggregate of all eligible gifts of objects that the Canadian Cultural Property Export Review Board has determined meet the criteria of the *Cultural Property And Import Act.*

4. **Total Ecological Gifts** is defined as all eligible gifts of land certified by the Minister of the Environment to be ecologically sensitive land, the conservation and protection of which is important to the preservation of Canada's environmental heritage. The beneficiary of the gift can be any level of government. The beneficiary can also be a registered charity, provided its primary purpose is the conservation and protection of Canada's environmental heritage.

11-155.   In addition to the items specified in the *Act*, under the U.S./Canada tax treaty, Canadians can claim gifts to any qualifying U.S. charity in amounts up to 75 percent of their net U.S. income (75 percent of their net world income if the Canadian resident lives near the U.S. border and commutes to a U.S. place of business or employment).

Eligible Amounts

11-156.   In the preceding material on the classification of donations, each of the definitions contains the term "eligible amounts". The term is defined as follows:

ITA 248(31)   The eligible amount of a gift or monetary contribution is the amount by which the fair market value of the property that is the subject of the gift or monetary contribution exceeds the amount of the advantage, if any, in respect of the gift or monetary contribution.

11-157.   ITA 248(32) defines "advantage" very broadly to include a benefit to the taxpayer that is in any way related to the gift, including benefits that are contingent on future events.

EXAMPLE   As an example of an advantage, consider a gift of real property with a fair market value of $300,000. If the charity receiving the gift were to assume a $100,000 mortgage on the property, this would be considered an advantage. The resulting eligible amount of the donation is $200,000 ($300,000 - $100,000).

11-158.   In addition to this eligibility requirement, ITA 248(30) includes the concept of "intention to give". The basic idea here is that, if the advantage to the taxpayer resulting from making the gift exceeds 80 percent of the value of the gift, the gift will be disallowed unless the taxpayer can convince the Minister that the transfer was made with a real intention to make a gift.

Deemed Fair Market Value

11-159.   In order to eliminate arrangements such as the art flip that was described in Paragraph 11-152, ITA 248(35) introduces the concept of "deemed fair market value". This Subsection indicates that, if a taxpayer acquires a property less than three years prior to its donation as a gift or, if a taxpayer acquires a property less than 10 years before the gift is made and it is reasonable to conclude that the taxpayer acquired the property with an intent to make a gift, the value of the gift will be based on the lesser of the cost to the taxpayer and the actual fair market value at the time of the gift. There is an exception to this rule for gifts made as a consequence of a taxpayer's death.

Gifts Of Capital Property - Transfer At Elected Value

11-160.   When an individual makes a charitable, Crown, or ecological (but not cultural) gift of capital property, an election is available under ITA 118.1(6). On such properties, there will usually be a difference between the tax cost of the property (i.e., adjusted cost base for non-depreciable properties or UCC for depreciable properties) and its fair market value. If the fair market value is the higher value, the taxpayer can elect to transfer the property at any value between the tax cost of the property and its fair market value. There are special rules applicable to gifts of publicly traded securities and ecologically sensitive land that will be covered in Paragraph 11-167.

11-161.   With respect to non-depreciable assets, if the fair market value of the donated asset exceeds the adjusted cost base of the asset, it is advisable to elect the fair market value. Any amount of elected value in excess of $200 will be eligible for a tax credit at either 29 percent or 33 percent. In contrast, only one-half of any capital gain that results from the disposition will be taxed.

EXAMPLE   Mr. Vignesh Menan has a piece of land with an adjusted cost base of $100,000 and a fair market value of $150,000. During 2020, he intends to gift this land to a registered Canadian charity and would like to know whether he should elect to make the donation at $100,000 or alternatively, at $150,000. Before consideration of any income resulting from making the gift, Mr. Menan has Taxable Income of more than $400,000. Given this, any amount of donations in excess of $200 will receive a credit based on the maximum tax rate of 33 percent.

ANALYSIS   The tax consequences of the two alternatives are as follows:

Elected Value	$100,000	$ 150,000
Tax Credit [(15%)($200) + (33%)($99,800)]	$ 32,964	
Tax Credit [(15%)($200) + (33%)($149,800)]		$ 49,464
Tax On Gain	N/A	
Tax On Gain [(1/2)($150,000 - $100,000)(33%)]		(8,250)
Credit Net Of Tax	$ 32,964	$ 41,214

11-162.   It should be noted that ITA 118.1(6) places a floor on this election. The elected value cannot be below the amount of any advantage received by the taxpayer as a consequence of the gift.

EXAMPLE - Extended   Mr. Vignesh Menan has a piece of land with an adjusted cost base of $100,000 and a fair market value of $150,000. In return for making this gift, he receives a cash payment from the registered charity of $110,000.

ANALYSIS   Mr. Menan cannot elect a value below $110,000. Assuming he elects to transfer the asset at the maximum value of $150,000, the eligible amount of his gift will be $40,000 ($150,000 - $110,000).

11-163.   The situation is not so clear when depreciable assets are involved. This results from the fact that an election at fair market value may create fully taxable recapture. The taxes on such recapture may be a bit more than the credit generated by the donation as the credit on the first $200 is at 15 percent. The analysis is further complicated by varying rates for the donations credit at the provincial level.

Gifts Of Capital Property - Income Limits

11-164.   In most cases, an individual's eligible donations are restricted to 75 percent of Net Income For Tax Purposes for the year (see Chapter 4). A potential problem with electing a value that creates income is that making a gift and electing to use the fair market value may result in income that cannot be eliminated with the related tax credit. In other words, making a gift could result in the payment of taxes. To avoid this problem, two other components are added to the Net Income base for charitable donations, resulting in a total base equal to:

- 75 percent of Net Income For Tax Purposes for the year; plus
- 25 percent of any taxable capital gain resulting from a gift; plus
- 25 percent of any recaptured CCA resulting from a gift.

11-165. An example will illustrate the importance of these additions to the overall limit:

EXAMPLE   In July 2020, Jonas Anderson gifts a customized bus that was used in his proprietorship to a registered Canadian charity. The bus has a fair market value of $130,000, a capital cost of $100,000, and a UCC of $65,000. He elects to make the gift at the fair market value of $130,000. He has no other source of income, other than amounts arising as a result of the gift.

ANALYSIS   The election to make the gift at the fair market value of $130,000 will result in a total increase in Net Income For Tax Purposes of $50,000. This is composed of a taxable capital gain of $15,000 [(1/2)($130,000 - $100,000)] and recaptured CCA of $35,000 ($100,000 - $65,000).

As Mr. Anderson has no other source of income, his basic limit for charitable donations would be $37,500 [(75%)($50,000)]. If his limit were $37,500, he would be faced with paying tax on $12,500 ($50,000 - $37,500) less his personal tax credits as a result of his generosity in making the gift. However, with the additions to the limit, his charitable donations credit base limit is as follows:

75 Percent Of Net Income For Tax Purposes [(75%)($50,000)]	$37,500
25 Percent Of Taxable Capital Gain [(25%)($15,000)]	3,750
25 Percent Of Recaptured CCA [(25%)($35,000)]	8,750
Total Limit (Equals Income From Donation)	$50,000

11-166.   As you can see, the additions to the limit serve the purpose of creating a base for charitable donations that includes 100 percent of any income resulting from gifts of capital property. Note, however, Mr. Anderson will not want to use the full $50,000 in 2019. As amounts over $200 will generate a credit at a rate of 29 percent (the 33 percent rate is not relevant as Mr. Anderson's Taxable Income is well below the $214,368 threshold for that rate) and all of Mr. Anderson's income will be taxed at a lower rate, use of the full $50,000 would produce a credit that is larger than his Tax Payable. In addition, he will want to make use of any non-refundable tax credits that are available for 2020. The following Exercise illustrates the determination of the amount of an available tax credit that should be taken in order to reduce Tax Payable to nil.

Exercise Eleven - 12

Subject: Donation Of Depreciable Property

Ms. Sally Felder donates some food preparation equipment to the local food bank, a registered Canadian charity. The assets have a fair market value of $85,000, a capital cost of $62,000, and a UCC of $28,000. She elects to make the donation at the fair market value of $85,000. She has no other source of income during the year and her only tax credit other than the charitable donations tax credit is her basic personal credit of $1,984. Determine her maximum charitable donations tax credit for 2020. In addition, determine the amount of the donation she should claim in 2020 in order to reduce her federal Tax Payable to nil. Calculate any carry forward of unused amounts that will be available in future years.

SOLUTION available in print and online Study Guide.

Gifts Of Publicly Traded Securities And Ecologically Sensitive Land

11-167.   Gifts of publicly traded securities and ecologically sensitive land benefit from special rules that make gifting these assets particularly attractive. While a donor can receive a donations tax credit based on the full fair market value of such assets, ITA 38(a.1) deems the capital gain on gifts of publicly traded securities to be zero. Using the same approach, ITA 38(a.2) deems the capital gain on gifts of ecologically sensitive land to be zero.

Exercise Eleven - 13

Subject: Donation Of Listed Shares

Mr. Saheed Radeem has employment income of $90,000. He owns shares that are listed on the Toronto Stock Exchange. These shares have a fair market value of $110,000 and an adjusted cost base of $30,000. During 2020, these shares are given to a registered Canadian charity. He has no deductions in the calculation of Taxable Income (i.e., his Taxable Income is equal to his Net Income For Tax Purposes). His tax credits, other than the charitable donations credit, total $4,000. Determine Mr. Radeem's maximum charitable donations tax credit for 2020 and the amount of the donation he should claim in 2020 in order to reduce his federal Tax Payable to nil. Calculate any carry forward of unused amounts that will be available in future years.

SOLUTION available in print and online Study Guide.

Gifts Of Publicly Traded Securities Acquired Through Stock Options

11-168.   Without special rules, there is a potential problem for donations of publicly traded shares purchased through stock options. You will recall from Chapter 3 that, in the case of these shares, any accrued gain that is present at the time the options are exercised is treated as an employment income inclusion. In order to give such gains effective capital gains treatment, a deduction of one-half is provided in the determination of Taxable Income.

EXAMPLE   Roberto Cerutti is provided with options to buy 1,000 of his employer's shares at an option price of $20 per share, the fair market value of the shares at the time the options are granted. Roberto exercises these options when the shares are trading at $32 per share. He gifts the shares immediately to a registered charity.

ANALYSIS   Roberto will have an increase in Taxable Income calculated as follows:

Employment Income [(1,000)($32 - $20)]	$12,000
Deduction Under ITA 110(1)(d) [(1/2)($12,000)]	(6,000)
Increase In Taxable Income	$ 6,000

11-169.   As this increase in Taxable Income is not a capital gain, it will not be deemed to be zero by ITA 38(a.1). In the absence of a further special provision, this $6,000 would be subject to tax. Fortunately, ITA 110(1)(d.01) contains a provision that acts to eliminate this tax. This paragraph provides an additional deduction equal to one-half of the Employment Income inclusion. Using this additional provision, the results would be as follows:

Employment Income [(1,000)($32 - $20)]	$12,000
Deduction Under ITA 110(1)(d) [(1/2)($12,000)]	(6,000)
Deduction Under ITA 110(1)(d.01) [(1/2)($12,000)]	(6,000)
Increase In Taxable Income	Nil

Canadian Cultural Property

11-170.   We have noted that, when an individual makes a charitable, Crown, or ecological gift of capital property, they can elect to have the proceeds of disposition be any value between the tax cost of the property and the fair market value. In the case of cultural gifts of capital property, ITA 118.1(10.1) deems the proceeds of disposition to be the fair market value of the property in all cases. Note, however, that this same Subsection indicates that the value established by the Canadian Cultural Property Export Review Board or the Minister of the Environment is deemed to be the fair market value of the donated asset.

11-171.   This fair market value rule must be considered in conjunction with the fact that a provision in ITA 39(1)(a)(i.1) indicates that, with respect to gifts of Canadian cultural property, the difference between the fair market value and the adjusted cost base of the asset does not fall within the meaning of capital gain. As a consequence, any gain on a gift of Canadian cultural property is not subject to tax. Losses, however, would be treated as normal capital losses. Given this, it is not unreasonable to require that the proceeds of disposition on cultural gifts of capital property be equal to the fair market value of the property.

Limits On Amount Claimed And Carry Forward Provisions

11-172.   As noted in Chapter 4, it is the policy of the government to limit charitable donations that are eligible for the tax credit to a portion of a taxpayer's Net Income For Tax Purposes. Note that, while corporations deduct their donations as opposed to receiving a credit against Tax Payable, the limits on the amount of eligible donations are the same for corporations as they are for individuals.

11-173.   The limit on eligible amounts of charitable gifts is 75 percent of Net Income For Tax Purposes, but there are exceptions to this general limit. For individuals, this limit is increased to 100 percent of Net Income For Tax Purposes in the year of death and the preceding year. In those situations where a gift of capital property resulted in a capital gain and/or recaptured CCA, the overall limit is increased by 25 percent of the taxable capital gain and 25 percent of any recaptured CCA resulting from such a gift. There is no income limit on the amount of Crown gifts, cultural gifts, or ecological gifts. Credits can be claimed for these gifts up to their full eligible amounts.

11-174.   The *Income Tax Act* does not require that charitable donations be claimed in the year that they are made. Unused charitable donations can be carried forward and claimed in the subsequent five year period (10 years for ecological gifts). In the carry forward period, the same income based limits will apply in determining eligible amounts.

Foreign Tax Credits Revisited

Rules For Corporations

11-175.   Corporations are allowed to use foreign non-business income and foreign business income tax paid as a basis for a credit against Canadian Tax Payable. The rules for corporations are somewhat different from those for individuals and, in addition, require an understanding of some concepts that have not been introduced at this stage in the material. As a result, the foreign tax credit rules applicable to corporations are discussed in Chapter 12.

Foreign Non-Business (Property) Income Tax Credit For Individuals

11-176.   ITA 126(1) provides for a tax credit in situations where a Canadian resident has paid foreign taxes on non-business income. We introduced coverage of foreign tax credits in Chapter 7, but could not fully discuss the calculations as we had not yet covered loss carry overs and the lifetime capital gains deduction.

11-177.   As was noted in Chapter 7, the full amount of foreign non-business income earned, including amounts withheld for taxes in the foreign jurisdiction, must be added to the taxpayer's Net Income For Tax Purposes. This 100 percent amount is then subject to Canadian taxes, with the amount withheld in the foreign jurisdiction being allowed as a credit against Canadian Tax

Payable. The objective of this procedure is to tax non-business income earned in a foreign juris-diction at the same overall rate as would apply to non-business income earned in Canada.

11-178.   There are a number of complications with this procedure. The first of these is that, for individuals, amounts withheld that exceed 15 percent of the total foreign non-business income must be deducted under ITA 20(11). If, for example, an individual earned $1,000 in a jurisdiction that withheld $200, $150 of this amount would serve as a credit against Tax Payable, with the remaining $50 being deducted under ITA 20(11).

11-179.   A further problem is that the Federal government wants to ensure that taxpayers do not receive a credit that is greater than the Canadian taxes that would have been paid on the foreign non-business income. This is accomplished by limiting the foreign non-business tax credit to the lesser of the amount withheld and the amount determined by multiplying the ratio of foreign non-business income to total income by Canadian Tax Payable. This approach is reflected in the following formula:

The **Foreign Non-Business Income Tax Credit** is the lesser of:

- The tax paid to the foreign government. For individuals, this is limited to 15 percent of foreign non-business income, and

- An amount determined by the following formula:

$$\left[\frac{\text{Foreign Non} - \text{Business Income}}{\text{Adjusted Division B Income}} \right] [\text{Tax Otherwise Payable}]$$

11-180.   The "Adjusted Division B Income" in this formula is defined as follows:

Division B Income (i.e., Net Income For Tax Purposes) less:
- net capital loss carry overs deducted under ITA 111(1)(b);
- any lifetime capital gains deduction taken;
- any amounts deductible for stock options under ITA 110(1)(d) and (d.1); and
- any amounts deductible under ITA 110(1)(f) for workers' compensation, social assistance, or exempt foreign income.

11-181.   "Tax Otherwise Payable" in this calculation consists of:

Part I Tax Payable before the deduction of:
- dividend tax credits;
- employment outside of Canada tax credits;
- political contributions tax credits;
- investment tax credits; and
- labour sponsored funds tax credits.

11-182.   You should note that the preceding definition of Adjusted Division B Income is unique to the calculation of foreign tax credits. It starts with Net Income For Tax Purposes (Division B Income), and proceeds to deduct some, but not all, of an individual's available Division C deduc-tions. The most important omission is the fact that non-capital losses are not deducted. As a result, "Adjusted Division B Income" is a figure that is neither Net Income For Tax Purposes nor Taxable Income.

11-183.   The preceding rules would have to be applied on a country by country basis if non-business income were received from more than one foreign source. If the amount of foreign non-business taxes withheld exceeds the amount determined by the formula, there is no carry over of the unused amount as a tax credit. However, ITA 20(12) allows a taxpayer to deduct such amounts in the determination of Net Income For Tax Purposes.

Foreign Business Income Tax Credit For Individuals

11-184.   If a Canadian resident has income from an unincorporated business in a foreign coun-try, ITA 126(2) provides for a credit for foreign taxes paid that is similar to that for non-business income. As is the case with foreign non-business income tax credits, individuals must include

100 percent of the foreign business income in their Net Income For Tax Purposes, with foreign taxes withheld being allowed as a credit against Tax Payable.

11-185.   While the amount of the credit that can be used does not have the 15 percent limit that is applicable to foreign non-business income tax credits, it is limited by a formula that is similar to the formula applicable to the foreign non-business income tax credit. One of the main differences between these two formulas is that, with respect to the foreign business income tax credit, there is an additional limit based on the tax otherwise payable for the year, reduced by any foreign non-business income tax credit deducted. The calculation of the foreign business income tax credit is as follows:

The **Foreign Business Income Tax Credit** is the least of:

- The tax paid to the foreign government (no 15 percent limit).

- An amount determined by the following formula:

$$\left[\frac{\text{Foreign Business Income}}{\text{Adjusted Division B Income}} \right] \text{[Tax Otherwise Payable]}$$

- Tax Otherwise Payable for the year, less any foreign tax credit taken on non-business income under ITA 126(1).

11-186.   A further important difference between the two foreign tax credits is that, when foreign business income taxes paid exceed the amount that can be used as a credit during the current year, there is a three year carry back and 10 year carry forward available. That is, if a taxpayer does not have sufficient Tax Payable to use all of the foreign business income tax credit during the current year, the excess can be claimed against Tax Payable in any of the three preceding years or in any of the 10 subsequent years. Note, however, that it can only be used in those years within the constraints provided by the formula in Paragraph 11-185.

Exercise Eleven - 14

Subject: Foreign Tax Credits

During 2020, Sarah Cheung has net rental income of $44,000, net taxable capital gains of $2,500, and foreign non-business income of $3,500. The foreign jurisdiction withheld 11 percent of this amount, resulting in a net receipt of $3,115. In calculating Taxable Income, she deducts a $4,000 non-capital loss carry forward and a $1,000 net capital loss carry forward. Her only tax credits are the basic personal credit and the credit for foreign tax paid. Calculate her federal Tax Payable for 2020. Include a detailed calculation of her foreign non-business income tax credit. Ignore the fact that Sarah could deduct any excess of the withholding amount ($385) over the actual credit in the determination of Net Income For Tax Purposes.

SOLUTION available in print and online Study Guide.

Alternative Minimum Tax

General Concept

11-187.   There is a strong public feeling that allowing wealthy individuals with high levels of income to pay little or no tax is not an equitable situation. While such cases usually involve no more than taking full advantage of the various provisions in the *Act* that allow individuals to reduce their Tax Payable, the government felt that it was necessary to have legislation in place to deal with this public relations problem. As a result, an alternative minimum tax (AMT) was introduced.

11-188. This tax is directed at individuals who take advantage of tax shelters and other "tax preference" items. The basic idea is that individuals who have certain types of income, deductions, or credits must calculate an adjusted taxable income by adding back all of the "tax preferences" that have been used in the calculation of regular taxable income. As will be discussed in Chapter 19, for income tax purposes, trusts are considered to be individuals. Given this, with a few exceptions, trusts are subject to the AMT.

11-189. After deducting a basic $40,000 exemption, a flat rate of 15 percent is applied to the remaining net adjusted taxable income. The resulting Tax Payable is reduced by some, but not all, of the individual's regular tax credits to arrive at a minimum tax. The taxpayer must pay the greater of the regular Tax Payable and the minimum tax. Again, as will be discussed in Chapter 19, the $40,000 exemption is not available to trusts in calculating their minimum tax. The one exception to this is a testamentary trust that is designated as a graduated rate estate.

Minimum Tax Calculation

Definition

11-190. The minimum tax is specified in ITA 127.51 as follows:

An individual's minimum amount for a taxation year is the amount determined by the formula

A (B - C) - D, where

A is the appropriate percentage for the year (15 percent for 2020);
B is his or her adjusted taxable income for the year determined under section 127.52;
C is his or her basic exemption for the year (currently $40,000); and
D is his or her basic minimum tax credit for the year determined under section 127.531.

Adjusted Taxable Income

11-191. The calculation of adjusted taxable income that is described in ITA 127.52 is illustrated in a somewhat more comprehensible fashion in Form T691. The basic idea behind this adjusted taxable income is to put back into regular taxable income those items that are felt to be "tax preferences". Examples of such preference items would be losses on tax shelters and the non-taxable portion of capital gains.

11-192. The calculation of adjusted taxable income described in ITA 127.52 is as follows:

Regular Taxable Income

Plus Additions:
- 30 percent of the excess of capital gains over capital losses (see Paragraph 11-193).
- 3/5 of the employee stock option deductions under ITA 110(1)(d) and (d.1).
- Amounts of CCA on Certified Canadian Films.
- The excess of CCA and interest charges claimed on rental and leasing property, over the net income or loss reported for such property.
- Amounts deducted for Canadian Exploration Expense (CEE), Canadian Development Expense (CDE), or depletion, net of certain resource related income.
- Losses deducted by limited partners and members of a partnership who have been specified members at all times since becoming partners, in respect of their partnership interests, net of certain gains allocated from the same partnership.
- Deductions related to investments identified or required to be identified under the tax shelter identification rules.

Less Deductions:
- The gross up of Canadian dividends.
- 60 percent of ABILs deducted (see Paragraph 11-194).
- 60 percent of net capital loss carry overs deducted.

Equals: Adjusted Taxable Income For Minimum Tax Purposes

11-193. Rather than require that all of the non-taxable component of capital gains be added back, which could result in an excessive number of taxpayers being exposed to alternative minimum tax, only 30 percent of the total capital gain is added in the Adjusted Taxable Income calculation. This brings the total inclusion of the excess of capital gains over capital losses to 80 percent (50 percent is already included in regular income, plus the additional 30 percent).

11-194. The government also decided that this 80 percent treatment was appropriate for ABILs. The adjusted taxable income calculation requires an additional deduction of 60 percent of any ABILs deducted in the year. Since 60 percent of an ABIL is equal to 30 percent of the total Business Investment Loss and 50 percent is already deducted from regular income, this effectively provides for a total deduction equal to 80 percent of the Business Investment Loss.

Tax Payable Before Credits

11-195. A basic exemption of $40,000 is subtracted from the adjusted taxable income figure. As noted, this $40,000 exemption is not available to trusts, other than those testamentary trusts that have been designated as graduated rate estates.

11-196. After subtraction of the basic exemption, a flat rate is applied to the resulting balance. This rate is referred to in the ITA 127.51 formula as the "appropriate percentage". Appropriate percentage is defined in ITA 248 as the lowest percentage applicable in calculating federal Tax Payable. Since 2007, this rate has been 15 percent. The resulting figure could be described as the alternative minimum tax before the deduction of tax credits.

Tax Credits For AMT

11-197. ITA 127.531 specifies the tax credits, as calculated for the determination of regular Tax Payable, which can be applied against the alternative minimum tax. The credits specified are as follows:

- Personal credits under ITA 118(1)
- Age credit under ITA 118(2), but not the transfer from a spouse
- Canada employment credit under ITA 118(10)
- Adoption expenses credit under ITA 118.01
- Home accessibility credit under ITA 118.041
- First time home buyer's credit under ITA 118.05
- Volunteer firefighters credit under ITA 118.06
- Volunteer search and rescue workers credit under ITA 118.07
- Charitable donations credit under ITA 118.1
- Medical expense credit under ITA 118.2
- Disability credit under ITA 118.3, but not the transfer from a spouse or other dependant
- Tuition credit under ITA 118.5, but not the transfer from a spouse or other dependant
- Interest on student loans credit under 118.62
- CPP and EI credits under ITA 118.7

11-198. The deduction of these credits will produce the alternative minimum tax payable. If this amount exceeds the regular taxes that are payable on the regular taxable income, the amount of alternative tax must be paid.

AMT Carry Forward - ITA 120.2

11-199. There will be individuals who become subject to this alternative minimum tax in only some taxation years. The most common example of this situation is the realization of a large capital gain that can be eliminated by the use of the lifetime capital gains deduction.

11-200. To provide for this, an excess of alternative minimum tax over regular Tax Payable can be carried forward for up to seven years to be applied against any future excess of regular Tax Payable over the alternative minimum tax.

Exercise Eleven - 15

Subject: Alternative Minimum Tax

Mr. Norton Blouson has Taxable Income for 2020 of $85,000. This includes taxable capital gains of $22,500 and taxable eligible dividends of $27,600 [(138%)($20,000)]. In addition, he received a $50,000 retiring allowance that was contributed to his RRSP. The full contribution was deductible. His only tax credits are the basic personal credit and the dividend tax credit. Determine whether Mr. Blouson would have a liability for alternative minimum tax and, if so, the total amount of such tax.

SOLUTION available in print and online Study Guide.

Sample Comprehensive Personal Tax Return

11-201.   In the separate Study Guide, there is a comprehensive example containing a completed personal tax return, as well as a Tax Software Self Study Problem included in the material for Chapter 11. The sample return illustrates tax savings possible through pension income splitting.

We suggest you work Self Study Problems Eleven-7 through Eleven-11.

Additional Supplementary Self Study Problems Are Available Online.

Key Terms Used In This Chapter

11-202.   The following is a list of the key terms used in this Chapter. These terms, and their meanings, are compiled in the Glossary located at the back of the Study Guide.

Active Business	Loss Carry Back
Active Business Income	Loss Carry Forward
Adjusted Taxable Income	Lump Sum Payments
Allowable Business Investment Loss	Net Capital Loss
Alternative Minimum Tax (AMT)	Net Income For Tax Purposes
Annual Gains Limit	Non-Capital Loss
Business Investment Loss	Ordering Rule
Carry Over	Personal Use Property
Charitable Donations Tax Credit	Purification Of A
Charitable Gifts	Small Business Corporation
Crown Gifts	Professional Corporation
Cultural Gifts	Qualified Farm Property
Cumulative Gains Limit	Qualified Fishing Property
Cumulative Net Investment Loss	Qualified Small Business Corporation
Ecological Gifts	Restricted Farm Loss
Excluded Business	Small Business Corporation
Excluded Shares	Source Individual
Farm Property	Specified Individual
Fishing Property	Split Income
Foreign Taxes Paid Credit	Stock Option
Lifetime Capital Gains Deduction	Taxable Income
Listed Personal Property	TOSI

References

11-203.   For more detailed study of the material in this Chapter, we would refer you to the following:

ITA 82(3)	Dividends Received By Spouse Or Common-Law Partner
ITA 110	Deductions Permitted
ITA 110.6	Lifetime Capital Gains Deduction
ITA 111	Losses Deductible
ITA 111.1	Order Of Applying Provisions
ITA 118.1	Charitable Gifts
ITA 120.2	Minimum Tax Carry Over
ITA 127.5-.55	Obligation To Pay Minimum Tax
IC 75-23	Tuition Fees And Charitable Donations Paid To Privately Supported Secular and Religious Schools
S4-F8-C1	Business Investment Losses
S5-F2-C1	Foreign Tax Credit
S7-F1-C1	Split-receipting and Deemed Fair Market Value
IT-113R4	Benefits To Employees — Stock Options
IT-226R	Gift To A Charity Of A Residual Interest In Real Property Or An Equitable Interest In A Trust
IT-232R3	Losses - Their Deductibility In The Loss Years Or In Other Years
IT-244R3	Gifts By Individuals Of Life Insurance Policies As Charitable Donations
IT-288R2	Gifts Of Capital Properties To A Charity And Others

IT-295R4   Taxable Dividends Received After 1987 By A Spouse
IT-322R   Farm Losses
IT-523   Order Of Provisions Applicable In Computing An Individual's
            Taxable Income And Tax Payable

Appendix - Returns For Deceased Taxpayers

Special Rules At Death

Coverage In Text

11A-1.   Filing requirements on the death of an individual can be very complicated and complex, especially if the individual left a significant amount of various types of assets. There are a number of special rules that are applicable when an individual dies. Some of these are covered in various Chapters in the text. The following is a short summary of the special rules covered in the text, as well as where more information related to the rules can be found in the text. This Appendix also covers the special filing requirements and elective returns for deceased taxpayers. Note that death benefits are income of the recipient and have no effect on the final return of the deceased. Death benefits are covered in Chapter 9.

Charitable Donations - Special Rules At Death

11A-2.   Charitable donations made in the year of death, or through bequests in the will and carried out by the executors of the will, can be claimed for tax credit purposes subject to a limit of 100 percent of Net Income, as opposed to the normal limit of 75 percent. Any charitable donations that are not claimed in the final return can be carried back to the immediately preceding year, subject to the 100 percent of Net Income limit.

Medical Expenses - Special Rules At Death

11A-3.   Medical expenses paid can normally be claimed for any 12 month period ending in the year to the extent they exceed a threshold amount (see Chapter 4). In the year of death, the time period is extended to the 24 month period prior to death.

Deemed Disposition Of Capital Property At Death

11A-4.   The deceased taxpayer is deemed to have disposed of capital property at fair market value immediately before his or her death. When the capital cost of a depreciable property for the deceased taxpayer exceeds its fair market value, the beneficiary is required to retain the original capital cost, with the difference being treated as deemed CCA.

11A-5.   An exception to the general rules is available where the transfer is to a spouse, a common-law partner, or a testamentary spousal or common-law partner trust. This is a rollover provision that allows the transfer of non-depreciable property at its adjusted cost base and depreciable property at its UCC. There are other tax free transfers involving specific types of farm and fishing assets. Deemed dispositions at death are covered in Chapter 9.

Deferred Income Plans At Death

11A-6.   In many cases, a deceased individual will have a Tax Free Savings Account (TFSA), a Registered Retirement Savings Plan (RRSP), or a Registered Retirement Income Fund (RRIF) at the time of death. There are a number of special rules associated with this situation and these are covered in Chapter 9 (TFSA) and Chapter 10 (RRSP and RRIF).

Capital Losses - Special Rules At Death

11A-7.   There are special rules that apply to both net capital losses from years prior to death and to allowable capital losses arising in the year of death. These accumulated losses can be applied against any type of income in the year of death, or the immediately preceding year. Any capital gains deductions claimed to the date of death reduce the net capital losses that can be claimed on an unrestricted basis. The treatment of capital losses at death is covered in this Chapter 11.

Appendix - Returns For Deceased Taxpayers

Representation

11A-8.   The deceased do not, of course, file tax returns. However, a considerable amount of filing and other tax work may need to be done by the legal representative of the deceased. This legal representative may be an executor. This is an individual or institution appointed in the will to act as the legal representative of the deceased in handling his or her estate.

11A-9.   In the absence of a will, or in situations where an executor is not appointed in the will, a court will generally appoint an administrator as the legal representative of the deceased. This administrator will normally be the spouse or next of kin of the deceased.

11A-10.   The basic tax related responsibilities of the legal representative of an estate are as follows:

- filing all necessary tax returns;
- paying all taxes owing;
- obtaining a clearance certificate from the CRA for all tax years, before property under his or her control is distributed to the beneficiaries (a failure to do this can result in a personal liability for taxes owing); and
- advising beneficiaries of the amounts of income from the estate that will be taxable in their hands.

11A-11.   In order to deal with the CRA in these matters, the legal representative will have to provide a copy of the deceased person's death certificate, as well as a copy of the will or other document identifying him or her as the legal representative of the deceased. Without this documentation, the CRA will not provide any of the deceased person's income tax information.

Procedures For Specific Returns

Ordinary Return(s)

11A-12.   As noted previously, the legal representative of the deceased is responsible for filing a return for the year of death (a.k.a., final return) and, if required, a return for the previous year. This return would contain the usual sources of income, including employment income, business income, property income, and net taxable capital gains. With respect to employment income, it would include salary or wages from the end of the last pay period to the date of death.

> **EXAMPLE**   A taxpayer dies on June 4. His last pay period is from May 16 through May 31, with the amount being payable on June 7.

> **ANALYSIS**   The accrual for the period from June 1, the first day after the end of his last pay period, through the June 4 date of his death must be included in his ordinary return for the year of death. With respect to the amount that is accrued but unpaid at his death, this can either be included in the taxpayer's ordinary return or, alternatively, in a separate "rights or things" return.

Rights Or Things Return

11A-13.   Rights or things are defined as unpaid amounts that would have been included in the deceased's income when they were realized or disposed of, had the taxpayer not died. Included would be:

- unpaid salaries, commissions, and vacation pay for pay periods that ended before the date of death (e.g., the salary for the period May 16 through May 31 in the example in Paragraph 11A-12)
- uncashed matured bond coupons, provided they were not required to be included in a previous year's income
- harvested farm crops and livestock on hand
- inventory and accounts receivable of taxpayers using the cash method
- declared but unpaid dividends

> **NOTE** Declared but unpaid dividends can provide a significant tax savings in the case of a descendent who controls a CCPC. Dividends in an amount of up to the beginning of the top tax bracket ($214,368 for 2020) can be declared just prior to the individual's death and paid subsequent to the death. This amount can then be included in a separate "rights or things" return, with none of it being subject to the maximum 33 percent federal rate.

11A-14. While some of these amounts could be included in the ordinary return of the taxpayer, it is generally advisable, provided the amounts are material, to file this separate return as it permits a doubling up of certain tax credits and, in many cases, will result in additional amounts being taxed at the lowest federal rate.

11A-15. Interest accrued at the time of death is somewhat problematical. If, at the time of his or her death, a taxpayer owns a term deposit or similar investment that pays interest on a periodic basis, ITA 70(1)(a) requires that interest accrued to the date of death be included in the taxpayer's ordinary return of income. This would be the case even if the taxpayer ordinarily used the cash basis of interest recognition. Under ITA 70(2), any accrued interest that is required to be included in the final ordinary return cannot be included in the rights or things return.

11A-16. In contrast, if the debt instrument does not pay periodic interest, the accrued interest can be treated as a right or thing. As examples of this, IT-210R2, "Income Of Deceased Persons — Periodic Payments", Paragraph 2 refers to a matured treasury bill that has not been realized and to matured but uncashed bond coupons as follows:

> If a deceased taxpayer owned a term deposit or other similar investment on which interest was payable periodically, interest accrued from the last date on which interest was payable up to the date of death would be included in income for the year of death under paragraph 70(1)(a). However, if the taxpayer also had on hand a matured investment (such as a matured Treasury Bill or uncashed matured bond interest coupons) at the date of death, any interest that was owing to the deceased taxpayer on the matured investment immediately before the date of death would be considered a right or thing for the purposes of subsection 70(2) to the extent the amount was not included or required to be included in the deceased's income for the year or a preceding year.
>
> For information about the tax treatment of "rights or things," refer to IT-212R3, Income of Deceased Persons — Rights or Things.

11A-17. As a final point, note that rights or things can be transferred to a beneficiary, provided this is done within the time limit for filing a separate rights or things return. If this election is made, the amounts will be included in the beneficiary's income when they are realized and should not be included in either the ordinary or the rights or things return of the deceased.

Other Elective Returns

11A-18. There are other elective returns that will be given limited attention in the following material.

Filing Requirements

Prior Year Returns

11A-19. If an individual dies between November 1 of the prior year and the normal due date for the prior year's return (April 30 of the current year or, if the individual or his or her spouse or common-law partner had business income, June 15 of the current year), it is likely that the deceased will not have filed the return for the prior year. In this situation, the due date for the prior year's return is the later of six months after the date of death and the normal filing date. For example, if an individual dies on January 31, 2020, it is unlikely that his or her 2019 tax return would have been filed. If his or her normal filing date was either April 30 or June 15, the legal representative would have until July 31, 2020, to file the 2019 tax return.

11A-20. Under ITA 111(2), a deceased taxpayer is allowed to deduct unused capital losses against any source of income in the year of death and the immediately preceding year.

However, any capital gains deductions claimed to the date of death reduce the net capital losses that can be claimed on an unrestricted basis. Charitable donations can also be carried back to the preceding year if not needed on the final return. If either item is applied to the preceding year, the prior year's return must be amended if it has been filed.

Multiple Returns

11A-21. Filing the appropriate tax returns in the most advantageous manner for a deceased taxpayer can be complicated as there are a number of exceptions to the normal rules. In addition, there are special rules for final returns.

11A-22. In fact, in some situations, more than one return will be filed on behalf of a deceased individual. Some of these are required by the ordinary provisions of the *Income Tax Act*. Other can be filed on the basis of an election and may or may not be filed in particular cases. The potential returns and their deadlines can be described as follows:

- **Ordinary Return - Year Of Death** The ordinary return for the year of death, also referred to as the final or terminal return, will be due on April 30 or June 15 of the subsequent year. However, if the death occurs between November 1 and December 31 of the current year, the deceased taxpayer's representative has until the later of the normal filing date and six months after the date of death to file the current year's return. For example, if a taxpayer died on December 1, 2020, and his or her normal filing date was April 30, 2021, his or her representative would have until June 1, 2021, to file the 2020 tax return. Alternatively, if the deceased taxpayer's return contained business income, his or her normal filing date of June 15, 2021, would be applicable.

- **Elective Return - Rights Or Things** Under ITA 70(2), this special return is due the later of one year from the date of death or 90 days after the mailing date of the notice of assessment of the final return. (See Paragraph 11A-13, which explains rights or things.)

- **Elective Return - Non-Calendar Fiscal Year End** If the deceased had business income from a partnership or proprietorship with a non-calendar taxation year, the taxpayer's death may or may not create a year end for the business. Usually, this will not be the case. However, if the taxpayer's death does create a deemed year end for the business, and that year end occurs after the end of the fiscal period of the business, ITA 150(4) provides for an elective return to include the income of the business for the period between the deemed year end and the end of the calendar year. This avoids having two years of business income accruing in a single taxation year.

  For example, if Mr. Samuel Rosen had a proprietorship with a June 30 year end and he died on November 23, 2019, his representative could file a separate return for the period July 1 through November 23, 2019. This would allow the representative to limit the business income in his final return to the 12 month period ending June 30, 2019. The filing deadline for this return is the same as the one applicable to the final return.

- **Elective Return - Graduated Rate Estate** Under ITA 104(23)(d), if the deceased is an income beneficiary of a Graduated Rate Estate that has a non-calendar taxation year, the representative may elect to file a separate return for the period between the end of the trust's fiscal year and the date of the taxpayer's death. The filing deadline is the same as the one applicable to the final return.

11A-23. There are two basic reasons for filing as many tax returns as possible. The first relates to the fact that the income tax rates are progressive and income starts at nil in each return. This means that the first $48,535 (for 2020) in each return has the advantage of being taxed at the lowest federal rate of 15 percent. If multiple returns are not filed, there may be amounts taxed at rates higher than 15 percent that would have been taxed at the lower rate if multiple returns had been filed.

11A-24. The second advantage of filing multiple returns is that some personal tax credits can be deducted in each return. As will be discussed in the following material, this could save the deceased taxpayer's estate several thousand dollars for each tax return filed.

Use Of Deductions And Credits

Multiple Usage

11A-25. The full amount of applicable personal credits is claimed, regardless of when the individual died in the year. As previously noted, one of the major advantages of being able to file multiple returns is that some personal tax credits can be used in all of the returns filed. It appears that the rationale for claiming certain tax credits on multiple returns is to recognize the fact that the income reported on the different returns could have been included in a later year's tax return if the deceased had lived. In that later year, personal tax credits would have been available to reduce Tax Payable.

11A-26. The CRA's Guide "Preparing Returns For Deceased Persons" (T4011) provides a great deal of information relevant to the returns of deceased taxpayers. In the Guide, it notes that there are three groups of amounts that can be claimed on optional returns. More specifically, the following non-refundable credits can be claimed in the final return and in each optional return filed:

- basic personal credit
- age credit
- spousal credit (including infirm amount if applicable)
- credit for an eligible dependant (including infirm amount if applicable)
- Canada caregiver for a child under 18 credit
- Canada caregiver credit

11A-27. The combined value of these federal tax credits, if applicable, can represent a significant tax savings if multiple tax returns can be filed. There are similar credits available in the various provinces. Achieving these savings is, of course, conditional on each of the individual returns having sufficient Tax Payable to make use of the credits.

Elective Usage

11A-28. Other non-refundable credits can be split between, or deducted in full, in any of the returns filed. However, the total claimed cannot exceed the amount that would be included in the ordinary return for the year of death. These credits include the following:

- adoption expenses
- disability amount for the deceased person
- disability amount for a dependant other than a spouse
- tuition amount for the deceased person
- tuition amount transferred from a child
- interest paid on certain student loans
- charitable donations, including amounts gifted in the will (limited to 100 percent of Net Income)
- first time home buyer's amount
- medical expenses (note that the total expenses must be reduced by the lesser of $2,397 (2019 figure) and 3 percent of the total Net Income reported on all returns)

Usage With Related Income

11A-29. With respect to the following deductions and non-refundable credits, they can only be claimed in the return in which the related income is reported:

- Canada or Quebec Pension Plan contributions credit
- Employment Insurance premiums credit
- Canada Employment credit
- pension income credit
- dividend tax credits
- stock option deduction
- social benefits repayment (clawback)

Usage With Ordinary Return

11A-30.   Deductions and credits that cannot be claimed on elective returns are claimed on the final return. The following deductions and non-refundable credits are listed in the CRA Guide as amounts that cannot be claimed on an optional return, but that can be claimed in the deceased's ordinary final return (it is not a complete list):

- Registered Pension Plan deduction
- Registered Retirement Savings Plan deduction
- annual union or professional dues
- amounts transferred from a spouse or common-law partner
- child care expenses
- carrying charges and interest expenses
- disability supports deduction
- allowable business investment losses
- moving expenses
- support payments made
- losses from other years
- lifetime capital gains deduction
- northern residents deduction
- exploration and development expenses

Payment Of Taxes

11A-31.   Regardless of the extension of filing dates for the final and elective returns, the tax owing is normally due on April 30 of the year following the year of death. We would also remind you that the due date for payment of taxes is unchanged by the deferral of the normal filing date to June 15 for taxpayers with business income.

11A-32.   However, if death occurs between November 1 of the prior year and April 30 of the current year, the due date for the payment of taxes is six months after the date of death.

11A-33.   With respect to income from the value of rights or things and from deemed dispositions of capital property at death, the legal representative for the deceased individual can elect to defer the payment of taxes. Under ITA 159(5), payment can be made in 10 equal annual instalments, with the first payment due on the regular payment due date of the final return. Security acceptable to the Minister must be furnished to guarantee payment of the deferred taxes. Interest will be charged on amounts outstanding and, as is the usual case, such interest is not deductible.

Sample Tax Return and Tax Software SS Problem

The Chapter 11 Sample Tax Return and the Tax Software Self Study Problem for Chapter 11 can be found in the print and online Study Guide.

Problems For Self Study (Online)

To provide practice in problem solving, there are Self Study and Supplementary Self Study problems available on MyLab Accounting.

Within the text we have provided an indication of when it would be appropriate to work each Self Study problem. The detailed solutions for Self Study problems can be found in the print and online Study Guide.

We provide the Supplementary Self Study problems for those who would like additional practice in problem solving. The detailed solutions for the Supplementary Self Study problems are available online, not in the Study Guide.

The .PDF file "Self Study Problems for Volume 1" on MyLab contains the following for Chapter 11:

- 11 Self Study problems,
- 6 Supplementary Self Study problems, and
- detailed solutions for the Supplementary Self Study problems.

Assignment Problems

(The solutions for these problems are only available in
the solutions manual that has been provided to your instructor.)

Assignment Problem Eleven - 1
(Loss Carry Overs - Individual)

Over a four year period ending on December 31, 2020, Ms. Brenda Breau had the following financial data:

	2017	2018	2019	2020
Business Income (Loss)	$18,000	($14,000)	$30,000	($19,000)
Farming Income (Loss)	(10,000)	2,000	3,150	(2,000)
Taxable (Grossed Up) Dividends	2,360	2,950	3,963	6,450
Capital Gains	1,200	2,000	4,000	4,500
Capital Losses	(4,200)	Nil	Nil	(14,500)

Because of the nature of her farming activities, Ms. Breau's farm losses are restricted. The dividend income is from taxable Canadian corporations and the amount includes the gross up.

When she has a choice, she would like to deduct the maximum amount of her net capital loss carry overs and carry back any losses to the earliest possible year. None of Ms. Breau's losses can be carried back before 2017.

Assume that Ms. Breau requires $14,000 in Taxable Income in each year to fully utilize her tax credits.

Required: Calculate Ms. Breau's minimum Net Income For Tax Purposes and Taxable Income for each of the four years. In applying carry over amounts, do not reduce Ms. Breau's Taxable Income below $14,000, the amount required to fully utilize her tax credits. Indicate the amended figures for any years to which losses are carried back. Also indicate the amount and types of loss carry overs that would be available at the end of each year.

Assignment Problem Eleven - 2
(Allowable Business Investment Losses)

In 2017, after several years of working part time at McDonald's, Lucinda McIvor was fortunate enough to win a lottery prize of more than $1,000,000. She quickly blew through over $100,000 of this on recreational drugs, alcohol, and luxury travel. However, in early 2018 after an overdose that very nearly ended her life, Lucinda checked herself into rehab and emerged from treatment a changed woman.

She embarked on a program of actively investing in rental properties and in the shares and debt of small private companies. Her investment income during the three years 2018 through 2020 were as follows:

2018 During this year she realized a large capital gain on the sale of shares in a wildly successful, qualified small business corporation. She used $156,000 of her lifetime capital gains deduction to reduce her 2018 Taxable Income to be equal to her Basic Personal Amount leaving her with a nil Tax Payable.

2019 During this year she had the following amounts of income:

Taxable Capital Gains	$ 17,300
Net Rental Income	91,450
Interest Income	38,275
Total	$147,025

2020 Income amounts during this year were as follows:

Taxable Capital Gains	$ 18,620
Net Rental Income	86,300
Interest Income	27,438
Total	$132,358

Assignment Problems

During 2020, Recovery Inc., a small business corporation to which she had extended a loan of $675,000, went into bankruptcy. Lucinda has been advised that it is extremely unlikely that she will recover any of this amount. Given this, Lucinda is writing off the entire balance.

The only tax credit available to Lucinda in 2019 or 2020 is the basic personal credit (basic personal amount of $12,069 in 2019 and $13,229 in 2020). For several years prior to 2018, Lucinda's Tax Payable was eliminated by various credits. She did not have any loss carry forwards from years prior to 2020.

Required: Determine Lucinda's optimum Taxable Income for the years ending December 31, 2019 and December 31, 2020. In your solution, consider the effect of the basic personal credit. Indicate any loss carry over that is present at the end of either year, and the rules applicable to claiming the loss carry over.

Assignment Problem Eleven - 3
(ABILs and the Capital Gains Deduction)
The following information is for David Foster for the taxation year ending December 31, 2020:

- David has been operating his own business of custom residential painting since 2008. His net business income for 2020 is $110,000.

- David purchased common shares of Abacus Ltd. for $33,000 in 2015 and sold the shares to an arm's length individual in December 2019 for $167,000. Selling expenses totaled $2,000. The shares met the definition of shares of a qualified small business corporation (QSBC) and therefore qualify for the capital gains deduction.

- Abacus Ltd. regularly declared annual dividends and David received $8,000 of non-eligible dividends in November 2020.

- David purchased common shares in Calculatrix Inc. in May 2018 for $82,000. He sold the shares for $21,000 in September 2019. Selling costs were $200. Calculatrix never paid any dividends during the period of ownership. The shares qualified as shares of a small business corporation, entitling David to a potential claim for an Allowable Business Investment Loss (ABIL). Since David did not own the shares for at least 24 months the shares would not have qualified for the capital gains deduction.

- David's Cumulative Net Investment Loss (CNIL) at the end of 2019 was $12,000. In 2020 there are no additions to the investment expense and the non-eligible dividend is the only addition to Investment income.

- David has a 2016 net capital loss of $5,500 [(1/2)($11,000)], which he has never deducted.

- David has used the capital gains deduction twice in his lifetime — once in 2011 to shelter a capital gain of $20,000 and a second time in 2015 to shelter a capital gain of $14,000. The capital gains deduction claimed was equal to the annual gains limit in each of those two years.

Required: Calculate David's Net income and Taxable income for 2020 minimizing taxable income to the extent possible. Provide all supporting calculations. In addition provide the necessary calculations to support the maximum deduction that may be claimed for the capital gains deduction under each of the following scenarios:

A.   David would prefer to maximize the use of his 2016 net capital loss balance before using the capital gains deduction.

B.   David would prefer to maximize use of the capital gains deduction only.

Assignment Problem Eleven - 4
(Tax On Split Income)
In the following five Cases, one or more taxpayers receive dividends from a private company. For each taxpayer, determine whether the dividends received will be classified as Split Income. Explain your conclusion.

CASE 1 Sam and Sandra are both 23 years old and have been married for five years. They each own 50 percent of the shares of Mobus, a corporation that is actively involved in mobile applications. The shares were acquired, in return for a nominal investment, when the corporation was formed. All of the shares have the same fair market value and the same voting rights.

Sam works full time for another corporation, while Sandra has a part time job in health care. They both spend time managing and operating Mobus. Neither Sam nor Sandra work more than 20 hours per week in the business. However, the nature of the corporation's business is such that additional employees are not required.

During 2020, because one of its applications has been very successful, Mobus is able to pay dividends of $200,000, with Sam and Sandra each receiving $100,000.

CASE 2 GoGreen is a Canadian private corporation that runs a seasonal landscaping business. The business operates from May 1 through September 30. Ninety percent of the shares are owned by John Go, with his twin children, Max and Mary Go, owning the remaining 10 percent (5 percent each).

The twins are 22 years old and attending university in another city during the period from mid-September until the end of April. During the period May through mid-September, they work full time with their father in operating the GoGreen business.

During 2020, each twin receives $10,000 in dividends from GoGreen.

CASE 3 Edward and Elsie Cole were married in 2007. Elsie has been the family's primary bread winner, a role she satisfied by operating Cole Industries, a Canadian private company involved in an active business. Elsie was the sole shareholder of this company and worked full time in its operations. In late 2019, citing irreconcilable differences, the couple divorced.

As part of the settlement agreement, Elsie was required to have Cole Industries issue a second class of shares to Edward. During 2020, as required by the divorce decree, these shares pay dividends to Edward in the amount of $50,000.

CASE 4 Larry and Louise Martin own respectively 95 percent and 5 percent of the shares of Musken Enterprises, a Canadian private company. Larry is 66 years old and Louise is 59 years old. They have been married for over 20 years.

From 2007, when Musken started operations, until 2019, Larry worked full time in the business. In 2019, Larry retired and turned the operation of the business over to a salaried manager. Louise has never been involved in the business.

During 2020, Musken pays dividends of $190,000 to Larry and $10,000 to Louise.

CASE 5 Donald Rump owned all of the shares of Dontar during the period 2012 through 2019. Dontar is a private Canadian company involved in an active business in manufacturing. Donald has worked full time in the business since its inception in 2012.

After graduating from high school at 18 years of age, Donald's son David worked full time in the business during the years 2017 through 2019. However, in January 2020, he enrolled in a full time university program and no longer spends any time working in the business. He is 22 years old at the end of 2019.

In late 2019, in order to assist David with the cost of attending university, Donald issues a second class of shares to his son. David uses his savings to acquire the shares. These new shares have a fair market value equal to 20 percent of the total value of all outstanding shares, pay dividends at an annual rate of 5 percent, and are non-voting. Assume that the basic prescribed rate is 2 percent throughout 2020.

During 2020, Dontar pays $105,000 in dividends to Donald and $6,000 in dividends to David.

Assignment Problem Eleven - 5

(Transfer Of Credits And Pension Income Splitting)

Mr. and Mrs. Bahry have been retired for several years. They are both in their early seventies, residents of Canada, and rely on pension income to provide for most of their needs. More specifically, the components of their income for the year ending December 31, 2020, are as follows:

	Mr. Bahry	Mrs. Bahry
Old Age Security Benefits	$ 7,400	$7,400
Receipts From Registered Pension Plan	12,340	820
Receipts From Registered Retirement Income Fund	N/A	1,000
Canada Pension Plan Receipts	3,690	830
Eligible Dividends Received From Canadian		
Public Corporations (100%)	1,600	336
Interest On Savings Accounts	1,239	3,500
Charitable Donations	1,210	300
Capital Gain On Sale Of Painting	N/A	500
Capital Loss On Sale Of Public Company Shares	3,975	820

Required:

A. Assume that Mr. and Mrs. Bahry do not elect to use the pension income splitting provisions. Determine the Taxable Income for both Mr. and Mrs. Bahry and the maximum federal tax credits that will be available to Mr. Bahry for the 2020 taxation year. Also indicate the amount and types of any loss carry overs that would be available to Mr. and Mrs. Bahry at the end of 2020.

B. If Mr. and Mrs. Bahry jointly elect to split the pension income, what objectives should they try to accomplish with the pension income split? (No calculations are required.)

Assignment Problem Eleven - 6

(Alternative Minimum Tax, RRSP Calculations, and Tax Planning)

Carol Duncan has been teaching introductory federal income tax at a college in Alberta for the last 10 years. At tax time, family and friends inundate her with requests for assistance with their personal income tax returns. As a rule, aside from answering a question or two, she has avoided involvement with assisting in preparing income tax returns. She has recently changed her mind, however, and agreed to prepare the returns of two part time students (Albert and Milana) and one family member (Therese) on condition that she can use the results as case studies in her income tax classes. She carefully selected the three individuals given their unique circumstances that allow her to focus on the alternative minimum tax (AMT), RRSPs, and related tax planning. The following information has been presented to Carol for the three individuals:

	Albert	Milana	Therese
Net Business Income	$ Nil	$120,000	$ Nil
Net Employment Income	$26,000	Nil	$60,000
Eligible Dividends Received	Nil	Nil	25,000
Dividend Gross Up (38%)	Nil	Nil	14,440
Non-Eligible Dividends Received	94,000	Nil	Nil
Dividend Gross Up (15%)	14,100	Nil	Nil
Taxable Capital Gains	180,000	140,000	500,000
Capital Gains Deduction Claimable	100,000	Nil	440,000[1]
Retiring Allowance	Nil	80,000	Nil
RRSP Contributions	5,000	46,000	24,000
Allowable Business Investment Loss (ABIL)	Nil	Nil	60,000
Non-Capital Losses Available	50,000	173,000	Nil

---

[1]The capital gains deduction is limited by the annual gains limit, which is equal to the ITA 3(b) amount of $500,000 less the ABIL realized of $60,000.

Albert had no unused RRSP deduction room or undeducted RRSP contributions at the end of 2019. His 2019 earned income was only $22,000.

Therese's T4 for 2019 indicates a Pension Adjustment (PA) of $11,600. Her earned income for 2019 was $120,000. In addition, at the end of 2019 she has unused RRSP deduction room of $21,000 and undeducted RRSP contributions of $8,000,

After 30 years of service, Milana retired from her employment in December 2019 and went into business for herself in January 2020. The terms of her employment provided her with a retiring allowance of $80,000, only part of which ($46,000) was eligible for a tax free rollover to her RRSP.

Albert and Therese's taxable capital gains relate to the sale of shares of a qualified small business corporation. Albert has used his capital gains deduction extensively in previous years and only had an available amount remaining of $200,000 of the maximum of $883,384. Milana's taxable capital gain arose as a result of the sale of a cottage that was not eligible for either the principal residence exemption or the capital gains deduction.

Albert is the sole shareholder in a Canadian controlled private corporation (CCPC) that is very profitable. He is flexible in terms of determining how he will be compensated by his company. Annually he requires $120,000 of income, which in 2020 he has decided should be paid as salary of $26,000 and dividends of $94,000.

Therese has been involved in searching for investment opportunities since she inherited a large sum of money years ago when her parents passed away. Most of her investments are in public companies, but a few years ago she decided to invest in up and coming small business corporations. While she experienced substantial capital gains on the sale of shares of one company she suffered a sizable loss on the sale of another, which fortunately qualified as an ABIL.

Ignore the EI, CPP, and Canada Employment tax credits. Assume that the only tax credits available to each of the three individuals are their basic personal credit and dividend tax credits.

Required: Calculate the minimum Part 1 federal tax payable for the 2020 year for each of the three individuals as well as each of their respective AMT liabilities, if any.

Bonus Question: What could Albert, Milana, and Therese have done differently to reduce or eliminate their AMT liability?

Assignment Problem Eleven - 7
(Death Of A Taxpayer)
Family Information
On July 7, 2020, Mrs. Rachelle Flax was killed in an automobile accident. At the time of her death, Rachelle was 47 years old. She is survived by her 44 year old husband, Martin Flax, and her 24 year old daughter, Roxanne Flax.

Martin has spent most of his adult life volunteering for worthy causes. During 2020, he has employment income of $2,100 that was paid to him for services performed for Rachelle's unincorporated business prior to her death, as well as $1,700 in interest income. This interest was earned on a guaranteed investment certificate that had been given to him by Rachelle several years ago.

Roxanne is a very successful home decorator and is not a dependant of Rachelle.

Business Income
For several years, Rachelle has been the proprietor of a dog boutique and restaurant. The business had a December 31 fiscal year end. Until the date of her death, the proprietorship had net business income for tax purposes of $69,400. At the time of her death, the fair market value of the business assets was $5,900 greater than their UCC. None of the individual assets had fair market values that exceeded their capital cost.

As noted, prior to her death, the business had paid her husband, Martin, a total of $2,100. This was for serving as bartender in the restaurant for discerning dogs. As Martin did not feel capable of carrying on the business on his own, he immediately sold the assets for their fair market value to a regular customer.

Rental Property

Rachelle had owned a residential rental property for five years prior to her death. In 2020, prior to her death, the property had rents of $46,300 and expenses other than CCA of $31,400. The property had been purchased for $312,000, of which $210,000 was allocated to the building and $102,000 to the land. An appraisal indicated that, at the time of her death, the total value of the property was $355,000, which was allocated $243,000 to the building and $112,000 to the land. At January 1, 2020, the building had a UCC of $174,795.

Rachelle's will leaves this property to her daughter, Roxanne.

Investments And Other Assets

Information related to the other assets that Rachelle owned at the time of her death is as follows:

Art Collection   Rachelle had collected Inuit art for a number of years. Her collection had an adjusted cost base of $23,400. At the time of her death, the fair market value of the collection was $57,000. The collection was left to her daughter, who immediately sold the collection for its fair market value of $57,000.

Jewelry   Over the years, Rachelle had spent $32,000 on various pieces of jewelry. At the time of her death, their fair market value was only $8,300. The collection was left to her daughter who immediately sold them for their fair market value of $8,300.

Shares In RAF Ltd.   RAF Ltd. is a Canadian public company. The common shares were purchased for $12,400 and, prior to her death, paid Rachelle eligible dividends of $860. At the time of her death, their fair market value was $28,600. Her will leaves these shares to the Humane Society. The Humane Society issues a charitable donation receipt for $28,600 on receiving the shares.

Shares In Flax Fittings Inc.   This is a company that was started by Rachelle's father with an investment of $20,000. He left all of the shares to Rachelle in his will. At that time, their fair market value was $72,000. Prior to her death, the shares paid Rachelle non-eligible dividends of $6,200. At the time of her death, their fair market value was $104,000. The shares are not eligible for the lifetime capital gains deduction. Her will leaves these shares to Martin.

RRSP   At the time of her death, Rachelle had an RRSP with a total fair market value of $1,123,000. Martin is named as beneficiary of the RRSP.

Family Residence   The family home is in Rachelle's name only. It had been purchased at a cost of $382,600. At the time of her death, the appraised value of the property was $507,000. This property is left to Martin.

Other Information

At the time of her death, Rachelle had a net capital loss carry forward of $89,400 and a listed personal property loss carry forward (100 percent) of $5,400. Rachelle has never claimed the lifetime capital gains deduction.

Due to her business income, Rachelle will pay the maximum CPP contributions for a self-employed proprietor.

The terms of Rachelle's will requires the executor of her estate to elect out of the ITA 70(6) spousal rollover in the case of all properties bequeathed to Martin.

Required: Calculate Rachelle's minimum Net Income For Tax Purposes for the 2020 taxation year, her minimum Taxable income for that year, and her 2020 federal Tax Payable.

Assignment Problem Eleven - 8
(Comprehensive Tax Payable With Donations)
Family Information

Lyla and Clark Beaston are both 45 years of age. They have been happily married for 23 years. When they first met, they found that they both shared a strong dislike for dogs, cats, and small children. Given this, they have no children and have never had a pet.

Both of them are lawyers and have had very successful careers in a variety of jobs. At this point, their net worth is over $5 million. Lyla is currently employed by a large public company. While Clark has been an employee in the past, he currently spends his time managing the family's investments. For a variety of reasons, all of these investments are solely owned by Clark.

While both Lyla and Clark enjoy generally good health, Clark has significant back problems related to a childhood accident. As these have worsened in recent years, in 2020, he decides to go to a clinic in the U.S. for surgery. The total cost of this surgery is US$52,000. At the time of this surgery, the exchange rate was US$1.00 = C$1.35, providing a translated value of $70,200. The travel costs associated with this surgery were US$8,000, resulting in a translated value of $10,800. Clark's Canadian doctor has provided a letter indicating that a similar surgery would have required a wait time of at least two years in Canada.

The couple have qualifying medical expenses in Canada consisting of prescriptions and regular dental work of $4,800.

Because they attribute much of their success to the excellent education they received at the University of Toronto, they make a 2020 donation of $175,000 to this institution when Clark receives a large and unexpected inheritance. As a result of this donation, they do not make their annual donation to the Canadian Cancer Society or any other donations during the year.

Lyla's Employment Information

Lyla's gross salary for 2020 is $270,000. Her employer withholds the maximum 2020 contributions to Employment Insurance ($856) and the Canada Pension Plan ($2,898). She does all of her work in her employer's office and is not required to travel. Given this, she has no deductible travel or other employment-related expenses.

Her employer sponsors a defined benefit pension plan. Her contribution, which is withheld from her salary payments, is $12,450. Her employer makes a matching contribution.

Her employer provides a group disability plan for its employees. The 2020 premium on this plan is $2,500, one-half of which is paid by Lyla through withholdings. Her employer also provides for a generous medical insurance plan that covers 100 percent of any prescription costs and dental fees paid in Canada by employees for themselves or their families.

Clark's Investment Results

During 2020, the results for the investments that Clark manages are as follows:

Interest	$ 28,600
Eligible Dividends From Canadian Public Companies	136,000
Net Taxable Capital Gains	77,000

In order to increase his investment holdings, Clark assumed a mortgage on the family residence. This residence had been purchased for cash and, at the time the mortgage was arranged, there was no debt on the property. The proceeds of the mortgage were immediately invested in shares of Canadian public companies. Interest on the mortgage for 2020 was $12,000.

Required:

A. Determine the combined federal Tax Payable for Lyla and Clark, assuming that Lyla claims all of the medical expenses and all of the charitable donations.

B. Determine the combined federal Tax Payable for Lyla and Clark, assuming that Clark claims all of the medical expenses and all of the charitable donations.

C. Determine whether there is an allocation of medical expenses and charitable donations that would produce a lower combined federal Tax Payable than either the Part A results or the Part B results. Show your calculations.

Assignment Problem Eleven - 9
(Comprehensive Personal Tax Payable)

On January 10, 2020, Ms. Arlene Arsenault formally separated from her husband and retained custody of her 15 year old son, Jerry. Jerry has no income during 2020. Ms. Arsenault is also responsible for her 20 year old daughter, Janine, who has a severe and prolonged disability (a medical doctor has certified her disability on Form T2201). Janine has 2020 income of $6,000, resulting from income on investments that were left to her by her grandmother.

In order to get a fresh start in life, Ms. Arsenault found a new job. She resigned from her position in Ottawa and moved to a similar position in Toronto. The move took place on October 31, 2020. She has asked for your assistance in preparing an estimate of her 2020 personal tax liability and, in order to assist you with your calculations, she has prepared the following list of transactions that occurred during 2020:

1. Her gross salary from her Ottawa employer, a large public company, for the first 10 months of the year was $82,000. Her employer withheld from this amount CPP contributions of $2,898, EI premiums of $856, and RPP contributions of $2,500. The employer also contributed $2,500 to the company's RPP on her behalf.

    Before leaving her Ottawa employer, she exercised stock options to acquire 2,000 of the company's shares at a price of $15 per share. The options were issued in 2019, when the market price of the shares was $12 per share. On August 12, 2020, the day that she exercised the options, the shares were trading at $20 per share. Ms. Arsenault sells the shares as soon as she acquires them. Brokerage fees totaled $350 on the sale.

2. During November and December, her gross wages with her Toronto employer amounted to $13,000. Her new employer withheld CPP contributions of $500, EI premiums of $390, and $650 in RPP contributions. Her Toronto employer also contributed $650 to the company's money purchase RPP on her behalf.

    Ms. Arsenault found a new home in Toronto during her September house hunting trip there. The legal arrangements for the house purchase were finalized on October 10. In Ottawa, she and her husband had lived for 10 years in a home that they rented. Her agreement with her new employer requires that they pay her moving costs. In order to simplify the record keeping, the employer paid her an allowance of $7,500 and did not require a detailed accounting of expenses. Her actual expenses were as follows:

Moving company charges	$3,800
Airfare for September Toronto trip to acquire new home	350
Meals and lodging on September Toronto trip	275
Gas for October 31 move to Toronto	65
Lodging in Ottawa on October 30	110
Meals on October 30 and October 31 While Moving	250
Charges for cancellation of lease on Ottawa home	935
Legal and other fees on acquisition of Toronto home	1,500
Total	$7,285

Ms. Arsenault did not use the simplified method of calculating vehicle expenses and moving costs.

3. In 2017, Ms. Arsenault's mother died, leaving her 5,000 shares of Linz Industries, a private company. These shares had cost her mother $50,000 and had a fair market value at the time of her death of $95,000. Ms. Arsenault received non-eligible dividends of $7,500 on these shares in May and, in December, she sells the shares for $105,000. Selling costs were $850.

4. Ms. Arsenault made $1,500 in donations to a registered Canadian charity and $900 in contributions to the Libcon Rebloc Party, a registered federal political party.

5. Ms. Arsenault incurred the following child care costs:

Payments To Individuals For Jerry And Janine	$ 7,160
Fees For Jerry To Attend Camp (4 Weeks At $200 Per Week)	800
Food And Clothing For The Children	6,400
Total	$14,360

6. Ms. Arsenault paid the following medical expenses:

For Herself	$ 9,700
Jerry	900
Janine	7,250
Total	$17,850

7. In previous years, Ms. Arsenault's husband took care of her financial affairs. She has no understanding of either RPPs or RRSPs, but will make the maximum deductible RRSP contribution for 2020 as soon as you have calculated it. Her RRSP Deduction Limit Statement from the CRA states that her 2019 Earned Income was $81,100 and that, at the end of 2019, she had no unused RRSP deduction room. Her 2019 T4 from her employer indicates a Pension Adjustment of $4,500. There are no undeducted contributions in her RRSP.

8. During the year, Ms. Arsenault paid legal fees of $2,500 in connection with her separation agreement. This settlement requires her husband to make a lump sum payment of $25,000 on March 1, 2020, as well as child support payments of $4,000 at the end of each month beginning on January 31, 2020. All required payments were received for the year.

9. In addition to her employment income, Ms. Arsenault operates an unincorporated mail order business with a December 31 year end. Her net business income for 2020 totaled $22,500.

Included in this amount is a deduction of $950 for interest that she paid on a demand loan taken out to finance inventory purchases. During the year ending December 31, 2020, Ms. Arsenault withdraws $27,000 from the bank account maintained by the business.

10. Ms. Arsenault's father owns and operates a very successful CCPC. In 2019, he gave Arlene a block of non-voting shares in his company. During 2020, these shares paid non-eligible dividends to Arlene in the amount of $10,000. Arlene has never been involved in this company's activities.

Required:

A. Determine Ms. Arsenault's minimum Net Income For Tax Purposes and her minimum Taxable Income for 2020. Ignore any HST considerations. In the Net Income For Tax Purposes calculation, provide separate disclosure of:

- Net Employment Income,
- Net Business And Property Income,
- Net Taxable Capital Gains,
- Other Sources Of Income, And
- Other Deductions From Income.

B. Based on your answer to Part A, calculate Ms. Arsenault's minimum federal Tax Payable and any other amounts owing to (refundable from) the CRA for 2020. Ignore any income tax withholdings that her employers would have made.

Assignment Problem Eleven - 10
(Comprehensive Tax Payable)

Jody Simpson turned 40 years of age in 2020. She has one child, Bert, who was 11 years of age at December 31, 2020. Jody was married in 2009 to her high school sweetheart, Michael Burns, but the marriage ended with a divorce that was finalized in November 2019. Jody obtained full custody of Bert following a court order issued shortly after the divorce. The court order entitles her to both child support in the amount of $15,000 annually and spousal support in the amount of $25,000 beginning January 1, 2020. All of the 2020 support payments were paid directly to her on a monthly basis.

Jody provides you with the following information concerning her 2020 income and expenses:

1. Jody's parents have been operating a CCPC for over 30 years that carries on a successful business commonly referred to as "pickers" – the company name is Pickers Ltd. The business involves travel across the country to identified locations where old items and collectibles can be found, including advertising signs, paintings, furniture, toys, cars, motorcycles, bicycles, comic books, and other various decades old items. When the business was incorporated Jody and her three siblings were all made shareholders. Each of them owns common voting shares that represents 12.0% of all of the voting shares and that represents 12.0% of the value of the company. Jody has never been actively involved in Picker Ltd.'s business nor has she made any financial or other contributions. In 2020 Jody received a non-eligible dividend of $40,000 from Pickers Ltd.

2. In 2016 Jody obtained an MBA and immediately decided to start a pawn shop business. Her parents agreed to sell her some of their surplus inventory on an ongoing basis at a discount and provided her with their many contacts allowing her to establish her own network for goods that her parents' company was not interested in. In 2019 Pickers Ltd. gross sales to Jody's business accounted for only 1.5 percent of their total gross sales. Jody operated the pawn shop as a sole proprietor until early 2019 at which time she incorporated the business in a CCPC she named PS World Inc. The company's taxation year is January 1 to December 31. Jody owns all of the 100 issued and outstanding common shares and Bert owns all 10

of the non-voting preferred shares. The ACB of Jody's common shares equal $100 ($1 per share). The ACB of Bert's shares are $10 ($1 per share), which he acquired with his own money earned mowing the lawns of neighbours.

3. Jody had learned in her MBA program that it was best to avoid incorporation until the business profits were sizable enough to warrant taking advantage of low corporate tax rates. As a result Jody has non-capital losses in each of 2016 to 2018 in the amounts of $32,000, $21,000, and $7,800, respectively. None of these losses have been claimed prior to 2020.

4. In 2020 PS World declared and paid non-eligible dividends in the amount of $84,000 to Jody and $34,000 to Bert. Jody also received a weekly salary of $1,500 on which the maximum CPP of $2,898 was paid. Since Jody's shareholding exceeds 40 percent of the voting shares she is ineligible for Employment Insurance and therefore pays no EI premiums nor does her company, except for other employees. The company regularly declares year end bonuses based on sales performance. The company declared a $60,000 bonus to Jody December 31, 2020, which was paid to her on April 15, 2021. She received a bonus of $50,000 on April 2, 2020, that represented a bonus declared by the company at the end of 2019.

5. In August 2020 Jody met Joe Abernathy, a like-minded individual who was very much interested in the pawn shop. He offered to purchase an interest in the company and Jody accepted, agreeing to sell him 25 of her common shares for $400,000 with half due at the signing August 1, 2020, and the balance due July 31, 2021. Interest was charged on the outstanding balance at the rate of 5 percent. Selling costs were $4,000.

6. In 2020 Jody received dividends from a U.S. public company in the amount of US$10,000. The exchange rate at the time was 1.282. U.S. withholding taxes were 15 percent, or US$1,500. Jody and her other siblings had inherited the shares on the passing of their grandmother in 2017.

7. Since Judy frequently travels to the U.S. she maintained, in Canada, a personal U.S. currency bank account from which she would draw sufficient funds when necessary. Due to ongoing cash needs she decided to transfer $20,000 of U.S. funds that had cost her C$26,100 to her Canadian currency account at a time when the exchange rate was 1.25.

8. Medical expenses for prescriptions and dental services (including braces for Bert) totaled $23,000 in 2020. Jody established a medical and dental plan in her company shortly after it was incorporated. The plans are equally available to all employees and their families. The plans covered 60 percent of the submitted claims or $13,800. In addition Jody personally paid premiums into both plans of $2,400 for the year.

9. In prior years Jody has claimed the capital gains deduction using $160,000 of the currently available $883,384 for 2020. Her CNIL account at the end of 2020 is $19,000.

10. In addition to the non-capital losses in #3, Jody has a 2017 net capital loss of $4,500 [(1/2) ($9,000)] and a 2018 Listed Personal Property Loss of $1,200 (100%).

11. Jody paid child care costs for Bert in the amount of $6,200. The costs cover daycare before and after school on weekdays throughout the year.

12. Jody learned at an early age to enjoy collectibles and is an avid collector to this day. When purchasing items for her company's pawn ship business she often comes across items that are perfect additions to her personal collections that are not suited for the business. As a result, purchasing excursions often result in a combination of personal and business purchases. To ensure she had additional funds to make new purchases Jody decided to let go of some of her collection and sold the following items: (1) a painting that had cost her $1,700 was sold for $8,700; (2) a stamp collection that cost her $9,500 was sold for $11,000;

and (3) a rare book about medical practices in the 1700s and 1800s that had cost her $250 was sold for $5,000.

13. Jody donates $1,000 every year to Plan Canada and another $1,000 to the Humane Society. In 2020 a local hospital was asking for donations to expand the Intensive Care Unit. In 2012 she had acquired a coin collection for $19,000 that she was certain was worth considerably more. An appraiser who works for her company advised her that it was only worth $11,000 and unlikely to increase in value. As a result Jody donated the collection to the local hospital, receiving a donation receipt for $11,000.

Jody currently lives with her son, Bert, in a spacious waterfront property that she has been renting since her divorce. The owner wants to sell and has offered her the opportunity to buy before the property is officially listed. The purchase price of $550,000 is a little more than she wants to spend, but she does not want to pass up the opportunity. She asks you for advice. She currently has $69,500 in her TFSA and $210,000 in her RRSP. She contributed $11,300 to her RRSP for the 2020 taxation year, all of which is fully deductible. She is not interested in carrying any debt and has asked you whether it is better to withdraw funds from her TFSA or RRSP should she require any additional cash to either avoid a mortgage altogether or to keep it as low as possible.

Required: Determine the minimum net income, taxable income, and federal Tax Payable for each of Jody and Bert. Include the alternative minimum tax (AMT) amount for Jody only. Where there is a potential TOSI (tax on split income), indicate whether or not it would apply and why. In addition detail the advice you would give to Jody regarding her questions to you about potential additional cash requirements should she go ahead and purchase the house she is currently living in.

Assignment Problem Eleven - 11
(Comprehensive Case Covering Chapters 1 to 11)
Family Information

Adam Huffer is 42 years old. His wife, Estelle Huffer, is 38 years old. They have been married for 19 years. They have a daughter, Portia, who is 15 years old and in good health.

Portia, who is very precocious, began attending university on a full time basis in September 2020. Her only income for the year is $3,400 that she earned in various part time jobs. Adam has paid her $5,400 tuition fee for the fall semester, as well as $450 for required textbooks and $2,400 for her residence fees. As her income is less than the basic personal tax credit, she has agreed to transfer her tuition credit to her father.

Adam and Estelle's only surviving parent is Adam's father, Jack. While he does not qualify for the disability tax credit, he is dependent on Adam and Estelle because of his limited mobility. He is 69 years old and lives with them. His 2020 Net Income For Tax Purposes is equal to $12,300, including OAS payments and a small pension from a former employer. Adam claims any available personal credit for Jack.

Adam serves as a volunteer firefighter. During 2020 he spent over 300 hours in this work, for which he received no compensation. Because he was convicted of arson when he was a juvenile, he feels that this volunteer work, at least partially, makes up for some of the damage he did in his teen years.

For many years, Adam has owned a small office building that he rented to the Red Cross. On January 1, 2020, he donates this building to that organization, receiving a tax receipt from them for its fair market value of $325,000. This estimated value is made up of $250,000 for the building and $75,000 for the land. Adam's capital cost for the property of $210,000 was made up of $150,000 for the building and $60,000 for the land. On January 1, 2020, the UCC of the building was $119,859. Adam would like to use the maximum amount of this credit during the current taxation year.

During 2020, Adam paid for medical and dental services as follows:

Root Canal Fee - Adam	$ 1,350
Teeth Cleaning - Adam And Estelle	360
Psychological Counseling For Portia	820
Teeth Whitening For Portia	625
Breast Enhancement Surgery For Portia	8,450
Prescription Glasses For Estelle And Portia	500
Electric Wheelchair For Jack	4,200
Total	$16,305

Estelle will claim the credit for qualifying medical expenses.

Adam's Employment Information
Adam works for a large Canadian public company. As CEO, his 2020 salary is $350,000, none of which is commissions. The amounts withheld by his employer during 2020 are as follows:

Registered Pension Plan Contributions*	$12,300
EI Premiums	856
CPP Contributions	2,898

*Adam's employer makes a matching contribution of $12,300.

As CEO, Adam is required to travel extensively by his employer. He uses his own vehicle for this travel. He purchased his current automobile, a BMW 750i, for $132,000 on January 1, 2020. During the year, he drove the automobile a total of 63,000 kilometres, of which 59,000 were employment related. Operating costs paid for the year totaled $11,300.

In addition to his automobile costs, his other 2020 employment-related travel were as follows:

Hotels	$16,000
Food	7,200

His employer provides him with the following allowances for his travel:

Hotels And Food ($700 Per Day)	$21,000
Use Of Personal Automobile ($300 Per Week)	15,600

On a regular annual basis, Adam's employer grants him options to buy the shares in the company at their trading value on the grant date. During 2020, he exercises options to acquire 1,000 shares at a price of $25 per share. On the exercise date the shares are trading at $28 per share. These shares paid no dividends during the year and Adam still holds the shares on December 31, 2020.

All of the family's other stock investments are owned by Estelle. As a consequence, Adam has no income other than his employment-related income and income that results from his charitable donation of real property.

Estelle's Investment Information
When Estelle's father died six years ago, he left her with shares in several small business corporations. Prior to 2020, she had the following two dispositions of small business corporation shares:

2015 In this year she sold shares in ABC, a qualified small business corporation, for $500,000. Her adjusted cost base for these shares was $275,000, resulting in a capital gain of $225,000. The taxable amount of this gain was eliminated using the lifetime capital gains deduction.

2017   In this year she sold shares in DEF, a qualified small business corporation, for $623,000. Her adjusted cost base for these shares was $216,000, resulting in a capital gain of $407,000. Once again, the taxable amount of this gain was eliminated using the lifetime capital gains deduction.

Estelle had no other dispositions of capital assets prior to 2020.

All of Estelle's income is derived from her corporate holdings. During 2020, she received a total of $32,000 in non-eligible dividends from these corporations.

In 2020, she had the following dispositions:

- Shares of GHI, a qualified small business corporation, for $662,000. Her adjusted cost base for these shares was $360,000, resulting in a capital gain of $302,000.

- Shares of JKL, a non-qualified small business corporation, for $230,000. Her adjusted cost base for these shares was $250,000, resulting in a capital loss of $20,000.

For several years, Estelle has been carrying forward a $15,000 net capital loss. In previous years, she has chosen not to use this carry forward in order to maximize her lifetime capital gains deduction. She would like to use this deduction in 2020, regardless of whether her lifetime capital gains deduction is maximized. Estelle has never had a CNIL balance.

Required: Ignore GST/HST/PST considerations in your solution.

A.   Determine Adam's federal Tax Payable for 2020.

B.   Determine Estelle's federal Tax Payable, including alternative minimum tax for 2020.

In both Part A and Part B, indicate any carry forward amounts available at the end of 2020.

Tax Software Assignment Problems

Tax Software Assignment Problem Eleven - 1

This problem is an expansion of the Chapter 4 problem.

DISCLAIMER: All characters appearing in this problem are fictitious. Any resemblance to real persons, living or dead, is purely coincidental.

Mr. Buddy Musician (SIN 527-000-061) was born in Vancouver on August 28, 1952. He has spent most of his working life as a pianist and song writer. He and his family live at 111 WWW Street, Vancouver, B.C. V4H 3W4, phone (604) 111-1111.

Mr. Musician's wife, Natasha (SIN 527-000-129), was born on June 6, 1994. She and Mr. Musician have four children. Each child was born on April 1 of the following years: Linda, 2014; Larry, 2015; Donna, 2016; and Donald, 2017. Natasha's only income during 2019 is $3,200 from singing engagements.

Buddy and Natasha Musician have two adopted children. Richard (SIN 527-000-285) was born on March 15, 2002, and has income of $2,800 for the year. Due to his accelerated schooling, he started full time attendance at university in September of 2019 at the age of 17. His first semester tuition fee is $3,000 and he requires books with a total cost of $375. These amounts are paid by Mr. Musician.

The other adopted child, Sarah, was born on September 2, 1999 and is in full time attendance at university for all of 2019 (including a four month summer session). Her tuition is $9,600 and she requires textbooks that cost $750. These amounts are also paid by Mr. Musician. Sarah has no income during the year.

Neither Richard nor Sarah will have any income in the next three years. They both have agreed that the maximum tuition amount should be transferred to their father.

Mr. Musician's mother, Eunice, was born on April 10, 1932, and his father, Earl, was born on November 16, 1930. They both live with Mr. Musician and his wife. While his father has some mobility issues, he is not infirm. His mother is legally blind. Eunice Musician had income of $9,500 for the year, while Earl Musician had income of $7,500.

Other information concerning Mr. Musician and his family for 2019 is as follows:

1. Mr. Musician earned $16,500 for work as the house pianist at the Loose Moose Pub. His T4 showed that his employer withheld $500 for income taxes and $287.30 for EI. No CPP was withheld as he has previously filed an election to stop contributing to the CPP.

2. During the year, Mr. Musician made his annual $3,000 donation to Planned Parenthood Of Canada, a registered Canadian charity.

3. Mr. Musician has been married before to Lori Musician (SIN 527-000-319). Lori is 52 years old and lives in Fort Erie, Ontario.

4. Mr. Musician has two additional children who live with their mother, Ms. Dolly Nurse (SIN 527-000-582), in Burnaby, British Columbia. The children are Megan Nurse, aged 12, and Andrew Nurse, aged 14. Neither child has any income during 2019. While Ms. Nurse and Mr. Musician were never married, Mr. Musician acknowledges that he is the father of both children. Although Buddy has provided limited financial aid by paying their dental and medical expenses, the children are not dependent on Buddy for support.

5. Mr. Musician wishes to claim all his medical expenses on a calendar year basis. On December 2, 2019, Mr. Musician paid dental expenses to Canada Wide Dental Clinics for the following individuals:

Himself	$1,200
Natasha (wife)	700
Richard (adopted son)	800
Sarah (adopted daughter)	300
Linda (daughter)	100
Earl (father)	1,050
Lori (ex-wife)	300
Dolly Nurse (mother of two of his children)	675
Megan Nurse (daughter of Dolly Nurse)	550
Total	$5,675

6. Mr. Musician signed a contract with Fred Nesbitt on January 13, 2019, to do permanent modifications to his house. The contract was for the installation of ramps with sturdy hand railings outside his front and back doors to give his parents easier access to the house and modifications to their bathroom so they would be less likely to fall when using the shower. The contract price was $5,800. As neither of his parents has a severe and prolonged mobility impairment, these expenditures are not eligible medical expenses.

7. Mr. Musician paid four quarterly instalments of $1,000 each (total of $4,000) for 2019, as requested on his Instalment Reminders from the CRA. He paid each instalment on the due date.

8. Mr. Musician receives $7,271.67 in Old Age Security payments and $5,500 in Canada Pension Plan "retirement benefit" payments over 12 months. There was no tax shown as withheld on his T4A(OAS) or his T4A(P).

9. Mr. Musician builds a state-of-the-art home theatre in a new extension of his home. In order to finance it, he sells stock in his RRSP and withdraws the funds from his RRSP. His T4RSP showed $52,000 in withdrawals from the House of Rock Bank (Box 22) and total tax of $15,600 deducted from these payments.

10. Several of Mr. Musician's songs, including his outstanding hit "Drop Kick Me Jesus Through The Goal Posts Of Life," have provided him with substantial royalty payments over the years.

In 2019, the Never Say Die Record Company paid him $78,000 in royalty payments. No T5 was issued by the company.

11. In order to ensure the financial security of his family, Mr. Musician decided to return to song-writing in earnest. On November 1, 2019, he rented a small, quiet studio for $700 a month and purchased a Roland electric piano for $7,750 that was delivered there. He does not plan to use the space or piano for personal enjoyment, only for composing.

12. The previous year, on January 2, 2018, Mr. Musician elected not to make any further CPP contributions on his self-employed income.

13. Mr. Musician is required by a court order to pay spousal support of $400 per month to his former spouse, Lori Musician. Mr. Musician made spousal support payments of $4,800 during 2019.

14. Mr. Musician is required by a court order to make child support payments of $350 per month to Dolly Nurse for his two children, Megan and Andrew Nurse. A total of $4,200 was paid during the year.

15. Mr. Musician made contributions to the federal Liberal Party in the amount of $610 during the year.

16. Mr. Musician made a $5,000 contribution to his TFSA during the year. Thanks to the excellent investing advice of his gardener, the balance in his TFSA account has grown to more than $175,000 by the end of the year.

Required: With the objective of minimizing Mr. Musician's Tax Payable, prepare Mr. Musician's 2019 income tax return using the ProFile tax software program assuming Natasha does not file a tax return. List any assumptions you have made and any notes and tax planning issues you feel should be placed in the file.

Tax Software Assignment Problem Eleven - 2

This problem is an expansion of the Chapter 4 problem.

DISCLAIMER: All characters appearing in this problem are fictitious. Any resemblance to real persons, living or dead, is purely coincidental.

George Pharmacy is a pharmaceutical sales rep who has been very successful at his job in the last few years. Unfortunately, his family life has not been very happy. Three years ago, his only child, Anna, was driving a car that was hit by a drunk driver. She and her husband were killed and their 14 year old son, Kevin, was blinded in the accident. He also suffered extensive injuries to his jaw that have required major and prolonged dental work.

George and his wife, Valerie, adopted Kevin. Valerie quit her part time job to care for him. She also cares for her mother, Joan Drugstore, who lives with them. Joan suffers from dementia, Parkinson's, and severe depression. The family doctor has signed a letter stating that she is dependent on George and Valerie because of her impairments. Joan does not meet the residency requirements necessary to qualify for Canadian Old Age Security payments.

Valerie's parents separated two years ago in Scotland after her father, David Drugstore, suffered enormous losses in the stock market. They were forced to sell their home and David moved to Chile. David phones periodically to request that money be deposited in his online bank account.

George's brother, Martin, completed an alcohol rehabilitation program after being fired for drinking on the job. He is also living with George and Valerie while he is enrolled as a full time student at Western University. George is paying his tuition and Martin has agreed to transfer any available education related amounts to George. Although Martin plans to file his 2019 tax return, he has not done so yet.

Kevin is taking several undergraduate psychology courses at Western University. After hearing a talk given by an expert blind echolocator (one who uses sound to locate objects), his goal is to become a researcher at the Brain and Mind Institute and study the use of echolocation.

Other information concerning George for 2019 is given on the following pages.

Required: Prepare the 2019 income tax return of George Pharmacy using the ProFile tax software program assuming Valerie does not file a tax return. List any assumptions you have made and any notes and tax planning issues you feel should be placed in the file. Ignore HST implications in your solution by assuming that George does not qualify for the GST/HST rebate.

Personal Information	Taxpayer
Title	Mr.
First Name	George
Last Name	Pharmacy
SIN	527-000-509
Date of birth (Y/M/D)	1955-07-02
Marital Status	Married
Canadian citizen?	Yes
Provide information to Elections Canada?	Yes
Own foreign property of more than $100,000 Canadian?	No

Taxpayer's Address
123 ZZZ Street, London, Ontario N0Z 0Z0
Phone number (519) 111-1111

Family Members	Spouse	Child	Mother-In-Law
First Name	Valerie	Kevin	Joan
Last Name	Pharmacy	Pharmacy	Drugstore
SIN	527-000-483	527-000-517	None
Date of birth (Y/M/D)	1954-12-30	2003-10-17	1934-02-24
Net income	$6,520 in CPP	Nil	$500

Family Members	Father-In-Law	Brother
First Name	David	Martin
Last Name	Drugstore	Pharmacy
SIN	None	527-000-533
Date of birth (Y/M/D)	1935-01-12	1972-06-02
Net income	Nil	$8,300

During September, David was arrested in Chile. Valerie had to spend three weeks in Chile and pay $2,000 in bribes before she could get him released from jail. George had to pay Nannies On Call $3,500 for in-home help to take care of Kevin while she was gone.

Tax Software Assignment Problems

T2202A - (Martin)	Box	Amount
Tuition fees - for Martin Pharmacy (brother)	A	8,000
Number of months in school - part time	B	0
Number of months in school - full time	C	8

T2202A - (Kevin)	Box	Amount
Tuition fees - for Kevin	A	3,600
Number of months in school - part time	B	8
Number of months in school - full time	C	0

Donor	Charitable Donation Receipts	Am't
Valerie	Mothers Against Drunk Drivers (MADD)	1,000
George	Canadian Institute For The Blind (CNIB)	3,000

T4	Box	Amount
Issuer - Mega Pharma Inc.		
Employment income	14	378,000.00
Employee's CPP contributions	16	2,748.90
Employee's EI premiums	18	860.22
Income tax deducted	22	114,000.00
Employment commissions	42	82,000.00
Charitable donations	46	400.00

During 2019, Mega reimbursed George $3,788 for meals and entertainment with clients, $2,268 for hotels and $4,925 for airline tickets.

In addition to George's salary, he also earns commissions. His employer requires him to have an office in his home and has signed the form T2200 each year to this effect.

During 2019, George purchased a new computer and software that will be used solely in his home office for employment-related uses. The computer cost $3,600 and the various software programs cost $1,250.

House Costs	
Area of home used for home office (square feet)	650
Total area of home (square feet)	5,000
Telephone line including high speed internet connection	620
Hydro	3,200
Insurance - House	4,000
Maintenance and repairs	3,800
Mortgage interest	6,200
Mortgage life insurance premiums	400
Property taxes	6,700

(Y/M/D)	Patient	Medical Expenses	Description	Am't
2019-12-31	George	Johnson Inc.	Out of Canada insurance	731.00
2019-08-31	George	Dr. Smith	Dental fees	155.40
2019-09-19	George	Optician	Prescription glasses	109.00
2019-11-07	Valerie	Pharmacy	Prescription	66.84
2019-06-07	Joan	Dr. Wong	Psychiatric counseling	2,050.00
2019-03-22	David	Tropical Disease Centre	Prescription	390.00
2019-12-20	Martin	Dr. Walker	Group therapy	6,000.00
2019-10-01	Kevin	Dr. Takarabe	Orthodontics and Dental	30,000.00

George paid $800 for the care and feeding of Kevin's seeing eye dog, Isis, during 2019.

At the beginning of 2019, George had a net capital loss carry forward of $10,500 from the sale of shares in 2018. He had not disposed of any capital assets prior to 2018.

Asset Dispositions	Asset 1	Asset 2	Asset 3
Description	Molson Inc. shares	Imperial Oil shares	Sailboat
Number of units	150	387	N/A
Year of acquisition	2016	2017	2017
Date of disposition	February 14	June 6	October 1
Proceeds of disposition	37,000	9,600	74,000
Adjusted cost base	27,600	12,100	72,000
Outlays and expenses	35	29	N/A

Asset Dispositions	Asset 4	Asset 5	Asset 6
Description	Motorcycle	Painting	Coin collection
Year of acquisition	2019	2012	2016
Date of disposition	November 17	August 28	March 24
Proceeds of disposition	14,000	1,100	700
Adjusted cost base	21,000	450	1,800
Outlays and expenses	N/A	N/A	N/A

Real Estate Rental - Commercial Property	Amount
Address - 888 YYZ Drive, Toronto, Ontario M0M 0M0	
Year of purchase	2015
Gross rents	16,000
Property taxes	5,128
Insurance	1,890
Interest on mortgage	3,175
Payment on principal	2,200
Furnace repairs	550
Maintenance contract	3,469
Building purchased for $120,100 - UCC beginning of year	107,441
Fixtures purchased for $8,500 - UCC beginning of year	4,651

The building and fixtures were purchased on August 28, 2015. At the time the building and fixtures were being used as a drugstore and Mr. Pharmacy has retained the same tenant.

George knows he should have been contributing to various savings plans over the years, but his increasing number of needy dependants required he spend all of his take home pay to support them and he has contributed to none. It was only in 2019 that his compensation had increased enough so that he had sufficient funds to consider savings plans.

His daughter had made contributions totaling more than $10,000 to an RESP for Kevin prior to her death, but George has made no RESP contributions to the plan since then.

George's 2019 RRSP deduction limit is $285,550.

Tax Software Assignment Problem Eleven - 3

This problem is an expansion of the Chapter 4 problem.

DISCLAIMER: All characters appearing in all versions of this problem are fictitious. Any resemblance to real persons, living or dead, is purely coincidental.

Information Related To Chapter 4 Material

Seymour Career and Mary Career are your tax clients. They have been married for two years. Mary has progressed quickly in MoreCorp, the large, publicly traded firm she is working for, due to her strong tax and accounting background. Her firm has an excellent health and dental plan that reimburses 100 percent of all medical and dental expenses.

Personal Information	Taxpayer	Spouse
Title	Ms.	Mr.
First Name	Mary	Seymour
Last Name	Career	Career
SIN	527-000-129	527-000-079
Date of birth (Y/M/D)	1981-12-08	1960-01-29
Marital status	Married	Married
Canadian citizen?	Yes	Yes
Provide information to Elections Canada?	Yes	Yes
Own foreign property of more than $100,000 Cdn?	No	No

Taxpayer's Address	
123 ABC Street, Saint John, N.B. E0E 0E0	
Phone number (506) 111-1111	
Spouse's address same as taxpayer? Yes	

Dependant	Child
First Name	William
Last Name	Career
SIN	527-000-319
Date of Birth (Y/M/D)	2012-02-24
Net Income	Nil

T4 - Mary	Box	Amount
Issuer - MoreCorp		
Employment Income	14	152,866.08
Employee's CPP Contributions	16	2,748.90
Employee's EI Premiums	18	860.22
RPP Contributions	20	Nil
Income Tax Deducted	22	48,665.11
Charitable Donations	46	1,000.00

Donor	Charitable Donation Receipts	Amount
Seymour	Canadian Cancer Foundation	500
Seymour	Salvation Army	250

Information Related To Chapter 6 Material

Tax Software Note   To create a return for Seymour that is coupled to Mary's, hit the F5 key with Mary's return open.

Seymour earns business income writing and editing instruction manuals on a contract basis. He has six different clients and operates under the business name Crystal Clear Communications from an office in their home. One of his clients issues him a T4A for the work that he has done for them.

During the year, Seymour is a part time student at Dalhousie University for three months. He is enrolled in the musicology program.

Tax Software Assignment Problems

Business or Professional Income - Seymour	
Revenues without T4A	41,603.17
T4A's issued (see T4A information)	20,000.00
Membership dues - Business Writers Association	231.00
Business insurance	126.16
Bank service charges	156.20
Cell phone air time	485.27
Postage and courier charges	110.00
Supplies	2,982.17
Separate business phone line charge	577.86
Fees for accounting and tax advice	500.00
Air fare (business travel)	526.97
Hotels (business travel)	1,240.91
Meals when traveling on business	607.14
Meals and drinks when entertaining clients	887.12
UCC of furniture - beginning of year	2,254.94
UCC of computer application software - beginning of year	219.15
UCC of computer hardware (Class 50) - beginning of year	426.00
Application software purchased May 12, 2018	525.00
Laptop computer purchased May 12, 2018	2,048.00

The mortgagee of Seymour's house, the Royal Bank, does not require life insurance.

House Costs	
Area of home used for business (square feet)	160
Total area of home (square feet)	1,500
Gas for heating	1,712.86
Hydro	1,641.18
Insurance - house	757.55
Snow plowing contract	440.00
Installation of new gas furnace	3,675.00
Painting of house interior	2,548.05
Mortgage interest paid to Royal Bank	8,456.22
Mortgage life insurance premiums	375.00
Mortgage principal paid	1,279.58
Property taxes	2,533.01
Interest on late property taxes	122.52

Tax Software Note   As the problem requires that you ignore GST/HST implications, enter all motor vehicle expenses as non-eligible for GST or HST.

Car Costs - Seymour	
Description - Subaru, cost = $35,000, bought 2016-02-15	
January 1 odometer	89,726
December 31 odometer	124,701
Business kilometres driven	8,412
Parking	321.71
Gas	2,582.12
Maintenance and repairs	458.63
Car insurance	779.00
Licence and registration fees	49.87
Interest on four year car loan granted on purchase date	597.89
UCC of Class 10.1 - beginning of year	15,470.00

T2202A - Seymour	Box	Amount
Tuition fees	A	2,200
Number of months in school - part time	B	3
Number of months in school - full time	C	0

T4A - Seymour	Box	Amount
Issuer - 3065 Canada Inc.		
Fee For Services (Professional)	48	20,000.00

Information Related To Chapter 7 Material

Seymour was previously married and has a 19 year old daughter from the previous marriage. As part of the property settlement, he received the house that he and his family had lived in. Since Mary already owned a much nicer home, he moved in with her when they were married in 2017 and rented out the property.

Seymour believed that in June he had paid an income tax instalment of $2,400 for 2019, but could find no record of it. You call the CRA and find that the June payment was toward his 2018 tax liability. Seymour had tax owing of more than $10,000 for 2018 and has not completely paid off the liability yet. He has paid no instalments for 2019.

Mary also paid no instalments for 2019. She has received tax refunds in the last two years.

During 2017, one of his clients convinced Seymour to take out a demand loan to purchase shares in the public company EEE Art Films Ltd. for $37,000. Later that year, the company's president was indicted for fraud. In 2018, Seymour sold his shares for $2,000 and used the proceeds to pay down his demand loan. During 2019, Seymour did not have sufficient funds to pay off the demand loan, but managed to reduce the principal by $10,000.

The interest and penalties paid by Seymour during 2019 were as follows:

Interest on credit cards for business expenses	$ 627.27
Interest on loan to buy laptop and software	104.24
Interest on loan to make 2017 RRSP contribution	162.15
Interest on loan to purchase EEE Art Films securities	1,372.52
Interest on late payment of 2018 income tax	233.72
Interest on insufficient tax instalments for 2018	52.81
Interest on late GST/HST payments	212.82
Penalty for late filing of 2018 tax return	303.92
Total	$3,069.45

Mary has invested in the stock market over the years and has done well. Seymour holds no securities outside of his RRSP during 2019. Mary has received her T3 and T5 information slips from her stockbroker and bank. The interest from the TD Bank is from a joint chequing account in the name of both Mary and Seymour.

Tax Software Note By inputting the joint T5 on Mary's return, the T5 information will appear on Seymour's Statement Of Investment Income (Schedule 4), but not on his T5 slip screen.

T5	Box	Slip 1	Slip 2
Issuer		Power Corp.	TD Bank
Recipient (Input both on Mary's return)		Mary	Joint 50% each
Actual amount of eligible dividends	24	950.00	
Taxable amount of eligible dividends	25	1,311.00	
Interest from Canadian sources	13		236.11

T3	Box	Amount
Issuer - TD Asset Management		
Recipient - Mary Career		
Foreign country - United States		
Foreign non-business income (Canadian dollars)	25	1,553.10
Foreign income tax paid - investment (Canadian dollars)	34	37.00
Other income - investment	26	214.50
Actual amount of eligible dividends	49	346.00
Taxable amount of eligible dividends	50	477.48

Real Estate Rental - Seymour	Amount
Address - 555 KKK Street, Moncton, NB, E0E 0E0	
Gross rents	12,000.00
Property taxes	3,610.00
Insurance	650.00
Interest on mortgage	4,207.25
Payment on principal	1,511.92
Wiring and furnace repairs	2,282.71
Snow removal and landscaping annual contract	1,070.00
Building purchased May 1, 2006 for $150,000 - UCC beginning of year	150,000.00
Appliances purchased June 6, 2017 for $1,700 - UCC beginning of year	1,350.00

Information Related To Chapter 8 Material

When Mary's grandmother died in 2017, she inherited some pieces of jewelry as well as a dining room set and a chandelier. Since the jewelry is not suited to Mary's relaxed style of dress, she sold some pieces during 2019. She sold the dining room set and chandelier to two colleagues from work.

Mary has purchased Extreme Wi-Fi Technologies stock over the years. Her transactions in this stock are as follows:

Acquisition Date	Shares Purchased (Sold)	Cost Per Share	Total Cost
April 1, 2017	1,500	$ 2	$ 3,000
October 1, 2017	2,000	12	24,000
April 1, 2018	(1,000)	?	
June 1, 2018	400	25	10,000
January 6, 2019	(800)	?	
February 1, 2019	800	20	16,000
March 14, 2019	(600)	?	

Mary Career provides you with the following information about her sales of securities and other items.

Asset Dispositions	Disposition 1	Disposition 2	Disposition 3
(All owned by Mary) Description	Extreme Wi-Fi Technologies	Extreme Wi-Fi Technologies	Fidelity Small Cap Fund
Number of units	800	600	258.92
Year of acquisition	2017	2017	2017
Date of disposition	January 6	March 14	February 17
Proceeds of disposition	11,806	13,465	2,982.31
Adjusted cost base	?	?	5,300.33
Outlays and expenses	29	29	Nil

Asset Dispositions	Disposition 4	Disposition 5	Disposition 6
Description	Diamond Pendant	Gold Ring	Pearl Brooch
Year of acquisition	2017	2017	2017
Date of disposition	July 20	July 20	July 20
Proceeds of disposition	4,000	750	1,300
FMV at grandmother's death	5,800	600	850

Asset Dispositions	Disposition 7	Disposition 8
Description	Dining room set	Crystal Chandelier
Year of acquisition	2017	2017
Date of disposition	July 20	July 20
Proceeds of disposition	200	1,500
FMV at grandmother's death	3,000	800

Information Related To Chapter 9 Material

Seymour has made all of the required payments to his ex-wife, Monica DeWitch (SIN 527-000-186), in 2019. In your files, you have noted that his 2016 divorce agreement requires Seymour to pay spousal support to his ex-wife of $200 per month. He also pays her child support of $250 per month for his 19 year old daughter, Faith.

Mary tells you that her parents have established an RESP for William in 2019 and are the sole contributors. They have contributed $300 in lieu of Christmas and birthday presents.

Mary has learned that Seymour's mother purchased a Guaranteed Investment Certificate (GIC) in William's name in 2019. The GIC paid interest of $120 in 2019, which Seymour had spent without advising her. She expects a T5 to be issued in William's name.

Mary registered William for art classes at the Da Vinci Institute on Saturdays. She provides you with the following receipts:

Child	Child Related Expenses (Organization or Name and SIN)	No. of weeks	Amount
William	No Worries Childcare (after school and summer)		3,100
William	Da Vinci Institute	16	1,000

On December 23, 2019, you receive a call from Mary Career with the terrible news that Seymour has just suffered a massive heart attack and died. Mary, his executor, inherits all of his assets except for the rental property and appliances in Moncton, which he has left to his daughter, Faith. Assume the transfer of the property and appliances takes place in 2019.

As Seymour was thinking of selling the property, he had it appraised in early December. The appraisal valued the land at $60,000, the building at $180,000, and the appliances at $700. Seymour had purchased the property on May 1, 2006, for $195,000 (land of $45,000 and building of $150,000) and lived in it until his marriage to Mary in 2017.

Tax Software Notes   On Seymour's "Info" page, input his date of death (under his birth date). Answer No to the question "Is this an Early Filed ...?". On Mary's return, check that her marital status has been changed to widowed and the date of change is included.

Answer Yes on the Info page on Seymour's return to the question "Did you dispose of a property ...?"

Complete the T2091, Designation Of Property As A Principal Residence, for Seymour's Moncton property and S3 Principal Residence Detail.

Information Related To Chapter 10 Material

On January 10, 2020, you receive a phone call from Mary Career. She has just received a T4RSP in the mail showing that Seymour had withdrawn virtually all the funds from his RRSP without her knowledge. She knows this could substantially increase Seymour's tax liability and is very concerned. At the moment, she cannot find any trace of the funds that were withdrawn.

Her stockbroker has told her that a spousal contribution can be made to her RRSP to utilize Seymour's unused contribution room. She would like you to calculate the maximum RRSP contribution that can be deducted on Seymour's return so that she can contribute that amount to her RRSP and have the RRSP receipt issued with Seymour's name as the contributor.

She would also like you to calculate the maximum RRSP contribution that can be deducted on her own return for 2019 and 2020. Since Mary has received more than $1 million in life insurance benefits, she will make the maximum RRSP contributions for Seymour and herself that you have calculated immediately (before the end of February 2020).

She provides you with the following T4RSP and RRSP receipts for the contributions that she has already made, as well as information related to her and Seymour's RRSP limits.

RRSP information - Mary	(Y/M/D)	Amount
Issuer of receipt - TD Asset Management	2019-12-10	5,400
Issuer of receipt - TD Asset Management	2020-01-05	35,191
Contributions made prior to 2020/03/03 and not deducted		Nil
Unused deduction room at the end of 2018		14,091
Earned income for 2018		180,000

T4RSP - Seymour	Box	Amount
Issuer of receipt - Royal Bank		
Withdrawal payments (in amounts of < $5,000 each)	22	126,000
Income tax deducted	30	12,600

RRSP information - Seymour	(Y/M/D)	Amount
Issuer of receipt - TD Asset Management		Maximum ?
Contributions made prior to 2020/03/03 and not deducted		Nil
Unused deduction room at the end of 2018		19,762
Earned income for 2018		45,000

Information Related To Chapter 11 Material

In checking Seymour's file, you find he has a net capital loss carry forward of $17,500 [(1/2)($35,000)] from the sale of his EEE Art Films Ltd shares in 2018. Mary has informed you that she has made all of the RRSP contributions as you had calculated.

On February 14, 2020, you receive a call from a very upset Mary Career. She has just received an amended T4. The original T4 had not included information on the stock options in her employer, MoreCorp (a public company), that she had exercised.

Mary had options to purchase 500 shares of MoreCorp at $42 per share. When she received the options, the shares were trading at $40 per share. On December 20, 2019, when the shares were trading at $125 per share, she exercised her options for 200 shares. She left verbal instructions for MoreCorp to immediately donate all of the shares to Tax Behind Bars, a Canadian registered charity whose volunteers provide extensive tax education to inmates in prisons across Canada.

Unfortunately for Mary, the employee she had given the donation instructions to was fired for falsifying her credentials so the donation was not done and she did not receive a 2019 charitable donation receipt.

Amended T4 - Mary	Box	Original Am't	Amended Am't
Issuer - MoreCorp			
Employment income	14	152,866.08	169,466.08
Employee's CPP contributions	16	2,748.90	2,748.90
Employee's EI premiums	18	860.22	860.22
RPP contributions	20	Nil	Nil
Income tax deducted	22	48,665.11	48,665.11
Stock option deduction 110(1)(d)	39	Nil	8,300.00
Charitable donations	46	1,000.00	1,000.00

Required: With the objective of minimizing the tax liability for the family, prepare Mary's 2019 income tax return and Seymour's final 2019 return. List any assumptions you have made and provide any explanatory notes and tax planning issues you feel should be placed in the files. Include in your solution Mary's maximum RRSP deduction for 2020.

CHAPTER 12

Taxable Income And Tax Payable For Corporations

Recent Developments In Corporate Taxation

Small Business Deduction Rate

For many years, the small business deduction reduced the federal tax rate on the qualifying income of Canadian controlled private corporations (CCPCs) to 11 percent. In 2016, the deduction was increased by one-half percent, reducing the federal rate to 10.5 percent, with further rate reductions scheduled for 2017 and 2018.

However, the government concluded that they could not afford the reductions scheduled for 2017 and 2018, resulting in a cancellation of these changes. This resulted in the relevant rate remaining at 10.5 percent for 2017 and, as originally proposed, for subsequent years.

However, for 2018 and 2019, the government has reinstated the reductions in the federal rate that were proposed in 2016. Increases in the deduction resulted in a 2018 rate of 10 percent and a 2019 rate of 9 percent on eligible Taxable Income. No further changes are planned at this point.

Tax Planning By Private Corporations

Problems

These reductions in the federal rate on the qualifying income of CCPCs reflected the government's policy of encouraging small business. This was based on the view that such businesses are very helpful to the Canadian economy in that they encouraged both additional investment in capital assets and the employment of Canadian individuals.

While providing these reduced rates to CCPCs, the government also recognized that these very favourable rates were being abused by wealthy Canadians to both reduce and defer taxes in situations that were not helpful to the Canadian economy. The two basic problems identified were:

- The sprinkling of dividend and other types of income to related individuals that were in low tax brackets, significantly reducing the amount of taxes that were paid on a given income stream.

- The accumulation of passive investments within the corporation with income that benefited from being taxed at the low rates applicable to the qualifying income of CCPCs. This resulted in both tax avoidance and tax deferral.

Based on this belief, the government introduced measures to correct these abuses. We will provide an overview of these measures in this note on recent developments.

Income Sprinkling

As discussed briefly in Chapter 1, income splitting is one of the most powerful weapons in a tax planner's arsenal. While the government finds the use of income splitting to be appropriate in certain situations (e.g., spousal RRSPs and pension income splitting), it believes that abusive use of income sprinkling creates an unfair element in our taxation system. This reflects the fact that the more sophisticated forms of income splitting are only available to wealthy Canadians.

The government's approach to dealing with this problem was the 2018 expansion of the application of the Tax On Split Income (TOSI). As this tax is related directly to individuals and involves business entities other than corporations, the changes in the TOSI were covered in Chapter 11. We will not provide additional direct coverage of the TOSI in this or subsequent Chapters. However, we will refer to this tax as required in material that deals with other types of taxable entities (corporations and trusts).

Private Companies Holding Passive Investments

It is not uncommon for a private corporation to be sufficiently successful that it is producing income that is larger than the current consumption needs of the owners, in some cases significantly larger. Given the desire to avoid taxation at the individual level, such owners will often invest this excess in passive investments to be held in the corporation. There are, in fact, many private companies that are holding millions of dollars in passive investments that have nothing to do with the corporation's business.

To the extent that passive investments are acquired with after tax funds to which full corporate rates have been applied, there is no real issue. As we shall find in Chapter 13, income on such investments is taxed at very high corporate rates, with a portion of this tax refunded when taxable dividends are paid to, and taxed in the hands of, the shareholders of the corporation.

However, a problem arises when such investments are acquired with after tax funds that have only been subject to the rates applicable to income that qualifies for the small business deduction. A simple example will serve to illustrate the issue.

> **EXAMPLE**   Sam and Ira Johnston are brothers, both of whom have employment income in excess of $250,000. Any additional income that they receive personally will be taxed at a combined federal/provincial rate of 52 percent.
>
> They both have a business that produces an additional $200,000 in business income, none of which is required to meet their families' financial needs. Sam's business is a proprietorship while Ira's business is operated inside a private company. On its active business income, Ira's private company is taxed at a combined federal/provincial rate of 15 percent.
>
> **ANALYSIS**   The amounts of after tax business income retained by the two brothers would be as follows:

	Sam	Ira
Before Tax Business Income	$200,000	$200,000
Tax Payable On Additional Income		
Sam At 52 Percent	(104,000)	
Ira At 15 Percent		(30,000)
After Tax Retention	$ 96,000	$170,000

Ira's corporation has $74,000 ($170,000 - $96,000) more in funds available for acquiring passive investments as compared to Sam's proprietorship. While subsequent earnings on Ira's investments will be taxed at corporate rates similar to those applicable to Sam, over time Ira will accumulate a much larger investment portfolio. There are, in fact, many cases where the additional investments have accumulated to millions of dollars. Not surprisingly, the government views this as an abuse of the favourable rates that are available to small businesses.

Given the variety of situations where small businesses are holding passive investments (e.g., they may be held to cover seasonal increases in costs), finding a solution to this problem has been difficult. While a number of approaches were considered, the final solution that was provided with the 2018 federal budget involved two components.

Small Business Deduction Limit Grind   A grind is a programmed reduction in some specified tax variable. For a number of years, the annual limit on income eligible for the small business deduction ($500,000) has been reduced by the amount of a CCPC's Taxable Capital Employed in Canada that is in excess of $10 million. For 2019, the limit will be ground down by the greater of this reduction and a new grind based on ADJUSTED Aggregate Investment Income in excess of $50,000.

While the taxation of corporate investment income is not covered until Chapter 13, this rather simple component of the solution to the passive investment income problem will be covered in this Chapter. This reflects the fact that it must be considered in conjunction with the Taxable Capital Employed in Canada grind, which is covered in this chapter.

Division Of The Refundable Dividend Tax On Hand Account (RDTOH)   This second component of the solution to the passive investment income problem is much more complex. Chapter 13, which deals with the taxation of corporate investment income, introduces the procedures associated with taxes that can be refunded when certain types of corporations pay dividends to their shareholders. The RDTOH account is used to track the availability of dividend refunds and, prior to 2019, all amounts in this account could be used to claim a dividend refund on the more favourably taxed eligible dividends (see Chapter 7). For 2019 and subsequent years, this account is divided into two components with a view to restricting the amount of the dividend refund that can be claimed on the payment of eligible dividends.

Both of these rules are effective for taxation years beginning after 2018.

Computation Of Net Income

12-1.   The day-to-day records of most corporations are kept in terms of accounting procedures and policies that are normally referred to as Generally Accepted Accounting Principles (GAAP). As noted in Chapter 6 on business income, many of the rules for computing business income under the *Income Tax Act* are identical to those used under GAAP. However, there are a number of differences that are specifically provided for and, as a result, the first step in the computation of Taxable Income for a corporation is to convert accounting Net Income as determined under GAAP into Net Income For Tax Purposes. Only then can we move from Division B's Net Income For Tax Purposes to Division C's Taxable Income.

12-2.   In making this conversion, there are many adjustments that could be required in particular circumstances. Some adjustments are necessary because of different allocation patterns that result in timing differences between accounting and tax income. Examples of this would be differences between accounting amortization and CCA, as well as alternative approaches to the determination of pension cost deductions. Other adjustments involve permanent differences between accounting and tax amounts. An example of this type of difference would be

---

Figure 12 - 1
Conversion Of Accounting Net Income To Net Income For Tax Purposes

Additions To Accounting Income:
- Income tax expense
- Amortization, depreciation, and depletion of tangible and intangible assets (accounting amounts)
- Recapture of CCA
- Tax reserves deducted in the prior year
- Losses on the disposition of capital assets (accounting amounts)
- Pension expense (accounting amounts)
- Scientific research expenditures (accounting amounts)
- Warranty expense (accounting amounts)
- Amortization of discount on long term debt issued (see discussion in Chapter 7)
- Foreign tax paid (accounting amounts)
- Excess of taxable capital gains over allowable capital losses
- Interest and penalties on income tax assessments
- Non-deductible automobile costs
- 50 percent of business meals and entertainment expenses
- Club dues and cost of recreational facilities
- Non-deductible reserves (accounting amounts)
- Charitable donations
- Asset write-downs including impairment losses on intangibles
- Fines, penalties, and illegal payments

Deductions From Accounting Income:
- Capital cost allowances (CCA)
- Incorporation costs (First $3,000)
- Terminal losses
- Tax reserves claimed for the current year
- Gains on the disposition of capital assets (accounting amounts)
- Pension funding contributions
- Deductible scientific research expenditures
- Deductible warranty expenditures
- Amortization of premium on long term debt issued
- Foreign non-business tax deduction [ITA 20 (12)]
- Allowable business investment losses
- Landscaping costs

---

the non-taxable one-half of capital gains. While accounting records include 100 percent of such gains, one-half of such gains will never be included in Net Income For Tax Purposes.

12-3.   A reconciliation between accounting Net Income and Net Income For Tax Purposes is a required part of the corporate tax return. The form that the CRA provides for this reconciliation is designated Schedule 1. The most common adjustments from this Schedule are listed in Figure 6-1 in Chapter 6, and that list has been duplicated as Figure 12-1.

12-4.   Chapter 6 on business income provided a detailed discussion of the conversion of Net Income for accounting purposes into Net Income For Tax Purposes. As that discussion is equally applicable to both corporations and unincorporated businesses, it will not be repeated here. However, if you are not familiar with the material in Chapter 6, we suggest that you review it before proceeding with these Chapters on corporate taxation. Exercise Twelve-1 provides a fairly simple illustration of how this reconciliation works.

Exercise Twelve - 1

Subject: Schedule 1 Reconciliation

Available information for the S1 Company for the year includes the following:

1. A capital asset was sold for $48,300. It had a cost of $120,700 and a net book value of $53,900. It was the last asset in its CCA class and the UCC balance in this class was $34,600 before the disposition. There were no other additions or dispositions during the year.
2. During the year, the company acquired goodwill at a cost of $180,000. Since there was no impairment of the goodwill during the year, no write-down was required for accounting purposes.
3. During the year, the company expensed charitable donations of $15,000.
4. Premium amortization on the company's bonds payable was $4,500 for the year.

You have been asked to prepare a Schedule 1 reconciliation of accounting Net Income and Net Income For Tax Purposes. Determine the addition and/or deduction that would be made in Schedule 1 for each of the preceding items.

SOLUTION available in print and online Study Guide.

We suggest you work Self Study Problem Twelve-1 at this point.

Computation Of Taxable Income

Deductions Available To Corporations

12-5.   The reconciliation schedule illustrated in Figure 12-1 is used to establish a corporation's Net Income For Tax Purposes. When this task is completed, certain specified items are deducted from the resulting Net Income For Tax Purposes figure in order to arrive at Taxable Income. These deductions are specified in Division C of the *Income Tax Act* and the relevant items for individuals were given detailed coverage in Chapters 4 and 11. However, there are significant differences in the Division C deductions available to individuals and those available to corporations.

12-6.   With respect to the Division C items that are available to individuals, the following are not available to corporations:

- employee stock option deduction
- deduction for payments (social assistance and workers' compensation benefits)
- lump sum payments
- lifetime capital gains deduction
- northern residents deductions

12-7.   A further significant difference relates to two items that, with respect to individuals, serve as a base for credits against Tax Payable. While these items are not available as a base for credits against corporate Tax Payable, they are available as deductions in the calculation of corporate Taxable Income. These items are:

Charitable Donations   Unlike the situation for individuals where charitable donations are the basis for a tax credit, corporations deduct charitable donations from Net Income For Tax Purposes in the determination of Taxable Income. While corporations have a deduction rather than a tax credit, the rules for determining which donations can be deducted by a corporation are essentially the same as the rules for determining which donations qualify for the tax credit for individuals. Further, corporations are subject to the same limits that

---

Figure 12 - 2
Conversion Of Corporate Net Income For Tax Purposes To Taxable Income

Net Income (Loss) For Tax Purposes

Less:
- Charitable donations (Limited to 75 percent of Net Income For Tax Purposes with a five year carry forward of unused amounts)
- Dividends received from taxable Canadian corporations
- Loss carry overs from subsequent or prior taxation years

Equals Taxable Income (Loss)

---

apply to individuals, with respect to the amount that can be deducted in the current taxation year. The five year carry forward provision is also applicable to corporations. These matters are given detailed consideration in Chapters 4 and 11 and will not be repeated here.

Dividends   As noted in previous Chapters, individuals must gross up dividends received from taxable Canadian corporations by 15 percent for non-eligible dividends or 38 percent for eligible dividends. This is accompanied by a federal dividend tax credit equal to either 9/13 of the gross up or 6/11 of the gross up. There is no corresponding gross up or tax credit with respect to dividends received by a corporation. However, a corporation is permitted to deduct the full amount of such dividends in the calculation of Taxable Income. Note that, while this deduction removes dividends from Taxable Income and the Tax Payable calculation, they must be included in determining Net Income For Tax Purposes.

12-8.   In addition to the two preceding deductions, corporations are allowed to deduct loss carry overs from previous or subsequent years in the calculation of Taxable Income. Other than in situations where a corporation has been the subject of an acquisition of control (see Chapter 14), the rules related to the deduction of loss carry overs by corporations are basically the same as those applicable to individuals. These general rules are covered in Chapter 11 and will not be repeated here.

12-9.   The calculation of corporate Taxable Income is outlined in Figure 12-2.

Dividends From Other Corporations

Deduction From Taxable Income
12-10.   ITA 112(1) permits a corporation to deduct, in the determination of Taxable Income, dividends that are received from taxable Canadian corporations.

12-11.   The reason for this deduction is fairly obvious. If taxes were levied on transfers of dividends between companies, it could result in taxes being repeatedly assessed on the same diminishing stream of income. That is, the paying corporation would be taxed on the income that provided the dividend and if, in addition, the receiving corporation had to include the amount received in its Taxable Income, double taxation of the same income would result. In more complex, multi-level corporate structures, this could extend to triple, quadruple, or even greater applications of tax to a single stream of income.

EXAMPLE   Mr. X owns 100 percent of the common shares of Company X, and Company X owns 100 percent of the common shares of Company Y. Both companies pay out all of their after tax income as dividends. Company Y has income of $1,000 for the year and Company X has no income other than dividends from Company Y. Assume both Company X and Company Y are subject to a combined federal/provincial tax rate of 30 percent and Mr. X is subject to a combined federal/provincial tax rate on non-eligible dividends received of 33 percent.

ANALYSIS   A comparison of the after tax flow through, with and without the intercompany dividend deduction, would be as follows:

	No Deduction	Deduction
Company Y Income	$1,000	$1,000
Corporate Taxes At 30 Percent	(300)	(300)
Dividends To Company X	$ 700	$ 700
Corporate Taxes At 30 Percent	(210)	Nil
Dividends To Mr. X	$ 490	$ 700
Personal Taxes At 33 Percent	(162)	(231)
After Tax Retention	$ 328	$ 469

12-12.   Without the deduction, the after tax retention is only $328. This means that the total tax rate on the $1,000 of income earned by Company Y is an almost confiscatory 67.2 percent. While the application of the dividend deduction provides a more reasonable level of taxation, you should note that the combined corporate and personal tax on the $1,000 income stream is $531 ($300 + $231). This heavy level of taxation reflects the fact that, with a corporate tax rate of 30 percent, flowing income through a corporation can result in the payment of higher taxes than would be the case with the direct receipt of income. This point is discussed more fully in Chapter 13, which provides detailed coverage of the concept of integration. The concept was introduced in Chapter 7 within our material on the taxation of dividend income.

Exercise Twelve - 2

Subject: Corporate Taxable Income

The Chapman Company had Net Income For Tax Purposes for the year ending December 31, 2020, of $263,000. This amount included $14,250 in taxable capital gains, as well as $14,200 in dividends received from taxable Canadian corporations. Also during 2020, the company made donations to registered charities of $8,600. At the beginning of the year, the company had available a non-capital loss carry forward of $82,000, as well as a net capital loss carry forward of $18,000 [(1/2)($36,000)]. Determine the company's minimum Taxable Income for the year ending December 31, 2020, and the amount and type of any carry forwards available at the end of the year.

SOLUTION available in print and online Study Guide.

Dividends From Untaxed Income

12-13.   While the preceding justifications for not taxing intercorporate dividends make sense in the majority of situations, problems can arise. One problem involves situations in which the corporation paying the dividend was not taxed on the funds prior to their distribution. Given the fact that, for most companies, accounting income is higher than Taxable Income, it would not be surprising to find cases where there is sufficient accounting income to warrant a dividend payment, combined with a tax loss for the period.

12-14.   In this case, there will be no taxation of the original income at the corporate level. This means that only personal taxes will be paid on the income stream and, as a consequence, the use of a corporation will result in a significantly lower level of taxation than would be the case if the income were received directly by the individual. In addition, because no tax will be assessed until the income is paid out in dividends, this situation may result in a significant deferral of the taxation that is applicable to the income stream.

Term And Other Preferred Shares

12-15.   A further problem arises when corporations attempt to achieve what is sometimes referred to as "after tax financing". Because of the favourable tax treatment given to both individual and corporate recipients of dividend income, rates that corporations will have to pay on preferred shares will sometimes be lower than rates paid on debt securities.

12-16. For most corporations, debt securities will continue to remain attractive because the tax deductibility of interest payments provides a lower after tax cost of funds than would be the case with the use of preferred shares. However, this is not the case when the corporation is in a loss position and, as a consequence, such companies have often issued preferred shares.

12-17. To make these preferred shares more attractive to investors, issuers add features such as redemption provisions. These features produce a preferred share that has most of the characteristics of debt. In fact, IAS 32, *Financial Instruments: Presentation*, may require that such preferred shares be treated as debt for accounting purposes.

12-18. Despite many debt-like features, the payments made on such preferred shares are, for tax purposes, dividend income. As previously discussed, this type of income is taxed very favourably in the hands of individual investors and is not taxed at all in the hands of corporate investors.

12-19. The loss of tax revenues on this type of security could be very high. To prevent this loss, the ITA either imposes special taxes under Part IV.1 and Part VI.1 or denies the dividend deduction to alter the treatment of dividends on these preferred shares. However, these provisions go beyond the scope of this material.

Dividends On Shares Sold For Loss (Stop Loss Rules)

12-20. As the declaration and payment of dividends by a corporation reduces the corporation's net assets, it would be expected that the value of the shares would fall by approximately the amount of any dividend declared and paid. Given this, it would be possible for one corporation to acquire shares in another corporation at a time when it was anticipated that a dividend would be paid on the acquired shares. The dividends on these shares could be received tax free and, if the value of the shares declined when they went ex-dividend, they could be sold to create a capital loss. The following example illustrates the problem that is created by this situation:

> **EXAMPLE** On June 30, 2020, Brian Company acquires 1,000 shares of Leader Company, a public company, at a cost of $20 per share. On July 1, 2020, Leader Company declares and pays its regular $3 per share dividend. Because this dividend had been anticipated by the market, the price of the Leader Company stock falls $3 per share to $17 per share. On July 15, 2020, Brian Company sells all of its Leader Company shares at a price of $17 per share.

> **ANALYSIS** In the absence of a special rule, the preceding situation would provide very favourable results for Brian Company. They would have received $3,000 in dividends which, because of the deduction for intercorporate dividends, would not be included in their Taxable Income. In addition, they would have a potentially deductible capital loss of $3,000 on the disposition of the shares.

12-21. To prevent this from happening, ITA 112(3) and (3.01) contain "stop loss" rules applicable to shares held as capital property, and ITA 112(4) and (4.01) contain similar rules for shares held as inventory. Under these rules, any loss resulting from a disposition of shares by a corporation must be reduced by the amount of dividends received that are eligible for deduction under ITA 112(1). These rules apply if:

- the shares are held for less than one year; or
- the corporation holding the shares, along with other non-arm's length persons, owns more than 5 percent of the class of shares on which the dividend was received.

12-22. In the preceding example, since Brian Company held the shares for less than one year, the $3,000 capital loss would be eliminated by the $3,000 dividend received. The second condition, whether Brian Company owns more than 5 percent of the class of shares, is not relevant given the length of time the shares were owned.

Exercise Twelve - 3

Subject: Stop Loss Rules

On June 16, 2019, Loren Ltd. acquires 1,000 of the 10,000 shares of Manon Inc. at a cost of $25.30 per share. On July 1, 2020, these shares pay a dividend of $2.16 per share. These are the only dividends that were received on these shares. Loren sells the shares on July 29, 2020, for $21.15 per share. Loren Ltd. has taxable capital gains of $50,000 in the year. What is the amount of the allowable capital loss that Loren Ltd. will include in its tax return for the taxation year ending December 31, 2020?

SOLUTION available in print and online Study Guide.

Foreign Source Dividends Received

12-23.   The situation for dividends received from non-resident corporations is more complex. The general rules are discussed in Chapter 7, which notes that foreign source dividends are included in income on a gross basis, before the deduction of any foreign taxes withheld. However, in Chapter 11 we introduced the foreign non-business tax credit provisions. These credits against federal Canadian Tax Payable are designed to compensate the recipient of foreign source non-business income for foreign taxes withheld at source, provided the income has been subject to a reasonable amount of Canadian taxation. You will recall that, in many situations, the credit against Canadian Tax Payable will be equal to the amount of foreign taxes withheld at source. Note that foreign source dividends are generally not deducted in the determination of Taxable Income (the exception to this general rule is foreign affiliate dividends, which are covered in Chapter 20).

We suggest you work Self Study Problem Twelve-2 at this point.

Non-Capital Loss Carry Over For A Corporation

Additional Issues

12-24.   As the general rules for loss carry overs are the same for all taxpayers, most of the relevant material on this subject is dealt with in Chapter 11 where we discuss the determination of Taxable Income for individuals. There is, however, an additional problem in calculating the amount of the current year non-capital loss carry over for a corporation. This problem relates to the fact that dividends received from taxable Canadian corporations can be deducted by a corporation in the determination of its Taxable Income. To illustrate this problem, consider the following:

> **EXAMPLE** During 2020 Marco Inc. has net taxable capital gains of $30,000 [(1/2)($60,000)], dividends of $25,000 received from taxable Canadian corporations, and a net business loss of $60,000. The company also has a net capital loss carry forward of $50,000 [(1/2)($100,000)].
>
> **ANALYSIS** Using the ITA 3 rules for calculating Net Income For Tax Purposes, the result would be as follows:

ITA 3(a)	Dividends Received	$25,000
ITA 3(b)	Net Taxable Capital Gains	30,000
ITA 3(c)	Subtotal	$55,000
ITA 3(d)	Net Business Loss	(60,000)
Net Income For Tax Purposes And Taxable Income		Nil

12-25.   From an intuitive point of view, it would appear that the non-capital loss for the year is $5,000, the ITA 3(c) subtotal less the net business loss. Further, as Net Income is nil, it appears that none of the net capital loss carry forward can be deducted, despite the $30,000 taxable capital gain. In addition, it does not appear that the company will get any benefit from the potential deduction of the $25,000 in dividends that were received during the year. Fortunately, the ITA 111(8) definition of non-capital loss solves both of these problems.

An Expanded Definition

12-26.   You may recall that the ITA 111(8) definition was discussed previously in Chapter 11. In that material, we explained how the definition permits a net capital loss carry over to be deducted even in cases where current year losses result in a nil Net Income For Tax Purposes. In effect, the definition allows a net capital loss carry over to be converted to a non-capital loss carry over.

12-27.   In the Chapter 11 discussion, we were dealing only with the Taxable Income of individuals. Given this, we did not consider the additional problem that arises with the fact that dividends received by a corporation can be deducted in the calculation of corporate Taxable Income. While this was not apparent from the simplified version of the non-capital loss definition that was presented in Chapter 11, a more complete version of the ITA 111(8) definition deals with this problem. The expanded definition is as follows:

> **ITA 111(8)**   The non-capital loss of a taxpayer for a taxation year means the amount determined by the formula:
>
> $$A - D, \text{ where}$$
>
> **A**   is the amount determined by the formula:
>
> $$E - F, \text{ where}$$
>
> **E**   is the total of all amounts each of which is the taxpayer's loss for the year from an office, employment, business, or property, the taxpayer's allowable business investment loss for the year, net capital loss carry overs deducted in the calculation of Taxable Income for the year (this amount cannot exceed the taxable capital gains for the year), and **dividends received from taxable Canadian corporations and deducted in computing Taxable Income.**
>
> **F**   is the amount of income determined under ITA 3(c). [Sum of ITA 3(a) non-capital positive sources and ITA 3(b) net taxable capital gains, less Division B, Subdivision e deductions.]
>
> **D**   is the taxpayer's farm loss for the year.

12-28.   The only difference in this definition from the one that was presented in Chapter 11 is the addition of "dividends received from taxable Canadian corporations and deducted in computing Taxable Income" in the E component. However, it is an important change in that it allows dividends that cannot be deducted because of insufficient Net Income For Tax Purposes to be added to the non-capital loss carry over balance.

Example

12-29.   All of these points can be illustrated by returning to the example presented in Paragraph 12-24. If we assume that Marco Inc. wishes to deduct the maximum amount of the net capital loss carry forward in 2020, the Net Income For Tax Purposes and Taxable Income would still be nil and the non-capital loss for the year would be calculated as follows:

Amount E:		
Net Business Loss		$ 60,000
Dividends Received And Deducted		25,000
Net Capital Loss Carry Forward Deducted		
(Limited To Net Taxable Capital Gains For The Year)		30,000
Total For Amount E		$115,000
Amount F - ITA 3(c) Income:		
Dividends Received	($25,000)	
Net Taxable Capital Gains	(30,000)	(55,000)
Non-Capital Loss For The Year		$ 60,000
Net Capital Loss Carry Forward ($50,000 - $30,000)		$ 20,000

12-30. Note the results of applying the non-capital loss definition. In effect, if there is not sufficient Net Income to allow their deduction in the calculation of Taxable Income, both dividends and net capital loss amounts deducted can be added to the non-capital loss carry over balance. Although subject to a 3 year carry back, 20 year carry forward limit, the loss carry over can be deducted against any type of income.

Exercise Twelve - 4

Subject: Non-Capital Loss With ABIL

For the taxation year ending December 31, 2020, Hacker Inc. has business and property income of $63,500. Also during this year, capital asset dispositions result in capital gains of $23,100 and capital losses of $38,400. The company experiences a further loss on the arm's length sale of shares of a small business corporation in the amount of $151,500. Determine Hacker Inc.'s Net Income For Tax Purposes for 2020. Indicate the amount and type of any loss carry overs available at the end of the year.

Exercise Twelve - 5

Subject: Non-Capital Loss Carry Forward

The following information is for Loser Ltd., a Canadian public company, for the taxation year ending December 31, 2020:

Capital Gains On Capital Asset Sales	$111,000
Capital Losses On Public Company Stock Sales	84,000
Allowable Business Investment Loss	5,250
Dividends Received From Taxable Canadian Corporations	48,000
Canadian Source Interest Income	27,200
Net Business Loss	273,000

The company has available a net capital loss carry forward of $19,000. It would like to deduct this loss during 2020. Determine the non-capital loss balance [ITA 111(8)] and net capital loss carry forward for Loser Ltd. at the end of the 2020 taxation year.

SOLUTIONS available in print and online Study Guide.

Ordering Of Taxable Income Deductions

12-31. Chapter 11 covered the specific ordering rules in ITA 111.1 for claiming deductions in the calculation of Taxable Income. However, these rules are directed at individuals and do not apply to corporations. The *Act* does not contain an equivalent provision for corporations and, as a consequence, there is a question as to how deductions should be ordered for a corporation.

12-32.   Charitable donations in excess of 75 percent of Net Income For Tax Purposes are not deductible in the current year, but can be carried forward for five years, subject to the same 75 percent limitation in those years. As this is shorter than the carry forward period for any other type of loss, this would suggest using these amounts prior to claiming loss carry forwards. However, in reaching this conclusion, it should also be noted that these donations can be deducted against any type of income.

12-33.   Turning to the deduction of loss carry overs, ITA 111(3) requires that losses within any single category must be deducted in chronological order. That is, if a corporation chooses to deduct a portion of its non-capital loss balance during the current year, the oldest losses of this type must be deducted first. However, there are no rules with respect to the order in which the individual types of loss carry forwards must be deducted.

12-34.   Farm loss carry forwards and non-capital loss carry forwards have restrictions on the time for which they are available. This would suggest that they be deducted first. However, while there is no restriction on the period of availability for capital loss carry forwards, these amounts can only be used to the extent that there are net taxable capital gains during the period.

12-35.   For a corporation that experiences only limited capital gains, these restrictions may be a more important consideration than the period of time during which the loss will be available. With the carry forward period for non-capital losses lasting 20 years, this would appear to leave plenty of time to recover this type of loss.

12-36.   An additional factor in making decisions on whether to deduct non-capital or farm losses is the period left to their expiry. Clearly, items that expire in the current year should be deducted immediately, with additional consideration given to items near the end of their carry forward period.

We suggest you work Self Study Problems Twelve-3 and 4 at this point.

Geographical Allocation Of Income

Permanent Establishments

12-37.   After Taxable Income is calculated, in order to determine the amount of provincial taxes that are payable and the province(s) to which they are due, it is necessary to allocate the income of the corporation to the various provinces. Given the variations in provincial tax rates on corporations, this can be a matter of considerable significance.

12-38.   The key concept here is the idea of a "permanent establishment". This concept is defined as follows:

> **ITR 400(2)**   Permanent establishment means a fixed place of business of the corporation, including an office, a branch, a mine, an oil well, a farm, a timberland, a factory, a workshop, or a warehouse.

12-39.   This meaning has been extended to include having an agent or employee in a province, if that agent or employee has the general authority to contract for a corporation or carries a stock of merchandise from which orders are regularly filled. The mere presence of a commission salesperson or an independent agent is not considered evidence of a permanent establishment. In addition, the presence of a controlled subsidiary in a province is not necessarily indicative of a permanent establishment.

12-40.   However, ITR 400(2)(d) indicates that where a corporation that has a permanent establishment anywhere in Canada owns land in a province, such land will be deemed to be a permanent establishment. In addition, ITR 400(2)(e) indicates that where a corporation uses substantial machinery or equipment in a particular place, that corporation shall be deemed to have a permanent establishment in that place.

Activity At Permanent Establishments

12-41.   Once the location of permanent establishments has been determined, income will be allocated on the basis of two variables. These are gross revenues from the permanent establishment and salaries and wages paid by the establishment.

12-42.   After these values are established, ITR 402(3) provides a formula for using these variables to allocate Taxable Income to provinces. It requires calculating, for each province, that province's gross revenues as a percentage of total corporate gross revenues, and that province's salaries and wages as a percentage of total corporate salaries and wages. A simple average of these two percentages, without regard to the relative dollar values associated with the corporate totals, is then applied to corporate Taxable Income to determine the amount of Taxable Income that will be allocated to that province.

12-43.   Note that, if the corporation has permanent establishments outside of Canada, not all of its Taxable Income will be allocated to a province. The presence of these foreign permanent establishments will be reflected in the calculation of the federal tax abatement (see Paragraph 12-46). If there are no permanent establishments outside of Canada, the federal tax abatement will be the full 10 percent, even if there is foreign investment income.

Example - Permanent Establishments

12-44.   The following example illustrates the process of allocating Taxable Income on a geographic basis:

EXAMPLE   Linford Company has permanent establishments in Alberta, Manitoba, and Ontario. The company's Taxable Income for the current year totaled $100,000, with gross revenues of $1,000,000 and salaries and wages of $500,000.

The following allocation of the gross revenues and the salaries and wages among the provinces occurred during the current year:

Province	Gross Revenues		Salaries And Wages	
	Amount	Percent	Amount	Percent
Alberta	$ 250,000	25.0	$100,000	20.0
Manitoba	400,000	40.0	200,000	40.0
Ontario	350,000	35.0	200,000	40.0
Totals	$1,000,000	100.0	$500,000	100.0

ANALYSIS   Using the average of the two percentages for each province, Linford Company's Taxable Income would be allocated to the three provinces as follows:

Province	Average Percent	Taxable Income	Amount Allocated
Alberta	22.5	$100,000	$ 22,500
Manitoba	40.0	100,000	40,000
Ontario	37.5	100,000	37,500
Totals	100.0	N/A	$100,000

We suggest you work Self Study Problem Twelve-5 at this point.

Federal Tax Payable

Basic Rate

12-45.   All corporations are initially subject to the same basic tax rate. This rate is specified in ITA 123 and, for many years, has been set at 38 percent.

Federal Tax Abatement

12-46.   ITA 124(1) provides a reduction of 10 percentage points in the federal tax rate. This is normally referred to as the federal tax abatement and it is designed to leave room for the provinces to apply their respective tax rates. When deducted from the basic rate of 38 percent, this leaves a net federal rate of 28 percent.

12-47.   Note that this 10 percentage point reduction in the federal tax rate is only applicable to income earned in a Canadian province or territory. When a corporation has foreign operations in permanent establishments outside of Canada, less than 100 percent of its income will be allocated to the various provinces and territories. When this is the case, the amount of abatement to be deducted is reduced by multiplying the 10 percent abatement by the total percentage of Taxable Income that was allocated to the provinces and territories. For example, if only 80 percent of a corporation's Taxable Income was allocated to one or more provinces, the abatement would effectively be reduced to 8 percent [(10%)(80%)].

General Rate Reduction

General Rate Reduction Percentage

12-48.   In implementing changes in the federal rate on corporations, the government has decided to use a process that maintains the basic rate of 38 percent. When changes are required, the desired result is accomplished by using a "general rate reduction percentage." This percentage is applied to what is referred to as "full rate taxable income" (see explanation that follows). Since 2011, the general rate reduction percentage has been 13 percent.

12-49.   In those situations where all of a corporation's income is both allocated to a province and eligible for the general rate reduction, the corporate rate at the federal level is 15 percent:

Basic Corporate Rate	38%
Less: Federal Tax Abatement	(10%)
Balance	28%
Less: General Rate Reduction	(13%)
General Federal Corporate Rate	15%

Full Rate Taxable Income

12-50.   As noted, the "general rate reduction percentage" must be applied to "full rate taxable income." In fairly simple terms, full rate taxable income is income that does not benefit from certain other tax privileges. The most common of these privileges are the small business deduction, the manufacturing and processing profits deduction (M&P deduction), and the refundability of certain types of taxes on the investment income of private companies.

12-51.   Both the small business deduction and the M&P deduction are discussed later in this Chapter. Full rate taxable income will also be considered in this Chapter. The coverage of refundable taxes on the investment income of private companies will not be dealt with until Chapter 13.

Exercise Twelve - 6

Subject: Geographical Allocation And Federal Tax Payable

Sundown Ltd., a Canadian public company, has Taxable Income for the taxation year ending December 31, 2020, in the amount of $226,000. It has Canadian permanent establishments in Ontario and Manitoba. The company's gross revenues for the 2020 taxation year are $2,923,000, with $1,303,000 of this accruing at the permanent establishment in Ontario and $896,000 accruing at the permanent establishment in Manitoba. Wages and salaries total $165,000 for the year. Of this total, $52,000 is at the permanent establishment in Ontario and $94,000 is at the permanent establishment in Manitoba. Sundown has sales to the U.S. through a U.S. permanent establishment. Calculate federal Tax Payable for the taxation year ending December 31, 2020. Ignore any foreign tax implications

SOLUTION available in print and online Study Guide.

Provincial Tax Payable

General Rules

12-52.   In calculating Tax Payable for individuals, a graduated rate structure is involved at both the federal and provincial levels. While limits on the brackets may differ from those used at the federal level, all of the provinces assess taxes on individuals using graduated rates applied to Taxable Income.

12-53.   In contrast, provincial corporate taxes are based on a flat rate applied to a Taxable Income figure. With the exception of Alberta and Quebec, the federal Taxable Income figure is used. While these two provinces collect their own corporate taxes, the Taxable Income figure that they use is normally similar to that used at the federal level.

General Rate

12-54.   As calculated in Paragraph 12-49, the general federal corporate rate is 15 percent. When the varying provincial rates are added to this percentage, Figure 12-3 shows that the general corporate tax rate ranges from a low of 26.5 percent in Ontario to a high of 31 percent in Nova Scotia and Prince Edward Island.

Manufacturing And Processing Rate

12-55.   For many years, manufacturing and processing (M&P) income has been eligible for a 13 percent deduction from Tax Payable at the federal level. More recently, a general rate reduction, providing the same 13 percent reduction in Tax Payable, was made available. As the base for the general rate reduction is reduced by any amounts on which the M&P deduction is claimed, there is little point in claiming the M&P deduction at the federal level. This situation is reflected in Figure 12-3, which indicates that, at the federal level, the general rate and the M&P rate are identical.

	General Rate	M&P Rate	Small Business Rate
Figure 12 - 3 **Combined Federal/Provincial Corporate Rates - March 2020**			
Federal Tax Only	15.0%	15.0%	9.0%
Combined Federal/Provincial			
Alberta	25.0%	25.0%	11.0%
British Columbia	27.0%	27.0%	11.0%
Manitoba	27.0%	27.0%	9.0%
New Brunswick	29.0%	29.0%	11.5%
Newfoundland	30.0%	30.0%	12.0%
Nova Scotia	29.0%	29.0%	11.5%
Ontario	26.5%	25.0%	12.2%
Prince Edward Island	31.0%	31.0%	12.0%
Quebec	26.6%	26.6%	14.0%
Saskatchewan	27.0%	25.0%	11.0%

12-56.   This is also the situation with all but three of the provinces. At one time, there were more provinces with reduced M&P rates, but now only Ontario, Quebec, and Saskatchewan apply reduced rates to this type of income. Because it is still relevant in these two provinces, we provide coverage of the M&P deduction in this Chapter.

Small Business Rate

12-57.   The lowest rates in Figure 12-3 are referred to as the small business rates. As will be discussed later in this Chapter, Canadian controlled private corporations (CCPCs) are eligible for a small business deduction that lowers the federal rate to 9 percent on a limited amount of income. In general, the availability of this reduced rate is limited to the first $500,000 of active business income earned in a year.

12-58.   All of the provinces, with the exception of Saskatchewan, also apply their small business rate to the first $500,000 of active business income. Saskatchewan uses an increased limit of $600,000.

12-59.   When the reduced federal and provincial rates are combined, the resulting rates range from a low of 9 percent in Manitoba, to a high of 15 percent in Quebec. You might note that the 15 percent rate for Quebec is significantly higher than the rates in other provinces. The next highest rate is 12.5 percent in Ontario and Prince Edward Island.

Investment Income Rates

12-60.   While this is not illustrated in Figure 12-3, different rates are applicable to certain types of investment income. We will provide coverage of these rates in Chapter 13.

Other Provincial Taxes

12-61.   At one time, provincial taxes on corporate capital were fairly common. However, though some provinces levy capital taxes on specific types of entities (e.g., financial institutions), none of the provinces has a general tax on corporate capital.

12-62.   Several provinces currently levy payroll taxes, often to fund the provincial health care system. For example, Ontario has a payroll tax on annual payrolls totaling more than $490,000.

Other Goals Of The Corporate Tax System

12-63.   If raising revenues was the only goal of the corporate taxation system, there would be nothing much to discuss with respect to this matter, and there would be little need for the Chapters on corporate taxation that follow. However, in addition to raising revenues, the Canadian corporate taxation system has been structured to accomplish a number of other objectives. These include:

- **Incentives For Small Business**   While there are several features of the tax system directed at encouraging small businesses, the major tax incentive for these organizations is the small business deduction.
- **Incentives For Certain Business Activities**   The Canadian tax system provides generous investment tax credits for scientific research as well as for the employment of apprentices. Support is also provided to the natural resource industries through a variety of programs.
- **Incentives For Certain Regions**   Certain regions of Canada are given assistance through investment tax credits and other programs.
- **Integration**   One of the goals of the Canadian tax system is to keep the level of taxes paid on a given stream of income the same, regardless of whether or not a corporation is placed between the original source of the income and the ultimate recipient.

12-64. The small business deduction and the manufacturing and processing profits deduction will be examined in this Chapter. Integration will be dealt with in detail in Chapter 13. Our material on scientific research and experimental development expenditures and investment tax credits can be found in Chapter 14.

Small Business Deduction

Introduction

12-65. It has been a longstanding goal of the Canadian taxation system to provide incentives to small business. The underlying assumption is that, particularly during their formative years, these businesses need some degree of tax relief in order to allow them to accumulate the capital required for expansion. In very simplified terms, the small business deduction provides a deduction against the Tax Payable of a Canadian controlled private corporation.

12-66. Over the last three years, the deduction has been increased from 17.5 percent in 2017, to 18 percent in 2018, and to 19 percent for 2019 and subsequent years.

12-67. The federal deduction is only available on the first $500,000 of active business income. While almost all provinces use the same $500,000 limit, we have noted previously the Saskatchewan limit is $600,000.

12-68. A simple example will serve to illustrate the application of this deduction.

EXAMPLE   A Canadian controlled private corporation has Taxable Income of $100,000 for the year ending December 31, 2020. All of this income is earned in Canada and eligible for the small business deduction. The provincial tax rate applicable to income eligible for the small business deduction is 3 percent.

ANALYSIS   The corporation's Tax Payable would be calculated as follows:

Base Amount Of Part I Tax [(38%)($100,000)]	$38,000
Federal Tax Abatement [(10%)($100,000)]	(10,000)
Small Business Deduction [(19%)($100,000)]	(19,000)
General Rate Reduction (Note)	Nil
Federal Tax Payable	$ 9,000
Provincial Tax Payable [(3%)($100,000)]	3,000
Total Tax Payable	$12,000

Note   As explained later in this Chapter, the general rate reduction is not available on income that is eligible for the small business deduction.

12-69. As can be seen in the example, when the small business deduction is available, it reduces the federal rate to 9 percent ($9,000 ÷ $100,000). We have also applied a provincial rate of 3 percent (roughly the average provincial rate). This produces a combined federal/provincial rate of 12 percent ($12,000 ÷ $100,000).

12-70. The small business deduction provides a significant incentive to businesses that qualify. Only certain types of corporations qualify for this deduction and it is only available on certain amounts and types of income. The criteria for qualification can be described in non-technical terms as follows:

Type Of Corporation   The availability of the small business deduction is restricted to Canadian controlled private corporations (CCPCs).

Type Of Income   The deduction is only available on income earned in Canada that qualifies as "active business income". This would include the income of professional corporations and management companies, provided they are private and Canadian controlled. However, the income of specified investment businesses and personal services corporations (see definitions later in this Chapter) does not qualify.

Limit On Amount   The federal deduction is available on the first $500,000 of active business income earned in a year. This amount is referred to as the annual business limit and, in some circumstances, it is subject to a reduction formula.

Associated Corporations   The $500,000 annual business limit must be shared among associated corporations.

12-71.   The issues associated with these criteria are discussed in the material that follows.

Canadian Controlled Private Corporation (CCPC)

12-72.   CCPCs are defined in ITA 125(7) as private corporations that are not controlled, directly or indirectly, by one or more non-resident persons, by one or more public corporations, or a combination of non-resident persons and public corporations. In addition, corporations that have shares listed on a designated stock exchange, in or outside of Canada, do not qualify as CCPCs.

Active Business Income

The General Idea

12-73.   ITA 125(7) contains the following definition of "active business":

Active business carried on by a corporation   means any business carried on by the corporation other than a specified investment business or a personal services business and includes an adventure or concern in the nature of trade.

12-74.   While the preceding defines active business, a further definition in ITA 125(7) defines income from an active business as follows:

Income of the corporation for the year from an active business   means ... the income of the corporation for the year from an active business carried on by it, including any income for the year pertaining to or incident to that business, other than income for the year from a source in Canada that is a property ... [The definition goes on to cover an amount under ITA 12(10.2) that is of no interest to users of this material.]

12-75.   While this definition is not a model of clarity, it expresses the basic idea that active business income involves "doing something" to produce income. The concept excludes what is usually referred to as property income. Property income is distinguished by the fact that it generally becomes available with little or no effort on the part of the recipient (e.g., interest earned on long term bonds).

The Problem With Defining Property Income

12-76.   As noted, the preceding definitions of active business and active business income are largely directed toward excluding property income such as interest, dividends, and rents from eligibility for the small business deduction. The Federal government does not wish to allow individuals to have access to the small business deduction by simply placing their passive investments in the shelter of a Canadian controlled private corporation. However, a blanket exclusion of property income is inappropriate since there are corporations that are "actively" involved in earning such income.

12-77.   The difficulty is in finding a way to distinguish between corporations that are simply being used as tax shelters for property or passive income, and corporations that engage in active property management. For example, if a corporation has a single residential rental property, the rents from this property would undoubtedly be viewed as passive income.

12-78.   Alternatively, a corporation that owns a chain of hotels with more than 10,000 rooms would certainly be entitled to view the rentals of these properties as an active business. The question is, at what point does the corporation cross the line between earning passive investment income and active business income?

12-79.   Similar but less obvious problems arise with interest income. If a corporation has no activity other than collecting interest on term deposits, the amounts that it earns would almost certainly be viewed as passive investment income. Alternatively, interest earned by a company actively involved in providing mortgage financing to corporate clients could be viewed as business income. Again, a problem exists in finding the point at which a crossover is made between the two situations.

The Solution - Specified Investment Business

12-80.   The concept of a "specified investment business" provides a somewhat arbitrary solution to this problem. The term is defined in ITA 125(7) as follows:

> **Specified Investment Business** carried on by a corporation in a taxation year, means a business (other than a business carried on by a credit union or a business of leasing property other than real or immovable property) the principal purpose of which is to derive income (including interest, dividends, rents and royalties) from property but, except where the corporation was a prescribed labour-sponsored venture capital corporation at any time in the year, does not include a business carried on by the corporation in the year where
>
> (i)   the corporation employs in the business throughout the year more than five full-time employees, or
>
> (ii)   any other corporation associated with the corporation provides, in the course of carrying on an active business, managerial, administrative, financial, maintenance or other similar services to the corporation in the year and the corporation could reasonably be expected to require more than five full-time employees if those services had not been provided.

12-81.   As the activities of these specified investment businesses are excluded from the definition of active business, it means that income from property generated by such businesses is not eligible for the small business deduction. Stated alternatively, for corporations that are primarily engaged in earning income from property, the *Act* specifies that only those with more than five full time employees involved in earning such income are considered to be earning active business income and eligible for the small business deduction.

12-82.   While this is an arbitrary solution to the problem of distinguishing between active and passive investment income from a business, it does serve to resolve most of the uncertainty in this area. With respect to interpreting this rule, IT-73R6 states that "more than five full-time employees" means that at least six employees are working full business days on each working day of the year. However, this interpretation has been overturned in a Tax Court of Canada Decision *(489599 B.C. Ltd. vs. The Queen).*

12-83.   In this decision, the court indicated that a combination of five full time employees and one part time employee would constitute "more than five full-time employees". While IT-73R6 is archived and will not be revised to reflect the results in this case, the CRA has indicated that they accept this decision and will rule accordingly in future applications of the specified investment business definition.

Incidental Property Income

12-84.   The definition of active business income includes incidental property income that is earned by a corporation engaged in an active business. In this regard, many corporations experience temporary excess cash balances, and these balances will usually be invested in interest bearing assets. Within reasonable limits, such interest can be included as a component of active business income. In similar fashion, revenues resulting from temporary rentals of excess space may be included in active business income.

Property Income Received From An Associated Corporation

12-85.   Income from a specified investment business and non-incidental property income earned by a CCPC do not qualify for the small business deduction. However, when a corporation derives income from holding property, and the income is received from an associated company that deducted the amounts in computing active business income, ITA 129(6)(b) deems the income to be active business income to the recipient.

12-86.   The logic behind this is that, while the amounts received by one of the associated companies must be considered property income, because of its legal form, the deduction by the payer corporation reduces the total active business income within the associated group.

> **EXAMPLE**   Lardin Inc. is associated with Dwarm Ltd. Lardin lends $100,000 to Dwarm to use in active business activities. During the current year, Dwarm pays $6,000 of interest to Lardin.
>
> **ANALYSIS**   Normally, Lardin could not classify the interest received as active business income. However, if Dwarm is earning active business income, the payment to Lardin reduced the amount of this income, as well as the total active business income of the associated group. In order to prevent this reduction, the recipient corporation is allowed to treat such interest as active business income.

Annual Business Limit

12-87.   The federal limit on the amount of active business income that is eligible for the small business deduction is $500,000 per taxation year. As discussed in the paragraph that follows, this annual limit must be shared by associated corporations. In addition, as will be discussed beginning at Paragraph 12-102, this $500,000 limit will be reduced for CCPCs with either Taxable Capital Employed in Canada in excess of $10 million or ADJUSTED Aggregate Investment Income in excess of $50,000 in the previous year. We have capitalized ADJUSTED to avoid confusion with Aggregate Investment Income (see Paragraph 12-142).

Allocation Among Associated Companies

12-88.   In the absence of special rules, it would be very easy to avoid the annual limit that applies to the small business deduction. This could be accomplished by dividing a single corporation's activities between two separate corporations, thereby doubling up on the annual business limit of $500,000. However, the *Act* prevents this by requiring that associated companies share their annual business limit.

12-89.   In some cases, association is fairly obvious. If, for example, a single individual owned all of the shares to two separate corporations, these corporations are clearly associated. However, a complete coverage of this subject becomes very complex. Because of this, we have allocated our detailed coverage of this subject to Chapter 14, "Other Issues In Corporate Taxation".

12-90.   While we are deferring our detailed coverage of this subject, we would note here that a group of associated companies can allocate the $500,000 limit in any manner that they wish. It can be divided equally among the group, allocated 100 percent to a single member of the group, or split in any proportions that the group chooses to use.

Calculating The Small Business Deduction

The General Formula

12-91.   After noting that to qualify for this deduction a corporation must be a CCPC throughout the year, ITA 125(1) specifies that the deduction from federal Tax Payable is equal to 19 percent of the least of three figures (note that for ease of reference, this formula is included at the front of this text in "Rates and Other Data"):

(a) Net Canadian active business income.

(b) Taxable Income, less:

   (i)   100/28 times the ITA 126(1) credit for taxes paid on foreign non-business income, calculated without consideration of the additional refundable tax under ITA 123.3 (see Chapter 13) or the general rate reduction under ITA 123.4; and

   (ii) 4 times the ITA 126(2) credit for taxes paid on foreign business income, calculated without consideration of the general rate reduction under ITA 123.4 (see Note)

(c) The annual business limit of $500,000, less any portion allocated to associated corporations, less any Taxable Capital Employed in Canada or ADJUSTED Aggregate Investment Income grind. (These grinds are explained later in this Chapter.)

Note   ITA 125(1)(b)(ii) actually has a more complicated calculation as follows:

... the amount determined by the formula

$$1 \div (A - B), \text{ where}$$

A   is the percentage set out in paragraph 123(1)(a) [the basic federal rate of 38 percent], and

B   is the percentage that is the corporation's general rate reduction percentage (as defined by section 123.4) for the taxation year [13 percent].

Given these numbers, ITA 125(1)(b)(ii) is calculated as $[1 \div (.38 - .13)] = 4$. We will use this number 4 in all of our examples and problems, without showing the complete calculation.

Constraints - Type Of Income And Annual Business Limit
12-92.   We have already noted that the deduction is only available on active business income earned in Canada, the item A constraint. We have also noted that the annual business limit of $500,000, the item C constraint, must be shared by associated companies.

Constraints - Taxable Income
12-93.   With respect to the limit that uses Taxable Income, we would note that active business income earned during the taxation year is included in Net Income For Tax Purposes. In many cases, this amount will also be included in full in Taxable Income. However, it is possible that large Division C deductions could eliminate all or part of this income from the Taxable Income total. Examples of such Division C deductions would be as follows:

- charitable donations
- non-capital loss carry overs
- farm loss carry overs

12-94.   You will notice that neither dividends nor net capital losses are included in this list. This reflects the fact that these amounts can only be deducted to the extent that either dividends or taxable capital gains are included in Net Income. Given this, they cannot serve to offset amounts of active business income that are included in Net Income For Tax Purposes.

12-95.   A simple example will illustrate the need for this Taxable Income constraint on the small business deduction:

EXAMPLE   During the current year, Allard Ltd. has active business income of $123,000, taxable capital gains of $15,000, and dividends received from taxable Canadian corporations of $50,000. At the beginning of the year, Allard Ltd. has a net capital loss carry forward of $35,000 and a non-capital loss carry forward of $105,000. The company will use the loss carry forwards to the extent possible during the current year. The calculation of Allard's Net Income For Tax Purposes and Taxable Income would be as follows:

Net Income For Tax Purposes	
($123,000 + $15,000 + $50,000)	$188,000
Dividends Received	(50,000)
(Limited To Taxable Capital Gains)	(15,000)
Subtotal (Equal To Active Business Income)	$123,000
Non-Capital Loss Carry Forward	(105,000)
Taxable Income	$ 18,000

12-96. Note that if only the net capital loss carry forward and dividends were deducted, Taxable Income would have been equal to the $123,000 in active business income. The problem is the non-capital loss carry forward. It has further reduced Taxable Income to $18,000, an amount well below the active business income.

12-97. If, in this case, the small business deduction were based on active business income, the amount would be $23,370 [(19%)($123,000)]. As this deduction is in excess of the Tax Payable on $18,000 of Taxable Income, this is not a reasonable outcome. The example clearly illustrates the need for the Taxable Income constraint on the small business deduction.

Constraints - Foreign Tax Credits

12-98. Another concern of the Federal government is to ensure that the small business deduction is not provided on income that has not been taxed in Canada. To prevent this from happening, the B component of the ITA 125(1) formula reduces Taxable Income by:

- 100/28 times the ITA 126(1) credit for taxes paid on foreign non-business income, calculated without consideration of the additional refundable tax under ITA 123.3 (see Chapter 13) or the general rate reduction under ITA 123.4; and
- 4 times the ITA 126(2) credit for taxes paid on foreign business income, calculated without consideration of the general rate reduction under ITA 123.4.

12-99. The 100/28 figure is based on the notional assumption that foreign non-business income will be subject to a federal tax rate of 28 percent (i.e., if the credit is equal to the taxes paid at 28 percent, 100/28 times the credit will equal the notional amount of income received).

12-100. In similar fashion, the 4 times figure that is applicable to foreign business income is based on the notional assumption that this income will be subject to a federal tax rate of 25 (1 ÷ 4) percent.

12-101. Based on the preceding analysis, subtracting these amounts from Taxable Income has the effect of removing from this figure the amounts of foreign income on which the foreign tax credit has eliminated the Canadian taxation at the assumed rates of 28 and 25 percent. A simple example can be used to clarify this point:

EXAMPLE A corporation earns $100,000 in foreign non-business income, with $18,000 being withheld by the foreign government.

If this income had been earned in Canada, it is assumed that the tax would be $28,000 (using the notional rate on this type of income of 28 percent). Being received from a foreign source, the $28,000 in Canadian Tax Payable will be offset by the $18,000 foreign tax credit. This will leave a net Canadian Tax Payable of $10,000.

Using the foreign tax credit of $18,000 and an assumed tax rate of 28 percent, the formula removes $64,286 [(100/28)($18,000)] from Taxable Income, leaving $35,714 ($100,000 - $64,286). If we multiply this $35,714 by the notional rate of 28 percent, the result is $10,000, the amount of Canadian tax remaining after the application of the foreign tax credit. This demonstrates how the formula ensures that the small business deduction is not available on Taxable Income on which foreign tax credits have eliminated Canadian taxation.

If the foreign tax withheld and the foreign tax credit had been $28,000 [(28%)($100,000)], the formula would have removed $100,000 [(100/28)($28,000)], or all of the foreign source income.

Exercise Twelve - 7

Subject: Amount Eligible For The Small Business Deduction

Kartoom Ltd. is a CCPC that began operations on January 1, 2019. It is not associated with any other corporation. For the year ending December 31, 2019, Kartoom has Net Income For Tax Purposes of $570,000. This amount is made up of dividends from taxable Canadian corporations of $85,000, active business income of $425,000, and foreign non-business income of $60,000. The foreign income was subject to withholding in the foreign jurisdiction at a rate of 15 percent. Kartoom receives a foreign tax credit against federal Tax Payable that is equal to the amount withheld. Kartoom has a non-capital loss carry forward of $160,000, which it intends to deduct during 2019.

Determine the amount eligible for the small business deduction for the year ending December 31, 2019.

SOLUTION available in print and online Study Guide.

Annual Business Limit Reduction

Problem I

12-102.   As the name implies, the small business deduction was designed to provide assistance to small corporations. For a variety of reasons, including the belief that such corporations have a positive impact on employment growth and the fact that small corporations often experience financing difficulties in their formative years, the generous tax advantages provided by this deduction were thought to be appropriate.

12-103.   However, in designing the small business deduction provisions, eligibility was based on the type of income earned (active business income) and the type of corporation (CCPCs). No consideration was given to the size of the corporation's income or assets. As a consequence, under its usual provisions, some very large private corporations received the benefit of the small business deduction on amounts of active business income that were below the annual business limit. This was clearly not in keeping with the intent of this legislation.

12-104.   To deal with this problem, there has been a grind (i.e., a programmed reduction) in the annual business limit for many years. For CCPCs that have Taxable Capital Employed in Canada (TCEC) in excess of $10 million, the annual business limit for the small business deduction is gradually reduced, with the basic $500,000 completely disappearing when the TCEC reaches $15 million.

Problem II

12-105.   A second and more recently identified problem was described in the introductory Note to this Chapter. This is the fact that the low small business rate allows those shareholders that do not need all of the income from their corporation to accumulate large portfolios of passive investments.

12-106.   As of 2019, a second grind is applied to the annual business limit. This grind is based on a CCPC's ADJUSTED Aggregate Investment Income. This unique version of investment income, defined in ITA 125(7), is used only for purposes of determining this grind of the small business deduction. In somewhat simplified terms it contains:

- interest, rents, and royalties;
- net taxable capital gains on the disposition of capital assets not used in the active business of the corporation;
- dividends received from taxable Canadian corporations with the exception of those from connected corporations (defined in Chapter 13); and
- dividends from foreign corporations with the exception of those from foreign affiliates (defined in Chapter 20).

12-107. This grind is accompanied by some very complex provisions related to the Refundable Dividend Tax On Hand (RDTOH) balance. As we do not cover investment income received by a CCPC or the determination of the RDTOH balance until Chapter 13, there is a case for deferring coverage of this grind until Chapter 13. However, the revised ITA 125(5.1) requires that the overall grind be based on the greater of the Taxable Capital Employed in Canada grind and the ADJUSTED Aggregate Investment Income grind. Because of this relationship, we are providing coverage of both grinds in this Chapter. Note, however, our coverage of the ADJUSTED Aggregate Investment Income grind will be limited to the calculation of the small business deduction. When investment income is involved, we cannot illustrate the determination of Tax Payable for a CCPC at this stage.

Taxable Capital Employed In Canada (TCEC) Grind - ITA 125(5.1)

12-108. The formula for this component of the annual business limit grind is as follows:

Taxable Capital Employed in Canada REDUCTION $= A \times \dfrac{B}{\$11,250}$ where,

A is the amount of the corporation's annual business limit for the year ($500,000 or less if shared with associated corporations).

B is 0.225 percent (.00225) of the excess over $10 million of the previous year end's total Taxable Capital Employed in Canada of the corporation and any associated companies.

NOTE This formula is for the **reduction** of the annual business limit, not for the available balance.

12-109. "Taxable capital employed in Canada" is defined in ITA 181.2. In somewhat simplified terms, it has the following meaning:

Taxable Capital Employed in Canada (TCEC) GAAP determined debt and equity capital of the corporation, less certain types of debt and equity investments in other corporations. When not all of the corporation's Taxable Income is allocated to a province, the resulting amount is multiplied by the same percentage that is applied to the abatement in order to determine the portion of the total capital that is employed in Canada.

12-110. The mechanics of this formula are easily understood. If a corporation has $10 million or less TCEC, B will equal nil ($10 million or less minus the $10 million specified deduction). This means the formula amount will be nil and there will be no reduction in the corporation's annual business limit.

12-111. When the amount of TCEC for the previous year reaches $15 million, B in the formula will be equal to $11,250 [(.00225)($15,000,000 - $10,000,000)]. The annual business limit will then be multiplied by one ($11,250 ÷ $11,250) and the reduction in the annual business limit will be 100 percent of the available amount.

12-112. Not surprisingly, a CCPC that is associated with one or more other corporations in a taxation year ending in a given calendar year will be required to take into account the TCEC of all of these firms.

Example Of The TCEC Grind

12-113.   The following example illustrates the reduction of the small business deduction for a large CCPC:

EXAMPLE   Largess Inc. is a CCPC with a December 31 year end. All of its income is earned in Canada, and it is not associated with any other corporation. On December 31, 2020, the following information is available:

2020 Active Business Income	$ 523,000
2020 Taxable Income	550,000
2019 Taxable Capital Employed In Canada	13,700,000
2019 ADJUSTED Aggregate Investment Income	Nil

ANALYSIS   For the preceding year, 2019, B in the reduction formula would be equal to $8,325 [(.00225)($13,700,000 - $10,000,000)]. Using this in the ITA 125(5.1) formula would produce the following reduction in the 2020 annual business limit:

$$\$500,000 \times \frac{\$8,325}{\$11,250} = \$370,000 \text{ \textbf{Reduction}}$$

Given this, the reduced annual business limit would be $130,000 ($500,000 - $370,000) and the small business deduction for 2020 would be 19 percent of the least of:

Active Business Income	$523,000
Taxable Income	550,000
Reduced Annual Business Limit ($500,000 - $370,000)	130,000

The reduced annual business limit is the least of the three figures and the 2020 small business deduction would be $24,700[(19%)($130,000)], a significant reduction from the $95,000 [(19%)($500,000)] that would have been available in the absence of the ITA 125(5.1) requirement for reducing the annual business limit for large CCPCs.

Exercise Twelve - 8

Subject: Taxable Capital Employed In Canada (TCEC) Grind

Largely Small Inc. is a Canadian controlled private corporation. For the year ending December 31, 2020, its Net Income For Tax Purposes is $1,233,000, all of which is active business income, except for $36,000 in foreign source non-business income. Fifteen percent of this amount was withheld in the foreign jurisdiction, and the corporation receives a foreign tax credit against federal Tax Payable that is equal to the amount withheld. The corporation's only deduction in the calculation of Taxable Income is for a non-capital loss carry forward of $914,000. The corporation had Taxable Capital Employed in Canada of $11,300,000 for the year ending December 31, 2019, and $11,600,000 for the year ending December 31, 2020. It is not associated with any other corporation. Determine the amount of Largely Small Inc.'s small business deduction for the year ending December 31, 2020.

SOLUTION available in print and online Study Guide.

ADJUSTED Aggregate Investment Income Grind - ITA 125(5.1)

12-114. The formula for the ADJUSTED Aggregate Investment Income grind is as follows:

ADJUSTED Aggregate Investment Income REDUCTION

$$= \left[\frac{D}{\$500,000} \right] [(5)(E - \$50,000)] \text{ where,}$$

D is the amount of the corporation's annual business limit for the year ($500,000 or less if shared with associated corporations).

E the total of all amounts each of which is the ADJUSTED Aggregate Investment Income of the corporation or of any corporation with which it is associated for the preceding year.

12-115. As we have noted, ADJUSTED Aggregate Investment Income is a unique concept that is only used for the purposes of determining this grind of the annual business limit.

12-116. As was the case with the TCEC grind formula, the ADJUSTED Aggregate Investment Income grind formula is fairly easy to understand. If the CCPC's ADJUSTED Aggregate Investment Income for the previous year is $50,000 or less, there is no reduction in its annual business limit.

EXAMPLE Before the grind, DOC Inc. has an annual business limit of $500,000 and ADJUSTED Aggregate Investment Income for the previous year of $50,000. Its TCEC for the previous year is less than $10 million.

ANALYSIS The required reduction would be calculated as follows:

[($500,000/$500,000)][(5)($50,000 - $50,000)] = Nil

This would leave the company's annual business limit at $500,000.

12-117. Alternatively, for every dollar of ADJUSTED Aggregate Investment Income in excess of $50,000, the company's annual business limit will be reduced by $5.

EXAMPLE Before the grind, Arc Ltd. has an annual business limit of $500,000 and ADJUSTED Aggregate Investment Income for the previous year of $75,000. Its TCEC for the previous year is less than $10 million.

ANALYSIS The required reduction would be calculated as follows:

[($500,000/$500,000)][(5)($75,000 - $50,000)] = $125,000 **Reduction**

This would leave an annual business limit of $375,000 ($500,000 - $125,000).

Exercise Twelve - 9

Subject: ADJUSTED Aggregate Investment Income Grind

Investco Ltd. is a Canadian controlled private corporation. For the fiscal year ending December 31, 2020, its Net Income For Tax Purposes and Taxable Income is made up of active business income of $350,000 plus ADJUSTED Aggregate Investment Income of $125,000. For 2019, its ADJUSTED Aggregate Investment Income was $105,000. Its TCEC was $9 million for 2020 and $8 million for 2019. Because of its association with Subco Ltd., its 2020 allocation of the annual business limit is $300,000. Subco's TCEC was $200,000 for 2020 and for 2019. Subco has no ADJUSTED Aggregate Investment Income in either year.

Determine the amount of Investco's small business deduction for the year ending December 31, 2020.

SOLUTION available in print and online Study Guide.

Economic Impact

12-118. As indicated previously, the actual reduction in the annual business limit will be the greater of the TCEC grind and the ADJUSTED Aggregate Investment Income grind. With respect to the TCEC grind, it will only have an effect on CCPCs that have TCEC in excess of $10 million. This means that the great majority of CCPCs would not be affected.

12-119. With respect to the new ADJUSTED Aggregate Investment Income grind, in its notes to the new legislation, the Department of Finance has indicated their belief that only about 3 percent of the companies claiming the small business deduction will be affected.

12-120. Even in those situations where there is a reduction in the annual business limit, this may have no impact on the company's small business deduction. There are many CCPCs that do not have sufficient active business income to fully use their annual business limit. In such situations, the application of these grinds will only increase Tax Payable in those situations where the annual business limit is reduced below the CCPC's active business income.

Exercise Twelve - 10

Subject: Annual Business Limit Reduction

Reduco Inc. is a Canadian controlled private corporation. For the fiscal year ending December 31, 2020, its Net Income For Tax Purposes of $540,000 is made up of active business income of $450,000 and $90,000 of ADJUSTED Aggregate Investment Income. For 2019, the Reduco's ADJUSTED Aggregate Investment Income was $72,000. Its only deduction in the determination of 2020 Taxable Income is a non-capital loss carry forward of $60,000. Because of its association with another company, Reduco's share of the annual business limit is $350,000. The associated company has no ADJUSTED Aggregate Investment Income for either 2019 or 2020.

Determine Reduco's small business deduction for the year ending December 31, 2020, assuming that the combined TCEC of Reduco and its associated company was:

Case 1 $11,000,000 for 2020 and $13,500,000 for 2019.

Case 2 $13,500,000 for 2020 and $11,000,000 for 2019.

SOLUTION available in print and online Study Guide.

Personal Services Corporations

12-121. The small business deduction represents a very significant reduction in corporate taxes and, as a consequence, taxpayers have a strong incentive to channel income into a corporation qualifying for this benefit.

12-122. At one point in time, this could be accomplished by having an executive of a corporation resign, establish a company, and immediately have his or her company sign a contract with the former employer to provide the same services as the individual was previously performing as an employee. Since this new corporation could then qualify for the small business deduction, the use of such personal services corporations provided significant tax deferral and, in some cases, significant tax avoidance for individuals such as executives, professional athletes, and entertainers.

12-123. Under the current rules, such blatant tax avoidance schemes are no longer possible. To begin, ITA 125(7) defines a "personal services business" as follows:

... a business of providing services where

    (a) an individual who performs services on behalf of the corporation (referred to as an incorporated employee), or

    (b) any person related to the incorporated employee

is a specified shareholder of the corporation and the incorporated employee would reasonably be regarded as an officer or employee of the person or partnership to whom or to which the services were provided but for the existence of the corporation, unless

(a) the corporation employs in the business throughout the year more than five full-time employees, or

(b) the amount paid or payable to the corporation in the year for the services is received or receivable by it from a corporation with which it was associated in the year.

12-124.   In less technical language, a corporation is classified as a personal services business when a "specified shareholder", or a person related to a "specified shareholder", is providing services to another business and the individual who is performing the services can reasonably be regarded as an officer or employee of the entity for which the services are performed. As the term is used in this definition, in general, "specified shareholder" refers to an individual who owns, directly or indirectly, not less than 10 percent of the shares of any class of the corporation that is providing the services.

12-125.   Being classified as a personal services corporation is costly in terms of tax. Such a corporation is not eligible for the small business deduction or the general rate reduction. In addition, due to the fact that the maximum individual federal rate is 33 percent, these corporations are subject to an additional tax of 5 percent, resulting in an overall federal rate of 33 percent (38% - 10% + 5%), which is equal to the maximum individual federal rate.

12-126.   In addition to this high rate, personal services corporations cannot deduct any expenses other than:

- salaries, wages, other remuneration and benefits paid in the year to the individual who performed the services on behalf of the corporation; and
- other expenses that would normally be deductible against employment income, for example, travel expenses incurred to earn employment income.

12-127.   These rules serve to make the use of a personal services corporation undesirable in situations where they were once used to save taxes on an executive's employment income. However, athletes, entertainers, and consultants may still find it attractive to incorporate. In many cases, they will qualify for the small business deduction either because they have sufficient diversity of income or more than five full time employees. In addition, there is an advantage in that all of the income of a personal services business is added to the GRIP balance (see Chapter 13), meaning that all of the income can be paid out as eligible dividends.

Professional Corporations And Management Companies

12-128.   In general terms, these two types of corporations can be described as follows:

Professional Corporations   This term is used where a corporation is established to carry on the practice of a profession specified in ITA 248(1). The ITA definition includes a corporation that carries on the professional practice of an accountant, dentist, lawyer, medical doctor, veterinarian, or chiropractor. Each province has different laws and rules as to which professions are allowed to incorporate. The incorporation of the professional practice of an engineer or architect would not meet the ITA definition.

Management Companies   This is a term that refers to corporations established to provide various management services, primarily to an unincorporated business. The unincorporated business is usually a professional practice, such as that of a doctor or dentist.

The services provided by this type of company include various personnel functions, such as payroll and accounting services, purchasing all supplies and equipment necessary to carry on the business, and providing the necessary office space required by the professional practice.

The unincorporated business pays fees to the company to cover the cost of providing management services and to provide for some income. A 15 percent markup for profit is usually allowed. The fees paid are deductible from the revenues of the professional practice. These companies are often used to transfer a portion of a professional's income to a lower income spouse or other related parties.

12-129.   Both types of companies are eligible for the small business deduction. However, the fact that medical services are exempt goods under the GST/HST legislation has made management companies unattractive for doctors and dentists. While GST/HST must be paid on services billed by the management company, these amounts cannot be recovered by medical professionals because their services are GST/HST exempt. (For coverage of GST/HST exempt services, see Chapter 21, "GST/HST".) Given this situation, and the fact that professionals can incorporate, management companies for medical professionals delivering GST/HST exempt services are not as common as they once were.

Manufacturing And Processing Profits Deduction

Introduction

12-130.   Given the importance of such activity to the Canadian economy, it is not surprising that the Federal government has provided tax assistance to enterprises that are involved in manufacturing and processing (M&P). As an example of this, in Chapter 5, "Capital Cost Allowances", we noted that the government is providing significantly enhanced CCA rates on both buildings used for M&P and for M&P machinery and equipment.

12-131.   A more general incentive is the M&P deduction available to some corporations for their M&P profits. IT Folio S4-F15-C1, "Manufacturing and Processing", discusses the calculation of this deduction and activities that are and are not considered to be manufacturing or processing.

12-132.   As was explained previously, the rate for this deduction is the same as the percentage for the general rate reduction. Since the general rate reduction does not apply to income that is eligible for the M&P deduction, the use of the M&P deduction does not provide any direct tax benefits at the federal level. Given this situation, it would seem logical for the government to eliminate the complex legislation related to the M&P deduction. However, this has not happened. The probable explanation for this is that three provinces, Ontario, Quebec, and Saskatchewan, provide special treatment for income that qualifies for the federal M&P deduction. Because of this, and the special CCA rates for M&P assets, we will continue to provide some coverage of the M&P rules.

Calculating The Deduction

General Formula

12-133.   ITA 125.1 provides for a deduction from Tax Payable equal to the general rate reduction of 13 percent times the company's M&P profits. Given that this amount is deducted from Tax Payable, it would be more consistent to refer to this "deduction" as a tax credit. However, ITA 125.1 uses the term deduction and, as a consequence, we will also use this terminology.

12-134.   While the basic idea is that the deduction is equal to the general rate reduction percentage applied to M&P profits, there are a number of other constraints on the amount that is eligible for this deduction. ITA 125.1(1) specifies that the deduction will be equal to the corporation's general rate reduction percentage multiplied by the lesser of:

A   Manufacturing and processing profits, less amounts eligible for the small business deduction; and

B   Taxable income, less the sum of:

   1.   the amount eligible for the small business deduction;

2. the relevant factor (see note) multiplied by the foreign tax credit for business income calculated without consideration of the general rate reduction under ITA 123.4; and

3. where the corporation is a Canadian controlled private corporation throughout the year, Aggregate Investment Income as defined in ITA 129(4).

Note The relevant factor is the same for both the small business deduction and the M&P deduction. While this is a simplification, we will use 4 as the relevant factor in our examples and problems (see Paragraph 12-91 for an explanation).

12-135.   Part A of this formula provides the basic limit based on the amount of M&P profits earned during the year. As will be noted subsequently, M&P profits is a technical term and must be calculated by a formula established in ITR 5200. In many cases, particularly for large public companies, this will be the factor that limits the amount of the M&P deduction.

12-136.   Like the small business deduction formula, for ease of reference, this M&P deduction formula is included at the front of this text in "Rates and Other Data".

Constraints - Small Business Deduction
12-137.   As was previously discussed, the small business deduction provides certain corporations with a deduction equal to 19 percent of the first $500,000 of their active business income. It appears that the government believes that granting both the 13 percent M&P deduction and the 19 percent small business deduction on the same income stream would be too generous. As a consequence, any amounts of income that are eligible for the small business deduction are not eligible for the M&P deduction. In the preceding ITA 125.1(1) formula, this is accomplished by removing amounts eligible for the small business deduction from both the A and B components. Note that it is the "amount eligible" for the small business deduction that is removed, not the deduction itself.

Constraints - Taxable Income
12-138.   As was explained in our discussion of constraints on the availability of the small business deduction, the government wants to ensure that credits are not given on amounts that are not included in Taxable Income. As was the case with the active business income that is eligible for the small business deduction, M&P profits that are included in Net Income For Tax Purposes may not find their way into Taxable Income.

12-139.   This can occur when the corporation has deductions for such items as charitable donations, non-capital loss carry overs, or farm loss carry overs. For reasons that were discussed and illustrated in the discussion of the small business deduction, amounts eligible for the M&P deduction are limited by the amount of Taxable Income for the year.

Constraints - Foreign Tax Credits
12-140.   As was the case with the Taxable Income constraint, the nature of the constraint created by deducting a multiple of foreign tax credits was explained in our discussion of the small business deduction. There is, however, one significant difference.

12-141.   In the ITA 125.1(1) formula for the M&P deduction, Taxable Income is reduced by a multiple of the foreign business income credit only. It is not adjusted for the foreign non-business income credit as was the case with the ITA 125(1) formula for the small business deduction. This probably reflects the fact that the M&P formula contains an extra deduction from Taxable Income for Aggregate Investment Income, an amount that includes foreign non-business income.

Constraints - Aggregate Investment Income
12-142.   This constraint is more difficult to explain at this stage of the text. It is based on the fact that part of the federal tax paid on the Aggregate Investment Income of a Canadian controlled private corporation can be refunded to the corporation (this procedure is discussed in detail in Chapter 13). As it would not be appropriate to provide a tax credit against taxes that are

intended to be refunded, these amounts are removed from the Taxable Income that is eligible for the M&P deduction.

12-143.   In the formula in Paragraph 12-134, note the reference to "Aggregate Investment Income as defined in ITA 129(4)". As discussed fully in Chapter 13, "Taxation Of Corporate Investment Income", this somewhat unusual concept of investment income is defined as follows:

Net Taxable Capital Gains	$xxx
Property Income (Including Foreign Source)	
Interest (That Is Not Active Business Income)	xxx
Rents	xxx
Royalties	xxx
Total Positive Amounts	$xxx
Net Capital Loss Carry Overs Deducted During The Year	(xxx)
ITA 129(4) Aggregate Investment Income	$xxx

Note that, in contrast to the usual concept of investment income, this definition does not include most dividends. Technically only dividends that are deductible in computing a corporation's Taxable Income are excluded. This calculation is included at the front of this text in "Rates and Other Data".

Also note that this definition is different from the ADJUSTED Aggregate Investment Income that is used in calculating the ADJUSTED Aggregate Investment Income grind on the annual business limit for the small business deduction.

Eligibility

12-144.   On the surface, eligibility for the M&P deduction appears to be easily determinable. Any corporation that derives 10 percent or more of its Canadian active business gross revenues from Canadian manufacturing or processing is eligible. The problem with this rule is the determination of what constitutes M&P activity.

12-145   The *Income Tax Act* does not define the terms manufacturing or processing. However, ITA 125.1(3) specifically excludes several types of activity from the designation of manufacturing or processing. These include logging, farming and fishing, construction, producing industrial minerals, and processing mineral resources.

M&P Profits Defined

12-146.   We have noted that the M&P deduction is calculated by multiplying the general rate reduction percentage by "M&P profits". The determination of M&P profits is based on a fairly complex calculation that is found in ITR 5200. Given that this is largely a mechanical process and the fact that the M&P deduction no longer has an effect on the amount of federal Tax Payable, we are not providing coverage of this calculation in our text.

Exercise Twelve - 11

Subject: Amounts Eligible For Small Business and M&P Deductions

Marion Manufacturing is a Canadian controlled private corporation throughout 2020 and is not associated with any other company. It has Net Income For Tax Purposes of $462,000, a figure that includes $411,000 in manufacturing and processing profits (as per ITR 5200). The $462,000 also includes foreign source business income of $21,000 and taxable capital gains of $30,000. Because of withholding on the foreign source business income, the company is entitled to a foreign tax credit of $3,150 [(15%)($21,000)].

The company's only deduction in the calculation of Taxable Income is donations to registered Canadian charities in the amount of $310,000. Marion anticipates large increases in Taxable Income in the next few years.

Determine the amount of Marion's small business deduction and M&P deduction for the year ending December 31, 2020, assuming that the company deducts all of the $310,000 of charitable donations. Do you believe that deducting all of the donations is the best alternative for Marion? Explain your conclusion.

SOLUTION available in print and online Study Guide.

General Rate Reduction - ITA 123.4(2)

Approach To Rate Reductions

12-147.   In our discussion of the basic federal tax rate for corporations, we noted that, in implementing reductions in corporate tax rates, the government has left the basic rate of 38 percent unchanged (see Paragraph 12-45). Instead of reducing the basic rate, they have created a deduction from this rate. This deduction is referred to as the "general rate reduction" percentage and the rate is currently 13 percent.

12-148.   While the government wished to reduce corporate tax rates through the use of this general rate reduction, they did not want it to be available on income that was already benefitting from some other tax privilege (e.g., the small business deduction). To deal with this potential problem, the government introduced the concept of Full Rate Taxable Income.

Full Rate Taxable Income

12-149.   In defining Full Rate Taxable Income, the goal was to develop a measure of income that did not benefit in a significant way from other legislative provisions. In particular, the government did not want this reduction to be applied to income that was eligible for:

- The small business deduction.   This deduction is only available to CCPCs.
- The M&P deduction.   This deduction is available to CCPCs, public companies, and private companies that are not Canadian controlled.
- Refundable Taxes.   Refundable taxes are applicable to the investment income of CCPCs and, in some applications to the investment income of private companies that are not Canadian controlled. They are not applicable to public companies. While we need to consider the impact of refundable taxes on Full Rate Taxable Income at this point, detailed procedures related to refundable taxes are discussed in Chapter 13.

12-150.   Since the availability of the relevant benefits depends on the type of company, we will have to give separate attention to the calculation of the Full Rate Taxable Income of CCPCs and to the Full Rate Taxable Income of companies that are not CCPCs (public companies and private companies that are not Canadian controlled).

Application To Companies Other Than CCPCs

12-151.   For these companies, the only adjustment to Taxable Income that is required to determine Full Rate Taxable Income is the removal of income eligible for the M&P deduction. Given this, for companies other than CCPCs, Full Rate Taxable Income is defined as follows:

Regular Taxable Income	$ x,xxx
Income Eligible For The M&P Deduction	(xxx)
Full Rate Taxable Income	$ x,xxx

12-152.   A simple example will serve to illustrate the relevant calculations:

EXAMPLE   For the year ending December 31, 2020, Daren Ltd., a Canadian public company, has Taxable Income equal to $100,000, with $40,000 of this amount eligible for the M&P deduction.

ANALYSIS   Full Rate Taxable Income is equal to $60,000 ($100,000 - $40,000). Given this, total federal Tax Payable for Daren Ltd. would be calculated as follows:

Base Amount Of Part I Tax [(38%)($100,000)]	$38,000
Federal Tax Abatement [(10%)($100,000)]	(10,000)
M&P Deduction [(13%)($40,000)]	(5,200)
General Rate Reduction [(13%)($100,000 - $40,000)]	(7,800)
Federal Tax Payable	$15,000

12-153.   For a corporation with income consisting entirely of M&P profits, there is no general rate reduction as there is no Full Rate Taxable Income. This is illustrated by revising the example in Paragraph 12-152:

EXAMPLE - Revised   Assume that the $100,000 in Taxable Income of Daren Ltd. was generated solely by M&P activities.

ANALYSIS   Total federal Tax Payable for Daren Ltd. would be calculated as follows:

Base Amount Of Part I Tax [(38%)($100,000)]	$38,000
Federal Tax Abatement [(10%)($100,000)]	(10,000)
M&P Deduction [(13%)($100,000)]	(13,000)
General Rate Reduction [(13%)($100,000 - $100,000)]	Nil
Federal Tax Payable	$15,000

12-154.   This calculation illustrates the fact that the overall federal rate on income that is eligible for the M&P deduction is 15 percent. This is, of course, identical to the overall rate on income that is eligible for the general rate reduction, illustrating the fact that the M&P deduction is not advantageous at the federal level.

Exercise Twelve - 12

Subject: Federal Tax Payable For A Public Company

For the year ending December 31, 2020, Marchand Inc., a Canadian public company, has Taxable Income of $320,000. Of this total, $180,000 qualifies for the M&P deduction. Calculate Marchand's federal Tax Payable for the year ending December 31, 2020. Include in your solution any M&P deduction available.

SOLUTION available in print and online Study Guide.

Application To CCPCs

12-155.   Not surprisingly, the calculation of Full Rate Taxable Income for a CCPC is somewhat more complex than it is for a public company. As we have noted, in addition to the M&P deduction, these companies may benefit from the small business deduction and the refundable tax provisions on investment income.

12-156.   Given the potential presence of these additional tax privileges, Full Rate Taxable Income for a CCPC is defined as follows:

General Rate Reduction - ITA 123.4(2)

Taxable Income, reduced by:

1. Income eligible for the small business deduction.

2. Income eligible for the M&P deduction.

3. The corporation's Aggregate Investment Income for the year as defined in ITA 129(4). [This is to remove income that will benefit from refundable taxes when it is distributed by the corporation. These taxes are explained in Chapter 13.]

12-157.   The definition of Aggregate Investment Income in ITA 129(4) was discussed in the coverage of the M&P deduction (see Paragraph 12-143). It includes both foreign and Canadian amounts of net taxable capital gains, interest, rents, and royalties, but not dividends that are deductible in computing Taxable Income. The balance is reduced by net capital loss carry overs deducted during the year.

12-158.   As is covered in Chapter 13, a portion of the Part I tax paid by CCPCs on their Aggregate Investment Income is refunded when dividends are paid. Because of this refund, Aggregate Investment Income is already taxed advantageously when it is flowed through a CCPC. Given this, it does not receive the benefit of the general rate reduction.

12-159.   The following example illustrates the application of the general rate reduction rules to a CCPC with no investment income.

> **EXAMPLE**   For the year ending December 31, 2020, Zaptek Ltd., a CCPC, has $200,000 in Taxable Income. This amount is made up entirely of active business income earned in Canada, none of which relates to M&P activity. Zaptek is associated with another company and, as per the agreement with that company, Zaptek is entitled to $100,000 of the annual business limit.

> **ANALYSIS**   The federal Tax Payable for Zaptek Ltd. would be calculated as follows:

Base Amount Of Part I Tax [(38%)($200,000)]	$76,000
Federal Tax Abatement [(10%)($200,000)]	(20,000)
Small Business Deduction [(19%)($100,000)]	(19,000)
General Rate Reduction [(13%)($200,000 - $100,000)]	(13,000)
Federal Tax Payable	$24,000

12-160.   The overall rate of federal tax in this example is 12 percent ($24,000 ÷ $200,000). This reflects a combination of a rate of 9 percent (38% - 10% - 19%) on the $100,000 of income that was eligible for the small business deduction, and a rate of 15 percent (38% - 10% - 13%) on income that was not eligible for this deduction.

Exercise Twelve - 13

Subject: Federal Tax Payable For A CCPC

Redux Ltd. is a Canadian controlled private corporation. For the year ending December 31, 2020, the company has Taxable Income of $200,000, all of which is active business income. Of this amount, $145,000 results from M&P activity. As it is associated with two other corporations, its share of the annual business limit is $140,000. Determine the company's federal Tax Payable for the year ending December 31, 2020. Include in your solution any M&P deduction available.

SOLUTION available in print and online Study Guide.

We suggest you work Self Study Problems Twelve-6, 7, 8, and 9 at this point.

Foreign Tax Credits For Corporations

Introduction

12-161. The foreign tax credits that are available to individuals earning foreign business or non-business income are discussed in detail in Chapter 11. Under rules that are very similar to those applicable to individuals, corporations are also allowed to use foreign taxes paid on business and non-business income as credits against Canadian Tax Payable. While the rules are similar to those for individuals, there are differences that will be discussed here. IT Folio S5-F2-C1, "Foreign Tax Credit", gives interpretations with respect to some of the most commonly encountered requirements contained in these foreign tax credit provisions.

Calculation Of Foreign Tax Credits

Foreign Non-Business (Property) And Business Tax Credits

12-162. The formula that limits the Canadian tax credit for foreign taxes paid on foreign source non-business income is as follows:

The **Foreign NON-BUSINESS Income Tax Credit** is the lesser of:

- The tax paid to the foreign government (for corporations, there is no 15 percent limit on the foreign non-business taxes paid by a corporation)
- An amount determined by the following formula:

$$\left[\frac{\text{Foreign } \mathbf{NON\text{-}BUSINESS} \text{ Income}}{\text{Adjusted Division B Income}}\right] [\text{Tax Otherwise Payable}]$$

12-163. The meaning of "Adjusted Division B Income" and "Tax Otherwise Payable" are explained beginning at Paragraph 12-166. Both of the foreign tax credit formulae are included at the front of this text in "Rates and Other Data".

12-164. The formula that limits the amount of foreign business income taxes paid that can be used as a foreign tax credit is as follows:

The **Foreign BUSINESS Income Tax Credit** is the least of:

- The tax paid to the foreign government
- An amount determined by the following formula:

$$\left[\frac{\text{Foreign } \mathbf{BUSINESS} \text{ Income}}{\text{Adjusted Division B Income}}\right] [\text{Tax Otherwise Payable}]$$

- Tax Otherwise Payable for the year, less any foreign tax credit taken on non-business income under ITA 126(1).

12-165. As was the case with individuals, there is an additional factor to consider in the case of foreign business income tax credits. This is the "Tax Otherwise Payable", reduced by any foreign non-business income tax credit deducted under ITA 126(1).

Adjusted Division B Income

12-166. While the general descriptions in the formulae (e.g., Adjusted Division B Income and Tax Otherwise Payable) are the same as those applicable to individuals, their meaning is somewhat different. More specifically, for a corporation, "Adjusted Division B Income" is determined as follows:

Division B Income (Net Income For Tax Purposes)	$x,xxx
Net Capital Loss Carry Overs Deducted Under ITA 111(1)(b)	(xxx)
Taxable Dividends Deducted Under ITA 112	(xxx)
Dividends From A Foreign Affiliate Deductible Under ITA 113	(xxx)
Adjusted Division B Income	$x,xxx

Tax Otherwise Payable

12-167.   The following table compares the components included in the calculation of Tax Otherwise Payable for foreign non-business tax credits with those used to calculate foreign business tax credits.

Tax Otherwise Payable Components	Non-Business	Business
Base Amount Of Part I Tax (38%)	Yes	Yes
Plus: Additional Refundable Tax (ART) On Investment Income Of CCPC (See Chapter 13)	Yes	No
Minus: Federal Tax Abatement	Yes	No
Minus: General Rate Reduction	Yes	Yes

12-168.   "Tax Otherwise Payable" is a particularly confusing term as its calculation is different for individuals and corporations. As shown in the table, adding to the confusion is the fact that its components differ depending on whether it is being used to calculate foreign non-business tax credits or foreign business tax credits for corporations.

12-169.   You will recall that the purpose of the 10 percent federal tax abatement is to leave room for the provinces to tax corporations. It is deducted in the formula for determining foreign non-business tax credits because non-business income will, in general, be taxed in a province. As a consequence, it is appropriate to deduct this abatement in determining the limit on the foreign non-business tax credit.

12-170.   In contrast, in the calculation of the foreign business income tax credit, "Tax Otherwise Payable" is not reduced by the 10 percent federal tax abatement, reflecting the fact that foreign business income will not be taxed in a province. Also different is the fact that this calculation of "Tax Otherwise Payable" does not include the additional refundable tax on investment income under ITA 123.3. (See Chapter 13.)

12-171.   You may recall that the foreign tax credit constraint in the small business deduction calculation uses foreign tax credit amounts that do not consider the general rate reduction (see Paragraph 12-98). The reason for this is a potentially circular calculation. Since the general rate reduction amount uses the amount eligible for the small business deduction and the small business deduction calculation uses the foreign tax credits, these amounts cannot all be calculated at the same time. As a result, the foreign tax credits used in calculating the small business deduction may not be equal to the actual foreign tax credits.

Foreign Tax Credit Carry Overs

12-172.   Unlike the situation with individuals, where the amount of foreign taxes that can be used as a credit is limited to 15 percent of the foreign source non-business income, the only limit for a corporation is the limit that is found in the second component of the formula. If the actual amount of foreign taxes paid is greater than this limit, there is no carry over of the excess as a tax credit. However, as was noted in Chapter 11, unclaimed amounts can be deducted under ITA 20(12) in the determination of Net Income For Tax Purposes.

12-173.   Unlike the case with foreign non-business income taxes paid in excess of amounts used as tax credits, unused foreign business taxes paid can be carried over as a tax credit to the 3 preceding taxation years or the 10 subsequent taxation years. In calculating the allowable tax credit for such carry overs, these unused amounts will be added to the foreign tax paid factor in the calculation of the foreign business income tax credit.

Exercise Twelve - 14

Subject: Foreign Tax Credits

Internat Inc. is a Canadian public company. For the year ending December 31, 2020, it has Net Income For Tax Purposes of $146,000, including foreign business income of $20,000. The foreign government withheld $3,000 in taxes on this income, resulting in a net remittance of $17,000. None of the company's income involves manufacturing and processing and, based on the ITR 402(3) formula, 88 percent of the company's income was allocated to a province. In calculating Taxable Income, the company deducts $30,000 in dividends received from taxable Canadian companies, a non-capital loss carry forward of $75,000, and a net capital loss carry forward of $25,000. Determine the company's Part I Tax Payable for the year ending December 31, 2020. Include in your answer any carry overs available at the end of the year.

SOLUTION available in print and online Study Guide.

We suggest you work Self Study Problem Twelve-10 at this point.

Refundable Journalism Labour Tax Credit

Described

12-174.   The March 29, 2019, budget introduced three provisions designed to encourage Canadian journalism organizations.

- A 25 percent refundable credit for salaries and wages paid to Eligible Newsroom Employees of a Qualifying Canadian Journalism Organizations. This credit is available for expenditures made after January 1, 2019.

- A non-refundable credit for individuals based on the cost of their subscriptions to digital news services. This credit is not available until 2020.

- A provision that allows some journalism organizations to register as qualified donees able to issue tax receipts for donations. These provisions are not applicable until 2020.

12-175.   The 25 percent credit is capped at $55,000 for each Eligible Newsroom Employee, providing a maximum credit of $13,750 [(25%)($$55,000)] for each such employee. The base for the credit will be reduced by any financial assistance received during the year from any level of government.

12-176.   It appears that, even though journalism organizations that qualify as registered donees do not pay income taxes, they will be eligible for this refundable credit.

Definitions - ITA 125.6

12-177.   As usual, the application of this credit requires an understanding of some technical definitions. These are as follows:

Qualifying Canadian Journalism Organization   To qualify, the organization must meet the following conditions:

- it must be primarily engaged in the production of written news content;
- it must not be carrying on a broadcasting operation;
- it does not receive any amount from the Canada Periodical Fund; and
  - if it is a public corporation, its shares must be listed on a designated stock exchange in Canada; or
  - if it is not publicly traded, at least 75 percent of its shares must be owned by Canadian citizens or a publicly traded qualifying journalism organization.

Eligible Newsroom Employee   This means an individual who:

- is employed by a Qualifying Canadian Journalism Organization;
- works a minimum of 26 hours per week throughout the portion of the taxation year in which the individual is employed;
- is employed for a minimum period of 40 consecutive weeks; and
- spends at least 75 percent of their time engaged in the production of news content, including researching, collecting information, verifying facts, photographing, writing, editing, designing, and otherwise preparing content.

Additional Supplementary Self Study Problems Are Available Online.

Key Terms Used In This Chapter

12-178.   The following is a list of the key terms used in this Chapter. These terms, and their meanings, are compiled in the Glossary located at the back of the Study Guide.

Active Business	Grind
Active Business Income	Loss Carry Back
Adjusted Active Business Income	Loss Carry Forward
ADJUSTED Aggregate Investment Income	Manufacturing And Processing Profits
Allowable Business Investment Loss	Deduction (M&P Deduction)
Allowable Capital Loss	Net Business Income
Annual Business Limit	Net Capital Loss
Associated Corporations	Non-Capital Loss
Business Income	Ordering Rule
Business Investment Loss	Permanent Establishment
Canadian Controlled Private Corporation	Personal Services Business
Carry Over	Preferred Shares
CCPC	Private Corporation
Common Shares	Professional Corporation
Corporation	Property Income
Designated Stock Exchange	Public Corporation
Disposition	Qualifying Canadian Journalism
Eligible Newsroom Employee	Organization
Federal Tax Abatement	Refundable Journalism Labour Tax Credit
Foreign Taxes Paid Credit	Small Business Deduction
Full Rate Taxable Income	Specified Investment Business
GAAP	Stop Loss Rules
General Rate Reduction	Taxable Capital Employed in Canada
	Term Preferred Shares

References

12-179.   For more detailed study of the material in this Chapter, we refer you to the following:

ITA 89(1)	Definitions (Private Corporation And Public Corporation)
ITA 110	Deductions Permitted
ITA 111	Losses Deductible
ITA 112	Deduction Of Taxable Dividends Received By Corporations Resident In Canada
ITA 113	Deduction In Respect Of Dividend Received From Foreign Affiliate
ITA 123	Basic Part I Rate For Corporations
ITA 123.3	Additional Refundable Tax On CCPC's Investment Income
ITA 123.4(2)	General Deduction From Tax
ITA 124	Federal Abatement
ITA 125	Small Business Deduction
ITA 125.1(1)	Manufacturing And Processing Profits Deductions
S3-F8-C1	Principal Business Corporation In The Resource Industries
S4-F15-C1	Manufacturing And Processing
S5-F2-C1	Foreign Tax Credit
IT-67R3	Taxable Dividends From Corporations Resident In Canada
IT-73R6	The Small Business Deduction
IT-177R2	Permanent Establishment Of A Corporation In A Province (Consolidated)
IT-189R2	Corporations Used By Practising Members Of Professions
IT-206R	Separate Businesses
IT-232R3	Losses — Their Deductibility In The Loss Year Or In Other Years
IT-391R	Status Of Corporations
IT-458R2	Canadian Controlled Private Corporation

Problems For Self Study (Online)

To provide practice in problem solving, there are Self Study and Supplementary Self Study problems available on MyLab Accounting.

Within the text we have provided an indication of when it would be appropriate to work each Self Study problem. The detailed solutions for Self Study problems can be found in the print and online Study Guide.

We provide the Supplementary Self Study problems for those who would like additional practice in problem solving. The detailed solutions for the Supplementary Self Study problems are available online, not in the Study Guide.

The .PDF file "Self Study Problems for Volume 2" on MyLab contains the following for Chapter 12:

- 10 Self Study problems,
- 5 Supplementary Self Study problems, and
- detailed solutions for the Supplementary Self Study problems.

Assignment Problems

(The solutions for these problems are only available in
the solutions manual that has been provided to your instructor.)

Assignment Problem Twelve - 1
(Corporate Taxable Income)

The Income Statement that has been prepared by Margo Ltd.'s accountant for the year ending December 31, 2020, is as follows:

Sales Revenue		$925,000
Cost Of Goods Sold (Note 1)		(717,000)
Gross Profit		$208,000
Operating Expenses:		
Salaries And Wages	($40,200)	
Rents	(22,200)	
Property Taxes (Note 2)	(8,800)	
Amortization Expense	(35,600)	
Write-Down Of Goodwill (Note 3)	(1,700)	
Charitable Donations	(19,800)	
Legal Fees (Note 4)	(2,220)	
Bad Debt Expense (Note 5)	(7,100)	
Warranty Provision (Note 6)	(5,500)	
Social Club Membership Fees	(7,210)	
Other Operating Expenses	(39,870)	(190,200)
Operating Income		$ 17,800
Other Revenues (Expenses):		
Gain On Sale Of Investments (Note 7)	$ 9,500	
Interest Revenue	2,110	
Interest On Late Income Tax Instalments	(1,020)	
Investment Counsellor Fees	(500)	
Foreign Interest Income (Note 8)	1,530	
Dividends From Taxable Canadian Corporations	3,000	14,620
Income Before Taxes		$ 32,420

Notes And Other Information:

1. The calculation of Cost Of Goods Sold was based on an opening inventory of $225,000 and a closing inventory of $198,600. In addition, the closing inventory was reduced by $15,000 for a reserve for future declines in value. This is the first year the company has used an inventory reserve.

2. Property Taxes include $1,200 for tax paid on vacant land. The company has held this land for five years in anticipation of relocating its head office.

3. As the result of a business combination on January 15, 2020, Margo Ltd. recorded $34,000 in goodwill. As of December 31, 2020, this goodwill was found to be impaired and a goodwill impairment loss of $1,700 was recorded.

4. The maximum CCA for the current year is $79,785. This includes the appropriate write-off of the goodwill described in Item 3.

5. The legal fees are made up of $1,200 paid to appeal an income tax assessment and $1,020 paid for general corporate matters.

6. The company bases its accounting Bad Debt Expense on the values used for tax purposes.

7. This is the first year that the company has deducted a provision for estimated warranties.

8. The gain on the sale of investments involved marketable securities with a cost of $21,000. The securities were sold for $30,500.

9. The gross foreign interest income of $1,800 was received net of $270 in foreign tax withholdings.

Required: Determine the minimum Net Income For Tax Purposes and Taxable Income of Margo Ltd., for the year ending December 31, 2020.

Assignment Problem Twelve - 2
(Corporate Taxable Income)

Cabrera Digital is a Canadian public company. It has always used a taxation year that ends on December 31. During the year ending December 31, 2020, it had operating revenues of $1,234,000 and operating expenses of $962,000, resulting in an operating income $272,000.

Also during 2020, it received the following dividends:

- Non-Eligible Dividends From 100 Percent Owned Subsidiary $23,600
- Eligible Dividends From Canadian Public Companies   61,300

The company's only other property income was a $312,000 capital gain on a holding of temporary investments. Because of this very fortunate investment result, the company decides to make a $241,000 donation to a registered Canadian charity. No other capital gains are anticipated in the foreseeable future.

At the beginning of the year ending December 31, 2020, the company had the following carry forward balances:

- Net Capital Losses $262,000
- Non-Capital Losses   193,000

Required: Calculate the minimum Net Income For Tax Purposes and Taxable Income for Cabrera Digital for the year ending December 31, 2020. Indicate the amount and type of any carry forwards that are available at the end of that year.

Assignment Problem Twelve - 3
(Corporate Net And Taxable Income)

Vertin Ltd. is a Canadian public company that has always used a December 31 year end. However, as December is a very busy time for their business activities, it has requested a change in their taxation year end to July 31, a date at which their business activity is at the low point for the year. They have presented this situation to the CRA and the Department has accepted their request for the change.

The change will be implemented during 2020, resulting in a short fiscal period ending July 31, 2020. The company's Income Statement, prepared in accordance with generally accepted accounting principles, for the period January 1, 2020, through July 31, 2020, is as follows:

Vertin Ltd.
Income Statement
7 Month Period Ending July 31, 2020

Sales (All Within Canada)		$1,796,600
Cost Of Sales		(973,400)
Gross Margin		$ 823,200
Other Expenses (Excluding Taxes):		
Wages And Salaries	($108,200)	
Cost Of Sales	(194,200)	
Amortization	(97,600)	
Rent	(113,400)	
Interest Expense	(13,200)	
Foreign Exchange Loss	(7,600)	
Travel And Promotion	(86,300)	
Bad Debt Expense	(6,200)	
Warranty Expense	(7,400)	
Charitable Donations	(8,100)	
Other Operating Expenses	(51,200)	(693,400)
Operating Income		$ 129,800
Gain On Sale Of Investments		7,800
Income Before Taxes		$ 137,600

Other Information:

1. Wages and salaries includes a $28,000 bonus to Vertin Ltd.'s CEO. Because she anticipates retiring at the end of 2020, this bonus will not be paid until January 2022.

2. In determining the Cost Of Sales, the company deducted a $23,400 reserve for inventory obsolescence.

3. Amortization is on a Class 1 building, Class 8 furniture and fixtures, and Class 10 delivery vehicles. The following information is relevant for the determination of CCA for the seven month period ending July 31, 2020:

    Building The January 1, 2020, UCC for the building was $872,000. During 2020, the company spent $42,000 on improved flooring in all areas of the property. The building was not a new building when it was acquired.

    Furniture And Fixtures The January 1, 2020, UCC balance for Class 8 was $285,000. During 2020, new furniture was acquired at a cost of $40,600. Old furniture with a capital cost of $28,200 was sold for $17,600.

    Delivery Vehicles On January 1, 2020, the Class 10 UCC balance was $198,300. There were no additions or disposals in this Class during the seven month period ending July 31, 2020.

4. The interest expense relates to a line of credit that was used to finance seasonal fluctuations in inventory.

5. The foreign exchange loss resulted from financing costs related to the purchase of merchandise in the United Kingdom.

6. The travel and promotion expense consisted of the following items:

Business Meals And Entertainment	$32,400
Hotels And Airfare	41,800
Golf Club Memberships	12,100
Total Travel And Promotion Expense	$86,300

7. For accounting purposes, the company establishes a warranty reserve based on estimated costs. On January 1, 2020, the reserve balance was $8,200. On July 31, 2020, a new reserve was established at $7,400.

8. The accounting gain on the sale of investments is equal to the capital gain for tax purposes.

9. During the period January 1, 2020, through July 31, 2020, the company declared and paid dividends of $31,400.

10. On January 1, 2020, the company has available a $24,600 non-capital loss carry forward and a $7,200 [(1/2)($14,400)] net capital loss carry forward.

Required: Calculate the minimum Net Income For Tax Purposes and Taxable Income for Vertin Ltd. for the seven month period ending July 31, 2020. Indicate the amount and type of any carry forwards that will be available for use in future years.

Assignment Problem Twelve - 4
(Corporate Loss Carry Forwards)

The following information relates to the operations of Notem Inc. for the taxation year ended December 31, 2020 (all amounts are based on the relevant tax rules):

Net Business Loss	$141,800
Dividends From Taxable Canadian Corporations	33,500
Taxable Capital Gains	9,600
Allowable Capital Losses	4,425
Charitable Donations	5,400

At the beginning of the taxation year, the company had a carry forward of unused charitable donations of $1,350 from the previous year and a net capital loss carry forward of $10,500 [(1/2)($21,000)].

It is the policy of the company to minimize net capital loss balances prior to using any other type of carry over balance.

Required: Calculate the corporation's minimum Net Income For Tax Purposes and Taxable Income for its 2020 taxation year. Indicate any balances available for carry forward to subsequent years.

Assignment Problem Twelve - 5
(Corporate Loss Carryovers - Four Years)

Lactor Ltd. (Lactor) commenced business in 2017. The company selected a calendar based taxation year that ends on December 31 of each year. Lactor's operations involve a dairy substitute to appeal to a growing number of children who are allergic to cow's milk. The company experienced a slow start in 2017 with small losses that quickly reached high profits in both 2018 and 2019 but only to experience debilitating losses in 2020. The company is uncertain of whether it will be able to continue into 2021. A relevant factor for the company's ability to survive is determining its income tax obligations, which depend on the ability to efficiently utilize losses it has incurred with the goal of minimizing its Taxable Income. The company has asked for your assistance and provided you with the following information:

	2017	2018	2019	2020
Business Income (Loss)	($75,000)	$38,000	$178,000	($200,000)
Net Capital Gains (Losses)	10,000	(27,000)	(9,000)	23,000
Dividends Received	11,000	21,000	33,000	42,000
Charitable Donations	25,000	15,000	20,000	14,000

All of the dividends have been received from taxable Canadian corporations and are therefore deductible to Lactor through ITA 112 in determining Taxable Income. It is the policy of the company to minimize its net capital loss carry forward balance first then donations second and non-capital losses last.

Required: For each of the four years calculate and determine:

- The minimum net and taxable income including the amount and type of any unused losses that are available to carry to other years.
- Apply any loss carryovers to the maximum extent possible to minimize Taxable Income in each year and then determine the loss carryover balances remaining that are available to carry to other years.
- Losses that are carried back require amending the previous year returns. Clearly indicate any year returns that require amending as a result.

Assignment Problem Twelve - 6
(Corporate Loss Carry Forwards - Four Years)

Metronet Inc. is a Canadian public company with a December 31 year end. It commenced operations in 2017 and has had mixed results since that time. In terms of its business income (loss), the results, determined using the relevant tax legislation, were as follows:

	2017	2018	2019	2020
Net Business Income (Loss)	$233,500	$34,000	($163,000)	$57,000

Other Information:

1. In each of the years 2017 through 2020, Metronet receives dividends from taxable Canadian companies of $13,500.

2. In 2017, Metronet made charitable donations of $4,800, followed by a donation of $15,600 in 2018. The donations declined to $7,400 in 2019. No contributions were made in 2020.

3. In 2017, Metronet realized a capital loss of $24,600, followed by a $45,600 capital gain in 2018. In 2019, there was a capital loss of $48,400. Things improved in 2020, during which Metronet realized a $33,200 capital gain.

It is the policy of the company to minimize its net capital loss carry forward balance prior to minimizing other types of carry forwards.

Required: For each of the four years 2017 through 2020, provide the following information:

- The minimum Net Income For Tax Purposes and Taxable Income that would be reported for Metronet Inc. Indicate the amount and type of any current year losses that are available for carry back or carry forward.
- The amended figures for any years to which losses are carried back.
- An analysis of the amount and type of carry forwards that would be available at the end of the year.

Assignment Problem Twelve - 7
(Geographical Allocation Of Income)

The Sundean Company has its national headquarters in Toronto, and all of its senior management people have their offices at this location. The company also has operations in Vancouver, Calgary, Saskatoon, and Halifax. In each of these cities, warehouse space is maintained and orders are filled. In addition, a sales staff operates out of office space in each warehouse, taking orders throughout the province in which the warehouse is located.

For the current taxation year, the company's Taxable Income totaled $1,546,000, on gross revenues of $10,483,000. Also during the current year, the company had salaries and wages totaling $1,247,000. These gross revenues and expenses were distributed among the provinces where the company has operations in the following manner:

	Gross Revenues	**Wages And Salaries Accrued**
Alberta	$ 1,886,940	$ 261,870
British Columbia	2,306,260	274,340
Nova Scotia	1,362,790	174,580
Saskatchewan	1,257,960	99,760
Ontario	3,669,050	436,450
Total	$10,483,000	$1,247,000

Required: Calculate the amount of Sundean Company's Taxable Income for the current year that would be allocated to each of the five provinces. Any percentages used in your calculations should be rounded to one decimal place.

Assignment Problem Twelve - 8
(Part 1 Tax with Reduced SBD)

Deckton Ltd. is a large successful Canadian controlled private corporation (CCPC) operating in multiple jurisdictions through permanent establishments in which it carries on the business of renovating residential homes. In 2020 Deckton's percentage of gross revenues and wages and salaries in each of the four jurisdictions in which they operate is as follows:

Province	**Revenues**	**Wages**	**Average**
Alberta	41%	48%	44.5%
British Columbia	20%	23%	21.5%
Saskatchewan	28%	22%	25.0%
U.S. Washington State	11%	7%	9.0%
Total	100%	100%	100.0%

Deckton's taxable income for 2020, which consists exclusively of active business income, is $2,447,000. Its Canadian operations account for $2,073,000 of its taxable income with the remainder of $374,000 attributable to its U.S. operations. The U.S. operations paid business and profits taxes in the amount of C$71,060.

Deckton Ltd. represents the western Canadian operations of a corporate group composed of three companies, all of which are associated. Deckton is allocated $200,000 of the business limit of the associated group for 2020. The three companies all have taxation years ending December 31 with no short taxation years. The companies have been associated for over 10 years.

All of the gross revenues of the three associated companies are derived from arm's length sales and there are no intercompany sales between them.

The combined Adjusted Aggregate Investment Income (Adjusted AII) of the associated group of companies is less than $50,000 in both 2019 and 2020.

The Taxable Capital Employed in Canada (TCEC) of the associated group in 2019 was $14,125,000 and was $13,754,000 in 2020.

Assume that Deckton's foreign tax credit is equal to the foreign taxes paid of $71,060.

Required: Determine Deckton's minimum federal Part I Tax Payable for the year ending December 31, 2020. Show all supporting calculations.

Assignment Problem Twelve - 9
(Corporate Tax Payable)

For the taxation year ending December 31, 2020, Lorne Inc., a Canadian controlled private company, has Net Income For Tax Purposes of $340,500. This is made up of $312,400 of active business income and $28,100 of dividends from various Canadian public companies. It has been determined that $211,300 of the active business income qualifies as manufacturing and processing profits.

During 2020, the company makes donations to registered charities totaling $31,400.

At the beginning of 2020, the company has a non-capital loss carry forward of $29,300. It intends to deduct all of this carry forward during 2020.

Lorne Inc. is associated with three other CCPCs. The companies have agreed that each company will claim one-quarter of the annual business limit. The combined Taxable Capital Employed in Canada for the four associated companies is less than $10 million in both 2019 and 2020. The combined Adjusted Aggregate Investment Income of the four companies was $45,000 in 2019.

Required: Determine the minimum Taxable Income and Part I federal Tax Payable for Lorne Inc. for the year ending December 31, 2020. Show all calculations, whether or not they are necessary to the final solution. As the corporation operates in a province that has a reduced tax rate for M&P activity, a separate calculation of the federal M&P deduction is required.

Assignment Problem Twelve - 10

Note to Instructors: There are two points: (1) We added a comment in the lease of the warehouse commentary clarifying that the expenditures fall within Class 13. This is to ensure that the expenditures are not treated as Class 1 costs as a result of ITR 1102(5). (2) Since the ART is not covered until Chapter 13 but is relevant to the tax calculations in this problem we have provided both the AII and the ART tax to be included.

(Comprehensive Corporate Tax Payable)

Kalex Inc, a Canadian controlled private corporation, was incorporated in 2018 and selected a December 31 taxation year end. Kalex is a family owned company with four equal shareholders, all of whom are siblings. The company employs in excess of 50 employees at its head office in Toronto, a further 80 employees at its manufacturing facility in Oshawa, Ontario, and a further 12 employees at its office in Syracuse, New York. The company is primarily involved in the manufacture and sale of storage shelving and pallets. You have been asked to prepare the corporate tax returns for 2020. The company provides you with its financial statements for the year ending December 31, 2020. The financial statements have been prepared using Accounting Standards for Private Enterprises (ASPE), which represents the application of generally accepted accounting principles. No attempt has been made to reconcile the net accounting income with Net Income For Tax Purposes. Through your own observations and by asking several questions you have uncovered the following information concerning the 2020 income and expenses of Kalex:

1.   Net income for accounting purposes is $2,481,986 after deducting $325,000 of current income tax expenses.

2.   Other amounts either deducted or added in the determination of net income for accounting purposes are as follows:

1. Bond premium amortization applied and reduced interest expenses	$ 8,800
2. Deducted amortization expense	615,000
3. Deducted loss from employee theft (60% recovered through insurance)	4,750
4. Deducted 10% of landscaping costs paid of $58,000	5,800
5. Deducted pre-paid advertising for 24 months (covers May 1, 2020, to April 30, 2022)	37,200

6.	Deducted donations to registered charities	17,400
7.	Deducted 100% of meal and entertainment expenses	62,500
8.	Deducted life insurance premiums for four shareholders	22,000
9.	Added capital dividend received from associated company	40,000
10.	Deducted all of the renovation costs of adding two offices to its head-quarters in Toronto	112,000
11.	Deducted all of the operating costs for an automobile for the shareholder/president who uses it 40% of the time for company business	11,700
12.	Deducted penalties on late income tax instalments	2,900
13.	Deducted interest on late municipal tax payments	1.835
14.	Added a court-ordered damage award for breach of contract. The company would have earned a profit of $37,000 had the contract been completed	33,500
15.	Deducted legal expenses incurred in the breach of contract	21,000
16.	Deducted annual golf club membership fees for the president to entertain customers	19,300
17.	Deducted reserve for estimated warranty expenses	16,275

3. Kalex estimates it's doubtful account receivables by applying an historical percentage of 7.5 percent to accounts that have been outstanding for more than 30 days. At December 31, 2020, those accounts totaled $450,000, resulting in a doubtful debt expense of $33,750 [7.5% of $450,000]. After a detailed evaluation of the accounts you determine that a reasonable reserve that would be acceptable to CRA would be $28,800. The 2019 reasonable reserve claimed was $30,900 – no adjustment has been made for this in 2020.

4. On January 1, 2020, Kalex had the following UCC balances:

Class 1 – Toronto Headquarters	$1,823,600
Class 1 – Oshawa Manufacturing	1,197,000
Class 8	648,000
Class 10	133,875
Class 13	119,000
Class 53	375,000

Elections were filed for each of the Class 1 buildings to be eligible for additional CCA. As a result the two buildings are in separate classes. The Oshawa building is used 100 percent for non-residential purposes that is manufacturing while the Toronto headquarters building is used exclusively (100 percent) for non-residential purposes that is not manufacturing. No capital expenditures were made for the Oshawa building, but capital renovations in the amount of $112,000 were made to the Toronto building. The amount included in each class represents the capital cost of the building only.

Class 8 depreciable property represents office furniture and fixtures for the two Class 1 buildings. The original cost when acquired in January 2018 was $800,000. Kalex was approached by a new business in February 2020 operating out of Niagara Falls, Ontario. The business leases refurbished office furniture and fixtures on long term leases. After a round of negotiations and running the numbers, Kalex has decided to replace all of their Class 8 property with leased property. Kalex signed a five year contract at $4,000 monthly. In exchange Kalex will receive $700,000 for all of its Class 8 property. Kalex correctly expensed the lease payments in 2020.

The Class 10 property is composed of three two-seater delivery vans with extra storage capacity. Each of the three vans cost $75,000. After hearing of the tax incentives for zero-emission vehicles and the expanding network of charging stations, the company decided to trade in the three existing vans for three zero-emission vans that cost

$95,000 each. The vans were purchased July 2, 2020. The company received $105,000 as a trade-in allowance for the three existing vans.

The company acquired a 2020 Tesla Model S in early January 2020 for $130,000. The car is used exclusively by the company president. It is estimated that the car is used by the president 40 percent of the time for company business.

Midway through 2018 the company realized that the Oshawa facility lacked the necessary storage space to accommodate its expanding inventory. They reached out to a local developer who agreed to lease the company a warehouse that had sat empty for a few years. A five year lease was signed with a renewal option for an additional five years. The lease provides that Kalex can make any improvements or renovations it considers necessary but that no payment will be made by the lessor at the end of the lease. The company spent $140,000 on modifications in 2018 and another $150,000 in July 2020. Assume that the expenditures are within Class 13.

In March 2020 Kalex acquired a client list from a local competitor who was on the verge of closing its doors. The company paid $80,000 for the client list.

In May 2020 the company acquired new manufacturing machinery that would double its output at the Oshawa facility. The equipment cost $900,000.

Company policy is to claim the maximum CCA it is entitled to in each year.

5. When the company began operations in early 2018 it acquired a vacant lot not far from the Oshawa facility for $150,000. The plan was to eventually build a warehouse, but the company opted to lease a warehouse instead. The company, as part of the leasing arrangement, agreed to sell the land to the lessor for $460,000. The arrangements required the purchaser to pay $175,000 on the closing date, February 1, 2020, with the remainder paid in three equal instalments of $100,000 each plus interest at 6 percent on January 31, 2021, 2022, and 2023. Kalex did not carry a mortgage on the vacant land but did incur municipal property taxes from the day it acquired the land to the day of sale in the amount of $11,700. No income was earned from the vacant land throughout its ownership. Selling costs of the land were $8,300. The only adjustment made by the company for this transaction was the addition of an accounting gain of $290,000. The capital gain and accounting gain are determined in the exact same manner and are identical.

6. In late 2018 Kalex acquired a 25 percent shareholding of Jennco Lrd., an arm's length "small business corporation" for $125,000. Kalex had plans to eventually acquire a controlling interest and combine the two companies, but larger competitive companies moved in, taking over the market and the share value began to decline rapidly. Kalex managed to sell the shares to an arm's length investor for $10,000 three months before the company declared bankruptcy. Selling costs were $1,600. Kalex deducted an accounting loss on the shares of $116,600. Jennco never paid any dividends while Kalex owned the shares.

7. The portion of Kalex's taxable income that is considered to be earned in Canada using the formula in section 400 of the ITR is 83.6 percent.

8. The U.S. business operations resulted in net profits of C$410,000. Kalex paid U.S. taxes on those profits of C$77,900. The Income Statement, however, only adds that portion of the U.S. profits in excess of the U.S. taxes, or $332,100 [$410,000 – $77,900].

9. Kalex has no non-capital losses but experienced a net capital loss of $52,000 in 2019 on the sale of share investments.

10. Kalex's active business income in 2020 is $1,815,000, $1,288,000 of which represents its Canadian manufacturing and processing profits eligible for the M&P credit.

11. Kalex has been associated with one other CCPC since its incorporation in 2018. Both com-panies have a December 31 taxation year end and have shared the small business limit equally and will continue to do so for 2020. The Taxable Capital Employed in Canada of the associated group in 2019 was $11 million and $12.2 million in 2020. In addition the Adjusted Aggregate Investment Income of the associated group in 2019 was $77,500 and $92,300 in 2020.

Required:

A. Calculate the minimum Net Income For Tax Purposes for Kalex for 2020 with a reconciliation that begins with the net accounting income of $2,189,000. Make all necessary adjustments, including CCA for each class of property together with the UCC balance as of January 1, 2021. Show all supporting calculations.

B. Calculate the minimum Taxable Income for Kalex for 2020. Indicate the amount and type of any carry overs that are available at the end of the year.

C. Calculate the minimum federal Part I Tax Payable for Kalex for 2020. The province of Ontario is one of three provinces and territories in Canada (Saskatchewan and Yukon are the others) that provides a reduced tax rate for M&P activity. The determination of the M&P credits in those jurisdictions uses the federal calculations and as a result a separate calculation of the federal M&P deduction is required.

D. Assume (1) that the foreign tax credit for foreign business income is equal to the foreign taxes withheld of $77,900 and (2) that the Additional Refundable Tax (ART) is equal to 10-2/3 percent of Aggregate Investment Income of $16,500.

CHAPTER 13

Taxation Of Corporate Investment Income

Note On Current Developments

As was discussed more extensively in a note at the beginning of Chapter 12, the government is concerned about the accumulation of passive investments resulting from the retention of the after tax income that has been taxed at low corporate rates. As a reflection of this concern, legislation related to the income on such passive investments becomes effective for years that begin after 2018.

In simple terms, when such passive income exceeds $50,000 per year, there will generally be a reduction (grind) in the annual business limit that is available to Canadian controlled private corporations (CCPCs). This annual business limit grind was covered in Chapter 12, along with the grind that occurs when a CCPC has Taxable Capital Employed in Canada (TCEC) in excess of $10 million.

As noted in that Chapter, there is a second component of the legislation related to passive investments. You will recall from Chapter 7 that dividends that are designated as eligible are taxed more favourably than non-eligible dividends. The new legislation does not change the ability to designate dividends as eligible. What has changed is the corporation's ability to access refundable taxes on the payment of eligible dividends. Corporations will be faced, in some situations, with the choice of giving up potential refunds if dividends are designated as eligible, and not designating eligible dividends in order to recover these taxes. This is likely to make the accumulation of investment income in private corporations less attractive.

We would note that this legislation will make the material in this Chapter much more complex, both in the text and in the majority of the problem material.

Integration

The Basic Concept

The Goal

13-1. An individual who is entitled to receive business or property income has the choice of:

• Receiving that income directly as an individual. If this approach is used, the only taxes that will be assessed are at the personal level.

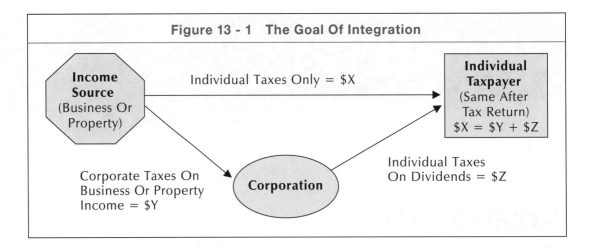

Figure 13 - 1 The Goal Of Integration

- Alternatively, the relevant assets can be transferred to a corporation. If this approach is used, there will be two levels of taxation. The income will be subject to corporate taxes prior to its distribution. Then, when the after tax amounts are distributed, they will be subject to a second level of tax at the personal level.

13-2. As depicted in Figure 13-1, the goal of integration is to ensure that the use of a corporation does not alter the total amount of taxes that will be paid on a given stream of business or property income. Stated alternatively, integration procedures are directed at equating the amount of taxes paid by an individual on the direct receipt of income with the combined corporate/individual taxes that would be paid if that same stream of income was channeled through a corporation.

Integration Procedures

13-3. As we will find in the various chapters dealing with corporate taxation, there are a number of procedures associated with achieving this goal. However, from the point of view of individual taxpayers, the dividend gross up and tax credit procedures are the primary tools used in building a system that integrates corporate and individual tax amounts.

13-4. As discussed in Chapter 7, the basic idea underlying the gross up and tax credit procedures is that the taxable amount of dividends received by an individual will be grossed up to reflect the amount of pre-tax income earned by the corporation. This will be accompanied by a credit against Tax Payable that will compensate the individual for the taxes that were paid at the corporate level. A simple example, using hypothetical rates, will serve to illustrate the fundamentals of this approach:

EXAMPLE Marion Fluery has a business that produces $100,000 of income in each year. If she receives this income directly from the business, it will be subject to tax at her marginal rate of 51 percent.

Alternatively, if she transfers this business to a corporation, the corporation will be subject to taxes at 20 percent.

When the after tax income of the corporation is distributed as dividends, it will be subject to a gross up of 25 percent. The combined federal/provincial dividend tax credit in Marion's province is equal to the amount of the gross up.

ANALYSIS If the business does not incorporate, Marion's after tax retention would be as follows:

Pre Tax Income	$100,000
Personal Taxes At 51 Percent	(51,000)
After Tax Retention	$ 49,000

If, alternatively, the business is transferred to a corporation, results at the corporate level would be as follows:

Corporate Income Before Taxes	$ 100,000
Corporate Taxes At 20 Percent	(20,000)
After Tax Income And Maximum Dividend Payable	$ 80,000

If the maximum dividend is paid by the corporation and a gross up of 25 percent is applied to this amount, the result would be as follows:

Dividends Received	$ 80,000
Gross Up [(25%)($80,000)]	20,000
Taxable Dividends = Pre-Tax Corporate Income	$ 100,000

As the amount of the gross up is equal to the corporate taxes paid, adding the gross up results in taxable dividends equal to the pre-tax corporate income.

Based on this amount, Marion's Tax Payable would be calculated as follows:

Taxable Dividends (After Gross Up)	$ 100,000
Marion's Tax Rate	51%
Tax Payable Before Dividend Tax Credit	$ 51,000
Dividend Tax Credit (Equal To Gross Up)	(20,000)
Marion's Tax Payable	$ 31,000

Based on the preceding calculation of Tax Payable, Marion's after tax retention would be calculated as follows:

Dividends Received	$ 80,000
Tax Payable	(31,000)
After Tax Retention - Use Of Corporation	$ 49,000

13-5.   You will note that this is exactly the same $49,000 of after tax retention that would result from Marion receiving the $100,000 in income directly and being taxed on it at 51 percent. This means that, in this example, the gross up and tax credit procedures have produced perfect integration. That is, Marion has retained exactly the same amount of after tax income, without regard to whether the pre-tax income is received directly or, alternatively, is channeled through a corporation.

AN IMPORTANT NOTE   An understanding of dividend gross up and tax credit procedures is essential to the material that follows in this Chapter and Chapters 14, 15, and 16. If you do not fully understand these procedures, you should review the material on dividends that is found in Chapter 7.

Eligible Vs. Non-Eligible Dividends

The Problem

13-6.   The preceding example illustrates the fact that, given the appropriate combination of corporate tax rate, gross up percentage, and dividend tax credit rate, the dividend gross up and tax credit procedures can provide perfect integration. In attempting to implement a system that provides for integration, all of the provinces use the federal gross up rates. However, there are significant variations in effective corporate tax rates, both because of the type of income earned by the corporation and the different rates applied at the provincial level. This means that there is no possibility that any single combination of gross up and tax credit rates could consistently provide integration for all corporations.

13-7.   For many years, the government ignored this issue, applying a single gross up rate and a single dividend tax credit rate, without regard to the differences in corporate tax rates. While it would not have been practical to have an array of gross up and credit rates that would reflect all of the different corporate tax rates, it was recognized that the single rate approach was not proving effective in providing for integration. In particular, the single rate that was being used was unfair to public companies that were subject to much higher rates than those applicable to CCPCs earning active business income (see Chapter 12).

13-8.   In response to this problem, a dual system of rates was developed. The two rate system was based on a split between dividends paid out of income that was taxed at full corporate rates and dividends paid out of income that benefitted from the small business deduction or refundable taxes. The former were referred to as eligible dividends, with the latter being referred to as non-eligible. In general terms, most of the dividends paid by public companies will be designated as eligible. In contrast, most of the dividends paid by CCPCs will not be designated as eligible and, as a result, will be non-eligible.

Eligible Dividends

13-9.   You may recall from Chapter 7 that ITA 89(1) defines eligible dividends as any taxable dividend that is designated as such by the company paying the dividend (designation procedures are covered in detail later in this Chapter). Dividends that are designated as eligible are grossed up by 38 percent and receive a federal dividend tax credit equal to 6/11 of the 38 percent gross up. As was discussed in Chapter 7, the application of these rates will result in the shareholder receiving these dividends being taxed at a more favourable tax rate than would be the case if the dividends were non-eligible. The term eligible dividends refers to the fact that such dividends are eligible for this "enhanced" dividend tax credit procedure.

13-10.   With the exception of capital dividends, all types of dividends may be designated as eligible dividends. This includes cash dividends, stock dividends, dividends in kind, and the various types of deemed dividends that will be introduced in Chapter 14 (e.g., ITA 84(3) dividends on redemption of shares).

Non-Eligible Dividends

13-11.   It is common terminology to refer to dividends that have not been designated as eligible as non-eligible dividends, and this is the term we use. (Unfortunately, the term used in tax returns is "other than eligible" dividends, which can cause confusion.) For 2020, these non-eligible dividends are grossed up by 15 percent and receive a federal dividend tax credit of 9/13 of the 15 percent gross up.

13-12.   Any taxable dividend that has not been designated as eligible will be considered to be non-eligible. This includes cash dividends, stock dividends, dividends in kind, and the various types of deemed dividends that are discussed in Chapter 14. Note, however, as capital dividends are not taxable dividends, they do not qualify for either the dividend gross up procedure or the tax credit procedure.

Importance

13-13.   The distinction between eligible and non-eligible dividends is extremely important. The reasons for this are as follows:

Effective Tax Rates   For an individual subject to maximum tax rates, the effective tax rates on non-eligible dividends can be over 10 percentage points higher than the rate on eligible dividends. Note, however, the size of this difference varies considerably from province to province, ranging from less than 5 percentage points to over 10 percentage points.

Tax Free Dividends   As we will discuss in Chapter 15, an individual with no other source of income can receive a substantial amount of dividends without paying any taxes. For a single individual receiving non-eligible dividends, the amount is just over $30,000.

In contrast, this same individual could avoid taxes on over $63,000 of eligible dividends. This is of great importance when a source of income is being split with low-income family members. Keep in mind, however, that this process is made much more difficult with the expansion of the Tax On Split Income (TOSI).

13-14.   Because of this importance, we will need to give attention to the rules for designating dividends as eligible. These rules will be covered after our discussion of Part I and Part IV refundable taxes. However, with the need to divide the Refundable Dividend Tax On Hand (RDTOH) account into eligible and non-eligible components, the material on designating eligible dividends will be covered prior to dealing with these accounts.

Rates Required For Integration

Corporate Rates And Provincial Dividend Tax Credits

13-15.   The goal of integration is to ensure that, if an individual chooses to channel an income stream through a corporation, he or she will retain the same after tax amount of funds that would have been retained if he or she had received the income directly. The procedures associated with integration are directed at equating the amount of taxes paid by an individual who does not incorporate an income source and pays taxes only at the individual level with the total amount of taxes that would be paid if the relevant assets were transferred to a corporation and the resulting income taxed at both the corporate level and at the individual level on distribution of the after tax corporate income.

13-16.   In Chapter 7, we also demonstrated that, for integration to work, certain assumptions were required with respect to both the combined federal/provincial tax rate on corporations and the combined federal/provincial dividend tax credit. As noted in that chapter, those assumptions are as follows:

Corporate Federal/Provincial Tax Rate For integration to work perfectly, the corporate rate must be such that the dividend gross up percent must restore the after tax corporate amount to the pre corporate tax amount. The relevant rates are as follows:

- For eligible dividends that have a 38 percent gross up, the required rate is 27.54 percent. For example, $10,000 of corporate income would result in corporate taxes of $2,754 and an after tax amount of $7,246 ($10,000 - $2,754). When the $7,246 is grossed up by 38 percent, the result is the original $10,000 [($7,246)(1.38)] of corporate earnings.

- For non-eligible dividends that have a 15 percent gross up, the required rate is 13.04 percent. For example, $10,000 of corporate income would result in corporate taxes of $1,304 and an after tax amount of $8,696 ($10,000 - $1,304). When the $8,696 is grossed up by 15 percent, the result is the original $10,000 [($8,696)(1.15)] of corporate earnings.

If the provincial dividend tax credit is at the level required for integration, combined corporate tax rates above 27.54 percent (for eligible dividends) and 13.04 percent (for non-eligible dividends) will result in higher taxation on income flowed through a corporation. This type of situation is referred to as under-integration.

Provincial Dividend Tax Credit For the total taxes on income flowed through a corporation to be equal to taxes that would be paid on the direct receipt of income, there must be a credit against personal taxes that is equal to the taxes paid at the corporate level. As you can see in our examples of the required rates for perfect integration, when the corporate tax rate is the one required for perfect integration, the gross up will be equal to the corporate taxes paid. Putting these two facts together leads to the conclusion that the combined dividend tax credit must be equal to the gross up of dividends received. The required rates are as follows:

- For eligible dividends, the federal dividend tax credit is equal to 6/11 of the gross up (54.5 percent). This means that, for the combined credit to equal the gross up, the provincial credit must be equal to 5/11 (45.5 percent) of the gross up.

Figure 13 - 2
Corporate Rates And Dividend Tax Credits Required For Integration

Type Of Dividends	Required Corporate Combined Tax Rate	Required Provincial Dividend Tax Credit
Eligible (38% Gross Up)	27.54%	5/11 ≈ 45.5%
Non-Eligible (15% Gross Up)	13.04%	4/13 ≈ 30.8%

- For non-eligible dividends, the federal dividend tax credit is equal to 9/13 of the gross up (69.2 percent). This means that, for the combined credit to equal the gross up, the provincial credit must be equal to 4/13 (30.8 percent) of the gross up.

If the corporate tax rate is at the level required for integration, provincial dividend tax credits below these rates will result in under-integration, (i.e., additional taxation because a corporation is used). These required tax and dividend credit rates are summarized in Figure 13-2.

Actual Vs. Required Corporate Tax Rates

13-17.   It is important to be aware of how closely actual corporate tax rates compare to the rates required to implement integration. The following general comments are relevant to this:

Eligible Dividends   For eligible dividends, integration requires a combined federal/ provincial corporate tax rate of 27.54 percent. As most eligible dividends will be paid by public companies, the relevant rate is the one applicable to these companies. The combined rates for such companies currently range from roughly 26 to 31 percent. As these rates are fairly close to the required 27.54 percent, integration is working reasonably well, with modest amounts of over- or under-integration in specific provinces.

Non-Eligible Dividends   For non-eligible dividends, integration requires a federal/ provincial tax rate on corporations of 13.04 percent. The situation here is more complex in that the source of such dividends may be either the income of CCPCs that have benefitted from the small business deduction or the investment income of such companies.

To the extent that the non-eligible dividends reflect income that has benefitted from the small business deduction, the appropriate combined federal/provincial rates range from 9 percent to about 12.5 percent (this ignores Quebec's unusually high rate on this income). As was the case with eligible dividends, these rates are close to the required 13.04 percent, suggesting that integration is working fairly well here.

There is a problem, however, when the source of the non-eligible dividends is investment income earned by CCPCs. As we shall discover in this Chapter, the combined federal/ provincial rates on this type of income are, in general, over 50 percent. While integration would clearly not work with overall corporate rates at this level, we will find that the effect of these rates is mitigated by the fact that a substantial portion of these taxes are refunded to the corporation when the investment income is paid out to shareholders as dividends.

13-18.   For both types of dividends, the preceding analysis makes it clear that the effectiveness of integration is very dependent on the province in which the corporation operates.

Actual Vs. Required Dividend Tax Credits

13-19.   Also of importance is the relationship between actual provincial dividend tax credit rates and those that currently exist. The following general comments are relevant here:

Eligible Dividends   For eligible dividends, the required provincial dividend tax credit is 45.5 percent of the gross up. There is currently a wide range of such credits, going from under 20 percent to just over 50 percent. However, the distribution is skewed to the low side, with the average rate being approximately 37 percent. Given this, there will generally be under-integration with respect to eligible dividends.

Non-Eligible Dividends   For non-eligible dividends, the required provincial dividend tax credit rate is 30.8 percent of the gross up. Here again, there is a wide range of actual rates. However, the average is just 21.5 percent, which suggests that integration is also not working well for this type of dividend.

13-20.   As is the case with corporate tax rates, variations in the dividend tax credit rates make it clear that the effectiveness of integration is highly dependent on the province in which the shareholder resides.

Exercise Thirteen - 1

Subject: Integration (Non-Eligible Dividends)

Jan Teason has a business that she estimates will produce income of $100,000 during the taxation year ending December 31, 2020. If she incorporates this business, all of the income would be eligible for the small business deduction and any dividends paid will be non-eligible. In the province where she lives, such corporate income is taxed at a combined federal/provincial rate of 15 percent. Ms. Teason has other income sources that place her in a combined federal/provincial tax bracket of 45 percent. In her province, the provincial dividend tax credit on non-eligible dividends is equal to 30 percent of the gross up. Would Ms. Teason save taxes if she were to channel this source of income through a corporation? Explain your result.

Exercise Thirteen - 2

Subject: Integration (Eligible Dividends)

John Horst has a business that he estimates will produce income of $100,000 during the taxation year ending December 31, 2020. Because he controls another corporation that fully utilizes $500,000 of its small business deduction, if he incorporates this business, none of this income will be eligible for the small business deduction and any dividends paid would be designated eligible. In the province where he lives, such corporate income is taxed at a combined federal/provincial rate of 30 percent. Mr. Horst has other income sources that place him in a combined federal/provincial tax bracket of 42 percent. In his province, the provincial dividend tax credit on eligible dividends is equal to 28 percent of the gross up. Would Mr. Horst save taxes if he were to channel this source of income through a corporation? Explain your result.

SOLUTIONS available in print and online Study Guide.

We suggest you work Self Study Problem Thirteen-1 at this point.

Alternative Calculations For Dividend Tax Credits

13-21.   Note that, while federal legislation calculates the dividend tax credit as a fraction of the gross up, you often see this credit expressed as a percentage of dividends received, or a percentage of the grossed up amount of the dividends.

13-22.   Because our focus is largely on federal legislation, we will generally present dividend tax credits as a fraction of the gross up. However, if needed, it is quite simple to convert different approaches to a uniform base. For example, if an eligible dividend of $100 is paid, the federal dividend tax credit of $20.73 can be calculated as:

- 6/11 (54.55%) of the $38 [(38%)($100)] gross up. (Which is our standard approach.)
- 20.73 percent of the $100 in dividends received, or
- 15.02 percent of the $138 of grossed up dividends.

Refundable Taxes On Investment Income

Meaning Of Aggregate Investment Income

Regular Meaning

13-23.   In the following material on refundable taxes, we will be using the term Aggregate Investment Income. For purposes of determining the amount of refundable taxes available, this term is defined in ITA 129(4) and has a very specific definition. You may recall that we provided this definition in Chapter 12 and it is also included at the front of this text in "Rates And Other Data". It is provided again here for your convenience.

ITA 129(4) Aggregate Investment Income

Net Taxable Capital Gains	$xxx
Interest	xxx
Rents	xxx
Royalties	xxx
Total Positive Amounts	$xxx
Net Capital Loss Carry Overs Deducted During The Year	(xxx)
ITA 129(4) Aggregate Investment Income	$xxx

13-24.   Note carefully the differences between this Aggregate Investment Income and what we normally think of as property or investment income. Unlike the normal definition of property or investment income, this concept includes net taxable capital gains for the current year, reduced by net capital loss carry overs deducted during the year.

13-25.   The other difference between Aggregate Investment Income and the usual definition of investment income is that it excludes most dividends from other Canadian corporations. This reflects the fact that dividends from Canadian corporations generally flow through a corporation without being subject to Part I corporate taxes. You should also note that Aggregate Investment Income includes income from both Canadian and foreign sources.

ADJUSTED Aggregate Investment Income

13-26.   Chapter 12 introduced an alternative definition of investment income, referred to as ADJUSTED Aggregate Investment Income [ITA 125(7)]. We have capitalized ADJUSTED to avoid confusion with Aggregate Investment Income. This ADJUSTED definition differs from the regular definition as follows:

- It includes dividends from taxable Canadian corporations with the exception of those from connected corporations. This can also be referred to as portfolio dividends.
- It only includes net taxable capital gains on the disposition of assets that are not used in an active business.
- There is no deduction for net capital loss carry overs that are deducted during the current year.

13-27.   It is important to note that this alternative ADJUSTED definition is only used for the determination of the annual business limit grind. In all other applications, the ITA 129(4) definition of Aggregate Investment Income is used.

Basic Concepts

The Problem

13-28.   As shown in Figure 13-3 (on the following page), when income is flowed through a corporation it is subject to two levels of taxation. It is taxed first at the corporate level and, if the after tax corporate amount is distributed to the individual shareholder, it will be taxed again in

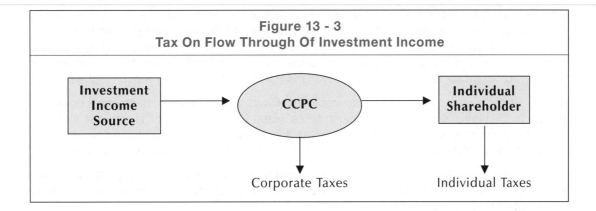

Figure 13 - 3
Tax On Flow Through Of Investment Income

the hands of that individual. If we assume that the corporate tax rate on the investment income of a CCPC is 52 percent and that the individual shareholder is taxed at a combined rate of 39 percent on non-eligible dividends received, the overall rate of taxation on investment income flowed through a corporation would be 70.7 percent [52% + (1 - 52%)(39%)].

13-29. This is significantly higher than the maximum federal/provincial tax rate on Canadian individuals of 54 percent. Such a large difference is clearly not consistent with the concept of integration. Given this, it was necessary to find some method of providing tax relief for shareholders of CCPCs earning investment income.

The Solution

13-30. The most obvious solution to this problem would be to lower the rate of corporate taxation on the investment income of a CCPC. For example, if the corporate rate was lowered to 22 percent, the overall rate on the flow through of income would be taxed at 52.4 percent [22% + (1 - 22%)(39%)]. This is within the range of rates that are applied to high net worth individuals who receive business or property income directly.

13-31. The problem with this solution is that it would provide for a significant deferral of taxes on investment income. If an individual received the investment income directly, the full amount of taxes must be paid when the income is earned. In contrast, when a corporation is used, only the first, or corporate, level of taxation is assessed when the income is earned. If the after tax amount is left in the corporation, the assessment of the individual level of tax can be deferred indefinitely.

13-32. For higher income individuals who do not require all of their investment income for current expenditures, this would present an outstanding opportunity for tax deferral, as well as for the accumulation of large portfolios of passive investments. This would be the case whenever the corporate tax rate on investment income is below the rate applicable to the individual on the direct receipt of income.

13-33. Given the opportunity for tax deferral that would result from the use of lower corporate tax rates, it is not surprising that a different solution to the problem of excessive tax rates on the flow through of a CCPC's investment income has been adopted. This solution involves leaving the corporate tax rate at a high level, but having a portion of the tax being designated as refundable. The refund of this portion of the corporate tax occurs when the income is distributed in the form of dividends that will be subject to the second level of taxation in the hands of the shareholders.

13-34. Consistent with this concept of keeping the basic rate high on the Aggregate Investment Income of a CCPC, this type of income is excluded from the definition of Full Rate Taxable Income and, as a consequence, is not eligible for the general rate reduction.

Refundable Tax Procedures

13-35. While the detailed procedures related to these refundable taxes are complex, the basic concept is not. A portion of the tax paid on investment income at the corporate level is refunded when the income is distributed to investors in the form of dividends. This keeps the combined corporate and personal tax rate in line with the rate that would be applicable to an individual on the direct receipt of income. The high rate of corporate tax discourages tax deferral, while at the same time, the refund procedures avoid the excessive rate of taxation that would occur if this high corporate tax rate was combined with individual taxes on the same income stream.

13-36.   Stated simply, the use of a refundable tax allows the government to charge a corporate tax rate that is high enough to remove much of the incentive for accumulating investment income in a corporation and, at the same time, provides a reasonable overall rate of taxation when the income is flowed through the corporation and taxed in the hands of the individual shareholder.

13-37.   In implementing this refundable tax approach, the *Income Tax Act* designates three different components of total taxes paid that can be refunded on the payment of dividends. They can be described as follows:

Ordinary Part I Tax   At this point, you should be familiar with the calculation of the regular Part I tax that is assessed on the Taxable Income of a corporation. A portion of this tax, conceptually the portion of the Part I tax that is applicable to investment income, will be designated as refundable on the payment of dividends. Note the fact that a portion of the Part I tax being designated as refundable does not change, in any way, the manner in which the Part I tax is calculated.

Additional Refundable Tax On Investment Income (ART)   The Additional Refundable Tax On Investment Income, a Part I tax, was introduced in order to ensure that the combined federal/provincial tax on investment income was sufficiently high that it would discourage the use of a corporation to defer taxes. To achieve this objective, this combined tax rate had to be at a level that was higher than the rate applicable to high net worth individuals.

The ART rate is 10-2/3 percent, resulting in a federal rate on investment income of 38-2/3 percent (38% - 10% + 10-2/3%). When the various provincial rates on this type of income are taken into consideration, applicable combined rates are all in excess of 50 percent, with the top rate at nearly 55 percent. As this is comparable to, or higher than, the maximum rate on individuals in all of the provinces, ART serves to discourage earning investment income that is retained within a corporation.

Part IV Tax   Even with the Part I refundable tax and ART in place, there is still the possibility of using a related group of corporations to defer taxation on investment income. Based on this, a Part IV tax is assessed at a rate of 38-1/3 percent on certain intercorporate dividends received by a private corporation.

13-38.   In dealing with this material, we will first consider the issues involved with a single corporation. In these single corporation situations, only the refundable Part I tax and the additional refundable tax on investment income will be considered.

Refundable Part I Tax On Investment Income
Additional Refundable Tax On Investment Income (ART)
Basic Calculations
13-39.   As was noted previously, tax legislation contains a refundable tax on the investment income of a Canadian controlled private corporation (CCPC). This additional refundable tax (ART) is assessed under ITA 123.3 (the definition is available at the front of this text in "Rates And Other Data"). The amount payable is equal to 10-2/3 percent of the lesser of:

• the corporation's "Aggregate Investment Income" for the year [as defined in ITA 129(4)]; and

• the amount, if any, by which the corporation's Taxable Income for the year exceeds the amount that is eligible for the small business deduction.

13-40.   The basic objective of this tax is to make it undesirable to shelter investment income within a corporate structure in order to defer full taxation of the amounts earned. As we have noted, when this additional 10-2/3 percent is added to the usual rates applicable to a CCPC's investment income, the combined rate is over 50 percent in all provinces.

13-41.   This means that, with the addition of the ART, rates on the investment income of a CCPC will generally be higher than the rates applicable to an individual receiving the same income directly. Given this, there is little or no tax incentive to use a corporation to defer taxation on this type of income.

13-42.   As described in Paragraph 13-39, the ART is based on the lesser of Aggregate Investment Income and the amount of Taxable Income that is not eligible for the small business deduction. The reason for the latter limit is to ensure that such deductions as charitable donations or non-capital loss carry overs have not totally or partially eliminated the investment income from the amount flowing through to Taxable Income. The goal is to prevent the ART from being inappropriately applied to active business income.

Exercise Thirteen - 3

Subject: Additional Refundable Tax On Investment Income

Zircon Inc. is a CCPC with a December 31 year end. Zircon is not associated with any other company. For the 2020 taxation year, its Net Income For Tax Purposes is equal to $281,000. This is made up of active business income of $198,000, dividends from taxable Canadian corporations of $22,000, interest income on long term investments of $15,000, and taxable capital gains on the disposition of capital assets used in the active business of $46,000.

The company has available a net capital loss carry forward of $26,000 [(1/2)($52,000)] and a non-capital loss carry forward of $23,000. The company intends to deduct both of these carry forwards in the 2020 taxation year. In 2019, the corporation's ADJUSTED Aggregate Investment Income was $13,000, and its Taxable Capital Employed in Canada was $6 million.

Determine Zircon's Taxable Income and its additional refundable tax on investment income for the 2020 taxation year.

SOLUTION available in print and online Study Guide.

ART And Foreign Tax Credit Calculations

13-43.   As discussed in Chapter 12, the use of foreign taxes paid as credits against Canadian Tax Payable is limited by a formula that includes the "tax otherwise payable." In the case of foreign taxes paid on non-business income, the "tax otherwise payable" in the formula adds the ART that is assessed under ITA 123.3.

13-44.   This creates a potential problem in that the calculation of the ART includes the amount eligible for the small business deduction. Since one of the factors limiting the small business deduction [ITA 125(1)(b)] is Taxable Income reduced by 100/28 of the foreign non-business income tax credit and 4 times the foreign business income tax credit, this could have created an insolvable circular calculation.

13-45.   As is explained in Chapter 12, there is a similar circularity issue involving the general rate reduction under ITA 123.4. The calculation of this amount also requires knowing the amount of income that is eligible for the small business deduction.

13-46.   To avoid both of these problems, for the purposes of calculating the small business deduction, ITA 125(1)(b)(i) permits the foreign tax credit for taxes paid on foreign non-business income to be calculated using a "tax otherwise payable" figure that does not include the ART under ITA 123.3 or the general rate reduction. ITA 125(1)(b)(ii) permits the foreign tax credit for taxes paid on foreign business income to be calculated using a "tax otherwise payable" figure that does not include the general rate reduction.

13-47.   This means that in situations where the small business deduction, foreign tax credits, and the ART are involved, the following procedures should be used:

1. Calculate the foreign non-business tax credit using a "tax otherwise payable" figure that excludes both ITA 123.3 (ART) and ITA 123.4 (general rate reduction). This initial version of the foreign non-business tax credit will be used only for the purpose of determining the small business deduction, with the actual credit available calculated after the ITA 123.3 and 123.4 amounts have been determined.

2. Calculate the foreign business tax credit using a "tax otherwise payable" figure that excludes ITA 123.4 (as business income is involved, ITA 123.3 is excluded by definition). However, this credit is limited by the amount of tax otherwise payable, reduced by the foreign non-business tax credit. As a consequence, it will be necessary to calculate an initial version of this foreign business tax credit, using the initial version of the foreign non-business tax credit. This initial version will be used only for the purpose of determining the small business deduction and the M&P deduction.

3. Calculate the amount eligible for the small business deduction and M&P deduction using the numbers determined in steps 1 and 2.

4. Using the amount eligible for the small business deduction and the M&P deduction determined in step 3, calculate the ART and the general rate reduction.

5. Calculate the actual foreign non-business tax credit using a "tax otherwise payable" figure that includes the ART and the general rate reduction determined in step 4.

6. Calculate the actual foreign business tax credit using the actual foreign non-business tax credit determined in step 5 and the general rate reduction from step 4.

Problem One: Excessive Tax Rates On The Flow Through Of A CCPC's Investment Income

13-48.   With the addition of the 10-2/3 percent ART on the investment income of a Canadian controlled private corporation, this investment income is taxed at a combined federal/provincial rate that is consistently over 50 percent (see Paragraph 13-40).

13-49.   All of these combined rates are far higher than the 13.04 percent rate required for perfect integration (the 13.04 percent rate for non-eligible dividends is used since the investment income of a CCPC cannot be used as a basis for paying eligible dividends). In the absence of some type of relieving mechanism, the objective of integrating corporate and individual tax rates would not be met.

13-50.   The problem of excessive rates of tax on investment income flowed through a corporation was discussed previously in Paragraph 13-28. This is a more complete example:

EXAMPLE   Mr. Monroe has investments that generate interest income of $100,000 per year. He is personally subject to a combined federal/provincial tax rate of 49 percent. The dividend tax credit for non-eligible dividends in his province of residence is equal to 4/13 of the gross up. Calculate the amount of cash Mr. Monroe will retain from this investment income under the following alternative assumptions:

Case A   He receives the $100,000 in interest income directly.

Case B   Mr. Monroe is the sole shareholder of a Canadian controlled private corporation that earns the $100,000 of investment income. The corporation is subject to a combined federal/provincial tax rate, including the ITA 123.3 tax on investment income, of 54 percent. The corporation pays out all of its after tax earnings as non-eligible dividends, resulting in a dividend to Mr. Monroe of $46,000. Ignore any refund of Part I tax paid.

13-51. The calculations comparing the investment income if it was received directly (Case A) and if it was earned through a corporation (Case B) are as follows:

Case A - Investment Income Received Directly

Investment Income - Direct Receipt	$ 100,000
Personal Tax At 49 Percent	(49,000)
After Tax Cash Retained Without Corporation	$ 51,000

Case B - Investment Income Flowed Through Corporation
Assume No Refundable Part I Tax

Corporate Investment Income	$ 100,000
Corporate Tax At 54 Percent (Includes The ART)	(54,000)
Non-Eligible Dividends Paid To Mr. Monroe	$ 46,000

Non-Eligible Dividends Received	$ 46,000
Gross Up Of 15 Percent	6,900
Personal Taxable Income	$ 52,900
Personal Tax Rate	49%
Tax Payable Before Dividend Tax Credit	$ 25,921
Dividend Tax Credit [(9/13 + 4/13)(Gross Up)]	(6,900)
Personal Tax Payable With Corporation	$ 19,021

Non-Eligible Dividends Received	$ 46,000
Personal Tax Payable	(19,021)
After Tax Cash Retained With Corporation	$ 26,979

Savings - Direct Receipt

Income Received Directly	$ 51,000
Income Flowed Through Corporation	(26,979)
Net Savings On Direct Receipt	$ 24,021

13-52. The results show that, in the absence of the refundable component of Part I tax, interest income flowed through a corporation is subject to an effective tax rate of over 73 percent [($100,000 - $26,979) ÷ $100,000]. This is significantly higher than the 49 percent rate that is applicable to the direct receipt of the investment income, an outcome that would represent a major failure in the government's attempt to achieve integration.

13-53. Before leaving this example you should note that, with the inclusion of the ART on investment income, there is no deferral advantage associated with using a corporation in this example. The corporate taxes alone are $54,000, well in excess of the $49,000 that would be paid if Mr. Monroe had received the income directly.

Solution To Problem One: Refundable Portion Of Part I Tax

Basic Concepts

13-54. The preceding example makes it clear that taxes on investment income earned by a CCPC and flowed through to its shareholders are potentially much higher than would be the case if the shareholders received the income directly. This major imperfection in the system of integration results from a federal/provincial tax rate on the investment income of CCPCs that is over 50 percent.

13-55. In those cases where the income is retained in the corporation, this is an equitable arrangement in that this high rate discourages the use of a CCPC to temporarily shelter passive income from a portion of the taxes that would be assessed on the direct receipt of the income by the individual. However, when the investment income is flowed through a CCPC and paid as dividends, the result is not consistent with the government's desire to tax CCPCs under the integration view of corporate taxation.

13-56.   As noted previously, the government could have dealt with this problem by reducing the corporate tax rate on the investment income of CCPCs. However, this would have allowed the owners of CCPCs to defer personal taxes on this income by leaving the investment income in the corporation. To avoid this, the refundable tax approach is used.

13-57.   Under this approach, the investment income of Canadian controlled private corporations is taxed at the usual high rates, including the ART on investment income. However, when the corporation distributes its after tax income in the form of dividends, a part of this tax is refunded. Under ITA 129(1), the refund is based on the amount of dividends paid by the corporation, with the refund being equal to 38-1/3 percent of dividends paid.

Concepts Illustrated

13-58.   For integration to work perfectly on non-eligible dividend payments, the overall corporate tax rate has to equal 13.04 percent (see Paragraph 13-16). In order to give you a better understanding of how the concepts associated with the refund of Part I tax work, we will use an example based on a pre-dividend refund tax rate that will provide a 13.04 percent tax rate after the refund has contributed to the total dividend. While we will not go through the calculation of this rate, the required rate is 46.375 percent, including the 10-2/3 percent ART. You should note that this rate is lower than any of the relevant combined federal/provincial rates that are currently available.

13-59.   With the initial corporate tax rate at 46.375 percent, a refund is necessary to reduce the rate to the required 13.04 percent. The rate that is specified in ITA 129(1) is 38-1/3 percent of the total dividends paid. As we will discuss later, this refund is limited by the corporation's balance in its Refundable Dividend Tax On Hand account.

13-60.   The following example, involving perfect integration, will illustrate the rates that we have just presented:

> **EXAMPLE**   Ms. Banardi has investments that generate interest income of $100,000 per year. You have been asked to advise her as to whether there would be any benefits associated with transferring these investments to her wholly owned Canadian controlled private corporation. Ms. Banardi is personally subject to a combined federal/provincial tax rate of 49 percent. The dividend tax credit on non-eligible dividends in her province of residence is equal to 4/13 of the gross up. Her corporation would be taxed on this income at a combined federal/provincial rate of 46.375 percent, including the ART on investment income.

> **Note**   In the calculations that follow, we have ignored some small rounding issues in order to avoid extending the required rates to more decimal places. This in no way defeats the objective of illustrating the conceptual basis for the Part I refundable tax.

13-61.   The calculations comparing the after tax investment income if it was earned in a corporation and if it was received directly are as follows:

After Tax Retention - Use Of A Corporation

Corporate Investment Income	$ 100,000
Corporate Tax At 46.375 Percent (Includes The ART)	(46,375)
After Tax Income	$ 53,625
Dividend Refund (See Analysis)	33,335
Non-Eligible Dividends Paid To Ms. Banard	$ 86,960

ANALYSIS   In this somewhat academic example of the dividend refund mechanism, we assume that all of the corporation's after tax income will be paid out as dividends. Given this, a bit of algebra is needed to determine the total dividend, and in the process, the amount of the refund. Specifically, we need to solve the following simple equation:

$X = \$53,625 + [(38\text{-}1/3\%)(X)]$
$X - [(38\text{-}1/3\%)(X)] = \$53,625$
$[(61\text{-}2/3\%)(X)] = \$53,625$
$X = \$86,960$

Where X = The total dividend, including the refund.

This provides a dividend refund of $33,335 ($86,960 - $53,625), an amount that is equal to 38-1/3 percent of $86,960.

In this example, we have provided a complete illustration of the conversion of available after tax income to a dividend that includes a refund equal to 38-1/3 percent of the total dividend. In future examples, we will use a condensed version of this process to do a direct calculation of the amount of the refund. The formula for the refund is as follows:

Refund = [(After Tax Funds Available ÷ .61667) - After Tax Funds Available]

Applying this to the current example gives the same result that was achieved by the more detailed calculation:

$$\$33,335 = [(\$53,625 \div .61667) - \$53,625]$$

Note that, at this point, the total corporate tax paid is equal to $13,040 ($100,000 - $86,960). This reflects the 13.04 percent rate ($13,040 ÷ $100,000) that is required for perfect integration.

The assumption that all after tax income will be paid out as dividends is not consistent with the real world approach in which the amount of the dividend is determined by a variety of factors (e.g., availability of cash or alternative investment opportunities) and very rarely, if ever, equals the after tax income plus the dividend refund.

Calculation of the after tax amounts retained follows:

Non-Eligible Dividends Received	$ 86,960
Gross Up Of 15 Percent	13,040
Personal Taxable Income	$ 100,000
Personal Tax Rate	49%
Tax Payable Before Dividend Tax Credit	$ 49,000
Dividend Tax Credit [(9/13 + 4/13)(Gross Up)]	(13,040)
Personal Tax Payable With Corporation	$ 35,960
Non-Eligible Dividends Received	$ 86,960
Personal Tax Payable	(35,960)
After Tax Cash Retained With Corporation	$ 51,000

After Tax Retention - Direct Receipt

Investment Income - Direct Receipt	$ 100,000
Personal Tax At 49 Percent	(49,000)
After Tax Cash Retained Without Corporation	$ 51,000

13-62.   While this example provides equal amounts of after tax cash, without regard to whether the income is flowed through a corporation or received directly, it is not a realistic example. All of the combined federal/provincial rates on the investment income of CCPCs are higher than the 46.375 percent rate used in our example. In addition, as we shall see in the next section of this Chapter, the amount of the refund is limited by the balance in the Refundable Dividend Tax On Hand (RDTOH). We have not taken that into consideration in this example. If we had, the dividend refund in this example would be limited to $30,677 [(30-2/3%)($100,000)].

Use Of Other Rates In Refundable Part I Tax Example

13-63.   In this example, we will use a corporate tax rate of 54-2/3 percent. This will illustrate that, when realistic corporate tax rates are used, using a CCPC to hold assets earning investment income will result in a lower after tax return than holding the investments directly.

> **EXAMPLE**   Mr. Leoni has investments that generate interest income of $100,000 per year. He has over $250,000 in other income and is subject to a combined federal/provincial tax rate of 51 percent. The provincial dividend tax credit for non-eligible dividends is equal to 4/13 of the gross up. Mr. Leoni is the sole shareholder of a CCPC and is considering the transfer of these investments to his corporation. His corporation would be taxed on this income at a combined federal/provincial rate of 54-2/3 percent, including the ART on investment income (38% - 10% + 10-2/3% + 16%).

13-64.   The calculations comparing the after tax investment income if it was earned through a corporation and if it was received directly are as follows:

After Tax Retention - Use Of A Corporation

Corporate Investment Income	$ 100,000
Corporate Tax At 54-2/3 Percent (Includes The ART)	(54,667)
After Tax Income	$ 45,333
Dividend Refund [($45,333 ÷ .61667) - $45,333]	28,180
Non-Eligible Dividends Paid To Mr. Leoni	$ 73,513
Non-Eligible Dividends Received	$ 73,513
Gross Up Of 15 Percent	11,027
Personal Taxable Income	$ 84,540
Personal Tax Rate	51%
Tax Payable Before Dividend Tax Credit	$ 43,115
Dividend Tax Credit [(9/13 + 4/13)($11,027)]	(11,027)
Personal Tax Payable With Corporation	$ 32,088
Non-Eligible Dividends Received	$ 73,513
Personal Tax Payable	(32,088)
After Tax Cash Retained With Corporation	$ 41,425

After Tax Retention - Direct Receipt

Investment Income - Direct Receipt	$ 100,000
Personal Tax At 51 Percent	(51,000)
After Tax Cash Retained Without Corporation	$ 49,000

13-65.   There are two things that should be noted here. First, when a 54-2/3 percent corporate tax rate is used, the taxes of $54,667 at the corporate level are significantly higher than the $51,000 that would have been paid if Mr. Leoni had received the income directly. While there are some combinations of provincial corporate and provincial individual tax rates that would provide for some deferral of taxes at the corporate level, that is clearly not the case with the rates used here.

13-66. With respect to the after tax flow through of investment income, using a corporation is clearly not a good idea. Mr. Leoni has $7,575 ($49,000 - $41,425) less after tax cash, as compared to the amount he would have retained on direct receipt of the $100,000 income. While this difference is particularly large when a 54-2/3 percent corporate tax rate is used, the basic result would be the same when any of the other available corporate tax rates are used. As a result, using a corporation would almost always produce less after tax cash.

Exercise Thirteen - 4

Subject: Flow Through Of Investment Income

Ms. Shelly Nicastro has investments that generate interest income of $100,000 per year. Due to her employment income, she is in the top tax bracket, with a combined federal/ provincial rate of 51 percent. She is considering the transfer of these investments to her CCPC, which would be subject to a tax rate on investment income of 52 percent (including the ART). The dividend tax credit for non-eligible dividends in her province is equal to 30 percent of the gross up. Any dividends paid by the CCPC out of investment income will be non-eligible. Advise her as to whether there would be any tax benefits associated with this transfer.

SOLUTION available in print and online Study Guide.

Refundable Part IV Tax On Dividends Received

Problem Two: Use Of Multi-Level Affiliations
To Defer Taxes On Investment Income

13-67. In the preceding section, we demonstrated how refund procedures applicable to Part I tax payable are used to lower the overall rate of taxation on the investment income of a CCPC, while at the same time preventing the use of a corporation to defer a portion of the overall taxation on such income. While varying provincial tax rates on corporations and individuals prevent these procedures from providing perfect results, they appear to produce results that come close to achieving the goal of integration of personal and corporate taxes.

13-68. The situation becomes more complex when a group of connected companies is involved. The refundable tax procedures that were previously described are not effective in preventing tax deferral in this case. As a result, there is a need for additional procedures.

EXAMPLE Eastern Inc. has a 100 percent owned subsidiary, Western Ltd. Both companies are Canadian controlled private corporations and have a December 31 year end. During the current year, Western has income of $100,000, made up entirely of interest and taxable capital gains. Assume that the combined federal/provincial tax rate for both companies is 50-2/3 percent, including the ART. Western pays out all of its after tax income in dividends to Eastern Inc. This situation is illustrated in Figure 13-4 (on the following page).

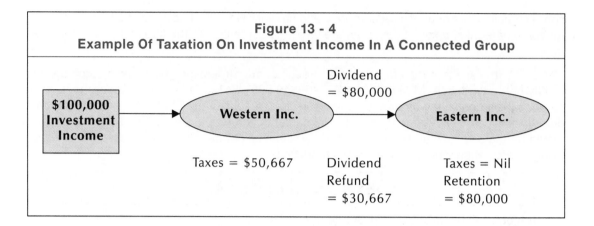

Figure 13 - 4
Example Of Taxation On Investment Income In A Connected Group

ANALYSIS   On receipt of the $100,000 of investment income, Western would pay taxes of $50,667 [($100,000)(50-2/3%)]. However, when the remaining $49,333 is paid out in dividends, a dividend refund of $30,667 (38-1/3% of the $80,000 total dividend) becomes available, resulting in a total dividend of $80,000 as shown in the following calculation:

Investment Income Of Western	$ 100,000
Corporate Tax At 50-2/3 Percent (Includes The ART)	(50,667)
Income Before Dividends	$ 49,333
Dividend Refund [($49,333 ÷ .61667) - $49,333]	30,667
Dividends Paid To Eastern	$ 80,000

As the dividends from Western will be received tax free by Eastern, they will have after tax retention of $80,000. Unless Eastern pays out taxable dividends to its individual shareholders, no additional Part I tax will be assessed. This means that, in the absence of additional procedures, there could be a significant deferral of taxes on investment income resulting from the use of two related corporations.

Solution To Problem Two: Refundable Part IV Tax

Corporations Subject To Part IV Tax

13-69.   To eliminate this potential flaw in integration, a Part IV tax is assessed on dividends received by a private corporation from certain other types of corporations. Note that this tax is assessed without regard to whether or not the private corporation is Canadian controlled.

13-70.   In general, only private corporations are liable for Part IV tax. However, there remains the possibility that a company that is controlled largely for the benefit of an individual, or a related group of individuals, might use a small issue of shares to the public in order to avoid this tax. Such corporations are referred to as "subject corporations" and they are defined in ITA 186(3) as follows:

> **Subject Corporation**   means a corporation (other than a private corporation) resident in Canada and controlled, whether because of a beneficial interest in one or more trusts or otherwise, by or for the benefit of an individual (other than a trust) or a related group of individuals (other than trusts).

13-71.   ITA 186(1) indicates that, for purposes of Part IV tax, subject corporations will be treated as private corporations. This means that both private corporations, as well as those public corporations that fall within the definition of subject corporations, will be liable for the payment of Part IV tax. In this Chapter, any subsequent references to private corporations should be considered to include subject corporations.

Rates

13-72. The Part IV rate is assessed at a rate of 38-1/3 percent. It is applicable to portfolio dividends as well as some dividends from connected corporations (both of these terms will be subsequently explained). The rate at which this tax is refunded is the same as the rate for refunds of Part I tax. Both refunds are at a rate of 38-1/3 percent of the total dividend.

Applicable Dividends

13-73. The Part IV tax is only applicable to certain types of dividends received by private corporations. Specifically, Part IV tax is payable on dividends received by private corporations in the following circumstances:

- A dividend is received from an unconnected company that is deductible in the calculation of the recipient's Taxable Income. While the *Income Tax Act* refers to such dividends as "assessable dividends", it is a common practice to refer to such dividends as "portfolio dividends", a practice we will follow in the remainder of this text.

- The dividend is received from a connected company that, as a result of making the dividend payment, received a dividend refund.

13-74. Each of these types of dividends will be given attention in the material that follows.

Part IV Tax On Portfolio Dividends Received

Portfolio Dividends And Connected Corporations Defined

13-75. A portfolio dividend is defined as a dividend received by a private corporation from a corporation to which it is not connected and that is deductible in the determination of the private corporation's Taxable Income. As with many *Income Tax Act* terms, the definition of a portfolio dividend includes another term that requires definition. This term is "connected corporation" and the definition is found in ITA 186(4). Under this definition, a connected corporation is either:

- a controlled corporation, where control represents ownership of more than 50 percent of the voting shares by any combination of the other corporation and persons with whom it does not deal at arm's length, or

- a corporation in which the other corporation owns more than 10 percent of the voting shares, and more than 10 percent of the fair market value of all of the issued shares of the corporation.

13-76. Given the definition of connected corporation, a 10 percent shareholding test is generally used to determine whether the dividends received are portfolio dividends or dividends from a connected corporation.

> **EXAMPLE** A dividend is received on an investment made by a private company in 500 shares of a large publicly traded company that has 15 million shares outstanding.

> **ANALYSIS** The 500 shares would be significantly less than 10 percent of the total shares outstanding and would not constitute control of the company. As a consequence, the dividends would be considered portfolio dividends and the Part IV tax would be applicable.

Portfolio Dividends And Integration

13-77. The tax policy issue with respect to portfolio dividends relates to integration. If such dividends are received by an individual, they are normally subject to taxation. For example, assume that an individual receives $100,000 in dividends. This individual is subject to a combined federal/provincial marginal rate of 45 percent and lives in a province with a dividend tax credit equal to 5/11 of the eligible dividend gross up and 4/13 of the non-eligible dividend gross up. The resulting Tax Payable would be calculated as follows:

Refundable Part IV Tax On Dividends Received

	Eligible Dividends	**Non-Eligible Dividends**
Dividends Received	$100,000	$100,000
Gross Up Of 38 or 15 Percent	38,000	15,000
Taxable Income	$138,000	$115,000
Personal Tax Rate	45%	45%
Tax Payable Before Dividend Tax Credit	$ 62,100	$ 51,750
Dividend Tax Credit:		
[(6/11 + 5/11)(Gross Up)]	(38,000)	
[(9/13 + 4/13)(Gross Up)]		(15,000)
Personal Tax Payable	$ 24,100	$ 36,750

13-78.   As an alternative, consider what would happen if the same $100,000 in dividends had been received by a corporation. Under the general rules for intercorporate dividends, the $100,000 would be deductible in the calculation of the corporation's Taxable Income, resulting in no Part I tax at the corporate level. While tax will ultimately be paid when the corporation distributes this income to its shareholders, there is a potential for significant deferral of taxes until such time as this corporation distributes the income as dividends.

13-79.   In order to correct this flaw in the corporate tax integration system, Part IV tax is applied as follows:

> **Part IV Tax - Portfolio Dividends**   When a private corporation receives a dividend on shares that are being held as a portfolio investment, the recipient company is liable for a Part IV tax of 38-1/3 percent of the dividends received. This Part IV tax is refundable, on the basis of 38-1/3 percent of dividends paid, when such dividends are passed on to the shareholders of the recipient corporation.

13-80.   We can see the reasoning behind the rate of this tax by referring back to the preceding example in Paragraph 13-76. You will notice that the effective tax rate on the eligible dividends received by the individual is 24.1 percent ($24,100 ÷ $100,000). By charging a Part IV tax of 38-1/3 percent at the corporate level, the tax paid by the corporation is in excess of the 24.1 percent effective tax rate that would apply to eligible dividends received by an individual with a tax rate of 45 percent. This makes it unattractive to use a private corporation as a shelter to defer the payment of taxes on dividend income. Again, however, by making the tax refundable, it allows the dividends to flow through the recipient corporation without assessing an unreasonable level of taxation on the income flowed through a corporation.

Dividends From A Connected Corporation

The Investment Income Problem

13-81.   It is the intent of the government to allow a Canadian controlled private corporation to be used to defer taxes on active business income. Earning such income entitles the corporation to the use of the small business deduction and this, in most situations, provides a rate of corporate taxation that will effectively defer taxes on income left in the corporation. To the extent that a connected corporation is paying dividends out of such income, there will be no dividend refund and no Part IV tax to be paid by the recipient corporation. This maintains the tax deferral on active business income as it moves between corporations.

13-82.   However, when the connected corporation is a private company (whether or not it is Canadian controlled) and the dividends are paid out of investment income, a problem arises. This problem was illustrated by the example presented in Paragraph 13-68.

13-83.   In that example, Western paid an $80,000 dividend to Eastern, a payment that included a $30,667 refund of taxes previously paid by Western. Under the general rules for dividends, the $80,000 dividend paid by Western would be included in the calculation of Eastern's Net Income For Tax Purposes and deducted in the determination of its Taxable Income, with the net result that no Part I taxes would be paid on the $80,000. This would, in effect, allow retention of 80 percent of the investment income within the corporate group, a result that is contrary to the general concept of integration.

The Solution

13-84. In order to correct this situation, a second application of Part IV tax is as follows:

Part IV Tax - Connected Companies When a private corporation receives dividends from a connected private corporation that has received a dividend refund under ITA 129(1) as a result of paying the dividends, the recipient company is liable for a Part IV tax equal to its share of the refund received by the paying corporation. If the dividend paid is eligible for a full 38-1/3 percent of the dividend paid, the Part IV tax can also be expressed as 38-1/3 percent of the dividends received.

However, the payor corporation may be earning both active business income and investment income. In such situations, if dividends reflect a distribution of both types of income, the dividend refund will not be at the full 38-1/3 percent rate. (See the Paragraph 13-92 example.) This is why the Part IV tax on dividends received from a connected corporation is expressed in terms of the recipient's share of the refund received by the paying corporation, not in terms of a specific rate.

As was the case with the Part IV tax on portfolio dividends, this Part IV tax is refundable on the basis of 38-1/3 percent of dividends paid by the assessed corporation.

Example Of Connected Corporation Dividends

13-85. Returning to the example presented in Paragraph 13-68, you will recall that Western has $100,000 in investment income and pays maximum dividends of $80,000 to Eastern. When the Part IV tax is taken into consideration, the tax consequences for the two companies are as follows:

Investment Income Received By Western	$ 100,000
Corporate Tax At 50-2/3 Percent (Including The ART)	(50,667)
Income Before Dividends	$ 49,333
Dividend Refund [($49,333 ÷ .61667) - $49,333]	**30,667**
Dividends Paid To Eastern	$ 80,000
Investment Income (Dividends Received From Western)	$ 80,000
Part IV Tax Payable (100% Of Western's Refund*)	**(30,667)**
Income Retained By Eastern	$ 49,333

*Because all of Western's income was from investments, Western's dividend refund is the full 38-1/3 percent of dividends paid. This means that Eastern's Part IV tax can also be calculated as 38-1/3 percent of the $80,000 in dividends received from Western.

13-86. As this simple example shows, after the application of the Part IV tax, the amount retained in Eastern is the same $49,333 that was retained in Western. This retention reflects a tax rate on the amount retained within the corporate group of 50-2/3 percent [($100,000 - $49,333) ÷ $100,000], about the same rate that would be paid by an individual taxpayer in the maximum federal/provincial tax bracket on the direct receipt of the $100,000 in investment income. Clearly, the application of Part IV tax has served to maintain integration in situations involving connected companies.

13-87. If Eastern decides to distribute the retained income to its shareholders, the results would be as follows:

Income Retained By Eastern	$49,333
Dividend Refund [($49,333 ÷ .61667) - $49,333]	**30,667**
Non-Eligible Dividend To Shareholders	$80,000

13-88.   In effect, the $100,000 of investment income has passed through two corporations and into the hands of individual shareholders, subject to corporate taxes of only 20 percent. This has been accomplished, despite the fact that the initial level of corporate taxation was sufficiently high to discourage allocating investment income to a multi-level corporate structure.

13-89.   Note, however, the effective corporate tax rate in this example is only 20 percent. It is for this reason that the Aggregate Investment Income of a CCPC is subtracted in the determination of Full Rate Taxable Income.

Applicability

13-90.   We would remind you again that the Part IV tax on dividends from a connected company is only applicable when the paying corporation has received a dividend refund. This means that dividends paid out of a corporation's Aggregate Investment Income or paid out of portfolio dividends received will be subject to Part IV tax. If the paying corporation was earning only active business income, no refund would be available when this after tax income was paid out as dividends. As a consequence, no Part IV tax would be assessed on the corporation receiving the dividend.

13-91.   This result is consistent with the goals of integration in that, when a corporation is earning active business income that is taxed at the low small business rate, tax deferral is permitted on income that is retained in the corporation and not paid out as dividends.

Dividends Paid Out Of Mixed Income Of A Connected Corporation

13-92.   In many cases, a corporation will be earning both investment income and active business income. This will result in a situation, unlike the example previously presented, where some part of the dividends paid by the corporation will be eligible for a refund and the remainder will not. In this type of situation, the Part IV tax will not be equal to 38-1/3 percent of the dividends received. An example will make this point clear:

> **EXAMPLE**   Lower Ltd. declares and pays a dividend of $45,000. As a result of paying this dividend, the company receives a dividend refund equal to $9,000 or 20 percent of the dividend. Upper Inc. owns 60 percent of the outstanding shares of Lower Ltd. and receives dividends of $27,000.

> **ANALYSIS**   In this case, the dividend refund is clearly less than 38-1/3 percent of the dividends paid, indicating that Lower's income is made up of a combination of investment income and other income. In this more realistic situation, the Part IV Tax Payable by Upper will be based on Upper's 60 percent share of the $9,000 dividend refund of Lower that resulted from paying the dividend. Upper's Part IV tax would be $5,400 [(60%)($9,000)].

Exercise Thirteen - 5

Subject: Part IV Tax

Opal Ltd., a Canadian controlled private corporation, received the following amounts of dividends during the year ending December 31, 2020:

Dividends On Various Portfolio Investments	$14,000
Dividends From Emerald Inc. [(100%)($41,500)]	41,500
Dividends From Ruby Inc. [(30%)($60,000)]	18,000

Opal Ltd. owns 100 percent of the voting shares of Emerald Inc. and 30 percent of the voting shares of Ruby Inc. The fair market value of the Ruby Inc. shares is equal to 30 percent of the fair market value of all Ruby Inc. shares. As a result of paying the $60,000 dividend, Ruby Inc. received a dividend refund of $15,000. Emerald Inc. received no dividend refund for its dividend payment.

Determine the amount of Part IV Tax Payable by Opal Ltd. as a result of receiving these dividends.

SOLUTION available in print and online Study Guide.

Other Part IV Tax Considerations

13-93.   The preceding material has dealt with the basic features of the Part IV tax on dividends received by private corporations. There are a few additional points to be made. First, you should note what kinds of dividends are not subject to Part IV tax. For a private or a subject company, the only dividends, besides capital dividends, that will not be subject to Part IV tax are those received from a connected corporation that does not get a dividend refund as a result of paying the dividend.

13-94.   A second point is that ITA 186(1)(c) and (d) allows a corporation to use unabsorbed non-capital losses to reduce any Part IV tax. The Part IV tax otherwise payable can be reduced by 38-1/3 percent of any non-capital or farm losses claimed for this purpose. However, if this option is chosen, the corporation has effectively used a possible permanent reduction in future taxes to acquire a reduction of Tax Payable that could otherwise ultimately be refunded. This would only make sense in situations where the non-capital loss carry forward was about to expire, or where the company did not expect to have Taxable Income in the carry forward period. With the non-capital loss carry forward period set at 20 years, this is unlikely to be a very useful strategy.

Designation Of Eligible Dividends

Basic Concepts

The Problem

13-95.   We have previously discussed the importance of the distinction between eligible and non-eligible dividends (see Paragraph 13-13). Given the significant difference in the taxation of the two types of dividends, tax planners will clearly have an incentive to maximize the amount of dividends that can be designated as eligible.

13-96.   We have also noted that, because of the availability of the small business deduction, most dividends declared by CCPCs will be non-eligible and most dividends declared by public companies will be designated as eligible.

13-97.   Given this, it would be very convenient to have a rule that says that all taxable dividends paid by non-CCPCs are eligible dividends, while all dividends paid by CCPCs are non-eligible. Unfortunately, this simple dichotomy does not work. This reflects the fact that:

- some CCPCs may have a portion of their income taxed at full rates (e.g., active business income in excess of the annual business limit of $500,000), and

- some public companies may have a portion of their income taxed at favourable rates (e.g., a CCPC that goes public with a retained earnings balance that contains amounts that benefitted from the small business deduction).

The Solution

13-98.   To deal with the problem, a system is required that recognizes the need for different procedures to be applied to CCPCs vs. non-CCPCs. In simplified terms, the system that has been developed is as follows:

CCPCs It is assumed that, in general, dividends paid by CCPCs are non-eligible. However, to track components of their income that have been taxed at full corporate rates, CCPCs have a notional account referred to as a General Rate Income Pool (GRIP). The balance in this account provides a basis for paying eligible dividends. Note, however, as will be discussed later in this Chapter, the ability to obtain a refund on eligible dividends is limited by the balance in the corporation's Eligible Refundable Dividend Tax On Hand (Eligible RDTOH).

Non-CCPCs In general, non-CCPCs are composed of public companies and private companies that are not Canadian controlled. For these companies, it is assumed that, in general, dividends paid are eligible. However, to track components of their income that have been taxed at low rates, they have to use a notional account referred to as a Low Rate Income Pool (LRIP). The balance in this account must be reduced to nil by the payment of non-eligible dividends prior to the payment of eligible dividends.

CCPCs And Their GRIP

Default Treatment

13-99.   While individual CCPCs may have some amount of Full Rate Taxable Income, most of the income earned by such corporations will benefit either from the small business deduction or the refund procedures that we have discussed. Given this, the majority of dividends paid by most CCPCs will be non-eligible. For these corporations, the default assumption is that their dividends will be so classified.

13-100.   However, it is still necessary to deal with the fact that, to the extent that a CCPC has Full Rate Taxable Income or has received eligible dividends, its dividends should benefit from the eligible dividend procedures. The mechanism to provide for this is the General Rate Income Pool (GRIP).

General Rate Income Pool (GRIP)

13-101.   The General Rate Income Pool is a notional account that is designed to track amounts of a CCPC's income that qualify as a basis for paying eligible dividends. As noted, the default treatment for CCPC dividends is to classify them as non-eligible. However, to the extent that there is a balance in the GRIP account of the corporation, CCPC dividends paid can be designated as eligible.

13-102.   The GRIP balance is defined in ITA 89(1). It is a very complex definition that consists of an A component and a B component. The content of the B component involves such things as loss carry overs and other future events that may influence the current year. The application of this component goes beyond the scope of this text and will be given no consideration in any of our material. The A component is defined as follows (also available at the front of this text in "Rates And Other Data"):

$$A = C + D + E + F - G, \text{ where}$$

C   is the CCPC's GRIP at the end of the preceding taxation year.

D   is 72 percent of the CCPC's adjusted taxable income for the year.
Adjusted Taxable Income is regular Taxable Income reduced by the amount eligible for the small business deduction and the lesser of the CCPC's Aggregate Investment Income and its Taxable Income for the year.

E   is the amount of eligible dividends received by the CCPC during the year.

F   involves a group of technical additions related to becoming a CCPC, amalgamations, and wind-ups.

G   is the amount of eligible dividends paid during the **preceding** year less the amount of any Excessive Eligible Dividend Designation (EEDD) made during the preceding year (see Paragraph 13-109).

13-103.   Several comments on this formula are relevant at this point:

- The D component calculates a Taxable Income that is adjusted to eliminate the types of income for which CCPCs receive favourable tax treatment. As dividends are paid out of after tax funds, the residual income is multiplied by 72 percent, reflecting a notional federal/provincial tax rate of 28 percent.

- If a CCPC receives eligible dividends, the addition in E allows these dividends to retain that status on their flow through to the shareholders of the CCPC.

- Note that the balance is reduced, not by eligible dividends paid in the current year, but by eligible dividends paid in the preceding year.

13-104.   A simple example will illustrate these provisions:

EXAMPLE   Norgrave Ltd., a CCPC, had no GRIP balance at the end of 2018. During 2019, the company received eligible dividends of $46,600 and designated $25,000 of its dividends paid as eligible. At the end of 2019, Norgrave has a GRIP of $46,600.

For 2020, Norgrave has Taxable Income of $225,000. This amount includes Aggregate Investment Income of $55,000. In addition, the company receives eligible dividends during the year of $50,000.

In determining 2020 Tax Payable, the company has a small business deduction of $28,500 [(19%)($150,000)]. During 2020, Norgrave pays dividends of $40,000, with $20,000 of this amount being designated as eligible.

ANALYSIS   The 2020 ending balance in GRIP will be calculated as follows:

C - GRIP Balance At End Of 2019		$ 46,600
D - Taxable Income	$ 225,000	
Amount Eligible For The Small		
Business Deduction	(150,000)	
Aggregate Investment Income		
(Less Than Taxable Income)	(55,000)	
Adjusted Taxable Income	$ 20,000	
Rate	72%	14,400
E - Eligible Dividends Received		50,000
G - Eligible Dividends Designated in 2019		(25,000)
GRIP At End Of 2020		$ 86,000

The eligible dividends paid during 2020 will be deducted from the GRIP in 2021.

Exercise Thirteen - 6

Subject: GRIP Balance

Lanson Inc., a CCPC, had no GRIP balance at its year end on December 31, 2018. During 2019, the company received eligible dividends of $35,000 and designated all of its $25,000 in dividends paid as eligible. At the end of 2019, Lanson has a GRIP of $35,000.

For 2020, Lanson has Taxable Income of $960,000. This amount includes net taxable capital gains of $65,000, mortgage interest received of $23,000, and a net capital loss carry forward deduction of $14,000. In addition, the company receives eligible dividends during the year of $85,000. In determining 2020 Tax Payable, the company has a small business deduction of $42,750. During 2020, Lanson pays dividends of $78,000, with $42,000 of this amount being designated as eligible. Determine the company's GRIP balance at the end of 2020.

SOLUTION available in print and online Study Guide.

Non-CCPCs And Their LRIP

Low Rate Income Pool (LRIP)

13-105. For non-CCPCs, their income will generally be taxed at full corporate rates. This means that, in general, their dividends can be designated as eligible. However, in some situations, a non-CCPC may have balances that have not been taxed at full corporate rates. This could include amounts of income retained by a CCPC before it became a public company, as well as non-eligible dividends received from a CCPC.

13-106. Such balances will be allocated to a notional account referred to as a Low Rate Income Pool (LRIP). This account, defined in ITA 89(1), is similar to the GRIP account in that it is used to track certain types of income. However, the two accounts serve different purposes:

- The GRIP account is used to track balances that can be used by a CCPC as the basis for designating eligible dividends. To the extent that a GRIP balance is present, CCPC dividends can be designated as eligible until such time as the balance is exhausted. Note, however, the presence of a GRIP balance does not require that dividends be designated as eligible. Designation as eligible is at the discretion of the corporation.

- The LRIP account is used to track balances that have not been subject to full corporate tax rates. When an LRIP balance is present, any dividends paid by the corporation will be considered non-eligible. Stated alternatively, a corporation with a positive LRIP balance cannot designate any of its dividends as eligible until the LRIP balance is exhausted. In this situation, the corporation has no discretion.

13-107. The definition of the LRIP balance, as found in ITA 89(1), is as follows:

$$(A + B + C + D + E + F) - (G + H), \text{ where}$$

- **A** is the non-CCPCs LRIP at the end of the preceding year.
- **B** is the amount of non-eligible dividends received by the non-CCPC from a corporation resident in Canada.
- **C** is a group of technical additions related to corporate reorganizations.
- **D** is an adjustment for a non-CCPC that was a CCPC in some preceding year.
- **E** is an adjustment for a non-CCPC that was a credit union in some preceding year.
- **F** is an adjustment for a non-CCPC that was an investment company in some preceding year.
- **G** is the amount of taxable dividends, other than eligible dividends, paid by the non-CCPC during the year.
- **H** is the amount of any EEDD made by the non-CCPC during the year.

13-108. A simple example will serve to illustrate this definition.

EXAMPLE At the end of 2019, Ovamp Ltd. has an LRIP balance of $450,000. During 2020, the company receives non-eligible dividends from a CCPC in the amount of $225,000. During 2020, the company pays dividends of $360,000.

ANALYSIS Given the presence of a positive LRIP balance in excess of the total dividends paid, none of the Ovamp dividends could be designated eligible.

Part III.1 Tax On Excessive Eligible Dividend Designations

Calculation

13-109. The enhanced dividend tax credit procedures are available on any dividend that the paying corporation has designated as eligible. This raises the possibility that a corporation might designate a dividend as eligible under circumstances where such a designation is not appropriate (e.g., a CCPC designating a dividend as eligible when it has no balance in its GRIP at the end of the year). To discourage this, the government has a Part III.1 tax on what is referred to as an Excessive Eligible Dividend Designation (EEDD).

13-110. If the EEDD is inadvertent, the Part III.1 tax is equal to 20 percent of the excess amount. In these circumstances, Part III.1 provides for an election that will allow the taxpayer to effectively undo the designation.

13-111. If the CRA concludes that the EEDD reflects an attempt to artificially manipulate either a GRIP or an LRIP, the Part III.1 tax rate goes to 30 percent. In addition, there are two other consequences:

- The tax applies to the entire dividend, not just the EEDD.
- No election is available to undo the excessive election.

13-112. In order to appropriately track all dividend payments, any resident Canadian corporation that pays a taxable dividend is required to file a return for the year under Part III.1.

13-113. ITA 89(1) defines EEDD differently for CCPCs and non-CCPCs. These definitions will be considered separately in the following material.

EEDD For A CCPC

13-114. If a CCPC designates an amount of eligible dividends that is in excess of its GRIP at the end of the year, it will be considered an EEDD and be subject to Part III.1 tax.

> **EXAMPLE** At its December 31, 2019, year end, Sandem Inc., a CCPC, has a GRIP of $45,000. It paid no dividends in 2019. During 2020, the company pays dividends of $100,000, of which $60,000 are designated as eligible. There are no additions to the company's GRIP during 2020.

> **ANALYSIS** The company has an EEDD of $15,000 ($60,000 - $45,000). Provided the CRA believes that this was an inadvertent result, this amount will be subject to a Part III.1 tax of 20 percent on the excess of $15,000. There is also the possibility of electing to have the EEDD treated as a non-eligible dividend.

> If the CRA concludes that the EEDD was a deliberate attempt to manipulate the company's GRIP, an additional 10 percent is added to the Part III.1 tax. In addition, the applicable 30 percent tax is assessed on the entire eligible amount of $60,000, not just the $15,000 EEDD amount, and no election is available to undo the excessive election.

EEDD For A Non-CCPC

13-115. In somewhat simplified terms, an EEDD for a non-CCPC is equal to the lesser of its eligible dividends paid and its LRIP at the time the dividend is paid. For example, if a non-CCPC paid an eligible dividend of $50,000 at a point in time that its LRIP was equal to $40,000, the EEDD would be $40,000. Note that, unlike the situation with EEDDs for CCPCs, where the amount is based on the end of year balance of the GRIP, the EEDD for a non-CCPC is based on the balance of the LRIP at the point in time when the eligible dividend is paid.

13-116. A simple example will illustrate these provisions:

> **EXAMPLE** Victor Ltd., a Canadian public company, receives $42,000 in non-eligible dividends from a CCPC on June 15, 2020. Its LRIP has a balance of nil prior to this. On September 23, 2020, Victor pays dividends of $100,000, with $30,000 of this amount being designated as eligible.

> **ANALYSIS** As at September 23, 2020, the balance in the LRIP would be $42,000. The lesser of this amount and the eligible dividend would be $30,000 and this would be the amount of the EEDD.

> This result seems somewhat counterintuitive in that a non-eligible dividend was paid in an amount sufficient to eliminate the LRIP. However, the legislation is clear that the LRIP is measured at a particular point in time and, if an eligible dividend is paid when there is a positive balance in this account, it creates an EEDD. We would note that this situation could have been avoided had the non-eligible dividend been paid before, even by one day, the payment of the eligible dividend.

Provided there were no further dividend transactions, the LRIP balance at the end of the year would be nil as the payment of $70,000 in non-eligible dividends would have eliminated the $42,000 balance created by the non-eligible dividends received.

With respect to the Part III.1 tax, a tax of 20 percent would normally be assessed on the EEDD of $30,000. However, if the CRA concludes that a deliberate attempt to manipulate the LRIP was involved, the tax rate will be increased to 30 percent.

A Final Word On Eligible Dividends

13-117. You should be aware that the preceding is a fairly simplified version of the provisions related to eligible dividends and their designation. The complete legislation is far more complex, dealing with a number of transitional situations, changes in a corporation's classification, as well as problems associated with corporate reorganizations. However, we feel that this version of the material is appropriate for an introductory text in taxation.

Refundable Dividend Tax On Hand (RDTOH)

Background

Pre-2019

13-118. As will be discussed in the material that follows, the RDTOH is an account that is used to track refundable taxes paid during the year. The balance is reduced by refunds claimed in the previous year, resulting in a balance that can be refunded when dividends are paid to shareholders.

13-119. Prior to 2019, each private corporation had a single RDTOH account. All refundable taxes, both Part I and Part IV, were added to this account. The resulting balance then provided a limit on the amount of dividend refund that could be claimed. As will be discussed later in this section, the dividend refund was limited to the lesser of:

- 38-1/3 percent of taxable dividends paid; and
- the balance in the RDTOH.

13-120. As was noted in the previous section of this Chapter, the amount of dividends that could be designated by a CCPC as eligible is limited to the balance in the corporation's GRIP account. (Note that private companies that are not Canadian controlled are not able to have a GRIP account.) Prior to 2019, any balance that was in the corporation's single RDTOH was available for a dividend refund. The entire balance could be used for a dividend refund on either eligible or non-eligible dividends paid.

2019 And Subsequent Years

13-121. As has been noted, the government believes that private corporations have an unfair advantage in their ability to accumulate large portfolios of passive investments using income that has been retained after being taxed at low small business rates. Given this concern, legislation has been put in place that will make this process less attractive.

13-122. We introduced the first of these legislative provisions in Chapter 12. As discussed in that Chapter, CCPCs that have ADJUSTED Aggregate Investment Income for the previous year in excess of $50,000 will see their annual business limit for the small business deduction ground down, with the full amount of the limit disappearing when ADJUSTED Aggregate Investment Income for the previous year reaches $150,000. As noted in Chapter 12, the Department of Finance has indicated their belief that only about 3 percent of the companies claiming the small business deduction will be affected.

13-123. A second, much more pervasive measure, is directed toward limiting the amount of dividend refunds that can be paid on dividends designated as eligible. This involves dividing the RDTOH account into two separate balances. We will refer to these two balances as the Eligible

RDTOH and the Non-Eligible RDTOH. When dividends are designated as eligible, a dividend refund is only available to the extent of the balance in the corporation's Eligible RDTOH. This means that, if dividends are designated as eligible when there is no balance in the corporation's Eligible RDTOH, no dividend refund is available. Stated alternatively, if a corporation maximizes the amount of dividends that the GRIP balance would allow to be designated as eligible, they may not be able to access all of the refundable taxes they have paid.

13-124.   What this means is that, in order to access all of the refundable taxes paid, a corporation may have to pay non-eligible dividends, even in situations where a GRIP balance would allow the designation of eligible dividends. This is very important in that individual tax rates are significantly higher on non-eligible dividends than is the case with eligible dividends. While the amount varies from province to province, the average difference is about 8 percentage points. Despite the favourable taxation of eligible dividends, this change will clearly discourage the use of eligible dividends in situations where the designation results in a less than maximum dividend refund.

Transitional Provision

13-125.   To implement this new regime, a transitional provision was required. At December 31, 2018, most private corporations had a single RDTOH balance that required division into its eligible and non-eligible components. The transitional provision served to facilitate this process.

13-126.   The application of this transitional provision was largely implemented during the 2019 taxation year. However, as you are aware, the content of this book is based on tax procedures for the 2020 taxation year. Given this, we will provide no coverage of this transitional process as it is not relevant to the years under consideration.

Part IV Tax Payable

13-127.   When we define both the eligible and non-eligible RDTOH accounts, we will have to add the amount of both Part I and Part IV taxes that are eligible for a refund. The situation with the Part IV tax paid is simple. All amounts paid during the year will be included in the RDTOH balances.

Refundable Part I Tax Payable

Basic Formula

13-128.   The situation is more complex with the Part I tax in that only a part of the amount paid is refundable. In simplified terms, only the Part I tax that is related to Aggregate Investment Income is eligible for a refund. However, the Tax Payable on this income can be reduced by deductions in the determination of Taxable Income (e.g., charitable contributions) or by credits against Tax Payable (e.g., foreign tax credits). Given this, it is necessary to take the amounts of Taxable Income and Tax Payable into consideration when determining the refundable portion of Part I tax. This is accomplished in the ITA 129(4) definition of Non-Eligible RDTOH. This definition places constraints on the refundable amount by indicating that it will be the least of three amounts:

- ITA 129(4)(a)(i)   An amount based on Aggregate Investment Income.
- ITA 129(4)(a)(ii)   An amount based on Taxable Income.
- ITA 129(4)(a)(iii)   An amount based on Tax Payable.

13-129.   We will give detailed attention to each of these constraints in the Paragraphs that follow.

Investment Income Constraint - ITA 129(4)(a)(i)

13-130.   The basic amount of Part I tax that should be considered refundable is based on the amount of Aggregate Investment Income for the year:

ITA 129(4)(a)(i)   the amount determined by the formula

A - B, where

A   is 30-2/3 percent of the corporation's Aggregate Investment Income for the year, and

B   is the amount, if any, by which the foreign non-business income tax credit exceeds 8 percent of its foreign investment income for the year.

13-131.   Aggregate Investment Income is as defined in ITA 129(4). As indicated previously, Aggregate Investment Income is the sum of:

- Net taxable capital gains for the year reduced by any net capital loss carry overs deducted during the year.

- Income from property reduced by any property losses. Dividends that are deductible in computing the corporation's Taxable Income are excluded.

13-132.   These amounts do not include interest or rents that are incidental to the corporation's efforts to produce active business income. As noted in Chapter 12, these amounts would be considered active business income. Note, however, the definition does include both Canadian and foreign sources of the types of income listed.

13-133.   If the corporation has no foreign source investment income, the ITA 129(4)(a)(i) amount is simply 30-2/3 percent of Aggregate Investment Income. The RDTOH legislation is based on the assumption that the federal/provincial rate on investment income, before any dividend refund, is 50-2/3 percent. This assumption is within the range of current combined federal/provincial rates on the investment income of private companies.

13-134.   With respect to foreign non-business income, the RDTOH legislation is based on the assumption that the Canadian tax rate on this foreign income is 38-2/3 percent (38% - 10% + 10-2/3%). Reflecting this assumption, the B component in the ITA 129(4)(a)(i) formula subtracts any amount of foreign tax credit that is in excess of 8 percent of foreign investment income for the year.

13-135.   The basic idea here is that a foreign tax credit of 8 percent will reduce the Canadian taxes paid to 30-2/3 percent (38-2/3% - 8% = 30-2/3 percent, the rate applicable to the refund). If the foreign tax credit exceeds 8 percent of the foreign investment income, the Canadian taxes paid would be less than the potential refund of 30-2/3 percent. In other words, without the 8 percent subtraction, the Canadian government would be providing a refund that is larger than the amount of Canadian tax paid on the foreign investment income.

> **EXAMPLE**   A CCPC earns $50,000 in foreign investment income. The government in the foreign jurisdiction withholds 15 percent of this amount and, as a consequence, the company receives a foreign non-business tax credit of $7,500.

> **ANALYSIS**   At the assumed rate of 38-2/3 percent, Canadian tax on this income would be $11,833 [(38-2/3%)($50,000) - $7,500]. This results in a Canadian tax rate on this income of only 23.7 percent ($11,833 ÷ $50,000). Without some type of adjustment, the refundable taxes on this $50,000 of income would be at a rate of 30-2/3 percent and would equal $15,333 [(30-2/3%)($50,000)], $3,500 more than the $11,833 in Canadian taxes that would be paid. This is clearly not appropriate.

> To correct this situation, the excess of the foreign non-business income tax credit over 8 percent of the foreign investment income is subtracted from the 30-2/3 percent refund on the foreign investment income. The 8 percent reflects the difference between the notional rate of 38-2/3 percent and the refund rate of 30-2/3 percent.

In our example, the calculations would be as follows:

30-2/3 Percent Of Foreign Investment Income		$15,333
Deduct Excess Of:		
Foreign Non-Business Tax Credit	($7,500)	
Over 8% Of Foreign Investment Income		
[(8%)($50,000)]	4,000	(3,500)
ITA 129(4)(a)(i)		**$11,833**

This procedure has, in effect, reduced the amount of the refund to $11,833. As calculated at the beginning of this analysis, this is equal to the notional amount of Canadian taxes paid on the foreign investment income.

Taxable Income Constraint - ITA 129(4)(a)(ii)

13-136.   A further problem with respect to determining the refundable portion of Part I tax payable is that the corporation's Taxable Income may include amounts that are not taxed at full corporate rates (e.g., amounts eligible for the small business deduction). Further, Taxable Income may be reduced by such items as non-capital loss carry overs to a level that is less than the amount of investment income on which ITA 129(4)(a)(i) would provide a refund. To deal with this, the refundable portion of the Part I tax is limited as follows:

ITA 129(4)(a)(ii)   30-2/3 percent of the amount, if any, by which the corporation's taxable income for the year exceeds the total of:

A   the amount eligible for the small business deduction;
B   (100 ÷ 38-2/3) of the tax credit for foreign non-business income; and
C   4 times the tax credit for foreign business income.

13-137.   Component B is designed to remove foreign investment income that is not taxed because of the foreign non-business tax credit. The elimination is based on the assumption that it is taxed at a notional rate of 38-2/3 percent (38-2/3 ÷ 100). In similar fashion, Component C is designed to remove foreign business income that is not taxed because of the foreign business income tax credit. The elimination here is based on the assumption that this type of income is taxed at a notional rate of 25 percent (1 ÷ 4). The factor of 4 in Component C is actually the result of a more complex calculation. See Chapter 12 for details of this calculation explained in the context of the small business deduction formula.

Tax Payable Constraint - ITA 129(4)(a)(iii)

13-138.   A final issue here relates to the fact that the dividend refund could exceed the corporation's actual Tax Payable for the year. This could happen if, for example, the company had large amounts of tax credits for scientific research and experimental development. To deal with this issue, the refundable portion of Part I tax is limited as follows:

ITA 129(4)(a)(iii)   the corporation's federal tax for the year payable under this Part (Part I).

Formula For Part I Tax Addition To RDTOH

13-139.   To summarize, the addition to the RDTOH for Part I tax (also available in the front of this text under "Rates And Other Data") is the least of:

ITA 129(4)(a)(i)   30-2/3 percent of Aggregate Investment Income, reduced by the excess, if any, of foreign non-business income tax credits over 8 percent of foreign investment income.

ITA 129(4)(a)(ii)   30-2/3 percent of the amount, if any, by which Taxable Income exceeds the sum of:

- the amount eligible for the small business deduction,
- (100 ÷ 38-2/3) of the foreign non-business tax credit, and
- 4 times the foreign business tax credit.

ITA 129(4)(a)(iii)   Part I tax payable.

Exercise Thirteen - 7

Subject: Refundable Part I Tax

Debut Inc. is a Canadian controlled private corporation. During the taxation year ending December 31, 2020, Debut Inc. has the following amounts of property income:

Dividends From Portfolio Investments	$22,000
Foreign Non-Business Income (Net Of 5 Percent Withholding)	14,250
Capital Gains	38,250
Net Rental Income	6,500
Interest Income On Ten Year Bond	9,200

The company's Net Income For Tax Purposes is $121,825. The only deductions in the calculation of Taxable Income are the dividends on portfolio investments and a net capital loss carry forward of $9,000 [(1/2)($18,000)]. A $9,500 small business deduction and a foreign tax credit of $750 served to reduce Tax Payable. Assume that the company's Part I Tax Payable has been correctly determined to be $19,536. Determine the refundable amount of Part I tax for 2020.

SOLUTION available in print and online Study Guide.

RDTOH Balances Defined

Eligible RDTOH Defined

13-140.   The definition for the Eligible RDTOH account is found in ITA 129(4). In somewhat simplified terms, this definition is as follows:

BEGINNING BALANCE   For 2020 and subsequent years, the calculation would begin with the balance in the Eligible RDTOH at the end of the previous taxation year.

ADDITIONS   In somewhat simplified terms, two items would be added to this beginning balance:

- Part IV taxes paid on eligible dividends from non-connected taxable Canadian corporations. These are commonly referred to as portfolio dividends.

- Part IV taxes paid on eligible dividends from connected corporations to the extent that such dividends included a refund from the paying corporation's Eligible RDTOH.

DEDUCTION   Deducted from this total would be any dividend refund claimed from the Eligible RDTOH account in the previous taxation year.

13-141.   It is important to note what is missing here. Prior to 2019, Part I refundable taxes were included in the single RDTOH account, all of which could be used for a dividend refund on eligible dividends. This is no longer the situation.

13-142.   As we shall see in our discussion of the Non-Eligible RDTOH account, all of the Part I refundable taxes are added to the Non-Eligible RDTOH account. This means that they can only be refunded through the payment of non-eligible dividends. We would remind you that shareholders who are individuals pay considerably higher rates of tax on non-eligible dividends when compared to eligible dividends. This represents a significant change in tax policy.

Non-Eligible RDTOH Defined

13-143.   The definition of the Non-Eligible RDTOH account is also found in the ITA 129(4). Again, in somewhat simplified terms, it is as follows:

BEGINNING BALANCE For 2020 and subsequent years, the calculation would begin with the balance in the Non-Eligible RDTOH at the end of the previous taxation year.

ADDITIONS There are three items that are added to the Non-Eligible RDTOH beginning balance:

- All of the Part I refundable tax for the year, determined as per the calculations discussed beginning at Paragraph 13-128.

- Part IV taxes paid on non-eligible dividends from connected corporations to the extent that such dividends included a refund from the paying corporation's Non-Eligible RDTOH.

- Part IV taxes paid on non-eligible dividends from non-connected taxable Canadian corporations. The situations where this would be applicable would be rare.

DEDUCTION Deducted from this total would be any dividend refund claimed from the Non-Eligible RDTOH account in the previous taxation year.

13-144. As you can see in the preceding paragraph, all of the Part I refundable taxes are added to the Non-Eligible RDTOH. This means that these taxes can only be recovered through the payment of non-eligible dividends. In contrast to the results when there was only a single RDTOH account, Part I refundable taxes cannot be recovered on the payment of eligible dividends.

An Important Difference

13-145. While this cannot be explained fully until we look at the legislative provision for dividend refunds, there is a significant difference in the use of the two RDTOH accounts. With respect to eligible dividends, a refund is only available to the extent that there is a balance in the Eligible RDTOH. No part of the Non-Eligible RDTOH can be used for a refund related to eligible dividends.

13-146. The situation is different with respect to non-eligible dividends. While refunds on these dividends must first come out of the Non-Eligible RDTOH, if the 38-1/3 percent of the non-eligible dividends exceed the balance in that account, the Eligible RDTOH can be accessed to bring the total refund up to the required 38-1/3 percent of dividends paid.

13-147. As will be illustrated in the next section of this Chapter, corporations may be faced with a choice between maximizing the amount of eligible dividends (more favourably taxed for individuals) and recovering all of the refundable taxes that have been paid. While shareholders receiving eligible dividends pay about 8 percentage points less in taxes than on the receipt of non-eligible dividends, giving up the dividend refund on such dividends would be even more costly to the dividend paying corporation.

Losses Used To Reduce Part IV Taxes

13-148. We have noted the possibility that non-capital and farm losses can be used to reduce Part IV taxes. To the extent that they are used for this purpose, they are not added to either RDTOH balance. This raises the question of how to allocate any remaining balance that is available. ITA 129(4.1) and (4.2), provide guidance on this allocation process. We do not believe that this is a common enough transaction to warrant coverage in a general text such as this.

The Dividend Refund

Dividend Refund On Eligible Dividends

13-149. When a CCPC declares dividends, an amount can be designated as an eligible dividend to the extent there is a balance in the corporation's GRIP account. The refund on these eligible dividends will then be the lesser of:

- 38-1/3 percent of the total of all eligible dividends paid by it in the year; and
- the end of year balance in the corporation's Eligible RDTOH.

13-150. A simple example will serve to illustrate this determination:

EXAMPLE Divor Ltd. is a CCPC with a December 31 year end. On December 31, 2019, the corporation has an Eligible RDTOH of $38,333. The balance on this date in the Non-Eligible RDTOH is $76,667. During 2020, the corporation pays dividends of $70,000, all of which are designated as eligible.

ANALYSIS As the GRIP balance is $100,000, there is no problem with designating all of the $70,000 in dividends as eligible. The refund is $26,833, the lesser of:

- $26,833 [(38-1/3%)($70,000)]; and
- $38,333, the balance in the Eligible RDTOH account at the end of the year.

The lesser figure would be $26,833, leaving $11,500 ($38,333 - $26,833) in the Eligible RDTOH account after the dividend refund has been subtracted in 2021. There would also be a $30,000 ($100,000 - $70,000) balance in the GRIP account after the 2020 eligible dividends paid have been subtracted in 2021.

Dividend Refund On Non-Eligible Dividends

13-151. If the amount of dividends paid during the year exceed the amount that is designated as eligible, the excess will be a non-eligible dividend. The refund here consists of two components. The purpose of Component 2 is to allow access to the Eligible RDTOH for dividend refunds on the payment of non-eligible dividends if there is no balance left in the Non-Eligible RDTOH.

Component 1 The lesser of:

- 38-1/3 percent of the total of all non-eligible dividends paid by it in the year; and
- the end of year balance in the corporation's Non-Eligible RDTOH.

Component 2 If 38-1/3 percent of the non-eligible dividends paid in the year exceeds the balance in the Non-Eligible RDTOH, this Component 2 is the lesser of:

- the amount of the excess; and
- any balance that remains in the Eligible RDTOH after subtracting the dividend refund on eligible dividends designated.

If there is no excess, this Component is nil.

13-152. An example will serve to illustrate this calculation.

EXAMPLE At the end of 2020, the balance in the Eligible RDTOH is $115,000 and the balance in the Non-Eligible RDTOH is $76,667. The corporation's GRIP balance on this date is $115,000.

During 2020, Lexy paid dividends of $500,000, with $300,000 of this amount being designated as eligible.

ANALYSIS The dividend refund on the $300,000 of eligible dividends is $115,000. This is equal to 38-1/3 percent of the $300,000 of eligible dividends paid and the balance in the Eligible RDTOH.

The dividend refund on the non-eligible dividends is $76,667. This is equal to 38-1/3 percent of the $200,000 ($500,000 - $300,000) of non-eligible dividends paid and the balance in the Non-Eligible RDTOH. As there is no excess of 38-1/3 percent of the non-eligible dividends paid over the end of year balance in the Non-Eligible RDTOH, Component 2 is equal to nil.

Exercise Thirteen - 8

Subject: Dividend Refund

Alesia Ltd. is a Canadian controlled private corporation with a taxation year that ends on December 31. On December 31, 2019, the balance in the Eligible RDTOH was $134,167, the balance in the GRIP account was $350,000, and the balance in the non-eligible RDTOH was $95,833.

During the year ending December 31, 2020, there were no additions to either RDTOH account or to the GRIP balance. During that year, the corporation paid dividends of $600,000. Only $200,00 of these dividends were designated as eligible.

Determine the amount of the dividend refund on the payment of (1) the eligible dividends and (2) the non-eligible dividends.

SOLUTION available in print and online Study Guide.

We suggest you work Self Study Problem Thirteen-2, 3, 4, and 5 at this point.

Economic Impact Of Changes

The Impact Illustrated

13-153.   We will use an example to illustrate the economic imact of these changes.

> **EXAMPLE** The following information relates to Sarco Inc., a CCPC with a December 31 year end:
>
> - December 31, 2020 GRIP $1,000,000
> - December 31, 2020 Eligible RDTOH   76,667
> - December 31, 2020 Non-Eligible RDTOH   306,667
>
> The combined RDTOH is $383,334 ($76,667 + $306,667). To recover the full amount of refundable taxes that have been paid, a dividend of $1,000,000 must be paid ($383,334 ÷ 38-1/3%). Determine the tax consequences related to each of the following alternatives.
>
> **Alternative 1**   Sarco pays a dividend of $1,000,000, with the entire amount being designated as eligible. Non-eligible dividends would be nil.
>
> **Alternative 2**   Sarco pays a dividend of $1,000,000, with none of the amount being designated as eligible, i.e., eligible dividends would be nil.
>
> **Alternative 3**   Sarco pays a dividend of $1,000,000, with $200,000 of the total paid designated as eligible.
>
> **ANALYSIS ALTERNATIVE 1** $1,000,000 is the maximum amount that can be designated as eligible. If this approach is used, the GRIP balance will be eliminated. However, the refund will only be $76,667, the balance in the Eligible RDTOH. In the absence of non-eligible dividends, Sarco will not have access to the Non-Eligible RDTOH as a source for a dividend refund.
>
> **ANALYSIS ALTERNATIVE 2**   Unlike the situation with Alternative 1, where the Non-Eligible RDTOH could not be used for a refund on eligible dividends, the refund legislation allows access to the Eligible RDTOH, despite the fact that no eligible dividends were paid. Specifically, in this case, the refund on the non-eligible dividends would be calculated as follows:

- **Component 1** This amount is $306,667, the lesser of $383,333 [(38-1/3%)($1,000,000)] and $306,667, the balance in the Non-Eligible RDTOH.

- **Component 2** This amount is $76,666, the excess of 38-1/3 percent of the non-eligible dividends paid over the balance in the Non-Eligible RDTOH ($383,333 - $306,667).

This provides a total refund of $383,333 ($306,667 + $76,666), the full amount of the refundable taxes paid.

ANALYSIS ALTERNATIVE 3   The dividend refund on the eligible dividends would be $76,667. This amount is 38-1/3 percent of the $200,000 in eligible dividends paid and the balance in the Eligible RDTOH. The refund on the non-eligible dividends paid would be $306,667. This amount is 38-1/3 percent of the $800,000 in non-eligible dividends paid and the balance in the Non-Eligible RDTOH. As in Alternative 2, the total refund is $383,333 (with a $1 rounding error).

SUMMARY   These results can be summarized as follows:

	Case 1	Case 2	Case 3
Eligible Dividends Paid	$1,000,000	Nil	$200,000
Non-Eligible Dividends Paid	Nil	$1,000,000	800,000
Total Dividend Refund	76,667	383,333	383,333
January 1, 2021:			
GRIP Balance	Nil	1,000,000	800,000
Eligible RDTOH	Nil	Nil	Nil
Non-Eligible RDTOH	306,667	Nil	Nil

13-154.   What this example illustrates is that there may be situations where none of the refund alternatives is completely satisfactory. Alternative 1 maximizes the amount of dividends designated as eligible, a very desirable result from the point of view of the shareholders. However, it leaves unrecovered refundable taxes of $306,667. Without this refund, the corporate taxes on the pre-dividend income would be around 50 percent. When this is combined with the taxes on the dividend distribution paid by individual shareholders, the overall tax rate could exceed 75 percent.

13-155.   Alternative 2 has the advantage of recovering all of the refundable taxes. However, shareholders will be taxed on non-eligible dividends only, rather than on the more favourably taxed eligible dividends.

13-156.   Alternative 3 improves on Alternative 2 in that, while recovering all of the refundable taxes paid, some of the dividends paid have been designated as eligible. While this is likely the best of the three alternatives, it still leaves an $800,000 balance in the GRIP balance, with no balance in the Eligible RDTOH to provide for a refund on any future dividends designated as eligible.

13-157.   You should note that this would not have been a problem under the old pre-2019 RDTOH system. With a single RDTOH balance, the full $1,000,000 of dividends could have been designated as eligible, while still recovering all of the refundable taxes paid.

Conclusion

13-158.   A variety of other results are possible, depending on the relationships that exist between the GRIP balance, the Eligible RDTOH balance, and the Non-Eligible RDTOH. However, the preceding example is sufficient to make it clear that the 2019 changes have made it less desirable to use a CCPC to accumulate passive investments.

Example Of RDTOH Calculations

13-159. The following simplified example illustrates the refundable tax calculations.

EXAMPLE Fortune Ltd. is a Canadian controlled private corporation. Based on the formula in ITR 402(3), 90 percent of the company's income is earned in a province. The following information is available for the year ending December 31, 2020:

Canadian Source Investment Income	
(Includes $25,000 In Taxable Capital Gains)	$ 100,000
Gross Foreign Non-Business Income (15 Percent Withheld)	20,000
Gross Foreign Business Income (15 Percent Withheld)	10,000
Active Business Income (No Associated Companies)	150,000
Portfolio Dividends Received	30,000
Net Income For Tax Purposes	$ 310,000
Portfolio Dividends	(30,000)
Net Capital Loss Carry Forward Deducted	(15,000)
Taxable Income	$ 265,000

2019 Taxable Capital Employed in Canada (TCEC)	$2,400,000
2019 ADJUSTED Aggregate Investment Income	32,000
Eligible RDTOH - January 1, 2020	$ 4,600
Non-Eligible RDTOH - January 1, 2020	18,400
Taxable Dividends Paid During 2020	60,000
GRIP - January 1, 2020	12,000

ANALYSIS Reflecting the fact that the 2019 TCEC was less than $10 million and the 2019 ADJUSTED Aggregate Investment Income was less than $50,000, there would be no grind of the annual business limit for the small business deduction.

The Part I Tax Payable would be calculated as follows:

Base Amount Of Part I Tax [(38%)($265,000)]	$100,700
Federal Tax Abatement [(10%)(90%)($265,000)]	(23,850)
Small Business Deduction (Note 1)	(28,500)
ART (Note 2)	11,200
General Rate Reduction (Note 3)	(1,300)
Foreign Non-Business Tax Credit (Note 1)	(3,000)
Foreign Business Tax Credit (Note 1)	(1,500)
Part I Tax Payable	$ 53,750

Note 1 In order to simplify the calculation of the small business deduction, the foreign tax credits are assumed to be equal to the amounts withheld (15 percent). Additional calculations would be required to support this conclusion.

The small business deduction would be equal to 19 percent of the least of:

1.	Active Business Income	$150,000

2.	Taxable Income		$ 265,000
	Deduct:		
	[(100/28)($3,000 Foreign Non-Business Tax Credit)]		(10,714)
	[(4)($1,500 Foreign Business Tax Credit)]		(6,000)
	Adjusted Taxable Income		$ 248,286

3.	Annual Business Limit	$500,000

The small business deduction is $28,500 [(19%)($150,000)].

Note 2 The Additional Refundable Tax (ART) is equal to 10-2/3 percent of the lesser of:

- Aggregate Investment Income, calculated as follows:

Canadian Source Investment Income	$100,000
Gross Foreign Non-Business Income	20,000
Net Capital Loss Carry Forward Deducted	(15,000)
Aggregate Investment Income	$105,000

- An amount calculated as follows:

Taxable Income	$265,000
Amount Eligible For the Small Business Deduction	(150,000)
Balance	$ 115,000

This results in an ART equal to $11,200 [(10-2/3%)($105,000)].

Note 3 The general rate reduction would be calculated as follows:

Taxable Income	$265,000
Amount Eligible For Small Business Deduction (Note 1)	(150,000)
Aggregate Investment Income	(105,000)
Full Rate Taxable Income (= Foreign Business Income)	$ 10,000
Rate	13%
General Rate Reduction	$ 1,300

13-160. Based on the preceding information, the refundable portion of Part I tax would be the least of the following three amounts:

30-2/3% Of Aggregate Investment Income		
[(30-2/3%)($105,000)]		$ 32,200
Deduct Excess Of:		
Foreign Non-Business Tax Credit	($3,000)	
Over 8% Of Foreign Investment Income		
[(8%)($20,000)]	1,600	(1,400)
Amount Under ITA 129(4)(a)(i)		**$ 30,800**

Taxable Income		$ 265,000
Deduct:		
Amount Eligible For Small Business Deduction	($ 150,000)	
[(100 ÷ 38-2/3)($3,000 Foreign Non-Business		
Tax Credit)]	(7,759)	
[(4)($1,500 Foreign Business Tax Credit)]	(6,000)	(163,759)
Total		$ 101,241
Rate		30-2/3%
Amount Under ITA 129(4)(a)(ii)		**$ 31,047**

Amount Under ITA 129(4)(a)(iii) = Part I Tax Payable	**$ 53,750**

The refundable portion of Part I tax is equal to $30,800, which is the least of the preceding three amounts.

13-161.   The Part IV tax would be $11,500, 38-1/3 percent of the $30,000 in portfolio dividends received.

13-162.   The ending balance in the Eligible RDTOH would be calculated as follows:

January 1, 2020, Balance	$ 4,600
Part IV Tax On Portfolio Dividends	11,500
December 31, 2020, Eligible RDTOH	$16,100

13-163.   The ending balance in the Non-Eligible RDTOH would be calculated as follows:

January 1, 2020, Balance	$18,400
Part I Refundable Tax	30,800
December 31, 2020, Non-Eligible RDTOH	$49,200

13-164.   The ending GRIP balance would be calculated as follows:

January 1, 2020, Balance	$12,000
Portfolio Dividends Received	30,000
December 31, 2020, GRIP Balance	$42,000

13-165.   Of the total dividends paid of $60,000, the amount that can be designated as eligible is limited to the GRIP balance of $42,000. The refund on these dividends is the lesser of:

- $16,100 [(38-1/3%)($42,000)]; and
- $16,100, the ending balance in the Eligible RDTOH.

13-166.   If the maximum designation is made, $42,000 would be subtracted from the ending 2020 GRIP in 2021. Similarly, the $16,100 refund would be subtracted from the ending 2020 Eligible RDTOH in 2021.

13-167.   With $42,000 of the dividends designated as eligible, the remaining $18,000 ($60,000 - $42,000) will be non-eligible. On these dividends, the refund will be the lesser of:

- $6,900 [(38-1/3%)($18,000)]; and
- $49,200, the ending balance in the Non-Eligible RDTOH.

13-168.   The $6,900 would be subtracted from the ending 2020 Non-Eligible RDTOH in 2021.

13-169.   The total refund is $23,000 ($16,100 + $4,900). Note that this is equal to 38-1/3 percent of the $60,000 in total dividends paid.

13-170.   Given the receding calculations, Fortune's total federal Tax Payable is as follows:

Part I Tax Payable	$ 53,750
Part IV Tax Payable	11,500
Dividend Refund	(23,000)
Federal Tax Payable	$ 42,250

Working Through Large Corporate Tax Problems

13-171. At this point we have completed our general coverage of Taxable Income and Tax Payable for corporations. As we are sure you are aware, there are a great many concepts and procedures involved in this process. While we have illustrated the concepts and procedures in individual examples, we have not provided a comprehensive example that encompasses all of these items.

13-172. You will find, however, that several of the Self Study and Assignment Problems involve fairly comprehensive calculations of corporate Taxable Income and Tax Payable. Given the complexity of these problems, it is useful to have a systematic approach to dealing with this type of problem. To fill that need, we would suggest you approach the required calculations in the following order (we are assuming that only federal taxes are being calculated as this is generally the case with the problem material in this text):

- Net Income For Tax Purposes. Depending on the problem, this may require converting an accounting Net Income figure into the required tax figure.

- Taxable Income. This would include making deductions for charitable donations, dividends from taxable Canadian corporations, and loss carry overs.

- Basic federal Part I Tax Payable at the 38 percent rate.

- Federal tax abatement. If there is foreign business income, this may require a calculation of the amounts that are to be allocated to Canadian provinces.

- If the corporation is a CCPC:

  - Determine Taxable Capital Employed in Canada (TCEC) and ADJUSTED Aggregate Investment Income **for the previous year**.

  - Small business deduction (without consideration of the general rate reduction or the ART in the foreign income tax credit constraints).

  - Aggregate investment income.

  - Additional refundable tax on investment income (ART). Note that this is an addition to Part I Tax Payable, not a deduction.

- Manufacturing and processing profits deduction (without consideration of the general rate reduction in the foreign income tax credit constraints).

- General rate reduction.

- Foreign non-business income tax credit.

- Foreign business income tax credit.

- If the corporation is a CCPC:

  - Refundable portion of Part I tax.
  - the GRIP balance.

- If the corporation is a CCPC or other private corporation:

  - Part IV tax payable.
  - Balance in the Eligible and Non-Eligible refundable dividend tax on hand accounts.
  - Dividend refund on eligible dividends and non-eligible dividends.

We suggest you work Self Study Problems Thirteen-6, 7, and 8 at this point.

Additional Supplementary Self Study Problems Are Available Online.

Key Terms Used In This Chapter

13-173.   The following is a list of the key terms used in this Chapter. These terms, and their meanings, are compiled in the Glossary located at the back of the Study Guide.

Additional Refundable Tax	General Rate Income Pool (GRIP)
On Investment Income (ART)	Integration
ADJUSTED Aggregate Investment Income	Low Rate Income Pool (LRIP)
Aggregate Investment Income	Non-Eligible RDTOH
ART	Over-Integration
Canadian Controlled Private Corporation	Part IV Tax
CCPC	Portfolio Dividend
Connected Corporation	Private Corporation
Dividend Gross Up	Public Corporation
Dividend Tax Credit	RDTOH
Dividends	Refundable Dividend Tax On Hand
Eligible Dividends	Refundable Part I Tax
Eligible RDTOH	Subject Corporation
Excessive Eligible Dividend Designation (EEDD)	Under-Integration

References

13-174.   For more detailed study of the material in this Chapter, we refer you to the following:

ITA 82(1)	Taxable Dividends Received
ITA 89(1)	Definitions (Canadian Corporations, GRIP, LRIP, and EEDD)
ITA 123.3	Refundable Tax On CCPC's Investment Income
ITA 123.4	General Rate Reduction
ITA 129(1)	Dividend Refund To Private Corporation
ITA 129(4)	Definition Of Eligible And Non-Eligible Refundable Dividend Tax On Hand
ITA 129(4)	Aggregate Investment Income
ITA 129(5)	2019 Transitional RDTOH
ITA 185.1	Tax On Excessive Eligible Dividend Designations
ITA 185.2	Election To Treat Excessive Eligible Dividend As An Ordinary Dividend
ITA 186	Part IV Tax
IT-67R3	Taxable Dividends From Corporations Resident In Canada
IT-243R4	Dividend Refund To Private Corporations
IT-269R4	Part IV Tax On Taxable Dividends Received By a Private Corporation Or A Subject Corporation
IT-391R	Status Of Corporations
IT-458R2	Canadian Controlled Private Corporation

Sample Corporate Tax Return For Chapter 13

The Sample Tax Return for this Chapter can be found in the print and online Study Guide.

Problems For Self Study (Online)

To provide practice in problem solving, there are Self Study and Supplementary Self Study problems available on MyLab Accounting.

Within the text we have provided an indication of when it would be appropriate to work each Self Study problem. The detailed solutions for Self Study problems can be found in the print and online Study Guide.

We provide the Supplementary Self Study problems for those who would like additional practice in problem solving. The detailed solutions for the Supplementary Self Study problems are available online, not in the Study Guide.

The .PDF file "Self Study Problems for Volume 2" on MyLab contains the following for Chapter 13:

- 8 Self Study problems,
- 4 Supplementary Self Study problems, and
- detailed solutions for the Supplementary Self Study problems.

Assignment Problems

(The solutions for these problems are only available in
the solutions manual that has been provided to your instructor.)

Assignment Problem Thirteen - 1
(Integration Example)

Assume the following with respect to an individual shareholder of a wholly owned CCPC:

- The corporation's only income is from an active business and totals $340,000 for the year.

- The corporation has no GRIP and therefore all of the dividends it declares and pays (other than capital dividends) will be non-eligible dividends.

- The individual's marginal federal tax rate is 33 percent and his marginal provincial tax rate is 15 percent.

- The provincial dividend tax credit on non-eligible dividends is equal to 34 percent of the gross up.

- The combined federal and provincial corporate tax rate on business income is 12.0 percent.

Required: Indicate, using these assumptions, whether integration is working perfectly and whether it is beneficial to use a corporation or not in this instance. Show all supporting calculations, including both the income tax comparison and after tax return comparison of (1) earning the income directly without the use of a corporation and (2) earning the income through a corporation and distributing all of the after tax corporate income as a non-eligible dividend to the sole individual shareholder. If integration is not working properly, briefly explain why.

Assignment Problem Thirteen - 2
(Part I and Part IV Refundable Taxes)

Burton Investments Ltd. is a Canadian controlled private corporation that sells office supplies. It owns 52 percent of the outstanding shares of Puligny Inc. On December 15, 2020, Puligny Inc. declared and paid a dividend of $122,000, of which Burton Investments Ltd. received $63,440 (52 percent). None of this dividend was designated as eligible by Puligny. As a result of paying the $122,000 dividend, Puligny Inc. received a dividend refund in the amount of $12,500.

Other 2020 income that was reported by Burton Investments consisted of the following amounts:

Capital Gain	$18,000
Eligible Dividends From Bank Of Montreal Shares	13,480
Interest	1,150

The capital gain was on the sale of land that had been used as an auxiliary parking lot but was no longer needed.

Burton's office supply business is seasonal and, as a consequence, temporary cash balances must be set aside for the purchase of inventories during the busy parts of the year. All of the $1,150 in interest was earned on such temporary cash balances.

At the beginning of 2020, the company's Non-Eligible RDTOH balance was $14,426. The balance in the Eligible RDTOH was nil. The corporation did not have a GRIP balance on January 1, 2020.

The company's Taxable Income for the year ending December 31, 2020, was $62,800. No foreign income was included in this total. Assume the Part I Tax Payable for the year ending December 31, 2020, was correctly calculated as $12,560. Because of its association with Puligny Inc., its share of the annual business limit on income eligible for the small business deduction is $40,000. Burton's active business income is more than its share of the annual business limit.

Burton Investments paid taxable dividends of $22,500 in 2020. It is the policy of the corporation to designate dividends as eligible only to the extent that a dividend refund will be available on their payment.

For 2019, Burton and Puligny had combined ADJUSTED Aggregate Investment Income of $23,000. Their combined Taxable Capital Employed in Canada was $1,600,000 for 2019.

Required:

A. Determine the refundable portion of Burton's Part I Tax Payable for 2020.

B. Determine Burton's Part IV Tax Payable for 2020.

C. Determine the December 31, 2020, balances in Burton's Eligible RDTOH and its Non-Eligible RDTOH.

D. Determine Burton's 2020 dividend refund, providing separate amounts for refunds on eligible dividends and refunds on non-eligible dividends.

Assignment Problem Thirteen - 3
(Dividend Refund)
Case 1

Ho Trading Company is a Canadian controlled private corporation with a December 31 year end. On December 31, 2020, it had the following balances in its accounts:

GRIP	$150,000
Eligible RDTOH	38,333
Non-Eligible RDTOH	76,667

During the year, the corporation paid taxable dividends of $250,000. The corporation would like to maximize the amount of this dividend that is designated as eligible.

Determine the amounts for the corporation's 2020 dividend refund on eligible dividends paid and the corporation's 2020 dividend refund on non-eligible dividends paid.

Case 2

Amadeus Ltd. is a Canadian controlled private corporation with a December 31 year end. On December 31, 2020, it had the following balances in its accounts:

GRIP	$400,000
Eligible RDTOH	95,833
Non-Eligible RDTOH	134,167

During the year, the corporation paid taxable dividends of $500,000. It is the policy of the corporation to designate dividends as eligible only to the extent that a refund is available.

Determine the amounts for the corporation's 2020 dividend refund on eligible dividends paid and the corporation's 2020 dividend refund on non-eligible dividends paid.

Assignment Problem Thirteen - 4
(Part I and IV, Refundable Taxes, RDTOH, & GRIP)

Rual Ltd. is a Canadian controlled private corporation with a December 31 year end. The components of its Net Income For Tax Purposes are as follows:

Active Business Income (Note 1)	$950,225
Net Taxable Capital Gains	112,900
Rental Loss from Investment Property (Note 2)	(27,550)
Foreign Source Interest (Note 2)	45,375
Dividends (Note 3)	583,750

Note 1   The active business income amount includes manufacturing profits of $774,100. This amount qualifies for the M&P deduction. Since the company operates in a province that provides a special rate for M&P profits, the company calculates the federal M&P deduction.

Note 2   Both of the investments that generate rental income or loss and foreign source interest have been made with funds that are no longer needed in the active business operations. In addition there are no foreign taxes required to be paid on the foreign source income as a result of an income tax treaty.

Note 3   Total dividends received in the 2020 year are made up of the following amounts:

Eligible Portfolio Dividends From Canadian Companies	$ 142,435
Non-Eligible Dividends From Dual Ltd. (Note 4)	230,000
Non-Eligible Dividends From Fual Ltd. (Note 5)	211,315
Total Dividends	$ 583,750

Note 4   Dual Ltd. is a wholly owned subsidiary of Rual Ltd. since Rual owns all of its shares. As a result, Dual is connected to Rual for the purposes of Part IV. In 2020 the payment of the dividend to Rual resulted in a dividend refund of $79,200, all of which was attributable to Dual's non-eligible RDTOH.

Note 5   Rual owns 60 percent of the voting shares of Fual Ltd. As a result, Fual is controlled by Rual and therefore connected to it for the purposes of Part IV. In 2020 the payment of the dividend to Rual resulted in a dividend refund of $62,700. Fual had no GRIP balance at year end, with the result that all of the dividends paid to Rual are non-eligible dividends. Fual had insufficient non-eligible RDTOH, however, and was forced to use up all of its eligible RDTOH to maximize its dividend refund. Assume that 20 percent of its dividend refund is attributable to its eligible RDTOH and 80 percent to its non-eligible RDTOH.

Additional Information

1.   On December 16, 2020, Rual paid taxable dividends to its shareholders totaling $315,000. No other dividends were paid during the year. It is the policy of the company to designate dividends as eligible only to the extent that their payment will result in a dividend refund.

2.   Rual has a 2016 net capital loss carry forward balance of $76,100. In addition, there is a 2018 non-capital loss carry forward balance of $40,600. Rual would like to deduct the maximum amount of these carry forward losses possible for their 2020 taxation year.

3. Rual has controlled both Dual and Fual since 2016, and as a result the three corporations are all associated in the 2020 year and in the immediately preceding year. The companies have agreed that Rual will be allocated $325,000 of the small business limit for 2020; Dual $100,000; and Fual $75,000. All three corporations use a December 31 year end.

4. The combined Adjusted Aggregate Investment Income for the three associated corporations for the 2019 year is $48,700 and will be $58,450 for 2020. The Taxable Capital Employed in Canada of the three associated corporations totals $9,125,000 for the 2019 year and will equal $11,660,000 for 2020.

5. At December 31, 2019, Rual had an eligible RDTOH balance of $26,875, a non-eligible RDTOH balance of $103,850, and a GRIP balance of $167,000. During 2019, Rual paid taxable dividends of $96,500, $16,500 of which were designated as eligible. As a result of paying the dividends, Rual received a dividend refund of $36,991 [(38-1/3%)($96,500)].

6. Assume for the purposes of the federal abatement that 97 percent of Rual's Taxable Income has been allocated to the provinces.

Required: Show all of the calculations used to provide the following required information, including those for which the result is nil.

For Rual Inc.'s 2020 taxation year, calculate the following items:

A. Part I Tax Payable.

B. The refundable portion of Part I Tax Payable.

C. Part IV Tax Payable.

D. The balance in the GRIP account on December 31, 2020.

E. The balance in both the Eligible RDTOH and Non-Eligible RDTOH on December 31, 2020.

F. The dividend refund, if any, showing separately the amount attributable to eligible dividends and the amount attributable to non-eligible dividends.

G. Total federal Tax Payable (net of any dividend refund).

Assignment Problem Thirteen - 5
(Comprehensive Corporate Tax Payable With CCA)
Oland Ltd. is a Canadian controlled private corporation with a December 31 year end. For the year ending December 31, 2020, the Income Statement of the company, prepared in accordance with generally accepted accounting principles, is as follows:

Revenues		$1,625,986
Expenses:		
Cost Of Goods Sold	($776,257)	
Selling And Administrative Costs	(394,672)	
Amortization Expense	(125,489)	
Charitable Donations	(27,000)	(1,323,418)
Operating Income		$ 302,568
Gain On Sale Of Property	$ 153,600	
Loss On Sale Of Vehicles	(55,000)	
Gain On Sale Of Investments	11,000	
Dividends Received (See Note)	123,400	233,000
Net Income Before Taxes		$ 535,568

Note   The components of the dividends received are as follows:

Eligible Dividends From Canadian Public Companies	$ 62,300
Non-Eligible Dividends From 80 Percent Owned Subsidiary (The Subsidiary Received A Dividend Refund Of $15,000 From Its Non-Eligible RDTOH)	48,000
Non-Eligible Dividends From Wholly Owned Subsidiary (No Dividend Refund)	13,100
Total Dividends Received	$ 123,400

Oland is associated with both of these companies. The two subsidiaries have each been allocated $125,000 of the small business deduction's annual business limit. The remaining $250,000 has been allocated to Oland.

Other Information:

1. Selling And Administrative Costs include $22,490 in business meals and entertainment.

2. Selling And Administrative Costs includes interest on late income tax instalments of $1,240 and on late municipal tax payments of $625.

3. Selling And Administrative Costs includes bond discount amortization of $3,850.

4. During 2020, Oland Ltd. acquired a competing business at a price that included goodwill of $110,400. For accounting purposes, there is no impairment or write-down of the goodwill in 2020.

5. Selling And Administrative Costs include membership fees for several employees in a local golf and country club. These fees total $7,285.

6. As the company expects to issue more shares during 2020, it made a number of amendments to its articles of incorporation and included the legal costs in Selling And Administrative Costs. These costs totaled $11,482.

7. On January 1, 2020, the company had the following UCC balances:

Class 1	$582,652
Class 8	575,267
Class 10	75,348
Class 13	88,600
Class 14.1	Nil

    The Class 1 balance relates to a single real property acquired in 2000 at a cost of $750,000. It is estimated that the value of the land at this time was $50,000. On February 1, 2020, this property is sold for $850,000. It is estimated that, at this time, the value of the land has increased to $80,000. In the accounting records, this real property was carried at $696,400, $646,400 for the building and $50,000 for the land.

    The old building is replaced on February 15, 2020, with a new building acquired at a cost of $923,000, of which $86,000 is allocated to land. As the building is used more than 90 percent for non-residential purposes, it qualifies for the special 6 percent CCA rate. In order to use this rate, the building is put into a separate CCA class. No elections are made with respect to the replacement of the building.

    During 2020, Class 8 assets were acquired at a cost of $226,000. Class 8 assets with a capital cost of $185,000 were sold for $210,000. These Class 8 assets were paintings by Canadian artists, and each was sold for an amount in excess of its cost. The accountant had not amortized them for accounting purposes as he could not determine an estimated useful life. Class 8 contains a large number of assets at the end of 2020.

As the company has decided to lease all of its vehicles in the future, all of the assets in Class 10 are sold during the year. The capital cost of these assets was $142,000 and the proceeds of disposition amounted to $43,000. The net book value of these assets was $98,000.

The Class 13 balance relates to a single lease that commenced on January 1, 2015. The lease has an initial term of seven years, with two successive options to renew for three years each. At the inception of the lease, the company spent $110,000 on leasehold improvements. On January 1, 2017, an additional $44,800 was spent on further improvements.

8. It is Oland's policy to deduct maximum amounts of CCA.

9. During 2020, Oland spends $18,500 landscaping the grounds of its new building. For accounting purposes this was treated as an asset. However, the company will not amortize this balance because it believes the work has an unlimited life.

10. Investments were sold during the year for $126,000. The adjusted cost base of these investments was $115,000.

11. On January 1, 2020, Oland had the following balances:

Eligible RDTOH	$ 39,660
Non-Eligible RDTOH	Nil
GRIP	$162,345

During 2019, Oland designated $12,350 of its dividends as eligible.

12. During 2020, Oland paid $42,300 in dividends. Of this total, $26,300 were designated as eligible.

13. At the beginning of 2020, Oland had a $23,000 net capital loss carry forward [(1/2)($46,000)]. It also had a non-capital loss carry forward of $36,400. The company would like to deduct as much as possible of these two carry overs during 2020.

14. All of Oland's Taxable Income will be allocated to a province.

15. It has been determined that Oland has $300,289 of active business income. Of this total, $43,000 results from manufacturing and processing activity. Because of special rates in the province in which it operates, Oland makes a separate calculation of the M&P deduction.

16. For 2019, Oland and its associated companies had combined ADJUSTED Aggregate Investment Income of $48,900. Their Taxable Capital Employed in Canada totaled $8,900,000 for 2019.

Required: Show all of the calculations used to provide the following required information, including those for which the result is nil.

A. Determine Oland's minimum Net Income For Tax Purposes and Taxable Income for the year ending December 31, 2020. Include in your solution the January 1, 2021, UCC balance for each CCA class.

B. Determine Oland's Part I Tax Payable for the year ending December 31, 2020.

C. Determine the refundable portion of Oland's Part I Tax Payable for 2020.

D. Determine Oland's Part IV Tax Payable for the 2020.

E. Determine the December 31, 2020, balance in Oland's GRIP.

F. Determine the December 31, 2020, balances in Oland's Eligible RDTOH and Non-Eligible RDTOH.

G. Determine Oland's dividend refund for 2020, separately identifying the refund related to eligible dividends and the refund related to non-eligible dividends.

H. Determine Oland's net federal Tax Payable for 2020.

Assignment Problem Thirteen - 6
(Comprehensive Corporate Tax Payable)

Fancom Inc. is an Alberta corporation that qualifies as a Canadian controlled private company. For the taxation year ending December 31, 2020, the components of its Net Income For Tax Purposes and Taxable Income are as follows:

Active Business Income (Note 1)	$ 328,000
Gross Foreign Business Income (Note 2)	40,800
Gross Foreign Non-Business Income (Note 2)	31,200
Interest On Long Term Investments	49,900
Taxable Capital Gains (Note 3)	16,500
Eligible Dividends Received On Portfolio Investment	21,000
Net Income For Tax Purposes	**$ 487,400**
Eligible Dividends Received	(21,000)
Charitable Contributions	(86,400)
Net Capital Loss Carry Forward Deducted	(13,900)
Non-Capital Loss Carry Forward Deducted	(263,000)
Taxable Income	**$ 103,100**

Note 1 As determined by the Income Tax Regulations, $152,000 of this active business income was manufacturing and processing profits. As these amounts are allocated to a province that has a special rate for M&P profits, the company calculates the federal M&P deduction.

Note 2 Foreign jurisdictions withheld $6,120 (15 percent) from the foreign business income and $7,800 (25 percent) from the foreign non-business income.

Note 3 The $6,500 is one-half of a capital gain of $33,000. The gain resulted from a disposition of passive investments.

Other Information:

1. During the year ending December 31, 2020, Fancom used its existing cash resources to pay taxable dividends of $223,200. Of this total, $49,300 were designated as eligible.

2. On January 1, 2020, Fancom had the following balances:

Eligible RDTOH	$14,000
Non-Eligible RDTOH	Nil
GRIP	$49,360

During 2019, Fancom designated $8,700 of its dividends as eligible.

3. For 2019, Fancom's ADJUSTED Aggregate Investment Income was $36,450. Its Taxable Capital Employed in Canada was $4,652,300 for 2019.

4. As determined by the Income Tax Regulations, 85 percent of Fancom's Taxable Income can be allocated to a Canadian province.

5. Assume that the foreign business and non-business tax credits are equal to the foreign taxes withheld.

Required: Show all of the calculations used to provide the following required information, including those for which the result is nil.

A. Determine Fancom's Part I Tax Payable for the year ending December 31, 2020.

B. Determine the refundable portion of Fancom's Part I Tax Payable for 2020.

C. Determine Fancom's Part IV Tax Payable for the 2020.

D. Determine the December 31, 2020, balance in Fancom's GRIP.

E. Determine the December 31, 2020, balances in Fancom's Eligible RDTOH and Non-Eligible RDTOH.

F. Determine Fancom's dividend refund for 2020, separately identifying the refund related to eligible dividends and the refund related to non-eligible dividends.

Assignment Problem Thirteen - 7
(Comprehensive Corporate Tax Payable)

Falko Ltd. is a Canadian controlled private corporation with a December 31 year end. For its year ending December 31, 2020, its accounting Net Income Before Taxes, as determined using generally accepted accounting principles, was $1,029,700. Relevant information for the 2020 year necessary to make the appropriate reconciliation adjustments to Net Income For Tax Purposes, Taxable Income, and federal Taxes payable is as follows.

1. Falko's amortization expense was $494,500. Maximum deductible CCA for the year was $713,000. Company policy has always been to deduct the maximum available CCA.

2. The company's revenues included foreign source investment income of C$44,000. The amount received, however, was only C$36,080 as a result of foreign withholding income taxes of 18 percent, or $7,920. The company only recorded the amount received as revenue.

3. Falko sold one of its buildings that required costly renovations in favour of leasing a building. The total sales price was $1,725,000 with $500,000 allocated to the land and $1,225,000 to the building. The original cost of the land and therefore its adjusted cost base was $650,000. The capital cost and adjusted cost base of the building was $1,000,000 and its UCC at the time of sale was $885,000. For accounting purposes the net book value of the building was $710,000. The company records accounting gains and accounting losses based on the net book value for the building and the original cost of the land.

4. During the year, the company earned the following amounts of Canadian source investment income, all of which have been included in net income for accounting purposes:

Interest On Long Term Investments	$28,700
Non-Eligible Dividends From A 100% Owned Subsidiary	77,500
Eligible Dividends On Bank of Nova Scotia Shares	53,300

5. Falko is only associated with one company – its wholly owned subsidiary Lands Inc. after acquiring all of its shares in 2016. Lands received a dividend refund of $26,475 as a result of the dividends paid to Falko in 2020. Since Lands' non-eligible RDTOH was insufficient to recover all of the dividend refund it was forced to partially rely upon its eligible RDTOH. Lands' GRIP account balance was nil at year end, preventing it from designating any of the dividends paid to Falko as eligible. Of the dividend refund, 43 percent was attributable to its eligible RDTOH and 57 percent to its non-eligible RDTOH.

6. Company expenses for accounting purposes included (1) $39,800 spent on business meals and entertainment; (2) a write-down of inventory (for obsolescence) beyond that permitted in valuing inventory for tax purposes; the excess amount is $11,400; (3) life insurance premiums totaling $14,375 paid on the life of two of the principal shareholders; and (4) bonuses to the same two shareholders for $75,000 each. The bonuses were never paid.

7. Falko's active business income for the year was $796,400, which includes $427,000 of Canadian manufacturing profits that qualify for the M&P deduction (ITA 125.1). Since the company operates in a province that provides a special rate for M&P profits, the company calculates the federal M&P deduction every year.

8. During the year ending December 31, 2020, the company used its existing cash resources to pay taxable dividends of $285,000. It is the policy of the company to only designate dividends as eligible to the extent they generate a dividend refund.

9. At December 31, 2019, Falko had an eligible RDTOH balance of $19,446, a non-eligible RDTOH balance of $73,670, and a GRIP balance of $24,000. During 2019, Falko paid taxable dividends of $118,800, $18,800 of which were designated as eligible. As a result of paying the dividends, Falko received a dividend refund of $45,540 [(38-1/3%)($118,800)]; $7,207 of the dividend refund [($18,800)(38/1/3%)] was attributable to the eligible RDTOH and the remainder of $38,333 [($100,000)(38/1/3%)] was attributable to its non-eligible RDTOH.

10. The combined Adjusted Aggregate Investment Income for the two associated corporations for the 2019 year is $47,190 and will be $62,770 for 2020. The Taxable Capital Employed in Canada of the two associated corporations totals $6,445,000 for the 2019 year and will equal $10,960,000 for 2020.

11. Falko has a 2016 non-capital loss carry forward balance of $112,000 and a 2018 net capital loss carry forward balance of $16,930. Falko's management has indicated that they wish to deduct the maximum amount of these losses possible for its 2020 taxation year.

12. Falko and its wholly owned subsidiary Lands have agreed to split the small business limit 50-50 for the 2020 taxation year.

Required: Show all of the calculations used to provide the following required information, including those for which the result is nil.

A. Calculate Falko's minimum Net Income For Tax Purposes and Taxable Income for the year ending December 31, 2020.

B. Assume the foreign non-business tax credit is equal to the foreign tax withheld. Calculate Falko's Part I Tax Payable for the year ending December 31, 2020. As the corporation operates in a province that has a reduced rate for M&P activity, a separate calculation of the federal M&P deduction is required.

C. Calculate the refundable portion of Falko's Part I Tax Payable for 2020

D. Calculate Falko's Part IV Tax Payable for the year ending December 31, 2020.

E. Determine the December 31, 2020, balance in Falko's GRIP account.

F. Determine the December 31, 2020, balances in Falko's Eligible RDTOH and the Non-Eligible RDTOH.

G. Calculate Falko's dividend refund for the year ending December 31, 2020, showing separately the amount attributable to eligible dividends and the amount attributable to non-eligible dividends.

Assignment Problem Thirteen - 8
(Comprehensive Tax Payable)

Industco Inc. is a Canadian controlled private corporation. It uses a taxation year that ends on December 31. It keeps its records in accordance with generally accepted accounting principles.

For the year ending December 31, 2020, the company's condensed Income Statement is as follows:

Operating Revenues In Canada		$ 2,937,500
Operating Expenses In Canada		(1,905,000)
Operating Income In Canada		$ 1,032,500
Other Income Items:		
Eligible Portfolio Dividends	$ 52,000	
Foreign Non-Business Income		
(Net Of 15 Percent Withholding)	25,500	
Foreign Business Income		
(Net Of 10 Percent Withholding)	45,000	
Canadian Source Interest	26,000	
Gain On Sale Of Class 8 Assets	225,000	373,500
Accounting Income Before Taxes		$ 1,406,000

Other information related to operating expenses follows.

Amortization And CCA   The operating income figure was reduced by a charge for amortization of $623,000.

At the beginning of 2020, the company has a balance in Class 1 of $1,000,000. The only asset in the Class is the company's headquarters building. The company has owned this building since 2001.

In general, other property is leased. However, in February 2020, a policy change results in the acquisition of a new building at a cost of $650,000, of which $125,000 is allocated to the land on which the building is situated. The building is used 100 percent for non-residential purposes and is allocated to a separate Class 1. One-half of the non-residential use is for manufacturing and processing.

The January 1, 2020, balance in Class 8 was $4,200,000. During 2020, there were additions to this class in the total amount of $700,000. Also, Class 8 assets with a cost of $400,000 were sold for proceeds of $550,000. The net book value of these assets in the accounting records was $325,000. There were numerous assets remaining in the class at the end of the 2020 taxation year.

At the beginning of 2020, the UCC in Class 10 was $800,000, reflecting the company's fleet of trucks. As the company is changing to a policy of leasing its trucks, all of these trucks were sold during the year for $687,000. The capital cost of the trucks was $1,200,000 and their net book value in the accounting records was equal to the sale proceeds of $687,000.

Landscaping   The company spent $95,000 on landscaping for its main office building. This amount was recorded as an asset in the accounting records and, because the work has an unlimited life, no amortization was recorded on this asset.

Advertising   The company spent $17,000 on advertisements in *Fortune* Magazine, a U.S. based publication. Over 90 percent of the magazine's non-advertising content is original editorial content. The advertisements were designed to promote sales in Canadian cities located on the U.S. border.

Travel And Entertainment   Included in the travel costs deducted in 2020 was $12,000 for airline tickets and $41,400 for business meals and entertainment.

The company paid, and deducted for accounting purposes, a $2,500 initiation fee for a corporate membership in the Highland Golf And Country Club.

Taxes On Vacant Land   The company paid, and deducted, property taxes of $15,000 on vacant land that is being held for possible future expansion of its headquarters site.

Other Information

1. Industco Inc. declared and paid taxable dividends of $83,000 during 2020. It is the policy of the corporation to only designate dividends as eligible to the extent that their payment will result in a dividend refund.

2. It has been determined that 92 percent of Industco's Taxable Income can be allocated to a province.

3. On January 1, 2020, Industco had the following balances:

Eligible RDTOH	$ 78,000
Non-Eligible RDTOH	Nil
GRIP	$298,000

4. During 2019, the company designated $64,000 of its dividends paid as eligible.

5. Industco Inc. is associated with two other Canadian controlled private corporations. Industco has been allocated $125,000 of the annual business limit.

6. Assume that the foreign tax credits for the foreign non-business and foreign business income are equal to the amounts withheld.

7. Industco's Canadian active business income is equal to its net business income for tax purposes. One-half of this Canadian active business income results from manufacturing and processing activity.

8. At the beginning of 2020, Industco has a net capital loss carry forward of $42,000 and a non-capital loss carry forward of $18,000. The company intends to deduct the maximum amount of these carry forwards during 2020.

9. For 2019, the ADJUSTED Aggregate Investment Income of Industco and its associated companies is $31,600. Their Taxable Capital Employed in Canada was $6,420,000.

Required: Determine the following amounts. You should show all of the calculations required to provide these amounts, even when the result of the calculations is nil.

A. Industco's Net Income For Tax Purposes and Taxable Income for the year ending December 31, 2020. As the company's active business income is based on its net business income for tax purposes, a separate calculation of this component of Net Income For Tax Purposes is required.

B. Industco's Part I Tax Payable for the year ending December 31, 2020. As the company operates in a province that has a reduced tax rate for manufacturing and processing activity, a separate calculation of the federal M&P deduction is required.

C. The refundable portion of Industco's Part I Tax Payable for 2020.

D. Industco's Part IV Tax Payable for 2020.

E. Industco's GRIP balance on December 31, 2020.

F. The balances in Industco's Eligible RDTOH and Non-Eligible RDTOH on Decembert 31, 2020.

G. Industco's dividend refund for 2020, showing separately the amount related to eligible dividends and the amount related to non-eligible dividends.

CHAPTER 14

Other Issues In Corporate Taxation

Introduction

14-1.   Chapters 12 and 13 dealt with basic issues associated with the determination of Taxable Income and Tax Payable for a corporation. Specifically, Chapter 12 described the basic adjustments associated with converting Net Income For Tax Purposes to corporate Taxable Income. This was followed by consideration of how this Taxable Income is allocated to specific provinces for the determination of provincial Tax Payable. With respect to Tax Payable, Chapter 12 dealt with the rates applicable to corporations, the small business deduction, the M&P deduction, foreign tax credits, and the general rate reduction. Included is material on the annual business limit grinds related to Taxable Capital Employed In Canada and ADJUSTED Aggregate Investment Income.

14-2.   After a fairly detailed discussion of the concept of integration, Chapter 13 focused on the taxation of investment income earned by Canadian controlled and other private corporations. Coverage includes the Additional Refundable Tax (ART) on investment income, refundable Part I and Part IV taxes, the designation of eligible dividends, dividend refunds, and both the Eligible RDTOH and the Non-Eligible RDTOH accounts.

14-3.   In presenting the material in Chapters 12 and 13, we focused on what we view as basic issues, skipping over some of the more technical considerations related to the determination of corporate Taxable Income and corporate Tax Payable. This was done in the belief that avoiding the more technical aspects would enhance your understanding of the basic procedures associated with these determinations.

14-4.   In this Chapter 14, we are turning our attention to these technical issues. In this Chapter we will provide coverage of:

- the acquisition of control rules;
- the associated company rules;
- investment tax credits;
- tax basis shareholders' equity; and
- distributions of corporate surplus, including capital dividends and deemed dividends.

Acquisition Of Control Rules

Economic Background

14-5.   Over a period of years, some corporations may experience sufficiently large losses that they have no hope of recovering their economic health. While they may have accumulated large amounts of net capital or non-capital loss carry forwards, they have no real prospect of being able to use these amounts. Such companies can become attractive takeover targets for profitable corporations, provided they can structure their business to make use of the tax benefits associated with these losses. For example, if a profitable company can acquire a company for $100,000 that has $1,000,000 in loss carry forwards that can be utilized in the future, it is clearly a bargain for the purchaser. Further, if the acquiree cannot make use of the losses, receiving the $100,000 may be a better alternative than declaring bankruptcy.

14-6.   This situation is of concern to the government in that there are billions of dollars of such benefits available in the economy at any point in time. If access to these benefits was relatively trouble-free, the cost to the government could be enormous. As a consequence, the government has enacted legislation that significantly restricts the use of loss carry forwards in situations where there has been an acquisition of control.

Acquisition Of Control Legislation

14-7.   ITA 111(4) through 111(5.5) contain rules that are applicable when there has been an acquisition of control by a person or group of persons. IT-302R3, which deals with the losses of a corporation, indicates that control requires ownership of shares that carry with them the right to elect a majority of the board of directors.

14-8A.   An acquisition of control most commonly occurs when a majority shareholder sells his or her shares to an arm's length person. However, it can also occur through the redemption of shares. For example, if Ms. A owns 75 percent of AB Ltd. and Ms. B, an unrelated person, owns the other 25 percent, there would be an acquisition of control by Ms. B if AB Ltd. were to redeem all of Ms. A's shares.

14-8B.   In recent years, several new anti-avoidance rules have been designed to address loss trading among trusts (ITA 251.2) and using de facto control to avoid the acquisition of control rules (ITA 256.1). The complexity of these rules is beyond the scope of this general text. We would also notes that the *Income Tax Act* now refers to acquisition of control situations as "loss restriction events".

Deemed Year End

14-9.   To prevent losses from being used prior to the end of the taxation year in which the acquisition of control took place, ITA 249(4) requires that the corporation have a deemed year end on the day preceding an acquisition of control.

14-10.   If the acquisition of control occurs prior to the corporation's normal year end, a short fiscal period will be created. For example, if the corporation's normal year end was December 31, and the acquisition of control took place on February 1, 2020, the deemed year end would create a fiscal year with only one month (January 1, 2020, through January 31, 2020). Further, if the corporation retains its old year end after the acquisition of control, there will be a second short fiscal year that runs from February 1, 2020 through December 31, 2020.

14-11.   Note, however, ITA 249(4) allows the corporation to change its year end when there is an acquisition of control. This means that the corporation could have avoided a second short fiscal period by establishing January 31 as the new year end. This means that the first fiscal year after the acquisition of control will end on January 31, 2021.

14-12.   The extra year end is of importance in that the non-capital losses that may be available after the acquisition of control are time limited. In our example, the deemed year end creates, in effect, an extra year end that shortens the period during which time-limited losses can be used.

However, with a 20 year carry forward period for non-capital losses, this is unlikely to be an important consideration.

14-13.   Other implications of such short fiscal periods include the need to base CCA calculations on a fraction of the year, the need to prorate the annual business limit for the small business deduction, as well as the usual year end procedures such as inclusions of reserves.

Restrictions On The Use Of Charitable Donations

14-14.   ITA 110.1(1.2) places two restrictions on the deduction of charitable donations:

- Undeducted amounts that are present at the time of the acquisition of control cannot be carried forward to taxation years subsequent to that date.

- No deduction is available on a gift made subsequent to the acquisition of control if the gifted property was acquired prior to the acquisition date in anticipation of the acquisition of control.

14-15.   An example of the latter restriction would be a situation where an individual, who does not have sufficient tax payable to use a credit on the donation of a particular property, transfers that property to a corporation he or she controls with the expectation that he or she will sell the shares in the corporation and the corporation will make the donation and take the deduction.

Restrictions On The Use Of Losses

General Rules

14-16.   The acquisition of control rules apply to any losses that have not been deducted at the deemed year end. This would include losses that have been carried forward from prior years, as well as any additional losses that accrue in the taxation year that is created by the deemed year end.

14-17.   As will be explained later, the losses in this deemed taxation year may be increased by provisions that require the recognition of unrealized losses on capital assets. They can also be reduced by gains resulting from an election to have one or more deemed dispositions.

Capital Losses

14-18.   The acquisition of control rules are particularly harsh in their treatment of net capital losses. ITA 111(4)(a) indicates that any net capital losses that are present at the deemed year end are simply lost. They cannot be carried forward to future years and, as a consequence, they will be of no benefit to the corporation subsequent to the acquisition of control. Note that this would include any unused Allowable Business Investment Losses that are present at the deemed year end.

14-19.   In addition, if there are capital gains in the three years before the deemed year end, ITA 111(4)(b) prevents net capital losses from years subsequent to the deemed year end from being carried back to those years.

Non-Capital Losses

14-20.   While non-capital losses can be carried forward, they too are subject to restrictions. These restrictions, found in ITA 111(5), are that:

- after the acquisition of control has taken place, the corporation must continue to carry on the business in which the loss occurred;
- there must be a reasonable expectation of profit in that business; and
- the losses can only be applied against future income generated by the same or a similar business.

14-21. A brief example can be used to illustrate these provisions:

EXAMPLE Bostox Ltd. operates two separate lines of business, manufacturing cameras and the sale of specialty food products. During the year ending December 31, 2019, the camera business experienced a loss for tax purposes of $5 million, while the food specialty products operation had business income for tax purposes of nil. The $5 million loss could not be carried back and, as a result, it became a loss carry forward. On January 1, 2020, Bostox Ltd. is acquired by another company. During the year ending December 31, 2020, the camera business lost an additional $1 million, while the food products business earned $7 million.

ANALYSIS If there was no acquisition of control, both the current 2020 loss of $1 million and the $5 million loss carry forward resulting from the camera business could be deducted against the income of the specialty food products business. This would have resulted in a 2020 Taxable Income of $1 million ($7 million profit on food products, offset by a current loss of $1 million on cameras and a non-capital loss carry forward of $5 million).

However, with the acquisition of control at the beginning of 2020, the loss carry forward can only be used against profits produced by the camera business. This means that none of the loss carry forward can be deducted in 2020, but the $1 million 2020 camera business loss can be netted against the $7 million food products income, resulting in a 2020 Taxable Income of $6 million. The $5 million loss carry forward will still be available, but can only be applied against future camera business income.

Exercise Fourteen - 1

Subject: Acquisition Of Control

India Inc. operates two separate lines of business, one of which sells fountain pens, while the other provides professional accounting services. In its first year of operations ending on December 31, 2019, the pen business had a loss of $192,000, and the accounting business had income of $57,000, resulting in a Net Income For Tax Purposes and Taxable Income of nil. This leaves a non-capital loss carry forward of $135,000. For the taxation year ending December 31, 2020, the pen business had income of $42,000, and the accounting business had income of $247,000, resulting in a Net Income For Tax Purposes of $289,000.

Determine the minimum Taxable Income for 2020 assuming (1) that there was no acquisition of control in either year and (2) that there was an acquisition of control on January 1, 2020. The company has no deductions from Net Income For Tax Purposes other than possible loss carry forwards from 2019.

SOLUTION available in print and online Study Guide.

Unrecognized Losses At Deemed Year End

The Problem

14-22. As previously indicated, the acquisition of control restrictions apply to losses that accrue in the taxation year that has been created by the deemed year end. As there has been a deemed year end, there may be a loss from normal operations for the fiscal period that has ended. In addition, there may be losses resulting from actual dispositions of capital assets during the period.

14-23. However, the acquisition of control rules are also concerned with accrued losses that have not been recognized at the deemed year end. The problem is that if such accrued losses are realized after that time, they will not be subject to the acquisition of control restrictions.

EXAMPLE A corporation owned a parcel of land with an adjusted cost base of $200,000 and a fair market value of $150,000. If the land was to be disposed of subsequent to the acquisition of control, the result would be an allowable capital loss of $25,000, which could be claimed against taxable capital gains in the years subsequent to the acquisition of control. This could be viewed as a way of avoiding the restrictions imposed by the acquisition of control rules.

Special Rules

14-24.   In recognition of this problem, the acquisition of control rules require a number of special procedures at the deemed year end. They are as follows:

Non-Depreciable Capital Property   ITA 111(4)(c) requires that non-depreciable capital property be written down to its fair market value if that value is below its adjusted cost base. ITA 111(4)(d) requires that the amount of the write-down be treated as a capital loss. The new lower value becomes the adjusted cost base of the property. The resulting allowable capital loss can be applied against available taxable capital gains or carried back. However, if it is not used at the deemed year end, or in the three year carry back period, it is lost forever.

Depreciable Capital Property   ITA 111(5.1) requires that depreciable capital property be written down to its fair market value if that value is below the UCC. The write-down amount is treated as CCA to be deducted in the deemed taxation year. This will reduce the income for that period and, in some cases, create or increase the loss for that year. For capital gains purposes, the property will retain the original capital cost.

Accounts Receivable   ITA 111(5.3) does not permit the deduction of a reserve for doubtful accounts under ITA 20(1)(l). Rather, amounts must be written off as specific bad debts on the basis of the largest possible amount. If a doubtful account is not written off at the time an acquisition of control occurs, no deduction is available if the account subsequently becomes uncollectible. This procedure will generally result in a larger deduction and will reduce income, increase a loss, or create a loss in the deemed taxation year.

Exercise Fourteen - 2

Subject: Write-Downs At Deemed Year End

On November 15 of the current year, Parkat Ltd. acquires control of Sparkat Ltd. On November 14, Sparkat Ltd. has the following assets:

- Land with an adjusted cost base of $293,000 and a fair market value of $215,000.

- Class 8 depreciable assets with a capital cost of $416,000, a UCC balance of $276,000, and a fair market value of $184,000.

Indicate the tax consequences of the procedures that will be applied to these assets in the deemed year end that results from the acquisition of control.

SOLUTION available in print and online Study Guide.

Deemed Disposition Election

The Problem

14-25.   The requirement that non-depreciable capital property be written down to fair market value at the deemed year end is particularly onerous in that the resulting capital losses may simply disappear. To offset the harshness of this requirement, ITA 111(4)(e) allows the corporation to elect, at the time of the deemed year end, to have a deemed disposition/reacquisition of any depreciable or non-depreciable capital property on which there is an accrued gain or recapture of CCA. This election can be used to trigger capital gains that will offset either unused losses of the current period or unused loss carry forwards from earlier periods.

14-26.   The election can also be used to trigger recapture, which can absorb non-capital losses from the current or previous years. This is a less important application in most situations as non-capital losses do not disappear at the deemed year end. However, as noted in Paragraph 14-20, there are restrictions on the use of such losses after the deemed year end. Given this, it may be desirable to minimize non-capital loss carry forwards when an acquisition of control occurs.

Procedures

14-27.   The elected value, which will serve as the deemed proceeds of disposition, cannot exceed the fair market value of the asset at the time of the deemed disposition. The minimum value for the election is the adjusted cost base or capital cost of the property. The elected value can be any amount between this minimum and maximum. This means that, in the case of property on which CCA has been taken, any election that will create a capital gain will also create recapture of CCA.

14-28.   If the corporation has net capital losses and there are non-depreciable properties with accrued gains, this election is clearly desirable in that it will generate capital gains, which can be used to offset the net capital losses that would disappear as a result of the acquisition of control.

14-29.   The situation is less clear cut when the gains are on depreciable capital property. While the deemed disposition will create the needed capital gains, it will generally result in recapture of CCA. This may or may not be a desirable situation.

Example

14-30.   The following example will illustrate the procedures associated with the ITA 111(4)(e) deemed disposition election:

> **EXAMPLE**   Burkey Ltd. has a December 31 year end. On June 1, 2020, a new investor acquires control of the company. While its basic operations have been profitable for many years, it has a net capital loss carry forward of $200,000 [(1/2)($400,000)]. On May 31, 2020, the company has non-depreciable capital assets with a fair market value of $800,000 and an adjusted cost base of $500,000. Its depreciable capital assets have a fair market value of $1,200,000, a capital cost of $1,100,000, and a UCC of $600,000.

> **ANALYSIS**   The ITA 111(4)(e) election is clearly desirable with respect to the non-depreciable capital property. It generates a taxable capital gain of $150,000 [(1/2)($800,000 - $500,000)]. Deducting a $150,000 carry forward against this 2020 gain will use up $150,000 of the net capital loss. This will leave an unused amount of $50,000 ($200,000 - $150,000).

> Using the ITA 111(4)(e) election on the depreciable capital property will create a $50,000 [(1/2)($1,200,000 - $1,100,000)] taxable capital gain. Deducting a $50,000 loss carry forward against this amount will use up the remaining $50,000 of the net capital loss balance. However, the election will also create recaptured CCA of $500,000 ($1,100,000 - $600,000), an amount on which it appears that tax would have to be currently paid. Given that, in the absence of this election, taxation on the recapture could be deferred indefinitely, the election may not be desirable with respect to the depreciable capital property. One other factor that should be considered is that the election would result in increased CCA in the future.

Adjusted Cost Base After Election

14-31.   In addition to serving as the deemed proceeds of disposition, the elected value also becomes the adjusted cost base or capital cost of the asset on which the election was made. If the elections were made at fair market value on both properties in the preceding example, the new adjusted cost base of the non-depreciable assets would be $800,000, while the capital cost of the depreciable assets would be $1,200,000.

14-32.   However, if the $1,200,000 value was allowed to be used for CCA purposes, the company would be able to deduct 100 percent of the $100,000 difference between the $1,200,000 elected value and the old capital cost of $1,100,000, despite the fact that they have, in effect, paid tax on only one-half of this amount.

14-33.   To prevent this from happening, ITA 13(7)(f) specifies that, when an election is made under ITA 111(4)(e), the new capital cost of the property for CCA purposes only is equal to the original capital cost of the asset, plus one-half of the excess of the elected value over the asset's original capital cost. In the example in Paragraph 14-30, this value would be $1,150,000 [$1,100,000 + (1/2)($1,200,000 - $1,100,000)]. You might recall that other paragraphs in ITA 13(7) contain the same rule for both non-arm's length transfers of depreciable property and for some changes in use.

14-34.   Future CCA would be based on this $1,150,000 figure and, in addition, if the assets were sold for more than $1,150,000, the $1,150,000 would be subtracted from the UCC to determine any recapture. However, any future capital gain would be based on the new adjusted cost base of $1,200,000.

Exercise Fourteen - 3

Subject: Election On Acquisition Of Control

Means Ltd. has a December 31 year end. On May 1, 2020, all of the company's shares are acquired by a new owner. For the period January 1, 2020, through April 30, 2020, the company has an operating loss of $45,000. On April 30, 2020, the company has available a net capital loss carry forward of $110,000 [(1/2)($220,000)]. Also at that time, the company has the following assets:

Asset Type	Adjusted Cost Base Or Capital Cost	UCC	Fair Market Value
Non-Depreciable	$500,000	N/A	$650,000
Depreciable	400,000	350,000	500,000

Advise the company with respect to the most appropriate elections to be made prior to the acquisition of control and explain your results.

SOLUTION available in print and online Study Guide.

We suggest you work Self Study Problems Fourteen-1 and 2 at this point.

Associated Companies

The Problem

14-35.   In the absence of special rules, it would be very easy to avoid the annual limit that applies to the small business deduction. This could be accomplished by dividing a single corporation's activities between two separate corporations, thereby doubling up on the annual business limit of $500,000. However, as was noted in Chapter 12, the *Act* makes this more difficult by requiring that associated companies share their annual business limit.

14-36.   For example, assume that Mr. Robards owns all of the outstanding voting shares of both the Mark Company and the Grand Company. These two companies would be considered to be associated and, as a consequence, would have to share the $500,000 annual business limit. As was indicated in Chapter 12, they can elect to allocate the annual limit in any proportion they wish, provided the total does not exceed $500,000. If the Mark Company has active business income and the Grand Company does not, it would be most advantageous to allocate the entire annual limit to the Mark Company, so that it could claim the maximum small business deduction.

14-37. The preceding example is very clear cut and results in an allocation of the small business deduction that reflects the goals of the relevant legislation. However, with a deduction that can be worth $95,000 [(19%)($500,000)] per year in federal tax alone, there is a significant incentive to develop arrangements that will avoid the intent of the legislation. Correspondingly, there is a need to have legislation that is sophisticated enough to frustrate these arrangements. As a consequence, the identification of associated companies can be very complex.

Definitions
Related Persons

14-38. ITA 251 provides definitions of related persons. The legislation for identifying associated companies makes much use of these definitions. Given this, working with the associated companies rules requires an understanding of the related persons rules. Note, however, that you are dealing with two different concepts. ITA 251 deals with all classes of related taxpayers, while ITA 256 deals only with corporations. Further, even with corporations, the terms related and associated have different meanings.

14-39. The more important of the related persons definitions are as follows:

ITA 251(2)(a) - Related Persons With respect to individuals, Paragraph (a) notes that individuals are related if they are connected by blood relationship, marriage, common-law partnership, or adoption. Various other Subsections in ITA 251 and 252 elaborate on this statement to point out that all of the following individuals would be "related" to the taxpayer:

- Parents and grandparents, as well as parents and grandparents of the taxpayer's spouse or common-law partner.
- The taxpayer's spouse or common-law partner, as well as the spouse or common-law partner's siblings and their spouses and common-law partners.
- Siblings of the taxpayer, as well as spouses or common-law partners of the taxpayer's siblings.
- Children, including those that are adopted or born outside of marriage. Also included here would be spouses and common-law partners of children and children of the taxpayer's spouse or common-law partner.

ITA 251(2)(b) indicates that a corporation is related to:
- a person who controls it, if it is controlled by one person;
- a person who is a member of a related group that controls it; or
- any person related to a person who controls it or who is related to a member of a related group that controls it.

ITA 251(2)(c) indicates that two corporations are related if:
- they are controlled by the same person or group of persons;
- each of the corporations is controlled by one person and the person who controls one of the corporations is related to the person who controls the other corporation;
- one of the corporations is controlled by one person and that person is related to any member of a related group that controls the other corporation;
- one of the corporations is controlled by one person and that person is related to each member of an unrelated group that controls the other corporation;
- any member of a related group that controls one of the corporations is related to each member of an unrelated group that controls the other corporation; or
- each member of an unrelated group that controls one of the corporations is related to at least one member of an unrelated group that controls the other corporation.

Associated Companies

14-40.   The definitions that relate directly to identification of associated companies are found in the ITA 256. The more important of these are as follows:

ITA 256(1.1) - Specified Class, Shares Of   In simplified terms, this definition refers to non-voting shares that have a fixed dividend rate and redemption amount. Such shares are commonly referred to as preferred shares.

ITA 256(1.2)(a) - Definition Of Group   For purposes of defining associated companies, a group is two or more persons, each of whom owns shares in the corporation in question. A related group involves a group of persons, each member of which is related to every other member. ITA 251(4) notes that a related group is a group of persons, each member of which is related to every other member. An unrelated group is any group, other than a related group.

ITA 256(1.2)(c) - Control   The definition of associated corporations also involves the concept of control. For purposes of determining association, a corporation is deemed to be controlled by another corporation, a person, or a group of persons if the corporation, person, or group of persons owns either:

- shares (common and/or preferred) of capital stock with a fair market value of more than 50 percent of all issued and outstanding shares of capital stock; or

- common shares with a fair market value of more than 50 percent of all issued and outstanding common shares.

This definition is based on legal control. Control can also be "Control In Fact" as described in ITA 256(5.1) or control through other corporations as described in ITA 256(6.1) and 256(6.2).

Deeming Rules   The most relevant deeming rules can be described as follows:

- **ITA 256(1.2)(d) - Holding Companies**   This provision indicates that where shares of a corporation are held by another corporation, a shareholder of the holding corporation is deemed to own the shares of the held corporation in proportion to his or her interest in the holding corporation. Similar provisions apply to shares held by partnerships and trusts. Note, however, if a holding corporation holds a controlling interest in an investee, the holding corporation is considered to control all of the shares held by that investee.

- **ITA 256(1.3) - Children Under 18**   This provision requires that shares of a corporation owned by a child under the age of 18 be deemed to be owned by a parent of the child for the purpose of determining whether the corporation is associated with any other corporation that is controlled by that parent or a group that includes that parent.

- **ITA 256(1.4) - Rights And Options**   This provision requires that rights to acquire shares be treated as though they were exercised for purposes of determining associated companies. This Subsection also indicates that, where a person has a right to require a shareholder to redeem, cancel, or acquire its own shares, for purposes of determining association, the corporation is deemed to have carried out the redemption, cancellation, or acquisition.

- **ITA 256(1.5) - Person Related To Himself, Herself, Or Itself**   This provision indicates that, where a person owns shares in two or more corporations, the person shall as shareholder of one of the corporations be deemed to be related to himself, herself, or itself as shareholder of each of the other corporations.

ITA 256(2) - Association Through A Third Corporation   This provision indicates that two corporations, both of which are associated with a third corporation, are deemed to be associated with each other. This Subsection also includes an election that can mitigate this rule. The third corporation can elect to not be associated with the other two corporations. A consequence of this is that the third corporation's annual business limit will be set at nil. However, the election will allow the other two corporations to be exempt from the association rules under ITA 256(2).

14-41.   Given these definitions and rules, we are now in a position to look at the definition of associated companies as it is found in ITA 256(1).

Examples - Associated Corporation Rules

14-42.   The preceding definitions are essential to the understanding of the associated corporation rules found in ITA 256(1). This Subsection contains five Paragraphs designated (a) through (e), with each Paragraph describing a relationship involving association. These five Paragraphs will be given individual attention in the material that follows.

14-43.   The first of these paragraphs indicates that one corporation is associated with another in a taxation year if, at any time in the year,

> **ITA 256(1)(a)**   one of the corporations controlled, directly or indirectly in any manner whatever, the other.

Figure 14 - 1   [ITA 256(1)(a)]

14-44.   This type of association can be illustrated by the situation shown in Figure 14-1 in which A Company owns 75 percent of the outstanding voting shares of B Company. In this situation, A Company and B Company are associated by virtue of ITA 256(1)(a).

14-45.   The second Paragraph in ITA 256(1) indicates that one corporation is associated with another in a taxation year if, at any time in the year,

> **ITA 256(1)(b)**   both of the corporations were controlled, directly or indirectly in any manner whatever, by the same person or group of persons.

Figure 14 - 2   [ITA 256(1)(b)]

14-46.   This type of association can be illustrated by the situation shown in Figure 14-2. In this situation, Mr. A owns 75 percent of the voting shares of both A Company and B Company. As a consequence, these two companies are associated by virtue of ITA 256(1)(b), in that they are both controlled by the same person.

14-47.   The third Paragraph in ITA 256(1) indicates that one corporation is associated with another in a taxation year if, at any time in the year,

> **ITA 256(1)(c)**   each of the corporations was controlled, directly or indirectly in any manner whatever, by a person and the person who so controlled one of the corporations was related to the person who so controlled the other and either of those persons owned, in respect of each corporation, not less than 25 percent of the issued shares of any class, other than a specified class, of the capital stock thereof.

14-48. This type of association can be illustrated by the situation shown in Figure 14-3. In this situation, Mr. A owns 70 percent of the voting shares of A Company and his spouse, Mrs. A, owns 70 percent of the voting shares of B Company. In addition, Mr. A owns not less than 25 percent of the shares of B Company. Provided that the B Company shares owned by Mr. A are not of a specified class, A Company and B Company are associated under ITA 256(1)(c). As the required cross ownership can be in either direction, the two companies would also be associated if the cross ownership was by Mrs. A in A Company.

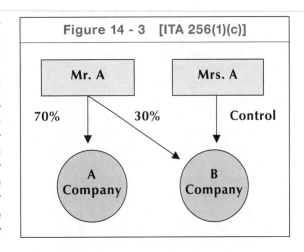

Figure 14 - 3   [ITA 256(1)(c)]

14-49. The fourth Paragraph in ITA 256(1) indicates that one corporation is associated with another in a taxation year if, at any time in the year,

> **ITA 256(1)(d)**   One of the corporations was controlled, directly or indirectly in any manner whatever, by a person and that person was related to each member of a group of persons that so controlled the other corporation, and that person owned, in respect of the other corporation, not less than 25 percent of the issued shares of any class, other than a specified class, of the capital stock thereof.

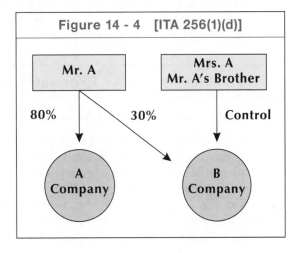

Figure 14 - 4   [ITA 256(1)(d)]

14-50. This type of association can be illustrated by the situation in Figure 14-4. In this situation, Mr. A owns 80 percent of the voting shares of A Company, while Mrs. A and Mr. A's brother each own 35 percent (70 percent in total) of the voting shares of B Company. This means that Mr. A is related to each member of a group that controls B Company. Mr. A also has the required cross ownership, in that he owns 30 percent of the shares of B Company. Provided that the shares of B Company owned by Mr. A are not of a specified class, A Company and B Company are associated by virtue of ITA 256(1)(d). Note that, under ITA 256(1)(d), the cross ownership has to be by Mr. A in B Company. If the cross ownership was in the other direction (e.g., Mrs. A owns 30 percent of A Company), the two companies would not be associated under ITA 256(1)(d). Note, however, that in such cases the two companies would be associated under ITA 256(1)(e), which is discussed in the next Paragraph.

14-51. The final Paragraph in ITA 256(1) indicates that one corporation is associated with another in a taxation year if, at any time in the year,

> **ITA 256(1)(e)**   Each of the corporations was controlled, directly or indirectly in any manner whatever, by a related group and each of the members of one of the related groups was related to all of the members of the other related group, and one or more persons who were members of both related groups, either alone or together, owned, in respect of each corporation, not less than 25 percent of the issued shares of any class, other than a specified class, of the capital stock thereof.

14-52. This type of association can be illustrated by the situation in Figure 14-5. Mr. and Mrs. A are a related group that control A Company, and Mr. and Mrs. B are a related group that control B Company. If we assume that Mrs. B is Mr. A's sister, then each member of one related group is related to all of the members of the other related group. Mr. and Mrs. A each own 50 percent of the voting shares of A Company, and Mr. and Mrs. B each own 30 percent of the voting shares of B Company. Mr. A owns the remaining 40 percent of the voting shares of B Company. In this situation, A Company and B Company are associated

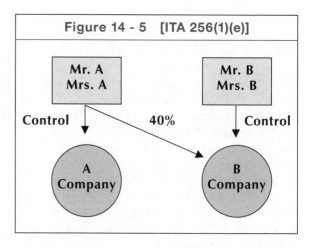

Figure 14 - 5   [ITA 256(1)(e)]

under ITA 256(1)(e). Once again, Mr. A's cross ownership has to be shares other than those of a specified class. However, if A Company shares were available, the cross ownership could be in the other direction (e.g., Mrs. B owns not less than 25 percent of A Company).

Exercise Fourteen - 4

Subject: Associated Companies

The Top Company owns 65 percent of the shares of Middle Company, as well as 10 percent of the shares of Bottom Company. Middle Company owns 35 percent of the shares of Bottom Company. Mr. Top, who owns all of the shares of Top Company, also owns 5 percent of the shares of Bottom Company and has options in those shares that would, if exercised, increase his ownership by another 10 percent. Mr. Top's 12-year-old son owns 15 percent of the Bottom Company shares. Indicate which of these companies are associated, citing the relevant provisions of the *Income Tax Act*.

SOLUTION available in print and online Study Guide.

We suggest you work Self Study Problems Fourteen-3 and 4 at this point.

Investment Tax Credits

Background

14-53.   In terms of directing economic incentives to specific regions or types of activities, investment tax credits are a very effective tax policy tool. They can be used to provide tax reductions that are specifically targeted (e.g., scientific research expenditures). In addition, by making some of them refundable, they can even provide benefits for enterprises with no Tax Payable.

14-54.   Despite their advantages in terms of targeting benefits, the use of investment tax credits has declined over the last 10 to 20 years. At one time, they were applicable to large classes of assets in broadly defined regions of Canada. At present, their use is confined to specific targeted areas. The ones that we will discuss in this Chapter are credits for salaries of eligible apprentices, current expenditures for scientific research, and the cost of qualified property.

Procedures

14-55.   Investment tax credits are tax incentives that are available to Canadian taxpayers who are earning business income or undertaking scientific research and experimental development.

With some exceptions, they are available on the same terms for corporations as they are for individuals.

14-56. In general terms, the procedures for investment tax credits, which are contained in ITA 127(5) through ITA 127.1(4), allow the taxpayer to deduct a specified percentage of the cost of certain types of current and capital expenditures from federal Tax Payable. The credits provide for a direct reduction in the amount of tax that is payable.

14-57. When capital expenditures are involved, the amount of the investment tax credit must be removed from the capital cost of the asset so that only the net capital cost is deductible through capital cost allowances (CCA). The legislation is such that the deduction from capital cost occurs in the taxation year following the year in which credit is claimed.

14-58. The capital cost must also be reduced by any government or non-government assistance received or receivable for the property, such as grants or subsidies. However, the reduction for these other types of assistance is made in the year in which the assistance is received or receivable.

14-59. When the investment tax credits are earned by making deductible current expenditures, the credits will be added to income in the following year.

14-60. In effect, the tax mechanism that is involved with investment tax credits is that the enterprise gives up $1 of current or future tax deductions in return for a $1 reduction in the amount of Tax Payable. This is clearly beneficial in that the cost of losing a $1 deduction is only $1 multiplied by the company's tax rate, a figure that could be below $0.15. By contrast, $1 of reduced tax payable is a cash flow savings of $1.

Eligible Expenditures

14-61. To provide a general picture of the applicability of investment tax credits, brief descriptions are provided of expenditures that qualify for these credits:

Salaries And Wages Of An Eligible Apprentice   An eligible apprentice is defined in ITA 127(9) and can be described as follows:

> **Eligible apprentice** means an individual who is employed in Canada in a prescribed trade (a trade currently listed as a "Red Seal Trade") in the first two years of their apprenticeship contract. This contract must be registered with a federal, provincial or territorial government under an apprenticeship program designed to certify or license individuals in the trade.

Qualified Property is defined in ITA 127(9) with further elaboration provided in ITR 4600 and 4601. As presented in this material, qualified property must be newly acquired primarily for use in Canada, and it must be available for use in specified activities. These activities include manufacturing and processing, logging, farming or fishing, and storing grain.

Qualified Scientific Research And Experimental Development (SR&ED) Expenditures includes current expenditures for basic or applied research, and for the development of new products and processes. (Capital expenditures do not qualify for SR&ED credits.) The rules related to SR&ED expenditures are extremely complex and the application of these rules goes beyond the scope of this introductory text. As a result, we provide very limited coverage of this topic and do not include coverage of what qualifies as SR&ED expenditures.

Rates

General

14-62. Current rates for the investment tax credits that we have described are as follows:

Type Of Expenditure	Rate
Salaries And Wages Of Eligible Apprentices	
(Limited To The First $20,000 Of Salaries And Wages For Each Apprentice)	10%
Qualified Property	
In Atlantic Provinces And Gaspe Peninsula	10%
Prescribed Offshore Regions (East Coast)	10%
Rest Of Canada	Nil
Scientific Research And Experimental Development	
Incurred By Any Taxpayer	15%
Incurred By CCPCs (See Paragraph 14-63)	35%

Exercise Fourteen - 5

Subject: Investment Tax Credit Procedures

During 2020, Colus Inc. pays salaries to five eligible apprentices totalling $125,000 ($25,000 per apprentice). In addition, it acquires $3,000,000 in Class 8 assets on which a 10 percent investment tax credit is available. Describe the 2020 and 2021 tax consequences associated with making these expenditures and claiming the related investment tax credits. Include in your solution the CCA for 2020 and 2021.

SOLUTION available in print and online Study Guide.

Special Rate On SR&ED Expenditures By CCPCs

14-63. With respect to the 35 percent rate for SR&ED expenditures, this overall rate results from providing an additional 20 percent for some expenditures made by a corporation that is a CCPC throughout a taxation year under ITA 127(10.1). Special provisions are available on up to $3 million in qualifying expenditures.

14-64. Prior to the March 19, 2019, federal budget, the $3 million limit could be reduced if the preceding year's Taxable Income was in excess of $500,000 and/or if the preceding year's Taxable Capital Employed In Canada was greater than $10 million. The 2019 budget eliminated the Taxable Income constraint. For taxation years that end after March 18, 2019, the ITA 127(10.2) limitation is as follows:

Annual Expenditure Limit = [$3,000,000][($40,000,000 − **A**) ÷ $40,000,000]

where **A** is

(a) nil, if the corporation's Taxable Capital Employed In Canada, along with the Taxable Capital Employed In Canada of any associated companies, is less than $10 million for the immediately preceding year.

(b) in any other case, the lesser of $40 million and the amount by which the corporation's Taxable Capital Employed In Canada, along with the Taxable Capital Employed In Canada of any associated companies, exceeds $10 million.

14-65. If a CCPC and its associated companies has previous year Taxable Capital Employed In Canada of less than $10 million, the limit on which the 35 percent investment tax credit will be applicable is $3 million. If the CCPC's Taxable Capital Employed In Canada for the preceding year exceeds $10 million, the limit will be reduced by $3 for every $40 of the excess. It will be completely eliminated when the Taxable Capital Employed In Canada for the preceding year reaches $50 million, as shown in the following calculation:

$$[\$3 \text{ Million}] \left[\frac{\$40 \text{ Million} - (\$50 \text{ Million} - \$10 \text{ Million})}{\$40 \text{ Million}} \right] = \text{Nil}$$

Exercise Fourteen - 6

Subject: SR&ED Credits For CCPCs

Anfax has been a CCPC since it began operations and has a taxation year ending on December 31. It has no associated companies. Its Taxable Capital Employed In Canada equaled $12,500,000 for 2019 and $11,500,000 for 2020. Determine its annual SR&ED expenditure limit for 2020.

SOLUTION available in print and online Study Guide.

Refundable Investment Tax Credits

General Rules - 40 Percent Refund

14-66. A problem with tax credits is that, in general, they have value only when the taxpayer has a tax liability. To deal with this problem, some tax credits are "refundable". What this means is that, when a taxpayer has earned a tax credit and does not have sufficient Tax Payable to use it in full, the government will pay ("refund") all or part of the unused amount to the taxpayer. We have encountered this type of situation previously for individuals with respect to the refundable medical expense supplement tax credit (see Chapter 4).

14-67. A refund can be made for up to 40 percent of the investment tax credits earned by a taxpayer, provided the taxpayer is:

- an individual;
- a "qualifying corporation", which is a Canadian controlled private corporation throughout the year with Taxable Income in the previous year, less an adjustment for Taxable Capital Employed In Canada (which is the same as the one illustrated in Paragraph 14-65), that is $500,000 or less before loss carry backs; or
- a trust where each beneficiary is an individual or a qualifying corporation.

14-68. This means that if an individual had $1,000,000 in SR&ED current expenditures, he or she would be eligible for a $150,000 [(15%)($1,000,000)] investment tax credit. If the individual did not have sufficient Tax Payable in the current year or the three previous years to use this credit, there would be a refund (payment) of up to $60,000 [(40%)($150,000)].

Additional Refund - 100 Percent Refund

14-69. In the case of a qualifying corporation, additional amounts are refundable. To the extent that current SR&ED expenditures are eligible for the 35 percent investment tax credit, the resulting credit is eligible for a 100 percent refund. This means that a qualifying corporation that spends $3,000,000 on current SR&ED expenditures is eligible for a refund payment of up to $1,050,000 [(35%)($3,000,000)] from the government (qualifying corporations are described in Paragraph 14-67).

14-70. The 100 percent refund is only available on the first $3,000,000 of expenditures that qualify for the 35 percent investment tax credit. We would remind you that capital expenditures do not qualify for SR&ED credits.

Carry Overs Of Investment Tax Credits

14-71. Under the definition of investment tax credit in ITA 127(9), unused investment tax credits may be carried back for up to 3 years and forward for 20 years. A taxpayer is required to claim all other available tax credits before calculating and claiming the investment tax credit for the year. Also, a taxpayer must reduce, to the fullest extent possible, federal Tax Payable for the current year before using investment tax credits to reduce previous years' federal Tax Payable.

Exercise Fourteen - 7

Subject:　Refundable Investment Tax Credits

Sci-Tech Inc. has made a number of expenditures that qualify for investment tax credits. They have invested $123,000 in Qualified Property in Nova Scotia. In addition, they have $1,200,000 in current expenditures for scientific research and experimental development. The company is a Canadian controlled private corporation and, for the previous taxation year, has Taxable Income of $176,000 and Taxable Capital Employed In Canada of $6,000,000. The company has no Tax Payable for the current year or the three previous years.

Determine the amount of the refund that Sci-Tech will receive as a result of earning these investment tax credits and any available carry forwards. Include in your answer any other tax consequences of these investment tax credits.

SOLUTION available in print and online Study Guide.

We suggest you work Self Study Problem Fourteen-5 at this point.

Effect Of Acquisition Of Control On Investment Tax Credits

14-72.　As was the case with companies having accumulated loss carry forwards, the government is concerned about the large amount of unused investment tax credits that are being carried forward in the tax records of Canadian corporations. The carry forwards reflect the fact that these corporations have experienced losses and, as a consequence, have not had a tax liability to which the non-refundable credits could be applied.

14-73.　While the government does not object to these credits being used against Tax Payable resulting from improved profitability for the corporations that have experienced losses, there is concern that these loss corporations will be acquired by profitable corporations in order to make use of these credits. As a consequence, there are acquisition of control rules that apply to the carry forward of investment tax credits.

14-74.　These rules are found in ITA 127(9.1) and (9.2). Their effect was described in the cancelled IT-151R5, Scientific Research and Experimental Development Expenditures, as follows:

> If control of a corporation has been acquired ... subsection 127(9) may apply to restrict the availability of the corporation's investment tax credits. In general, these provisions limit the application of investment tax credits to the tax on the income from a particular business carried on by the corporation before the acquisition of control or any other business substantially all the income of which is from the sale, leasing, rental, or development of properties or the rendering of services similar to those of the particular business carried on by the corporation before the acquisition of control.

14-75.　As you can see, the effect of these provisions is to treat investment tax credits in a manner similar to the treatment of non-capital loss carry forwards when there is an acquisition of control.

Tax Basis Shareholders' Equity

Shareholders' Equity Under GAAP

14-76.　In this Chapter, we will be considering various distributions to shareholders. In order to comprehend this material, some understanding of the tax basis components of shareholders' equity is required.

14-77.　You should be familiar with the components of Shareholders' Equity as they appear in a Balance Sheet prepared using generally accepted accounting principles (GAAP). The two basic components of the total balance disclosed are:

Contributed Capital   This is the amount that has been paid by investors in return for shares issued. In jurisdictions where par value shares can still be used, this balance may be divided into par value amounts and an excess over par amount, commonly designated contributed surplus.

Earned Capital (Retained Earnings)   This component reflects amounts that have been earned by the corporation and retained in the business. While this balance is sometimes referred to as earned surplus, the more common designation is retained earnings. In some situations, part of this balance may be designated as reserves.

14-78.   This segregation into contributed and earned capital is based on the general legal requirement that dividends cannot be paid out of contributed capital. By using this disclosure, investors are informed as to the legal basis for payment of dividends by the corporation. However, this legal basis may not be supported by the cash resources that would be needed to, in fact, pay cash dividends.

Paid Up Capital (Tax Basis Contributed Capital)

14-79.   ITA 89(1) defines paid up capital, normally referred to as "PUC". This Subsection indicates that the amount should be calculated without reference to the *Income Tax Act*, telling us that PUC should be based on legal stated capital as determined under the legislation governing the particular corporation (*Canada Business Corporations Act* or relevant provincial legislation). As contributed capital under GAAP is also based on legal stated capital, the initial PUC for shares issued will generally be equal to contributed capital under GAAP. However, as will be discussed in this and subsequent Chapters, there will be adjustments to PUC that have no equivalent adjustment under GAAP.

14-80.   PUC is applied on an average per share basis to each class of shares. This means, for example, that if a corporation issues 100,000 shares to one individual at $10 per share and, at a later point in time, issues an additional 100,000 shares of the same class to a different individual at $15 per share, the per share PUC will be $12.50 for all of the shares of that class. Stated alternatively, all shares of a particular class will have the same per share PUC value.

14-81.   Note the difference between the PUC value per share and the adjusted cost base (ACB) of a share. The ACB of a share is the average cost of the shares held by a particular shareholder. In the example in Paragraph 14-80, the taxpayer acquiring the first issue has an adjusted cost base of $10 per share, while the purchaser of the second issue has an adjusted cost base of $15 per share.

14-82.   The importance of PUC lies in the fact that it is a capital contribution and does not reflect accumulated earnings of the corporation. Because of this, it can be distributed to shareholders as a return of capital (subject to any restrictions imposed by corporate law), without tax consequences for either the corporation or the shareholder. This may not be the case, however, when capital distributions are made to shareholders of public corporations.

Exercise Fourteen - 8

Subject: Determination Of PUC And Adjusted Cost Base

Halide Ltd. has one class of shares. The company issued its first 100,000 shares at a price of $1.10 each. Two years later, an additional 50,000 shares were issued for $1.35 per share. During the current year, a further 30,000 shares were issued for $1.82 per share. One of the investors in the company acquired 2,400 shares of the first group of shares issued and an additional 3,850 shares from the most recent issue. Determine the adjusted cost base per share, as well as the total PUC of this investor's shares.

SOLUTION available in print and online Study Guide.

Tax Basis Retained Earnings

Amount

14-83.   The situation with respect to Retained Earnings is much more complex. To begin, we will be dealing with a different total for tax purposes. As you are aware, there are significant differences between accounting Net Income and Net Income For Tax Purposes.

14-84.   While the accounting literature defines accounting/tax differences as temporary differences with reference to Balance Sheet accounts (e.g., the difference between the Net Book Value and the UCC of a depreciable asset), most of these Balance Sheet differences are created by Income Statement differences (e.g., the difference between Amortization Expense and CCA). As a result, total Retained Earnings as determined under GAAP will, in most cases, be a significantly different number than the corresponding tax figure.

14-85.   A further point here relates to terminology. In general, the term Retained Earnings has replaced Earned Surplus in accounting literature and in published financial statements. However, the term surplus is still alive and well in tax work. As evidence, we would note that the *Income Tax Act* contains only five references to Retained Earnings, in contrast to 44 references to Surplus.

Basic Components

14-86.   Moving beyond the differences in the total amount, we encounter further problems in relating tax and GAAP figures. Under GAAP, Retained Earnings is often a single homogeneous balance. While some companies still segregate parts of this balance into reserves, such components have no formal meaning beyond assisting with disclosure.

14-87.   In contrast, the corresponding tax balance has four components, each with a well defined role in tax work. The four components are as follows:

- Capital Dividend Account (private companies only)
- Post-1971 Undistributed Surplus
- Pre-1972 Undistributed Surplus (no longer covered in this text)
- Pre-1972 Capital Surplus On Hand (no longer covered in this text)

14-88.   The Capital Dividend Account is only available to private companies. It is discussed in detail in this Chapter beginning at Paragraph 14-92.

14-89.   "Post-1971 Undistributed Surplus" tracks the earnings retained after 1971 that do not have any special tax status.

14-90.   In Chapter 8 we noted that, prior to 1972, capital gains were not subject to tax in Canada. The 1972 introduction of capital gains taxation resulted in the need to have a complex set of transitional rules to avoid taxation of gains accrued prior to that date. Although at one time these rules were very important, with the passage of time this is no longer the case.

14-91.   "Pre-1972 Undistributed Surplus" is simply earnings that accrued prior to 1972 that are retained in the corporation. The "Pre-1972 Capital Surplus On Hand" tracks capital gains and losses that accrued prior to 1972, but were realized after 1971. Such transactions are no longer of sufficient importance to warrant coverage in a general text such as this.

Capital Dividend Account (CDA)

Objective

14-92.   The objective of the Capital Dividend Account (CDA) is to track items that can be distributed on a tax free basis to the shareholders of the corporation. While a number of different items can be included in this account, the reason for its use can best be understood in the context of capital gains.

EXAMPLE During 2017, Uval Ltd. acquires land at a cost of $150,000. During 2020, the land is sold for $190,000, resulting in a capital gain of $40,000 ($190,000 - $150,000).

ANALYSIS It is the intent of tax legislation to assess tax on only one-half of capital gains. This means that Uval will have a taxable capital gain of $20,000 [(1/2)($40,000)]. However, the remaining $20,000 is still being held by the corporation. While the goal of tax legislation is not to have taxes assessed on this balance, in the absence of some special provision, its distribution would be subject to tax in the hands of the recipient shareholders.

14-93. The CDA provides the required relief in this situation. The untaxed balance of $20,000 will be added to the CDA. This balance can then be used to pay a capital dividend, a special type of dividend that can be distributed tax free to the shareholders of the corporation. Such dividends will be discussed in more detail at a later point in this Chapter.

14-94. While this analysis would appear to be relevant to all types of corporations, only private corporations can have a CDA. Note, however, the use of this account is available to private corporations, without regard to whether they are Canadian controlled.

Procedures

14-95. As indicated in the preceding section, there are a number of different items that can be allocated to the capital dividend account. The complete definition of these items is found in ITA 89(1) and is very complex. Without becoming involved in some of the more complex issues found in that Subsection, the basic components of the CDA are as follows:

Capital Dividends Received Capital dividends received from other corporations are added to the CDA. This preserves the tax free status of non-taxable amounts that pass through more than one corporation.

Capital Gains The non-taxable portion of realized net capital gains are accumulated in the CDA account, with this balance being reduced by the non-deductible portion of realized capital losses (this would include 100 percent of the gain on publicly traded shares that have been gifted to a registered Canadian charity).

Note that this component of the CDA cannot become negative and reduce the aggregate amount of the other CDA components, like capital dividends received.

EXAMPLE In 2015, a resident private corporation realizes a capital loss of $15,000, the non-deductible portion of which is $7,500. In 2017, it realizes a capital gain of $10,000, the non-taxable portion of which is $5,000. In 2020, it receives a capital dividend of $1,000.

ANALYSIS While the net of the capital gains component of the CDA is a negative amount of $2,500, the balance of this component in the CDA would be nil. The overall balance in the CDA is $1,000 (the capital dividend received).

Life Insurance Proceeds Life insurance proceeds received by the corporation are added to the account, net of the adjusted cost base of the policy. This can be an important addition when the company insures the life of one or more of its shareholders. This is a common procedure in owner-managed businesses, where life insurance proceeds are sometimes used to finance the buyout of the shares from the estate of a deceased shareholder.

Capital Dividends Paid The account is reduced by capital dividends paid. As will be discussed in Paragraph 14-111, an ITA 83(2) election is required.

Exercise Fourteen - 9

Subject: Capital Dividend Account

The following transactions involve the Knerd Corporation's capital dividend account:

- In 2018, they sold land with an adjusted cost base of $86,000, for cash of $108,000.

- During the year ending December 31, 2019, the company received a capital dividend of $8,200.

- On July 15, 2020, they sold goodwill for proceeds of $43,000. The goodwill had been internally developed and was not reflected in the company's records. On January 1, 2020, there was a nil balance in the company's Class 14.1 UCC.

- On October 31, 2020, the company paid an ITA 83(2) capital dividend of $16,000. The appropriate election was made.

Determine the balance in the capital dividend account at December 31, 2020.

SOLUTION available in print and online Study Guide.

We suggest you work Self Study Problems Fourteen-6 and 7 at this point.

Distributions Of Corporate Surplus

Introduction

14-96.   Corporate surplus, generally referred to by accountants as Retained Earnings, forms the basis for various distributions to shareholders of a corporation. This happens most commonly through the cash dividends that are paid by most Canadian companies. Less commonly, we encounter stock dividends and dividends in kind (distributions of corporate assets other than cash).

14-97.   These fairly routine types of dividends were given coverage in Chapter 7 in our material on property income. However, they will be reviewed at this point as an introduction to the various types of deemed dividends that are under consideration here. We will also give further attention to ITA 83(2) capital dividends.

14-98.   In addition to these various types of actual dividends, several types of deemed dividends can occur. The specific types of deemed dividends that will be covered in this section of Chapter 14 are as follows:

- ITA 84(1) Deemed Dividend on Increase of PUC
- ITA 84(2) Deemed Dividend on Winding Up or Reorganization of a Business
- ITA 84(3) Deemed Dividend on Redemption, Acquisition, or Cancellation of Shares
- ITA 84(4) and (4.1) Deemed Dividend on Reduction of PUC

14-99.   With the exception of capital dividends, all of the dividends considered here are subject to taxes when they are actually received or deemed to be received by an individual. This means that, provided they are received from a taxable Canadian corporation, they will generally be subject to the dividend gross up and tax credit procedures. In those situations where they are designated as such by the payor, they will be treated as eligible dividends.

14-100.   When such dividends are received by a corporation, rather than by an individual, there will be no gross up of the amount, nor any credit against corporate tax payable. The recipient corporation will include only the amount received in their Net Income For Tax Purposes. Further, this amount will generally be deducted in the determination of Taxable Income.

Regular Cash Dividends

14-101.   Regular cash dividends are paid out of a corporation's unrestricted surplus balances. The payment of cash dividends serves to reduce these balances. Unlike the payment of interest on debt, the payment of cash dividends does not create a tax deduction for the corporation. In effect, they are paid out of after tax funds.

14-102.   If cash dividends are received by an individual or a trust, they are subject to the usual gross up and tax credit procedures. In contrast, if they are paid to another corporation, they are included in the corporation's Net Income For Tax Purposes, but deducted in the determination of the corporation's Taxable Income.

14-103.   A further point here relates to the accounting treatment of dividends on certain types of preferred shares. IAS 32, *Financial Instruments - Presentation*, recommends that shares which require mandatory redemption by the issuer be classified as liabilities. Consistent with this, the dividend payments on these shares must be disclosed as interest, resulting in the amount of the distribution being deducted in the determination of accounting net income.

14-104.   To date, this treatment has not been recognized by the CRA. From a tax point of view, the dividends paid on preferred shares with mandatory redemption provisions will be given the same treatment as any other dividend. This means that, even if the GAAP based financial statements of the enterprise present preferred dividends as interest expense, they will not be deductible to the paying corporation. This difference will require adjustment in converting accounting income to a corporation's Net Income For Tax Purposes.

Stock Dividends

14-105.   From an accounting perspective, a stock dividend is a pro rata distribution of new shares to the existing shareholder group of the corporation, normally accompanied by a capitalization of Retained Earnings equal to the fair market value of the shares issued.

EXAMPLE   Jessica Rabin owns 100 shares of Fergis Ltd. She acquired these shares several years ago for $2,500 ($25 per share). On January 1, 2020, the Shareholders' Equity of Fergis Ltd. is as follows:

No Par Common Stock (1,000,000 Shares)	$ 7,500,000
Retained Earnings	12,500,000
Total Shareholders' Equity	$20,000,000

On December 31, 2020, the publicly traded shares of Fergis have a fair market value of $30 per share. On this date, the company declares a 10 percent stock dividend (100,000 shares). This dividend is not designated as eligible.

ANALYSIS - Fergis Ltd.   At the time of the stock dividend, Fergis would transfer an amount equal to the $3,000,000 [($30)(10%)(1,000,000)] fair market value of these shares from Retained Earnings to the contributed capital account. Subsequent to this transfer, the Shareholders' Equity of Fergis would be as follows:

No Par Common Stock (1,100,000 Shares)	$10,500,000
Retained Earnings ($12,500,000 - $3,000,000)	9,500,000
Total Shareholders' Equity	$20,000,000

From a tax point of view, the $3,000,000 increase in contributed capital would generally be an increase in PUC, reflecting an increase in the amount that could be distributed to the shareholders of the company on a tax free basis.

ANALYSIS - Jessica Rabin   As a result of the stock dividend, she will receive 10 shares [(10%)(100)] of stock worth $300 [(10)($30)]. This dividend will be taxable to the extent that it reflects an increase in PUC. Provided the increase in the Fergis Ltd. PUC is equal to the $3,000,000 increase in Contributed Capital (the usual case), Jessica will have a dividend of $300 [($3,000,000)(100 ÷ 1,000,000)]. This non-eligible dividend will be grossed up to a taxable amount of $345 [($300)(115%)].

With respect to the adjusted cost base of the new shares, ITA 52(3) will deem her to have acquired 10 additional shares at a cost of $300. With this addition, the average per share adjusted cost base would be $25.45 [($2,500 + $300) ÷ 110].

Note On PUC   In most accounting and tax texts, the usual procedure is to transfer an amount equal to the fair market value of the dividend shares issued to Retained Earnings. However, this may not be the case. In some provinces, the amount of legal stated capital to be assigned to the dividend shares is discretionary. If the assigned amount is a value that is lower than fair market value, the corresponding transfer to PUC will be lower. This results in a lower taxable value for the stock dividend and a smaller addition to the adjusted cost base of the shares.

14-106.   These stock dividend rules create an unfortunate situation for the taxpayer. An individual receiving stock dividends will require a cash outflow (taxes on the dividend received) with no corresponding cash inflows (the dividends are not received in cash). This approach to the taxation of stock dividends serves to significantly discourage their use in Canada, particularly in the case of large publicly traded companies.

14-107.   As noted, however, it is possible for a company to issue shares with a legal stated capital and a PUC that is less than fair market value. When this is the case, the negative tax effect that was described in the preceding paragraph can be reduced.

Exercise Fourteen - 10

Subject: Stock Dividends

On June 30, 2020, the Shareholders' Equity of Sturgis Inc. is as follows:

Common Stock (23,400 Shares Outstanding)	$351,000
Retained Earnings	462,000
Total Shareholders' Equity	$813,000

On this date, the company declares a 5 percent stock dividend. This dividend is not designated as eligible. At this time, the shares are trading at $25 per share. The company increases its PUC by the fair market value of the new shares issued.

Jean Tessier is holding 1,000 of the Sturgis, shares which he acquired several years ago at a cost of $18 per share. Determine the effect of this transaction on Jean's 2020 Net Income For Tax Purposes and 2020 federal Tax Payable. In addition, determine the adjusted cost base per share of his Sturgis Inc. holding.

SOLUTION available in print and online Study Guide.

Dividends In Kind

14-108.   While somewhat unusual, corporations do sometimes declare dividends that are payable in assets other than cash or the corporation's own shares. An example of this might be a situation in which a corporation has a major holding of another corporation's shares and wishes to dispose of them. If the block is large, sale on the open market could significantly depress the proceeds received. A possible alternative is to distribute the shares on a pro rata basis to the corporation's existing shareholders.

14-109.   From the point of view of the corporation, the dividend is treated as a disposition of the distributed property. Under ITA 52(2), the proceeds of disposition will be deemed to be the fair market value of the property distributed. Depending on the type of property, this could result in a capital gain, capital loss, recapture, or terminal loss for the corporation.

14-110.   Also under ITA 52(2), the shareholders are deemed to have acquired the assets at their fair market value. This amount is considered to be a taxable dividend subject to the usual gross up and tax credit procedures for eligible and non-eligible dividends.

> **EXAMPLE**   Hold Ltd. owns shares in Bold Inc. These shares have an adjusted cost base of $800,000 and a fair market value of $3,500,000. Hold Ltd. decides to distribute the Bold Inc. shares as a dividend in kind to its shareholders, all of whom are individuals.
>
> **ANALYSIS**   The tax consequences of this dividend are as follows:
>
> - Based on deemed proceeds of $3,500,000, Hold Ltd. will have a taxable capital gain of $1,350,000 [(1/2)($3,500,000 - $800,000)].
>
> - Hold Ltd. will have declared a dividend of $3,500,000.
>
> - The shareholders will have received a taxable dividend of $3,500,000, subject to either the eligible or non-eligible dividend gross up and tax credit procedures.
>
> - The adjusted cost base of the Bold Inc. shares to the Hold Ltd. shareholders will be $3,500,000.

Exercise Fourteen - 11

Subject: Dividends In Kind

Sandrine Cloutier owns 15 percent of the 500,000 outstanding shares of Cloutier Ltd. Cloutier Ltd. owns 150,000 shares of Botan Inc. The Botan Inc. shares were acquired at a cost of $42 per share and have a current fair market value of $51 per share. On June 30, 2020, Cloutier Ltd. declares a non-eligible dividend involving the distribution of all of the Botan shares on a pro rata basis to its existing shareholders.

Determine the effect of the payment of this dividend on Cloutier Ltd.'s 2020 Net Income For Tax Purposes. In addition, determine the effect of the payment of this dividend on Sandrine Cloutier's 2020 Net Income For Tax Purposes and 2020 federal Tax Payable.

SOLUTION available in print and online Study Guide.

Capital Dividends Under ITA 83(2)

14-111.   As we have previously indicated, the balance in the capital dividend account reflects amounts that can be distributed on a tax free basis to the shareholders of the private corporation. However, this tax free status does not happen automatically. When a corporation makes a distribution, an amount not in excess of the balance in the capital dividend account can be designated as a capital dividend. This is accomplished through an election under ITA 83(2), using Form T2054. Note that, provided there is a balance in the capital dividend account, this election can be made for any dividend, including deemed amounts.

14-112.   Distributing a capital dividend reduces the balance in the capital dividend account. It will be received by the taxpayer, whether the taxpayer is a corporation, a trust, or an individual, on a tax free basis with no reduction in the adjusted cost base of their shares. You will also recall that, if the recipient of the capital dividend is a private corporation, the amount of the dividend will be added to the recipient corporation's capital dividend account.

14-113.   If an election is made to pay a capital dividend in excess of the balance in the capital dividend account, a tax equal to 60 percent of the excess will be assessed under ITA 184(2) of the *Income Tax Act*. This will not affect the tax free nature of the dividend to the recipient.

14-114.   In some circumstances, an excess election can occur inadvertently. For example, the non-taxable portion of a capital gain may be added to the capital dividend account and, at a subsequent point in time, a reassessment will cause the capital gain to be recharacterized as business, rather than capital. This in turn means that the capital dividend account will be reduced through the reassessment process. If this happens, ITA 184(3) and 184(4) contain provisions that allow for a revision of the election in order to avoid the 60 percent penalty.

14-115.   As a final point, the fact that capital dividends are not taxable dividends means that they are not subject to the dividend gross up and tax credit procedures. In turn, this means that they cannot be classified as either eligible or non-eligible dividends under any circumstances.

Deemed Dividends Under ITA 84(1) - Increase In PUC

General Rules

14-116.   ITA 84(1) dividends involve a situation where there has been an increase in the corporation's PUC, accompanied by a smaller increase in the fair market value of the corporation's net assets (e.g., increase in assets or decrease in liabilities). This would include situations where the increase in PUC is accompanied by no increase in the net assets of the corporation.

14-117.   The most common example of this type of deemed dividend would involve situations where a corporation issues shares to settle a debt obligation that has a carrying value that is smaller than the fair market value of the shares.

EXAMPLE   A corporation issues shares with a PUC of $500,000 to a creditor, in settlement of $450,000 that is owed to a creditor. The creditor has agreed to repayment only if the shares have a value greater than the amount that he is owed.

ANALYSIS   This transaction would result in an ITA 84(1) deemed dividend of $50,000 ($500,000 - $450,000).

14-118.   The reason for treating this $50,000 as a form of income to the shareholders is that it represents an increase in the amount that can be distributed to them on a tax free basis. As a group, their economic position has clearly been improved as a result of this transaction.

14-119.   It is important to note that, because the extra $50,000 in PUC will be allocated to all of the shareholders of the particular class, a corresponding treatment will be given to the deemed dividend. That is, the $50,000 dividend will be allocated on a pro rata basis to all of the shareholders of the class, not just the new shareholder who acquired his shares by giving up $450,000 in debt securities.

14-120.   In order to provide equity in this situation, the amount assessed as a dividend will be added to the adjusted cost base of the shares. For the new shareholder, his or her share of the $50,000 ITA 84(1) deemed dividend is added to the adjusted cost base of the shares that were issued to him or her, resulting in an adjusted cost base for these shares of $450,000 plus his or her share of the deemed dividend. Note that this will not be the PUC of these shares, since PUC is calculated as an average value for all of the outstanding shares on a class by class basis.

EXAMPLE   Lantin Inc. has 250,000 shares outstanding at the beginning of the current year. These shares were sold for $12 each, resulting in a PUC of $3,000,000. Jeanne Moreau owns 25,000 of these shares, which she acquired at the time of their issue for $12 each.

During the current year, the company issues 50,000 new shares with a market value of $750,000 ($15 per share) in order to retire debt with a fair market value of $675,000.

Shortly after the 50,000 new shares were issued, Ms. Moreau sells her 25,000 shares for $450,000 ($18 per share).

ANALYSIS   The ITA 84(1) deemed dividend will be calculated as follows:

PUC Of New Shares [(50,000)($15)]	$750,000
Increase In Net Assets (Carrying Value Of Debt Retired)	(675,000)
ITA 84(1) Deemed Dividend	$ 75,000

This would be allocated to all of the outstanding shares in the amount of $0.25 ($75,000 ÷ 300,000) per share. This would be a taxable dividend, subject to either the eligible or non-eligible dividend gross up and tax credit procedures.

With respect to Ms. Moreau's holding, this $0.25 per share dividend would increase her per share adjusted cost base to $12.25 ($12.00 + $0.25). Given this, the tax consequences of her sale would be calculated as follows:

Proceeds Of Disposition [(25,000)($18)]	$450,000
Adjusted Cost Base [(25,000)($12.25)]	(306,250)
Capital Gain	$143,750
Inclusion Rate	1/2
Taxable Capital Gain	$ 71,875

Exercise Fourteen - 12

Subject: ITA 84(1) Deemed Dividends

At the beginning of the current year, Unilev Inc. has 126,000 shares of common stock outstanding. The shares were originally issued at $10.50 per share for total proceeds of $1,323,000, with this amount constituting the PUC. During the current year, a creditor holding $450,000 of the company's debt agrees to accept 40,000 newly issued common shares of the company in exchange for settlement of the debt obligation. At the time of this exchange, the shares are trading at $12.70 per share.

Subsequent to the exchange, Mr. Uni, who had purchased 5,000 Unilev Inc. shares at the time of their original issue, sells the shares for $13.42 per share.

Describe the tax consequence(s) to all of the shareholders of Unilev Inc. as a result of the exchange of debt for common shares. In addition, describe the tax consequences to Mr. Uni resulting from the sale of his Unilev Inc. shares.

SOLUTION available in print and online Study Guide.

Excluded Transactions

14-121.   There are a number of transactions involving increases in PUC that are specifically excluded from the ITA 84(1) deemed dividend treatment. The most important of these are:

- **Stock Dividends**   While there will be an increase in PUC in excess of the increase in net assets when a stock dividend is declared, such dividends are not considered to be an ITA 84(1) deemed dividend. Rather, they are taxed under ITA 82(1) as regular dividends. From the point of view of the recipient of the dividend, this distinction is of no consequence.

- **Shifts Between Classes**   When the PUC of one class of shares is decreased and, at the same time, the PUC of a different class is increased by a corresponding amount, there is no ITA 84(1) deemed dividend.

- **Conversion Of Contributed Surplus**   In situations where the consideration received for shares issued is in excess of the amount added to PUC, for tax purposes a contributed surplus balance is created. This contributed surplus balance can generally be converted to PUC, without the increase in PUC being treated as a deemed dividend under ITA 84(1).

Deemed Dividends Under ITA 84(2) - On Winding-Up

14-122. When there is a winding-up of a Canadian corporation under the provisions of ITA 88(2), the corporate assets will be sold and the liabilities, including taxes on the various types of income created by the sale of the assets, will be paid. The remaining cash will then be distributed to the shareholders of the corporation. Subsequent to this distribution, the shares of the corporation will be canceled. This process is covered in detail in Chapter 17.

14-123. In this Chapter, we would note that ITA 84(2) indicates that the excess of the fair market value of the amount distributed over the PUC of the shares that are canceled is considered to be a deemed dividend. While ITA 84(2) defines this entire amount as a deemed dividend, some components of this total are, in effect, redefined under ITA 88(2)(b). Specifically, ITA 88(2)(b) indicates that the ITA 84(2) dividend will be dealt with as follows:

Capital Dividend   To the extent that the corporation has a balance in its capital dividend account, ITA 88(2)(b) indicates that this amount of the distribution will be considered a separate dividend, which will be received on a tax free basis under ITA 83(2). As was noted in our discussion of capital dividends, this treatment will only apply if an appropriate election is made.

Distribution Of Pre-1972 Capital Surplus On Hand   As mentioned previously in this Chapter, the importance of Pre-1972 Capital Surplus On Hand has diminished greatly over time and is no longer of importance to most users of a general text such as this. However we would point out here that if the corporation has pre-1972 Capital Surplus On Hand, the distribution of this amount will be deemed not to be a dividend.

Taxable Dividend   Any remaining distribution will be treated as a taxable dividend under ITA 84(2), subject to either the eligible or non-eligible dividend gross up and tax credit procedures.

14-124. To illustrate these provisions, consider the following:

EXAMPLE   After selling its assets and paying all of its liabilities, a corporation has cash of $1,200,000 available for distribution to its only shareholder. The PUC of the company's shares is $100,000, and this is also their adjusted cost base. The balance in the capital dividend account is $175,000. The company makes the appropriate election to have the distribution of the $175,000 treated as a capital dividend [ITA 83(2)].

ANALYSIS   The analysis of the $1,200,000 distribution would be as follows:

Cash Distributed	$1,200,000
PUC Of Shares	(100,000)
ITA 84(2) Deemed Dividend	$1,100,000
ITA 83(2) Capital Dividend	(175,000)
ITA 88(2)(b) Taxable Dividend	$ 925,000

Depending on whether or not the $925,000 wind-up dividend, or some portion of it, is designated as eligible, it would be subject to either the eligible or non-eligible dividend gross up and tax credit procedures.

14-125. From the point of view of the shareholder, there has been a disposition of his or her shares, an event that requires the determination of a capital gain or loss. In the absence of a mitigating provision, this capital gain or loss would be calculated using the $1,200,000 as the proceeds of disposition, an approach that would double count $1,100,000 of this amount as both a deemed dividend and a capital gain or loss.

14-126. Fortunately, this problem is resolved by the ITA 54 definition of "proceeds of disposition". This definition indicates that, to the extent that an amount received is considered to be a deemed dividend under ITA 84(2), it is excluded from the proceeds of disposition. This means that the capital gain on the disposition of the shares in the example would be calculated as follows:

Cash Distributed	$1,200,000
Less: ITA 84(2) Deemed Dividend	(1,100,000)
ITA 54 Proceeds Of Disposition	$ 100,000
Adjusted Cost Base	(100,000)
Capital Gain	Nil

Exercise Fourteen - 13

Subject: ITA 84(2) Deemed Dividends

After selling its assets and paying all of its liabilities, a corporation has cash of $2,350,000 available for distribution to its only shareholder. The corporation was established 20 years ago with an investment of $250,000. This figure is both the PUC and the adjusted cost base of the shares. The balance in the capital dividend account is $340,000, and the company makes the appropriate election to have the distribution of this amount be treated as a capital dividend under ITA 83(2). What are the tax consequences of distributing the $2,350,000 to the corporation's only shareholder?

SOLUTION available in print and online Study Guide.

Deemed Dividends Under ITA 84(3) - On Redemption, Acquisition, Or Cancellation Of Shares

14-127.   An ITA 84(3) deemed dividend occurs most commonly when a corporation redeems some of its outstanding shares. Such dividends can also occur when the corporation acquires or cancels some of its outstanding shares. To the extent that the redemption amount paid by the corporation exceeds the PUC of the shares redeemed, a deemed dividend is assessed under ITA 84(3).

14-128.   For the corporation, this is a distribution of their unrestricted surplus balance. From the point of view of the person receiving the redemption proceeds, the deemed dividend component of the proceeds will be treated as an ordinary taxable dividend, subject to either the eligible or non-eligible dividend gross up and tax credit procedures.

14-129.   However, there is a problem here. As a redemption of shares is also a disposition of the redeemed shares, the proceeds of redemption will also be used as the proceeds of disposition. As was the case with the ITA 84(2) deemed dividends on winding up, this creates the possibility that some amount of the proceeds will be double counted as both a deemed dividend and a capital gain.

14-130.   The solution to this problem is similar to the one we described in our discussion of ITA 84(2) deemed dividends. The ITA 54 definition of proceeds of disposition excludes any amounts received that are deemed to be ITA 84(3) dividends.

EXAMPLE   Mr. Jonas owns all of the preferred shares of Jonas Ltd. They were issued with a PUC of $75,000. However, their adjusted cost base to Mr. Jonas is $25,000. They are redeemed by the corporation for $200,000.

ANALYSIS   The analysis of this transaction is as follows:

Cash Distributed	$200,000
PUC Of Shares Redeemed	(75,000)
ITA 84(3) Deemed Dividend	$125,000

This deemed dividend would be subject to either the eligible or non-eligible dividend gross up and tax credit procedures.

The capital gain on the disposition would be calculated as follows:

Proceeds Of Redemption	$200,000
Less: ITA 84(3) Deemed Dividend	(125,000)
ITA 54 Proceeds Of Disposition	$ 75,000
Adjusted Cost Base	(25,000)
Capital Gain (PUC - ACB)	$ 50,000
Inclusion Rate	1/2
Taxable Capital Gain	$ 25,000

We would note that, in situations where the PUC and adjusted cost base are equal, these calculations will result in no capital gain or loss. If the PUC exceeds the adjusted cost base, the result will be a capital gain. Alternatively, if the PUC is less than the adjusted cost base, a capital loss will result from the disposition. Note that, if the individual shareholder receiving redemption proceeds is affiliated with the corporation immediately after the redemption, any capital loss arising on the disposition will be disallowed.

Exercise Fourteen - 14

Subject: ITA 84(3) Deemed Dividends

When first incorporated, Tandy Ltd. issued 233,000 common shares in return for $1,922,250 in cash ($8.25 per share). All of the shares were issued to Ms. Jessy Tandy, the founder of the company. Except for 15,000 shares, she is still holding all of the originally issued shares. The 15,000 shares were sold to Ms. Tandy's brother, Jesuiah, for $7.90 per share, the estimated market value of the shares at that time. Because of ongoing difficulties between the two siblings, Ms. Tandy has arranged for Tandy Ltd. to redeem all of her brother's shares at a price of $11.75 per share during the current year. Any dividends resulting from the redemption will be non-eligible. Determine the tax consequences of this redemption to Ms. Tandy and Jesuiah.

SOLUTION available in print and online Study Guide.

Deemed Dividends Under ITA 84(4) And ITA 84(4.1)

14-131.   This type of dividend is not as common as the other deemed dividends we have discussed. It arises when a corporation resident in Canada distributes a part of its invested capital to its shareholders, without redeeming or canceling any of its shares. It might occur, for example, if a corporation divested itself of a major division and did not wish to reinvest the proceeds from the sale in other corporate assets. In this type of situation, the proceeds may be distributed to shareholders. Such distributions are commonly referred to as liquidating dividends.

14-132.   In order to make all, or part, of the distribution tax free, it is usually accompanied by a reduction in PUC. However, if the distribution exceeds the PUC reduction, an ITA 84(4) deemed dividend is created. Note that ITA 84(4.1) contains a different set of rules for public companies. Under these alternative rules, a deemed dividend can arise, even if the distribution does not exceed the PUC reduction.

EXAMPLE   Jong Ltd., a CCPC, has shares with a PUC of $5,000,000 and a nil balance in its capital dividend account. As it has accumulated excess cash, it will distribute $1,000,000 to its shareholders. In order to limit the tax effects of this distribution, the PUC of the shares will be reduced by $700,000.

ANALYSIS   Under ITA 84(4), $700,000 of the total distribution will be a tax free distribution of PUC. The remaining $300,000 is treated as a deemed dividend, subject to the usual gross up and tax credit procedures. The adjusted cost base of the shares would be reduced by $700,000, the amount of the tax free distribution to shareholders. However, there would be no reduction in the adjusted cost base for the $300,000 distribution as it would be subject to tax as a deemed dividend.

14-133.   ITA 84(4.1) provides a different rule that overrides ITA 84(4) in the case of public companies. For these companies, if a payment is made to shareholders in conjunction with a reduction of PUC that is not part of a reorganization of the corporation's business or its capital, and there is no redemption, acquisition, or cancellation of shares, the entire distribution is generally treated as a deemed dividend. Note that ITA 84(3) would be applicable if there was a redemption, acquisition, or cancellation of shares.

14-134.   With respect to our example, this means that, if Jong Ltd. is a public company, the entire $1,000,000 distribution will be considered to be a deemed dividend under ITA 84(4.1). As the $1,000,000 amount will be subject to tax, the adjusted cost base of the shares will not be reduced by this distribution.

14-135.   There is an exception to this general rule for public corporations. If the payment can reasonably be considered to be derived from a transaction that is outside the ordinary course of business for the corporation, it can be considered a tax free return of capital to the extent that it is accompanied by a PUC reduction.

14-136.   An example of this would be where the company disposes of a business unit of the corporation and does not wish to reinvest the proceeds in some other line of business activity. The distribution would have to be made within 24 months of the occurrence of the non-ordinary transaction and the exception would only apply to the first such payment made. If there is more than one payment, the second and any subsequent payments would come under the general ITA 84(4.1) deemed dividend rule.

Exercise Fourteen - 15

Subject: ITA 84(4) Deemed Dividends

Mr. Jondo owns all of the outstanding shares of Jondo Ltd., a CCPC. The shares have a PUC of $450,000 and an adjusted cost base of $625,000. Because it has accumulated excess cash, Jondo Ltd. pays a liquidating dividend of $330,000, accompanied by a PUC reduction of $225,000. What are the tax consequences of this distribution to Mr. Jondo?

SOLUTION available in print and online Study Guide.

We suggest you work Self Study Problem Fourteen-8 at this point.

Additional Supplementary Self Study Problems Are Available Online.

Key Terms Used In This Chapter

14-137.   The following is a list of the key terms used in this Chapter. These terms, and their meanings, are compiled in the Glossary located at the back of the Study Guide.

Acquisition Of Control	Liquidating Dividend
Annual Business Limit	Paid Up Capital
Apprenticeship Job Creation Tax Credit	Preferred Shares
Associated Corporations	PUC
Capital Dividend	Qualified Property
Capital Dividend Account	Qualifying Corporation
CCPC	Redemption Of Shares
Common Shares	Refundable Investment Tax Credit
Contributed Capital	Related Persons
Control [ITA 256(1.2)(c)]	Retained Earnings
Corporation	Scientific Research And
Deemed Dividends	Experimental Development (SR&ED)
Deemed Disposition	Shareholders' Equity
Dividends	Specified Class ITA 256(1.1)
Dividends In Kind	Specified Shareholder ITA 248(1)
Earned Capital	Stock Dividend
Earned Surplus	Taxable Capital Employed In Canada
Group Of Persons	Winding-Up Of A Canadian Corporation
Investment Tax Credit	

References

14-138.   For more detailed study of the material in this Chapter, we refer you to the following:

ITA 52(2)	Cost Of Property Received As Dividend In Kind
ITA 52(3)	Cost Of Stock Dividends
ITA 82(1)	Taxable Dividends Received
ITA 83(2)	Capital Dividend
ITA 84	Deemed Dividend
ITA 88(2)	Winding Up Of A Canadian Corporation
ITA 127(5) to	
127.1(4)	Investment Tax Credits
ITA 249(4)	Year End On Change In Control
ITA 251	Arm's Length
ITA 252	Related Persons
ITA 256	Associated Corporations
ITR 4600	Investment Tax Credit - Qualified Property
ITR 4601	Investment Tax Credit - Qualified Transportation Equipment
ITR 4602	Certified Property
IC 78-4R3	Investment Tax Credit Rates

S1-F5-C1	Related Persons And Dealing At Arm's Length
S3-F2-C1	Capital Dividends

IT-64R4	Corporations: Association And Control (Consolidated)
IT-149R4	Winding Up Dividend
IT-302R3	Losses Of A Corporation
IT-463R2	Paid-Up Capital

Problems For Self Study (Online)

To provide practice in problem solving, there are Self Study and Supplementary Self Study problems available on MyLab Accounting.

Within the text we have provided an indication of when it would be appropriate to work each Self Study problem. The detailed solutions for Self Study problems can be found in the print and online Study Guide.

We provide the Supplementary Self Study problems for those who would like additional practice in problem solving. The detailed solutions for the Supplementary Self Study problems are available online, not in the Study Guide.

The .PDF file "Self Study Problems for Volume 2" on MyLab contains the following for Chapter 14:

- 8 Self Study problems,
- 5 Supplementary Self Study problems, and
- detailed solutions for the Supplementary Self Study problems.

Assignment Problems

*(The solutions for these problems are only available in
the solutions manual that has been provided to your instructor.)*

Assignment Problem Fourteen - 1
(Acquisition Of Control Rules - Losses)

For many years, Janice Virtue had been a professor of Business Ethics in the Faculty of Business at a major Canadian university. In 2018, while continuing to teach one section of Business Ethics, she established Virtue Ltd. (VL) in order to market her numerous publications and online courses involving the application of ethical principles to business situations.

While the company experienced a net operating loss of $128,000 in the fiscal period ending December 31, 2018, VL experienced rapidly increasing sales during 2019. Because Janice believed the improvement was indicative of the success to come, VL moved to larger premises that were purchased for $423,000. Of this total, $100,000 related to the land, with the remaining $323,000 allocated to the building. Because the building was to be used exclusively for non-residential purposes, it was allocated to a separate Class 1. In selling the previous premises in 2019, VL experienced an allowable capital loss on the land of $36,000. The building was sold at its UCC value.

The Net Income For Tax Purposes of VL for the year ending December 31, 2019, after deducting CCA on the Class 1 building, was $16,000. VL realized no capital gains during the year.

In early 2020, a joint CRA/RCMP operation found that Janice was the mastermind and guiding force behind a network of illegal aliens working throughout Canada. They were selling stolen weapons and preparing thousands of tax returns with large fictitious charitable donations. The fee for the tax return preparation was always paid for in cash, which was not reported to the CRA.

Various charges were laid and, while Janice remains free on bail, a court date has been set for September.

By May 2020, Janice's lawyer indicated that it is likely that she will be convicted on multiple charges and will spend a significant amount of time in prison. She has also been advised by her employer that her contract to teach Business Ethics will not be renewed in the fall.

Given these circumstances, Janice decides to sell her VL shares. She finds a corporate buyer who is willing to acquire the shares on June 1, 2020. This buyer, Peerzon Books, is a large publicly traded Canadian company. The VL assets include the copyrights to all of her publications. While sales of these publications have fallen off precipitously in 2020, Peerzon believes its crack marketing team will be able to put the proper spin on Janice's life experiences and sales will take off.

As this acquisition of control resulted in a deemed year end, VL prepared an Income Statement for the period January 1, 2020, through May 31, 2020. This short fiscal period statement showed an additional business loss of $34,000 for this period. There were, however, no further capital losses.

On May 31, 2020, the values of the company's assets were as follows:

Asset	Cost	UCC	Fair Market Value
Temporary Investments	$ 32,000	N/A	$ 7,000
Accounts Receivable	123,000	N/A	110,000
Land	100,000	N/A	115,000
Building	323,000	$313,310	352,000
Equipment	46,000	33,120	5,000
Vehicles (Class 10)	36,000	21,420	25,000
Copyrights	Nil	Nil	42,000

VL will make all possible elections to minimize any net capital and non-capital loss balances.

Shortly after taking over VL, Peerzon Books decided that some of the extra space in VL's facilities could be used for manufacturing electronic reading devices. VL's income (loss) from the two separate businesses for the period June 1 through December 31, 2020, and for the 2021 taxation year was as follows:

Business	June 1 to Dec. 31, 2020	2021 Year
Electronic Reading Devices	$123,000	($ 26,000)
Janice's Publications	(53,000)	185,000

Required:

A. Determine the amount of the non-capital loss balance that will be carried forward after the acquisition of control by Peerzon Books, and calculate the amount of the net capital losses that will be lost as a result of this change in ownership, if any.

B. Indicate the maximum amount of the non-capital loss carry forward that can be used during the period June 1 through December 31, 2020, and the amount remaining at December 31, 2020.

C. Indicate the maximum amount of the non-capital loss carry forward that can be used during 2021, and the amount remaining at December 31, 2021.

Assignment Problem Fourteen - 2
(Acquisition Of Control Rules)
Boudin Inc. was incorporated 10 years ago in New Brunswick. At its formation, all of the shares were issued to Andre Boudin. The company's business involved the distribution of

health food products throughout the Maritime provinces. The company's taxation year ends on December 31.

The company operated successfully for a number of years. However, late in 2017, a local newspaper found that many of the claims made by the products that they distributed were either misleading or false. Widespread publication of this information resulted in a steep decline in the sales of Boudin Inc.

Because of this the company had an operating loss of $42,000 in 2018 and $123,000 in 2019. In addition, there was a 2019 allowable capital loss of $32,000 on the disposal of some temporary investments.

In early 2020, seeing no real hope for a return to profitable operations, Mr. Boudin begins a search for a buyer for his company's shares. On May 1, 2020, all of the shares are sold to Healthy Bites Ltd., a manufacturer of health food products. This company hopes to be able to revive the fortunes of Boudin Inc.

For the period January 1, 2020, through April 30, 2020, Boudin Inc. experienced a business loss of $48,000. This figure includes a write-down of inventories to their fair market values on April 30, 2020, and a deduction for uncollectible receivables, calculated as per the provisions of ITA 111(5.3). It does not include any taxable capital gains, allowable capital losses, Allowable Business Investment Losses, or property losses.

On April 30, 2020, Boudin Inc.'s assets had the following values:

Asset	Cost	UCC	Fair Market Value
Long Term Investments*	$ 47,000	N/A	$ 82,000
Land	207,000	N/A	305,000
Building	465,000	$360,000	485,000
Equipment	350,000	190,000	150,000

*Healthy Bites intends to sell these investments as soon as possible.

Required:

A. Indicate the amount of any non-capital and net capital loss carry forwards that would remain after the May 1, 2020, acquisition of control, using the assumption that Healthy Bites Ltd. elects to have a deemed disposition of all eligible assets at their fair market values.

B. If Healthy Bites Ltd. decides to only use the election(s) required to eliminate those losses that would expire at the acquisition of control, indicate the assets on which the elections should be made and the amounts that should be elected.

C. Advise Healthy Bites Ltd. as to which course of action (Part A or B) they should take.

Assignment Problem Fourteen - 3
(Associated Corporations)
The following situations are **independent** of each other. All of the corporations involved are Canadian controlled private corporations and have only one class of shares.

A. Circle Ltd. owns 51 percent of the shares of Loop Ltd., which in turn owns 51 percent of the shares of Ring Ltd.

B. Gerald Stone owns 75 percent of the shares of Rock Ltd. and 85 percent of the shares of Boulder Ltd.

Assignment Problems

C. The percentage share ownership of Jukebox Ltd. and Vending Ltd. are as follows:

	Jukebox	Vending
Jewel Cunningham	35.0	45.0
Roger Takahashi	15.0	15.0
Kari Fisher	5.0	8.0
Ming Chen	45.0	-
Kelly Clerkson	-	32.0
Total	100.0	100.0

None of the individuals are related to each other.

D. Rainer Gosling owns 100 percent of the shares of Fowl Ltd. Beatrice Owlet, Rainer's sister, owns 100 percent of the shares of Capon Ltd. Rainer, Beatrice, and their mother and father each own 25 percent of the shares of Pullet Ltd.

E. Ryan McLain owns 62 percent of the shares of McLain Ltd. and 40 percent of the shares of Chatelaine Ltd. McLain Ltd. owns 18 percent of the shares of Chatelaine Ltd.

F. Melissa Andrews owns 75 percent of the shares of Andrews Ltd. and 25 percent of the share of Statler Ltd. Jeremy Statler, Melissa's brother, owns 75 percent of the shares of Statler Ltd. and 25 percent of the shares of Andrews Ltd.

Required: For each of the preceding situations, indicate whether the corporations are associated and explain your conclusion with reference to the *Income Tax Act*. In order to assist you in answering this question, we have provided you with the content of ITA 256(1).

ITA 256(1) Associated corporations — For the purposes of this Act, one corporation is associated with another in a taxation year if, at any time in the year,

(a) one of the corporations controlled, directly or indirectly in any manner whatever, the other;

(b) both of the corporations were controlled, directly or indirectly in any manner whatever, by the same person or group of persons;

(c) each of the corporations was controlled, directly or indirectly in any manner whatever, by a person and the person who so controlled one of the corporations was related to the person who so controlled the other, and either of those persons owned, in respect of each corporation, not less than 25 percent of the issued shares of any class, other than a specified class, of the capital stock thereof;

(d) one of the corporations was controlled, directly or indirectly in any manner whatever, by a person and that person was related to each member of a group of persons that so controlled the other corporation, and that person owned, in respect of the other corporation, not less than 25 percent of the issued shares of any class, other than a specified class, of the capital stock thereof; or

(e) each of the corporations was controlled, directly or indirectly in any manner whatever, by a related group and each of the members of one of the related groups was related to all of the members of the other related group, and one or more persons who were members of both related groups, either alone or together, owned, in respect of each corporation, not less than 25 percent of the issued shares of any class, other than a specified class, of the capital stock thereof.

Assignment Problem Fourteen - 4
(Associated Companies)
Each of the following is an **independent** Case involving the ownership of voting shares of Canadian controlled private corporations. All of the corporations have taxation years that end on December 31 and have only one class of shares.

A. Mr. Bond owns 55 percent of Sarnen Inc. Sarnen Inc. owns 40 percent of Barxo Ltd. Mr. Bond also owns 14 percent of Hax Ltd., which in turn owns 54 percent of the shares of Barxo Ltd. Mr. Bond's 10 year old daughter owns 6 percent of the shares of Barxo Ltd.

B. Mr. Jones, Mr. Knight, and Mr. Long are three unrelated individuals.

*   Mr. Jones owns 50 percent of the shares of Anix Inc. and 25 percent of the shares of Brex Ltd.
*   Mr. Knight owns 50 percent of the shares of Brex Ltd.
*   Mr. Long owns 50 percent of the shares of Anix Inc. and 25 percent of the shares of Brex Ltd.

C. Sam Scully owns 60 percent of Scully Inc. His sister, Susan Wilson, owns 80 percent of Wilson Ltd. and 30 percent of Scully Inc. Sam Scully also owns 10 percent of Wilson Ltd.

D. Joan and Sarah Lartch are sisters. Joan owns 100 percent of the shares of JL Inc. and 31 percent of the shares of Meadow Ltd. Her sister Sarah owns 60 percent of the shares of SL Inc., with the remaining 40 percent of the shares held by her mother. Sarah also owns 39 percent of the shares of Meadow Ltd. The remaining shares of Meadow Ltd. are held by an unrelated party.

E. John and May Carp each own 30 percent of the shares of Jomay Inc. Serge and Beth Carp each own 45 percent of the shares of Besa Ltd. John and Serge Carp are brothers. Beth Carp owns 40 percent of the shares of Jomay Inc. and May Carp owns 10 percent of the shares of Besa Ltd.

Required: For each of the preceding Cases, determine whether the corporations are associated. Support your conclusions with references to specific provisions of ITA 256. In order to assist you in answering this question, we have provided you with the content of ITA 256(1).

ITA 256(1) Associated corporations — For the purposes of this Act, one corporation is associated with another in a taxation year if, at any time in the year,

(a) one of the corporations controlled, directly or indirectly in any manner whatever, the other;

(b) both of the corporations were controlled, directly or indirectly in any manner whatever, by the same person or group of persons;

(c) each of the corporations was controlled, directly or indirectly in any manner whatever, by a person and the person who so controlled one of the corporations was related to the person who so controlled the other, and either of those persons owned, in respect of each corporation, not less than 25 percent of the issued shares of any class, other than a specified class, of the capital stock thereof;

(d) one of the corporations was controlled, directly or indirectly in any manner whatever, by a person and that person was related to each member of a group of persons that so controlled the other corporation, and that person owned, in respect of the other corporation, not less than 25 percent of the issued shares of any class, other than a specified class, of the capital stock thereof; or

(e) each of the corporations was controlled, directly or indirectly in any manner whatever, by a related group and each of the members of one of the related groups was related to all of the members of the other related group, and one or more persons who were members of both related groups, either alone or together, owned, in respect of each corporation, not less than 25 percent of the issued shares of any class, other than a specified class, of the capital stock thereof.

Assignment Problem Fourteen - 5
(Investment Tax Credits)
Case A

In 2020, Gypsy Ltd., a Canadian controlled private corporation with a December 31 taxation year end, hired 18 eligible apprentices – six were hired at the beginning of January, six more August 1, and the remaining six November 1. Each of the apprentices began with an annual salary of $45,000, all of which qualified for the Apprenticeship Tax Credit. Based on the hiring dates the first group of six, each earned $45,000 for the year while the second group each earned $18,750 and the third group each earned $7,500. The total amount paid to these individuals in 2020 is $427,500.

Gypsy Ltd. also acquired Class 53 machinery for $640,000 on the November 27, 2020, to be used in New Brunswick. The machinery was delivered to the company site in early December and immediately began to be used. Assume that the machinery is qualified property for investment tax credit purposes.

Required: Describe the 2020 and 2021 income tax consequences of the salary and wages to apprentices and the acquisition of the Class 53 machinery. Specifically, determine whether the amounts qualify for any investment tax credit and, if so, the amount of that tax credit and the 2021 implications of claiming any available tax credit in 2020. Assume that the company will claim the maximum CCA possible on the Class 53 machinery in 2020, that the opening UCC in Class 53 for 2020 is nil, that no additions will be made to the class in 2021, and that the company will have sufficient Part 1 Tax Payable to fully utilize any investment tax credits in 2020.

Case B

Taurus Ltd., a Canadian controlled private corporation with a December 31 taxation year end, has been conducting Scientific Research and Experimental Development (SRED), which qualifies for additional federal investment tax credit (ITC) incentives based upon its "SRED expenditure limit". Taurus has never been associated with another corporation since its incorporation in 2014. The company has provided the following information for its 2019 and 2020 taxation years:

	2019	2020
Taxable Income	$ 735,000	$ 850,000
Taxable Capital Employed In Canada	16,900,000	21,440,000

Required: Determine Taurus's SRED expenditure limit for its 2020 taxation year.

Case C

Libra Ltd. is a Canadian controlled private corporation (CCPC) with a December 31 taxation year end. The company was incorporated in 2017 and has conducted Scientific Research and Experimental Development (SRED) since its incorporation. The company has only realized non-capital losses in each year from 2017 up to and including the 2020 taxation year. As a result its Taxable Income for 2019 and 2020 is nil. The company has never applied any non-capital losses. As a result of its nil Taxable Income the company has no Tax Payable for the 2019 and 2020 taxation years.

Because of the potential success of its SRED efforts the company has received and continues to receive considerable funding in the form of share capital and long term financing. As a result the TCEC of the company was $21,350,000 in 2019 and $24,730,000 in 2020. The company is not associated with any other corporation.

During 2020, the company acquired the following property and incurred the following SRED expenditures that qualify for investment tax credits:

- $220,000 for the purchase of qualified property to be used in New Brunswick

- $3,110,000 in current expenditures for SRED

- $1,890,000 in capital expenditures for SRED

Assume that the company deducts all of its SRED expenditures rather than accumulate them in a SRED expenditure pool.

Required: Determine the maximum amount of refundable ITC that Libra Ltd. will be entitled to receive. In addition, determine the amount of any ITC carry forwards and how they could be applied. Finally, identify any other related income tax consequences that occur as a result of the refund.

Assignment Problem Fourteen - 6
(Capital Dividend Account)

Since its incorporation in 2009, Park Inc. has qualified as a Canadian controlled private corporation. During the period since incorporation until December 31, 2020, the company has had the following transactions that might involve the capital dividend account:

1. In 2011, the company sold a depreciable asset with a capital cost of $225,000. It was the last asset in its class and the balance in the class at the time of the sale was $129,600. The proceeds from the sale were $275,000. No assets were added to the class during 2011.

2. In 2013, the company received a capital dividend of $46,000.

3. In 2014, the company received life insurance proceeds, net of the adjusted cost base of the policy, in the amount of $27,500.

4. In 2015, the company paid a capital dividend of $38,000 and eligible dividends of $19,000. The required election was made.

5. In 2015, the company sold a parcel of land for $100,000. The adjusted cost base of this land was $145,000.

6. In January 2020, Park acquired all of the shares of a small incorporated business at a cost of $850,000. This total cost was allocated as follows:

Non-Depreciable Assets	$150,000
Depreciable Assets (See Note)	500,000
Goodwill	200,000
Total Cost	$850,000

Note   The capital cost of the non-depreciable assets to the acquired business was $100,000. The capital cost of the depreciable assets was $450,000 and their UCC was $375,000. The goodwill was internally generated and was not reflected on the books of the acquired business. Park does not use a rollover provision to transfer the assets.

While Park intended to integrate this business into its other operations, they received an unsolicited offer to purchase the shares of this business for $965,000. Finding this offer too attractive to resist, it was accepted and the business was sold on October 1, 2020. On January 1, 2020, Park had no UCC balance in Class 14.1. The total proceeds were allocated as follows:

Non-Depreciable Assets	$175,000
Depreciable Assets	550,000
Goodwill	240,000
Total Proceeds	$965,000

7. In 2020, the company received a capital dividend of $17,800. They paid a capital dividend of $21,600 and eligible dividends of $8,000. The required election was made.

Required: Determine the balance in the company's capital dividend account as of December 31, 2020.

Assignment Problem Fourteen - 7
(Corporate Surplus Distributions)

Grado Ltd. is a Canadian controlled private corporation with a December 31 taxation year end that was incorporated in 2011. All of the existing shareholders are individuals. The company's condensed Balance Sheet, prepared in accordance with generally accepted accounting principles, as of December 31, 2019, is as follows:

Total Assets		$858,000
Current Liabilities		$122,000
Long Term Liabilities		384,000
Shareholders' Equity:		
700 Preferred Class A (Paid Up Capital)	$ 14,000	
1,000 Common Shares (Paid Up Capital)	87,000	
Retained Earnings	251,000	352,000
Total Equities		$858,000

Required: Determine the income tax consequences of each of the following **independent** transactions. Income tax consequences are considered to include the amount of taxable dividends, the dividend tax credit, any taxable capital gains and allowable capital losses, and any changes to the adjusted cost base (ACB) of relevant property and the Paid-Up Capital (PUC) of a class of shares. Any dividends paid or deemed to be paid by Grado Ltd. would be non-eligible.

A. (i) Mr. McDuff holds $200,000 of the currently outstanding long term liabilities. The debt does not allow Mr. McDuff the right to convert to shares, but in an effort to restructure, the company made a proposal to Mr. McDuff to convert to preferred shares, which he has accepted. Given the favourable terms and conditions it is estimated that the value of the debt is $230,000. Grado will create a new class of preferred shares (e.g., Class B) that will be used to make the conversion. Grado will issue 500 Class B preferred shares that are redeemable at the option of the holder for $460 each. Assume that the PUC of the Class B preferred shares increased by $230,000 as a result of the conversion.

   (ii) Using the same facts as described in A(i), explain what would have happened had Grado not created a new class of preferred shares to make the conversion with the debtholder but instead issued $230,000 of existing Class A preferred shares. Assume that 2,300 additional Class A shares would be issued on the conversion.

B. The company declared and distributed a 15 percent stock dividend on the common shares. The PUC of the common shares increased by $15,000 with a corresponding reduction in Retained Earnings.

C. Mr. William Bristle owns 25 percent of the common shares, which he acquired in 2013 for $60 each. In April 2020 the company announced that there would be a distribution to all common shareholders following the shutdown of one of its operations. A payment of

$68,000 was made shortly thereafter with $57,000 of that distribution considered a partial return of capital (e.g., PUC). In early December 2020 Mr. Bristle decided to sell all of his common shares to an arm`s length individual who agreed to pay him $100 per share.

D. (i) Mrs. Wiebe owns 100 of the common shares. She purchased the shares for $18 a share in 2012. The company redeems these shares for $90 per share in June 2020.

    (ii) Mrs. Wilbury purchased 200 of the Class A preferred shares for $36. The company redeemed all of her shares in September 2020 for $25 per share. Assume that she owns no other shares in Grado and has no capital gains in 2020.

Tax Software Assignment Problem

Tax Software Assignment Problem Fourteen - 1

RadionFaux Industries Ltd. (RIL) is a Canadian controlled private corporation, located at 123 ABC Street in Ottawa, Ontario K4E 1A1. Its Ontario corporation tax account number is 1234567. Its phone number is (613) 111-1111. It was incorporated on February 24, 1990, in Ottawa.

The government's Crown Copyright no longer permits us to use fake Business Numbers in software problems. To reduce the number of ProFile's error messages because of this, enter NR (for not registered) in the Business Number field.

The company has 1,000 shares of common stock issued and outstanding, all of which are held by Ms. Margaret Ottawa (SIN 527-000-301).

Ms. Ottawa, the president and director of the company, is the person who should be contacted with respect to matters concerning the company's books and records. She is the authorized person as well as the signing officer.

RIL is a retailer of pet supplies. All of its sales occur within Canada. It has net assets of $235,000 on December 31, 2019. This includes a few investments that Ms. Ottawa inherited from her father two years earlier.

RIL owns all of the 500 common shares of OttawaFaux Inc., which holds most of the investments Ms. Ottawa inherited from her father. The common shares have a book value of $1,200,000. OttawaFaux Inc. has the same location and phone number as RadionFaux Industries Ltd. OttawaFaux Inc. has a December 31 fiscal year end. Enter NR (for not registered) in the Business Number field for OttawaFaux Inc.

OttawaFaux Inc. is also involved in earning active business income through the breeding and sale of championship dogs. It has total assets of $2,000,000 and total revenues for 2019 of $200,000. Its Taxable Capital Employed In Canada was $350,000 as at December 31, 2018, and $365,000 as at December 31, 2019.

The following information applied to RIL:

Taxable Capital Employed In Canada - 2018	$328,000
Taxable Capital Employed In Canada - 2019	411,000
Total Assets As At December 31, 2019	750,000
RDTOH As At December 31, 2018	5,200
Dividends Declared And Paid During 2018	Nil
GRIP Balance As At December 31, 2018	11,750
Capital Dividend Account As At December 31, 2018	6,000

RIL does not use International Financial Reporting Standards (IFRS). For the taxation year ending December 31, 2019, RIL's Income Statement, before any deduction for income taxes, was as follows:

Tax Software Assignment Problem

Sales Revenues	$580,000
Interest On Long Term Debt	27,500
Interest Received On Foreign Bank Account (Note 1)	18,000
Eligible Dividends On Royal Bank Shares	17,500
Non-Eligible Dividends From OttawaFaux Inc. (Note 2)	42,000
Gain On Sale Of Shares (Note 3)	27,000
Total Revenues	$712,000
Cost Of Goods Sold	$208,000
Amortization Expense	122,000
Other Operating Expenses	147,000
Total Expenses (Excluding Taxes)	$477,000
Net Income (Before Taxes)	$235,000

Note 1   This interest is net of $2,000 in taxes withheld in Ireland.

Note 2   As a result of paying this $42,000 in dividends to RIL, OttawaFaux Inc. received a dividend refund of $14,000.

Note 3   On March 23, 2019, RIL sold 2,700 shares of Canadian Imperial Bank of Commerce. The common shares had cost $118,800 on June 6, 2016, and were sold for net proceeds of $145,800.

Other Information:

1. Expenses include a deduction for charitable donations to the Ottawa Civic Hospital in the amount of $5,000.

2. RIL's expenses include penalties of $3,500 resulting from a judgment in the Tax Court of Canada.

3. RIL reimbursed Ms. Ottawa $34,000 for business meals and entertainment for clients and suppliers during the year.

4. During the year, RIL incurred $20,000 in landscaping costs. For accounting purposes these are being treated as a capital asset, to be amortized using the straight-line method over 10 years. The related amortization is included in the Amortization Expense shown on the Income Statement.

5. The opening UCC balances were $246,000 for Class 1, $135,000 for Class 8, and $90,000 for Class 10. The only fixed asset disposition during the year was the sale of a delivery truck. The truck had cost $35,000 and was sold for its net book value of $12,000. The only fixed asset acquisition was $52,000 in office furniture on April 1, 2019.

6. During 2019, RIL paid taxable dividends of $92,000. Of these dividends, $25,000 were designated as eligible. On September 1, 2019, RIL also elects to pay the maximum capital dividend allowable.

7. RIL allocates $60,000 of the annual business limit to OttawaFaux Inc. This is $5,000 more than OttawaFaux Inc. can utilize in 2019, but RIL cannot use the excess.

8. RIL paid quarterly income tax instalments of $8,000 each on the 20th of March, June, September, and December during 2019.

9. RIL has a website describing the products it carries, but no income is generated from the website.

10. Assume that the adjusted aggregate investment income (AAII) of both companies is nil in the 2018 preceding year.

Required: Prepare the federal corporate tax return for RIL for the 2019 taxation year using the ProFile T2 corporate software program. Determine the eligible and non-eligible RDTOH and comment on whether the designation of $25,000 of eligible dividends was a good idea. If not indicate the designation that you would have made. On the ProFile schedule titled "Info", the Filing question "Complete return from GIFI?" is answered Yes by default, click No. Ignore the GIFI requirements except as follows:

On GIFI Schedule 125:

- Input the total revenues less the Gain On Sale Of Shares ($685,000) on the line "Total Sales Of Goods And Services" (Code 8000).

- Choose "Realized gains / losses on sale of investments" (Code 8211) from the drop down menu under Code 8089 and input the Gain On Sale Of Shares.

- Choose "Purchases / cost of materials" (Code 8320) from the drop down menu under Cost of Sales and input the Cost of Goods Sold.

- Choose "Amortization of tangible assets" (Code 8670) from the drop down menu under Operating Expenses and input the amortization expense.

- Choose "Other expenses" (Code 9270) from the drop down menu under Operating Expenses and Other Operating Expenses.

On GIFI Schedule 100:

- Input the Net Income figure as "Cash and deposits" (Code 1000) in order to make the total assets equal to the total liabilities and equity.

Although this will not properly complete the GIFI statements, it will eliminate the warning messages that would otherwise be generated when the Net Income figure and Amortization Expense are input on Schedule 1. These GIFI entries will have no effect on the calculations in the tax return.

In addition, to prevent audit warnings, S141, "Notes Checklist", has to be completed. Assume there are no notes to the financial statements and answer "No" to any other relevant questions.

CHAPTER 15

Corporate Taxation And Management Decisions

The Decision To Incorporate

Basic Tax Considerations

Deferral And Reduction

15-1. One of the more important decisions facing the owner of a business is deciding whether or not the business should be incorporated. There are, of course, a number of non-tax considerations involved in this decision, and these factors will be reviewed in this Chapter. At this point, however, we are concerned with the influence of corporate taxation on this decision.

15-2. The decision to incorporate, from both a legal and a tax point of view, has the effect of separating the business from its owners. This means that, in order for incorporated business income to be made available to the owner, it must go through two levels of taxation. First, the amount of Tax Payable applicable to the corporation will be determined. Then, when any after tax amounts are distributed to the owner, additional personal taxes will be payable on the amounts received.

15-3. This dual system of taxation may or may not be advantageous to the owner of the business. In terms of the types of tax advantage that can result from an individual incorporating business income, there are two possibilities:

Tax Reduction In some situations, the total taxes that would be paid at the combined corporate and personal level will be less when the business is incorporated than would be the case if the individual had earned the business income directly as an individual proprietor.

Tax Deferral As was noted in Paragraph 15-2, getting income from its source through a corporation and into the hands of a shareholder involves two levels of taxation. If the shareholder does not require all available income for his or her personal needs, after tax funds can be left in the corporation, resulting in a postponement of the second level of taxation. If the rate at which the corporation is taxed is lower than the rate at which the individual would be taxed on the direct receipt of the income, the use of a corporation provides tax deferral.

15-4.   As you probably discerned while proceeding through the earlier chapters on corporate taxation, whether the presence of a corporation will provide a deferral or reduction of taxes depends on both the type of corporation and the type of income that is being earned by that business entity. An additional important factor, as will be discussed in this Chapter, is the province in which the individual and the corporation pay income taxes.

15-5.   This means that there is no one answer to the question of whether incorporation will provide tax reduction and/or tax deferral. Because of this, we will devote a major section of this Chapter to examining the various possible combinations of income types and corporate classifications in order to provide you with a general understanding of the availability of these two tax features. This material begins in Paragraph 15-12.

Using Imperfections In The Integration System

15-6.   We have previously noted that the integration provisions that are contained in Canadian tax legislation are based on the assumption that certain corporate and personal tax rates prevail. Even at the federal level, actual corporate tax rates vary from the notional rates required for effective integration.

15-7.   In addition, there are significant variations in the corporate tax rates used by the provinces. This means that it is unlikely that the combined federal/provincial rate in any given province will be equal to the notional combined rates assumed in the integration model. As it may be possible to use incorporation to take advantage of these imperfections in the integration system, it is important for you to understand how the imperfections can influence the decision to incorporate. We will provide a section that deals with this issue later in this Chapter.

Income Splitting

15-8.   Even in situations where the use of a corporation neither reduces nor defers significant amounts of taxes for a single individual, incorporation may be attractive to a family or other related group of individuals. In a typical family situation, it is fairly common to find some individuals earning amounts far in excess of the amount required to put them in the maximum personal tax bracket while, at the same time, other members of the group have incomes that leave them in a lower bracket or free of taxes altogether.

15-9.   As was discussed in Chapter 1, if some method can be found to redistribute the aggregate family or group income from high-income to low-income individuals, the tax savings can be significant. While we did not discuss this in Chapter 1, using a corporation can be one of the most effective approaches to achieving income splitting goals. Given this, this Chapter will provide a section that deals with this possibility. You should note, however, that the Tax On Split Income (TOSI) makes using a private corporation for income splitting much more difficult. (See coverage in Chapter 11.)

Other Advantages And Disadvantages

Advantages

15-10.   Other advantages that are normally associated with the use of a corporation are as follows:

Limited Liability   Because a corporation is a separate legal entity, the shareholders' liability to creditors is limited to the amount that they have invested. That is, creditors of the corporation can look only to the assets of the corporation for satisfaction of their claims. However, for smaller corporations, obtaining significant amounts of financing will almost always require the owners to provide personal guarantees on any loans, making this advantage somewhat illusory for this type of company. Note, however, limited liability may still be important for a smaller corporation if it is exposed to significant product or environmental claims.

Lifetime Capital Gains Deduction   Individuals who dispose of the shares of a qualified small business corporation are eligible to claim the lifetime capital gains deduction ($883,384 for 2020). To qualify, a business must be a Canadian controlled private corporation with substantially all of the fair market value of its assets (at least 90 percent) used in an active business carried on primarily in Canada (at least 50 percent) at the time of disposition. In addition, no one other than the seller, or related persons, can own the shares during the 24 months preceding the sale. During this 24 month period, more than 50 percent of the fair market value of the assets must have been used in active business carried on primarily in Canada. For a more complete discussion of this provision, see Chapter 11.

Flexibility On Timing, Type, And Distribution Of Income   In the case of a corporation with a single shareholder, the owner can determine when his or her compensation will be paid and the form that it will take (e.g., salary vs. dividends). As mentioned previously, the owner may also be able to use the corporate form to split income with family members.

Foreign Taxes   Foreign estate taxes can often be avoided by placing foreign property in a Canadian corporation.

Estate Planning   A corporation can be used in estate planning, particularly with respect to freezing the asset values of an estate (see Chapter 19).

Disadvantages

15-11.   Disadvantages that are normally associated with incorporation include the following:

Use Of Losses   An individual can deduct business and unrestricted farm losses against any other source of income, including employment and property income. If the business or farm is incorporated, such losses can only be deducted against past or future corporate income. The corporation's losses belong to the corporation and cannot be used to offset income earned by the individual shareholder. This is of particular importance to operations that are just getting started, as they will frequently experience significant losses in their formative years.

Tax Credits   A corporation is not eligible for personal tax credits, such as the basic personal, tuition fee, age, pension, and disability tax credits.

Charitable Donations   Charitable donations provide the basis for a tax credit for individuals, largely at 29 or 33 percent at the federal level. In contrast, they are a deduction in calculating Taxable Income for a corporation. In general, this deduction will not be as valuable as the tax credit that an individual would receive for donations.

Additional Maintenance Costs   The legal, accounting, and other costs associated with maintaining a business operation will be significantly higher in the case of a corporation (e.g., the cost of filing a corporate tax return on an annual basis).

Winding Up Procedures   The complications associated with the termination of an incorporated business will be greater than would usually be the case with a proprietorship or partnership. In addition, there may be adverse tax effects on winding up.

We suggest you work Self Study Problems Fifteen-1 and 2 at this point.

Tax Reduction And Deferral

Approach

15-12.   As we have noted, whether the use of a corporation will result in a reduction or deferral of taxes will depend on the type of income being earned, as well as the type of corporation. In this section, we will examine this issue by using a basic example to consider this issue in the following situations:

- A public corporation.

- A CCPC earning active business income that is eligible for the small business deduction, and business and property income that is not eligible for the small business deduction.

- A CCPC earning investment income (net taxable capital gains and other property income, excluding dividends).

- A CCPC earning both eligible and non-eligible dividend income.

15-13. These cases should serve to provide you with a good understanding of the ability of incorporation to provide either tax reductions or tax deferral for an individual taxpayer under current rates of corporate taxation.

15-14. To assist you in understanding this material (which is covered in detail in Chapter 13), we remind you that eligible dividends include:

- Designated dividends paid by CCPCs with a positive General Rate Income Pool (GRIP) at the end of the taxation year in which the dividend is paid.

- Designated dividends paid by non-CCPCs that do not have a positive Low Rate Income Pool (LRIP) balance at the time the dividend is paid.

Basic Example

Data On The Individual Taxpayer

15-15. In order to consider the various results that can be achieved by incorporating a source of income, we will use a simple example in which an individual, Mr. Renaud, has access to $100,000 in income that he can either receive directly or channel through a corporation. We will assume that, before any consideration of this additional $100,000, Mr. Renaud has sufficient Taxable Income to place him in the maximum federal tax bracket of 33 percent (amounts over $214,368 for 2020). The Tax Payable on his other income is sufficient to absorb all of his personal and other tax credits.

15-16. To illustrate the effects of incorporating different types of income, several cases will be presented with varying assumptions as to the source of this income and the type of corporation that will be established. However, before turning to these cases, we will give consideration to the various personal and corporate tax rates that will be used.

Personal Tax Rates And Tax Payable

15-17. In these examples, we will assume that Mr. Renaud lives in a province where the maximum provincial tax rate on individuals is 18 percent. As all of Mr. Renaud's additional income will be subject to this maximum rate, his combined federal/provincial marginal rate will be 51 percent (33% + 18%). The 18 percent provincial rate that we are using is approximately the 2020 average for the nine provinces other than Quebec, which has a different tax system. However, it is significantly below the maximum rate of 21 percent.

15-18. This 51 percent rate is applicable to the direct receipt of income. This means that, if Mr. Renaud receives the $100,000 in income without channeling it through a corporation, taxes of $51,000 will be paid and $49,000 will be retained.

15-19. If the income is channeled through a corporation, the situation becomes more complex. Taxes must be paid at the corporate level, leaving only part of the total income available for distribution to shareholders. When this after tax amount is distributed to the shareholders, the amount of dividends received must be grossed up, with this amount providing a basis for a credit against Tax Payable. The amounts involved will depend on whether the dividends are non-eligible (e.g., paid by a CCPC out of income that has benefited from the small business deduction) or eligible (e.g., paid by a non-CCPC out of fully taxed income):

Non-Eligible Dividends   These dividends are grossed up by 15 percent and benefit from a federal dividend tax credit of 9/13 of the gross up. We will assume that Mr. Renaud lives in a province where the dividend tax credit on non-eligible dividends is 20 percent of the dividend gross up. This is just below the 2020 average for the nine provinces excluding Quebec of 21.5 percent.

Eligible Dividends   These dividends are grossed up by 38 percent and benefit from a federal dividend tax credit of 6/11 of the gross up. We will assume that Mr. Renaud lives in a province where the dividend tax credit on eligible dividends is 36 percent of the dividend gross up. This is approximately the 2020 average for the nine provinces excluding Quebec of 36.8 percent.

15-20.   Using these gross up and tax credit amounts, the rates applicable to Mr. Renaud on eligible and non-eligible dividends can be calculated as follows:

Personal Tax On Dividends	Non-Eligible Dividends	Eligible Dividends
Provincial Dividend Tax Credit	20.0%	36.0%
Dividends Received	100.0%	100.0%
Gross Up	15.0%	38.0%
Taxable Dividends	115.0%	138.0%
Times The Combined Federal/Provincial Tax Rate	51.0%	51.0%
Equals: Combined Federal/Provincial Tax Rate On Dividends Received	58.7%	70.4%
Less: Dividend Tax Credit [(9/13 + 20%)(15%)]	(13.4%)	
Less: Dividend Tax Credit [(6/11 + 36%)(38%)]		(34.4%)
Effective Personal Tax Rate On Dividends Received	45.3%	36.0%

15-21.   For use in our examples, we will round the non-eligible rate to 45 percent. For eligible dividends, we will use 36 percent.

Corporate Tax Rates

15-22.   In making the required calculations, we will use the corporate federal tax rates that apply for the 2020 calendar year. With respect to provincial rates, we will use 2.5 percent for income eligible for the small business deduction and 13.5 percent for other income. Both of these rates are close to the average rates applicable in the nine provinces excluding Quebec. When these provincial rates are added to the corresponding federal rates, the combined rates are 11.5 percent (9% + 2.5%) for income eligible for the small business deduction and 28.5 percent (15% + 13.5%) for other income. The following table provides the rates that will be used in our examples:

General Part I Tax Rate	38%
Federal Tax Abatement	10%
General Rate Reduction (GRR)	13%
Refundable Tax On Investment Income Of A CCPC (ART)	10-2/3%
Federal Small Business Deduction	19%
Provincial Tax Rates	
Income Eligible For Federal Small Business Deduction	2.5%
Income Not Eligible For Federal Small Business Deduction	13.5%
Refundable Portion Of Part I Tax On Investment Income	30-2/3%
Refundable Part IV Tax	38-1/3%

15-23. Note that the general rate reduction is not applicable to income that benefits from either the small business deduction or the M&P deduction. In addition, it is not applicable to Aggregate Investment Income of a CCPC, which attracts the 10-2/3 percent additional refundable tax (see Chapter 13).

15-24. We will apply this basic information, in a number of different situations, in order to examine the question of whether the incorporation of $100,000 in income will serve to either reduce or defer taxes for an individual taxpayer.

Public Corporation

M&P Deduction

15-25. As discussed in Chapter 12, both the M&P deduction and the GRR are at the same rate. As these two provisions cannot be used simultaneously, the effective federal tax rate will not be altered by the use of the M&P deduction. Given this, we will not give separate attention to situations where a public corporation is earning income that is eligible for the M&P deduction. Keep in mind, however, that companies will continue to make the M&P calculation in those provinces where there is a favourable provincial rate for this type of income.

General Results

15-26. With only $100,000 of income, there is no possibility that Mr. Renaud would be in a position to establish a public company. However, this case does serve to illustrate a simple calculation of corporate taxes. In addition, this same tax calculation would apply to a CCPC on amounts of active business income in excess of the CCPC's allocated annual business limit.

15-27. As discussed in Chapter 13, dividends paid by non-CCPCs, a category that includes public companies, will generally be designated as eligible. There will be situations, however, where a public corporation has an LRIP. While this raises the possibility that at least some of the dividends paid by such a company would be non-eligible, we do not feel that this situation is of sufficient importance that an illustration of the tax reduction and deferral results is warranted. It should be fairly obvious to you that for non-eligible dividends, the tax reduction results would be significantly worse than those illustrated in the following calculations:

Public Corporation

Federal Tax [(38%)($100,000)]	$38,000
Federal Tax Abatement [(10%)($100,000)]	(10,000)
General Rate Reduction [(13%)($100,000)]	(13,000)
Federal Tax Payable	$15,000
Provincial Tax Payable [(13.5%)($100,000)]	13,500
Corporate Tax Payable	$28,500
Corporate Business Income	$100,000
Corporate Tax Payable	(28,500)
Maximum Eligible Dividend Payable	$ 71,500
Personal Tax On Eligible Dividends [(36%)($71,500)]	(25,740)
Income Retained By The Individual	$ 45,760
After Tax Retention - With Corporation	$ 45,760
After Tax Retention - Without Corporation	(49,000)
Advantage (Disadvantage) With Corporation	($ 3,240)

Analysis

15-28. If the $100,000 had been received directly, $49,000 [($100,000)(1 - .51)] would be retained, an amount greater than the $45,760 that is retained when the $100,000 is flowed through a public corporation. In terms of total taxes, incorporation is clearly not desirable.

15-29. However, there is a deferral of tax on income that is left within the corporation. Taxes at the corporate level are $28,500, significantly less than the $51,000 that would be paid on the direct receipt of income. There is some question as to whether this amount of deferral would justify the payment of an additional $3,240 in taxes.

15-30. More to the point is that, in real world terms, deferral is not an issue for shareholders of publicly traded companies. In the case of private corporations with a single shareholder or a small shareholder group, these individuals can control the extent to which their corporation distributes resources. If they do not have an immediate need for funds, tax deferral can be achieved by leaving resources in their corporation.

15-31. This is not the case with large publicly traded companies. Their dividend decisions are based on a large number of factors, including corporate cash needs and the maximization of share values. The cash flow needs of individual shareholders would rarely be at the top of this list.

Integration And Eligible Dividends

15-32. The preceding example is based on the public corporation paying eligible dividends. The government's stated goal in bringing in the eligible dividends legislation was to improve integration by lowering the total corporate and personal taxes paid on income flowed through a public company. The calculations in Paragraph 15-27 make it clear that, at current corporate tax rates, this stated goal has not been achieved.

15-33. As discussed in Chapter 7, the gross up and tax credit procedures on eligible dividends are based on a notional corporate tax rate of 27.54 percent. As the combined federal/provincial rates for 2020 average 36.8 percent, which is well above the required rate for integration to be effective, corporate tax rates are not the main problem.

15-34. The problem is with the dividend tax credit rates. Effective integration requires the combined federal/provincial tax credit to be equal to the gross up. This means that, given the federal rate of 6/11, the provincial dividend tax credit would have to be 5/11 or 45.5 percent. In actual fact, most of the provincial dividend tax credit rates are below this level, ranging from a low of 19.6 percent to a high of 50.8 percent. The average, however, at 36.8 is well below the required 45.5 percent.

Exercise Fifteen - 1

Subject: Eligible Dividends And Integration

Ms. Jennifer Ashley is the owner of a number of successful CCPCs. For 2020, she has sufficient income that any additional personal income will be taxed at a combined federal/provincial rate of 45 percent. She lives in a province where the provincial tax credit on eligible dividends is equal to 47.1 percent of the gross up. Ms. Ashley has made an investment in a business venture that she anticipates will generate $100,000 of active business income during the coming year. If she retains personal ownership of this investment, she will retain $55,000 [($100,000)(1 - 45%)] after taxes. If she transfers this investment to a new private corporation, it would not be allocated any amount of the small business deduction and its income would be taxed at a combined federal/provincial rate of 26.5 percent (15% + 11.5%). She has asked your advice as to whether she should retain the investment personally or transfer it to a new corporation. Provide the information required by Ms. Ashley.

SOLUTION available in print and online Study Guide.

CCPC - Active Business Income

General Results

15-35. A CCPC can be subject to two different tax rates on its active business income. A low rate is available on up to $500,000 of income that is eligible for the small business deduction, with a higher tax rate assessed on income that is not eligible for this valuable deduction. With respect to the provinces, there is a similar dual rate system. In addition, we will have to take into consideration the fact that dividends that have been paid out of income that has benefitted from the small business deduction cannot be designated as eligible dividends.

15-36. We will continue to use the Mr. Renaud example from Paragraph 15-15 to illustrate the tax consequences of applying these two rates. While using the basic data from this example, we will consider two different cases:

Case One In Case One, we will assume that the corporate income is eligible for the small business deduction. This means that dividends that are received by Mr. Renaud will be non-eligible and subject to tax at a rate of 45 percent (see Paragraph 15-21).

Case Two In Case Two, we will assume that none of the corporate income is eligible for the small business deduction (the full amount has been allocated to an associated corporation). This means that the dividends that are received by Mr. Renaud can be designated as eligible and subject to tax at a rate of 36 percent. You will note that the results in this case are identical to those for a public corporation (see Paragraph 15-27).

Active Business Income Of CCPC	Case One SBD Deduction	Case Two No SBD
Federal Tax [(38%)($100,000)]	$ 38,000	$ 38,000
Federal Tax Abatement [(10%)($100,000)]	(10,000)	(10,000)
Small Business Deduction [(19%)($100,000)]	(19,000)	N/A
General Rate Reduction [(13%)($100,000)]	N/A	(13,000)
Federal Tax Payable	$ 9,000	$ 15,000
Provincial Tax Payable:		
At 2.5 Percent	2,500	N/A
At 13.5 Percent	N/A	13,500
Corporate Tax Payable	$ 11,500	$ 28,500
Corporate Business Income	$100,000	$ 100,000
Corporate Tax Payable	(11,500)	(28,500)
Maximum Dividend Payable	$ 88,500	$ 71,500
Personal Tax At 45 Percent (Non-Eligible)	(39,825)	N/A
Personal Tax At 36 Percent (Eligible)	N/A	(25,740)
Income Retained By The Individual	$ 48,675	$ 45,760
After Tax Retention - With Corporation	$ 48,675	$ 45,760
After Tax Retention - Without Corporation	(49,000)	(49,000)
Advantage (Disadvantage) With Corporation	($ 325)	($ 3,240)

Analysis

15-37. As can be seen in the preceding table, there is a disadvantage for income flowed through a corporation, even when that income is eligible for the small business deduction. In the absence of the small business deduction, the corporate choice results in a $3,240 disadvantage. Note that this is identical to the results found in our analysis of public corporation taxation (see Paragraph 15-27).

15-38. In both cases the use of a corporation results in deferral of taxes. In the small business deduction case the corporate taxes are only $11,500, as compared to $51,000 when the income is received directly. When this significant amount of deferral is combined with the small tax disadvantage associated with this alternative, using the corporate route when the small business deduction is available seems advantageous. Note, however, the benefit of the deferral can only be achieved if the funds are left in the corporation.

15-39. The situation is less clear when the small business deduction is not available. As corporate taxes are only $28,500, well below the $51,000 that would be paid on direct receipt of income, there is significant deferral. However, the price that is paid for this is $3,240 in extra taxes to be paid when the income is distributed by the corporation. If Mr. Renaud is in a position to leave the funds in the corporation for some length of time, it seems likely that he would find this to be a worthwhile trade-off.

15-40. A further point related to tax deferral is sometimes overlooked. Any income that is left in the corporation should not be left idle. If it is not needed in the principal activities, it is likely that it will be invested in assets that will produce investment income. If this income is taxed as investment income, the result will be prepayment of taxes at the corporate level. This will be illustrated in a later example when we look at the taxation of investment income received by a Canadian controlled private corporation.

Exercise Fifteen - 2

Subject: Incorporation Of Active Business Income

Keith Slater has an unincorporated business that he anticipates will have active business income of $126,000 for the taxation year ending December 31, 2020. He has employment income in excess of $300,000, with additional amounts subject to a provincial tax rate of 16 percent. The provincial dividend tax credit is equal to 27 percent of the dividend gross up for non-eligible dividends. Also in his province of residence, the corporate tax rate is 3 percent on income eligible for the small business deduction and 12 percent on other income. Mr. Slater has asked your advice as to whether he should incorporate this business. Advise him with respect to any tax deferral that could be available on income left in the corporation and on any tax savings that could be available if all of the income is paid out as dividends.

SOLUTION available in print and online Study Guide.

"Bonusing Down" Active Business Income

15-41. A traditional tax planning technique for owners of CCPCs that have active business income in excess of their annual business limit is to "bonus down". As our example has shown, income that is eligible for the small business deduction benefits from significant tax deferral, and only a small tax cost. In contrast, if a CCPC's Taxable Income does not benefit from the small business deduction, a tax cost is incurred. As shown in Paragraph 15-36, the after tax retention on $100,000 of income that is not eligible for the small business deduction is $3,240 less than if the income is received directly.

15-42. When it is likely that a CCPC will have Taxable Income in excess of its annual business limit ($500,000 if there are no associated companies and no applicable grinds), the simple solution is for the owner of the CCPC to pay him or herself sufficient additional salary that the corporation's Taxable Income will be reduced to the amount of income that is eligible for the small business deduction.

EXAMPLE In our example, if Mr. Renaud had a CCPC with active business income of $600,000, paying additional salary of $100,000 would result in after tax retention of $49,000 on receipt of this salary. This is, of course, $3,240 higher than the $45,760 that would be paid if the $100,000 ($600,000 - $500,000) that is not eligible for the small business deduction was taxed at the corporate level, with the residual amount being paid to Mr. Renaud as eligible dividends.

15-43.   Tax practitioners sometimes find it difficult to convince some individuals that bonusing down is a good idea. The problem is that bonusing down involves paying taxes out of the owner-manager's personal funds. It is not uncommon to encounter individuals who, even in situations where there is a clear cut tax advantage to using this procedure, will simply refuse to make the required salary payments. While this is usually not a rational decision, it appears to reflect a greater level of comfort for an owner-manager when he or she does not have to pay the taxes directly out of his or her personal assets.

Electing Out Of The Small Business Deduction

15-44.   ITA 89(11) allows a CCPC to make an election not to be a CCPC. A related provision, ITA 89(12), allows a corporation to revoke the ITA 89(11) election and return to being a CCPC. Note that the use of either of these provisions creates a deemed year end. In some circumstances, this may have adverse tax consequences (e.g., shortened loss carry forward periods).

15-45.   The good news is that making this election will allow the corporation to designate its dividends as eligible. The bad news is that it will lose the small business deduction. While there may be some situations where this election may be useful, the fact that it appears to have a significant tax cost would suggest that its application would be rare.

CCPC - Investment Income Other Than Dividends

15-46.   As was discussed in Chapter 13, the Aggregate Investment Income of a CCPC is taxed at full corporate rates. Neither the small business deduction nor the general rate reduction is available to offset these rates. In addition, there is an additional refundable tax under ITA 123.3 (the ART) equal to 10-2/3 percent of Aggregate Investment Income.

15-47.   To offset this high level of taxation, a dividend refund is available at a rate of 38-1/3 percent of dividends paid. Note, however, investment income that is eligible for a refund does not add to the corporation's GRIP balance. This means that it does not contribute to the corporation's ability to pay eligible dividends.

15-48.   Continuing our Mr. Renaud example from Paragraph 15-15, if Mr. Renaud incorporates, as it is greater than $50,000, his $100,000 in investment income would likely result in a grind of his small business limit. However, as his corporation would have no other income, this would not be relevant in this example. Given this, his after tax retention on $100,000 of investment income received by a CCPC, compared to the direct receipt of investment income, would be as follows:

Investment Income Of CCPC

Federal Tax [(38%)($100,000)]	$ 38,000
Additional Refundable Tax [(10-2/3%)($100,000)]	10,667
Federal Tax Abatement [(10%)($100,000)]	(10,000)
Federal Tax Payable	$ 38,667
Provincial Tax Payable [(13.5%)($100,000)]	13,500
Corporate Tax Payable	$ 52,167
Non-Eligible RDTOH Balance [(30-2/3%)($100,000)]	$ 30,667
Corporate Investment Income	$100,000
Corporate Tax Payable	(52,167)
Net Corporate Income Before Dividend Refund	$ 47,833
Dividend Refund (See Note)	29,734
Maximum Dividend Payable	$ 77,567
Personal Tax On Non-Eligible Dividends At 45 Percent	(34,905)
Income Retained By The Individual	$ 42,662

After Tax Retention - With Corporation	$ 42,662
After Tax Retention - Without Corporation	(49,000)
Advantage (Disadvantage) With Corporation	($ 6,338)

Note   The dividend refund is the lesser of the balance in the Non-Eligible RDTOH account ($30,667) and 38-1/3 percent of taxable dividends paid. The available cash of $47,833 would support a dividend of $77,567 ($47,833 ÷ .61667), which includes a potential dividend refund of $29,734 [(38-1/3%)($77,567)]. This is less than the balance in the Non-Eligible RDTOH, so a dividend refund of $29,734 is available, which leaves a Non-Eligible RDTOH balance of $933.

15-49.   As the corporate taxes of $52,167 exceed $51,000 that would be paid on direct receipt of the $100,000, there is no deferral of taxes through the use of a corporation. When this fact is combined with the $6,338 reduction in after tax retention, it is clear that the use of a corporation in this situation would be a bad idea.

Exercise Fifteen - 3

Subject: Incorporation Of Interest Income

David Slater has investments that he anticipates will earn interest income of $126,000 for the year ending December 31, 2020. He has employment income in excess of $300,000, with additional amounts subject to a provincial tax rate of 18 percent. The provincial dividend tax credit is equal to 27 percent of the dividend gross up for non-eligible dividends. Also in his province of residence, the corporate tax rate is 3 percent on income eligible for the small business deduction and 12 percent on other income. Mr. Slater has asked your advice as to whether he should transfer these investments to a corporation in which he would own all of the shares. Advise him with respect to any tax deferral that could be available on income left in the corporation and on any tax savings that could be available if all of the income is paid out as dividends.

SOLUTION available in print and online Study Guide.

We suggest you work Self Study Problem Fifteen-3 at this point.

CCPC - Dividend Income

Possible Sources Of Dividend Income

15-50.   A CCPC can only designate dividends as eligible to the extent that it has a balance in its GRIP. Dividend receipts that increase this balance enable the CCPC to designate its dividends as eligible. In general, dividends received by a CCPC will be subject to Part IV tax. The exception to this is if the dividend is received from a connected company that did not claim a dividend refund as a result of paying the dividend. Dividend income effects for a CCPC can be summarized as follows:

Eligible Dividends   Any dividends received (portfolio or connected company) that have been designated eligible will be added to the CCPC's GRIP balance and to the Eligible RDTOH. Non-eligible dividends have no effect on the CCPC's GRIP balance.

Portfolio Dividends   These dividends will be subject to Part IV tax regardless of whether they are eligible or non-eligible.

Connected Company Dividends   These dividends can be eligible or non-eligible and may be subject to Part IV tax depending on:

- If a dividend refund results from the dividend payment, the dividends will be subject to Part IV tax. The fact that there is a dividend refund generally means that the connected company had investment income.

- If no dividend refund results from the dividend payment, the dividends will not be subject to Part IV tax. The fact that there is no dividend refund generally means that the connected company had income that benefitted from the small business deduction.

Analysis

15-51.   Recalling that Mr. Renaud would pay taxes on:

- eligible dividends received at a rate of 36 percent (see Paragraph 15-21), his after tax retention on the direct receipt of $100,000 of these dividends would be $64,000 [($100,000)(1 - .36)], and

- non-eligible dividends received at a rate of 45 percent (see Paragraph 15-21), his after tax retention on the direct receipt of $100,000 of these dividends would be $55,000 [($100,000)(1 - .45)].

A comparison of this retention with the after tax results from using a corporation, assuming the connected company paid non-eligible dividends, would be as follows:

Dividend Income Of CCPC	Eligible Portfolio Dividends	Non-Eligible Portfolio Dividends	Connected With Refund	Connected No Refund
Corporate Dividend Income	$100,000	$100,000	$100,000	$100,000
Part IV Tax Payable At 38-1/3%	(38,333)	(38,333)	(38,333)	N/A
Net Corporate Income Before Dividend Refund	$ 61,667	$ 61,667	$ 61,667	$100,000
Dividend Refund At 38-1/3%	38,333	38,333	38,333	N/A
Maximum Dividend Payable	$100,000	$100,000	$100,000	$100,000
Personal Tax On:				
Eligible Dividends At 36%	(36,000)			
Non-Eligible Dividends At 45%	N/A	(45,000)	(45,000)	(45,000)
Income Retained By Individual	$ 64,000	$ 55,000	$ 55,000	$ 55,000
After Tax Retention:				
With Corporation	$ 64,000	$ 55,000	$ 55,000	$ 55,000
Without Corporation	(64,000)	(55,000)	(55,000)	(55,000)
Advantage (Disadvantage)	Nil	Nil	Nil	Nil

15-52.   In all cases, the dividends that can flow through to the investor total the full $100,000 that was received by the corporation. As a result, the total Tax Payable on dividends is the same whether the investment is held personally or in a corporation.

15-53.   The Part IV tax does, however, influence the conclusions on tax deferral. If the dividends are subject to Part IV tax, this 38-1/3 percent tax is higher than the 36 percent tax rate on eligible dividends received by Mr. Renaud, and less than the 45 percent tax rate applicable to non-eligible dividends. As a result, there is a prepayment of taxes on eligible dividends that are flowed through a corporation.

15-54.   The situation is different in the absence of a Part IV tax in that no taxes will be assessed on dividends received at the corporate level. This, of course, provides for a significant deferral of Tax Payable on dividends not subject to Part IV tax.

Conclusions On Tax Reductions And Deferrals

15-55. The results from the preceding cases can be summarized as follows:

	Corporate Taxes Before Dividend Refund	After Tax Retention On Flow Through
Public Corporation ($100,000 Of Income) (Paragraph 15-27):	$28,500	$45,760
CCPC ($100,000 Of Active Business Income):		
Eligible For SBD (Paragraph 15-36)	$11,500	$48,675
Not Eligible For SBD (Paragraph 15-36)	28,500	45,760
CCPC ($100,000 Of Interest Income):		
Investment Income (Paragraph 15-48)	$52,167	$42,662
CCPC ($100,000 Of Dividend Income):		
Eligible Portfolio Dividends (Paragraph 15-51)	$38,333	$64,000
Non-Eligible Portfolio Dividends (Paragraph 15-51)	38,333	55,000
Connected With Refund (Paragraph 15-51)	38,333	55,000
Connected No Refund (Paragraph 15-51)	Nil	55,000

15-56. The conclusions reached can be summarized as follows:

Tax Reduction Available As illustrated previously, Mr. Renaud is subject to taxes on the direct receipt of income, other than dividends, at a rate of 51 percent, while his rate on the direct receipt of dividends is 36 percent (eligible) or 45 percent (non-eligible). This means that his after tax retention resulting from the direct receipt of income would be:

- $49,000 On $100,000 Of Business Or Interest Income
- $64,000 On $100,000 Of Eligible Dividend Income
- $55,000 On $100,000 Of Non-Eligible Dividend Income

Comparing these amounts to those in the preceding table, there is no case where there is a reduction in taxes through the use of a corporation. The least unfavourable scenario is where a CCPC is earning active business income. In this case, the tax cost of $325 is relatively small.

When a public company is involved, the use of a corporation results in the payment of $3,240 more taxes and correspondingly less retention ($45,760 vs. $49,000). The same $3,240 shortfall results when a CCPC is earning active business income that is not eligible for the small business deduction. The situation is even worse for investment income earned by a CCPC. The shortfall here is $6,338 ($42,662 vs. $49,000).

In the case of dividend income received by a CCPC, the after tax results are the same whether the income is received directly or flowed through a corporation.

Tax Deferral Available Tax deferral occurs when income is not distributed to shareholders and taxes paid at the corporate level are less than those that would be paid if the income was received directly by the shareholder. On direct receipt of relevant amounts, Mr. Renaud would pay the following amounts in income tax:

- $51,000 On $100,000 Of Business Or Interest Income
- $36,000 On $100,000 Of Eligible Dividend Income
- $45,000 On $100,000 Of Non-Eligible Dividend Income

Comparing these amounts to the corporate tax amounts in the preceding table, we find that there is tax deferral in some, but not all, cases.

There is deferral in the case of public companies, with taxes on business or interest income of only $28,500 at the corporate level.

The worst case scenario is when a CCPC earns interest income. Corporate taxes are $52,167, as compared to $51,000 on direct receipt of income.

In the cases where Part IV tax is applicable, the $38,333 that would be required when that tax is assessed, is larger than the $36,000 that would be paid on the direct receipt of eligible dividends, but smaller than the $45,000 that would be paid on the direct receipt of non-eligible dividends.

The most significant amounts of deferral are available to a CCPC earning active business income eligible for the small business deduction, or dividend income that is not subject to Part IV tax. In the case of income eligible for the small business deduction, taxes at the corporate level are $11,500, $39,500 less than the $51,000 that would have been paid on the direct receipt of this income.

Even if a CCPC has active business income that is not eligible for the small business deduction, taxes on $100,000 of this additional income would only be $28,500, $22,500 less than the $51,000 payable on direct receipt of this amount of income.

There is also deferral in the case of dividend income when it is not subject to Part IV tax. However, for dividends to not be subject to Part IV tax, they must be received from a connected corporation that did not receive a dividend refund as a result of their payment. This would generally involve payment from a CCPC earning business income. This means that deferral would have been available at the level of the paying corporation, without the use of an additional corporation to receive the dividends.

15-57. These conclusions are based on assumed provincial personal and corporate tax rates as outlined previously. While the rates we have used are within the range of current actual rates, the use of other rates will produce different results. As these differences can be important, we will give some attention to this issue in the next section of this Chapter.

Exercise Fifteen - 4

Subject: Incorporation Of Interest And Dividend Income

One of your clients has asked your advice on whether he should transfer a group of investments to a new Canadian controlled private corporation that can be established to hold them. He anticipates that the transferred investments will have the following amounts of income during the 2020 taxation year:

Eligible Dividends On Portfolio Investments	$46,000
Non-Eligible Dividends From 100 Percent Owned Subsidiary	
(A Dividend Refund Of $29,000 Will Be Received by The Payor)	87,000
Interest Income	32,000

Although he has employment income of over $250,000, your client needs all of the income that is produced by these investments as he has newborn quintuplets. On additional amounts of income, your client is subject to a provincial tax rate of 18 percent. The provincial dividend tax credit is equal to 5/11 of the dividend gross up for eligible dividends and 4/13 of the dividend gross up on non-eligible dividends. The corporation will be subject to a provincial tax rate of 2.5 percent on income eligible for the small business deduction and 12 percent on other income. The corporation will make the maximum eligible dividend designation. Provide the requested advice and explain your conclusions.

SOLUTION available in print and online Study Guide.

Exercise Fifteen - 5

Subject: Incorporation Of Capital Gains

One of your clients has asked your advice on whether she should transfer a group of investments to a new corporation that can be established to hold them. The corporation will be a Canadian controlled private corporation and she anticipates that, during the coming year, the market value of these investments will increase by $92,000. No other income will be generated by the investments.

For the year ending December 31, 2020, your client has employment income in excess of $250,000 and will sell these investments by the end of the year to finance her trip across Canada by bicycle. None of these investments are eligible for the lifetime capital gains deduction. The corporation will be subject to a provincial tax rate of 3.5 percent on income eligible for the small business deduction and 12 percent on other income. On additional personal income, your client is subject to a provincial tax rate of 16 percent. The provincial dividend tax credit is equal to 4/13 of the dividend gross up for non-eligible dividends.

Provide the requested advice, including an explanation of your conclusions.

SOLUTIONS available in print and online Study Guide.

We suggest you work Self Study Problem Fifteen-4 at this point.

Provincial Taxes And Integration

Introduction

15-58. We have presented a number of different cases dealing with the question of whether it is better, both in terms of tax reduction and tax deferral, for an individual to receive income directly or, alternatively, channel that income through a corporation. In doing so, we have given consideration to both the type of income being earned and whether the corporation is eligible for the small business deduction on the income.

15-59. The conclusions that we reached were presented in Paragraph 15-56. We found that, while there were several cases the use of a corporation provided some degree of tax deferral, there were no scenarios that provided a reduction in taxes.

15-60. It is important to note, however, that all of our conclusions were based on calculations that used average provincial tax rates. As discussed in other Chapters of this text, there are wide variations in all of these provincial amounts. Further, these variations can provide results that are different than those summarized in Paragraphs 15-55 and 15-56. For example, if a province legislates a tax free period of time for corporations that operate within its jurisdiction, this will make the use of a corporation more attractive in that province.

15-61. This section will be concerned with how variations in provincial tax rates can influence the decision to incorporate. In doing so, we will not attempt to delineate every possible combination of rates and type of income. With 10 provinces and 3 territories, several different types of income, and various corporate, individual, and dividend tax credit rates to consider, there are literally hundreds of possible combinations. Given this, our goal will be to help you understand how changes in each of the provincial rates will act to influence conclusions on the use of a corporation for tax deferral or tax reduction purposes.

Tax Deferral

15-62.   The analysis of using a corporation to provide tax deferral is very straightforward. If the combined federal/provincial tax rate on corporations is less than the combined federal/provincial tax rate on individuals, the use of a corporation provides for deferral. Some examples of this analysis are as follows:

Alberta CCPC Earning Active Business Income   The combined federal/provincial tax rate on the corporation would be 11 percent. For an Alberta resident individual in the maximum tax bracket, the combined federal/provincial rate would be 48 percent. In this case, the use of a corporation would clearly provide deferral.

Manitoba CCPC Earning Investment Income   The combined federal/provincial tax rate on the corporation would be 50.7 percent. For a Manitoba resident individual in the maximum tax bracket, the combined federal/provincial rate would be 50.4 percent. In this case, there would be no deferral and small tax pre-payment.

British Columbia Public Corporation (or CCPC Earning Over $500,000 In Active Business Income)   The combined federal/provincial tax rate on the corporation or income would be 27 percent. For a British Columbia resident individual in the maximum tax bracket, the combined federal/provincial rate would be 49.8 percent. In this case, the use of a corporation would clearly provide deferral.

15-63.   We would remind you not to look at the deferral issue in isolation from other considerations. If the income will be distributed out of the corporation in the future, both tax deferral and tax reduction must be considered. If all of the income will be distributed immediately, tax deferral is irrelevant.

Tax Reduction

Introduction

15-64.   The question of whether a corporation can be used to reduce tax involves a more complex analysis. In looking at the after tax retention when income is received directly, only the combined federal/provincial tax rate on individuals is relevant. However, in looking at after tax retention of income that is flowed through a corporation, three factors must be considered:

1.   The combined federal/provincial tax rate on individuals.
2.   The combined federal/provincial tax rate on corporations.
3.   The combined federal/provincial dividend tax credit.

15-65.   As we will demonstrate in the next section, the first of these factors is not influential in this analysis. For any given combination of corporate tax rates and dividend tax credit rates, the conclusion on whether a corporation can be used to reduce taxes will be the same, without regard to the tax rate on individuals.

15-66.   The real determinate here is the relationship between the combined corporate tax rate and the combined dividend tax credit. As our later analysis will show, if the combined dividend tax credit exceeds the combined corporate taxes paid, the use of a corporation will reduce taxes. Alternatively, if the credit is less than the corporate taxes, direct receipt of income will be preferable.

Provincial Rates On Individuals

15-67.   Maximum combined federal/provincial tax rates on individuals range from a low of 47.5 percent in Saskatchewan to a high of 54 percent in Nova Scotia. Note, however, variations in the combined rate influence both the direct receipt of income and the amounts that are flowed through a corporation. That is, a high tax rate on individuals will reduce after tax retention on both the direct receipt of income as well as on the after tax retention of income flowed through a corporation. Correspondingly, a low tax rate on individuals will increase both types of after tax retention.

15-68. What this means is that, for any specific combination of corporate tax rate and dividend tax credit rate, the tax rate applicable to individuals will not alter the conclusion on whether the use of a corporation will serve to reduce taxes. While the amount of the advantage or disadvantage associated with the use of a corporation will vary with the tax rate on individuals, the conclusion on the ability of a corporation to reduce taxes will not. This is illustrated by the following example.

EXAMPLE A CCPC has $100,000 of active business income that will be taxed at a combined federal/provincial rate of 11.5 percent (9.0% + 2.5%). The provincial dividend tax credit on non-eligible dividends is equal to 4/13 of the gross up. We will consider two cases, the first based on the assumption that Niko Parma is taxed at a combined federal/provincial rate of 48 percent (33% federal, plus 15% provincial), the second based on the assumption that Nela Parma is taxed at a combined federal/provincial rate of 54 percent (33% federal, plus 21% provincial).

ANALYSIS If the individuals received the $100,000 directly, Niko's after tax retention would be $52,000 [($100,000)(1 - .48)] and Nela's would be $46,000 [($100,000)(1 - .54)]. The after tax retention if the income is flowed through a corporation would be as follows:

Comparison - Rates For Individuals	Niko (48%)	Nela (54%)
Corporate Income	$100,000	$100,000
Corporate Taxes At 11.5 Percent	(11,500)	(11,500)
Available For Dividends	$ 88,500	$ 88,500
Non-Eligible Dividends Received	$ 88,500	$ 88,500
Gross Up (15%)	13,275	13,275
Taxable Dividends	$101,775	$101,775
Individual Tax Rate	48%	54%
Taxes Before Dividend Tax Credit	$ 48,852	$ 54,959
Dividend Tax Credit (Equal Gross Up)	(13,275)	(13,275)
Individual Taxes	$ 35,577	$ 41,684
Dividends Received	$ 88,500	$ 88,500
Individual Taxes	(35,577)	(41,684)
After Tax Retention With Corporation	$ 52,923	$ 46,816
After Tax Retention With Corporation	$ 52,923	$ 46,816
Direct Receipt After Tax Retention	(52,000)	(46,000)
Advantage With Corporation	$ 923	$ 816

15-69. Despite using individual tax rates that vary significantly, the result is the same for both Niko and Nela. The use of a corporation provides tax reduction for both individuals. As an average corporate rate was used in this example, the saving is fairly modest. Note that the conclusion on tax reduction would be the same if a lower or higher corporate tax rate were used. However, the amount would be larger (lower rate) or smaller (higher rate).

Provincial Dividend Tax Credit And Provincial Corporate Tax Rates

15-70. As can be seen in the preceding example, the major determinate of whether the use of a corporation will provide tax reduction is the relationship between the combined federal and provincial taxes paid at the corporate level, and the combined federal/provincial dividend tax credit. As the federal components of these values do not vary, the provincial rates become the determining factor.

15-71.   The rules here can be stated fairly simply:

Favourable To Incorporation   If the combined federal/provincial dividend tax credit exceeds the combined taxes paid at the corporate level, the use of a corporation will reduce taxes and provide a higher level of after tax retention. This is sometimes referred to as over-integration.

Unfavourable To Incorporation   If the combined federal/provincial dividend tax credit is less than the combined taxes paid at the corporate level, the use of a corporation will increase taxes and reduce the amount of after tax retention. This is sometimes referred to as under-integration.

Examples - Effects Of Provincial Rates On Integration

Data

15-72.   The range of values in the nine provinces, excluding Quebec, for provincial corporate tax rates and provincial dividend tax credit rates are as follows:

Corporate Tax Rates   The provincial rates for public companies (which would also apply to CCPCs whose active business income is not eligible for the small business deduction) range from 11.6 percent to 16 percent. When these are combined with the federal rate of 15 percent, the combined rates range from 26.6 percent to 31 percent.

The provincial rates for CCPCs earning income eligible for the small business deduction range from zero percent to 6 percent. When these are combined with the federal rate of 9 percent, the combined rates range from 9 percent to 15 percent.

Dividend Tax Credit Rates   The provincial rates for eligible dividends range from 19.6 percent of the gross up to 50.8 percent of the gross up. When combined with the federal rate of 6/11 (54.5 percent) of the gross up, the combined rates range from 74.1 percent of the gross up to 105.3 percent of the gross up.

The provincial rates on non-eligible dividends range from 6 percent of the gross up to 36.6 percent. When combined with the federal rate of 9/13 (69.2 percent) of the gross up, the combined rates range from 75.2 percent to 105.8 percent of the gross up.

15-73.   The following two examples illustrate the effects of provincial corporate tax rates and provincial dividend tax credit rates on the after tax retention for individuals. They both use the following information:

EXAMPLE   The company has $100,000 in business income. The shareholders will be taxed at a combined federal/provincial rate of 45 percent. If the $100,000 of income is received directly by the individuals, they will retain $55,000 [($100,000)(1 - .45)].

Public Company Paying Eligible Dividends

15-74.   Dealing first with public companies that are paying eligible dividends, we will consider the following three alternative cases:

Perfect Integration   For a public company paying eligible dividends, perfect integration occurs when the combined federal/provincial tax rate on corporations is 27.53623 percent (for this example, we have rounded this to 27.536) and the dividend tax credit is equal to one (6/11 + 5/11).

Worst Case   Here we will use a combination of the highest corporate tax rate (31 percent) and the lowest dividend tax credit rate (74.1 percent).

Best Case   Here we will use a combination of the lowest corporate tax rate (26.6 percent) and the highest dividend tax credit rate (105.3 percent).

ANALYSIS   If the income is flowed through a corporation, the after tax retention under the three cases described would be as follows:

Public Company Eligible Dividends	Perfect Integration	Worst Case (31%/74.1%)	Best Case (26.6%/105.3%)
Corporate Income	$100,000	$100,000	$100,000
Corporate Taxes:			
At 27.536 Percent	(27,536)		
At 31 Percent (Worst)		(31,000)	
At 26.6 Percent (Best)			(26,600)
Available For Dividends	$ 72,464	$ 69,000	$ 73,400
Eligible Dividends Received	$ 72,464	$ 69,000	$ 73,400
Gross Up (38%)	27,536	26,220	27,892
Taxable Dividends	$100,000	$ 95,220	$ 101,292
Individual Tax Rate	45%	45%	45%
Taxes Before Dividend Tax Credit	$ 45,000	$ 42,849	$ 45,581
Dividend Tax Credit:			
[($27,536)(1)]	(27,536)		
[($26,220)(74.1%)] (Worst)		(19,429)	
[($27,892)(105.3%)] (Best)	N/A		(29,370)
Individual Taxes	$ 17,464	$ 23,420	$ 16,211
Eligible Dividends Received	$ 72,464	$ 69,000	$ 73,400
Individual Taxes	(17,464)	(23,420)	(16,211)
After Tax Retention With Corporation	$ 55,000	$ 45,580	$ 57,189
After Tax Retention With Corporation	$ 55,000	$ 45,580	$ 57,189
Direct Receipt After Tax Retention	(55,000)	(55,000)	(55,000)
Advantage (Disadvantage)	Nil	($ 9,420)	$ 2,189

ANALYSIS - Continued   This example clearly illustrates the influence of varying provincial rates for corporate taxes and dividend tax credits. The results range from a $9,420 reduction in after tax retention with the use of a corporation, to a $2,189 increase in after tax retention with the use of a corporation. Considering that only $100,000 of income was involved, this represents a significant difference in the results achieved through using a corporation.

CCPC Paying Non-Eligible Dividends
15-75. This example calculates the after tax retention of non-eligible dividends paid by a CCPC. We will consider the following three alternative cases:

Perfect Integration   As you may recall from earlier examples in the text, for a CCPC paying non-eligible dividends, perfect integration occurs when the combined federal/provincial tax rate on corporations is 13.043 percent and the dividend tax credit is equal to one (9/13 + 4/13).

Worst Case   Here we will use a combination of the highest corporate tax rate (15 percent) and the lowest dividend tax credit rate (75.2 percent).

Best Case   Here we will use a combination of the lowest corporate tax rate (9 percent) and the highest dividend tax credit rate (105.8 percent).

CCPC - Non-Eligible Dividends	Perfect Integration	Worst Case (15%/75.2%)	Best Case (9%/105.8%)
Corporate Income	$100,000	$100,000	$100,000
Corporate Taxes:			
At 13.043 Percent	(13,043)		
At 15 Percent (Worst)		(15,000)	
At 9 Percent (Best)			(9,000)
Available For Dividends	$ 86,957	$ 85,000	$ 91,000
Non-Eligible Dividends Received	$ 86,957	$ 85,000	$ 91,000
Gross Up (15%)	13,043	12,750	13,650
Taxable Dividends	$100,000	$ 97,750	$104,650
Individual Tax Rate	45%	45%	45%
Taxes Before Dividend Tax Credit	$ 45,000	$ 43,988	$ 47,093
Dividend Tax Credit:			
[($13,043)(1)]	(13,043)		
[($12,750)(75.2%)] (Worst)		(9,588)	
[($13,650)(105.8%)] (Best)	N/A		(14,442)
Individual Taxes	$ 31,957	$ 34,400	$ 32,651
Non-Eligible Dividends Received	$ 86,957	$ 85,000	$ 91,000
Individual Taxes	(31,957)	(34,400)	(32,651)
After Tax Retention With Corporation	$ 55,000	$ 50,600	$ 58,349
After Tax Retention With Corporation	$ 55,000	$ 50,600	$ 58,349
Direct Receipt After Tax Retention	(55,000)	(55,000)	(55,000)
Advantage (Disadvantage)	Nil	($ 4,400)	$ 3,349

ANALYSIS   The results for the best and worst cases for both eligible and non-eligible dividends can be compared as follows:

Advantage (Disadvantage) Of Using A Corporation	Eligible Dividends	Non-Eligible Dividends
Worst Case	($9,420)	($4,400)
Best Case	2,189	$3,349

In both cases the results are skewed toward the disadvantage side, particularly in the case of eligible dividends. That is, the worst case scenario has a larger negative result than the positive result that comes from the application of the best combination of corporate tax rates and dividend tax credits. This would suggest that, on the average, the effect of provincial variations in corporate tax rates and dividend tax credits do not result in a reduction in taxes when compared to the direct receipt of income.

Summary: Tax Deferral And Tax Reduction

15-76.   The preceding examples make it clear that the province in which the corporation and the individual is taxed (which may not be the same province) is a significant factor in deciding whether the use of a corporation will be advantageous. Depending on the type of corporation and the type of income, whether tax deferral is possible depends heavily on the province in which the income is taxed. In a similar fashion, the applicable combination of corporate tax rate and dividend tax credit will determine whether the use of a corporation will serve to reduce taxes.

We suggest you work Self Study Problem Fifteen-5 at this point.

Tax Free Dividends

Tax Rates On Dividends

15-77.   In this Chapter we are concerned with owner-managed businesses, and these will typically be CCPCs. In most cases, the bulk of their income will either be active business income that benefits from the small business deduction or, alternatively, investment income that qualifies the corporation for a refund of taxes paid. While such corporations may have a positive GRIP account that will allow them to pay eligible dividends, most of their dividends will be non-eligible. Given this, our analysis will focus on non-eligible dividends that are subject to the gross up of 15 percent.

15-78.   For an individual in the 33 percent federal tax bracket, subject to an 18 percent provincial tax rate on Taxable Income, and living in a province where the dividend tax credit is equal to 4/13 of the gross up on non-eligible dividends and 5/11 on eligible dividends, the combined federal/provincial rate is:

- 43.7 percent on non-eligible dividends received [(33% + 18%)(115%) - (9/13 + 4/13)(15%)],
- 32.4 percent on eligible dividends received [(33% + 18%)(138%) - (6/11 + 5/11)(38%)], and
- 25.5 percent on capital gains [(33% + 18%)(1/2)].

15-79.   The rate on non-eligible dividends is well above that applicable to eligible dividends and capital gains. However, it is well below the maximum 51 percent rate (33% + 18%) that would be applicable to most other types of income. In addition to the fact that dividends are taxed at favourable rates, the structure of the dividend tax credit system is such that a substantial amount of dividends can be received without incurring any taxation. This very desirable result will be explained and illustrated in this section on tax free dividends.

Use Of Tax Credits

Credits In General

15-80.   For 2020, every individual has a personal credit against federal Tax Payable based on $13,229 multiplied by the 15 percent rate applicable to the lowest federal tax bracket. This means that the first $13,229 of an individual's income can be received tax free.

15-81.   Extending this analysis, it can be said that, for most types of income, the amount that can be received tax free is limited to the total tax credit base amounts available to the individual. That is, for every dollar of tax credit amount, one dollar of income can be received on a tax free basis. There are two exceptions to this:

Dividends   An individual with only the basic personal credit of $1,984 [(15%)($13,229)] can receive tax free dividends more than double the $13,229 base for this credit. More specifically, such an individual can receive $28,899 in non-eligible dividends without incurring any liability for federal tax. (See the calculations in Paragraph 15-86.) Note that, depending on the amount of the provincial dividend tax credit, this amount may or may not be totally free of provincial tax.

Charitable Donations   The tax credit on amounts of charitable donations over $200 is based on 29 or 33 percent, rather than the 15 percent applicable to other credit amounts. Since the 33 percent rate is applicable if income is taxed at 33 percent, we will only consider the credit rate of 29 percent in this analysis. This means that a dollar of charitable donations in excess of $200 will allow an individual in the lowest tax bracket to receive $1.93 in tax free income. More specifically, a $1 contribution in excess of $200 is eligible for a tax credit of $0.29. This $0.29 would eliminate $0.29 of tax payable, the amount of tax that an individual in the lowest bracket would pay on $1.93 of income [(15%)($1.93) = $0.29]. This is unlikely to be an important exception in that it would be unusual for someone in the 15 percent federal tax bracket to be making significant charitable donations.

Special Rules For Dividends

15-82.   How can an individual receive such a large amount of dividends without paying federal tax? The answer lies in the dividend gross up and tax credit mechanism. For an individual in the lowest tax bracket, the increase in tax associated with one dollar of non-eligible dividends received compared to one dollar of interest income can be calculated as follows:

Tax Increase Per $1	Dividend	Interest
Cash Received	$1.0000	$1.0000
Gross Up At 15 Percent	.1500	N/A
Taxable Income	$ 1.1500	$1.0000
Federal Tax Payable At 15 Percent	$ 0.1725	$ 0.1500
Federal Dividend Tax Credit [(9/13)($0.15)]	(0.1038)	N/A
Increase In Federal Tax Payable	$0.0687	$ 0.1500

15-83.   For each dollar of non-eligible dividends received, an individual must add a taxable dividend of $1.15 ($1 + $0.15 gross up) to Taxable Income. For individuals in the lowest federal tax bracket, the federal tax on this amount will be $0.1725 [($1.15)(15%)]. However, there will be a federal credit against this tax payable equal to 9/13 of the gross up, or $0.1038 [(9/13)($0.15)]. This means that there is only a $0.0687 increase in federal tax for each one dollar increase in non-eligible dividends. This is in contrast to an increase in federal tax of $0.15 for each one dollar increase in interest income (i.e., a 15 percent rate of increase). As the preceding calculations demonstrate, dividend income uses up an individual's available tax credits at a much lower rate than most other types of income, i.e., a 6.87 percent rate.

15-84.   For example, one dollar of interest income will use up one dollar [($1.00)($.15 ÷ $.15)] of an individual's personal tax credit base of $13,229. In contrast, one dollar of non-eligible dividends received will use up only $0.458 of this base [($1.00)($.0687 ÷ $.15)]. This means that, in comparison with other types of income, a much larger amount of dividends can be received before an individual's tax credits are absorbed and taxes will have to be paid.

15-85.   The amount of dividends that can be received tax free by an individual with no other source of income is a function of the total amount of personal tax credits available and can, in fact, become a fairly large amount.

Tax Free Amounts For 2020

15-86.   For 2020, ignoring possible tax credits other than the basic personal and spousal credits, the amount of non-eligible dividends that can be received free of federal tax by a single individual and by an individual with a dependent spouse (or eligible dependant) with no other source of income is calculated in the table that follows. Note that, in the dependent spouse case, the grossed up amount of the dividends exceeds $48,535, the top of the 15 percent federal tax bracket. This means that some of this dividend will be taxed at a higher federal rate of 20.5 percent.

	Single Individual	Dependent Spouse
Non-Eligible Dividends Received	$28,899	$50,322
Gross Up Of 15 Percent	4,335	7,548
Taxable Income	$33,234	$57,870
Taxed At 15%	(30,319)	(48,535)
Taxed At 20.5%	$ Nil	$ 9,335
Federal Tax At 15%	$ 4,985	$ 7,280
Federal Tax At 20.5%	Nil	1,914
Dividend Tax Credit (9/13 Of Gross Up)	(3,001)	(5,226)
Basic Personal Credit [(15%)($13,229)]	(1,984)	(1,984)
Spousal Credit [(15%)($13,229)]	N/A	(1,984)
Federal Tax Payable	Nil	Nil

Note   While this is not relevant to our analysis in this section, you might wish to note that, with respect to eligible dividends, the tax free amount for a single individual would be $61,534, and $81,160 for an individual with a dependent spouse.

15-87.   There may or may not be provincial tax payable on the amounts in the preceding table. A number of provincial factors would have to be considered. These include the provincial tax rates, the provincial tax brackets, the provincial personal tax credit amounts, and the provincial dividend tax credit rates.

15-88.   The alternative minimum tax is not a factor in determining the amount of non-eligible dividends that can be received on a tax free basis. As the dividend tax credit is not available in the calculation of the alternative minimum tax payable, the dividend gross up is deducted in the calculation of adjusted taxable income for alternative minimum tax purposes. Given this, the $40,000 basic exemption that is provided by the alternative minimum tax legislation, combined with the $13,229 basic personal tax credit (plus the $13,229 spousal credit in the dependent spouse example), would serve to eliminate the alternative minimum tax on the tax free non-eligible dividends calculated in Paragraph 15-86. However, alternative minimum tax may be a consideration when a large amount of eligible dividends are involved. See Chapter 11 for our coverage of alternative minimum tax.

Income Splitting

Basic Concept

15-89.   In Chapter 1 we provided a very simple example of income splitting. As illustrated in that example, if an individual can find a way to share a large block of income with related parties in lower tax brackets, the result can be a significant reduction in taxes, not just in the current year, but on an ongoing basis.

15-90.   While the examples presented earlier in this Chapter suggested that there are limits on an individual's ability to reduce or defer taxes through the use of a corporation, these examples did not take into consideration that a corporation could be used to effectively implement income splitting. This possibility is further enhanced by the fact that, as discussed in the preceding section, individuals without other sources of income can receive substantial amounts of dividends without paying any taxes at the federal level.

15-91.   Note, however, income splitting only works when the Tax On Split Income (TOSI) does not apply to the recipient of the split income. The 2018 extension of the TOSI to related adults has made it much more difficult to effectively use a corporation in an income splitting strategy.

We suggest you work Self Study Problem Fifteen-6 at this point.

Shareholder Benefits Including Loans

The Owner-Manager Environment

15-92.   Much of the material in this Chapter deals with owner-managed corporations. These are typically CCPCs with either a single shareholder or a small group of shareholders. When there is a shareholder group, the group often consists of members of a single family.

15-93.   Unlike the situation with publicly traded companies, in this environment the owner-manager is subject to few constraints on the use of the corporate assets. In effect, he or she is in a position to provide significant benefits to him or herself and other related individuals.

15-94.   This situation is complicated by the fact that some things that might be considered benefits are, in fact, necessary to the operation of the business. For example, the owner-manager may need an automobile to use in carrying out the business of the corporation. If he or she provides him or herself with a $30,000 Honda, this cost would appear to be a legitimate business expense. However, if the car provided is a $450,000 Bentley, there is some question as to whether calling on clients really requires this type of vehicle.

15-95.   As was discussed in earlier Chapters, the CRA deals with potential abuses in the area of corporate ownership and leasing of vehicles by:

- restricting the corporation's ability to deduct the costs of owning or leasing vehicles; and
- assessing taxable benefits for personal use of corporate vehicles.

15-96.   Another problem area is travel costs. Most owner-managers have legitimate reasons to travel on matters related to corporate business. However, there is always the temptation of trying to find some business reason for spending a week in a luxury resort in Phoenix. In fact, there is a thriving industry that encourages such behaviour. It is not difficult to find a 30 minute seminar on human resource management that is conveniently conducted just before the ski lifts open at Whistler.

15-97.   Unlike the situation with automobiles, there are no provisions that deal specifically with travel costs. Such costs are only subject to the general constraint that requires a business purpose for their incurrence. In addition, they must be reasonable in the circumstances. Not surprisingly, there are frequent disputes in this area.

Shareholder Benefits Other Than Loans

15-98.   ITA 15(1) deals with situations where a corporation has provided a benefit to a shareholder that does not appear to have a business purpose. Examples of this type of situation would include:

- a corporation providing a shareholder with a jet for personal use;
- a corporation building a swimming pool at a shareholder's personal residence; or
- a corporation selling assets to a shareholder at prices that are substantially below fair market value.

15-99.   When any of these events occur, the shareholder is required to include the value of these benefits or appropriations in his or her income. Such amounts will not be considered dividends and, as a consequence, they will not be eligible for the dividend tax credit.

15-100.   A further point here is that, when an amount is included in a shareholder's income under ITA 15(1), IT-432R2 indicates that the corporation is not allowed to deduct the amount that has been included in the shareholder's income.

> **EXAMPLE**   A corporation provides a shareholder with a $10,000 holiday trip to Italy.
>
> **ANALYSIS**   ITA 15(1) requires the inclusion of the $10,000 cost of the trip in the shareholder's income. Despite the fact that this amount is being taxed in the hands of the shareholder, the corporation would not be able to deduct the cost of the trip.

15-101.   It would seem clear, given this non-deductibility, that corporations should avoid providing benefits that will be assessed to shareholders under ITA 15(1).

Shareholder Loans

General Rule

15-102.   ITA 15(2) is applicable when a corporation makes a loan to a shareholder or an individual connected to, or affiliated with, a shareholder. Under ITA 15(2.1), persons are connected for this purpose if they do not deal with each other at arm's length. When such loans are made, this general rule requires that the full principal amount of the loan be included in the Net Income For Tax Purposes of the recipient of the loan (the shareholder or the person connected to the shareholder) in the taxation year in which the loan is made.

15-103.   This general rule applies without regard to the amount of interest paid on the loan. Note, however, in periods subsequent to the inclusion of the principal amount of the loan in the income of the shareholder, there is no imputed interest benefit, even in cases where the loan is on an interest free basis.

15-104.   Under this general rule, the granting of the loan to a shareholder has the same tax consequences as the payment of an equivalent amount of salary to the shareholder. However, there are two important differences:

- Taxes paid on salary cannot normally be recovered by repaying the salary. In contrast, when all or part of a shareholder loan that has been included in the taxpayer's income under ITA 15(2) is repaid, the amount of the repayment can be deducted from Net Income For Tax Purposes under ITA 20(1)(j).

- Unlike salary payments, the corporation cannot deduct the loan even when the shareholder must include the loan in income. If the shareholder is going to be taxed on the principal of a loan, it is generally preferable for the corporation to pay salary, rather than to extend a loan.

Exceptions To The General Rule

15-105.   There are three exceptions to this general rule that are available to shareholders, without regard to whether or not they are also employees of the corporation. They can be described as follows:

Non-Resident Persons   ITA 15(2.2) indicates that the general rule does not apply to indebtedness between non-resident persons. This means that, if both the corporation and the shareholder receiving the loan were non-residents, the principal amount of any loan would not have to be included in income.

Loans In Ordinary Course Of Business   ITA 15(2.3) indicates that the general rule does not apply when the loan is in the ordinary course of the corporation's business. Included in this exception would be such situations as a customer, who is also a shareholder, taking advantage of an ongoing promotion by a furniture store that provides interest free loans to purchase furniture. In addition, ITA 15(2.3) notes that this would apply to loans made by a corporation that is in the business of making loans. This covers situations where, for example, an individual happens to be a shareholder of the bank that provides him or her with a personal loan.

Repayment Within One Year   ITA 15(2.6) indicates that the general rule does not apply when the loan is repaid within one year after the end of the taxation year of the lender or creditor in which the loan was made, or the indebtedness arose. If, for example, a corporation with a June 30 year end extended a $100,000 loan to a shareholder on January 1, 2020, the $100,000 would not have to be included in income if it is repaid, in full, by June 30, 2021. Any part of the balance that is unpaid on that date would, in fact, have to be included in the taxpayer's 2020 income.

A further point with respect to this exception is that IT-119R4 indicates that this exception is not available when the repayment is part of a series of loans and repayments. The primary evidence of this type of situation would be a repayment near the end of a corporate taxation year, followed by a loan for a similar amount early in the following corporate taxation year.

15-106.   Additional exceptions to the general rule requiring the principal of shareholder loans to be included in income involve situations where the shareholder is also an employee of the corporation making the loan. These exceptions are found in ITA 15(2.4) and can be described as follows:

Not Specified Employee   ITA 15(2.4)(a) indicates that loans made to a shareholder, who is an employee, are not subject to the general rule if the shareholder is not a specified employee. This exception applies without regard to the purpose of the loan. A specified employee is one who, at any time of the year, owns 10 percent or more of any class of the shares of the corporation, or who does not deal at arm's length with the corporation. For example, an arm's length employee who owns less than 1 percent of the shares purchased through stock options.

Dwelling Loans   ITA 15(2.4)(b) indicates that loans made to a shareholder, who is an employee or the spouse or common-law partner of the employee, to acquire a dwelling to live in are not subject to the general rule.

Stock Acquisition Loans   ITA 15(2.4)(c) indicates that loans made to a shareholder, who is an employee, to acquire shares in the lending corporation or a corporation related to the lending corporation are not subject to the general rule.

Motor Vehicle Loans   ITA 15(2.4)(d) indicates that loans made to a shareholder, who is an employee, to acquire a motor vehicle to be used in employment duties are not subject to the general rule.

15-107.   In order for these exceptions to apply, the following conditions must be met:

- the loan must be made to the individual because he or she is an employee, not because he or she is a shareholder [ITA 15(2.4)(e)]; and

- at the time the loan is made, bona fide arrangements must be made to repay the loan within a reasonable period of time [ITA 15(2.4)(f)].

15-108.   The first of these conditions can create significant problems for owner-managers of private corporations wishing to obtain loans from their corporations. In order to avoid having the principal amount of the loan included in Net Income For Tax Purposes, the owner-manager must demonstrate that he or she received the loan because of his or her role as an employee.

15-109.   In order to do this, the owner-manager will likely have to make similar loans available to all employees with duties similar to those of the owner-manager. That is, if the company gives the owner-manager a $100,000, low interest loan to purchase a residence, such loans would have to be made available to all employees with duties similar to those of the owner-manager. If this is not the case, the CRA is likely to conclude that the owner-manager received the loan because of his or her role as a shareholder.

15-110.   A further problem would arise if, as would not be uncommon in owner-managed situations, there are no other senior employees of the business, or no other employees at all. It is not clear in this case whether the owner-manager would be able to demonstrate that he or she received a loan in his or her capacity as an employee. However, the CRA will look at the loan practices of other similar corporations as an approach to making this determination.

Imputed Interest Benefit

15-111.   It was previously noted that, if the principal amount of a shareholder loan is included in the taxpayer's income, there is no imputed interest benefit related to a low rate or interest free loan. However, if the loan is exempted from the general inclusion in income rule by one of the exceptions described in Paragraphs 15-105 and 15-106, ITA 80.4(2) is applicable and a benefit may be assessed. The analogous benefit for employees, which was discussed in Chapter 3, is assessed under ITA 80.4(1).

EXAMPLE On July 1, 2020, Andros Ltd., a CCPC with a taxation year that ends on December 31, extends a $100,000 loan to its only shareholder, George Andros. The loan is interest free and, because it will be repaid in January 2021, the $100,000 principal amount does not have to be included in his income. Assume the prescribed rate throughout 2020 is 2 percent.

ANALYSIS For 2020, Mr. Andros will be assessed a taxable benefit under ITA 80.4(2) equal to $1,000 [(2% - Nil)($100,000)(6/12)]. In the examples in IT-421R2, "Benefits To Individuals, Corporations, And Shareholders From Loans Or Debt", interest is calculated on the basis of the number of months the loan is outstanding. While not illustrated, calculations could also be based on the number of days the loan is outstanding. We would remind you that, if the loan proceeds are invested in income producing assets, the imputed interest that is assessed on the loan will be deductible.

15-112. In the fairly common situation where the shareholder also works as an employee of the business, the benefit may be assessed under either ITA 80.4(1) or ITA 80.4(2). If the benefit is assessed under ITA 80.4(1), it will be classified as employment income. In contrast, if it is assessed under ITA 80.4(2), it will be considered property income. There are additional differences when the loan is made to assist an employee/shareholder with the purchase of a home.

15-113. In the case of a home purchase loan, for the first five years the loan is outstanding the benefit assessed to an employee under ITA 80.4(1) will use a rate no higher than the prescribed rate that prevailed when the loan was made. Should the rate go down, the employee is entitled to use the lower prescribed rate for the benefit calculation (see Chapter 3 for examples of this procedure). Alternatively, in the case of a home purchase loan to a shareholder, the ITA 80.4(2) benefit must be calculated using the actual quarterly prescribed rates that prevail over the term of the loan.

Exercise Fifteen - 6

Subject: Shareholder Loans - Car Purchase

Ms. Martha Rourke is an employee of Rourke Inc., a large private company in which her husband owns 70 percent of the outstanding shares. Ms. Rourke owns the remaining 30 percent of the shares. On July 1, 2020, she receives a $50,000 interest free loan that will be used to purchase an automobile to be used in her employment duties. The loan is to be repaid on June 30, 2024. Assume the prescribed rate for all of 2020 is 2 percent. What are the tax implications of this loan for Ms. Rourke in 2020?

Exercise Fifteen - 7

Subject: Shareholder Loans - Term Outstanding

On June 1, 2020, Generic Inc. loans $162,000 to its principal shareholder, Ms. Jan Fisk, in order to finance her gambling debts. Generic Inc. has a taxation year that ends on June 30. The loan is interest free. Assume that, during all periods, the relevant prescribed rate is 2 percent. What are the tax consequences to Ms. Fisk if the loan is repaid (1) on January 1, 2021, and (2) on December 31, 2021?

SOLUTIONS available in print and online Study Guide.

Exercise Fifteen - 8

Subject: Shareholder Loans - Home Purchase

On November, 1, 2020, Hasid Ltd. loans Mr. Aaron Hasid, the CEO and principal shareholder of the company, $123,000 in order to assist in his purchase of a principal residence. The company has a taxation year that ends on December 31. The loan does not bear interest and, during all periods, assume that the relevant prescribed rate is 2 percent. The loan is to be repaid in four equal annual instalments, the first occurring on October 31, 2021. What are the tax consequences of this loan to Mr. Hasid? State any assumptions that you have made in providing your answer.

SOLUTIONS available in print and online Study Guide.

We suggest you work Self Study Problems Fifteen-7 and 8 at this point.

Management Compensation

General Principles

Salary As The Bench Mark

15-114.   The most obvious and straightforward way to compensate managers is to pay salaries. Provided they are reasonable, the amounts are a deductible expense to the corporation. At the same time, they are fully taxable to the recipient, rendering such payments neutral in terms of tax planning. For large publicly traded corporations, where the managers are not the principal owners of the business, salary is the usual starting point in negotiating management compensation. However, for some high-income executives, stock based compensation may be of greater importance than salary.

15-115.   Even with a public corporation, however, the tax effects of various methods of compensation should not be ignored. By paying salaries, a corporation receives a deduction from Taxable Income in the year of accrual, while the recipient employee receives an equal addition to Taxable Income in the year of payment.

15-116.   Any form of compensation that creates an excess of the corporation's deductions over the employee's inclusions creates an aggregate tax savings. In addition, any form of compensation that is deductible to the corporation prior to inclusion in the income of the employee involves tax deferral. These considerations can allow for improved after tax benefits to the employee or, alternatively, a lower after tax cost to the corporation.

Tax Effective Alternatives

15-117.   Some simple examples of compensation features that can be used to defer or reduce the payment of taxes are as follows:

- **Registered Pension Plans**   Within prescribed limits, a corporation can deduct contributions to Registered Pension Plans in the year of contribution. These contributions will not become taxable to the employee until they are received as a pension benefit, resulting in an effective tax deferral arrangement. In addition to tax effectiveness, such plans can promote loyalty and reduce employee turnover.

- **Deferred Profit Sharing Plans**   In a fashion similar to Registered Pension Plans, amounts that are currently deductible to the corporation are deferred with respect to inclusion in the employee's Taxable Income. As with registered pension plans, these plans can also promote loyalty and reduce employee turnover.

- **Provision Of Private Health Care Plans**   The premiums paid by the corporation for such benefits as dental plans can be deducted in full by the corporation and will not be considered a taxable benefit to the employee.

- **Stock Options**   Stock options provide employees with an incentive to improve the performance of the enterprise. In addition, for CCPCs, taxation of any benefits resulting from the options is deferred until they are exercised or sold (for a full discussion of the deferral of stock option benefits, see Chapter 3). Further, the value of the employment benefit received is enhanced by the fact that, in general, one-half of the amount can be deducted in the calculation of Taxable Income.

  From the point of view of the corporation, evaluation of stock option compensation is more complex. Discouraging the use of options is the fact that no tax deduction is available for the granting of options. However, IFRS 2, *Share-Based Payment*, requires that the estimated value of options be charged to expense for accounting purposes when they are granted, despite the fact that the cost of issuing stock options is not deductible for tax purposes.

15-118.   Changes in tax legislation over the years have served to restrict the tax benefits associated with employee compensation. Perhaps most importantly, the rules related to taxable benefits on employer provided automobiles can be quite unfavourable, in some cases resulting in a taxable benefit that exceeds the value derived from having use of the vehicle. The rules related to employee fringe benefits and employee stock options were covered in Chapter 3. Chapter 10 contained coverage of deferred compensation plans and this Chapter included coverage of shareholder loans.

Salary Vs. Dividends

15-119.   For large public corporations, there is little point in considering the tax benefits related to salary/dividend trade-offs. The dividend policy of public corporations is normally based on considerations that extend well beyond the compensation that is provided to the management group of the company.

15-120.   In situations where the manager of the business is also an owner, such an individual is in a position to receive compensation in the form of either salary or dividends. If there are no other owners involved in the decision, the choice is completely at the discretion of the owner-manager and tax factors will generally be an important consideration in making this decision. The choice between compensation in the form of salary or in the form of dividends, the salary vs. dividend decision, is the subject of the remainder of this Chapter.

Salary Vs. Dividends For The Owner-Manager

The Basic Trade-Off

Example - Data

15-121.   To illustrate the basic trade-off that is involved in salary vs. dividend decisions, assume that Ms. Olney owns all of the shares of a corporation that has $100,000 in Taxable Income, and that she has sufficient property income from other sources to place her in the 51 percent federal/provincial tax bracket (33 percent federal rate plus 18 percent provincial rate).

15-122.   If the full $100,000 of corporate income is paid to Ms. Olney in the form of salary, it can be deducted by the corporation and will reduce the corporation's Taxable Income to nil. This means that no Part I taxes will be paid at the corporate level. However, the $100,000 will be taxed at Ms. Olney's marginal rate of 51 percent. This means that she will pay tax of $51,000 and be left with after tax funds of $49,000.

15-123.   If no salary is paid to Ms. Olney, corporate taxes will be assessed and any remaining amount, after adjustments for any refundable taxes, will be paid in dividends. This amount will be subject to personal tax and the resulting after tax cash flow to her can be determined. These amounts, which are dependent on the type of corporation and the type of income earned, were calculated earlier in this Chapter. The results of those calculations were summarized in Paragraph 15-55. You may wish to refer to this summary as you work through the remainder of this Chapter.

Analysis Of The Example

15-124.   In looking at the question of whether or not to incorporate an income source, we looked at the possibilities for both tax deferral and tax reduction through the use of a corporation. In salary vs. dividend decisions, we are not concerned with deferral. The question we need to answer here is:

> "What is the most tax effective way to have a corporation provide its owner-manager with a required amount of after tax income?"

15-125.   There is, of course, no deferral available on amounts that are to be removed from the corporation.

15-126.   In comparing Ms. Olney's $49,000 retained with the various results listed in Paragraph 15-55, in all cases flowing business or property income through a corporation resulted in lower after tax retention. Even in the case of a CCPC earning income that is eligible for the small business deduction, the after tax retention was $48,675, which is lower than the $49,000 that would be retained through direct receipt of the $100,000.

15-127.   This would suggest that, in general, salary should be used. However, the preceding analysis is based on a number of assumptions with respect to provincial tax rates on personal and corporate income. In addition, other factors, such as RRSP contributions, CPP contributions, and payroll tax costs, have been ignored. These factors will be considered in the following material.

Other Considerations

Provincial Tax Rates And Credits

15-128.   The results that were presented in Paragraph 15-55 assumed a provincial tax rate on individuals of 18 percent, a provincial dividend tax credit on non-eligible dividends equal to 20 percent of the gross up, and provincial rates on corporations for income eligible for the small business deduction and other types of income of 2.5 and 13.5 percent, respectively. While these numbers are fairly representative, they are not the only possible rates.

15-129.   In assessing the importance of these differences, you should recognize that the payment of salaries is analogous to the direct receipt of income. That is, if a corporation has $100,000 in income and pays this entire amount in salaries, there will be no corporate Tax Payable. Further, the taxes paid by the individual on the salary will be similar to the taxes that would be paid if the income were received directly. This means that the comparison of salary payments with dividends involves the same type of analysis as the comparison of the after tax retention from the direct receipt of income with the after tax retention resulting from channeling income through a corporation.

15-130.   Given this, we can discuss the effect of varying provincial tax rates on the salary vs. dividend decision by using the conclusions reached in the comparison of the direct receipt vs. flow through decisions. Direct receipt vs. flow through decisions were considered in Paragraphs 15-58 through 15-76. Applying that analysis to salary vs. dividend decisions, the following statements can be made:

> **Tax Rates For Individuals**   In the analysis contained in Paragraphs 15-67 through 15-69, we noted that higher tax rates on individuals made the use of a corporation more attractive from the point of view of deferring taxes on income retained within the corporation. Here, however, we are concerned only with amounts that will be distributed either in the form of dividends or in the form of salary and, as a consequence, tax deferral is not an issue. This means that the level of individual tax rates is not a major issue in this type of decision. This point is illustrated with the example found in Paragraph 15-68.

> **Dividend Tax Credit And Corporate Tax Rates**   For integration to work, the combined federal/provincial dividend tax credit must be equal to the combined corporate taxes paid.

- **Eligible Dividends**   For eligible dividends subject to a 38 percent gross up, this would require a combined corporate tax rate of 27.54 percent and a dividend tax credit equal to the gross up. This in turn would require a provincial corporate tax rate of 12.54 percent [27.54 - (38 - 10 - 13)] and a provincial dividend tax credit of 5/11 of the gross up (1.0 - 6/11).

- **Non-Eligible Dividends**   For non-eligible dividends (the type usually paid by a CCPC) subject to a 15 percent gross up, this would require a combined corporate tax rate of 13.043 percent and a dividend tax credit equal to the gross up. This requires a provincial corporate tax rate of 4.043 percent [13.043 - (38 - 10 - 19)] and a provincial dividend tax credit equal to 4/13 of the gross up (1.0 - 9/13).

The examples in Paragraphs 15-74 and 15-75 illustrate the results of applying the current range of values for corporate tax rates and dividend tax credit rates in all of the Canadian provinces. While these examples were designed to illustrate the desirability of using a corporation, they can also be used to evaluate salary vs. dividend decisions. As noted, paying salary is, from a tax point of view, the equivalent of direct receipt of income.

Analyzing these examples in the context of salary/dividend decisions, it is clear that, in situations where the dividend tax credit exceeds the corporate taxes paid, paying dividends will result in lower taxes than would be the case with paying salary. Similarly, when the dividend tax credit is less than the corporate taxes paid, the payment of salary, all other things being equal, will result in lower taxes.

Dividend Benefit - Income Splitting

15-131.   When a corporation is used for income splitting purposes, amounts may be distributed to individuals with little or no other source of income. As was noted in Paragraph 15-86, $28,899 in non-eligible dividends can be paid to such an individual without any federal tax liability being incurred. The fact that this is a much larger amount than can be distributed tax free in any other form clearly favours the use of dividends for distributions of corporate assets in these circumstances.

15-132.   A constraint on this approach is the Tax On Split Income (TOSI). If TOSI is applicable, amounts received by a specified individual will have all of this income subject to tax at the maximum federal rate of 33 percent. This will often make it difficult to implement an income splitting strategy involving corporate dividends.

Dividend Benefit - CNIL Reduction

15-133.   An individual's Cumulative Net Investment Loss (CNIL) is the cumulative amount by which investment expenses exceed investment income since 1987 (see Chapter 11 for an explanation of this amount, as well as the general provisions of the lifetime capital gains deduction). An individual's ability to make a deduction under the provisions of the lifetime capital gains deduction is reduced, on a dollar-for-dollar basis, by the balance in the CNIL account. This means that, if an individual contemplates selling shares of a qualified small business corporation, or an interest in a qualified farm or fishing property, sensible tax planning would suggest the elimination of any CNIL balance.

15-134.   For an individual whose income is provided by his or her owner-managed corporation, dividends can assist with this problem. The receipt of dividends reduces the CNIL by $1.15 for each $1.00 of non-eligible dividends received. In contrast, salary payments leave this balance unchanged. Another possibility, if the corporation has an amount owing to the shareholder, is to pay interest to the shareholder on the balance outstanding. This interest would also decrease any CNIL.

Salary Benefit - Earned Income For RRSP And CPP

15-135.   One of the most attractive features of the Canadian income tax system is the fact that individuals can make deductible contributions to RRSPs. Not only are the contributions deductible at the time that they are made, once inside the plan they enjoy the tremendous benefits associated with tax free compounding over what may be a period of many years. Most individuals will want to take advantage of these provisions.

15-136.   Dividends do not constitute Earned Income for the purposes of determining the maximum RRSP contributions, nor do they count as pensionable earnings on which CPP contributions can be based. As a result, if the owner-manager has no other source of Earned Income (e.g., employment income from a source other than the corporation), it will be necessary for the corporation to pay salary if the individual wishes to make RRSP and CPP contributions.

15-137.   The maximum for CPP pensionable earnings for 2020 is $58,700. In order to be eligible for the maximum CPP payments at retirement, salary of at least the maximum pensionable earnings for the year should be paid. With the 2021 RRSP limit at $27,830, if the owner-manager has no other source of Earned Income, a 2020 salary of at least $154,611 will be required to make the maximum RRSP contribution for 2021 [(18%)($154,611)= $27,830]. Note that RRSP deduction room can be carried forward, but there is no equivalent carry forward for the CPP program.

Salary Benefit - Earned Income For Child Care Costs

15-138.   If an individual is in a position to deduct child care costs, they are limited to two-thirds of earned income. Salary payments would add to this limit while dividends would not. For a detailed discussion of the deductibility of child care costs, see Chapter 9.

Salary Benefit - Corporate Tax Savings Carry Over

15-139.   In a particular year, an owner-manager may wish to withdraw amounts in excess of the earnings of the corporation. If this happens, there will be no current tax savings associated with the payment of salaries, a fact that would tend to make the payment of such amounts less attractive.

15-140.   However, payment of salaries in this situation would serve to create a loss carry over and, if we assume that the loss carry over can be used in some past or future year, the corporate tax savings associated with the payment of salaries would not be lost. The savings, however, will be deferred in the case of a carry forward and this means that, to properly evaluate the payment of salaries in this situation, consideration would have to be given to the time value of money.

Salary Cost (Possible) - Provincial Payroll Taxes

15-141.   With respect to provincial payroll taxes, five provinces and two territories assess such taxes. A summary of the various rates are as follows:

British Columbia   (Employer Health Tax) No tax on the first $500,000 of payroll. Excess is taxed at up to 1.95 percent with the maximum rate of 1.95 percent applied to total payroll of $1.5 million or more.

Ontario   (Employer Health Tax) No tax on the first $490,000 of payroll. Excess is taxed at up to a maximum of 1.95 percent

Manitoba   (Health And Post-Secondary Education Levy) No tax on the first $1.25 million of payroll. Excess is taxed 4.3 percent.

Newfoundland/Labrador   (Health And Post-Secondary Education Levy) No tax on the first $1.3 million of payroll. Excess is taxed at a rate of 2 percent.

Quebec   (Health Services Fund) Quebec has a complex system that includes exemptions for certain employers. When applicable the tax rate ranges from 1.65 percent to 4.26 percent of payroll.

Territories   (Payroll Tax) Nunavut and the Northwest Territories tax all payroll at a rate of 2 percent. This tax is employee paid, unlike the employer paid preceding payroll taxes listed. There is no payroll tax in the Yukon.

Salary Costs - CPP And EI

15-142.   In our example from Paragraph 15-121, we ignored the fact that salaries cannot be paid without contributions being made to the CPP. In addition, some provinces levy a payroll tax on salaries and wages as described in the preceding paragraph. These costs can constitute a significant reduction in the after tax cash flow associated with the payment of salaries.

15-143.   With respect to CPP contributions, 2020 employee contributions are based on 5.25 percent of $58,700 (maximum pensionable earnings), less a basic exemption of $3,500. This results in a maximum employee contribution for 2020 of $2,898. The employer is required to withhold and remit this contribution from salary paid and contribute an amount that is equal to the employee's contribution. This brings the total CPP cost of paying salaries of $58,700 or more to $5,796.

15-144.   As covered in Chapter 4, if an individual pays more CPP contributions than is required, perhaps because he or she has changed employers, he or she is refunded the excess through his or her tax return. Form PD24, Application for a Refund of Overdeducted CPP Contributions or EI Premiums, provides a way for employers who have made excess contributions for an employee to recover the excess.

15-145.   If an owner-manager owns more than 40 percent of the voting shares of the corporation, he or she cannot participate in the Employment Insurance (EI) program. While generally not relevant in the situations covered here, an employee's maximum EI premium for 2020 is 1.58 percent of $54,200 (maximum insurable earnings), with no exemption, an amount of $856. The employer must contribute 1.4 times the employee's premium, an amount of $1,198. This results in a total cost of $2,054 for an employee with maximum insurable earnings in excess of $54,200.

Salary Benefit - CPP And Canada Employment Tax Credits

15-146.   While CPP is an added cost of choosing the salary alternative, the payment of these costs provides a benefit to the individual in the form of future CPP benefit payments, as well as a benefit from the CPP tax credit. You will recall from Chapter 4 that this credit is equal to 15 percent of the basic payment . This provides a maximum credit of $410 on the payment of the 2020 basic CPP amount of $2,732 [(4.95%)($58,700 - $3,500)]. Note that this would not be a consideration if the individual has other sources of income that required the payment of maximum CPP.

> **NOTE**   We would remind you that, as of 2020, the amount of CPP paid by an employee is different from the base for that taxpayer's tax credit. While an employee's contribution for 2020 is $2,898, the base for the credit is only $2,732. The difference of $166 is a deduction in the determination of Net Income For Tax Purposes. If you do not understand this, please review this subject in Chapter 4.

15-147.   A further benefit of paying salary is the Canada employment credit of $187 [(15%) ($1,245)] for 2020. Unless the individual has other sources of employment income in excess of the base amount for this credit, the Canada Employment credit is only available on the payment of salary by the corporation.

Example Extended

15-148.   Returning to our example of Ms. Olney from Paragraph 15-121, as the owner of 100 percent of the shares of the corporation, she is not eligible to participate in the EI program. In addition, assume the province in which she lives assesses a 2 percent payroll tax to finance its health care program and provides a provincial credit for CPP contributions at a 6 percent rate. Her corporation is a Canadian controlled private corporation and all of its $100,000 in income is eligible for the small business deduction. Given this income and the costs associated with paying salary, the maximum salary that could be paid to Ms. Olney would be $95,198, a figure that would result in no corporate Tax Payable.

Pre-Tax Corporate Income	$ 100,000
Employer's CPP Contribution	(2,898)
Gross Salary [($100,000 - $2,898) ÷ 1.02]	(95,198)
Payroll Tax [(2%)($95,198)]	(1,904)
Corporate Taxable Income	Nil

15-149.   If $95,198 is paid to Ms. Olney as salary, her personal taxes are as follows:

Combined Tax Before Credits	
[(33% + 18%)($95,198 - $166 Deductible CPP)]	$ 48,466
Credit For Employee's CPP Contribution	
[(15% + 6%)($2,732)]*	(574)
Canada Employment Credit [(15%)($1,245)]	(187)
Personal Tax Payable	$ 47,705

*We have assumed that Ms. Olney has sufficient property income to place her in the maximum federal tax bracket. This income would absorb other tax credits and, as a consequence, only the CPP and Canada employment credits that result from the payment of salary are included in this analysis.

15-150.   With this amount of taxes payable, Ms. Olney's after tax retention would be calculated as follows:

Salary Received	$ 95,198
Employee's CPP Contribution - Maximum	(2,898)
Personal Tax Payable	(47,705)
After Tax Cash Retained	$ 44,595

15-151.   This more realistic result provides considerably less cash than the $49,000 [($100,000) (1 - 0.51)] that was left when CPP, payroll taxes, and the Canada employment credit are ignored. Note, however, while they would not be easy to quantify, the payment of CPP does provide the owner-manager with future benefits. Using the numbers in Paragraph 15-55, this makes payment of salary, if these additional factors are considered, less desirable than dividends paid out of:

- income eligible for the small business deduction (retention was $48,675),
- business income ineligible for the small business deduction (retention was $45,760).

Exercise Fifteen - 9

Subject: Salary And Dividend Compensation

For the year ending December 31, 2020, Broadmoor Inc., a Canadian controlled private corporation has Taxable Income, before consideration of dividends or salary paid to its sole shareholder, of $550,000. All of this income is from active business activities. The cash balance of the company, prior to any payments on the current year's taxes, is also equal to this amount. The company makes the maximum eligible dividend designation each year. Its only shareholder, Ms. Sarah Broad, has no income other than dividends or salary paid by the corporation and has combined federal/provincial personal tax credits of $5,000.

In her province of residence, assume:

- the corporate tax rate is 3 percent on income eligible for the small business deduction and 14 percent on other income
- her combined federal/provincial Tax Payable totals $75,000 on the first $214,368 with additional amounts of income taxed at a combined federal/provincial rate of 51 percent

- the dividend tax credit is 30 percent of the gross up for all dividends
- there is no payroll tax

Determine the amount of after tax cash that Ms. Broad will retain if (1) the maximum salary is paid by the corporation out of the available cash of $550,000 and (2) the maximum amount of eligible and non-eligible dividends are paid. Ignore the required CPP contributions and the Canada employment tax credit.

> **SOLUTION available in print and online Study Guide.**

Use Of Tax Credits

15-152. Our example in this section has involved an individual with other sources of income that placed her in the maximum federal tax bracket. This amount of income would generally be sufficient to absorb any tax credits available to the individual. However, there may be situations where a salary vs. dividend decision is being made with respect to an individual with no other source of income. This would be a fairly common situation when a corporation is being used for income splitting purposes, or for a corporation with only a limited amount of income to distribute.

15-153. If the individual has no other source of income and provincial tax rates favour the use of dividends, there may be a problem with the full use of available tax credits. We noted earlier in this Chapter that dividend payments use up tax credits at a much lower rate than other types of income, such as salary. If only limited amounts of income are being distributed, the use of dividends may leave a portion of the individual's tax credits unused. When this is the case, some combination of salary and dividends may provide the optimum solution.

15-154. A further potential complication stems from the fact that provincial tax credits can only be deducted against the provincial tax liability and federal tax credits can only be deducted against the federal tax liability. In our examples and problems we have not taken this into consideration and have given a single figure for combined federal/provincial tax credits.

15-155. In the real world, it would be possible to have a situation where an individual would have to pay some federal tax in order to use up all of his or her provincial tax credits, or alternatively, pay some provincial tax in order to use up all of his or her federal tax credits. Given this text's focus on federal income taxes, no further attention will be given to this complication of the issue.

15-156. The following example illustrates the salary vs. dividend issue when the full utilization of tax credits is a consideration.

> **EXAMPLE** Mr. Eric Swenson is the sole shareholder of Swenson Sweets, a Canadian controlled private corporation. The company has a December 31 year end and, for 2020, it has Taxable Income, before consideration of salary or dividends to Mr. Swenson, of $29,500, all of which results from active business activities. This amount is available in cash, prior to the payment of any salary or dividends. Mr. Swenson has combined federal/provincial personal tax credits of $3,920.
>
> The corporation operates in a province with a corporate tax rate on active business income of a CCPC of 3 percent and no payroll taxes. The provincial tax rate on personal income is 10 percent of the first $48,535 of Taxable Income, with a provincial dividend tax credit on non-eligible dividends that is equal to 4/13 of the gross up. In solving this problem, we will ignore CPP contributions and the Canada employment tax credit.

15-157. If the full $29,500 is paid out in salary, corporate Taxable Income would be nil and there would be no corporate tax payable. Mr. Swenson's after tax cash retention would be as follows:

Salary Vs. Dividends For The Owner-Manager

Salary Received		$29,500
Personal Tax Payable		
Personal Taxes At 25% (15% + 10%)	($7,375)	
Personal Tax Credits (Given)	3,920	(3,455)
After Tax Cash Retained (All Salary)		$26,045

15-158. As dividends are not tax deductible, corporate tax must be paid prior to any dividend distribution. The combined federal/provincial tax rate would be 12 percent (38% - 10% - 19% + 3%), resulting in corporate taxes of $3,540 [(12%)($29,500)]. This means that the maximum dividend that can be paid will be $25,960 ($29,500 - $3,540). The after tax retention in this case is as follows:

Non-Eligible Dividends Received	$25,960
Gross Up Of 15%	3,894
Taxable Dividends	$29,854
Personal Tax Rate	25%
Personal Tax Payable Before Tax Credits	$ 7,464
Personal Tax Credits (Given)	(3,920)
Dividend Tax Credit [(9/13 + 4/13)($3,894)]	(3,894)
Tax Payable ($350 In Unused Credits)	Nil

Non-Eligible Dividends Received	$25,960
Personal Taxes (See Paragraph 15-86	
- No Taxes Would Be Paid On This Amount)	Nil
After Tax Cash Retained (All Dividends)	$25,960

15-159. While the low federal/provincial tax rate on corporations suggests that dividends should be the best alternative, the preceding results do not confirm this view. The problem is that dividend income absorbs available tax credits at a much lower rate than other types of income. The fact that the all dividend solution leaves $350 of unused tax credits suggests that a better solution might be to pay a lesser amount of dividends plus sufficient salary to absorb these unused credits.

15-160. To investigate this possibility, we need to determine the salary/dividend mix that will fully utilize all of Mr. Swenson's credits. To begin, consider what would happen when we add a $1,000 salary payment to the all dividends case. As the salary will be fully deductible, the after tax cost of making this payment is $880 [($1,000)(1.0 - 0.12)]. As a result, in this type of situation, where the goal is to distribute all of the available corporate income, dividends will only have to be reduced by this $880 per $1,000 of salary increase.

15-161. The resulting increase in taxes payable can be calculated as follows:

Increase In Salary		$1,000.00
Decrease In Dividends	(	880.00)
Decrease In Dividend Gross Up [(15%)($880)]	(	132.00)
Decrease In Taxable Income	($	12.00)
Personal Tax Rate		25%
Decrease In Tax Payable Before Dividend Tax Credit	($	3.00)
Decrease In Dividend Tax Credit		
= Increase In Tax Payable [(9/13 + 4/13)($132)]		132.00
Net Increase In Personal Tax Payable	$	129.00

15-162. This analysis demonstrates that each $1,000 increase in salary results in an increase in personal Tax Payable of $129. Alternatively, this can be stated as an increase in personal Tax

Payable of $0.129 for every dollar of increase in salary. This means that to utilize Mr. Swenson's $350 in unused tax credits, he will have to receive salary of $2,713 ($350 ÷ 0.129). This results in the following amount being available for dividends:

Corporate Taxable Income Pre-Salary	$29,500
Salary	(2,713)
Corporate Taxable Income	$ 26,787
Corporate Tax At 12%	(3,214)
Available For Dividends	$23,573

15-163.   When this dividend is paid out to Mr. Swenson, his after tax retention is as follows:

Non-Eligible Dividends Received	$23,573
Gross Up Of 15%	3,536
Taxable Dividends	$ 27,109
Salary	2,713
Taxable Income	$29,822
Personal Tax Rate	25%
Personal Tax Payable Before Tax Credits	$ 7,456
Personal Tax Credits (Given)	(3,920)
Dividend Tax Credit [(9/13 + 4/13)($3,536)]	(3,536)
Personal Tax Payable (Salary And Dividends)	Nil

Comparison	All Salary	All Dividends	Salary And Dividends
Non-Eligible Dividends Received	N/A	$25,960	$23,573
Salary Received	$29,500	N/A	2,713
Personal Tax Payable	(3,455)	Nil	Nil
After Tax Cash Retained	$26,045	$25,960	$26,286

15-164.   As shown in the preceding calculations, this mix of salary and dividends is such that it utilizes all of Mr. Swenson's tax credits and leaves Tax Payable of nil. This results in a solution that not only improves on the $25,960 that was retained in the all dividend scenario, it also improves on the $26,045 that was retained in the all salary case. It would appear to be the optimum solution for this example where only tax effects are considered.

Optimizing A Limited Payment Of Cash

15-165.   A similar analysis could be done if the corporation had limited cash. Assume that, while the corporation in the example (Paragraph 15-156) had Taxable Income of $29,500, it had only $16,000 in cash. To determine the maximum salary that can be paid (X), it is necessary to solve the following equation:

$$X = \$16,000 - [(12\%)(\$29,500 - X)]$$

$$X - 0.12X = [(\$16,000 - (12\%)(\$29,500) = \$14,159$$

15-166.   Based on this amount of salary, the amount of after tax cash retained would be calculated as follows:

Corporate Cash Before Taxes	$ 16,000
Corporate Taxes [(12%)($29,500 - $14,159)]	(1,841)
Corporate Cash Available For Salary	$ 14,159

Salary Received		$14,159
Personal Tax Payable:		
Personal Tax On Salary [(25%)(14,159)]	($3,540)	
Personal Tax Credits (Given)	3,920	Nil
After Tax Cash Retained ($380 In Unused Credits)		$14,159

15-167. Alternatively, if maximum dividends are paid, the amount of after tax cash retained would be calculated as follows:

Corporate Cash Before Taxes	$16,000
Corporate Taxes [(12%)($29,500)]	(3,540)
Corporate Cash Available For Dividends	$12,460

Non-Eligible Dividend Received	$12,460
Personal Taxes (See Paragraph 15-86 - No Taxes Would Be Paid)	Nil
After Tax Cash Retained	$12,460

15-168.   It is clear that the salary approach results in a considerably larger after tax retention than the dividend approach. This result would be expected given that the corporate cash was insufficient to utilize the personal tax credits in either approach.

Exercise Fifteen - 10

Subject: Salary vs. Dividends

For the year ending December 31, 2020, Mortell Inc., a Canadian controlled private corporation, has Taxable Income, before consideration of dividends or salary paid to its sole shareholder, of $198,000. The company's cash balance is over $200,000. It is subject to a combined federal/provincial tax rate of 12 percent. Ms. Mortell, the company's only shareholder, has employment income of $150,000 and, under normal circumstances, does not make withdrawals from the corporation. However, she needs an additional $30,000 in cash to create the home theatre of her dreams. Ms. Mortell's combined federal/provincial tax rate on additional income is 45 percent. She lives in a province where the provincial dividend tax credit is equal to 25 percent of the dividend gross up for non-eligible dividends. She has asked your advice as to whether the payment of salary or, alternatively, the payment of non-eligible dividends would have the lowest tax cost. Provide the requested advice.

Exercise Fifteen - 11

Subject: Salary vs. Dividends - Limited Corporate Cash

For the year ending December 31, 2020, Fargo Ltd. has Taxable Income, before consideration of dividends or salary paid to its sole shareholder, of $21,500. The company's cash balance prior to the payment of any taxes for the year is $18,500. The company's Taxable Income is subject to a combined federal/provincial tax rate of 12 percent. There is no payroll tax in this province.

Mr. Fargo, the company's president and sole shareholder, is 71 years of age and has no other source of income (he is not eligible for OAS). He has combined federal/provincial personal tax credits of $3,950 and lives in a province that has a personal tax rate on the first $48,535 of Taxable Income equal to 10 percent. The provincial dividend tax credit is 30 percent of the gross up for non-eligible dividends.

Mr. Fargo would like to remove all of the cash from the corporation and has asked your advice as to whether it would be better to take it out in the form of all non-eligible dividends or all salary. As Mr. Fargo is over 70 years old, no CPP contributions are required. Ignore the Canada employment tax credit. Provide the requested advice.

SOLUTIONS available in print and online Study Guide.

Conclusion

15-169. As the preceding discussion makes clear, the salary vs. dividend decision is complex. Determination of the total tax consequences of the two alternatives does not necessarily resolve the issue. In addition to important factors already discussed in the chapter such as income splitting and bonusing down, consideration should be given to:

- the administrative costs related to withholding and remitting income tax and CPP premiums when salary is paid
- the ability to defer personal taxation to the subsequent calendar year if the payment of salary is deferred and the corporation's year end is within 180 days of December 31
- the effect of the gross up on dividends if the OAS clawback is relevant
- if the owner-manager is applying for a mortgage or loan, it will be more advantageous to have a history of salary received rather than dividends received

15-170. The preceding material does not give you a comprehensive approach to solving these problems on a quantitative basis. In actual fact, there are problems here that are probably not subject to quantitative solutions. For example, whether or not an individual feels a need for retirement income involves many subjective considerations. With an issue such as this, a tax advisor can only outline the various possible outcomes.

We suggest you work Self Study Problems Fifteen-9 to 11 at this point.

Additional Supplementary Self Study Problems Are Available Online.

Key Terms Used In This Chapter

15-171. The following is a list of the key terms used in this Chapter. These terms, and their meanings, are compiled in the Glossary located at the back of the Study Guide.

Active Business Income	Low Rate Income Pool (LRIP)
Aggregate Investment Income	Manufacturing And Processing
Annual Business Limit	Profits Deduction (M&P Deduction)
Bonusing Down	Over-Integration
Canadian Controlled Private Corporation	Private Corporation
Charitable Donations Tax Credit	Public Corporation
Eligible Dividends	Specified Employee
Estate Planning	Tax Avoidance
General Rate Income Pool (GRIP)	Tax Deferral
Income Splitting	Tax Planning
Integration	Taxable Benefit
Lifetime Capital Gains Deduction	TOSI (Tax On Split Income)
Limited Liability	Under-Integration

References

15-172. For more detailed study of the material in this Chapter, we refer you to the following:

ITA 6(1)	Amounts To Be Included As Income From Office Or Employment
ITA 15(1)	Benefit Conferred On Shareholder
ITA 15(2)	Shareholder Debt
ITA 18(1)	General Limitations (On Deductions)
ITA 20(1)(j)	Repayment Of Loan By Shareholder
ITA 67	General Limitation Re Expenses
ITA 80.4	Loans - Imputed Interest
ITA 80.5	Deemed Interest
ITA 82(1)	Taxable Dividends Received
ITA 121	Deduction For Taxable Dividends
ITA 123 To 125.5	Rules Applicable To Corporations
ITA 146	Registered Retirement Savings Plans
ITA 147	Deferred Profit Sharing Plans
S3-F6-C1	Interest Deductibility
IT-67R3	Taxable Dividends From Corporations Resident In Canada
IT-119R4	Debts Of Shareholders And Certain Persons Connected With Shareholders
IT-124R6	Contributions To Registered Retirement Savings Plans
IT-307R4	Spouse Or Common-Law Partner Registered Retirement Savings Plans
IT-421R2	Benefits To Individuals, Corporations, And Shareholders From Loans Or Debt
IT-432R2	Benefits Conferred On Shareholders
IT-487	General Limitation On Deduction Of Outlays Or Expenses

Problems For Self Study (Online)

To provide practice in problem solving, there are Self Study and Supplementary Self Study problems available on MyLab Accounting.

Within the text we have provided an indication of when it would be appropriate to work each Self Study problem. The detailed solutions for Self Study problems can be found in the print and online Study Guide.

We provide the Supplementary Self Study problems for those who would like additional practice in problem solving. The detailed solutions for the Supplementary Self Study problems are available online, not in the Study Guide.

The .PDF file "Self Study Problems for Volume 2" on MyLab contains the following for Chapter 15:

- 11 Self Study problems,
- 5 Supplementary Self Study problems, and
- detailed solutions for the Supplementary Self Study problems.

Assignment Problems

(The solutions for these problems are only available in
the solutions manual that has been provided to your instructor.)

Assignment Problem Fifteen - 1
(Advantages Of Incorporation)

Philip Caron is in his mid-fifties and he is married with two teenaged children. For over 15 years
he has worked as an unincorporated welder. The business is currently netting approximately
$250,000 per year. In recent years, Mr. Caron has been using about half of the business earnings
for personal living expenses.

In the last five years, he has been refining a fork lift that can be attached to half-ton trucks. He
has a product that is selling well with few malfunctions, and he is in the process of patenting
the design. As a result, his welding business is now predominantly manufacturing these fork
lift units.

Some of his welding equipment is old and he is faced with the need to replace it. Also, he
needs to acquire larger welders and pipe benders to mass manufacture the fork lift. The business expansion will require substantial capital investment for which external financing will be
required.

Required: Briefly discuss whether Mr. Caron should incorporate his business.

Assignment Problem Fifteen - 2
(Example Of Integration)

One of your longstanding clients, Mr. Carson Jones, has operated a successful unincorporated
business for 10 years. This business is something of a sideline for him in that he has employment and investment income of over $250,000 per year. Further, these latter sources of income
are more than adequate to meet his personal needs and absorb all of his available tax credits.

However, he has an intense dislike for paying taxes, particularly since the government has
increased the top federal tax rate to a near obscene (in his opinion) 33 percent. When this maximum federal rate is combined with the top rate of 20 percent in his province, the result is an
overall rate of 53 percent.

Given this, he is looking for ways to save taxes. One approach that he would like to consider is
transferring the income from his business, as well as a group of publicly traded securities, to a
new corporation. The new corporation would be named Carjon Ltd.

He has asked your advice on this approach and, to assist you in providing this advice, he has
provided you with the following relevant data:

Taxable Income of business (Active Business Income)	$115,000
Eligible portfolio dividends	133,000
Federal corporate tax rate after federal abatement	28%
Federal Small Business Deduction	19%
General Rate Reduction	13%
Provincial rate on Active Business Income of CCPCs	2%
Provincial dividend tax credits on:	
Eligible dividends	40% of dividend gross up
Non-eligible dividends	23% of dividend gross up

Required:

A. Assume no corporation is used and the income is received directly. Calculate Carson's personal Tax Payable, showing separately the Tax Payable on the active business income and the dividends.

B. Assume the income and dividends are received by Carjon Ltd. Calculate corporate Tax Payable, after tax income available for distribution, and personal taxes that would be payable on the distribution. Your calculations should show separately the Tax Payable on the active business income and any eligible or non-eligible dividends.

C. Compare the Tax Payable with and without the use of Carjon Ltd. and explain why the Tax Payable amounts are different. Advise Carson as to whether he should make the proposed transfers to a new corporation.

Assignment Problem Fifteen - 3
(Flow Through Of Interest Income)

As an employee of a public company, Maxine Ashley has an annual salary of $155,000.

After years of purchasing losing tickets, Maxine wins $500,000 in the provincial lottery. As her employment income is more than adequate for her current needs, she plans to invest all of these winnings in a debt security for the year ending December 31, 2020. The security pays annual interest at a rate of 5 percent.

The following information is applicable to the province in which Maxine is a resident:

- The provincial marginal tax rate for Maxine is 13 percent.
- The provincial dividend tax credit on non-eligible dividends is 28 percent of the gross up.
- The provincial tax rate on the investment income of CCPCs is 12 percent.

Other than the interest earned on her investment in the debt security, Maxine has no other source of investment income.

Required: Prepare calculations that will compare the after tax retention of income that will accrue to Maxine for 2020 if:

A. The investment is owned by her as an individual.

B. The investment is owned by a CCPC in which she is the sole shareholder and which pays out all available income in dividends.

Assignment Problem Fifteen - 4
(Flow Through Of Dividend Income)

As an employee of a public company, Thomas Nance has an annual salary of $300,000.

After years of purchasing losing tickets, Thomas wins $650,000 in the provincial lottery. As his employment income is more than adequate for his current needs, he plans to invest all of these winnings in public company preferred shares for the year ending December 31, 2020. These securities pay eligible dividends of 6 percent each year.

The following information is applicable to the province in which Thomas is a resident:

- The provincial marginal tax rate for Thomas is 19 percent.
- The provincial dividend tax credit on eligible dividends is 22 percent of the gross up.
- The provincial tax rate on the investment income of CCPCs is 11 percent.

Other than the preferred share dividends, Thomas has no other source of investment income.

Required: Prepare calculations that will compare the after tax retention of income that will accrue to Thomas in 2020 if:

A. The investment is owned by him as an individual.

B. The investment is owned by a CCPC in which he is the sole shareholder and which pays out all available income in eligible dividends.

Assignment Problem Fifteen - 5
(Incorporation Of Investment Income)

The following information provides tax information for the province in which Jason Tegue lives for 2020:

- The combined federal and provincial corporate tax rate on the investment income of CCPCs is 50-2/3 percent (including the ART).

- The provincial dividend tax credit on eligible dividends is equal to 40 percent of the gross up on these dividends.

- The provincial dividend tax credit on non-eligible dividends is equal to 30 percent of the gross up on these dividends.

- Provincial tax payable on an individual's first $97,069 of Taxable Income is $12,817. Amounts in excess of this are subject to provincial tax at a rate of 17.4 percent.

Jason owns the following investments and anticipates the following Canadian source income for 2020:

	Value At 31/12/2019	Type Of Income	Expected Income For 2020
Powor Corp Bonds	$ 78,000	Interest	$ 8,600
Larch Company Shares	312,000	Dividends	17,400
Inbridge Inc. Shares	36,000	Capital Gains	6,200
Calgary Dominion Bank Shares	38,000	Dividends	3,600
Calgary Dominion Bank Shares		Capital Gains	2,800
Totals	$464,000	N/A	$38,600

Jason only invests in the shares and debt of large, publicly traded companies. He does not own more than 1 percent of the shares or debt in any of these corporations. All of the dividends received were designated as eligible by the paying corporation.

In 2020, in addition to the above investment income, Jason expects to earn $92,000 in employment income. He has combined federal/provincial personal tax credits of $3,491. The total adjusted cost base for his investments is $450,000.

Jason asks you whether it is financially more attractive for him to have his investments owned by a corporation or to own them directly, as he currently does. Assume that he and his investments will generate the anticipated amounts of income.

Jason's lifestyle requires him to use all available income. As a consequence, he would like you to assume that, if the investments are transferred to his corporation, the corporation will pay out all available funds as dividends.

Required: Provide an appropriate analysis for Jason Tegue.

Assignment Problem Fifteen - 6
(Partner As Individual Or Corporation)

Having worked as an individual management consultant, Mellisa Fox has enjoyed a great deal of success. Her effectiveness has generated a fairly long list of potential clients who would like to use her services. Recognizing the opportunities involved in this situation, Mellisa has decided to join Consulting Unlimited (CU) as a fourth partner.

Her entrance into the partnership will be effective January 1, 2020. She is giving consideration to three different approaches, the first two of which require the establishment of a new Canadian controlled private corporation (CCPC) in which she will be the sole shareholder. If she adopts one of these alternatives, the other partners in CU have agreed to allocate 25 percent ($125,000) of the small business deduction annual limit to her corporation.

> **Alternative 1** Her new corporation will pay corporate tax on its full share of the partnership income, with the after tax funds being paid to Mellisa as dividends.

> **Alternative 2** Mellisa will receive sufficient salary from her corporation to reduce the corporation's income to its $125,000 share of the annual business limit. Corporate taxes will be paid on the remaining Taxable Income.

> **Alternative 3** Mellisa will join the partnership as an individual. Her share of the partnership income will be taxed as business income.

Mellisa lives in a province where the provincial tax payable on the first $214,368 of Taxable Income is $22,150, with additional amounts being taxed at a provincial rate of 18 percent. In this province, the provincial dividend tax credit is equal to 40 percent of the gross up for eligible dividends and 30 percent of the gross up for non-eligible dividends. Mellisa's tax credits for 2020 total $4,241.

If she forms a new corporation it would be subject to a combined federal/provincial tax rate on income eligible for the small business deduction of 12.5 percent. The rate on other active business income would be 27 percent.

During the CU's taxation year ending December 31, 2020, it is expected to have Taxable Income of $930,000. All of this income will be active business income and Mellisa or her corporation will be entitled to 25 percent of the total.

Because she has no other source of income, she requires all of the income that is generated by her participation in CU.

Required: Calculate the after tax personal retention of Mellisa's share of the partnership income for each of the three approaches. Ignore CPP considerations and the Canada employment tax credit in your calculations. Which approach would you recommend? Briefly explain why this alternative is the best and any other factors she should consider.

Assignment Problem Fifteen - 7
(Shareholder Loans)

Brewers Ltd. is a Canadian controlled private corporation (CCPC) with a December 31 taxation year end. The company was incorporated in 2014 by four unrelated individuals, Jamie, Spencer, Heather, and Pablo, all of whom (with the exception of Pablo) met in university while working toward their Masters of Business Administration (MBA). They quickly realized that their business ideas were quite similar and agreed to work together to create a new business. Spencer recommended they speak with a friend of his, Pablo, who had a degree in chemical engineering. Together the four individuals came up with the idea to operate their own micro-breweries. Pablo created unique mixtures that have been used to produce very successful beers in three provinces with very strong sales and brand loyalty.

In 2020 the company employs 200 people. In an effort to retain staff the company provides a generous package of benefits to its employees. Part of the benefit package includes participation in a stock option plan and the availability of interest free loans. In 2020, 150 employees own shares in the company. The company has issued two classes of shares. Jamie, Spencer, Heather, and Pablo each own 25 percent of the common shares, and the employees own all of the Class A preferred shares, which are non-voting but offer a participating cumulative dividend. No single employee owns more than 1.5 percent of the preferred shares.

Three types of interest free loans are offered for specific purposes once an employee has passed a probationary period of six months. Once a loan has been approved, quarterly payments are required throughout the term of the loan, although early repayments are allowed. If employment is terminated the loan must be paid in full within 30 days of termination. Interest free loans are permitted for the following:

- **Housing Loan**   To purchase a principal residence in which the employee and his or her family will live on a continual basis. Loans for cottages and other vacation properties do not qualify. The company will advance between $50,000 and $200,000 depending on the number of years the employee has worked for the company and the nature of their job – managers, for example, are entitled to larger amounts. The loan period cannot exceed 10 years.

- **Automobile Loan**   To purchase an automobile, the company will loan up to $30,000 and does not require that the automobile be used in their employment. The loan period is limited to three years.

- **Vacation Loan**   Once every three years an employee who has passed his or her probationary period is entitled to a vacation loan of $12,000. Quarterly loan payments are required with a maximum loan period of 18 months.

Additional Information:

- Quarterly loan payments are made through payroll withholdings.
- The company does not permit loans to family members of employees or shareholders.
- Jamie, Spencer, Heather, and Pablo are all on the Board of Directors of the company and work in the daily operations in senior management positions.
- All approved loan agreements are in writing.
- The company is not in the business of lending money and, aside from employee loans, has never made loans to anyone else.
- Quarterly payments are required to be made on the first day of the fourth month following the receipt of the loan and every three months thereafter. Early payments may be made.
- Assume that the prescribed interest rate is 2.0 percent at all times.

During 2020 the company made the following loans listed in points 1 to 5 and an unusual payment in point 6:

1. On April 1, Heather borrowed $200,000 to purchase shares in three separate public companies to increase her personal investment holdings. She has agreed to repay the loan with five annual payments of $40,000 beginning January 1, 2021. She received $18,000 of eligible dividends in December 2020 from these additional investments.

2. Francois and Danielle Gagnon are brother and sister. They have been employed with the Quebec operations since the fall of 2019 and completed their six month probationary period in March 2020. On June 1, 2020, they each borrowed $30,000 to purchase a new car. Danielle will use the car in her employment duties that include meeting with clients. Francois' duties do not require him to use a car for his employment. Both Francois and Danielle acquired preferred shares of the company in April 2020 under the employee stock option plan. Assume that Danielle calculates that for the period June 1 to December 31, 2020, she used her car 32 percent of the time for employment purposes.

3. On September 1, Pablo borrows $350,000 from the company to assist in the finance of a new home. He has agreed to make equal annual payments of $17,500 over the next 20 years beginning September 1, 2021.

4. Jacob Abernathy is a senior manager in the Toronto operations who has been renting an apartment since he began working for the company in 2014. Jacob has received a loan of $200,000 on May 1 that he will use to purchase a home. The loan will be for 10 years and require quarterly payments of $5,000 [$200,000 ÷ (10 years)(4 quarterly payments)]. Jacob owns preferred shares in the company, which he acquired through the company stock option plan.

5. Two employees (Safwan and Melody) have been working for the Vancouver operations since 2016. They are long-time friends and have regularly taken vacations together with their families. They each plan on requesting the maximum vacation loans, which they will use for a fall/winter 2020 and spring 2021 vacation. They each borrow $12,000 on July 1. Safwan is a shareholder as a result of the company stock option plan, but Melody is not.

6. On October 1, Spencer received $280,000 from the company that he used to build an addition to his Vancouver home. No payments have been made nor have any loan agreements been written.

With the exception of point 6, assume that all repayments have been made as scheduled.

Required: For the five loans indicated in points 1 to 5, determine the income tax consequences of each of the amounts received as loans under ITA 15(2) and ITA 20(1)(j) for the 2020, 2021, and 2022 taxation years. Only show the ITA 80.4 calculations for the 2020 and 2021 taxation years. Provide your analysis, together with any calculations, to identify specific amounts that are required to be included in the net income of the recipients together with any other income tax implications including loan repayments.

Discuss the implications of the payment to Spencer in point 6. Did he receive a loan?

Assignment Problem Fifteen - 8
(Bonusing Down)

Debee Ltd. is a Canadian controlled private corporation (CCPC) with a December 31 taxation year end. The company was incorporated in New Brunswick in 2013 by its sole shareholder, Rene Debee, who lives in Saint John, New Brunswick. The company only earns income from an active business that would qualify for the small business deduction, and it has never been associated with any other corporation. The company's Taxable Income prior to 2020 has never exceeded its small business limit of $500,000. The company is not subject to any reduction to its small business limit attributable to either of its Taxable Capital Employed in Canada or its Adjusted Aggregate Investment Income.

In 2018 and 2019 Rene was paid employment income from Debee of $20,000 a month, or $240,000 for each of the two years. As a result of the addition of a significant new client and resulting long term contract, Debee estimates that its taxable income for 2020 will be $700,000, which takes into consideration the $240,000 of employment income paid to Rene. Rene's accountant has informed him that the additional $200,000 of taxable income above the $500,000 small business limit will be subject to tax at a rate of 29.0 percent instead of the 11.5 percent rate that would have applied to the first $500,000. The result is that the additional income will result in an additional $35,000 of corporate tax [($700,000 - $500,000)(0.29 - 0.115)].

Rene is not pleased with the additional corporate income tax and has asked his accountant if there was some way to reduce that amount. He adds that he is planning on building his dream home overlooking the ocean over the next few years and he will need the additional cash earned by the company as a result of the new client contract. The accountant tells him that he could "bonus down", explaining that this is an acceptable tax planning strategy. When Rene enquires further the accountant explains that the options are to (i) have the company pay him additional salary of $200,000 to reduce the taxable income to $500,000, avoiding the high level of corporate tax on income above the small business limit or (ii) have the corporation pay tax on its Taxable Income of $700,000 and to distribute the additional $200,000 after tax income as a dividend. Assume that the company balance in its GRIP account at the beginning of 2020 is nil.

In 2020 the following information is relevant to New Brunswick:

- The provincial tax rate on active business income (ABI) eligible for the small business deduction is 2.5 percent and is 14.0 percent on ABI in excess of the small business deduction. The federal equivalent rates are 9.0 percent and 15.0 percent, respectively.

- The highest provincial personal income tax rate is 20.3 percent, which applies to Taxable Income in excess of $160,776. The equivalent federal rate applies to Taxable Income in excess of $214,368 at a rate of 33.0 percent.

- The dividend gross up will be 38 percent for eligible dividends and 15 percent for non-eligible dividends.

- The federal dividend tax credit will be 6/11 of the gross up for eligible dividends and 9/13 of the gross up for non-eligible dividends.

- The provincial dividend tax credit will be 50.8 percent of the gross up for eligible dividends and 21.1 percent of the gross up for non-eligible dividends.

Required: As Rene's income tax consultant, advise him whether bonusing down with additional salary of $200,000 in 2020 is preferable to not bonusing down and withdrawing the additional after tax cash as dividends. Justify your conclusions with supporting calculations applying a marginal analysis that focuses on the additional $200,000 of corporate income. Add at least three other considerations that should be brought to Rene's attention that may influence his decision, and comment on any tax deferral should Rene not require the funds immediately.

Assignment Problem Fifteen - 9
(Salary Vs. Dividends - Required Amount)

Linda Cross is the sole shareholder of Cross Ltd., a Canadian controlled private corporation (CCPC) incorporated in Alberta in 2010. The company taxation year end is December 31. The company business is conducted in Edmonton, Alberta, where Linda resides.

All of the income earned by Cross Ltd. is from an active business and is eligible for the small business deduction. The Taxable Income of the company has never exceeded its annual small business limit of $500,000, and this trend will continue into 2020. In 2020 the company will be subject to a provincial tax rate on income eligible for the small business deduction of 2.0 percent, which when combined with the federal rate on that same income of 9.0 percent will equal 11.0 percent.

The income of Cross Ltd. began to stabilize at the end of 2017 due to a solid customer base, and as a result Linda purchased a new home and re-evaluated her future cash needs. Working with her accountant, she decided that an annual salary of $158,000 would provide her sufficient after tax cash to meet all of her personal needs. The company began to pay her an annual salary of $158,000 in 2018 with no plan to make any changes to that amount in 2020.

In the spring of 2020 Linda decided that it was time to put in a pool since the summers seemed to becoming warmer each year. She obtained a number of quotes and has decided on an in-ground pool that will cost her $25,000. She spoke to her accountant about the additional cash she would need and the best way to draw the funds from the company as either additional salary or dividends.

Additional Information

(i)   Assume that Linda's salary is her only income and that it also equals her taxable income.

(ii) Cross Ltd.'s GRIP account at the beginning of 2020 is nil and no amount will be added to it in 2020.

(iii) The Alberta personal income tax rate in 2020 is 13.0 percent for Taxable Income between $157,464 and $209,952 and 14.0 percent for Taxable Income between $209,953 and $314,928.

(iv) The Federal personal income tax rate in 2020 is 29.0 percent for Taxable Income between $150,473 and $214,368 and 33.0 percent for Taxable Income in excess of $214,368.

(v)   In 2020 Alberta provides a dividend tax credit on non-eligible dividends of 16.7 percent, and 36.3 percent on eligible dividends.

Required: As Linda's accountant, determine the additional amount that would be required if Linda were to receive sufficient salary or dividends to leave her with the $25,000 cash she needs to put in an in-ground pool. Provide all supporting calculations and determine which of the two alternatives is most cost effective considering the income tax consequences to both Linda and Cross Ltd.

Assignment Problem Fifteen - 10
(Salary Vs. Dividends - Required Amount)

Simon Fahrquest is the sole shareholder of Dawg Ltd., a very successful business that was incorporated a number of years ago. The company has always qualified as a CCPC and uses a December 31 year end.

Simon has never been particularly fond of people, but has always loved dogs, particularly those of mixed breed. While he has no family, he currently owns 12 dogs, none of which are purebred.

While Dawg Ltd. has always been very profitable, Simon has chosen to live modestly in a dog friendly residential property that he has owned for many years. Each year, he estimates the amount of cash that he will need for his living expenses, which vary year to year, and looks to his corporation to provide the needed cash.

Since after meeting Simon's financial needs, Dawg Ltd. always has cash that isn't required for operations, it donates at least $100,000 per year to the Society For The Prevention Of Cruelty To Animals (SPCA), a registered charity. The donations specify that the funds must be used for the protection, maintenance, and placement of mixed breed dogs.

For 2020, Simon estimates that he will need $50,000 in after tax cash to meet his personal needs. He expects Dawg Ltd. will have Taxable Income of $350,000 before any payments to him, all of which will qualify for the small business deduction. The provincial tax rate on such income is 3 percent.

In Simon's province of residence, the provincial taxes on the first $48,535 of Taxable Income total $4,528. Additional income will be taxed at a provincial rate of 12 percent. Also in this province, the provincial dividend tax credit for non-eligible dividends is equal to 32 percent of the dividend gross up.

For the 2020 taxation year, Simon estimates that his personal tax credits will total $3,260.

Required:

A.   Determine the tax cost of providing Simon with the required $50,000 in after tax cash using only salary payments.

B.   Determine the tax cost of providing Simon with the required $50,000 in after tax cash using only dividend payments.

C. Given the information in this problem, do you believe that better results could be achieved with a combination of salary and dividends? Would your answer be different if Simon's personal tax credits totaled $10,000 instead of $3,260? Calculations are not required in answering this Part C.

D. Simon would like to increase his donations to the SPCA and has asked your advice on the most tax advantageous way to do this. What factors should be considered when analyzing this issue?

Ignore CPP contributions and the Canada employment credit in your solution.

Assignment Problem Fifteen - 11
(Salary Vs. Dividends - Optimum Mix)

Robert Lorca is the only shareholder of Rolorc Ltd., a Canadian controlled private company with a taxation year that ends on December 31. His only source of income is either dividends or salary provided by Rolorc. For 2020, because of extensive medial costs, he has available tax credits of $9,500.

While Rolorc's 2020 taxable income before any salary or dividend payments is $185,000, large capital expenditures has left the company with only $89,000 in cash that is available for distribution.

Relevant information with respect to Robert's province of residence is as follows:

- In order to simplify calculations, assume that all of Robert's Taxable Income will be taxed at a combined federal/provincial rate of 24 percent.

- The provincial dividend tax credit is equal to 33 percent of the gross up on non-eligible dividends.

- All of the company's activities are confined to a province in which the applicable corporate rate of taxation is 3 percent on income eligible for the small business deduction. The province does not levy a payroll tax.

Required: Ignore the required CPP contributions and the Canada employment tax credit when answering Parts A to D in this problem.

A. Determine the after tax amount of cash that Robert will retain if all of the company's cash is used to pay taxes and salary.

B. Determine the after tax amount of cash that Robert will retain if the company pays the maximum possible dividend.

C. Can Robert improve his after tax cash retention by using a combination of salary and dividends? Explain your conclusion.

D. If your answer to Part C is positive, determine the combination of salary and/or dividends that will produce the maximum after tax cash retention for Robert. Calculate the amount of this after tax cash retention.

CHAPTER 16

Rollovers Under Section 85

Rollovers Under Section 85

Introduction

16-1. Chapter 15 gave detailed consideration to the question of whether it would be advantageous to establish a corporation in order to reduce, defer, or redistribute the amount of Tax Payable. If the results of this analysis favour the use of a corporation, Section 85 of the *Act* provides an attractive basis for the transfer of property to the new corporation.

16-2. The problem that is involved with such a transfer is that the assets may have been owned by the transferor for some period of time. In these circumstances, it is possible that their fair market values may be well in excess of their adjusted cost base and/or their undepreciated capital cost. As a transfer by a taxpayer to a corporation would be considered a disposition by that taxpayer, the incorporation of an existing business could result in a need to include both capital gains and recapture in the transferor's Taxable Income. In a typical situation, where the owner of an operating business decides to transfer all of its assets to a newly formed corporation, the resulting tax liability could be significant.

> **EXAMPLE** Joanne Browski has an unincorporated business that is using assets with a fair market value of $572,000. The tax values for these assets total $225,000. Ms. Browski would like to transfer these assets to a corporation and continue her operations in that legal form (note that while we have treated the group of assets like a single asset in order to simplify this example, in actual practice each asset would have to be treated individually).

> **ANALYSIS** Under the general tax rules, asset dispositions must be recorded at fair market value. If this applied to Ms. Browski's transfer, the amount of taxation would be significant and could be a deterrent to the incorporation of her business.

16-3. Section 85 of the *Income Tax Act* is designed to provide relief in this type of situation. In somewhat simplified terms, it permits Ms. Browski's property to be transferred to a corporation on either a tax free basis or with a level of taxation that is determined at her discretion. As noted in earlier Chapters, such transactions are referred to in tax work as rollovers.

16-4. Of the rollovers that are available, the content of Section 85 provides for one of the most important and widely used. In this Chapter we will provide detailed coverage of the application of this Section. Other rollovers involving corporations will be given coverage in Chapter 17.

General Rules For The Transfer

Transferor And Transferee

Transferors

16-5.   As indicated in the introduction, we are concerned here with transfers of property to a corporation at a value that can be jointly elected by the transferor and the corporation. There are several possibilities with respect to the identity of the transferor:

- The transferor may be an **individual** who wishes to incorporate his or her proprietorship.
- The transferor may be a **corporation** that wishes to transfer some of its assets to a different corporation.
- The transferor may be a **trust** that wishes to transfer some of its assets to a corporation.
- The transferor may be a **partner** who wishes to incorporate his or her partnership interest.

16-6.   ITA 85(1) refers to taxpayers, and this subsection covers the rules related to transferors who are individuals, corporations, and trusts. As partnerships are not "taxpayers" for income tax purposes, a separate ITA 85(2) provides for the transfer of partnership assets to a corporation.

Transferees

16-7.   With respect to transferees, Section 85 requires that they be taxable Canadian corporations. A "Canadian corporation" is defined in ITA 89(1) as a corporation that is currently resident in Canada and that was either incorporated in Canada or has been a resident continuously since June 18, 1971. ITA 89(1) also defines a "taxable Canadian corporation" as a Canadian corporation that was not, by virtue of a statutory provision, exempt from taxation under Part I of the *Income Tax Act*.

Eligible Property

16-8.   Only "eligible property," the components of which are defined in ITA 85(1.1), can be transferred under Section 85. The major items listed in the Subsection include:

- both depreciable and non-depreciable capital property, generally not including real property owned by non-residents;
- Canadian resource properties;
- foreign resource properties;
- inventories, other than inventories of real property; and
- real property owned by a non-resident person and used in the year in a business carried on by that person in Canada.

16-9.   The general exclusion of real property owned by non-residents reflects the fact that this type of property is Taxable Canadian Property and gains on its disposition are subject to Canadian taxes, without regard to the residency of the seller. The exclusion is designed to prevent a non-resident who owns Canadian real estate from being able to transfer the property on a tax free basis to a corporation, and subsequently selling the shares in the corporation on a tax free basis. As explained in Chapter 20, gains on such dispositions are typically exempted from Canadian tax by international tax treaties.

16-10.   The second exclusion from assets eligible for the Section 85 rollover would be Canadian resident owned real property that constitutes an inventory. That is, if a group of real property assets is being actively traded, rather than being held for their income producing ability, they are not eligible for a tax free rollover under ITA 85.

16-11.   This latter exclusion of inventories of real property can be a particularly troublesome provision due to the fact that, in practice, some taxpayers may not be certain as to the status of their real estate holdings. If a taxpayer was to go through the Section 85 rollover procedures and then, after the fact, find that the transferred real estate holdings were considered inventory by the CRA, the tax consequences would be very severe. In this type of situation, it would be advisable to delay the transfer to the corporation until such time as any uncertainty regarding the status of the real estate could be clearly established.

Consideration To Transferor

16-12.   In return for the property transferred to the corporation, the corporation may provide various types of consideration to the transferor. The one requirement that is specified in ITA 85(1) is that some part of this consideration must consist of shares of the transferee corporation.

16-13.   The shares issued may be either preferred, common, or some combination of the two types. Further, the requirement for share consideration to be used can be satisfied by the issuance of as little as one share to the transferor. For reasons that will become evident later in this Chapter, the usual Section 85 transaction involves the use of a combination of shares and non-share consideration (e.g., cash or debt securities). In this context, the non-share consideration is usually referred to as the "boot".

16-14.   A further point here is that, without regard to the values that are elected for the exchange, the fair market value of the consideration provided to the transferor should be equal to the total fair market value of the assets transferred to the corporation. As will be discussed later in this Chapter, if these amounts are not equal, the difference may be viewed as a benefit to the transferor, or a gift to a related party.

Making The Election

16-15.   Both the transferor and the transferee corporation must elect to have the Section 85 provisions apply. This joint election is accomplished by filing Form T2057 (transfers from individuals, trusts, and corporations) or T2058 (transfers from partnerships), on or before the earliest of the dates on which the normal tax returns are due for the two taxpayers.

16-16.   A late election may be filed for up to three years after this date and, with the permission of the CRA, a late election will be accepted after the end of this three year period. Whenever there is a late election, a penalty of one-quarter of 1 percent of the difference between the fair market value and the agreed upon amount for each month beyond the normal filing date is assessed. The maximum penalty is $100 per month to a maximum of $8,000.

16-17.   In making the election, it is crucial that the taxpayer list all of the properties that are to be covered. If a property is omitted from the forms, the normal rules associated with dispositions will apply. This could result in the need to recognize capital gains, recapture, or business income on the transfer, an outcome that might require needless payment of taxes.

Selecting The Transfer Price

Importance

16-18.   One of the most significant features of ITA 85 is that it provides for the transfer of various properties to a corporation at values that are jointly elected by the transferor and transferee. Careful consideration must be given to the election of an appropriate transfer price in that, in general, this elected value establishes three important values. These are:

Transferor   The deemed proceeds of disposition for the property given up.

Transferor   The adjusted cost base or capital cost of the consideration received from the corporation.

Transferee   The tax cost of the property received by the corporation (adjusted cost base, capital cost, or UCC).

16-19.   As will be discussed at a later point in this Chapter, the elected value is also influential in determining the PUC of the newly issued shares.

The Usual Section 85 Scenario

16-20.   A simple example will serve to illustrate the basic Section 85 application:

EXAMPLE   Mr. Thompson owns land with a fair market value of $750,000 and an adjusted cost base of $500,000. On the transfer of this asset to a corporation, he will receive cash (non-share consideration) of $500,000 and shares with a fair market value of $250,000.

16-21.   In the usual application of Section 85, the transferor wishes to avoid recognizing any income at the time of the transfer. While the transfer price that provides this result varies with the type of asset being transferred (see the next Section of this Chapter, which deals with the detailed rules for various types of assets), we will deal here only with transfers of land.

16-22.   In the case of this asset, avoiding current taxation requires that the elected value be equal to the adjusted cost base of the land being transferred. In our Example, this value is $500,000 and its use as the transfer price will have the following tax consequences for the transferor and the transferee:

- The $500,000 will be the proceeds of disposition for the land. As this is equal to Mr. Thompson's adjusted cost base for the asset, there will be no capital gain on the transfer.

- The adjusted cost base of the land to the corporation will be $500,000. This means that, if the corporation were to sell the land immediately for its fair market value of $750,000, a capital gain of $250,000 ($750,000 - $500,000) would have to be recognized. This reflects the fact that the gain on the assets at the time of transfer was only deferred, not eliminated, by the use of the ITA 85 rollover.

- The election of $500,000 as the transfer price means that the adjusted cost base of the consideration will be this amount. This will be less than the $750,000 fair market value of the consideration. As will be explained later in this Chapter, all of this will have to be allocated to the non-share consideration.

16-23.   You should note that this scenario raises the possibility of double taxation on the $250,000 gain. The adjusted cost base of the property transferred and the consideration received by the transferor is $500,000. If the corporation sells the assets for their fair market value of $750,000, there will be a $250,000 gain at the corporate level. If the consideration received by the transferor is in the form of shares, a sale of these shares at their fair market value of $750,000 would result in the $250,000 gain being taxed a second time at the individual level. This would suggest that, if either the asset transferred or the consideration received by the transferor are to be sold, the election should be made at the fair market value of $750,000.

Using Other Values For The Election

16-24.   The majority of Section 85 transactions will use the scenario described above in order to avoid current taxation. However, there may be situations where the use of other values may be desirable. Before considering this, you should recognize the following limits for transfer values on non-depreciable assets:

- The elected value cannot exceed the $750,000 fair market value of the land transferred.

- The elected value cannot be lower than $500,000, the adjusted cost base of the land and the fair market value of the non-share consideration.

16-25.   The election can be made for any amount between these two values.

16-26.   Two possible situations where the taxpayer may wish to elect a value other than the $500,000 adjusted cost base of the land can be described as follows:

Unused Net Capital Losses   Consider a situation where the transferor in our Example has unused net capital losses of $75,000 [(1/2)($150,000)] that he wishes to use in the current year. This could be accomplished by electing a value of $650,000 for the Section 85 transfer. The election value would be the proceeds of disposition for the transfer, resulting in a capital gain of $150,000.

Need For More Cash   A second possibility would arise if the transferor is in need of more than $500,000 in cash, for example $625,000. While this will be explained in more detail in the next section, the elected value cannot be less than the amount of non-share consideration received. This means that the transferor, in order to receive $625,000 in cash, would have to elect this value. As this value would become the proceeds of disposition for the land, the result would be a taxable capital gain of $62,500 [(1/2) ($625,000 - $500,000)]

Transfer Prices - Detailed Rules

Rules Applicable To All Assets

Proceeds And Cost

16-27. ITA 85(1)(a) establishes the first basis rule. It makes the point that the amount elected by the taxpayer and corporation shall be deemed to be the taxpayer's proceeds of disposition, as well as the cost of the property to the corporation.

Boot As A Floor

16-28. The term "boot" is commonly used to refer to non-share consideration given to the transferor in an ITA 85 rollover. It would include cash paid to the transferor and new debt of the transferee corporation issued to the transferor. In those cases where an existing business is being transferred under these provisions, boot would include the assumption by the transferee corporation of any debt of the existing business that is being transferred.

16-29. Other types of non-share consideration (e.g., capital assets) could be used in an ITA 85 rollover and, if this were the case, the term boot would still be appropriate. However, in almost all situations, boot is restricted to cash, new debt issued by the transferee corporation, or existing debt of the transferor assumed by the transferee corporation.

16-30. Boot is of considerable significance in that, if the rollover is properly structured, it constitutes an amount of cash or cash equivalent that will be received by the transferor on a tax free basis. Because of this, a further general rule is as follows:

> **ITA 85(1)(b)**   Subject to Paragraph 85(1)(c), where the amount that the taxpayer and corporation have agreed on in their election in respect of the property is less than the fair market value, at the time of the disposition, of the consideration therefor (other than any shares of the capital stock of the corporation or a right to receive any such shares) received by the taxpayer, the amount so agreed on shall, irrespective of the amount actually so agreed on by them, be deemed to be an amount equal to that fair market value;

16-31. This establishes that, regardless of the type of asset being transferred, the elected value cannot be less than the boot.

Fair Market Value As A Ceiling

16-32. Finally, a further general provision limits the upper value for the election to the fair market value of the property transferred:

> **ITA 85(1)(c)**   Where the amount that the taxpayer and the corporation have agreed on in their election in respect of the property is greater than the fair market value, at the time of the disposition, of the property so disposed of, the amount so agreed on shall, irrespective of the amount actually so agreed on, be deemed to be an amount equal to that fair market value.

Summary

16-33. These general rules apply to all assets transferred, thereby establishing a range for the election. This range can be outlined as follows:

Ceiling Value   Fair market value of the assets transferred to the corporation.

Floor Value   The floor value will be equal to the greater of:
- the fair market value of the non-share consideration (boot) given to the transferor in return for the assets transferred; and
- the tax values (adjusted cost base or UCC) of the assets transferred.

16-34.   The application of the term "tax values" in the preceding outline of the rules will vary with the type of asset involved. Attention will be given to these differences in the material that follows.

Accounts Receivable

16-35.   As was discussed in Chapter 6, when accounts receivable are transferred in conjunction with all of the other assets of a business, under the usual rules the disposition will be treated as a capital transaction, with any resulting loss being only one-half deductible. Further, as the transferee has not included these amounts in income, no deduction can be made for bad debts. If the transferee collects less than the transfer amount, the difference must be treated as a capital loss and, again, only one-half of this loss will be deductible.

16-36.   To avoid these results, the usual procedure is to use a joint election under ITA 22. This election allows any loss to be treated as a fully deductible business loss and permits the transferee to deduct bad debts after the transfer. You may recall that this election was discussed in Chapter 6. If you do not recall the application of ITA 22, you should review that material now as this election will be commonly used in the problem material in this Chapter.

16-37.   While accounts receivable can be transferred under ITA 85, taxpayers are not permitted to elect under both ITA 85 and ITA 22. In general, it will be to the advantage of the taxpayer to make the ITA 22 election and, as a result, accounts receivable will usually not be one of the assets listed in the ITA 85 election.

16-38.   Note, however, this does not prevent these assets from being transferred. Using the ITA 22 joint election, they can be transferred at fair market value, with any resulting loss being fully deductible to the transferor. The corporation will have to include the difference between the face value and the price paid in income, but any difference between the face value and the amounts collected will be 100 percent deductible.

Inventories And Non-Depreciable Capital Property

16-39.   Unlike the situation with accounts receivable, when inventories are disposed of in conjunction with the sale of a business, any difference between fair market value and cost is automatically treated as business income or loss, not as a capital gain or loss. This is specifically provided for in ITA 23, with no election being required to bring this provision into effect.

16-40.   Non-depreciable capital property of a business would include land, temporary investments, and long-term investments. As capital property is involved, any gain or loss on their disposition would be treated as a capital gain or loss.

16-41.   In making the election here, the highest value will be the fair market value of the assets transferred to the corporation. The minimum election cannot be below the amount of the boot received by the transferor. However, a further floor limit is specified for the inventories and non-depreciable capital property in ITA 85(1)(c.1) to ensure that artificial losses cannot be created. This limit is the lesser of the fair market value of the property and its tax cost. For non-depreciable capital assets, the tax cost would be the adjusted cost base of the property. For inventory, tax cost would be either cost or market, depending on how the inventory balance is carried for tax purposes.

16-42.   Putting these limits together means that the minimum elected value for the floor, as specified in ITA 85(1)(e.3), will be the greater of:

A. The fair market value of the boot (the general floor for all assets); and

B. The lesser of:
   - the tax cost of the property; or
   - the fair market value of the property.

16-43. These rules can be illustrated using the three examples that follow:

	Example One	**Example Two**	**Example Three**
Fair Market Value Of Property	$15,000	$10,000	$20,000
Adjusted Cost Base	12,000	12,000	14,000
Fair Market Value Of The Boot	5,000	5,000	17,000

16-44. In Example One, the maximum transfer value is the fair market value of $15,000, and the minimum value is the cost of $12,000. The normal election value would be $12,000. Also note that up to $12,000 of boot, an additional $7,000, could have been taken out without changing the minimum election or creating immediate tax consequences.

16-45. In Example Two, the $10,000 fair market value is both the floor and the ceiling. If the property is inventories, this required election will result in a fully deductible business loss of $2,000 ($12,000 - $10,000). Alternatively, if the election was made on non-depreciable capital property, the result would be an allowable capital loss of $1,000 [(1/2)($12,000 - $10,000)]. As explained beginning in Paragraph 16-50, this capital loss may be disallowed.

16-46. In Example Three, the maximum value is again the fair market value. While the $14,000 cost is lower than the $20,000 fair market value, it is also lower than the boot. This means that, in this example, the minimum value that can be elected is the boot of $17,000. If this property is inventory, this election will result in fully taxable business income of $3,000 ($17,000 - $14,000). If the election was made on non-depreciable capital property, the result will be a taxable capital gain of $1,500 [(1/2)($17,000 - $14,000)].

16-47. If the goal is to structure the rollover to avoid any gain on the transfer of assets, Example Three will not accomplish this objective. In order to avoid a gain, the usual procedure is to limit the non-share consideration to the minimum elected value as otherwise determined ($14,000 in Example Three).

Exercise Sixteen - 1

Subject: Elected Value For Non-Depreciable Property

Jean Doan's unincorporated business has inventories with a fair market value of $125,000 and a tax cost of $140,000. In addition, he owns land with a fair market value of $350,000 and a tax cost of $110,000. He intends to transfer these assets to a new corporation, taking back $125,000 in cash for the inventories. For the land, he receives $150,000 in cash and $200,000 in securities. If he uses ITA 85 for the transfer, what is the possible range of values that can be elected for the two properties? Assume he elects the lowest possible value in each case. What are the tax consequences for Mr. Doan?

SOLUTION available in print and online Study Guide.

Non-Depreciable Capital Property - Disallowed Capital Losses
General Rules
16-48. The special rules described in the following material apply only to non-depreciable capital assets. They do not apply to either inventories or depreciable capital assets as it is not possible to have capital losses on these types of assets.

16-49.   While we are discussing these rules in the material related to Section 85 rollovers, you should note that they are applicable to transfers to affiliated persons, without regard to whether Section 85 is being used. The discussion is located here because, when a non-depreciable capital asset is transferred under ITA 85, the recognition of a loss may be unavoidable because of the rules limiting the elected values. This was the case in Example Two in Paragraph 16-45.

16-50.   The basic rule applicable to these situations is found in ITA 40(2)(g), which indicates that a taxpayer's loss, to the extent that it is a "superficial loss", is deemed to be nil. As with other concepts related to capital assets, the definition of "superficial loss" is found in ITA 54:

> **"superficial loss"** of a taxpayer means the taxpayer's loss from the disposition of a particular property where
>
> (a) during the period that begins 30 days before and ends 30 days after the disposition, the taxpayer or a person affiliated with the taxpayer acquires a property (in this definition referred to as the "substituted property") that is, or is identical to, the particular property, and
>
> (b) at the end of that period, the taxpayer or a person affiliated with the taxpayer owns or had a right to acquire the substituted property.

16-51.   Read together, these provisions deem to be nil any capital loss arising on a transfer to an affiliated person. While the allocation of the loss will depend on whether the transferor is an individual, a trust, or a corporation, the denial of the loss is applicable to all taxpayers. The actual allocation of the denied loss will be dealt with after our discussion of affiliated persons.

Affiliated Persons

16-52.   The term "affiliated person" is defined in ITA 251.1(1) as follows:

> A. An individual is affiliated to another individual only if that individual is his or her spouse or common-law partner.
>
> B. A corporation is affiliated with:
>   1. a person who controls the corporation;
>   2. each member of an affiliated group of persons who controls the corporation; and
>   3. the spouse or common-law partner of a person listed in (1) or (2).
>
> C. Two corporations are affiliated if:
>   1. each corporation is controlled by a person, and the person by whom one corporation is controlled is affiliated with the person by whom the other corporation is controlled;
>   2. one corporation is controlled by a person, the other corporation is controlled by a group of persons, and each member of that group is affiliated with that person; or
>   3. each corporation is controlled by a group of persons, and each member of each group is affiliated with at least one member of the other group.

16-53.   ITA 251.1(3) contains definitions that are required in the application of these rules. The two that are of importance here are:

> **Affiliated group of persons** means a group of persons each member of which is affiliated with every other member.
>
> **Controlled** means controlled, directly or indirectly, in any manner whatever. This definition refers to both legal control and de facto control, which does not necessarily require majority ownership of all shares.

16-54.   As was previously noted, if a capital loss arises on a transfer to an affiliated person, it is deemed to be nil. This rule applies to all taxpayers, including individuals, trusts, and corporations. In contrast to the normal use of the term, for purposes of the affiliated person rules, the term "person" includes partnerships. You should also note that, for transfers involving ITA 85, the transferee and the transferor will almost always be affiliated (e.g., the transferor will typically control the transferee corporation).

Allocation Of Disallowed Capital Loss

16-55.   When the transferor is an individual, the disallowed loss is allocated to the adjusted cost base of the transferred property. This requirement is dictated by ITA 53(1)(f), which describes adjustments to the cost base of a transferred property.

> **EXAMPLE - Individual**   Ms. Hannah Howard, the sole shareholder of HH Ltd., transfers land with an adjusted cost base of $50,000 and a fair market value of $40,000 to HH Ltd. The transfer is made under Section 85 at an elected value of $40,000.
>
> **ANALYSIS**   The $10,000 loss ($40,000 - $50,000) on the transfer is disallowed. As the transferor is an individual, the loss will be allocated to the adjusted cost base of the land in the tax records of HH Ltd. This means that the adjusted cost base to HH Ltd. will be the same $50,000 ($40,000, plus the $10,000 loss) that was the adjusted cost base to Ms. Howard.

16-56.   When the transferor is a corporation, trust, or partnership, the allocation of the disallowed loss is covered under ITA 40(3.4). In effect, this provision keeps the loss in the tax records of the transferor, to be recognized when one of the following events occurs:

- the transferee disposes of the property to a non-affiliated person (includes deemed dispositions);
- if the transferor is a corporation,
  - it is subject to an acquisition of control; or
  - it is subject to an ITA 88(2) winding up.

> **EXAMPLE - Not An Individual**   HC Ltd. transfers land with an adjusted cost base of $50,000 and a fair market value of $40,000 to HCSub, a corporation controlled by HC Ltd. (i.e., an affiliated person). Two years later, HCSub sells the land for $35,000 to a non-affiliated person.
>
> **ANALYSIS**   The $10,000 ($40,000 - $50,000) loss on the transfer to HCSub will be disallowed at the time of the transfer. However, when the land is sold by HCSub for $35,000, HC Ltd. will recognize the disallowed loss of $10,000 ($50,000 - $40,000). In addition, HCSub will recognize a $5,000 ($40,000 - $35,000) loss at the time of sale. The result is a total loss for the two companies of $15,000 ($50,000 - $35,000).

Tax Planning

16-57.   To the extent that the asset with the unrealized loss is necessary to the continued operations of the business, for example land on which the enterprise's factory is located, it makes no difference whether it is transferred under the provisions of ITA 85 or outside the election. In either case, the loss will be disallowed at the time of the transfer.

16-58.   If an asset is not essential to the operations of the corporation, a preferable course of action may be to sell it to a non-affiliated person. This will permit the immediate recognition of any loss on its disposition. However, if the asset is an integral part of the operations of the transferor this is not a viable alternative.

16-59.   The other basic point here is that if the asset in question has an unrealized loss, there is no reason to elect to transfer it under Section 85. The objective that the taxpayer is attempting to achieve in using Section 85 is to defer the taxation of income. When losses are involved on particular assets, including those assets in the Section 85 rollover complicates the election without contributing to the taxpayer's desired goals.

Depreciable Property

General Rules

16-60.   As with other assets, the ceiling for the election is the fair market value of the asset and the general floor is the fair market value of the non-share consideration received by the transferor.

However, as was the case with inventories and non-depreciable capital property, a further lower limit is specified in the *Income Tax Act*.

16-61.   ITA 85(1)(e) indicates that for depreciable property, the lower limit is the least of the UCC for the class, the fair market value of each individual property, and the cost of each individual property. This means that the overall lower limit for the election, as specified in ITA 85(1)(e.3), is the greater of:

A.   The fair market value of the boot (general floor for all assets), and

B.   The least of:
  - the balance of the UCC for the class;
  - the cost to the taxpayer of each individual property; and
  - the fair market value of each individual property.

Examples - Elected Values

16-62.   These rules can be illustrated by the following two examples, each involving the transfer of the only asset in a CCA class:

	Example One	Example Two
Fair Market Value Of The Property	$50,000	$18,000
UCC Of Class (Last Asset In Class)	20,000	20,000
Cost Of The Property	27,000	30,000
Fair Market Value Of The Boot	15,000	15,000

Example One Analysis   In Example One, the range of the election would extend from the UCC of $20,000 as the floor to the fair market value of $50,000. Note that any election in between the UCC of $20,000 and the cost of $27,000 would result in recapture of CCA. The normal election here would be the UCC of $20,000, which results in the transferor not recognizing a capital gain or recapture of CCA. In addition, the transferor would usually take out $20,000 in boot. In Example One, $5,000 more boot could be taken out without creating immediate tax consequences.

Example Two Analysis   In Example Two, using the limits specified in ITA 85(1)(e.3) the ceiling value and the floor value would be the $18,000 fair market value of the property. With the ceiling and floor at the same value, the general rules would indicate that only this $18,000 value could be elected. In Example Two, $3,000 more boot could be taken out without creating immediate tax consequences. Since the transfer of the property removes the last asset in this CCA class, the fact that the elected value is below the UCC suggests a terminal loss. However, as will be discussed beginning in Paragraph 16-70, ITA 85 does not apply to this transfer and this terminal loss will be disallowed.

Example - Order Of Disposition

16-63.   An additional problem arises in the case of depreciable assets in situations where a number of different assets that belong to the same CCA class are being transferred at the same time. This problem can be illustrated by the following example:

EXAMPLE   An individual owns two assets in a particular CCA class, and the UCC for that class is $28,000. Data on the two assets is as follows:

	Asset One	Asset Two
Cost Of Asset	$15,000	$30,000
Fair Market Value	20,000	25,000

16-64.   The problem here is that the wording of the transfer price rules for depreciable assets requires the floor to be based on the least of the cost of each individual asset, fair market value of each individual asset, but UCC for the class as a whole. This determination has to be made with respect to each asset in the class, with the resulting figures summed for purposes of the election floor.

16-65.   This means that, if the general rules were applied, the floor values would be $15,000 for Asset One plus $25,000 for Asset Two. This reflects the fact that both of these individual values are less than the $28,000 UCC for the class. However, if these values are elected, a total of $40,000 would be subtracted from the class. Since the UCC balance for the class is only $28,000, this would result in recapture of $12,000.

16-66.   To alleviate this problem, ITA 85(1)(e.1) allows an assumption that the properties are transferred one at a time. This means that for the transfer of Asset One, if the floor value of $15,000 were elected (this assumes that the non-share consideration provided to the transferor does not exceed this amount), this $15,000 would be subtracted from the UCC of $28,000.

16-67.   The resulting UCC balance would be $13,000, and when the depreciable asset rules are applied to Asset Two, this UCC balance of $13,000 would become the floor. If the taxpayer again elected to use the floor value, the $13,000 would be deducted from the UCC and this would reduce the UCC balance to nil without triggering recaptured CCA.

Exercise Sixteen - 2

Subject: Elected Value For Depreciable Property

Eric Li has two depreciable assets - a Class 1 building and a Class 10 vehicle. The assets are to be transferred to a corporation using ITA 85. Relevant information on the assets is as follows:

	Class 1	Class 10
Fair Market Value Of The Property	$475,000	$12,000
UCC Of Class (Last Asset In Class)	150,000	8,000
Cost Of The Property	220,000	28,000
Fair Market Value Of The Boot	250,000	10,000

What is the possible range of values that can be elected for the two properties? Assume he elects the lowest possible value in each case. What are the tax consequences for Mr. Li?

SOLUTION available in print and online Study Guide.

Depreciable Property - Disallowed Terminal Losses

General Rules

16-68.   In Paragraph 16-62, we noted that the terminal loss resulting from the required election on the asset in Example Two will be disallowed. More specifically, if a depreciable property with a fair market value that is less than its UCC is transferred by a person (individual, trust, or corporation) or a partnership to an affiliated person (see Paragraph 16-54), ITA 13(21.2) indicates that:

- ITA 85 does not apply;
- the proceeds of the disposition are deemed to be the UCC amount, thereby disallowing the terminal loss; and
- the transferee's capital cost for the property is deemed to be the transferor's capital cost, with the excess of that amount over the UCC of the asset deemed to be CCA deducted in previous periods.

16-69.   In Example Two from Paragraph 16-62, the property had a capital cost of $30,000, a UCC for the class of $20,000, and a fair market value of $18,000. As the $18,000 fair market value was less than the $20,000 UCC of the class, this means that ITA 85 does not apply to this transfer. In addition, ITA 13(21.2) would disallow this loss on any transfer to an affiliated person by deeming the proceeds of disposition to be equal to the UCC.

16-70. If, however, the property is sold to the corporation for its fair market value, the property will have a deemed capital cost to the transferee of $30,000 and a UCC value of $18,000. The $2,000 disallowed loss will be deemed to be a depreciable property that is owned by the transferor. It will be allocated to the same class as the transferred property for CCA purposes and will be subject to the usual CCA procedures. However, it will be kept in a separate class so that any unamortized amount can be recognized when one of the following events occurs:

- the transferee disposes of the property to a non-affiliated person (includes deemed dispositions);
- the use of the property is changed from income earning to non-income earning;
- if the transferor is a corporation,
  - it is subject to an acquisition of control; or
  - it is subject to an ITA 88(2) winding up.

Tax Planning

16-71. As was noted in our discussion of capital losses on transfers of non-depreciable capital property, Section 85 is normally used in order to defer the taxation of various types of income. If there is a terminal loss present on a depreciable property, ITA 85 cannot be used. This means that, if the asset is necessary to the continued operations of the business, it will be sold to the corporation at fair market value, with any terminal loss on the transaction being disallowed by ITA 13(21.2). If the asset is not necessary to the continued operations of the business, it would be preferable to sell it to a non-affiliated person.

Summary Of Transfer Price Rules

16-72. Figure 16-1 provides a summary of the transfer price rules that have been discussed in this section.

We suggest you work Self Study Problems Sixteen-1 and 2 at this point.

Allocation Of The Elected Value

Consideration Received By The Transferor (Shareholder)

16-73. As noted previously, the elected value for the assets transferred is used to establish the adjusted cost base of all consideration received by the transferor. The rules for allocating this total to the various types of consideration that may be used are found in ITA 85(1)(f), (g), and (h). They involve a sequential process that can be outlined as follows:

	Inventory And Non-Depreciable Assets	Depreciable Assets
Figure 16 - 1 **Summary Of Section 85 Transfer Price Rules**		
Ceiling (FMV Of Asset)	X	X
Floor - Greater Of:		
A. FMV Of Boot	X	X
B. Least Of:		
Tax Cost Of Asset	X	—
Cost Of Asset (Not Tax Cost)	—	X
FMV Of Asset	X	X
UCC Balance	—	X

Elected Value (Total Adjusted Cost Base Of All Consideration)	$xxx
Less: Adjusted Cost Base Of Non-Share Consideration (Fair Market Value)	(xxx)
Adjusted Cost Base Of All Shares Issued (Usually Nil)	$xxx
Less: Adjusted Cost Base Of Preferred Stock Issued	
(Usually Nil, But Limited To Fair Market Value)	(xxx)
Adjusted Cost Base Of Common Stock Issued (A Residual - Usually Nil)	$xxx

EXAMPLE   In transferring his proprietorship assets to a new corporation, Jason Browning elects a value of $972,000 for the assets transferred. As the fair market value of these assets is $1,650,000, he receives the following consideration:

- Cash of $220,000.
- Preferred shares of the new corporation with a fair market value of $345,000.
- Common shares of the new corporation with a fair market value of $1,085,000.

ANALYSIS   The $972,000 elected value would be allocated as follows:

Elected Value (Total Adjusted Cost Base Of All Consideration)	$972,000
Less: Adjusted Cost Base Of Non-Share Consideration (Fair Market Value)	(220,000)
Adjusted Cost Base Of All Shares Issued (Usually Nil)	$752,000
Less: Adjusted Cost Base Of Preferred Stock Issued	
(Usually Nil, But Limited To Fair Market Value)	(345,000)
Adjusted Cost Base Of Common Stock Issued (A Residual - Usually Nil)	$ 407,000

16-74.   The preceding example has been designed to illustrate the allocation of the elected value to all three types of consideration. However, in the usual ITA 85 scenario, minimum asset values will normally be elected in order to avoid the recognition of income on the transfer. Boot will then be taken out in an amount equal to these minimum values. This means that in the usual situation, non-share consideration will be equal to the elected value and, in terms of the preceding allocation process, both preferred and common shares will have an adjusted cost base of nil.

Exercise Sixteen - 3

Subject: Transfers Under Section 85 - ACB Of Consideration

Using ITA 85, Mrs. Jennifer Lee transfers non-depreciable capital property to a corporation at an elected value of $62,000. The property has an adjusted cost base of $62,000 and a fair market value of $176,000. As consideration, she receives a note for $51,000, preferred shares with a fair market value of $53,000, and common shares with a fair market value of $72,000. Indicate the adjusted cost base of the individual items of consideration received by Mrs. Lee.

SOLUTION available in print and online Study Guide.

Assets Acquired By The Corporation

General Rules

16-75.   With respect to the assets acquired by the transferee corporation, the basic rules are as follows:

Allocation Of The Elected Value

Non-Depreciable Property   The elected transfer price becomes the tax cost of these assets to the corporation.

Depreciable Property   Where the transferor's capital cost exceeds the elected value for the property, ITA 85(5) requires that the capital cost to the transferee be equal to the amount that was the capital cost to the transferor. In most cases, the elected value will be equal to the transferor's UCC. ITA 85(5) requires that the difference between these two values be treated as deemed CCA. To illustrate this, consider the following asset:

Cost	$100,000
UCC	67,000
Fair Market Value	105,000
Non-Share Consideration	67,000
Elected Value	67,000

The capital cost of the asset to the transferee will be $100,000, there will be deemed CCA taken of $33,000, and future CCA will be based on the elected value of $67,000. The reason for requiring the transferee to retain the transferor's capital cost is to avoid having the transferor convert potential recaptured CCA into a capital gain, only one-half of which would be taxed.

You should also note that, in the usual situation where the transferor is not dealing at arm's length with the transferee corporation, the half year rules do not apply to the calculation of CCA by the transferee. This is the case as long as the transferor has owned the asset for at least 364 days before the end of the taxation year of the transferee in which the property was acquired and used it as a capital property to earn business or property income.

16-76.   What these rules mean is that, in cases where the election has been made at an amount equal to the transferor's tax cost, the transferee corporation essentially assumes the tax position of the transferor.

Capital Gains On Transfers Of Depreciable Property

16-77.   The objective of using ITA 85(1) is usually to avoid tax consequences when assets are transferred to a corporation. This means that, in general, the elected values will be equal to the transferor's tax values (adjusted cost base or UCC).

16-78.   There are, however, circumstances in which the transferor may wish to generate a capital gain through the transfer of assets to a corporation. An example of this might be an individual who has large losses in the current year, or who has unused net capital or non-capital loss carry forwards that he or she wishes to claim.

16-79.   This creates a problem with respect to depreciable assets in that, under the general ITA 85 rules, the elected value becomes the basis for calculating future CCA amounts. An election on a depreciable asset at a value in excess of the capital cost would result in a capital gain, only one-half of which would be taxable. Under the usual disposition rules, this same excess would become part of the UCC, the basis for calculating fully deductible amounts of CCA. The following example will illustrate this problem.

EXAMPLE   Jan Harding plans to transfer a depreciable asset to a Canadian controlled private corporation in which she is the only shareholder. The relevant values are as follows:

Cost	$ 80,000
Fair Market Value	120,000
UCC	75,000
Elected Value	120,000

ANALYSIS   The election at $120,000 would create the following amounts of income:

Recaptured CCA ($80,000 - $75,000)	$ 5,000
Taxable Capital Gain [(1/2)($120,000 - $80,000)]	20,000
Total Income	$25,000

In the absence of a special rule, the cost and UCC of this asset to the corporation would be $120,000. This value would create $45,000 more CCA for the corporation than would have been available to the transferor ($120,000 - $75,000). This has been accomplished through an increase in the transferor's Taxable Income of only $25,000, clearly not an equitable situation from the point of view of the government.

16-80.　ITA 13(7)(e) acts to correct this situation. You may recall that this provision was discussed in some detail in Chapter 9. It is a general provision that applies to all non-arm's length transfers of depreciable assets, including those where ITA 85(1) has been used.

16-81.　When such transfers occur, ITA 13(7)(e) limits the capital cost of the asset for CCA purposes to the transferor's cost, plus one-half of any capital gain that results from the transfer. As applied to the example in Paragraph 16-79, the capital cost to the transferee under ITA 13(7)(e) for CCA, recapture, and terminal loss purposes only would be as follows:

Transferor's Cost		$ 80,000
Elected Transfer Price	$120,000	
Transferor's Cost	(80,000)	
Capital Gain	$ 40,000	
Taxable Portion	1/2	20,000
Capital Cost To The Transferee For CCA Purposes		$100,000

16-82.　Based on this capital cost, the increase in the CCA base to the corporation is only $25,000 ($100,000 - $75,000), the same amount the transferor recognized as income as a result of the transfer. Note, however, that for future capital gains calculations, the capital cost of the asset to the transferee is the elected value of $120,000.

Paid Up Capital (PUC) Of Shares Issued

General Rules

16-83.　Establishing the Paid Up Capital (PUC) of the shares received is important as it represents an amount that can be distributed to the shareholders as a tax free return of capital. In general, the amount of PUC for tax purposes is equal to the amount attributed to the shares under the appropriate corporate laws (legal stated capital).

16-84.　While there are some complications in those provinces that still permit the issuance of par value shares, the legal stated capital of a corporation is generally based on the fair market value of the consideration received in return for issued shares. In the case of shares issued in an ITA 85 rollover, this amount would be equal to the fair market value of the assets transferred.

16-85.　In the usual ITA 85 scenario, in order to defer taxation on the asset transfer, assets that have increased in value will be transferred at elected values that are below their respective fair market values. Again, in the usual ITA 85 scenario, the elected values will be equal to the non-share consideration, leaving the adjusted cost base of the shares issued at nil. At this point, the PUC of the shares, which is based on the fair market value of the assets transferred, will exceed the adjusted cost base of the assets by the amount of the deferred gains. If PUC was left at this value, it would provide the investor with an opportunity to distribute the deferred gains on a tax free basis. To prevent this from happening a PUC reduction is required.

Paid Up Capital Reduction

16-86.　The need for a PUC reduction, as well as the procedure for calculating the reduction, can be illustrated using the following example.

> **EXAMPLE**   A non-depreciable capital asset with a fair market value of $200,000 and an adjusted cost base of $150,000 is transferred under ITA 85 using an elected value of $150,000.
>
> While the usual ITA application would have the transferor receiving non-share consideration of $150,000, in order to better illustrate the mechanics of the PUC reduction we will assume that the consideration consists of cash of $120,000 and shares with a legal stated capital of $80,000.

16-87.   If the asset had been sold to an arm's length party, the vendor would have had an immediate capital gain of $50,000 ($200,000 - $150,000). As is the intent of the legislation, these amounts of income are deferred when Section 85 is used properly. The problem is that if the $80,000 legal stated capital of the shares issued is used as their PUC, this amount can be withdrawn from the corporation on a tax free basis. This would mean the potential capital gain could permanently escape taxation.

16-88.   Given this problem, ITA 85(2.1) requires that the PUC of issued shares be reduced by an amount equal to the total increase in legal stated capital, less any excess of the elected value over non-share consideration given. Continuing with our example, a summary of the facts and the resulting PUC reduction would be as follows:

Asset: Fair market value = $200,000, Adjusted cost base = $150,000

Consideration: Cash = $120,000, Legal stated capital of shares = $80,000

Elected Value (Total amount that can be withdrawn tax free) = $150,000

Increase In Legal Stated Capital		$80,000
Less Excess, If Any, Of:		
Total Elected Value	($150,000)	
Over The Non-Share Consideration	120,000	(30,000)
Reduction In Paid Up Capital (PUC)		$50,000
PUC Of Shares ($80,000 - $50,000)		$30,000

16-89.   It is easy to see the conceptual basis for this reduction. The amount of PUC that can be removed by the transferor on a tax free basis is reduced to $30,000, the same amount ($150,000 - $120,000) of consideration he could have received on a tax free basis at the time of the transfer. If the shares were redeemed at their fair market value of $80,000, there would be an ITA 84(3) deemed dividend of $50,000 ($80,000, less a PUC of $30,000). While the taxation of the two amounts is different, this deemed dividend is the same amount as the capital gain that would have resulted from an arm's length sale of the asset. If the non-share consideration had been equal to the elected value of $150,000 (the usual ITA 85 scenario), the PUC would be reduced to nil {$80,000 PUC - [$80,000 - ($150,000 - $150,000)]}.

16-90.   A further tax policy problem, which is not resolved by the PUC reduction, relates to the lifetime capital gains deduction. If the asset in the Paragraph 16-86 example is transferred to a corporation at an elected value of $150,000, this would be the adjusted cost base of the shares. If the shares were later sold for their fair market value of $200,000, the result would be a $50,000 capital gain that could be eligible for the lifetime capital gains deduction if it met the requirements. In effect, the use of the ITA 85(1) rollover could result in the complete elimination of tax on the $50,000 capital gain that was present on the asset prior to its transfer.

More Than One Class Of Shares

16-91.   In most Section 85 rollovers, the ITA 85(2.1) formula will reduce the PUC of all shares issued to nil. This reflects the fact that the non-share consideration taken will equal the elected value, resulting in the PUC reduction being equal to the increase in legal stated capital. If this is the case, having more than one class of shares does not create any difficulties.

16-92. If, however, the non-share consideration is less than the elected value, the PUC reduction must be allocated to the various classes of shares. You will recall that, when we allocated the adjusted cost base, it was a sequential process (see Paragraph 16-73). The total adjusted cost base (i.e., the elected value) was allocated first to non-share consideration, then to preferred shares to the extent of their fair market value, and finally to the common shares if a residual remained.

16-93. This is not the case with the PUC reduction. The formula in ITA 85(2.1) is such that the reduction is allocated to different classes of shares on the basis of the relative increases in the legal stated capital of the two classes of shares.

> **EXAMPLE** Joan Creek transfers non-depreciable capital assets with a fair market value of $1,600,000 to a corporation under the provisions of ITA 85(1). The elected value is equal to the $900,000 cost of the assets and, as consideration, she receives cash of $600,000, redeemable preferred shares with a fair market value of $250,000, and common shares with a fair market value of $750,000.

> **ANALYSIS** The total adjusted cost base for the consideration would be allocated as follows:

Elected Value (Total Adjusted Cost Base Of All Consideration)	$900,000
Non-Share Consideration (Fair Market Value)	(600,000)
Adjusted Cost Base Of All Shares Issued	$300,000
Less: Adjusted Cost Base Of Preferred Shares Issued	
(Limited To Fair Market Value)	(250,000)
Adjusted Cost Base Of Common Shares Issued (Residual)	$ 50,000

The PUC reduction would be calculated as follows:

Increase In Legal Stated Capital		
($250,000 + $750,000)		$1,000,000
Less Excess, If Any, Of:		
Total Elected Value	($900,000)	
Over The Non-Share Consideration	600,000	(300,000)
Reduction In PUC		$ 700,000

The PUC of the two classes of shares, reduced by a pro rata allocation of the $700,000 PUC reduction on the basis of relative fair market value, would be as follows:

$$\text{PUC Of Preferred Stock} \left[\$250,000 - \left(\frac{\$250,000}{\$1,000,000} \right) (\$700,000) \right] = \underline{\underline{\$75,000}}$$

$$\text{PUC Of Common Stock} \left[\$750,000 - \left(\frac{\$750,000}{\$1,000,000} \right) (\$700,000) \right] = \underline{\underline{\$225,000}}$$

16-94. Note that the total PUC of the two classes is equal to $300,000 ($75,000 + $225,000). As you would expect, this is equal to the total adjusted cost base of the two classes ($250,000 + $50,000) as well as the difference between the elected value of $900,000 and the non-share consideration of $600,000. The fact that the individual amounts are different reflects the difference between the sequential allocation process for the adjusted cost base amount and the pro rata allocation of the PUC reduction.

Exercise Sixteen - 4

Subject: Transfers Under Section 85 - PUC Reduction

Using ITA 85, Mr. Rob McCleen transfers non-depreciable capital property to a corporation at an elected value of $114,000. The property has an adjusted cost base of $114,000 and a fair market value of $234,000. As consideration he receives a note for $83,000, preferred shares with a fair market value and legal stated capital of $97,000, and common shares with a fair market value and legal stated capital of $54,000. Indicate the adjusted cost base and the PUC of the preferred and common shares that were issued to Mr. McCleen.

SOLUTION available in print and online Study Guide.

We suggest you work Self Study Problem Sixteen-3 at this point.

Comprehensive Example - Section 85 Rollovers

Basic Information

16-95.   John Martin has been operating an unincorporated business. On January 1, 2020, the tax costs (UCC or adjusted cost base) and fair market values for its assets and liabilities are as follows:

	Tax Value	Fair Market Value
Cash	$ 20,000	$ 20,000
Accounts Receivable	50,000	49,000
Inventories	100,000	105,000
Prepaid Expenses	10,000	10,000
Land	50,000	70,000
Building (Capital Cost = $150,000)	110,000	140,000
Equipment (Capital Cost = $70,000)	40,000	35,000
Goodwill	Nil	50,000
Total Assets	$380,000	$479,000
Liabilities	$100,000	$100,000

Excluded Assets

16-96.   The rollover would involve a new corporation, the Martin Company, assuming all of Mr. Martin's liabilities and acquiring all of his business assets except the following:

Excluded Asset	Tax Value	Fair Market Value
Cash	$ 20,000	$ 20,000
Accounts Receivable	50,000	49,000
Prepaid Expenses	10,000	10,000
Equipment	40,000	35,000
Total Values For Excluded Assets	$120,000	$114,000

16-97.   With respect to the Cash and Prepaid Expenses, they are not eligible assets as described under ITA 85(1.1) and cannot be transferred under this rollover provision. However, as their fair market values are equal to their tax values, this is of no consequence.

16-98.   The Accounts Receivable could be transferred under ITA 85. However, the $1,000 ($50,000 - $49,000) loss would have to be treated as a capital loss, which would be disallowed as a superficial loss by ITA 40(2)(g). Further, any additional bad debts incurred by the corporation would also have to be treated as capital losses.

16-99.   The alternative is a joint election under ITA 22. This allows the $1,000 current loss to be treated as a fully deductible business loss. While the corporation will have to include this $1,000 in income, it will then be able to deduct the full amount of any additional bad debts. Taxpayers are not permitted to simultaneously use both the ITA 22 and the ITA 85 elections for their accounts receivable, so we have excluded it from the ITA 85 election.

16-100.   With respect to the equipment, its fair market value is less than the UCC for the class. In this case, ITA 13(21.2) indicates that ITA 85 does not apply and the proceeds of disposition are deemed to be the UCC amount of $40,000 thereby disallowing the terminal loss. There will be no tax consequences associated with the transfer and the corporation will retain Mr. Martin's original capital cost of $70,000 with the difference between the capital cost and the UCC considered deemed CCA. While a terminal loss could have been recognized if the property had been transferred to a non-affiliated person, it would have been disallowed if it was part of the ITA 85 transaction because Mr. Martin's corporation is an affiliated person.

Implementing The Election

16-101.   Mr. Martin is interested in deferring all of the capital gains that are present on his assets and, as a consequence, he elects tax values for most of the assets that are to be transferred under ITA 85. The one exception to this is goodwill, which is transferred at a value of $1 to ensure that it is listed in the election. In Mr. Martin's proprietorship's tax records, the proceeds of $1 will be subtracted from Class 14.1, leaving a negative balance in that Class. If there are no additions to this Class prior to the end of 2020, this amount will be treated as recapture and included in Mr. Martin's income. The $1 will also be added to Class 14.1, restoring the balance to nil. In Martin Company's records, the $1 will be added to Class 14.1.

16-102.   Mr. Martin's total elected value of $260,001 is calculated as follows:

Tax Values Of Total Assets	$380,000
Tax Value Of Excluded Assets (Paragraph 16-98)	(120,000)
Nominal Value To Goodwill	1
Total Elected Value	$260,001

16-103.   With respect to the consideration to be given to Mr. Martin, it must equal the fair market value of the assets transferred. This amount would be $365,000 ($479,000 total, less the $114,000 fair market value of the excluded assets listed in Paragraph 16-98).

16-104.   The normal procedure would be to take back non-share consideration, in this example debt, with a fair market value equal to the elected value of $260,001, along with shares with a fair market value equal to the $104,999 ($365,000 - $260,001) excess of the fair market values of the assets transferred over their elected values. The $260,001 in debt consideration is made up of $100,000 in debt of the existing business that has been assumed by the corporation, plus $160,001 in new debt issued by the corporation.

16-105.   The ITA 85(1) election is made on an asset-by-asset basis, requiring both an elected value and specified consideration (which must include some shares) for each asset transferred. In the schedule that follows, non-share consideration is allocated to each asset up to a maximum of its elected value, with share consideration allocated to the asset to reflect the excess of the fair market value of the asset over its elected value. For example, the fair market value of the inventories is $105,000. Reflecting the fact that the elected value for this asset is its tax value of $100,000, $100,000 of non-share consideration is allocated to this asset. The $5,000 in share consideration allocated to this asset is based on the excess of its fair market value over the elected value.

Comprehensive Example - Section 85 Rollovers

		Consideration At Fair Market Value	
	Elected Value	Non-Share	Share
Inventories	$100,000	$100,000	$ 5,000
Land	50,000	50,000	20,000
Building (Capital Cost = $150,000)	110,000	110,000	30,000
Goodwill	1	1	49,999
Total Assets	$260,001	$260,001	$104,999

16-106.   In this example, the total non-share consideration is equal to the total elected value. If it were less (it cannot be more as the non-share consideration is the general floor for the values to be elected), the amount of non-share consideration allocated to some assets would be less than the full elected value.

16-107.   From the point of view of the corporation, the elected values would become the tax values to be used in subsequent periods of operation. The adjusted cost base of the shares that were issued to Mr. Martin would be determined as follows:

Total Elected Value	$260,001
Non-Share Consideration	(260,001)
Adjusted Cost Base Of Shares	Nil

16-108.   The initial PUC of these shares would be their legal stated capital, an amount equal to their fair market value of $104,999. However, there would be an ITA 85(2.1) reduction in this balance as follows:

Increase In Legal Stated Capital		$104,999
Less Excess, If Any, Of:		
Total Elected Value	($260,001)	
Over The Non-Share Consideration	260,001	Nil
Reduction In PUC		$104,999

16-109.   At this point, both the adjusted cost base and the PUC of the shares are nil ($104,999 PUC - $104,999 PUC reduction). If they were redeemed at their $104,999 fair market value, Mr. Martin would have to recognize an ITA 84(3) deemed dividend of $104,999. This deemed dividend would reduce the proceeds of disposition for capital gains purposes to nil, resulting in no capital gain or loss on the redemption.

16-110.   Alternatively, if he were to sell the shares at their fair market value, the result would be a capital gain of $104,999. Unlike the redemption scenario, which would result in the deferred gain being taxed as a dividend, a sale of shares could completely avoid taxation on the deferred gain. This would happen if the gain resulting from the sale of shares fully qualified for the lifetime capital gains deduction.

Exercise Sixteen - 5

Subject: Transfers Under Section 85 - Tax Consequences

Jasmine Wiens has operated her alternative medicine pharmacy as an unincorporated business for a number of years. The tangible assets of this business have a fair market value of $850,000 and a tax cost of $275,000. In addition to the tangible assets, because the business has been extremely profitable, Jasmine estimates that it has goodwill of $300,000, resulting in a total value for the business of $1,150,000. The total liabilities of the business amount to $83,000. As she no longer needs all of the income that the business is producing, she would like to transfer the business to a new corporation and, in order to defer taxation, she would like to use the provisions of ITA 85(1) for the transfer.

On January 20, 2020, she will make the transfer at an elected value of $275,000. The corporation will assume the $83,000 in business liabilities and, in addition, issue a note payable to Ms. Wiens in the amount of $17,000. Other consideration will be made up of redeemable preferred shares with a fair market value of $125,000 and common shares with a fair market value of $925,000. Any dividends paid by the corporation will be non-eligible. Determine the following:

1. The adjusted cost base of each type of consideration received by Ms. Wiens.
2. The Paid Up Capital of each type of share issued by the new corporation.
3. The tax consequences to Ms. Wiens of the new preferred shares being redeemed at their fair market value immediately.

SOLUTION available in print and online Study Guide.

We suggest you work Self Study Problems Sixteen-4 to Sixteen-7 at this point.

Gift To Related Party - Section 85

General Rules

16-111. If the transferor of the assets is the only shareholder of the transferee corporation, the indirect gift rules in ITA 85(1)(e.2) are not applicable. However, Section 85 rollovers are often used for income splitting purposes, and this usually means that other members of the transferor's family will be involved as shareholders in the transferee corporation. The indirect gift rules are designed to ensure that, while other family members will be permitted to share in the future growth and income of the corporation, they are not permitted to receive a portion of the current values of the transferred assets in the form of a gift.

16-112. ITA 85(1)(e.2) is applicable if the fair market value of the transferred property exceeds the greater of:

1. the fair market value of all consideration received from the corporation; and
2. the amount elected for the transfer;

and it is reasonable to regard that excess as a gift made by the taxpayer for the benefit of any related shareholder. In any situation where a party related to the transferor is a shareholder of the transferee corporation, it would be reasonable to regard the excess as a gift.

16-113. If ITA 85(1)(e.2) is applicable, the tax consequence is that, except for purposes of determining the adjusted cost base of any shares provided to the transferor, the gift amount will be added to the elected value for the transfer to create a deemed elected value. As this deemed elected value becomes the deemed proceeds of disposition for the transferor and the deemed adjusted cost base of the property to the transferee corporation, this will usually result in a capital gain and/or business income on the rollover.

16-114. A less direct consequence is that the fair market value of the shares held by the related person will be increased by the amount of the gift. As there will be no corresponding increase in the related person's adjusted cost base, the sale of these shares will result in a taxable capital gain.

Example

16-115. The following example will serve to illustrate the application of ITA 85(1)(e.2).

EXAMPLE Mr. Pohl owns a non-depreciable capital property with an adjusted cost base of $30,000. He estimated its fair market value was $130,000. A new corporation is formed with all of the common shares being issued to Mr. Pohl's adult son for $1,000 in cash. Using the provisions of ITA 85(1), Mr. Pohl then transfers his non-depreciable property to the corporation at an elected value of $30,000.

The corporation issues a $30,000 note payable and preferred shares with a fair market value and a legal stated capital of $100,000 to Mr. Pohl. By taking back $130,000 ($30,000 + $100,000) in total consideration, Mr. Pohl is filing the election on the basis that the fair market value of the non-depreciable property is also $130,000 and there is no capital gain on this transaction. However, on review, the CRA reassesses him on the basis that the actual fair market value of the property is $180,000. Mr. Pohl, after a heated exchange with his accountant, agrees to accept this value.

16-116. Based on the reassessed value, the fair market value of the property transferred exceeds the fair market value of the consideration received as shown in the following calculation:

Fair Market Value Of Property Transferred (Reassessed Value)	$180,000
Less The Greater Of:	
• FMV Of Consideration Received = $130,000	
• Elected Amount = $30,000	(130,000)
Excess (Gift)	$ 50,000

16-117. As Mr. Pohl's son is the only common shareholder of the new corporation, it would be reasonable to regard this $50,000 as a gift to his son. This would make ITA 85(1)(e.2) applicable to this transaction and Mr. Pohl would have a taxable capital gain determined as follows:

Deemed Elected Value = Deemed Proceeds Of Disposition	
($30,000 + $50,000 Gift)	$80,000
Adjusted Cost Base	(30,000)
Capital Gain	$50,000
Inclusion Rate	1/2
Taxable Capital Gain	$25,000

16-118. Any CRA reassessment of the fair market values will involve specific assets. In this example, only one non-depreciable asset is involved and this means that the result will be a capital gain on that asset. If depreciable assets or inventories were involved, there could also be recapture or business income.

16-119. We noted in Paragraph 16-113 that the ITA 85(1)(e.2) deemed elected value does not apply in determining the adjusted cost base of the shares received by the transferor. Given this, the adjusted cost base of Mr. Pohl's preferred shares would be calculated as follows:

Elected Value (Original)	$30,000
Non-Share Consideration	(30,000)
Adjusted Cost Base Of Preferred Shares	Nil

16-120. Note, however, the deemed elected value does apply to the cost figure that is used in the following PUC reduction calculation under ITA 85(2.1). This would be relevant if there was a share redemption.

Increase In Legal Stated Capital		$100,000
Less The Excess, If Any, Of:		
Deemed Elected Value	($80,000)	
Over The Non-Share Consideration	30,000	(50,000)
PUC Reduction		$ 50,000
PUC Of Shares ($100,000 - $50,000)		$ 50,000

16-121.   The other relevant fact here is that the transferee corporation, in addition to the $1,000 invested by Mr. Pohl's son, has an asset with a fair market value of $180,000. Given this, the fair market value of the son's shares would be $51,000 ($181,000 - $30,000 - $100,000). As there has been no change in the adjusted cost base of the son's shares, a subsequent sale of the shares would result in a capital gain of $50,000 ($51,000 - $1,000).

16-122.   The actual and potential gains resulting from the application of ITA 85(1)(e.2) to this transaction are as follows:

Actual Capital Gain On Transfer	$ 50,000
Potential Gain On Mr. Pohl's Preferred Shares ($100,000 - Nil)	100,000
Potential Gain On Son's Common Shares ($51,000 - $1,000)	50,000
Total Gain	$200,000

16-123.   If Mr. Pohl had simply sold his property, the total gain would have been only $150,000 ($180,000 - $30,000), $50,000 less than the total gain in the preceding table. In effect, the $50,000 amount of the gift will be subject to double taxation.

16-124.   This example illustrates the importance of taking great care in establishing the fair market value of the property being transferred. A failure to do so can result in the double taxation that is illustrated here.

16-125.   Once that fair market value has been established, the transferor should take back a non-growth security such as preferred shares for the difference between the fair market value of the property and its tax value. Common shares can then be issued to the other family members at a nominal value. While the initial value of these shares will be nominal, it will be these shares that will have growth in value in the future.

Exercise Sixteen - 6

Subject: Gift To Related Party - Section 85

Janice Bellows establishes a new CCPC, arranging to have all of its common shares issued to her adult daughter for cash of $1,000. Ms. Bellows then transfers, using ITA 85, non-depreciable capital property with an adjusted cost base of $50,000 and an estimated fair market value of $65,000. The transfer is made at an elected value of $50,000. As consideration for this property, the corporation gives Ms. Bellows a note for $50,000 and preferred shares with a fair market value and a legal stated capital of $15,000.

A CRA reassessment of this transaction determines that the actual fair market value of the property transferred is $110,000. Ms. Bellows reluctantly accepts this value. After the reassessment, Ms. Bellows and her daughter sell their shares for their fair market value.

Taking into consideration the reassessment, describe the tax consequences of these transactions for both Ms. Bellows and her daughter. How would these tax consequences differ if Ms. Bellows had simply sold the non-depreciable capital property for its post-reassessment value of $110,000?

SOLUTION available in print and online Study Guide.

We suggest you work Self Study Problem Sixteen-8 at this point.

Excess Consideration - Section 85

Introduction

16-126.   In the previous section we considered the tax consequences of the transferor receiving consideration that is less than the fair market value of the property transferred. In this section we are concerned with the opposite case. Here we are concerned with situations in which the value of the consideration received exceeds the value of the assets transferred. When this is the case, the result will be a taxable benefit assessed to the transferor under ITA 15(1). Note that ITA 15(1), which is discussed in detail in Chapter 15, is a provision that covers a broad variety of transactions that can create taxable benefits to the recipient shareholder.

16-127.   In situations where ITA 85 is used to roll assets into an existing corporation that has assets other than those transferred in, share consideration or a combination of share consideration can result in an excess consideration situation. However, if the transfer is to a new corporation with no other shareholders, an ITA 15(1) benefit can only arise if the non-share consideration exceeds the value of the assets transferred. This reflects the fact that any shares issued, when combined with the value of the non-share consideration, cannot have a value in excess of the fair market value of the assets transferred to the new corporation.

> **EXAMPLE**   An asset with a fair market value of $100,000 is transferred to a new corporation using ITA 85(1). The transferor receives $100,000 in non-share consideration as well as preferred shares. (To use Section 85, at least one share must be issued by the transferee.)

> **ANALYSIS**   As the $100,000 in non-share consideration is equal to the fair market value of the assets transferred, the shares can only have a nominal value. Given this, they cannot create an excess consideration situation. Note that on transfers to a new corporation, if the non-share consideration is equal to, or greater than, the fair market value of the assets transferred, the shares that will be issued will have both an adjusted cost base and a PUC of nil.

> In order to simplify our coverage of this fairly minor topic of excess consideration, we will limit our examples and problems to situations involving transfers to new corporations where the fair market value of the non-share consideration exceeds the fair market value of the assets transferred.

16-128.   Excess consideration situations do not usually involve a deliberate attempt by the taxpayer to receive an inappropriate amount of consideration. Rather the typical scenario involves the taxpayer filing an ITA 85 election using an estimated fair value for the assets transferred, with the CRA later reassessing based on a lower value for the assets. This is illustrated in the example in the next section.

Shareholder Benefit - ITA 15(1)

16-129.   The following example illustrates a situation in which the use of ITA 85(1) results in a taxable benefit to the transferor.

> **EXAMPLE**   In 2019, Ms. Sally Swit transfers non-depreciable capital property to a new corporation in which she owns 100 percent of the shares using ITA 85(1). The property has an adjusted cost base of $65,000 and she believes it has a fair market value of $200,000. She takes back debt with a fair market value of $200,000 and preferred shares with a nominal value. In her 2019 tax return, she shows a taxable capital gain of $67,500 [(1/2)($200,000 - $65,000)].

> In 2020, the CRA reassesses on the basis that the fair market value of the property was only $150,000 at the time of the transfer. Ms. Swit accepts this reassessed value and does not file an objection.

> **ANALYSIS**   Based on the original estimated fair market value for the property transferred, there was no excess consideration. However, with the reassessment value of $150,000 there is an excess, resulting in the following ITA 15(1) benefit:

Fair Market Value Of Consideration	$200,000
Reassessed Fair Market Value Of The Property	(150,000)
ITA 15(1) Shareholder Benefit	$ 50,000

With the value of the property transferred reassessed to $150,000, the elected value cannot exceed this amount. Based on this, there would be a revised taxable capital gain on the transfer, calculated as follows:

Elected Value Of Property After Reassessment	$ 150,000
Adjusted Cost Base	(65,000)
Capital Gain	$ 85,000
Inclusion Rate	1/2
Taxable Capital Gain On Property After Reassessment	$ 42,500

The reassessment increases 2019 Net Income For Tax Purposes from $67,500 to $92,500 ($50,000 + $42,500), an increase of $25,000 as shown in the following:

Taxable Capital Gain After Reassessment	$42,500
Shareholder Benefit After Reassessment	50,000
Reversal Of Reported Taxable Capital Gain	(67,500)
Total Addition To Net Income For Tax Purposes	$25,000

The reason for this increase is that $50,000 of the capital gain, only one-half of which would be taxed, was converted to a 100 percent taxable shareholder benefit of $50,000. Because a $50,000 benefit will be included in Ms. Swit's income as a result of a property acquisition, ITA 52(1) requires that this amount be added to the adjusted cost base of the non-share consideration. Given this, the adjusted cost base of the non-share consideration would be as follows:

Elected Value	$150,000
ITA 15(1) Shareholder Benefit	50,000
Adjusted Cost Base Of Non-Share Consideration	$200,000

As explained in Paragraph 16-127, both the adjusted cost base and the PUC of the preferred shares issued is nil.

Exercise Sixteen - 7

Subject: Benefit To Transferor (Excess Consideration) - Section 85

In 2019, Mr. Larry Custer uses ITA 85 to transfer non-depreciable capital property to a new CCPC in which he owns 100 percent of the shares. The adjusted cost base of the property is $123,000 and he believes that its fair market value is $270,000. In consideration for this property, Mr. Custer receives a note for $270,000 and preferred shares with a nominal value.

In 2020, Mr. Custer is reassessed on the basis that the fair market value of the transferred property was only $217,000. He accepts the reassessment without objection.

Describe the tax consequences of the transfer and the reassessment. Indicate the adjusted cost base of the consideration, and the adjusted cost base and the PUC of the preferred shares after the reassessment.

SOLUTION available in print and online Study Guide.

We suggest you work Self Study Problem Sixteen-9 at this point.

Dividend Stripping — ITA 84.1

Background

The General Concept

16-130. The term dividend stripping is applied to two types of situations, depending on when the relevant shares were issued by the corporation. In simple terms, both scenarios involve an individual who is attempting to remove assets from a corporation on a tax free basis.

16-131. Attaining this goal can be accomplished if the individual is willing to give up control by selling his or her shares to an arm's length party. However, when this is not the case and the individual retains control, the dividend stripping rules will often prevent the tax free removal of assets.

16-132. One approach to removing assets from a corporation while still retaining control would be to pay dividends. However, dividends will be taxed in the hands of the recipient and, being a rational individual, the owner of the corporation would prefer to receive the assets on a tax free basis.

16-133. Currently, the usual approach to accomplishing the goal of removing funds from a controlled corporation on a tax free basis is to convert what is, in effect, a dividend payment into a capital gain that would be eligible for the lifetime capital gains deduction. This is the origin of the term "dividend stripping". ITA 84.1 is a provision that is intended to thwart such efforts.

Pre-1972 Shares

16-134. At an earlier point in time, the most important application of ITA 84.1 was to prevent the conversion of pre-1972 earnings into a pre-1972 capital gain. As we noted in Chapter 8, prior to 1972, capital gains were not subject to tax in Canada. Given this, such a conversion could have resulted in the tax free receipt of a considerable amount of assets. While such situations still arise, they are not of sufficient importance to cover in a general text such as this. As a consequence, the application of ITA 84.1 in this type of situation will not receive further attention.

Qualified Small Business Corporation Shares

16-135. The most important current application of the dividend stripping rules from ITA 84.1 involves shares of a qualified small business corporation. The capital gains on dispositions of such shares are eligible for the lifetime capital gains deduction. This means that, if an individual can remove the retained earnings of such a corporation in the form of a capital gain, a very large amount of income can be received on a tax free basis. In general, ITA 84.1 serves to make such conversions difficult. The text and problems in this section will focus on this application of the dividend stripping rules that are found in ITA 84.1.

Applicability Of ITA 84.1

16-136. ITA 84.1(1) specifies the conditions under which the dividend stripping rules become applicable. These conditions are as follows:

- there is a disposition by a resident Canadian taxpayer (other than a corporation) of shares of a resident Canadian corporation (the subject corporation);
- the taxpayer held the shares as capital property (i.e., the shares were held to produce income, not for resale at a profit);
- the disposition is made to a corporation with which the taxpayer does not deal at arm's length; and
- the subject corporation must be connected with the purchaser corporation after the disposition of shares (i.e., the purchaser corporation must control the subject corporation or own more than 10 percent of the voting shares and 10 percent of the fair market value of all shares).

16-137. When these conditions are present, the provisions of ITA 84.1 will generally serve to eliminate the individual's ability to achieve their dividend stripping goals.

Figure 16 - 2
Application Of ITA 84.1 To Post-1971 Shares

Dividend Stripping Example

Basic Example

16-138.   A simple example will serve to illustrate the application of ITA 84.1 to post-1971 shares. As shown in Figure 16-2, Ms. Barton is the only shareholder of Barton Industries (BI), a Canadian controlled private corporation. The company was established in 1986 with an investment of $25,000 on the part of Ms. Barton. There has been no additional investment in the company and, as a consequence, $25,000 is the adjusted cost base of her shares as well as their PUC. The shares have a fair market value of $900,000. Because of her previous use of the lifetime capital gains deduction, Ms. Barton's available balance for the year is limited to $650,000. The shares of BI are qualified small business corporation shares. The company has no opening balance in its GRIP account.

16-139.   Ms. Barton could, of course, make use of her lifetime capital gains deduction by selling the BI shares to an arm's length party and realizing a capital gain of $875,000 ($900,000 - $25,000). However, this approach would result in tax payable as the capital gain of $875,000 exceeds the $650,000 deduction that she has available. In addition, and perhaps more importantly, she would lose control of BI.

16-140.   Given these considerations, she chooses to transfer the BI shares to a new company, Barton Holdings Ltd. (BHL), using the provisions of ITA 85(1). Ms. Barton uses an elected value for the transfer of $675,000, in order to limit her capital gain to $650,000 ($675,000 - $25,000). She takes back $675,000 in new debt of BHL, along with the common shares of the new company. These shares have a fair market value of $225,000 ($900,000 - $675,000) and an adjusted cost base of nil.

16-141.   Through this procedure, Ms. Barton appears to have realized the required $650,000 of the accrued capital gain on the BI shares and, at the same time, retained control of the company. However, Ms. Barton:

- is an individual, resident in Canada;
- held the shares as capital property;
- has made a disposition of shares to a corporation with which she does not deal at arm's length; and
- has created connected corporations subsequent to the transaction since BHL owns all of the shares of BI.

16-142.   Given these facts, the dividend stripping provisions of ITA 84.1 would be applicable to this transaction.

ITA 84.1 Procedures

16-143.   The ITA 84.1 procedures begin with a reduction in the PUC of any shares of the subject corporation that are received by Ms. Barton. Note that, when both ITA 85 and ITA 84.1 are involved, the PUC reduction rules specified in ITA 84.1(1)(a) must be used. They would apply as follows in this situation:

Increase In Legal Stated Capital Of BHL Shares		$ 225,000
Less Excess, If Any, Of:		
PUC Of Barton Industries Shares (Note One)	($ 25,000)	
Over The Non-Share Consideration	675,000	Nil
ITA 84.1(1)(a) PUC Reduction (Note Two)		$225,000

Note One   This amount is technically the greater of the PUC of the subject shares and their adjusted cost base. In this example, the two amounts are equal.

Note Two   In those cases where the boot is equal to or exceeds the greater of the PUC and the adjusted cost base of the subject corporation shares, the PUC reduction will be 100 percent of the PUC of the new shares.

16-144.   This would leave the PUC of the new shares at nil ($225,000 - $225,000). Given this, the ITA 84.1(1)(b) deemed dividend would be calculated as follows:

Increase In Legal Stated Capital Of BHL Shares		$225,000
Non-Share Consideration		675,000
Total		$900,000
Less The Sum Of:		
The Greater Of The PUC And ACB Of Barton		
Industries (Subject) Shares	($ 25,000)	
PUC Reduction Under ITA 84.1(1)(a)	(225,000)	(250,000)
ITA 84.1(1)(b) Deemed Dividend (Non-Eligible)		$650,000

16-145.   The results from Ms. Barton's disposition of her BI shares would be as follows:

Elected Proceeds Of Disposition	$675,000
ITA 84.1(1)(b) Deemed Dividend (See Note)	(650,000)
ITA 54 Deemed Proceeds Of Disposition	$ 25,000
Adjusted Cost Base Of Barton Industries Shares	(25,000)
Capital Gain	Nil

Note   The definition of proceeds of disposition in ITA 54 indicates that it does not include any amount that is deemed by ITA 84.1(1) to be a dividend. In the absence of this exclusion, the deemed dividend could be taxed a second time as part of a taxable capital gain.

16-146.   As the preceding example makes clear, the effect of ITA 84.1 in this situation is to convert the $650,000 capital gain on the BI shares into an ITA 84.1 deemed dividend. This means that Ms. Barton will not be able to make use of her lifetime capital gains deduction and that she will be subject to taxation on the deemed dividend. ITA 84.1 has clearly served to make this type of transaction unattractive.

16-147.   As a final point, you should note that Ms. Barton could have achieved her goal of triggering a capital gain for purposes of the lifetime capital gains deduction. Her problem was that she also wanted to remove the gain in the form of non-share consideration. If, as an alternative, she had elected the same transfer price of $675,000, but limited the non-share consideration to the $25,000 PUC amount, she would have had her $650,000 capital gain without creating an ITA 84.1 deemed dividend. Note, however, that she does not have the $650,000 in cash. She would be holding shares with a value of $875,000 and an adjusted cost base of $650,000, and a PUC of nil. In order to have the cash and take advantage of the lifetime capital gains deduction, she would have to sell the shares to an arms' length party and lose control of the corporation.

Exercise Sixteen - 8

Subject: Dividend Stripping

Miss Sarah Cole owns 100 percent of the outstanding shares of Cole Inc., a qualified small business corporation. The shares have a PUC and an adjusted cost base of $125,000 and a fair market value of $767,000. The company has no balance in its GRIP account. On February 1, 2020, Miss Cole uses ITA 85(1) to transfer these shares to Sarah's Holdings Ltd. at an elected value of $767,000. As consideration, she receives a note for $450,000 and preferred shares with a fair market value and a legal stated capital of $317,000. Miss Cole owns all of the shares of Sarah's Holdings Ltd. and has never made use of her lifetime capital gains deduction. What are the tax consequences of this transaction to Miss Cole?

SOLUTION available in print and online Study Guide.

We suggest you work Self Study Problem Sixteen-10 at this point.

Capital Gains Stripping — ITA 55(2)

The Problem

16-148.   A problem similar to that involved in dividend stripping arises when a corporation owns shares in a different corporation. If there is an accrued capital gain on these shares, a disposition of the shares will result in the recognition of that gain. Further, corporations are not eligible to use the lifetime capital gains deduction. This means that a disposition of the shares of the investee corporation for a gain will result in an increase in Taxable Income for the selling corporation.

16-149.   While capital gains are subject to corporate income taxes, dividends received from taxable Canadian corporations can escape corporate taxes. This means that, if the investor corporation can devise some method of disposing of its investment so that the accrued gain can be received in the form of dividends rather than as a taxable capital gain, the payment of corporate taxes can be avoided.

16-150.   In the absence of an anti-avoidance provision, this could be accomplished in a variety of ways. To illustrate this, assume the following:

* The Investee Company is a wholly owned subsidiary of the Investor Company.
* There is an accrued capital gain on the Investee Company shares.
* There is an arm's length purchaser who is prepared to buy the Investee Company shares at their fair market value.

16-151.   There are several approaches that could be used in an attempt to convert the accrued capital gain into dividends that could be received by the Investor Company on a tax free basis. The two approaches that we will consider here can be described as follows:

* **Approach One**   ITA 85(1) could be used to roll the Investee Company shares to a purchaser corporation at an elected value equal to the adjusted cost base of the Investee Company shares, resulting in no increase in Taxable Income for the Investor Company. As consideration, the purchaser corporation would issue preferred shares that are redeemable at the fair market value of the Investee Company shares. When the

preferred shares are redeemed, the result will be an ITA 84(3) deemed dividend, which can be received by the Investor Company on a tax free basis. Once again, it would appear that the Investor Company has disposed of the Investee Company shares without any increase in Taxable Income or Tax Payable.

- **Approach Two**   The Investee Company could assume debt equal to the accrued gain on its shares. This company would then, using the borrowed funds, pay a dividend equal to the accrued gain. This would reduce the fair market value of the Investee Company shares by the amount of the accrued gain, leaving the Investee Company shares with a fair market value equal to their adjusted cost base. They could then be sold with no tax consequences. As the dividend would be received by the Investee Company on a tax free basis, it would appear that the Investor Company has disposed of the Investee Company shares without any increase in Taxable Income or Tax Payable.

16-152.   Such procedures are referred to as capital gains stripping, reflecting the fact that it is an attempt to "strip" out a capital gain in the form of a non-taxable, intercorporate dividend. ITA 55(2) is an anti-avoidance provision designed to prevent such conversions of capital gains to dividends by a corporation disposing of an investment in shares.

Application Of ITA 55(2)

Conditions For ITA 55(2) To Apply

16-153.   In somewhat simplified terms, the provisions of ITA 55(2) act to prevent capital gains stripping when the following conditions are present:

- An Investor Company receives dividends that are deductible in the determination of its Taxable Income as part of a transaction, or series of transactions, involving a disposition of Investee Company shares owned by the Investor Company.

- It is determined that one of the purposes of the dividend was to significantly reduce the capital gain on Investee Company shares that would have been included in the Net Income For Tax Purposes of the Investor Company in the absence of the dividend.

- The disposition of the Investee Company shares was to an arm's length party. While we will not illustrate this in our coverage of this subject, ITA 55(2) would also be applicable if there was a significant increase in an unrelated person's interest in either the Investor Company or the Investee Company.

Application Of ITA 55(2)

16-154.   If the conditions specified in Paragraph 16-153 are present, the following rules apply to the dividend:

ITA 55(2)(a)   This provision indicates that the dividend received by the Investor Company will be deemed not to be a dividend except to the extent that the Company has a Safe Income balance (see following description). To the extent that a Safe Income balance is available, the dividend will retain its status as a dividend.

In simplified terms, Safe Income is income that has accrued after 1971 or, if the acquisition of the shares was after that date, after the date on which the shares were acquired. We would note that recent amendments to ITA 55, which required the determination of safe income, have made the application of ITA 55(2) more complex.

Note that this provision only serves to remove the dividend status from the payment received by the Investor Company. It does not indicate the tax status of the payment subsequent to its removal from the dividend category. This is accomplished using ITA 55(2)(b) or ITA 55(2)(c).

ITA 55(2)(b)   If shares are cancelled, an ITA 84(2) dividend can arise. Similarly, if shares are redeemed, an ITA 84(3) dividend can arise. If the conditions for the application of

Figure 16 - 3
Application Of ITA 55(2) - Example One (Approach One)

ITA 55(2) are present, ITA 55(2)(a) deems all or part of the dividend to not be a dividend and ITA 55(2)(b) deems the disallowed portion of the payment to be proceeds of disposition, except to the extent that it is otherwise included in computing such proceeds.

ITA 55(2)(c)   If the conditions for the application of ITA 55 are present and ITA 55(2) (b) does not apply, the portion of the payment that is deemed not to be a dividend by ITA 55(2)(a) is deemed to be a capital gain of the Investor Company.

Capital Gains Stripping - Example One

16-155.   This first example depicts Approach One that is described in Paragraph 16-153. It is diagramed in Figure 16-3.

16-156.   In this example, ITA 85(1) is used to roll the Lee Ltd. shares into the purchaser corporation at an elected value equal to the $200,000 adjusted cost base of the shares. As consideration for the shares, Lor Inc. takes back $800,000 in redeemable preferred shares. These shares have a PUC and an adjusted cost base of $200,000.

16-157.   As you may recall from Chapter 14, a redemption is also a disposition. This requires the calculation of both a proceeds of redemption and a proceeds of disposition. Such transactions can result in an ITA 84(3) dividend, a capital gain or loss, or both. The relevant calculations in this example are as follows:

Proceeds Of Redemption	$800,000
PUC Of Shares	(200,000)
ITA 84(3) Deemed Dividend [Absence Of ITA 55(2)]	$600,000
Proceeds Of Disposition	$800,000
Less The ITA 84(3) Dividend	(600,000)
Adjusted Proceeds Of Disposition	$200,000
Adjusted Cost Base	(200,000)
Capital Gain [Absence Of ITA 55(2)]	Nil

16-158.   In the absence of ITA 55(2), the ITA 84(3) dividend would be deducted in determining Lor's Taxable Income and Lor would have succeeded in disposing of the Lee shares for $800,000, without incurring any taxation. The provisions of ITA 55(2) will act to prevent this result from being realized.

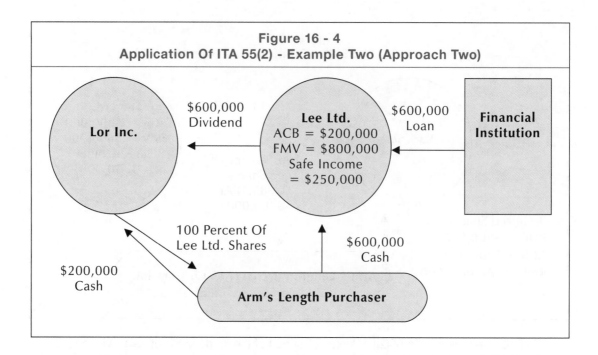

Figure 16 - 4
Application Of ITA 55(2) - Example Two (Approach Two)

16-159. ITA 55(2)(a) will deem any dividend that is not from Safe Income to not be a dividend. In this example, that amount would be $350,000 ($600,000 - $250,000). While $250,000 would retain its status as an ITA 84(3) dividend, under ITA 55(2)(b), the $350,000 would be deemed to be proceeds of disposition. As a result, the tax consequence to Lor would be calculated as follows:

Adjusted Proceeds Of Disposition	
(See Calculation In Paragraph 16-157)	$200,000
Deemed Proceeds Of Disposition - ITA 55(2)(b)	350,000
Total Proceeds Of Disposition	$550,000
Adjusted Cost Base	(200,000)
Capital Gain	$350,000

16-160. As can be seen in the preceding calculation, ITA 55(2) has served to convert $350,000 of the ITA 84(3) dividend into a capital gain of $350,000. The $250,000 dividend from Safe Income can be deducted under ITA 112 in the determination of Lor's Taxable Income, resulting in no tax cost.

Capital Gains Stripping - Example Two

16-161. This second example depicts Approach Two that is described in Paragraph 16-151. It involves the same two companies that were used in Example One. The only difference is in the approach that they use in attempting to convert the capital gain into a tax free dividend. It is diagramed in Figure 16-4.

16-162. In this example, Lor Inc. owns 100 percent of the shares of Lee Ltd. The shares have a fair market value of $800,000, an adjusted cost base of $200,000, and a potential capital gain of $600,000. Lee Ltd. has Safe Income of $250,000. An arm's length purchaser is willing to pay $800,000 for these shares. In order to implement this sale, Lor Inc. arranges the following:

- Lee Ltd. borrows $600,000 from a financial institution.

- The borrowed funds are used to pay a $600,000 tax free dividend to Lor Inc. This reduces the fair market value of Lee Ltd. to $200,000 ($800,000 - $600,000).

- Lor Inc. sells the shares to the arm's length purchaser for $200,000 in cash. As this is the adjusted cost base of the shares, there will be no capital gain.

- The arm's length purchaser invests $600,000 in Lee Ltd., with the funds being used to retire the $600,000 loan.

16-163.   In the absence of ITA 55(2), Lor Inc. would have managed to dispose of its interest in Lee Ltd. in a series of transactions for $800,000 ($200,000 received directly from the purchaser and $600,000 of tax free dividends financed indirectly by the purchaser) without the recognition of a capital gain. However, ITA 55(2) will prevent this from happening.

16-164.   Under ITA 55(2)(a), the portion of the $600,000 dividend that is not from Safe Income will be deemed not to be a dividend to Lor Inc., the dividend recipient. Under ITA 55(2)(c), this portion of the dividend will be treated as a capital gain on the disposition of capital property. This result is shown in the following calculation:

Dividends Received	$600,000
Dividend Attributable To Safe Income - Retains Status As A Dividend	(250,000)
Amount Deemed By ITA 55(2)(a) To Not Be A Dividend And By ITA 55(2)(c) To Be A Capital Gain	$350,000

16-165.   As was the result in Example One, ITA 55(2) has served to convert the portion of the dividend not paid from Safe Income into a capital gain, which will be taxed. The $250,000 portion of the dividend attributable to Safe Income will retain its status as a dividend and can be deducted in the determination of Lor's Taxable Income.

Exercise Sixteen - 9

Subject: Capital Gains Stripping

Markem Ltd. owns 100 percent of the outstanding common shares of Larkin Ltd. The shares of Larkin have an adjusted cost base of $75,000 and a fair market value of $840,000. Included in its Retained Earnings balance is $225,000 of income that has been earned since its acquisition by Markem Ltd. Markem Ltd. would like to sell its shares in Larkin Ltd. In order to implement this sale, Markem Ltd. has instructed Larkin Ltd. to borrow $750,000 from its bank and use all of these funds to pay a dividend on the shares held by Markem Ltd. The shares are then sold to Mr. J. Leaner for $90,000. Mr. Leaner is not related to Markem Ltd. or Larkin Ltd. What are the tax consequences to Markem Ltd. of these transactions?

SOLUTION available in print and online Study Guide.

We suggest you work Self Study Problem Sixteen-11 at this point.

Key Terms Used In This Chapter

16-166.   The following is a list of the key terms used in this Chapter. These terms, and their meanings, are compiled in the Glossary located at the back of the Study Guide.

Adjusted Cost Base	Non-Share Consideration
Affiliated Group Of Persons	Paid Up Capital
Affiliated Person - ITA 251.1(1)	PUC
Boot	Recapture Of CCA

Capital Cost	Rollover
Capital Gains Stripping	Safe Income
Controlled - ITA 251.1(3)	Subject Corporation
Corporation	Superficial Loss - ITA 54
Depreciable Capital Property	Taxpayer
Dividend Stripping	Terminal Loss
Eligible Capital Property	Transfer
Gift	Transferee
Individual	Transferor
Non-Depreciable Capital Property	Undepreciated Capital Cost (UCC)

References

16-167.   For more detailed study of the material in this Chapter, we would refer you to the following:

ITA 13(21.2)	Loss On Certain Transfers
ITA 15(1)	Benefits Conferred On A Shareholder
ITA 40(2)(g)	Superficial Losses
ITA 40(3.4)	Loss On Certain Properties
ITA 54	Definitions (Proceeds Of Disposition And Superficial Loss)
ITA 55(2)	Deemed Proceeds Or Capital Gain
ITA 84.1(1)	Non-Arm's Length Sale Of Shares
ITA 85	Transfer Of Property To Corporation By Shareholders
ITA 89(1)	Definitions
ITA 251.1	Affiliated Persons
IC 76-19R3	Transfer Of Property To A Corporation Under Section 85
S4-F3-C1	Price Adjustment Clauses
IT-188R	Sale of Accounts Receivable
IT-291R3	Transfer Of Property To A Corporation Under Subsection 85(1)
IT-489R	Non-Arm's Length Sale Of Shares To A Corporation

Problems For Self Study (Online)

To provide practice in problem solving, there are Self Study and Supplementary Self Study problems available on MyLab Accounting.

Within the text we have provided an indication of when it would be appropriate to work each Self Study problem. The detailed solutions for Self Study problems can be found in the print and online Study Guide.

We provide the Supplementary Self Study problems for those who would like additional practice in problem solving. The detailed solutions for the Supplementary Self Study problems are available online, not in the Study Guide.

The .PDF file "Self Study Problems for Volume 2" on MyLab contains the following for Chapter 16:

- 11 Self Study problems,
- 6 Supplementary Self Study problems, and
- detailed solutions for the Supplementary Self Study problems.

Assignment Problems

(The solutions for these problems are only available in
the solutions manual that has been provided to your instructor.)

Assignment Problem Sixteen - 1
(Transfers To A Corporation Vs. Direct Sale)
For a number of years, Brett Manson has owned an apartment building in the city of London, Ontario. Information on its acquisition is as follows:

Acquisition Cost	$1,355,000
Estimated Cost Of The Land	(462,000)
Estimated Cost Of The Building	$ 893,000

At the beginning of the current year, values related to the property are as follows:

Estimated Fair Market Value Of Property	$1,610,000
Estimated Fair Market Value Of Land	(574,000)
Estimated Fair Market Value Of The Building	$1,036,000
UCC Of The Building	$ 685,022

At this time, Brett transfers the property to a corporation using a Section 85 rollover. The value elected for the transfer is $1,147,022 ($462,000 + $685,022). The only consideration received by Brett is common shares in the new corporation.

Later in the year, all of the common shares are sold to Jason Border, an arm's length party, for $1,610,000.

Required:

A. Describe the tax consequences for Brett of using Section 85 and selling the common shares.

B. How do these results compare with the tax consequences of simply selling the building directly to Jason Border for $1,610,000?

Assignment Problem Sixteen - 2
(Section 85 Rollovers - Short Cases)
The following **independent** Cases involve transfers of assets under ITA 85.

Case One   Depreciable assets with a fair market value of $183,400 are transferred to a corporation in exchange for non-share consideration of $140,000, preferred shares with a fair market value of $22,000, and common shares with a fair market value of $21,400. The assets had a capital cost of $130,000. They were the only assets in their class and the UCC balance in the class was $59,904.

Case Two   Inventories of merchandise are transferred to a corporation in exchange for $93,000 in non-share consideration and $27,000 in common stock (fair market value and legal stated capital). The inventories have a cost of $87,000 and a fair market value of $120,000.

Case Three   Land is transferred to a corporation in exchange for $72,000 in non-share consideration and $751,000 in common stock (fair market value and legal stated capital). The land cost $617,000 and has a current fair market value of $823,000.

Required: For each of the three Cases provide the following information:

A. The minimum and maximum transfer prices that could be elected under the provisions of ITA 85.

B. Assuming the minimum value is elected, the amount of capital gain or business income to be included in the income of the transferor.

C. Again assuming that the minimum transfer value is elected, determine the adjusted cost base and PUC of the preferred and common stock consideration. Your answer should include the determination of any shareholder benefit under ITA 15(1) or deemed dividend under ITA 84(1) that will arise on the transfer, or explain why there is no benefit or deemed dividends.

Assignment Problem Sixteen - 3
(ACB Of Consideration And PUC)

Lily Haring has owned a depreciable property for a number of years. The property had an original capital cost of $623,000. It is the only asset in its class and, at the present time, the UCC for the class equals $229,663. The current fair market value of the asset is $946,000.

Lily would like to transfer this asset to a new corporation using the provisions of Section 85(1). She is considering the following alternative consideration packages, all of which total $946,000:

Package One   Lily will take back debt with a fair market value of $229,663, along with common shares with a fair market value of $716,337.

Package Two   Lily will take back debt with a fair market value of $100,000, preferred shares with a fair market value of $100,000, and common shares with a fair market value of $746,000.

Package Three   Lily will take back debt with a fair market value of $700,000 and preferred shares with a fair market value of $246,000.

Required: For each of the three packages, determine:

- The minimum transfer value that Lily can elect and the amount and type of income that will result from electing this value.

- The adjusted cost base of each of the items of consideration received by Lily.

- The Paid Up Capital for the preferred and/or common shares issued.

Assignment Problem Sixteen - 4
(ITA 85 Transfer Of Depreciable Asset)

During the current year, Mr. Rob Banting transfers a depreciable capital property to a new corporation. Rob owns all of the shares in the new corporation and it will have a December 31 year end.

The depreciable asset was purchased several years ago for $343,000. The asset has a current fair market value of $420,000. At the time of transfer, it is the only asset in its class and, prior to the transfer, the balance in the class was $213,790.

Rob has been carrying forward a $52,000 capital loss on a stock sale. In order to absorb this loss, he elects to transfer the property at a value of $395,000.

As consideration, Rob takes back a note for $175,000, preferred shares with a fair market value of $90,000, and common shares with a fair market value of $155,000.

Required: Describe the income tax implications resulting from this transaction. Your answer should include both current tax implications and the determination of values that will have future tax implications.

Assignment Problem Sixteen - 5
(Short Cases With Gift And Shareholder Benefit)

Peter Kowalski owns a rental property that was acquired years ago at a cost of $1,200,000. At the time, he estimated the value of the land to be $200,000 and the value of the building to be $1,000,000.

Peter estimates that the current value of the property is $1,500,000, with $300,000 of this amount being allocated to the land and $1,200,000 of this amount allocated to the building. As of this date, the UCC of the building is $460,800.

Peter has decided to transfer this property to a corporation using the provisions of Section 85. He is considering three possible scenarios. Consider each of the three scenarios as completely independent.

Scenario 1 Peter transfers the property to a new corporation in which he will be the sole shareholder. He has a net capital loss carryforward of $50,000. As he has no other assets with accumulated capital gains, he would like the transfer of the rental property to create a $100,000 capital gain against which he can apply his capital loss. To accomplish this, he elects a transfer value of $300,000 for the land. The elected value for the building will be $460,800. As consideration, he will receive a note payable for $760,800 and preferred shares with a legal stated capital and redemption value of $739,200.

Scenario 2 Peter transfers the property to a new corporation in which he will be the sole shareholder. The land is transferred at an elected value of $200,000 and the building is transferred at an elected value of $460,800. As consideration he will receive a note payable for $660,800, and preferred shares with a fair market value (their redemption value) of $939,200. The legal stated capital of the preferred shares will be $839,200.

Scenario 3 Peter's daughter, Stella, establishes a new corporation with an investment of $10,000 of her own money for the corporation's common shares. Peter transfers the rental property to this corporation with an elected value of $200,000 for the land and $460,800 for the building. As he would like to provide financial assistance for his daughter, in his election he claims that the fair market value of the land is $200,000, hoping that the CRA will not look at the fact that this value is too low. Based on this, he only takes back $1,400,000 in consideration, a note payable for $400,000, and preferred shares with a legal stated capital and a redemption value of $1,000,000.

On review, the CRA discovers the undervaluation and reassesses Peter on the basis that the land actually had a fair market value of $300,000. Peter does not object to this reassessment.

Required: For each of the preceding scenarios, determine for Mr. Kowalski:

- The tax consequences of the transfer for him.
- The tax cost of the land and building in the hands of the corporation.
- The adjusted cost base of the shares issued to him by the corporation.
- The PUC of the shares issued to him by the corporation.

In your solution for Scenario 3, include the effects of the CRA reassessment.

Assignment Problem Sixteen - 6
(ITA 85 Transfer With Sale/Redemption Of Shares)

Three years ago, Connie Bright acquired a commercial property consisting of land and a building at a total cost of $1,475,000. At the acquisition date, an appraisal concluded that the respective values for the two components of the property were $300,000 for the land and $1,175,000 for the building. The acquisition was facilitated by a $550,000 mortgage on the property.

During 2018 and 2019, she operated the property as a proprietorship with good success, realizing a substantial profit in each year. Given this, she would like to transfer the property to a corporation as of January 1, 2020. On that date, the relevant facts about the property are as follows:

	Land	Building
Fair Market Value	$475,000	$1,300,000
Adjusted Cost Base/Capital Cost	300,000	1,175,000
UCC	N/A	1,071,365
Mortgage Balance	N/A	525,000

Connie will elect a transfer value for the land of $475,000. The corresponding figure for the building will be $1,100,000.

The corporation will assume the $525,000 mortgage on the building and, in addition, will issue a note to Connie for $1,050,000. The corporation will also issue common shares to Connie with a fair market value of $200,000 and legal stated capital of $200,000.

The new corporation does not have a balance in its General Rate Income Pool (GRIP) account in any of the years under consideration.

Required:

A. What are the tax consequences of making this transfer at the elected value of $1,575,000 ($475,000 + $1,100,000)? Your answer should include amounts to be included in Connie's income as a result of the transfer, as well as the corporation's tax values for the assets.

B. Compute the adjusted cost base of each component of the consideration that Connie has received from the corporation.

C. Compute the PUC of the corporation's newly issued common shares.

D. What amounts would be included in Connie's Net Income For Tax Purposes if, during 2020, she sells her common shares for $400,000?

E. What amounts would be included in Connie's Net Income For Tax Purposes if, during 2020, the corporation redeems her common shares for $400,000?

Assignment Problem Sixteen - 7
(Transfer Of Land And Building To A Corporation)
Howard Foster has owned and operated his own professional income tax preparation and book-keeping business as a sole proprietorship for many years. The business is quite successful and has gradually grown to the point where Howard employs over 40 individuals full time, which doubles with the addition of part time staff to help at tax time. The business offices are located in a building in downtown Halifax that Howard purchased a few months before he began the business.

Recently, a relatively new client threatened legal action against Howard on learning that the bookkeeping services provided had not produced accurate and current books and records, resulting in a reassessment as a result of a CRA audit of the client. Howard personally worked with the client to resolve the issue but was sufficiently worried about the impact of a lawsuit that he decided to speak with his lawyer. The lawyer advised that the land and building be separated from the business to remove it from the reach of creditors should a lawsuit ever materialize. Howard agreed with the advice and a new corporation, 123789 Ltd., was incorporated in Nova Scotia. Howard will be the only shareholder and has acquired 100 common shares for $100.

Howard purchased the land and building for $4,100,000 using $775,000 of his own personal funds and financing the remainder with a mortgage of $3,325,000. Five years ago Howard spent $500,000 on major renovations to add a dozen new offices, which he financed by renegotiating the existing mortgage. The original cost of the property of $4,100,000 was split between the land, which was valued at $680,000, and the building at $3,420,000.

Howard will sell/transfer the land and building to the new company on December 9, 2020, for a total of $7,615,000, which represents the value of the property according to a recent valuation. The company will assume the mortgage balance. Once the property is transferred Howard and the company will enter into a rental agreement for the continued use of the property in Howard's business. Howard plans to file an election under ITA 85(1) with respect to the sale/transfer. Since Howard has realized allowable capital losses of $52,000 in 2020 he wishes to create sufficient taxable capital gains, as part of the ITA 85(1) election, to offset those losses.

Information relevant to the land and building is as follows:

- Fair Market Value Of The Land $ 915,000
- Adjusted Cost Base Of The Land   680,000
- Fair Market Value Of The Building   6,700,000
- Capital Cost Of The Building   4,600,000
- UCC Of The Building   2,764,600
- Mortgage Balance Owing   2,335,000

Howard wishes to get paid as quickly as possible and prefers promissory notes/debt to shares, which can be troublesome to redeem. Since Howard is not all that familiar with ITA 85 he has approached you, his tax advisor, to handle the election. He initially proposes the following breakdown of how the company will pay him:

Assumption of the Mortgage	$ 2,335,000
Promissory Note	3,000,000
Preferred Shares	2,280,000
Total Sale Price of the Property	$ 7,615,000

Howard proposes to elect to transfer the land for $784,000, to provide sufficient capital gains to offset his capital losses, and the building for $4,551,000. Together these two amounts equal the assumed mortgage and promissory note.

There will be no additions to 123789 Ltd.'s General Rate Income Pool (GRIP) in 2020.

Required:

A. Determine the income tax consequences of a sale by Howard to 123789 Ltd. if ITA 85(1) is not used.

B. Determine the income tax consequences of Howard's ITA 85(1) proposal. Your answer should include (i) the proceeds of disposition of the land and building, (ii) the tax cost to the company of the land and building, (iii) the tax cost of the promissory note, (iv) the tax cost (ACB) of the preferred shares, and (v) the PUC of the preferred shares. Comment on whether Howard's proposed elected amounts are within the acceptable range for ITA 85(1) purposes.

C. Using the tax values determined in Part B above, what amounts would be included in Howard's net income if, during 2021, he were to (i) sell all of the preferred shares for $2,500,000 or (ii) redeem the shares for $2,500,000?

D. As his tax advisor, determine the best use of ITA 85(1) that would result in no immediate income tax consequences other than a capital gain sufficient to offset his $52,000 of allowable capital losses. Your answer should include (i) the proceeds of disposition of the land and building, (ii) the tax cost to the company of the land and building, (iii) the tax cost of the promissory note, (iv) the tax cost (ACB) of the preferred shares, and (v) the PUC of the preferred shares. Assume that Howard wishes to maximize the amount of new debt he can receive.

E. Using the tax values determined in Part D above, what amounts would be included in Howard's net income if, during 2021, the corporation redeems all of the preferred shares for $4,500,000? Indicate the amount of any federal dividend tax credit.

Show all supporting calculations.

Bonus Question: Howard plans to pay rent to 123789 Ltd. and continue operating the business as a sole proprietor. 123789 Ltd. will have only one employee. Is there a better way that would be much more tax effective for the business and 123789 Ltd.? Explain your answer. **Hint:** This was discussed in Chapter 12 and relates to active business income.

Assignment Problem Sixteen - 8
(Transfers To A Corporation And Share Redemption)

Ms. Martha Fleck owns an unincorporated business that she operates out of leased premises. In order to simplify record keeping, her general accounting information is the same as that which she uses for tax purposes. On December 31, 2019, the business has the following assets and liabilities.

	Tax Value	Fair Market Value
Accounts Receivable	$132,000	$ 127,500
Inventory	261,000	312,000
Equipment (Cost = $420,000)	351,000	475,500
Goodwill	Nil	525,000
Total Assets	$744,000	$1,440,000
Liabilities	(142,500)	(142,500)
Net Assets	$601,500	$1,297,500

All of the assets of the unincorporated business will be transferred to Rollex Inc., a new corporation established for the purpose of this transfer. The accounts receivable have a face value of $132,000 and will be transferred using the ITA 22 joint election.

The remaining assets will be transferred under the provisions of ITA 85(1). The total consideration received by Ms. Fleck will have a value of $1,312,500 ($1,440,000 - $127,500), the fair market value of the assets other than accounts receivable. The consideration is made up of new debt of $112,500, assumption of the old debt of $142,500, preferred stock with a fair market value of $337,500, and common stock with a fair market value of $720,000. The new corporation does not have a balance in its General Rate Income Pool (GRIP) account in any of the years under consideration.

Ms. Fleck wishes to incorporate her business in a manner that minimizes or eliminates any tax effects resulting from the transaction.

Required: Ignore the lifetime capital gains deduction in your solution.

A. Do you agree with the decision to transfer the accounts receivable using ITA 22? Explain your conclusion and determine the tax consequences of this decision.

B. Given that Ms. Fleck wishes to minimize or eliminate current taxes, indicate the values that should be elected for each of the assets to be transferred.

C. Determine the adjusted cost base of the debt, preferred stock, and common stock that would be received by Ms. Fleck on the rollover.

D. Determine the Paid Up Capital of the common stock and preferred stock that were issued by the new corporation to Ms. Fleck.

E. Determine the tax consequences to Ms. Fleck if the preferred and common stock that she received in the rollover were immediately redeemed in January 2020 by the new corporation at fair market values.

Assignment Problem Sixteen - 9
(Gift To Related Party - Section 85)

Ms. Martine Renaud has operated an unincorporated business for over 25 years. The business has been very successful and, on January 1, 2020, its assets and liabilities have tax values and estimated fair market values as follows:

	Tax Value	Fair Market Value
Accounts Receivable (No Reserve Taken)	$ 60,000	$ 57,000
Inventories	825,000	840,000
Depreciable Assets - CCA Class 8 (Note One)	1,725,000	1,780,000
Land	923,000	1,450,000
Building (Note Two)	1,760,000	2,436,000
Total Assets	$5,293,000	$6,563,000
Liabilities	(430,000)	(430,000)
Net Assets (Owner's Equity)	$4,863,000	$6,133,000

Note One   The capital cost of the assets in Class 8 total $1,960,000.

Note Two   The capital cost of the Building is $3,600,000.

Ms. Renaud has two daughters, Alma aged 26 and Amanda aged 28. Currently, they are both unemployed but, thanks to Ms. Renaud's generosity over the years, they both have significant assets and a comfortable lifestyle.

Ms. Renaud would like to transfer the future growth in her business to her daughters. To accomplish this, in December 2019 she arranges for them to establish a new corporation through the investment of $10,000 each. Each daughter receives 100 common shares. The new corporation is named Almand Inc. and at this point, the corporation has no assets other than the $20,000 invested by the two daughters.

On January 1, 2020, Ms. Renaud transfers all of the assets of her unincorporated business to Almand Inc. The accounts receivable are transferred to the corporation using the ITA 22 joint election. The remaining assets are transferred under the provisions of ITA 85(1). The business does not have goodwill.

Ms. Renaud transfers the assets at an elected value of $5,233,000 ($5,293,000 - $60,000), the total tax value of the assets other than accounts receivable. Almand Inc. assumes all of the $430,000 in liabilities of Ms. Renaud's unincorporated business and issues new debt to her in the amount of $1,570,000. In addition, she receives redeemable preferred shares with a fair market value and legal stated capital of $4,506,000, a total of $6,506,000.

The CRA issues a reassessment related to the rollover transaction in November 2020. It is based on a fair market value for the land of $1,850,000, $400,000 more than Ms. Renaud's estimate of $1,450,000. Ms. Renaud does not file an objection to the reassessment as her father, a retired appraiser, has advised her she would ultimately lose after paying outrageous accounting fees.

Required: Ignore the lifetime capital gains deduction in your solution.

A. Taking into consideration the effect of the reassessment, determine the tax consequences to Ms. Renaud that result from the transfer of her business assets to Almand Inc. Your answer should include amounts to be included in Ms. Renaud's income as a result of the transfer and the reassessment, as well as the adjusted cost base and PUC of her preferred shares.

B.   Determine the tax consequence to Ms. Renaud if Almand Inc. redeems her preferred shares for $4,506,000 immediately after the reassessment.

C.   Alma finds that she cannot tolerate being a 50 percent shareholder in a corporation with her sister. She sells her Almand Inc. shares to an arm's length party for $275,000 immediately after the reassessment. Determine the tax consequences of this sale for Alma.

Assignment Problem Sixteen - 10
(Excess Consideration)

Moe Granite incorporated his residential construction business 15 years ago. The company, Bedrock Ltd., has been very successful and very profitable to the point that it has excess cash that it has been regularly investing.

Moe and his family live in a home he purchased a few years before he was married. Moe also acquired two plots of land – one located along the lakefront of an expanding area that has grown in popularity since he purchased it and a second in an area that Moe expected would one day become a growing commercial sector given its proximity to a major city.

The family home is his only principal residence. Moe had always planned to build a luxurious home on the vacant land but he has been so busy with the company he never had a chance to begin the construction of that lakefront home.

Moe recently sat down with his accountant, telling him about his plans and adding that he needed additional cash from the company to realize his dreams. He estimated that the construction of the lakefront home would take almost a full year given its location and would likely cost in excess of $1 million. He was unwilling to sell the current family home until the construction of the lakefront home was complete. He also was unwilling to sell the second piece of land, telling his accountant that the time was not right and he expected the value to increase substantially in the next few years.

Moe told his accountant that he was in a quandary as to how to come up with the cash he would need given he was unwilling to borrow from commercial lenders or his own company, did not want to sell his current family home or the second plot of land or pay any additional income taxes by drawing additional salary or dividends since he was already paying tax at the highest tax bracket. Given the expanded tax on split income (TOSI) he was also unwilling to entertain any family income splitting planning with his spouse and their three minor children.

Moe's accountant told him that he had a plan that would accomplish his objectives at minimum cost. The accountant explained that Moe could sell both the current family home and the second piece of land to his company. This, explained the accountant, would keep the current home and the land "in the family" while giving him all the funds necessary to complete the lakefront construction and avoiding the payment of any additional income taxes. Moe agreed. The plan is to sell/transfer the current family home and the second piece of land to the company. ITA 85(1) will be used to transfer both properties. The accountant added that while ITA 85(1) is not necessary for a fair market value sale of the family home since none of the gain will be taxable, he advised that the additional flexibility provided made it worthwhile to include it in the election. The sale agreements are all dated November 18, 2020. The two properties and their relevant values on the date of transfer are as follows:

	Tax Cost (ACB)	Fair Market Value (Moe)
Principle Residence	$450,000	$1,000,000
Vacant Land	115,000	500,000

The fair market value (FMV) for each property was estimated by Moe. Assume that no professional valuation was done. There is an existing mortgage on the principal residence of $160,000.

The company will pay Moe the following amounts for each property:

Assumption of the Mortgage	$ 160,000
Promissory Note	840,000
Preferred Shares	Nominal
Total Sale Price of the Principal Residence	$1,000,000

Note: The reference to "nominal" means $1 or other negligible amount, which you can ignore in your answer.

Assumption of the Mortgage	$ Nil
Promissory Note	115,000
Preferred Shares	385,000
Total Sale Price of the Principal Residence	$500,000

Total consideration for ITA 85(1) purposes is as follows:

Assumption of the Mortgage	$ 160,000
Promissory Note	955,000
Preferred Shares	385,000
Total Sale Price of the Principal Residence	$1,500,000

The ITA 85(1) elected amount for the principal residence will be $1,000,000 and $115,000 for the land.

Assume that in 2022, the 2020 ITA 85 election is audited and reassessed by the CRA on the basis that the FMV pf the principal residence is $750,000 and $250,000 for the vacant land.

Required:

A. Calculate the effect on Moe's net income that will result from the ITA 85(1) election as originally filed.

B. Determine the ACB and PUC of the preferred shares and ACB of the promissory note received by Moe on the transfer.

C. Determine the tax consequences of the reassessment by the CRA. Be sure to include in your answer revisions to the ACB of the promissory notes and ACB and PUC of the preferred shares after the reassessment.

D. Could Moe have done anything different to avoid the CRA reassessment?

Assignment Problem Sixteen - 11
(Dividend Stripping)
Sandrine Hoskirk incorporated her successful business 10 years ago. The corporation, Hoskirk Ltd., is a Canadian controlled private corporation (CCPC) with a December 31 taxation year end. Sandrine is the only shareholder and, on incorporation, acquired 1,000 common shares for $100 each. No new shares have been issued since incorporation. As a result the ACB and PUC of the shares are both $100 each, or $100,000 in total for the single class of shares.

The incorporated business has enjoyed great success and with eligibility for low corporate tax rates has grown considerably in value to a point that a valuation recently estimated the common shares were worth $2,770,000 or $2,770 per share.

Sandrine's only child is her 33 year old daughter, Debra Hoskirk Stephenson who recently gave birth to her first child. Sandrine would like to provide her daughter and her growing family with financial security and has spoken to her accountant to discuss the best way to accomplish that goal. A variety of options are discussed, but Sandrine decides on using a freeze transaction with a new corporation that will result in her daughter benefitting from the future increase in value of Hoskirk Ltd.

The tax plan is to first have Debra incorporate her own corporation. Debra will be the only common shareholder with her spouse and newborn child owning preferred shares. The next step is to have Sandrine sell her common shares in Hoskirk Ltd. to her daughter's corporation.

The day after Labour Day, September 8, 2020, Debra incorporated HS Ltd., a CCPC with a December 31 taxation year end. At the end of September an agreement will be drawn up that will have Sandrine selling some or all of her common shares of Hoskirk Ltd. to HS Ltd.

Sandrine has never used any of her capital gains deduction and has never realized allowable business investment losses (ABIL). In addition she will have no Cumulative Net Investment Loss (CNIL) in 2020. The result is that she has full access to the 2020 capital gains deduction limit of $883,384, which will eliminate income tax on $411,692 in taxable capital gains [(50%) ($883,384)] with the exception of any alternative minimum tax (AMT).

Sandrine's accountant explains that by structuring the share sale using ITA 85(1) three objectives/ benefits are achieved: (i) her capital gains deduction is immediately utilized, resulting in an increased ACB of any shares issued by HS Ltd. to Sandrine, which will reduce future capital gains; (ii) the freeze is accomplished, allowing her daughter and family to acquire shares in her company for minimal cost and to benefit from future growth; and (iii) any immediate income taxes are avoided. Sandrine has made it clear that she does not want to have to pay any additional income taxes as a result of these transactions.

Since HS Ltd. has no cash or other assets it can only acquire the shares from Sandrine by issuing either interest bearing debt (e.g., a promissory note), shares, or a combination of both. Because using ITA 85(1) requires that shares be issued as consideration and deferring tax means limiting non-share consideration, HS Ltd. will acquire Sandrine's shares for a combination of a promissory note and redeemable preferred shares.

After careful consideration Sandrine proposes the following alternatives to her accountant:

Proposal 1:   HS Ltd. will acquire all of Sandrine's common shares of Hoskirk Ltd. for $2,770,000 with payments of a promissory note of $2,000,000 bearing interest of 3.0 percent and redeemable preferred shares for the balance of $770,000. ITA 85(1) will be used.

Proposal 2:   Sandrine sells just enough of her shares to HS Ltd. to use all of her capital gains deduction. Sandrine would continue to keep any remaining shares. ITA 85(1) will be used.

Proposal 3:   Sandrine sells enough of her shares to Debra directly to use all of her capital gains deduction. Debra would provide Sandrine with a promissory note with interest at 3.0 percent. Debra would be issued regular dividends large enough to pay down both the principal and interest in subsequent years.

Assume that neither Hoskirk Ltd. nor HS Ltd. would have a positive balance in their General Rate Income Pool (GRIP) account at any time in 2020.

Required:

A. As her accountant, advise Sandrine on whether her first proposal is a good idea given her objectives. Show the results if ITA 84.1 did not apply and the results with ITA 84.1.

B. Indicate how Sandrine's first proposal could be modified to produce a better result that avoids any immediate income tax to her. Assume that Sandrine wants to maximize the non-share consideration.

C. Evaluate Sandrine's second proposal and add the necessary numbers to ensure it results in no income tax consequences.

D. Discuss the merits of Sandrine's third proposal. Is it workable? What are the advantages or disadvantages.

Provide your analysis and all supporting calculations.

Assignment Problem Sixteen - 12
(Dividend Stripping)

Daryl Foster has operated Foster's Fasteners Inc. for the last 15 years. It is a Canadian controlled private corporation that is involved in the sale of luxury hardware items. His original invest-ment when the company was established was $780,000. Daryl is the only shareholder and the $780,000 is both the adjusted cost base and the PUC of his shares.

As the company has been very profitable since its inception, its shares have a current fair market value of $6,200,000.

As Daryl is nearing retirement age, he would like to extract a significant amount of funds from his corporation without incurring a great deal of taxation. He has discussed this matter with Thornton Brockton, his self-trained accountant of many years. While Thornton has never imple-mented such a strategy, he indicates that he has heard of a procedure called a Section 85 roll-over that will allow Daryl to transfer his shares to a new corporation using an elected value that will create a capital gain of $600,000. As this is the amount of Daryl's unused lifetime capital gains deduction, Thornton advises Daryl that he can receive the original cost of his shares, plus a $600,000 capital gain on a tax free basis.

Using Section 85, Daryl will transfer all of the shares of Foster's Fasteners to Foster Invest-ments, a new company in which Daryl will hold all of the shares. The elected value for the trans-fer will be $1,380,000.

In return, Daryl will receive a non-interest bearing note for $1,380,000, plus Foster Investment shares with a redemption value of $4,820,000. Given the cash resources of Foster's Fasteners, this company's shares should be able to pay sufficient dividends to Foster Investments to allow the payment of the note within one or two years.

Neither of the companies have a balance in their General Rate Income Pool (GRIP) account in any of the years under consideration.

Required:

A. In the absence of ITA 84.1, indicate the tax consequences of the transfer of the shares of Foster's Fasteners to Foster Investments.

B. Determine whether ITA 84.1 would be applicable in this case. Assuming that ITA 84.1 is applicable, calculate the deemed dividend that would arise on this transfer. In addition, indi-cate the net economic effect that would result from this transfer combined with a redemp-tion of the Foster Investments shares at their fair market value of $4,820,000.

Assignment Problem Sixteen - 13
(Capital Gain Strips)

Dolteck Ltd. (Dolteck) is an operating company involved in commercial construction. It was incor-porated in Alberta 20 years ago and has been a Canadian controlled private corporation (CCPC) with a December 31 taxation year end ever since. Dolteck was authorized to issue multiple classes of shares, but the only shares it issued were common shares issued on incorporation to its sole corporate shareholder, Holdteck Ltd. (Holdteck), which is also a CCPC incorporated in Alberta with a December 31 taxation year end. Holdteck's role is as a strict holding company offering administrative, financing, managerial, and other support services to Dolteck for which it charges an annual fee based on the level of services provided.

The shares of Dolteck owned by Holdteck were acquired three years after its incorporation for $900,000, which currently remains the ACB. The PUC of the Dolteck shares is only $100,000.

A large arm's length publicly listed construction company, Giant Co., with a track record of buying up small competitors recently approached Holdteck with an offer to purchase all of the Dolteck shares for $7,000,000. The offer has been accepted with a closing date of December 31, 2020. Safe income on hand attributable to the common shares of Dolteck owned by Holdteck is $2,200,000.

Assume that Dolteck will not have any balance in its eligible RDTOH, non-eligible RDTOH, or General Rate Income Pool (GRIP) account at the beginning of 2020. In addition, assume that the provincial tax rate on investment income including taxable capital gains is 12.0 percent.

Required: Indicate the tax consequences of each of the following independent situations, specifically indicating whether ITA 55(2) applies, supported with explanations. Also comment on the application of Part IV, RDTOH, corporate tax rates, and the capital dividend account. Show all supporting calculations.

A. Holdteck sells all of the Dolteck shares to Giant Co. for $7,000,000.

B. Holdteck sells all of the Dolteck shares to Giant Co. for $4,800,000 after Dolteck declares and pays a safe income dividend of $2,200,000 to Holdteck. Assume that Dolteck has sufficient cash to pay the dividend in full.

C. Assume that Dolteck has no cash or borrowing power to raise additional cash to pay any dividends. Giant Co. loans Dolteck $6,100,000 on December 28, 2020. On December 29, 2020, Dolteck declares and pays a dividend to Holdteck of $6,100,000. On December 30, 2020, Holdteck sells all of its common shares in Dolteck to Giant Co. for $900,000.

D. Using ITA 85(1), Holdteck transfers all of the common shares it owns in Dolteck to Giant Co. The elected amount will be $900,000 and Holdteck will receive $7,000,000 of a newly created class of retractable preferred shares of Giant Co. The Giant Co. shares will be redeemed in early January 2021 for cash of $7,000,000. Ignore any Part IV implications in this case.

CHAPTER 17

Other Rollovers And Sale Of An Incorporated Business

Introduction

17-1. The preceding Chapter gave detailed consideration to the Section 85 rollover provisions, which provide for a tax deferred transfer of property to a corporation. In addition, Chapter 9 dealt with rollovers involving transfers to a spouse and transfers of farm property to children. There are a number of other rollover provisions in the *Income Tax Act* that will be discussed in this Chapter.

17-2. These additional rollover provisions cover share for share exchanges among corporations, share exchanges in the process of the reorganization of a corporation, amalgamations of existing corporations, the winding-up of a 90 percent or more owned subsidiary, and conversions of debt to shares. The winding-up of a Canadian corporation that is not a 90 percent owned subsidiary is also covered. This latter transaction does not involve a rollover, but is dealt with in the same Section of the *Income Tax Act* as the winding-up of a 90 percent or more owned subsidiary.

Share For Share Exchanges - ITA 85.1

Background

17-3. ITA 85.1 provides for a rollover in which a shareholder (vendor) exchanges his or her shares for shares of an acquiring corporation (purchaser). When there are many diverse shareholders, a share for share exchange is easier to accomplish than a Section 85 rollover, because there is no need for each shareholder to file an election. Further, the provisions of ITA 85.1 apply automatically, unless the vendor includes any gain or loss on the transaction in his or her income tax return. Given these features, an ITA 85.1 exchange is an important arrangement in business combination transactions.

General Rules

17-4. The general rules for this rollover apply automatically unless the vendor opts to include a gain or loss from the transaction in his or her income tax return. These general rules are as follows:

ITA 85.1(1)(a)   The vendor (acquiree) is deemed to have:

(i)   disposed of the exchanged shares for proceeds of disposition equal to their adjusted cost base.
(ii) acquired the shares of the purchaser at a cost to the vendor equal to the adjusted cost base to the vendor of the exchanged shares immediately before the exchange.

ITA 85.1(1)(b)   The cost to the purchaser (acquirer) of each of the acquired shares is deemed to be the lesser of:

(i)   its fair market value immediately before the exchange, and
(ii) its Paid Up Capital immediately before the exchange.

ITA 85.1(2.1)   The PUC of the purchaser shares that have been issued to the vendor is limited to the PUC of the shares given up by the vendor.

17-5.   You should note that the ITA 85.1(1)(b) provision may be problematic for the purchaser in situations where the adjusted cost base of the vendor's shares exceeds their PUC. If the shares are later sold by the purchaser, that excess of the adjusted cost base over the PUC will be subject to tax as a capital gain since the purchaser's adjusted cost base will be equal to the PUC. This would suggest that, in situations where the adjusted cost base of the shares exceeds their PUC, it might be better to use ITA 85(1) for the transfer.

Conditions For The Application Of ITA 85.1

17-6.   The conditions required for this rollover to be applicable are found in ITA 85.1(1) and (2). To begin, the vendor's shares must be held as capital property. Additional conditions for the applicability of the rollover are as follows:

ITA 85.1(2)(a)   The vendor and purchaser must be dealing with each other at arm's length.

ITA85.1(2)(b)   The vendor, or persons with whom he or she does not deal at arm's length, cannot control the purchaser immediately after the exchange. Likewise, he or she cannot own shares having a fair market value in excess of 50 percent of the total fair market value of the purchasing corporation's outstanding shares.

ITA 85.1(2)(c)   The vendor and purchaser cannot have filed an election under ITA 85(1) with respect to the exchanged shares.

ITA 85.1(2)(d)   The vendor must not have received any consideration, other than shares of the purchaser, in return for the shares given up in the exchange.

17-7.   You should note that this last condition under ITA 85.1(2)(d) does not prevent the vendor from selling additional shares to the purchaser for non-share consideration.

Example

Application Of ITA 85.1
17-8.   A brief example will serve to illustrate the basic provisions of ITA 85.1:

EXAMPLE   Ms. Cowper is the sole shareholder of Cowper Inc., owning a total of 1,000 shares with a Paid Up Capital (PUC) and an adjusted cost base of $10,000. The shares of Cowper Inc. have a current fair market value of $125,000.

Mega Holdings Ltd. acquires these shares in return for 5,000 of its common shares. The Mega Holdings shares are currently trading at $25 per share, resulting in a total value for the 5,000 shares of $125,000.

ANALYSIS   The information in the example is presented graphically in Figure 17-1 (on the following page).

In the absence of the share for share exchange provisions in ITA 85.1, Ms. Cowper would have a capital gain of $115,000 ($125,000 - $10,000). However, under the rollover provisions of ITA 85.1, the following results apply:

Figure 17 - 1
ITA 85.1 Example

Mega Holdings Ltd.

1,000 Cowper Inc. Shares
PUC = ACB = $10,000
FMV = $125,000

5,000 Mega Holdings Shares
At $25 Per Share
FMV = $125,000

Ms. Cowper

- Ms. Cowper is deemed to have disposed of her shares for an amount equal to the $10,000 adjusted cost base of the Cowper Inc. shares. This means that there is no capital gain on the disposition. [ITA 85.1(1)(a)(i)]

- Ms. Cowper is deemed to have acquired the shares in Mega Holdings Ltd. at a cost equal to the adjusted cost base of the Cowper Inc. shares, or $10,000. [ITA 85.1(1)(a)(ii)]

- The adjusted cost base of the Cowper shares acquired by Mega Holdings Ltd. is deemed to be equal to $10,000, the lesser of their fair market value of $125,000 and their PUC of $10,000 [ITA 85.1(1)(b)]. You should note that this limit applies, even in situations where the vendor opted to forego the rollover under ITA 85.1 by including the gain in income (see Paragraph 17-9).

- The PUC of the Mega Holdings Ltd. shares that have been issued to Ms. Cowper is limited to the $10,000 PUC of the Cowper shares that have been given up. [ITA 85.1(2.1)]

Opting Out Of ITA 85.1

17-9.   As we have noted, ITA 85.1 applies automatically unless the vendor opts out in his or her income tax return. In this example, Ms. Cowper could opt out of ITA 85.1 by including the taxable capital gain of $57,500 [(1/2)($125,000 - $10,000)] in her income tax return. Note that, unlike the situation when ITA 85(1) is used in a rollover, there is no flexibility on the transfer value. With respect to the shares that are exchanged, opting out requires that 100 percent of the capital gain on the exchanged shares be included in income. This could be a problem if, for example, Ms. Cowper only wanted to recognize part of the gain on her shares.

17-10.   There are two possible solutions to this problem. The transfer of Ms. Cowper's shares could be made using the provisions of ITA 85(1). This would allow the use of an elected value that would limit the amount of gain that would be recognized.

17-11.   An alternative, perhaps simpler solution, would be to sell a portion of her shares to Mega Holdings for cash. This would allow the recognition of the desired amount of capital gain. The remaining shares could then be exchanged on a tax free basis under ITA 85.1.

Exercise Seventeen - 1

Subject: Share For Share Exchange

Ms. Aly Alee is the sole shareholder of Aayee Ltd., a Canadian controlled private corporation that is not a qualified small business corporation. The corporation was established several years ago by Ms. Alee with an investment of $450,000. It has identifiable net assets with a fair market value of $2,200,000. The shares of her company are acquired by a large publicly traded company, Global Outreach Inc., through the issuance of 50,000 new shares. At the time of this business combination, the Global Outreach Inc. shares are trading at $49 per share. Indicate the tax consequences of this transaction to both Ms. Alee and Global Outreach Inc.

SOLUTION available in print and online Study Guide.

ITA 85.1 In Practice

17-12.   We have illustrated ITA 85.1 using an example that involves a large public company acquiring a corporation with a single shareholder. This is not the usual application of ITA 85.1. ITA 85.1 was designed to be used in situations where a public company acquires a widely held corporation with a large number of shareholders.

17-13.   As noted in Paragraph 17-3, Section 85 can be used as an alternative to Section 85.1. However, in situations where the acquiree has a large number of shareholders, this approach would require the filing of numerous, in some cases hundreds, of separate Section 85 elections. The use of Section 85.1 avoids this by making its application automatic, unless the acquiree includes any gain or loss in income. This is a much more efficient procedure in most business combination situations.

We suggest you work Self Study Problems Seventeen-1 and 2 at this point.

Exchange Of Shares In A Reorganization - ITA 86

BYRD/CHEN NOTE   ITA 86 has been widely used in the implementation of estate freezes, a procedure used to transfer the future growth in a private corporation to the spouses, children, or other parties related to the principal shareholder of a CCPC. The 2018 expansion of the applicability of the Tax On Split Income (TOSI) has made this a much more difficult procedure to implement effectively. When the TOSI is applicable, both dividends and capital gains received as a result of this procedure may be subject to taxation at the maximum federal rate, removing most or all of the incentive for undertaking an estate freeze.

More specifically, the TOSI will always be applicable to income received by children under 18. In addition, it will be generally applicable to other related individuals unless the income they receive is an Excluded Amount. If they are 18 or over and actively involved in the business, the income can escape the TOSI as the corporation may be an Excluded Business. If they are 25 or over and own at least 10 percent of the CCPC's outstanding shares in terms of both fair market value and voting rights, the income can escape the TOSI as their holding will be viewed as Excluded Shares. See Chapter 11 for a more detailed discussion of these concepts.

There are other applications of ITA 86, a common one being transfers of ownership to a key employee or group of employees. In general, these other procedures will generally not result in the application of the TOSI.

In our coverage of ITA 86, we will assume that the TOSI is not applicable. To make this more realistic we will avoid applications involving minor children and non-voting shares. However, it is important that you recognize that the use of Section 86 in estate freezes is limited by the possible application of the TOSI.

Application Of ITA 86(1)

Basic Procedure

17-14.   ITA 86(1) applies when there has been a reorganization involving an exchange of shares within a single corporation. In the usual application, a shareholder of a corporation exchanges shares held in at least one class of existing shares for authorized shares in the same company or for authorized shares in the same company combined with non-share consideration (note that the authorized shares must be of a different class than the existing shares). In effect, there is a redemption of the taxpayer's current shareholding, combined with an acquisition of a new shareholding. As long as non-share consideration is within acceptable limits, ITA 86(1) allows this transaction to take place without tax consequences to the taxpayer whose shares are being redeemed.

Use In Estate Freeze

17-15. One of the most common applications of ITA 86(1) is in an estate freeze, where an owner of a business wishes to pass on the future growth of the business to adult family members who have been actively engaged in the business.

> **EXAMPLE** A father holds all of the outstanding common shares of a corporation. These shares have a fair market value in excess of their adjusted cost base and, as a consequence, their sale or redemption would normally result in a deemed dividend and/or a capital gain or capital loss. Further, if the father continues to hold the shares, future growth in the corporation will accrue to him.

> **ANALYSIS** To avoid this situation, the father will exchange his common shares for newly issued preferred shares of the corporation. The preferred shares will have a fixed redemption value equal to the fair market value of the common shares given up. The fact that their value is fixed will serve to freeze the value of the father's interest in the corporation. If the father wishes to retain control of the corporation, the preferred shares can be structured to provide voting rights sufficient to achieve this objective. Common shares will then be issued to a spouse, a child, or some other related person.

17-16. As the preferred shares held by the father reflect the full fair market value of the company, the new common shares can be issued to the related person at a fairly nominal value. However, any future growth in the value of the company will accrue to these common shares. ITA 86(1) provides for the father's exchange of shares to take place on a rollover or tax free basis (see Chapter 19 for a more detailed discussion of estate freezes). Note that the ITA 86 rollover differs from the ITA 85(1) rollover in that there are no elected amounts and no election form to be filed.

Conditions For The Reorganization

General Conditions

17-17. For the provisions of ITA 86(1) to apply, several conditions must be met.

> **Shares Must Be Capital Property** First, the original owner's shares must be capital property to the owner. They cannot be part of an inventory of securities that is being held for trading purposes.

> **All Shares Held By Transferor In A Particular Class** A second condition is that the transaction must result in an exchange of all of the outstanding shares of a particular class that are owned by the transferor. For example, all Class A common shares that are owned by the transferor must be exchanged for some other type of share. Note that there is no requirement that Class A common shares that are held by other shareholders be exchanged as part of the transaction. Further, it is not necessary that other classes of shares owned by the transferor be exchanged for new shares.

> **Reorganization Of Capital** A third condition is that the share exchange must be integral to a reorganization of the capital. This will often require that the articles of incorporation be amended to authorize the addition of new classes of shares.

> **Transferor Must Receive Shares** A final condition is that the transferor must receive shares of the capital stock of the corporation. While this does not preclude the transferor from receiving non-share consideration, such non-share consideration should not exceed the adjusted cost base or the PUC of the shares transferred. If it does, the excess will have to be taken into income as a deemed dividend and either a taxable capital gain or an allowable capital loss.

Establishing Market Value For Preferred Shares

17-18.   In the more common applications of ITA 86(1), the new shares received by the transferor will usually be preferred shares. These shares must be designed in such a fashion as to clearly establish their fair market value. If this is not the case, a subsequent dispute with the CRA could result in some of the benefits of using ITA 86(1) being lost. Adding the following characteristics to the preferred shares will serve to establish a defensible fair market value:

- The preferred shares must be redeemable at the option of the shareholder. The CRA rigorously enforces this requirement to protect the fair market value of the preferred shares.

- The preferred shares should be entitled to a dividend at a reasonable rate. Without a reasonable dividend entitlement to the original shareholder, the incoming shareholders could benefit by receiving a disproportionate share of the corporation's future profits. However, there is no requirement for the entitlement to be cumulative.

- The corporation must guarantee that dividends will not be paid on any other class of shares if the payment would result in the corporation having insufficient net assets to redeem the preferred shares at their specified redemption price.

- The preferred shares must become cumulative if the fair market value of the net assets of the corporation falls below the redemption value of the preferred shares or if the corporation is unable to redeem the shares on a call for redemption.

- The preferred shares may or may not have normal voting rights. However, they should carry votes on any matter regarding the rights attached to the preferred shares.

- The preferred shares should have preference on liquidation of the corporation. While the very nature of preferred shares tends to guarantee preference, the CRA requires additional assurance that the normal provisions for such shares will not be avoided.

Procedures

General Rules

17-19.   As noted previously, an ITA 86(1) reorganization involves a redemption (disposition) of a given shareholder's holding of a particular class of shares (old shares, hereafter). In return, the shareholder acquires shares of a different class (new shares, hereafter) and, in some reorganizations, non-share consideration. ITA 86(1) specifies a number of rules that apply in such a reorganization of capital. These are as follows:

Non-Share Consideration   ITA 86(1)(a) indicates that the cost to the shareholder of this consideration is deemed to be its fair market value.

Cost Of New Shares   ITA 86(1)(b) indicates that the cost of the new shares to the shareholder is equal to the cost of the old shares less any non-share consideration received.

Proceeds Of Redemption For Old Shares   Because there is a redemption of shares, there is the possibility of an ITA 84(3) deemed dividend. ITA 84(3)(a) defines such dividends as the excess of the "amount paid" over the PUC of the shares being redeemed. This "amount paid" clearly includes any non-share consideration and, when shares are included in the redemption payment, ITA 84(5)(d) indicates that their value is based on any increase in PUC resulting from the issuance of these shares. Putting this together leads to the conclusion that the total proceeds for the redemption will be equal to the non-share consideration plus the PUC of any new shares issued. Note that, in the usual ITA 86(1) scenario, the PUC of the new shares will often be reduced by a PUC reduction under ITA 86(2.1)(a). (See Paragraph 17-20.)

Proceeds Of Disposition For Old Shares   As the redemption of the old shares is a type of disposition, there is also the possibility of a capital gain or loss. For the purposes of determining the capital gain or loss on this disposition, ITA 86(1)(c) defines the proceeds of disposition for the old shares as being equal to the cost of the new shares (the cost of the old shares, less non-share consideration), plus any non-share consideration received by the taxpayer.

In our general discussion of ITA 84(3) redemptions in Chapter 14, we discuss the possibility that the combination of redemption procedures and disposition procedures could result in the double counting of all or part of any gain on the transaction. As we noted there, this possibility is eliminated by the fact that the ITA 54 definition of proceeds of disposition excludes ITA 84(3) dividends.

PUC Reduction Calculation

17-20.   As noted in the preceding rules, a PUC reduction may be required on the new shares. This is specified in ITA 86(2.1)(a). This reduction is calculated as follows:

Increase In Legal Stated Capital Of New Shares		$xx,xxx
Less The Excess, If Any, Of:		
PUC Of Old Shares	($x,xxx)	
Over The Non-Share Consideration	x,xxx	(x,xxx)
ITA 86(2.1)(a) PUC Reduction		$xx,xxx

17-21.   In reviewing this PUC reduction formula, note that where the non-share consideration is equal to or greater than the PUC of the old shares, the amount subtracted from the increase in the legal stated capital of the new shares will be nil. This means that the PUC reduction will be equal to the increase in legal stated capital for the new shares. In common sense terms, if the shareholder takes back the full amount of the old PUC in the form of non-share consideration, the PUC of the new shares will be nil.

17-22.   As was the case with rollovers to a corporation under Section 85, if the PUC reduction applies to more than one class of shares, it will generally be allocated to the individual classes on the basis of the relative fair market value of each class.

Example Using ITA 86(1) In An Estate Freeze

Basic Data

17-23.   An example will serve to illustrate the ITA 86(1) procedures. You might note that the example illustrates the manner in which an ITA 86(1) reorganization of capital can be used to freeze the value of an individual's estate. The example is illustrated graphically in Figure 17-2 (on the following page).

> **EXAMPLE**   Mr. David Jones owns all of the outstanding shares of Jones Inc. These common shares have an adjusted cost base of $50,000 and a PUC of $75,000. Because of the successful operations of the company, the current fair market value of these common shares is $500,000.
>
> Mr. Jones would like to have future growth in the value of the corporation accrue to his daughter, Ms. Veronica Jones. Veronica is 30 years old and has been actively and substantially involved in the business for over five years. To accomplish this, Mr. Jones first exchanges his common shares for a $150,000 note payable from the corporation and preferred shares with a fair market value and a legal stated capital of $350,000. Common shares are then purchased by Veronica Jones for $1,000. These are the only Jones Inc. common shares outstanding subsequent to these transactions.

PUC Reduction

17-24.   The first step in applying the ITA 86(1) rules in this situation would be to calculate the required PUC reduction and the resulting PUC value for the preferred shares. As the non-share consideration of $150,000 exceeds the $75,000 PUC of the shares given up, we would expect the PUC reduction formula to reduce the PUC of the preferred shares to nil. The following calculations support this expected result:

Figure 17 - 2 ITA 86(1) Example

Cost Of Non-Share Consideration (Note Payable)	$150,000

Legal Stated Capital Of Preferred Shares Less The Excess, If Any, Of:		$350,000
PUC Of Shares Given Up	($ 75,000)	
Over The Non-Share Consideration	150,000	Nil
ITA 86(2.1)(a) PUC Reduction		$350,000

Legal Stated Capital Of Preferred Shares	$350,000
ITA 86(2.1)(a) PUC Reduction	(350,000)
PUC Of Preferred Shares	Nil

Other Calculations

17-25.   Other required values can be calculated as follows:

Adjusted Cost Base Of Shares Given Up	$ 50,000
Non-Share Consideration	(150,000)
Adjusted Cost Base Of Preferred Shares	Nil

PUC Of Preferred Shares	Nil
Plus Non-Share Consideration	$150,000
Proceeds Of Redemption - ITA 84(5)(d)	$150,000
PUC Of Shares Given Up	(75,000)
ITA 84(3) Deemed Dividend	$ 75,000

Adjusted Cost Base Of Preferred Shares	Nil
Plus Non-Share Consideration	$ 150,000
Proceeds Of Disposition - ITA 86(1)(c)	$ 150,000
Less ITA 84(3) Deemed Dividend	(75,000)
Adjusted Proceeds Of Disposition	$ 75,000
Adjusted Cost Base Of Shares Given Up	(50,000)
Capital Gain	$ 25,000
Inclusion Rate	1/2
Taxable Capital Gain	$ 12,500

Economic Analysis

17-26.   The shares held by David's daughter, Veronica, will have an adjusted cost base and a PUC of $1,000 and this will also be their initial fair market value. However, if the corporation prospers, all future increases in its value will accrue to her. In other words, by exchanging his common shares for non-growth preferred shares, Mr. Jones has frozen the value of his interest in Jones Inc.

17-27.   In reviewing this example, you should note that Mr. Jones' potential gain has not disappeared. If he had simply sold his shares without the reorganization, he would have realized a gain of $450,000 ($500,000 - $50,000). As a result of the reorganization, he has recognized $100,000 ($75,000 dividend + $25,000 capital gain). This gain reflects the excess of the $150,000 non-share consideration received by Mr. Jones over the $50,000 adjusted cost base of the original shares.

17-28.   This reorganization has left an unrecognized gain of $350,000 ($500,000 - $150,000). This gain will remain unrecognized until such time as Mr. Jones' holding of preferred shares is either redeemed or sold for its fair market value of $350,000. As these shares have a PUC of nil, a subsequent redemption would result in an ITA 84(3) deemed dividend of $350,000. As the adjusted cost base of the shares is also nil, a subsequent sale of the shares would result in a capital gain of $350,000, the taxable amount of which would be one-half, or $175,000.

17-29.   A final point here is that this example does not represent a typical ITA 86(1) estate freeze. While it does accomplish the goal of transferring future growth in the corporation to a related party, the approach used has resulted in current Tax Payable for Mr. Jones. This could have been avoided by limiting the non-share consideration to $50,000, the lesser of the $75,000 PUC and the $50,000 adjusted cost base of the old shares. It is this approach that would be used in a typical ITA 86(1) transaction.

Exercise Seventeen - 2

Subject: Exchange Of Shares In Reorganization (ACB = PUC = Boot)

Mr. Sam Samson is the sole shareholder of Samdoo Ltd. It is a Canadian controlled private corporation and its common shares have a fair market value of $2,300,000, an adjusted cost base (ACB) of $1,000,000, and a Paid Up Capital (PUC) of $1,000,000. At this time, Samdoo Ltd. has no balance in its GRIP account. Mr. Samson exchanges all of his Samdoo Ltd. shares for cash of $1,000,000 and preferred shares that are redeemable for $1,300,000. Determine the ACB and the PUC of the redeemable preferred shares. Indicate the amount and type of any income that will result from this transaction.

Exercise Seventeen - 3

Subject: Exchange Of Shares In Reorganization (ACB > PUC, PUC = Boot)

Mr. Sam Samson is the sole shareholder of Samdoo Ltd. It is a Canadian controlled private corporation and its common shares have a fair market value of $2,300,000, an adjusted cost base (ACB) of $1,250,000, and a Paid Up Capital (PUC) of $1,000,000. At this time, Samdoo Ltd. has no balance in its GRIP account. Mr. Samson exchanges all of his Samdoo Ltd. shares for cash of $1,000,000 and preferred shares that are redeemable for $1,300,000. Determine the ACB and the PUC of the redeemable preferred shares. Indicate the amount and type of any income that will result from this transaction.

SOLUTION available in print and online Study Guide.

Exercise Seventeen - 4

Subject: Exchange Of Shares In Reorganization (ACB > Boot > PUC)

Mr. Sam Samson is the sole shareholder of Samdoo Ltd. It is a Canadian controlled private corporation and its common shares have a fair market value of $2,300,000, an adjusted cost base (ACB) of $1,250,000, and a Paid Up Capital (PUC) of $1,000,000. At this time, Samdoo Ltd. has no balance in its GRIP account. Mr. Samson exchanges all of his Samdoo Ltd. shares for cash of $1,200,000 and preferred shares that are redeemable for $1,100,000. Determine the ACB and the PUC of the redeemable preferred shares. Indicate the amount and type of any income that will result from this transaction.

SOLUTION available in print and online Study Guide.

We suggest your work Self Study Problem Seventeen-3 at this point.

Gift To Related Person - ITA 86(2)

Background

17-30.   ITA 86(2) contains a rule designed to prevent a taxpayer from using the reorganization of capital rollover provision to confer a benefit on a related person. This rule is applicable whenever the fair market value of the old shares exceeds the sum of the fair market value of the new shares and the fair market value of the non-share consideration received, and it is reasonable to regard all, or part, of this excess as a gift to a related person. You might wish to note that this provision is similar to the provision that is applicable when the use of an ITA 85(1) rollover involves a gift to a related person (see Chapter 16).

17-31.   In situations where ITA 86(2) applies, the rules for the reorganization of share capital are as follows:

Proceeds Of Disposition   Under ITA 86(2)(c), the proceeds of the disposition for capital gains purposes on the old shares will be equal to the lesser of:

- the non-share consideration, **plus the gift**; and
- the fair market value of the old shares.

This compares to the proceeds of disposition under ITA 86(1)(c), which is equal to the cost of the new shares plus any non-share consideration.

Capital Losses   Under ITA 86(2)(d), any capital loss resulting from the disposition of the old shares will be deemed to be nil.

Cost Of New Shares   Under ITA 86(2)(e), the cost to the taxpayer of the new shares will be equal to:

- the cost of the old shares; less
- the sum of the non-share consideration, **plus the gift.**

This compares to a cost for the new shares under ITA 86(1)(b) equal to the cost of the old shares less any non-share consideration.

17-32.   To illustrate these procedures, we will modify the example in Paragraph 17-23 by decreasing the amount of consideration received to create a $100,000 gift. The revised example is as follows:

EXAMPLE   Mr. David Jones owns all of the outstanding shares of Jones Inc. These common shares have an adjusted cost base of $50,000 and a Paid Up Capital of $75,000. Because of the successful operations of the company, the current fair market value of these common shares is $500,000.

Mr. Jones would like to have future growth in the value of the corporation accrue to his daughter, Ms. Veronica Jones. Veronica is 30 years old and has been actively and substantially involved in the business for over five years. To accomplish this, Mr. Jones first exchanges his common shares for a $150,000 note payable from the corporation and preferred shares with a fair market value and a legal stated capital of $250,000. Common shares are then purchased by Veronica Jones for $1,000. These are the only Jones Inc. common shares outstanding subsequent to these transactions.

Calculation Of Gift

17-33. The gift involved in this approach is calculated as follows:

Fair Market Value Of Shares Given Up		$500,000
Less Fair Market Value Of Consideration:		
Non-Share Consideration	($150,000)	
Fair Market Value Of Preferred Shares	(250,000)	(400,000)
Gift		$ 100,000

17-34. As his daughter is the only holder of common shares, this $100,000 gift would accrue to her. As she is clearly a related person, ITA 86(2) would be applicable.

PUC Reduction

17-35. The PUC reduction and PUC of the preferred shares is calculated as follows:

Cost Of Non-Share Consideration (Note Payable)		$150,000

Legal Stated Capital Of Preferred Shares		$250,000
Less The Excess, If Any, Of:		
PUC Of Shares Given Up	($ 75,000)	
Over The Non-Share Consideration	150,000	Nil
ITA 86(2.1)(a) PUC Reduction		$250,000

Legal Stated Capital Of Preferred Shares	$250,000
ITA 86(2.1)(a) PUC Reduction	(250,000)
PUC Of Preferred Shares	Nil

Other Calculations

17-36. The remaining calculations that would be required under ITA 86(2) are as follows:

Adjusted Cost Base Of Common Shares Given Up		$ 50,000
Less:		
Non-Share Consideration	($150,000)	
Gift (See Paragraph 17-33)	(100,000)	(250,000)
Adjusted Cost Base Of Preferred Shares		Nil

PUC Of Preferred Shares	Nil
Plus Non-Share Consideration	$150,000
Proceeds Of Redemption - ITA 84(5)(d)	$150,000
PUC Of Common Shares Given Up	(75,000)
ITA 84(3) Deemed Dividend	$ 75,000

Proceeds Of Disposition Under ITA 86(2)(c) - Lesser Of:
- Fair Market Value Of Shares Given Up = $ 500,000
- Non-Share Consideration Plus Gift

($150,000 + $100,000) = $250,000	$250,000
Less ITA 84(3) Deemed Dividend	(75,000)
Adjusted Proceeds Of Disposition - ITA 54	$175,000
Adjusted Cost Base Of Common Shares Given Up	(50,000)
Capital Gain	$125,000
Inclusion Rate	1/2
Taxable Capital Gain	$ 62,500

17-37.   At the time of the reorganization, the potential gain on David's shares was $450,000 ($500,000 - $50,000). In the original version of this example (Paragraph 17-23), a gain of $100,000 was recognized ($75,000 + $25,000) at the time of the reorganization, leaving $350,000 of the gain deferred until David's preferred shares are redeemed or sold (the shares had a fair market value of $350,000, with both their PUC and adjusted cost base equal to nil).

17-38.   In this version of the example, the gain that is recognized at the time of the reorganization is $200,000 ($75,000 + $125,000), $100,000 larger than in the original version of the example. This reflects the fact that the amount of the gift was added to the ITA 86(2)(c) proceeds of disposition, resulting in a capital gain that is $100,000 larger. It is important to note, however, the total gain, current and deferred, is unchanged at $450,000. While the current gain is increased to $200,000, the deferred amount is reduced to $250,000 (the preferred shares have a fair market value of $250,000, with both their PUC and adjusted cost base equal to nil). While the gift resulted in current taxation that could have been deferred, it did not involve a penalty in the form of additional taxation.

17-39.   ITA 86(2) does, however, involve a penalty to his daughter Veronica. The new common shares issued to Veronica will have a fair market value equal to $101,000, the $1,000 she paid plus the $100,000 gift. The $100,000 additional value will not be reflected in the adjusted cost base of her shares and, as a consequence, this amount will be taxed when she disposes of the shares.

17-40.   In effect, the granting of the benefit has increased the amount that will be subject to taxation in the hands of Veronica by the $100,000 amount of the gift, without reducing Mr. Jones' total current and deferred income on the shares. This makes it clear that ITA 86 reorganizations should be structured in a manner that avoids such benefits being granted.

Exercise Seventeen - 5

Subject: Gift To A Related Party - ITA 86(2)

Janrev Inc. is a Canadian controlled private corporation. Its shares have a fair market value of $1,600,000 and a Paid Up Capital (PUC) of $250,000. Ms. Jan Reviser owns 80 percent of the shares. Her shares have an adjusted cost base of $200,000. The remaining 20 percent of the shares are held by her 19 year old daughter and they have an adjusted cost base of $50,000. On May 1, 2020, Ms. Reviser exchanges all of her Janrev Inc. shares for cash of $300,000 and preferred shares that are redeemable for $800,000. At this time, Janrev has no balance in its GRIP account. Indicate the amount and type of any income that will result from this transaction.

SOLUTION available in print and online Study Guide.

Using ITA 86(1) - Tax Planning Considerations

General Usage

17-41. The major advantages of using ITA 86(1), as compared to using ITA 85(1), can be described as follows:

- An ITA 86(1) share reorganization may be simpler to implement than a Section 85 rollover as it does not involve a transfer between two persons.
- The corporate law steps are easier, only requiring shares to be exchanged, and possibly new share classes to be formed.
- The use of ITA 86(1) does not require an election to be filed with the CRA.

17-42. The disadvantages associated with using ITA 86(1) are as follows:

- When only a single corporation is used, it is difficult to segregate investment income from active business income.
- A single corporation exposes all of the assets to any operating risk, and limited liability protection is reduced.
- In an ITA 86(1) reorganization, all of the taxpayer's shares of a particular class have to be exchanged. This can be a problem if the original shareholder wishes to retain some of the common or growth shares.
- ITA 86 does not provide the range of elected values that are available under ITA 85(1).

17-43. It is usually possible to get around the last disadvantage by re-issuing common shares to the original shareholder after the reorganization is completed.

Use In Key Employee Successions

17-44. In addition to its use in estate freezes, an exchange of shares can be very effective when arranging for gradual succession to a key employee. For example, consider a situation where an employee has little personal equity but has a good work record with the company and excellent owner-manager potential.

17-45. An ITA 86(1) reorganization could be used to convert common shares owned by the existing shareholder into preferred shares. The employee could then purchase the common shares over some agreed upon succession period. The annual investments in common shares would likely be modest, as most of the company's value would be reflected in the preferred shares, making the investments feasible for the incoming shareholder. The original owner could continue to be involved in the business throughout the succession years.

17-46. Eventually, when the original owner is ready to sell the common shares, the incoming shareholder will have the benefit of several years of management experience and should be able to obtain funding to acquire the preferred shares from the original owner.

We suggest you work Self Study Problems Seventeen-4 and 5 at this point.

Amalgamations - ITA 87

The Nature Of An Amalgamation

17-47. ITA 87 provides for a tax deferred rollover in situations where there is an amalgamation of corporations. This may involve two or more independent corporations wishing to merge and continue their business affairs on a combined basis. Alternatively, associated or related corporations may amalgamate to pursue common corporate goals.

17-48. If the two corporations want to transfer their assets to a new corporation on a tax free basis, the rollover provisions of ITA 87 would apply. The following simple example will illustrate this kind of situation.

Figure 17 - 3
ITA 87 Amalgamation Example

EXAMPLE The shareholders of Alpha Inc. have shares with an adjusted cost base of $1,000,000 and a fair market value of $5,000,000, while the shareholders of Beta Inc. have shares with an adjusted cost base of $1,700,000 and a fair market value of $5,000,000. All of the assets and liabilities (except intercompany balances) of Alpha Inc. and Beta Inc. are transferred to a new company, Alpha-Beta Ltd. The shareholders of Alpha Inc. and Beta Inc. exchange their shares for shares in Alpha-Beta Ltd. This example is illustrated in Figure 17-3.

17-49. In the absence of a rollover provision, the exchange of shares would be viewed as a disposition of the Alpha Inc. shares and the Beta Inc. shares, combined with an acquisition of the Alpha-Beta Ltd. shares. The fact that the share dispositions could result in taxable capital gains and the asset transfers could result in taxable capital gains and recapture could serve to discourage the combination of the two companies.

17-50. Fortunately, ITA 87 contains rollover provisions for both the transfer of assets to the amalgamated corporation and for the exchange of shares. The conditions necessary for this rollover to apply are as follows:

- All of the predecessor corporations must be taxable Canadian corporations.

- All shareholders of the predecessor corporations must receive shares of the amalgamated corporation due to the amalgamation.

- All of the assets and liabilities of the predecessor corporations, other than intercompany balances, must be transferred to the amalgamated corporation in the amalgamation.

- A formal amalgamation procedure, supported by the relevant corporate legislation, is required. The transfer cannot simply be a normal purchase of property or involve the distribution of assets on the winding-up of a corporation.

Position Of The Amalgamated Company

17-51. The tax values for the amalgamated corporation's assets will simply be the sum of the tax values of the assets that were present in the records of the predecessor corporations. In addition, all types of loss carry forwards (capital, non-capital, and farm) of the predecessor corporations flow through and become available to the amalgamated corporation.

17-52. The predecessor corporations will be deemed to have a taxation year that ends immediately before the amalgamation and, in most situations, this will result in an extra taxation year that will count toward the expiration of losses with a limited carry forward period. The amalgamated corporation is deemed to have been formed on the date of the amalgamation and may choose any year end it wishes. We would also note that, while this may not be consistent with corporate law, the *Income Tax Act* treats the amalgamated company as a brand new company and the predecessor companies as if they have come to an end.

17-53. With respect to assets, reserves, loss carry forwards, and other tax accounts of the predecessor companies, ITA 87 provides rollover provisions as follows:

Rollover Provisions In ITA 87 Amalgamations

Item	Rollover Effect
Inventories	At Cost
Depreciable Capital Property	At UCC
Non-Depreciable Capital Property	At ACB
Reserves	Flowed Through
Non-Capital Losses	Flowed Through
Net Capital Losses	Flowed Through
Restricted Farm Losses	Flowed Through
General Rate Income Pool (GRIP) (See Note 1)	Flowed Through
Low Rate Income Pool (LRIP) (See Note 2)	Flowed Through
Capital Dividend Account (See Note 3)	Flowed Through
Refundable Dividend Tax On Hand (See Note 3)	Flowed Through

Note 1 If a CCPC is formed as the result of an amalgamation, ITA 89(5) may be applicable. In situations where a predecessor corporation was a CCPC, this subsection provides for the flow through of its GRIP account to the amalgamated company. Where the predecessor was a non-CCPC, a notional GRIP is calculated and flows through to the amalgamated company.

Note 2 If a non-CCPC is formed as the result of an amalgamation, ITA 89(9) may be applicable. In situations where a predecessor corporation was a non-CCPC, this subsection provides for the flow through of its LRIP account to the amalgamated company. Where the predecessor was a CCPC, a notional LRIP is calculated and flowed through.

Note 3 The amalgamated company is treated as a public company if, prior to the amalgamation, any of the predecessor companies were a public company. If this is the case, the amalgamated company will no longer have access to any capital dividend accounts, or Refundable Dividend Tax On Hand accounts of the predecessor companies.

17-54. As can be seen in the preceding table, ITA 87 basically provides for a summing of the relevant tax values of the assets of the two companies that are amalgamating. The amalgamated corporation will be liable for taxes on future recapture and capital gains on the same basis as the predecessor corporations.

17-55. With respect to loss carry forwards, the limitations that were discussed in Chapter 14 are applicable if there is an acquisition of control. As noted, the deemed year end of the predecessor corporations will count as one year in any carry forward period. However, losses carried forward may qualify for deduction in the first taxation year of the amalgamated company.

Position Of The Shareholders

17-56. The shareholders of the predecessor corporations are deemed to dispose of their shares for proceeds equal to the adjusted cost base of the shares, and they are deemed to acquire the shares of the amalgamated company at the same value. For these general provisions to apply, ITA 87(4) specifies the following conditions:

- The shareholders must not receive any consideration other than shares in the amalgamated company.

- The original shares must be capital property of the shareholders.

- The amalgamation must not result in a deemed gift to a person related to the shareholders.

Vertical Amalgamations

17-57.   In situations where there is a desire to combine a parent and its subsidiary, a choice of rollovers may be available. The alternative to ITA 87, "Amalgamations", is the use of ITA 88(1), "Winding-Up". However, ITA 88(1) is only applicable to situations where the parent company owns 90 percent or more of the shares of each class of capital stock of a subsidiary. In contrast, ITA 87 can be used without regard to the percentage of ownership.

Asset Bump-Ups

17-58.   You may recall from an advanced financial accounting course that the cost of acquiring a subsidiary will usually exceed both the carrying values and the sum of the fair values of the acquired identifiable assets.

> **EXAMPLE**   Placor Inc. acquires 100 percent of the outstanding voting shares of Lacee Ltd. at a cost of $1,000,000. At this time the net identifiable assets of Lacee had carrying values of $700,000 and tax values of $650,000. The fair value of these assets totaled $900,000.

17-59.   The excess of the $1,000,000 investment cost over the tax values total of $650,000 creates a problem when there is an amalgamation involving either ITA 87 or ITA 88(1). Both of these provisions transfer assets to either an amalgamated company or a parent company at tax values. In the absence of a special legislative provision, the $350,000 excess of the investment cost over tax values of the assets will be lost.

17-60.   Fortunately, there is a provision that provides a limited amount of relief from this adverse tax consequence. As will be discussed in our coverage of winding-up (Paragraph 17-82), ITA 88(1) provides for a "bump-up" in certain asset values to reflect the parent company's excess of its investment cost over the subsidiary's tax values.

17-61.   ITA 87 provides for the same bump-up under ITA 87(11) by referring to the ITA 88(1) provision. However, there is a difference. Under ITA 88(1), the bump-up is available in situations where the parent owns 90 percent or more of the issued shares. Under ITA 87(11), the bump-up is only available when the parent owns 100 percent of the subsidiary's issued shares. Note that no bump-up is available under either provision when the ownership percentage is less than 90 percent.

Non-Tax Considerations

17-62.   While a statutory amalgamation does not involve a new company, there are likely to be significant legal complications. Each of the predecessor companies will have contracts with employees, suppliers, and customers. While they are still legally in force, modifications may be required to make the terms more compatible throughout the organization. There may also be problems with creditors. In fact, it is not uncommon for debt covenants to have a provision requiring the approval of debt holders before an amalgamation can take place. These factors may add considerable complexity to the amalgamation process.

Amalgamations - Tax Planning Considerations

17-63.   A Section 87 amalgamation offers a number of opportunities for tax planning. Some of the possibilities include:

- The utilization of loss carry forward amounts that the predecessor corporation(s) might not be able to absorb. Note, however, that if there is an acquisition of control, the usual restrictions on the use of loss carry forwards apply.

- With respect to acquisitions of control in the amalgamation process, we would note that, if the two predecessor corporations are related, an amalgamation will not result in an acquisition of control. However, if they are not related and the shareholders of one of the predecessor companies owns the majority of the voting shares in the amalgamated company, that company will be considered to have acquired control of the other predecessor company prior to the amalgamation.

- Current year losses of one predecessor corporation can effectively be utilized against Taxable Income of the other. Note, however, that corporate law in Canada does not generally allow a corporation to amalgamate if its financial health is in question. For example, a company that is insolvent is not allowed to amalgamate with another company.

- Bringing together a profitable and an unprofitable corporation may allow for a faster write-off of capital assets (through CCA) than would otherwise be possible by the unprofitable predecessor corporation.

- The amalgamation may provide for an increase in the amount of the manufacturing and processing profits tax deduction.

17-64. The timing of an amalgamation can be an important tax planning issue. As the amalgamation transaction results in a deemed year end, the company may have a short fiscal year for purposes of calculating CCA. In addition, outstanding reserves may have to be brought into income sooner, and the short fiscal period will count as a full year in the eligible loss carry forward years.

17-65. For income tax instalments there is a look through provision. While the amalgamated company does not have a previous tax year on which to base instalment payments of income tax, prepayments continue to be required based on the instalment history of the predecessor corporations.

Exercise Seventeen - 6

Subject: ITA 87 Amalgamations

During its taxation year ending December 31, 2019, Downer Ltd. incurs a non-capital loss of $93,000 and a net capital loss of $150,000. Neither loss can be carried back. On January 1, 2020, using the provisions of ITA 87, the company is amalgamated with Upton Inc., an unrelated company that also has a December 31 year end. The combined company is named Amalgo Inc. and it elects to use a December 31 year end. The terms of the amalgamation give 20,000 Amalgo Inc. shares to the Downer Ltd. shareholders and 150,000 Amalgo Inc. shares to the Upton Inc. shareholders. Amalgo Inc. was established with only one class of shares. This means that all of the newly issued shares are identical. During the year ending December 31, 2020, Amalgo Inc. has Net Income For Tax Purposes of $1,200,000, including over $300,000 in taxable capital gains. During its 2020 taxation year, will Amalgo Inc. be able to deduct the losses incurred by Downer Ltd. prior to the amalgamation? Explain your conclusion.

SOLUTION available in print and online Study Guide.

Winding-Up Of A 90 Percent Owned Subsidiary

The Nature Of A Winding-Up

Winding-Up Of Corporations In General

17-66. IT-126R2 states that a corporation is considered to have been "wound up" where:

(a) it has followed the procedures for winding-up and dissolution provided by the appropriate federal or provincial companies *Act* or winding-up *Act*, or

(b) it has carried out a winding-up, other than by means of the statutory procedures contemplated in (a) above, and has been dissolved under the provisions of its incorporating statute.

17-67.   In general, a winding-up operation requires that all outstanding creditor claims be satisfied and that all corporate property be distributed to the shareholders before the winding-up is undertaken. IT-126R2 also notes that, where there is substantial evidence that dissolution procedures will be completed within a short period of time, Section 88(1) can be used prior to the completion of the wind-up. Note, however, that losses cannot be accessed until the actual wind-up takes place.

17-68.   A winding-up may be undertaken for several reasons. As with amalgamations, a winding-up allows for the losses of a subsidiary to be flowed through to the parent corporation. Winding-ups are also undertaken to simplify an organizational structure, or when a subsidiary is ceasing its business operations.

90 Percent Owned Subsidiary

17-69.   The two major Subsections of ITA 88 can be described as follows:

ITA 88(1)   This Subsection is a rollover provision, providing for the tax free combination of the assets of a 90 percent or more owned subsidiary with those of its parent.

ITA 88(2)   This Subsection deals with the general winding-up of corporations, other than those to which ITA 88(1) is applicable. It is not a rollover provision.

17-70.   At this point we are concerned only with the provisions contained in ITA 88(1). The content of ITA 88(2) will be considered beginning in Paragraph 17-94.

17-71.   To use the ITA 88(1) rollover, the parent corporation must own at least 90 percent of each class of the subsidiary's shares. Therefore, not all winding-ups of subsidiaries qualify for the treatment described in ITA 88(1). A winding-up involving a subsidiary where a parent corporation has control but owns less than 90 percent of the issued shares would be implemented under the provisions of ITA 88(2). This provision would not allow for a tax free transfer of assets.

17-72.   If the parent has the required 90 percent or more ownership, it is permitted to exchange the subsidiary's shares for the assets of the subsidiary on a tax deferred basis. This transaction is very similar to an amalgamation, as it allows the assets of the two companies to be combined without recognizing any accrued capital gains or recaptured CCA on the transfers required to effect the combination. Note again that this rollover provision only applies to ITA 88(1) transactions. It does not apply when an ITA 88(2) wind-up takes place.

17-73.   As with other rollovers, there are two components to a winding-up transaction. The first is the acquisition of the subsidiary's assets and the assumption of its liabilities by the parent, and the second is the deemed disposition of the subsidiary's shares by the parent. We will now turn our attention to these components.

Acquisition Of Assets

General Rules

17-74.   In an ITA 88(1) winding-up, the subsidiary is deemed to have disposed of its assets and the parent is deemed to have acquired the assets on the following basis:

- A cost of nil in the case of Canadian or foreign resource property.

- The "cost amount" to the subsidiary in the case of other property. Cost amount is defined in ITA 248(1) as UCC for depreciable property and adjusted cost base for non-depreciable capital property.

GRIP Balances

17-75.   ITA 89(6) applies to situations in which a CCPC has wound up a subsidiary under ITA 88(1). If the subsidiary was also a CCPC, this provision provides for a flow through of the subsidiary's GRIP balance to the GRIP balance of the parent company.

17-76.   A second, much more complex provision in ITA 89(6), applies when the subsidiary is a non-CCPC. This provision attempts to measure what the subsidiary's GRIP would have been at the end of its last taxation year had it been a CCPC at that time. This amount will also be included in the parent company's GRIP.

LRIP Balances

17-77.   ITA 89(10) applies when a non-CCPC has wound up a subsidiary under ITA 88(1). If the subsidiary was also a non-CCPC, this provision provides for a flow through of the subsidiary's LRIP balance to the LRIP balance of the parent company.

17-78.   Once again, a second and much more complex provision applies when the subsidiary is a CCPC. This provision attempts to measure what the subsidiary's LRIP would have been at the end of its last taxation year had it been a non-CCPC at that time. This amount will also be transferred to the parent company's LRIP.

Deferral Of Loss Carry Forwards

17-79.   As indicated previously, an ITA 88(1) winding-up is very similar to an amalgamation. There is, however, one important difference between an amalgamation under ITA 87 and the winding-up of a subsidiary under ITA 88(1) and this involves loss carry forwards.

17-80.   As is generally the case under ITA 87, non-capital losses and net capital losses of the subsidiary will be available to the parent company when ITA 88(1) is used. However, under ITA 88(1.1), they will not become available until the first taxation year of the parent that begins after the date that the winding-up period commences.

> **EXAMPLE**   If a parent's fiscal year begins on February 1 and the winding-up commences on February 15, 2020, the losses of the subsidiary will not be available to the parent until its fiscal year beginning February 1, 2021.

17-81.   In those situations where the subsidiary has a different year end than the parent, subsidiary losses are deemed to have occurred in the parent's fiscal year that includes the subsidiary's year end.

> **EXAMPLE**   A parent has a June 30 year end, while its subsidiary has a September 30 year end. A winding-up commences on August 15, 2020, and is completed by August 31, 2020. The subsidiary has a non-capital loss for the period that is terminated on August 31, 2020, by the winding-up.

> **ANALYSIS**   The loss will be deemed to have occurred in the parent's year ending June 30, 2021. This would suggest that the loss would not expire until the parent's year ending June 30, 2041. However, ITA 88(1.1)(b) limits the carry forward period to the period that would have been available to the subsidiary if it had not been wound up. This means that, in actual fact, the loss expires on June 30, 2040. The losses of the subsidiary are not available to the parent until its fiscal year beginning on July 1, 2021.

Exercise Seventeen - 7

Subject: Losses In A Winding-Up

Park Inc. has a September 15 year end, while its 100 percent owned subsidiary, Side Ltd., has an October 31 year end. There is a winding-up of Side Ltd., using the rollover provision found in ITA 88(1), on June 30, 2020. Side Ltd. has a non-capital loss of $50,000 for the period November 1, 2019, to June 30, 2020. What is the earliest taxation year in which the $50,000 loss can be deducted? If it is not deducted then, in what taxation year will it expire?

SOLUTION available in print and online Study Guide.

Asset Bump-Up

17-82.   As we pointed out in our discussion of amalgamations, ITA 88(1) provides for a transfer of all or part of the excess of the purchase price of a 90 percent or more owned subsidiary's shares over the tax values of the subsidiary's assets. As noted, this bump-up is also available under ITA 87 when the parent owns 100 percent of the subsidiary. Under either of these provisions, the amount of this bump-up in tax values is limited by two amounts:

1. The basic amount of the bump-up is found in ITA 88(1)(d)(i) and (i.1). This amount is the excess of the adjusted cost base of the subsidiary shares held by the parent over the sum of:

    -   the tax values of the subsidiary's net assets at the time of the winding-up; and

    -   dividends paid by the subsidiary to the parent since the time of the acquisition (including capital dividends).

2. ITA 88(1)(d)(ii) further limits the amount that can be recognized to the excess of the fair market value of the subsidiary's non-depreciable capital property over their tax values at the time the parent acquired control of the subsidiary.

17-83.   The following example will illustrate these procedures:

EXAMPLE   On December 31, 2010, ParentCo acquires 100 percent of the outstanding shares of SubCo for $5,000,000. At that time, the only non-depreciable capital property owned by SubCo was land with a fair market value of $2,000,000 and a cost of $1,000,000. Between December 31, 2010, and December 31, 2020, SubCo pays dividends of $150,000 to ParentCo. On December 31, 2020, when the tax values of SubCo's assets total $4,200,000, SubCo is absorbed in a Section 88(1) winding-up.

ANALYSIS   The amount of the available asset bump-up will be the lesser of the two amounts described in Paragraph 17-82:

Adjusted Cost Base Of SubCo Shares		$5,000,000
Tax Values Of SubCo Assets At Winding-Up	($4,200,000)	
Dividends Paid By SubCo Since Its Acquisition	(150,000)	(4,350,000)
Excess		$ 650,000

Fair Market Value Of Land At Acquisition	$2,000,000
Cost Of Land At Acquisition	(1,000,000)
Excess	$1,000,000

17-84.   In this situation, the write-up of the land is restricted to the lower figure of $650,000. As a result, the subsidiary is deemed to have disposed of the land for $1,000,000 with no gain or loss. However, the parent is deemed to have acquired the same land for $1,650,000.

Exercise Seventeen - 8

Subject: Winding-Up Of A 90 Percent Or More Owned Subsidiary

On January 1, 2016, Procul Ltd. acquired 100 percent of the outstanding shares of Lorne Inc. at a cost of $1,200,000. At this point in time, the fair market value of Lorne's identifiable net assets was $850,000, including $270,000 for land. The tax values of the net assets at that time totaled $410,000.

On December 31, 2020, there is a winding-up of Lorne Inc. under the provisions of ITA 88(1). Lorne Inc. has paid no dividends since its acquisition by Procul Ltd. On December 31, 2020, the condensed Balance Sheet of Lorne Inc. is as follows:

Cash	$ 120,000
Land - At Cost (Purchased In 2012)	140,000
Depreciable Assets - At UCC (Purchased In 2012)	240,000
Total Assets	**$500,000**
Liabilities	$ 75,000
Shareholders' Equity	425,000
Total Equities	**$500,000**

Determine the tax values that will be recorded for Lorne Inc.'s assets after they have been incorporated into the records of Procul Ltd.

SOLUTION available in print and online Study Guide.

Disposition Of Shares

17-85.   The disposition of shares component of the winding-up is straightforward. In general, the parent is deemed to have disposed of its shares of the subsidiary for proceeds equal to the adjusted cost base of the shares. As an example, assume the parent had paid $4,000,000 for the subsidiary's shares. This amount would also be the deemed proceeds of the disposition and there would be no capital gain.

17-86.   An exception to this general rule will arise if the tax values of the subsidiary's net assets transferred and the Paid Up Capital of the subsidiary's shares is more than the amount paid for the shares by the parent. In this case, the deemed proceeds of disposition will be the lesser of the PUC and the tax values of the net assets transferred. As a result, a capital gain can arise in these situations.

> **EXAMPLE**   Prawn Ltd. owns 100 percent of the outstanding shares of Shrimp Inc. The cost of these shares was $4,000,000. This subsidiary is being wound up under the provisions of ITA 88(1). At the time of the winding-up, the tax values of the subsidiary's net assets total $4,800,000 and the PUC of the subsidiary's shares is $4,500,000.

> **ANALYSIS**   Given these facts, the exception applies and the deemed proceeds of disposition would be the greater of the $4,000,000 cost of the shares and $4,500,000. This latter figure is the lesser of the $4,800,000 tax value of the subsidiary's net assets and the $4,500,000 PUC of the subsidiary's shares. This gives proceeds of disposition of $4,500,000 and a capital gain of $500,000 ($4,500,000 - $4,000,000). It is expected that such gains situations would be fairly rare and, because the proceeds are defined using cost except when it is less than the alternative values, there is no possibility of a capital loss.

Tax Planning Considerations - Amalgamation Vs. Winding-Up

17-87.   Figure 17-4 (on the following page) contains a comparison of the features of an amalgamation under ITA 87 and the winding-up of a subsidiary that is at least 90 percent owned under ITA 88(1). A discussion of several of the items follows.

17-88.   A significant consideration in deciding between an amalgamation under ITA 87 and a winding-up under ITA 88(1) is the ability to recognize all or part of the excess of investment cost over tax values. In the case of an ITA 87 amalgamation, recognition is possible only in cases involving a parent and a 100 percent owned subsidiary. Under ITA 88(1), recognition can occur as long as the parent owns 90 percent or more of each class of the subsidiary's issued shares.

Figure 17 - 4 Comparison Of Amalgamation Under ITA 87 And Winding-Up Under ITA 88(1)		
Factor	**Amalgamation - ITA 87**	**Winding-Up Of 90% Owned Subsidiary - ITA 88(1)**
Valuation of assets	Tax values of assets of predecessor corporations carried forward to amalgamated company.	Tax values of subsidiary's assets carried forward to parent.
Recognition of some of the excess of investment cost over tax values	Recognition only if 100% owned subsidiary. If 100% owned, same treatment as ITA 88(1).	Write-up allowed if excess is associated with values of non-depreciable capital property.
Capital cost allowances	Claim in last year of predecessor and first year of amalgamated corporation.	No claim by subsidiary in year of winding-up, but available to parent in year of winding-up.
Loss carry forwards	Carried forward. However, their use may be limited if the amalgamation results in an acquisition of control.	Carried forward, but only available to parent beginning in the taxation year after winding-up.
Year end	Deemed year end before amalgamation, counts one year for loss carry forwards.	Year end of parent corporation continued. Subsidiary has a terminal year end that counts as one taxation year.

17-89.   Under either provision, it is possible that substantial tax values will disappear in the transaction. This would suggest that, when the adjusted cost base of the parent's investment is significantly greater than the tax values of the subsidiary's net assets, it may be better to continue to operate the subsidiary as a separate legal entity.

17-90.   Under the amalgamation procedures, the predecessor corporations will have a deemed year end, which will count toward the expiry of time-limited non-capital loss carry forwards. However, subject to the acquisition of control rules, the amalgamated company will be able to use the losses immediately.

17-91.   In contrast, the parent company that is using ITA 88(1) to absorb a 90 percent owned subsidiary will have its usual year end. However, it will not be able to use subsidiary loss carry forwards until the first taxation year beginning subsequent to the winding-up. In addition, the wind-up will count as an additional year in the expiry of time-limited loss carry forwards. The analysis of this situation may be complicated by differing year ends for the two corporations.

17-92.   In considering CCA claims, ITA 87 creates a deemed year end for both predecessor corporations, requiring them to take pro rata CCA claims for what will normally be a short fiscal period. Under the ITA 88(1) procedures, the subsidiary disposes of its assets prior to its year end and, as a consequence, there will be no claim for CCA in the subsidiary's final year. However, CCA may be claimed on these assets by the parent company, subsequent to their being acquired under the winding-up procedures.

17-93.   If the subsidiary is not 100 percent owned, ITA 88(1) cannot be used unless the minority shareholder group is at arm's length with the parent company. If the minority shareholders are at arm's length and ITA 88(1) can be used to transfer the assets belonging to the controlling interest, an application of this Subsection will generally have tax consequences for the non-controlling interest. A winding-up will require reporting of capital gains and recaptured CCA on property distributed by the subsidiary to the minority shareholders. Further, any liquidating dividend paid to the minority shareholders will be a taxable dividend.

We suggest you work Self Study Problem Seventeen-6 at this point.

Winding-Up Of A Canadian Corporation

The Nature Of The Transaction

Wind-Up (Liquidation) Vs. Rollover

17-94.   The winding-up procedures for a Canadian corporation, as described in ITA 88(2), are applicable where a corporation is being liquidated. If, for example, owners of a corporation decide that the business is no longer viable, winding-up procedures can be used in the disposition of the corporation's assets and the distribution of the resulting proceeds to the shareholders.

17-95.   In distinguishing the winding-up of a 90 percent or more owned subsidiary from a liquidating winding-up, you should note that the liquidation of a business has quite different objectives. In the case of the winding-up of a 90 percent or more owned subsidiary, we are usually not disposing of the business but, rather, are transferring its assets to a different legal entity that is controlled by the same investor or group of investors that previously had indirect control of its operations. This explains why a rollover is available on the winding-up of a 90 percent or more owned subsidiary, and no equivalent provision is available for the winding-up when a liquidation is under way.

Distributions To Shareholders

17-96.   While a winding-up can be implemented by distributing corporate assets directly to the shareholders, it is generally simpler for the corporation to liquidate its assets, pay off its creditors, pay any taxes that are applicable at the corporate level, and distribute the after tax proceeds to the shareholders.

17-97.   The distribution to shareholders becomes a fairly complex issue when a corporation is liquidated, as the proceeds available for distribution will consist of a combination of capital being returned, earnings that can be distributed on a tax free basis, and earnings that can only be distributed in the form of taxable dividends. A further complication is that there may be a combination of eligible and non-eligible dividends.

Disposition Of An Incorporated Business

17-98.   Later in this Chapter we will discuss the transfer of an incorporated business to a different group of owners. This can be accomplished through a sale of shares or, alternatively, through a sale of the corporation's assets. If the sale of assets is the more advantageous approach, the provisions of ITA 88(2) apply. That is, the sale of assets will be followed by a winding-up, with the after tax proceeds of the winding-up being distributed to the shareholders. While the business itself will continue to operate, the assets will now be on the books of a different legal entity.

Example

Basic Data

17-99.   The ITA 88(2) procedures will be illustrated in the following example.

> **EXAMPLE**   The Marker Company, a Canadian controlled private corporation, has been in operation for 20 years. It has a December 31 year end. On January 1, 2020, the following Balance Sheet, based on tax values, has been prepared in contemplation of liquidating the company:

Winding-Up Of A Canadian Corporation

The Marker Company
Balance Sheet - As At January 1, 2020 (Tax Values)

Accounts Receivable	$ 12,000
Non-Eligible RDTOH	8,000
Land - At Cost (Note One)	250,000
Building - At UCC (Note Two)	195,000
Total Assets	**$465,000**

Liabilities	Nil
Common Shares - No Par (Note Three)	$ 10,000
Retained Earnings (Note Three)	455,000
Total Equities	**$465,000**

Note One　The current fair market value of the Land is $300,000.

Note Two　The cost of the building was $320,000. Its current fair market value is $350,000.

Note Three　The Paid Up Capital and adjusted cost base of the common shares is $10,000. The Retained Earnings includes $75,000 in the capital dividend account. The company's GRIP balance is nil.

The assets of the company are sold for their fair market values, which total $662,000 ($12,000 + $300,000 + $350,000). The company has no other income for the taxation year. The provincial corporate tax rates are 2.5 percent on income eligible for the small business deduction and 14 percent on other corporate income. No reserves were deducted in 2019.

Cash Available For Distribution

17-100.　At the corporate level, the proceeds from the disposition of the individual assets and the related tax effects are as follows:

Asset	Proceeds	Taxable Capital Gain	Active Business Income
Accounts Receivable	$ 12,000	Nil	Nil
Land	300,000	$25,000	Nil
Building	350,000	15,000	$125,000
Totals	$662,000	$40,000	$125,000

The Tax Payable on Marker's Taxable Income of $165,000 ($40,000 + $125,000) would be calculated as follows:

Federal Tax On Active Business Income [(38% - 10% - 19%)($125,000)]	$11,250
Federal Tax On Investment Income [(38% - 10% + 10-2/3%)($40,000)]	15,467
Part I Tax Payable	$26,717
Provincial Tax On Active Business Income [(2.5%)($125,000)]	3,125
Provincial Tax On Investment Income [(14%)($40,000)]	5,600
Total Corporate Tax Payable	$35,442

17-101.　The only 2020 addition to an RDTOH balance would be the refundable portion of Part I Tax Payable. This amount would be the least of:

- 30-2/3% Of Investment Income [(30-2/3%)($40,000)] $12,267

- 30-2/3% Of Taxable Income, Less Amount EligibleFor
  Small Business Deduction [(30-2/3%)($165,000 - $125,000)] $12,267

- Part I Tax Payable $26,717

17-102. This amount would also be allocated to the Non-Eligible RDTOH, resulting in the following balance in that account:

Opening Balance	$ 8,000
Part I Refundable Tax	12,267
Non-Eligible RDTOH	$20,267

17-103. The after tax amount of cash that is available for distribution to shareholders is calculated as follows:

Gross Proceeds	$662,000
Corporate Tax Payable	(35,442)
Non-Eligible RDTOH*	20,267
Available For Distribution	$646,825

*Given the size of the gross proceeds, the balance in the Non-Eligible RDTOH is clearly going to be less than 38-1/3 percent of the dividends that will be declared.

Distribution To Shareholders

17-104. The balance in the capital dividend account can be distributed to the shareholders as a tax free capital dividend. This balance is calculated as follows:

Balance Before Dispositions (Balance Sheet Note Three)	$ 75,000
Disposition Of Land	25,000
Disposition Of Building	15,000
Capital Dividend Account - Ending Balance	$115,000

17-105. Prior to the sale of assets, the company's GRIP balance was nil. As all of the income resulting from the sale of assets was either Aggregate Investment Income or income eligible for the small business deduction, there would be no addition to the GRIP account resulting from the sale of assets. This means that all dividends paid that are subject to tax would be non-eligible. The non-eligible taxable dividend component of the total distribution to the shareholders is calculated as follows:

Total Distribution	$646,825
Paid Up Capital	(10,000)
ITA 84(2) Deemed Dividend On Winding-Up*	$636,825
Capital Dividend Account (Balance In Account)	(115,000)
Non-Eligible Dividend Subject To Tax	$521,825

*As explained in Chapter 14, in a winding up, when the total distribution to shareholders exceeds the PUC of the shares being canceled, the excess is an ITA 84(2) deemed dividend. This deemed dividend is treated first as a capital dividend, if the appropriate election is filed. Any excess is treated as an eligible or non-eligible taxable dividend.

17-106. Treatment of the $115,000 as a capital dividend is conditional on the appropriate election being made under ITA 83(2). The remaining taxable non-eligible dividend will be grossed up to $600,099 [(115%)($521,825)]. The dividend will provide a federal dividend tax credit of $54,190 [(9/13)(15%)($521,825)].

17-107.   In the ITA 54 definition of "proceeds of disposition," Paragraph j indicates that amounts that are deemed to be a dividend under ITA 84(2) are not included in this amount. As a consequence, in determining the capital gain resulting from the distribution to the shareholders, the ITA 84(2) dividend will be subtracted as follows:

Total Distribution to Shareholders	$646,825
ITA 84(2) Deemed Dividend	(636,825)
Deemed Proceeds Of Disposition	$ 10,000
Adjusted Cost Base Of Shares	(10,000)
Capital Gain	Nil

Exercise Seventeen - 9

Subject: Winding-Up Of A Canadian Corporation

Windown Inc. is a Canadian controlled private company. After disposing of all of its assets and paying all of its liabilities, including Tax Payable resulting from the asset dispositions, the company is left with cash of $865,000. The PUC of the company's shares is equal to their adjusted cost base, an amount of $88,000. After the sale of assets, the company has combined eligible and non-eligible RDTOH accounts of $47,000, a capital dividend account balance of $26,000, and a GRIP of nil. Determine the tax consequences to the shareholders associated with making the maximum distribution of cash to shareholders on the winding-up of Windown Inc. on June 1, 2020. Assume that appropriate elections will be made to minimize the taxes that will be paid by the shareholders.

SOLUTION available in print and online Study Guide.

We suggest you work Self Study Problem Seventeen-7 at this point.

Convertible Properties

Application

17-108.   There is one more rollover that you should be familiar with. ITA 51 contains a provision that permits a holder of shares or debt of a corporation to exchange those securities for shares of that corporation on a tax free basis. For this rollover provision to apply, the following two conditions must be met:

- The exchange must not involve any consideration other than the securities that are being exchanged.

- The exchange must not be part of a reorganization of capital or a rollover of property by shareholders to a corporation under ITA 85 or ITA 86.

17-109.   In practical terms, this provision is designed to accommodate a tax deferred conversion of debt or preferred shares of a corporation into preferred or common shares of the same corporation.

EXAMPLE   An investor acquires convertible bonds with a par value of $10,000 at a price equal to par value. The bonds are convertible into 500 shares of the issuing company's common shares and, at the time of purchase, these common shares are trading at $18 per share (the conversion value of the bonds is $9,000). The bonds are converted when the common shares are trading at $22 per share.

ANALYSIS   The conversion of the bonds is a disposition and, in the absence of a special provision, the tax consequences would be as follows:

Proceeds Of Disposition [(50)($22)]	$11,000
Adjusted Cost Base	(10,000)
Capital Gain	**$ 1,000**

17-110. The ITA serves to provide relief in this type of situation. ITA 51(1)(c) deems such exchanges not to be a disposition. Given this deeming provision, no gain will be recognized.

17-111. Going with this provision, ITA 51(1)(d) deems the cost of the acquired shares to be equal to the cost of the shares or debt given up. In effect, ITA 51 allows convertible securities to be converted with no immediate tax consequences. No gain or loss is recorded and the adjusted cost base of investors' securities remains unchanged.

Other Considerations

17-112. A conversion provision can assist corporations seeking to add an equity kicker to enhance the marketability of their debt or preferred shares. In addition, conversion arrangements can be used to facilitate income splitting within a corporation. Different classes of shares can be used to allow the redistribution of income and, with the ability to convert different classes of shares on a tax deferred basis, an additional element of flexibility is introduced into such arrangements.

17-113. ITA 51.1 contains a similar provision to cover situations under which bondholders of a particular company are allowed to convert their holdings into a different debt security of that company. Here again, there is a tax deferred rollover with the adjusted cost base of the old bond holding becoming the creditor's adjusted cost base for the new debt security.

17-114. We would call your attention to the fact that the accounting rules on debt that is convertible into common or preferred shares require that the proceeds from its issuance be divided between the amount paid by investors for the liability component of the financial instrument and the amount paid for the equity option (see IAS 32, *Financial Instruments: Presentation*). This important issue has not, at this point in time, been given recognition in tax legislation. For tax purposes, the full amount received for convertible debt must be allocated to the debt component of the security.

Sale Of An Incorporated Business

Alternatives

17-115. Assume that you are the sole shareholder of an incorporated business and that you have decided to dispose of your company. If the business has a value that extends beyond your personal services, it should be possible to arrange a sale of the business. In approaching the problem of selling an incorporated business, you are usually confronted with the following three alternatives:

- Sale of the individual assets of the corporation, on a piecemeal basis.
- Sale of the total net assets of the corporation, including any unrecorded intangibles such as goodwill.
- Sale of the shares of the corporation.

17-116. In the next section, consideration will be given to the advantages and disadvantages as well as to the tax effects that are associated with each of these alternatives. However, before turning our attention to these alternatives, some attention must be given to the tax treatment of restrictive covenants.

Restrictive Covenants (a.k.a. Non-Competition Agreements)

General Rules

17-117. Restrictive covenants are arrangements under which a taxpayer agrees to have his or her ability to provide goods or services restricted in one or more ways. Such agreements may relate to particular products or services (e.g., the taxpayer will not provide audit services) and may refer to specific geographic areas (e.g., the taxpayer will not provide audit services in the greater Calgary area). They may or may not be limited in terms of time. It is not uncommon, particularly in the case of owner-managed businesses, for the purchaser to require the seller to sign a restrictive covenant.

17-118.   ITA 56.4(2) requires that, in general, 100 percent of payments made to a taxpayer for agreeing to a restrictive covenant be included in income as an "other source" under Subdivision d. Fortunately for taxpayers, ITA 56.4(3) contains three important exceptions to this general rule.

Exceptions To 100 Percent Income Inclusion

17-119.   These exceptions are as follows:

ITA 56.4(3)(a) - Employment Income   In cases where the payment relates to past employment with the payor, the receipt will be treated by the recipient as employment income. While 100 percent of the amount would still be subject to tax, classification as employment income would mean that it does not have to be included in the recipient's income until it is received (employment income is on a cash basis). When this exception is applicable, ITA 56.4(4)(a) allows the payor to treat the payment as wages paid or payable.

ITA 56.4(3)(b) - Class 14.1   Provided the payor and recipient file a joint election, the restrictive covenant payment can be treated as an acquisition of a Class 14.1 asset by the payor, and as Class 14.1 proceeds of disposition by the recipient.

From the point of view of the payor, this is an unfavourable treatment. Instead of being a fully deductible expense, the payment is added to Class 14.1 where it will only be deductible on a 5 percent declining balance basis.

However, from the point of view of the recipient, this is a very favourable approach. As the intangible asset that is reflected in the restrictive covenant payment will normally have a capital cost of nil, the entire proceeds of disposition will be treated as a capital gain, only one-half of which will be taxable. In the absence of this treatment, the full amount of the restrictive covenant payment would be taxable to the recipient.

ITA 56.4(3)(c) - Sale Of An Eligible Interest   An eligible interest is an interest in shares in a corporation that carries on business or in a partnership that carries on business. In a situation where a restrictive covenant is sold in conjunction with an eligible interest, the amount received can be added to the proceeds of disposition. As was the case with the ITA 56.4(3)(b) exception, the payor and the recipient must file a joint election for this exception to apply. When this exception is applicable, ITA 56.4(4)(c) requires the purchaser to treat the payment as a cost of the purchase.

If this addition creates or increases a capital gain, only one-half of this amount will be subject to tax. Note that the application of this provision is more complex when there is more than one restrictive covenant involved in the sale of a single eligible interest.

17-120.   The first of these exceptions, treatment of the restrictive covenant payment as employment income, is not relevant to the material in this Chapter. However, the other two exceptions are very significant when a business is being sold and will be given further attention in our discussion of the alternative ways in which a business can be sold.

Sale Of Individual Assets

General Procedures

17-121.   Disposing of a business via a piece-by-piece sale of individual assets would only occur in certain situations. These could be described as follows:

- The business has not been successful in producing an adequate rate of return on the assets invested. In such situations, the most reasonable course of action may be the sale of individual assets.

- Some owner-managed businesses have income producing activities that are so closely tied to the skills of the owner-manager that the sale of the business independent of those skills would not be feasible.

17-122.   This type of disposition would only be appropriate in limited circumstances. Given that the circumstances associated with the particular business will dictate whether this approach will be used, there is no need to devote any attention to the advantages or disadvantages of this alternative.

Restrictive Covenants - Sale Of Individual Assets

17-123.   In the situations that are involved here, it is unlikely that a restrictive covenant will be used. However, if this were to occur, treatment of the amount involved as an acquisition/disposition of a Class 14.1 asset would be possible. This treatment will be discussed in the next section dealing with the sale of total assets as a going concern.

Sale Of Assets As A Going Concern

General Procedures

17-124.   In contrast to a liquidation, where the assets are sold on an individual basis, the purchaser in this situation would acquire the corporation's assets as a going concern and, in so doing, would acquire any goodwill or other intangible assets that might be associated with the enterprise.

17-125.   As was the case with the piece-by-piece sale of individual assets in a liquidation, the sale of all assets as a going concern may result in a combination of business income, capital gains, recapture, and terminal losses.

17-126.   In both types of asset sales, you should note that there are really two transactions involved. The first transaction involves the sale of assets and the payment of liabilities at the corporate level. Included in this process will be the determination of any tax liability resulting from the sale of the assets. At this point, the corporate assets would consist entirely of the after tax proceeds resulting from the disposition of the tangible and other assets of the corporation. In most situations, the owner will choose to distribute these assets and wind-up the corporation.

17-127.   This distribution of the after tax proceeds of the sale of corporate assets is the second transaction and, in general, it will involve income tax effects for the recipient shareholders. Given this two transaction process, a complete analysis of the alternatives of selling the assets of the business versus disposing of the shares will require dealing with both taxation on the corporation as a result of disposing of the assets and personal taxation as a result of distributing the after tax proceeds of this sale.

17-128.   In dealing with the sale of corporate assets, an understanding of the tax effects associated with such dispositions is required. These effects can be outlined as follows:

Cash   In most circumstances, the cash of the business will be retained in the business. If it is "sold", there will be no tax consequences associated with its disposition.

Accounts Receivable   In the absence of any special election, the sale of accounts receivable as a component of the sale of a business will be treated as a capital transaction. This means that any difference between the face value and the consideration received will be treated as a capital loss, only one-half of which will be deductible.

However, ITA 22 provides for a joint election to treat the sale of receivables as an income transaction. This allows the purchaser to treat any difference between the amount paid for the receivables and the amount actually collected as a bad debt expense. A more detailed description of this election is presented in Chapter 6.

Inventories   Even when inventories are sold as part of the sale of a business, any difference between the sales price and the vendor's cost will be treated as ordinary business income. This is provided for in ITA 23 and, unlike the situation with the ITA 22 treatment of receivables, no election is required. For the purchaser, the transfer price becomes the tax cost that will eventually be allocated to cost of goods sold.

Prepayments The *Income Tax Act* does not recognize prepayments as an asset. This means that some amounts that are treated as prepayments in the accounting records have, for tax purposes, been deducted as expenses. As a result of this, when such balances are sold for their fair market value, the proceeds will be included in income.

Non-Depreciable Capital Assets The most common non-depreciable capital assets of a business are land and investments. Depending on the amount of consideration received for these assets, the transferor will have a capital gain or loss. With respect to capital losses, in general they can only be deducted from capital gains.

If some of the consideration being paid for these assets is deferred, the corporation can use capital gains reserves to defer part of the applicable taxation. However, the use of this technique would require continuing the corporation through the deferral period, and this may not be in keeping with the objectives of the vendor.

For the purchaser, the adjusted cost base of non-depreciable capital assets will be the purchase price, which presumably is the fair market value.

Depreciable Assets The disposition of a depreciable asset can result in recapture, a terminal loss, or some combination of recapture and a capital gain. Unlike capital gains, recapture and terminal losses will be subject to 100 percent inclusion in, or deduction from, active business income and will be included in income eligible for the small business deduction.

As was the case with non-depreciable capital assets, if some of the consideration for these assets is not received immediately, reserves can be used to defer the taxation of capital gains.

For the purchaser, the capital cost of depreciable assets will be the purchase price, which presumably is the fair market value.

Goodwill If goodwill is present, some amount of the consideration received for the going concern will be allocated to goodwill. Any allocated amount will be treated as proceeds of disposition for a Class 14.1 asset. As the capital cost of goodwill will most commonly be nil, when the lesser of the proceeds of disposition and the capital cost of the goodwill is subtracted from any Class 14.1 balance, it commonly results in the entire proceeds of disposition allocated to goodwill being treated as a capital gain.

The purchaser of the going concern will add the allocated cost of the goodwill to Class 14.1 where it will be subject to CCA on a 5 percent declining balance basis. The AccII provisions are applicable to this class.

Restrictive Covenants - Sale Of Total Assets

17-129.   Restrictive covenants may take one of two different forms when there is a sale of the total assets of the corporation. If it is anticipated that the corporation will continue in business, the agreement can be between the purchaser of the assets and the corporation. In contrast, if the corporation is to be liquidated, the agreement will likely be between the purchaser and the former owner(s) of the shares. It is also possible that the purchaser will require both the corporation and the former shareholders to sign a restrictive covenant.

17-130.   This election is available only between the purchaser and the business (corporation or, in the case of a proprietorship, an individual). It could not be between the purchaser and the shareholders of the relevant corporation. This approach is conditional on the parties being prepared to make the required joint election.

17-131.   If the election is made, the consideration given for the restrictive covenant will be treated as the proceeds of disposition of a Class 14.1 asset. As previously discussed, in most situations this will result in the amount being treated as a capital gain.

17-132.   If the payment is eligible for the joint election and the election is made, the purchaser will treat the payment for the restrictive covenant as the acquisition cost of a Class 14.1 asset. However, if the payment is not eligible, or if no joint election is filed, ITA 56.4 provides no specific guidance for the purchaser.

17-133   This means that the purchaser will have to apply basic principles from other Sections of the *Income Tax Act*. Without regard to the fact that the vendor will be taxed on the full amount of the payment under ITA 56.4(2), the purchaser's treatment may involve a deduction of the full amount of the payment or an addition of the payment to one or more assets. The specific treatment by the purchaser will depend on the nature of the payment as determined under general tax principles.

Sale Of Shares

General Procedures

17-134.   In terms of accounting, legal, and tax considerations, this is the simplest way to sell a business. The calculation of the gain on the sale only requires the adjusted cost base of the shares to be subtracted from the proceeds received from their disposition. Any resulting difference will be a capital gain or loss and will be subject to the usual treatment accorded to share dispositions.

17-135.   In preparing for the sale of shares, a corporation will declare tax free capital dividends to the extent of its capital dividend account and taxable dividends for any additional amount, which will generate a dividend refund if there is an RDTOH balance.

Lifetime Capital Gains Deduction

17-136.   If the corporation is a "qualified small business corporation" as defined in ITA 110.6(1), the disposition of shares may qualify for the lifetime capital gains deduction. The conditions associated with the designation "qualified small business corporation" are discussed in Chapter 11. Note here, however, that this deduction is only available on the sale of shares by an individual. If the shares are sold by a corporation, this valuable deduction is not available.

Restrictive Covenants - Sale Of Shares

17-137.   In cases where a business disposition involves a sale of shares, any restrictive covenant that is required will involve an agreement between the purchaser of the shares and the vendor of the shares. In this situation the exception under ITA 56.4(3)(c) (see Paragraph 17-119) becomes important. The sale of shares would be a disposition of an eligible interest, and this would allow the taxpayer receiving payment for the restrictive covenant to include it as part of the proceeds of disposition. As such, it would serve to create or increase a capital gain on the sale, only one-half of which would be taxable.

17-138.   Note that this treatment requires the vendor and purchaser to file a joint election and, if they fail to do so, the vendor will have to include the full amount of the payment in income when it is received or becomes receivable. If the election is filed, the purchaser will include the payment in the cost of his or her purchase. If the election is not filed, the treatment by the purchaser will require the application of general tax principles.

Evaluation Of Alternatives

Advantages Of Selling Shares

17-139.   Generally speaking, the vendor of a business will favour selling shares over selling assets. Factors favouring this alternative are as follows:

- The sale of shares offers the simplicity of a single transaction. In contrast, in a sale of assets, the vendor must deal with the legal and tax consequences arising at the corporate level. In addition, the vendor must steer the corporation through a winding-up procedure and deal with the personal tax consequences of these procedures. The greater complexity will require additional personal efforts on the part of the vendor. Also, the legal and accounting fees associated with these transactions are likely to be significant.

Sale Of An Incorporated Business

- Any income produced by the sale of shares will usually be reported as capital gains. At worst, only one-half of such gains are taxable. At best, the taxable gains may be reduced or eliminated through the use of the lifetime capital gains deduction. If assets are sold by the corporation, some of the resulting income could be recaptured CCA, which must be included in income in full. In addition, if capital gains arise on the sale of assets, they will be treated as investment income to the corporation and will not be eligible for the small business deduction.

- If the enterprise has an unused non-capital loss carry forward, it will still be available to the enterprise if shares are sold. Any non-capital loss carry forwards are, of course, subject to the acquisition of control rules, requiring that they be applied against income earned in the same business in which the losses were incurred. However, if the sale of assets alternative is chosen, such loss carry forward balances will be completely unavailable to the purchaser.

- When a payment for a restrictive covenant is a component of the sale of shares, the vendor may be able to treat the amount received as an addition to his or her proceeds of disposition, rather than an amount that has to be fully included in income. This treatment is conditional on the vendor and purchaser filing a joint election, in which case the purchaser will add the amount paid to his or her acquisition cost.

- A sale of assets could result in the payment of land transfer taxes that would not be applicable if shares are sold.

Advantages Of Purchasing Assets

17-140.   As just described, there are a number of advantages that can be associated with selling shares, most of them benefitting the vendor. From the point of view of the purchaser, a purchase of assets is generally more desirable than a purchase of shares. Some of the advantages of purchasing assets are as follows:

- In acquiring assets, the purchaser acquires a completely new, and usually higher, set of tax values for the assets transferred. For example, consider a depreciable asset with a capital cost of $100,000, a UCC of $40,000, and a fair market value of $400,000. If shares are acquired, the CCA deductions available to the corporation will continue to be based on $40,000 and, if the assets are subsequently disposed of, capital gains will be determined from the original capital cost of $100,000. In contrast, if the asset were purchased in an arm's length transaction for its fair market value of $400,000, this amount would be the capital cost and UCC to the purchaser. This bump-up in asset values and the availability of higher CCA claims can significantly reduce the tax liabilities of the purchaser.

- Goodwill can be recognized when assets are acquired. The CCA deductions related to Class 14.1 are not available if shares are acquired.

- In situations where the purchaser has an existing corporation, he or she may prefer to have that corporation acquire the assets, rather than acquiring the shares of an additional corporation and incurring the administrative costs associated with maintaining a second corporation.

- If shares are acquired, all of the assets must be acquired. In a sale of assets, redundant assets can be left out of an acquisition of assets. Note, however, if there are unwanted assets, it is fairly common for these assets to be disposed of prior to the sale of shares.

- If shares are acquired, the existing liabilities of the corporation will continue to be in place. It is possible that the purchaser can obtain financing on more favourable terms, in which case he or she would prefer to acquire assets.

- If shares are acquired, the purchaser may become responsible for any future tax reassessments. While this exposure could occur because the purchased corporation continues to operate, it is usually covered in the buy and sell agreement for the transaction. This agreement is normally written to protect the purchaser from future problems in this area.

- A further problem relates to potential non-tax liabilities related to product or environmental liabilities. Again, because the purchased corporation is continuing to operate, it could be responsible for such liabilities. However, this is another issue that is normally dealt with in the buy and sell agreement.

- Most of the preceding discussion has implicitly assumed that the corporation's assets have fair market values in excess of their related tax values. If this is not the case and unrealized losses are present, selling assets may be advantageous to the vendor as well as the purchaser. This is based on the fact that the vendor would prefer to have fully deductible terminal or business losses, rather than capital losses that are only one-half deductible against taxable capital gains.

Conclusion

17-141.   While each situation needs to be evaluated on the basis of the specific assets and values involved, in general, a vendor will wish to sell shares while a purchaser will wish to acquire assets. As a result, negotiations will usually involve higher prices being offered for the assets of the business than are offered for the shares of the incorporated business.

Example

17-142.   To illustrate the sale of an incorporated business, we will use the following example.

EXAMPLE   Mr. O'Leary owns all of the outstanding shares of O'Leary Ltd., a Canadian controlled private corporation with a December 31 year end. Mr. O'Leary has reached retirement age and wishes to dispose of the business. He has received an offer to buy the shares for $180,000 or, alternatively, the assets of the business for $200,000. All of the liabilities of the business have been settled in preparation for the sale.

The cost of Mr. O'Leary's original investment was $50,000. As no additional investment has been made, this is also his adjusted cost base and Paid Up Capital for the outstanding shares. The provincial tax rate on business income eligible for the small business deduction is 2.5 percent. The provincial rate on all other income is 14 percent. The corporation has no balance in its RDTOH accounts, its capital dividend account, or its GRIP account. Mr. O'Leary is subject to a combined federal/provincial rate of 46 percent on non-dividend income and 31 percent on non-eligible dividends received.

Relevant information on the January 1, 2020, values for the assets of the business is as follows:

Asset	Cost	Fair Market Value
Cash	$ 5,000	$ 5,000
Receivables	10,000	10,000
Inventories	55,000	60,000
Land	20,000	40,000
Plant And Equipment (UCC = $45,000)	95,000	60,000
Goodwill	Nil	25,000
Total	$185,000	$200,000

Sale Of Shares For $180,000

17-143.   With respect to the sale of shares, the tax consequences are as follows:

Proceeds Of Disposition	$180,000
Adjusted Cost Base	(50,000)
Capital Gain	$130,000
Inclusion Rate	1/2
Taxable Capital Gain (For Mr. O'Leary)	$ 65,000

17-144.   The after tax results for Mr. O'Leary are as follows:

Proceeds Received	$180,000
Tax Payable [(46%))($65,000)]	(29,900)
Cash Retained	$150,100

17-145.   While this might be the result, it is likely that O'Leary Ltd. is a qualified small business corporation. If this is the case, the lifetime capital gains deduction could be used to eliminate all of the taxes on this disposition of shares, resulting in Mr. O'Leary retaining the entire $180,000 proceeds. Alternative minimum tax might be applicable if the capital gain is sheltered through the lifetime capital gains deduction.

Sale Of Assets For $200,000

17-146.   The tax consequences resulting from selling the assets are calculated as follows:

Account		Taxable Income
Inventories ($60,000 - $55,000)		$ 5,000
Plant And Equipment - Recaptured CCA ($60,000 - $45,000)		15,000
Active Business Income		$20,000
Taxable Capital Gains		
Land [(1/2)($40,000 - $20,000)]	$10,000	
Goodwill [(1/2)($25,000)]	12,500	22,500
Corporate Taxable Income		$42,500

17-147.   The resulting Tax Payable would be calculated as follows:

Federal Tax On:	
Active Business Income [(38% - 10% - 19%)($20,000)]	$ 1,800
Investment Income [(38% - 10% + 10-2/3%)($22,500)]	8,700
Part I Tax	$10,500
Provincial Tax On Active Business Income [(2.5%)($20,000)]	500
Provincial Tax On Investment Income [(14%)($22,500)]	3,150
Total Corporate Tax Payable	$14,150

17-148.   The GRIP and RDTOH balances at the beginning of the year are both nil. This means that the only amount available for a dividend refund would be the addition to the Non-Eligible RDTOH for the refundable portion of the Part I tax paid on the asset dispositions. This amount would be the least of:

- 30-2/3% Of Investment Income [(30-2/3%)($22,500)] $ 6,900

- 30-2/3% Of Taxable Income, Less Amount Eligible For
  Small Business Deduction [(30-2/3%)($42,500 - $20,000)] $ 6,900

- Part I Tax Payable $10,500

17-149. The allocation to the capital dividend account would be as follows:

Non-Taxable Portion Of Capital Gain On:

Land [(1/2)($20,000)]	$10,000
Goodwill [(1/2)($25,000)]	12,500
Capital Dividend Account	$22,500

17-150. Given the preceding analysis of the liquidation of the corporate assets, the net cash retained by Mr. O'Leary after the distribution of corporate assets can be calculated as follows:

Proceeds Of Disposition - Sale Of Assets	$200,000
Corporate Tax Payable (Before Dividend Refund)	(14,150)
Dividend Refund (Note)	6,900
Funds Available for Distribution	$192,750
Paid Up Capital	(50,000)
ITA 84(2) Deemed Dividend	$142,750
Capital Dividend (Balance In Account - Election Required)	(22,500)
Deemed Taxable Dividend	$120,250
Tax Rate (On Non-Eligible Dividends Received)	31%
Personal Tax Payable On Non-Eligible Dividend	$ 37,278

Note Technically, the dividend refund is the lesser of the $6,900 balance in the Non-Eligible RDTOH account and 38-1/3 percent of taxable dividends paid. However, given the size of the distribution in this example, it is clear that $6,900 will be the lower figure.

17-151. There would be no capital gain on the distribution as shown in the following:

Total Distribution	$192,750
ITA 84(2) Deemed Dividend	(142,750)
Deemed Proceeds Of Disposition	$ 50,000
Adjusted Cost Base Of The Shares	(50,000)
Capital Gain	Nil

17-152. Based on the preceding calculations, Mr. O'Leary's after tax retention from the sale of assets would be calculated as follows:

Amount Distributed	$192,750
Tax On Deemed Dividend	(37,278)
Cash Retained	$155,472

17-153. This amount is larger than the $150,100 that would be retained from a sale of shares if the resulting capital gain were subject to tax. However, it is significantly smaller than the $180,000 that would be retained from a sale of shares if the lifetime capital gains deduction could be used to eliminate the entire gain on the sale.

We suggest you work Self Study Problem Seventeen-8 at this point.

Additional Supplementary Self Study Problems Are Available Online.

Key Terms Used In This Chapter

17-154.   The following is a list of the key terms used in this Chapter. These terms, and their meanings, are compiled in the Glossary located at the back of the Study Guide.

Adjusted Cost Base	Parent Company
Amalgamation	Proceeds Of Disposition
Business Combination	PUC
Canadian Corporation	Qualified Small Business Corporation
Control (IAS 27)	Recapture Of CCA
Convertible Property	Redemption Of Shares
Corporation	Reorganization Of Capital (ITA 86)
Disposition	Restrictive Covenant
Exchange Of Shares In A	Rollover
Reorganization (ITA 86)	Share For Share Exchange (ITA 85.1)
Gift	Small Business Corporation
Goodwill	Subsidiary
Legal Stated Capital	Taxable Canadian Corporation
Lifetime Capital Gains Deduction	Terminal Loss
Merger	Vertical Amalgamation
Non-Share Consideration	Winding-Up Of A 90% Owned Subsidiary
Paid Up Capital	Winding-Up Of A Canadian Corporation

References

17-155.   For more detailed study of the material in this Chapter, we refer you to the following:

ITA 22	Sale Of Accounts Receivable
ITA 23	Sale Of Inventory
ITA 24	Ceasing To Carry On Business
ITA 51	Convertible Property
ITA 51.1	Conversion Of Debt Obligation
ITA 54	Definitions (Proceeds Of Disposition)
ITA 84(2)	Distribution on Winding-Up, Etc.
ITA 84(3)	Redemption Of shares
ITA 84(5)	Amount Distributed Or Paid Where A Share ...
ITA 85	Transfer Of Property To Corporation By Shareholders
ITA 85.1	Share For Share Exchange
ITA 86	Exchange Of Shares By A Shareholder In Course Of Reorganization Of Capital
ITA 87	Amalgamations
ITA 88(1)	Winding-Up (Of A 90 Percent Owned Subsidiary)
ITA 88(2)	Winding-Up Of A Canadian Corporation
ITA 110.6	Capital Gains Exemption
S4-F3-C1	Price Adjustment Clause
S4-F5-C1	Share For Share Exchange
S4-F7-C1	Amalgamations of Canadian Corporations

IT-115R2	Fractional Interest In Shares
IT-126R2	Meaning Of "Winding-Up"
IT-140R3	Buy-Sell Agreements
IT-142R3	Settlement Of Debts On The Winding-up Of A Corporation
IT-146R4	Shares Entitling Shareholders To Choose Taxable Or Capital Dividends
IT-149R4	Winding-Up Dividend
IT-188R	Sale Of Accounts Receivable
IT-243R4	Dividend Refund To Private Corporations
IT-287R2	Sale Of Inventory
IT-302R3	Losses Of A Corporation - The Effect That Acquisitions Of Control, Amalgamations, And Windings-Up Have On Their Deductibility - After January 15, 1987
IT-444R	Corporations — Involuntary Dissolutions

Problems For Self Study (Online)

To provide practice in problem solving, there are Self Study and Supplementary Self Study problems available on MyLab Accounting.

Within the text we have provided an indication of when it would be appropriate to work each Self Study problem. The detailed solutions for Self Study problems can be found in the print and online Study Guide.

We provide the Supplementary Self Study problems for those who would like additional practice in problem solving. The detailed solutions for the Supplementary Self Study problems are available online, not in the Study Guide.

The .PDF file "Self Study Problems for Volume 2" on MyLab contains the following for Chapter 17:

- 8 Self Study problems,
- 5 Supplementary Self Study problems, and
- detailed solutions for the Supplementary Self Study problems.

Assignment Problems

(The solutions for these problems are only available in
the solutions manual that has been provided to your instructor.)

Assignment Problem Seventeen - 1
(Section 85.1 Share For Share Exchange After ITA 85 Rollover)

In 2012, Sandy O'Brien opened a business, Sandy's Frames, that specialized in providing frames for high end paintings and drawings. From 2012 through 2015, he operated the business as a proprietorship. He did not incorporate because he needed all of the income produced by the business to cover his living expenses.

However, by 2015 his profits had increased to the point where he no longer needed all of the income produced by the business. Given this, he decided to incorporate.

His accountant advised him that he could avoid current taxation by using the provisions of ITA 85(1) to transfer his business assets to the new corporation. To facilitate this, on January 1, 2016, the following values were established for the assets of the business:

| Tax Values Of The Business Assets | $1,820,000 |
| Fair Market Value Of The Business Assets | $3,140,000 |

On this date, the assets are transferred to a new corporation, Frames Ltd., at an elected value of $1,820,000. As consideration, Sandy took back a note payable for $900,000, redeemable preferred shares with a fair market value of $920,000, and 6,950 common shares with a fair market value of $1,320,000. No other shares were issued during the years under consideration.

Over the next few years, the business continues to expand and prosper and, on January 1, 2020, he receives an offer from Conglomerate Inc., a large public company, for all of the common shares. Under terms of this offer, Sandy will give up all of the common shares of Frames Ltd. in return for a separate class of shares issued by Conglomerate Inc. These shares have a fair market value of $1,970,000. In addition, subsequent to the exchange transaction, Sandy's preferred shares will be redeemed for $920,000. Frames Ltd. does not have GRIP balance or an RDTOH balance at this time. Sandy and the controlling shareholders of Conglomerate Inc. deal with each other at arm's length.

While Sandy has been very successful with his business, he has made a number of very bad real estate investments. As a consequence, as of January 1, 2020, he has a $420,000 net capital loss carry forward.

Assume that Frames Ltd. does not meet the criteria for qualification as a small business corporation.

Required:

A. Advise Sandy with respect to the tax consequences that would arise for him from the redemption of his preferred shares and the acceptance of the offer from the public company for the exchange of shares. Your answer should consider both the application of ITA 85.1 and opting out of this provision.

B. Indicate the adjusted cost base of the Frames Inc. common shares on the books of Conglomerate Ltd.

C. Advise Sandy as to the alternative approaches that could be used to utilize his net capital loss carry forward in conjunction with the share exchange.

Assignment Problem Seventeen - 2
(ITA 85(1) and ITA 86(1) Share Exchange)
Homer Parsons opened an unincorporated retail business in 2013. This business, known as Parsons' Paranormal Services, provides services related to helping individuals make contact with dead loved ones.

Homer quickly gains a reputation for success in such matters and, by 2016, he has opened several locations in the city and retained a number of very wealthy clients. As a result, the business is producing income far in excess of his current needs. At this time, in order to defer current taxation, Homer decides to incorporate. His accountant advises him that he can do this on tax free basis by using the provisions of ITA 85(1).

On January 1, 2016, the assets of the business have tax values (adjusted cost base or UCC) totaling $1,986,000. The estimated fair market value of these assets is $2,950,000. On this date the assets are transferred to a new corporation at an elected value of $1,986,000. As consideration for the business assets, Homer takes back a note payable for $1,500,000 and common shares with a fair market value of $1,450,000. The new company, named Parsons Paranormal Inc. (PPI), will have a December 31 year end.

In its corporate form, the business continues to operate very successfully and, on January 1, 2020, the assets have tax values of $7,347,000. Their fair market value total $8,450,000.

Homer has an adult son who appears to have paranormal skills superior to his own. His name is Orpheus and, since 2016, he has become increasingly active in the business. As Homer now has sufficient resources to retire comfortably, he would like to transfer the future growth of the business to Orpheus.

To accomplish this, he is going to exchange his common shares in PPI for $5,000,000 in cash, plus redeemable preferred shares with a fair market value of $3,450,000. Subsequent to this exchange, Orpheus will acquire 200 common shares in PPI at a total cost of $20,000.

PPI does not have a GRIP balance or an RDTOH balance on January 1, 2020.

Required:

A. Determine the tax consequences for Homer that will result from his exchange of shares. As part of your answer, you should indicate both the adjusted cost base and the PUC of his preferred shares.

B. Determine the tax consequences for Homer that would result from the redemption of his preferred shares on February 1, 2020, for their fair market value of $3,450,000.

Assignment Problem Seventeen - 3
(Section 86 Reorganization With Gift)
Lartex Inc. was incorporated in 2011 to produce cutting edge sports clothing. At this time, the company issued 20,000 common shares for cash of $50 per share. Of these shares, 15,000 were purchased by Lara Text, with the remainder being purchased by Bentley Rolls, an arm's length individual who was her mentor.

In 2015, Bentley dies suddenly while running a marathon. Lara acquires the 5,000 shares that were purchased by Bentley Rolls from his estate for $90 per share. In order to finance the firm's rapidly expanding operations, the company issues an additional 5,000 shares to Lara for the same $90 per share price.

Lara has a son, Lance Text, whose dream is to make Lartex a household name. Starting in 2016, he seeks out the most challenging and rigorous courses in the business program at his university. During the following two years, he excels at his courses, especially his tax courses, which he considers the most interesting and rewarding. To encourage him in his studies, during 2018, when the estimated fair market value of a share was $100, Lara gives Lance a gift of 2,500 shares of Lartex Inc.

On January 1, 2020, the fair market value of the Lartex Inc. shares has increased to $120 per share. By this time, Lance has become increasingly active in helping her with the operations of Lartex Inc. Given this, she would like to transfer the future growth in Lartex Inc. to Lance using the provisions of ITA 86.

In order to implement this transfer, she exchanges her 22,500 shares of Lartex Inc. for a $500,000 note and redeemable preferred shares with a fair market value of $2,000,000. The only remaining common shares will be the 2,500 shares owned by Lance. At this time, the company does not have a GRIP balance.

Required:

A. Describe the immediate tax consequences of this transaction to Lara Text, including the following:

- the amount of any gift that Lara has made to Lance;
- the PUC of the new preferred shares;
- the adjusted cost base of the new preferred shares;
- the amount of any deemed dividends arising on the exchange; and
- any capital gain or loss resulting from the exchange of the common shares.

B.   Describe the tax consequences of this transaction to Lance Text.

C.   Describe the tax consequences of this transaction to Lara Text that would result from the immediate redemption of her newly issued preferred shares at their fair market value of $2,000,000. Ignore the possible use of the lifetime capital gains deduction.

Assignment Problem Seventeen - 4
(ITA 86(1) And 86(2))

Squire Ltd. Is a very successful Canadian controlled private corporation (CCPC) that was incorporated in Manitoba in 1985 by its sole shareholder and incorporator, Mr. Larry Squire. Squire Ltd uses a December 31 taxation year end. The company was initially authorized to issue an unlimited number of two classes of common shares (Class A and B). Mr. Squire acquired 1,000 of the Class A common shares for $10.00 each, or $10,000, for that class of common shares. Mr. Squire initially financed the company with a combination of bank financing (which he had to give a personal guarantee) and an interest free shareholder loan.

In 2016 on the advice of his accountant, Mr. Squire undertook a crystallization transaction to utilize $290,000 of his capital gains deduction to recognize the increasing value of the company. The result of this acceptable tax planning was that Mt. Squire gave up all of his Class A common shares for Class B common shares. The 1,000 Class B common shares now owned by Mr. Squire have a PUC of $10.00 per share ($10,000 for the class of shares) and an adjusted cost base (ACB) of $300 per share. By mid-2020 the value of the company has increased to the point that the fair market value (FMV) of the Class B common shares is $930 per share for a total FMV of $930,000.

Mr. Squire wishes to retire and pass on the incorporated business to his only daughter, Amanda, who has worked alongside him since 2001 and is well versed in all aspects of the company business. He has spoken to his accountant about a business succession plan that will pass control of the company to Amanda with the least tax cost possible while allowing him to gradually remove the $930,000 value of his shares over the next five years. He has advised his accountant that he wishes to maximize any non-share consideration such as promissory notes. Mr. Squire advises that the company currently needs all of its existing cash for working capital purposes but will generate excess cash later in 2020 and subsequent years that will be sufficient to pay him out.

Squire Ltd. does not meet all of the conditions to qualify as a qualified small business corporation (QSBC), and therefore the capital gains deduction is not a consideration in the succession planning. In addition the company balance at year end in its General Rate Income Pool (GRIP) account is expected to be nil and remain so into the foreseeable future.

As the accountant for Mr. Squire and the company you recommend a business succession plan that will result in an estate freeze share exchange under ITA 86 that would (i) require amending the articles of incorporate to add a new class of fixed value preferred shares that will be exchanged for all of Mr. Squire's Class B common shares, (ii) maximize the non-share consideration (e.g., a promissory note) received by Mr. Squire on the share exchange without income tax implications, (iii) allow Amanda to acquire Class A common shares at a minimal cost, and (iv) allow Mr. Squire to receive his investment value of $930,000 over the next five years through a combination of preferred share redemptions and payments on any promissory note. Assume that Amanda acquired 100 Class A common shares for $10 each, or $1,000 in total, once the estate freeze was completed.

Required:

A.   If it were not for rollovers such as ITA 86, what would the tax consequences have been had Squire Ltd. redeemed all of Mr. Squire's Class B shares?

B.   Determine both the maximum amount of non-share consideration and the FMV of the preferred shares that Mr. Squire can take back on the share exchange without triggering any income tax consequences.

C. Determine the ACB and PUC of the preferred shares received by Mr. Squire on the share exchange.

D. Determine both the proceeds of redemption and proceeds of disposition as a result of Mr. Squire's giving up his Class B common shares on the share exchange.

E. Determine whether the ITA 86 share exchange avoided any income tax consequences such as capital gains, capital losses, and deemed dividends using the numbers from Part D above.

F. Calculate the income tax consequences to Mr. Squire if he were to redeem all of the preferred shares received on the exchange in 2021 for their FMV.

G. Assume that in 2022 the CRA decides to review the ITA 86 exchange and determines that the FMV of the Class B common shares owned by Mr. Squire was $1,500,000. Determine the same income tax implications as determined in Parts B to F above to both Mr. Squire and his daughter.

Assignment Problem Seventeen - 5
[Section 87 vs. Section 88(1)]

Hubble Inc. owns 100 percent of the shares of Palomar Ltd. Hubble has decided that it does not want Palomar to continue as a separate legal entity. It has asked for your assistance on whether to absorb Palomar into its operations using ITA 87 or, alternatively, ITA 88(1).

At the time of this decision, Palomar Ltd. has the following asset values:

Asset	Capital Cost	Tax Value	FMV
Equipment	$ 11,000	$ 3,300	$ 700
Land	154,000	154,000	192,000
Goodwill	Nil	Nil	22,000

There are no liabilities and no tax loss carry forwards.

Hubble acquired the shares of Palomar several years ago for $231,000. At that time, the equipment was valued at its capital cost of $11,000 and the land was valued at $209,000, for a total of $220,000. At that time, goodwill was estimated to be $1,000.

Palomar has paid $5,000 in dividends since its acquisition by Hubble.

Required: Outline what the tax consequences would be if:

A. Palomar was amalgamated into Hubble Inc. using Section 87.

B. Palomar was rolled into Hubble Inc. using a Section 88(1) winding-up.

Assignment Problem Seventeen - 6
(Section 88(1) Winding-Up)

In 2016, Acme Ltd. purchased all of the outstanding shares of Cross Industries for cash of $1,400,000. The assets of Cross Industries at the time of the acquisition had tax values of $1,250,000 and included a piece of land that was being held as a location for a possible second manufacturing facility. This land had been acquired in 2011 for $640,000 and, at the time Acme acquired the Cross shares, it had a fair market value of $705,000.

Acme believes that the operations of Cross Industries have become so integrated with its own that it no longer makes sense to operate Cross as a separate entity. As a consequence, they are considering the possibility of absorbing Cross using an ITA 88(1) winding-up. At January 1, 2020, the tax values of the assets of Cross Industries total $1,270,000. The company is still holding the land for the additional manufacturing facility and it now has a fair market value of $790,000. Cross Industries has paid Acme Ltd. dividends totaling $20,000 since its acquisition.

Required: Explain the tax implications of the proposed winding-up from the point of view of both Acme Ltd. and Cross Industries.

Assignment Problem Seventeen - 7
(Winding up of a Corporation)

Hoxey Ltd. is a Canadian controlled private corporation (CCPC) with a December 31 taxation year end that was incorporated in Saskatchewan in 1997 by its incorporator/founder and sole shareholder, Spencer Richmond. Spencer was somewhat of a child protégé, quickly becoming conversant in computer technology at an early age, including writing advanced computer code. He quickly developed, created, and produced some of the first online video games that still remain popular. In an attempt to come up with new gaming ideas to deal with ever increasing competition Spencer suffered a heart attack in September 2020 and has decided to dissolve the business, wind-up the company, and enjoy life rather than working all the time. Spencer is not interested in selling his shares to anyone or selling the rights to the business to any one purchaser.

Spencer has spoken to his long-time accountant about an exit strategy. Since he has never married or lived common-law there is no one to continue the business. He explains that he simply wants to sell it all and move on with his life. The accountant explains that the plan will be to have the company sell all of its assets, pay any outstanding liabilities (including any income tax), and distribute the remaining cash to Spencer.

Spencer's accountant has prepared the following information to assist Spencer in determining how much he will have remaining once the company makes its final distribution to him. The assets will all be sold in the first half of December 2020 at the fair market values indicated on the statement of net assets shown below. The company is formally dissolved and wound up on December 31, 2020. Assume that net active business income (ABI) from ongoing operations throughout 2020 is $410,000 and that taxable capital gains are $62,700 without considering the effect of the sale of the company assets. The company did not receive any dividends on any of its investments and therefore was not liable to any Part IV taxes.

Hoxey Ltd.
Statement Of Net Assets
At December 15, 2020

	Tax Values	Fair Market Values
Accounts Receivable	$ 121,000	$ 89,000
Public Co Investments	774,000	1,125,000
Private Co Investment	946,000	381,000
Inventory	697,000	510,000
Office Building (Class 1)	2,458,000	6,000,000
Office Building Land	725,000	1,000,000
Office Furniture (Class 8)	300,720	380,000
Computers (Class 50)	54,675	28,000
Total Assets	$6,076,395	$9,513,000
Liabilities	(217,400)	(217,400)
Net Assets	$5,858,995	$9,295,600

Based on tax values, the components of the net asset tax value balance are as follows:

Paid Up Capital	$ 1,000
Capital Dividend Account	10,000
Income Retained (Surplus)	5,847,995
Total Net Asset Balance	$5,858,995

Other Information:

1. The tax values shown for each of Class 1, 8, and 50 are the Undepreciated Capital Cost (UCC) as of January 1, 2020.

2. The capital cost of the Building is $3,800,000, the Office Furniture $537,000, and the Computers $600,000.

3. Since all of the depreciable assets are sold prior to the final company taxation year end as a result of the dissolution on December 30, 2020, no CCA can be claimed for 2020.

4. The investment in a private company is for an arm's length CCPC that qualifies as a small business corporation.

5. The adjusted cost base of the common shares is $501,000 as a result of a capital gains crystallization transaction a few years ago.

6. On January 1, 2020, the company has a balance in its General Rate Income Pool (GRIP) account of $74,500.

7. The provincial corporate tax rate on income that qualifies for the small business deduction is 2 percent and is 12 percent on all other income including investment income and capital gains.

8. The January 1, 2020, balance in the company's Eligible RDTOH is $76,700, while the balance in the Non-Eligible RDTOH is $194,500

9. Assume that the capital dividend account balance of $10,000 has already been adjusted for the $62,700 of taxable capital gains realized in the year prior to the sale of all of the company's assets.

10. The company has no non-capital losses but has a 2018 net capital loss balance of $71,000 at the beginning of 2020.

11. No dividends were paid during the previous two years.

12. Assume that there are no reductions to the small business limit for Adjusted Aggregate Investment Income or Taxable Capital Employed in Canada.

13. No ITA 22 election was filed for the transfer of the accounts receivables.

Required:

A. Calculate the amount that will be available for distribution to Spencer after the sale of all of the company's assets. This will require calculating the company's net and Taxable Income, federal and provincial taxes payable, RDTOH account balances including any eligible and non-eligible dividend refund(s), the capital dividend account, and the GRIP balance. Show all supporting calculations.

B. Determine the eligible and non-eligible dividend and capital gain components of the distribution to Spencer that will accrue as a result of the winding-up of Hoxey Ltd. Ignore the possibility that Spencer might be subject to the alternative minimum tax. Assume that all appropriate elections, designations, and filings will be made on a timely basis to minimize his personal taxes.

C. Determine Spencer's net personal Tax Payable on the taxable dividends received after considering federal and provincial dividend tax credits. Assume that (i) Spencer is subject to the highest federal rate of 33 percent and the highest Saskatchewan rate of 14.5 percent and (ii) that the provincial dividend tax credit on eligible dividends equals 40 percent of the gross up and is equal to 26 percent of the gross up on non-eligible dividends.

Assignment Problem Seventeen - 8
(Sale of Assets vs. Shares)

Naimo Ltd. is a Canadian controlled private corporation (CCPC) that was incorporated in British Columbia in 2006 by its incorporator and sole shareholder, Mr. Roger Naimo. The company's taxation year end is December 31. Naimo Ltd. operates a very successful restaurant on Vancouver Island that includes catering. Roger had first opened the restaurant as a sole proprietor in 1997. His accountant convinced him in late 2005 that it was time to incorporate, which led to the creation of the company in early 2006. The business and all of its assets and liabilities were transferred to the company under the rollover rule of ITA 85(1). Roger acquired 100 common shares for $15,000 at the time of incorporation. No other shares have been issued since.

In recent years there has been an acceleration in new residential and commercial construction followed by a proliferation of new restaurants and plenty of competition. Roger has been approached by two different investors – one proposes to acquire all of the shares of the corporation for $800,000 and the second to acquire all of the assets including assuming any outstanding liabilities for a net payment of $953,800. If the assets are sold, Roger plans on winding-up the company after paying off any outstanding corporate taxes and distributing any remaining cash to him.

Roger has decided to sell and move somewhere else where it is a little quieter. He has asked his accountant for advice on which offer he should accept. The accountant has prepared the following statement dated December 1, 2020, which contains a list of assets and liabilities, their tax values, and fair market values (FMV) as of that date determined by a local business valuator. The FMVs will serve as the basis for the asset sale and assumption of corporate liabilities. If there is a sale of shares the transaction will close on December 31, 2020. If Roger decides on a sale of assets all sales and assumption of liabilities will be concluded by December 18, 2020, with the company being formally dissolved December 31, 2020.

Naimo Ltd. has never owned investments and therefore has no investment income. All of its income is from an active business, which has never exceeded its small business limit. There are no associated companies and, in 2019, its Adjusted Aggregate Investment Income was nil and its Taxable Capital Employed in Canada was less than $1 million. Assume that its net active business income for 2020 prior to the sale of shares or assets is $284,000.

Naimo Ltd.
Statement Of Net Assets
At December 1, 2020

	Tax Values	Fair Market Values
Accounts Receivable	$ 22,700	$ 19,000
Inventory	46,500	57,700
Restaurant Building	284,000	755,000
Restaurant Building Land	134,000	217,000
Kitchen Equipment	34,100	62,900
Kitchen Utensils	Nil	5,200
Delivery Van	1,800	17,000
Goodwill	Nil	220,000
Total Assets	$ 523,100	$1,353,800
Accounts Payable	(94,100)	(94,100)
Mortgage Payable	(306,000)	(306,000)
Net Assets	$ 123,000	$ 953,700

Based on tax values, the components of the net asset tax value balance are as follows:

Paid Up Capital	$ 15,000
Capital Dividend Account	Nil
Income Retained (Surplus)	108,000
Total Net Asset Balance	**$123,000**

Other Information:

A. The tax values shown for each of the restaurant building, the kitchen equipment, kitchen utensils, and the delivery van are the Undepreciated Capital Cost (UCC) as of January 1, 2020.

B. The capital cost of the Building is $466,000, the kitchen equipment $115,000, the kitchen utensils $16,300, and the delivery van $44,000.

C. If the assets are sold no CCA can be claimed in 2020 since the company will have no depreciable assets on hand on the last day of its final taxation year as a result of the dissolution on December 31, 2020.

D. The shares of the company qualify for the capital gains deduction. Roger's available capital gains deduction immediately prior to a sale of shares or assets is $116,472 and his Cumulative Net Investment Loss (CNIL) account is nil.

E. The adjusted cost base (ACB) and Paid Up Capital (PUC) of the common shares are both $15,000.

F. On January 1, 2020, the company has a nil balance in its General Rate Income Pool (GRIP) account.

G. The provincial corporate tax rate on income that qualifies for the small business deduction is 2 percent and is 12 percent on all other income, including investment income and capital gains.

H. The company has nil balances at January 1, 2020, in both its Eligible and Non-Eligible RDTOH.

I. The company's capital dividend account balance at the time of a sale of shares or assets is nil.

J. The company has a 2018 non-capital loss of $49,600 and no net capital losses at the beginning of 2020.

K. No dividends were paid during the previous two years.

L. The 2020 provincial dividend tax credit rate on non-eligible dividends is 15 percent of the gross up and 36.3 percent of the gross up for eligible dividends.

M. Assume that any income received by Roger as dividends and capital gains will be subject to the highest federal personal tax rate of 33 percent and that the BC rate is 20.5 percent.

N. Assume that on a sale of assets no ITA 22 election will be filed for the accounts receivables since the amounts are not considered significant enough.

Required:

1. Determine which of the two offers Roger should accept in terms of maximizing after tax cash retention. For the sale of assets you will have to calculate the company's net and Taxable Income, federal and provincial taxes payable, RDTOH account balances including any eligible and non-eligible dividend refund(s), the capital dividend account, and the GRIP balance. You will also have to determine the eligible and non-eligible dividend and capital gain components of the distribution to Roger as a result of the winding-up of Naimo Ltd. Ignore any alternative minimum tax implications and assume that all appropriate elections, designations, and filings will be made on a timely basis to minimize personal taxes. On the sale of shares, consider that Roger will maximize the use of his capital gains deduction.

2. What non-tax advantages and disadvantages should you, as Roger's accountant, communicate to him that may influence his ultimate decision.

Assignment Problem Seventeen - 9
(Sale Of Assets vs. Shares)
Mr. Nathan Naper is the president and only shareholder of Nepean Ltd., a Canadian controlled private corporation. The company's fiscal year ends on December 31. Mr. Naper established the company 15 years ago by investing $265,000 in cash. There have been no other shares issued since then.

Mr. Naper is considering selling the corporation and, in order to better evaluate this possibility, he has prepared a special Statement Of Assets. In this special statement, comparative disclosure is provided for the values included in his accounting records, values that are relevant for tax purposes, and fair market values. This statement is as follows:

Nepean Ltd.
Statement Of Assets
As At January 1, 2020

	Accounting Net Book Value	Tax Value	Fair Market Value
Cash	$ 54,500	$ 54,500	$ 54,500
Accounts Receivable	406,000	406,000	372,250
Inventories	869,750	869,750	976,000
Land	201,500	201,500	405,000
Building (Note One)	538,000	469,250	2,061,000
Equipment (Note Two)	434,000	294,000	171,250
Goodwill	Nil	Nil	811,000
Totals	$2,503,750	$2,295,000	$4,851,000

Note One   Mr. Naper built this building on the land for a total cost of $1,281,000.

Note Two   The equipment had a cost of $807,500.

At the same time that this Statement Of Assets was prepared, a similar Statement Of Equities was drawn up. This latter statement contained the following accounting and tax values:

	Accounting Book Value	Tax Value
Current Liabilities	$ 697,000	$ 697,000
Loan From Shareholder	137,500	137,500
Future Income Tax Liability	542,000	N/A
Common Shares- No Par	265,000	265,000
Capital Dividend Account	N/A	164,500
Other Income Retained	N/A	1,031,000
Retained Earnings	862,250	N/A
Totals	$2,503,750	$2,295,000

In addition to the information included in the preceding statements, the following other information about the company is available:

- The company has available non-capital loss carry forwards of $83,000.
- The company has available a net capital loss carry forward of $129,650 [(1/2)($259,300)].
- Nepean Ltd. is subject to a provincial tax rate of 3 percent on income that qualifies for the federal small business deduction and 14 percent on income that does not qualify for this deduction.

- On December 31, 2019, the company has no balance in either its RDTOH account or its General Rate Income Pool (GRIP) account.

- Nepean Ltd. is not a qualified small business corporation.

Mr. Naper has received two offers for his company, and he plans to accept one of them on January 2, 2020. The first offer involves a cash payment of $3,508,000 in return for all of the shares of the company. Alternatively, another investor has expressed a willingness to acquire all of the assets, including goodwill, at a price equal to their fair market values. This investor would assume all of the liabilities of the corporation and has agreed to file an ITA 22 election with respect to the Accounts Receivable. If the assets are sold, it is Mr. Naper's intention to wind-up the corporation.

Mr. Naper will have over $300,000 in income from other sources and, as a consequence, any income that arises on the disposition of this business will be taxed at the maximum federal rate of 33 percent, combined with a provincial rate of 18 percent. He lives in a province where the provincial dividend tax credit on eligible dividends is 5/11 of the gross up, and on non-eligible dividends is equal to 4/13 of the gross up.

Required: Determine which of the two offers Mr. Naper should accept. Ignore the possibility that Mr. Naper might be subject to the alternative minimum tax. Assume that appropriate elections or designations will bemade to minimize the taxes that will be paid by Mr. Naper.

CHAPTER 18

Partnerships

Introduction

Taxable Entities In Canada

18-1. As is noted in Chapter 1, the *Income Tax Act* (ITA) is applicable to individuals (human beings), corporations, and trusts. In the case of individuals and corporations, these taxable entities have a separate legal existence. In contrast, trusts are simply arrangements for transferring property and, as such, are not separate legal entities. Partnerships are similar to trusts in that they do not have a legal existence separate from the participating partners. More to the point here is the fact that, under the provisions of the *Income Tax Act,* partnerships are generally not defined as taxable entities. An exception to this is "SIFT Partnerships", which are taxable under Part IX.1 of the *Act* (see discussion at the end of this Chapter).

18-2. The *Income Tax Act* deals with the fact that partnerships are generally not taxable entities through the use of a deeming rule. A deeming rule is a statutory fiction that requires an item or event be given a treatment for tax purposes that is not consistent with the actual legal nature of the item or event. We have encountered several such rules in previous chapters:

- A member of the Canadian Armed Forces is deemed to be a resident of Canada even if he or she does not set foot in the country during the year.

- A change in use is deemed to be a disposition of an asset combined with its immediate re-acquisition.

- The death of an individual results in a deemed disposition of all of his or her capital property.

18-3. The deeming rule that is applicable to partnerships is that, for purposes of determining the income or loss of its members, such organizations are considered to be a person resident in Canada. Note that this rule applies only for the purpose of calculating the income or loss of members. It does not make a partnership a taxable entity and there is no requirement that these organizations file a separate income tax return.

18-4. In general terms, a partnership is treated as a flow through entity. The preceding deeming rule requires that an income figure be determined at the partnership level using the usual rules for various types of income (e.g., business income, property income, capital gains). Then the income or loss of the partnership is allocated to the taxable entities (i.e., individuals, trusts, or corporations) based on the amounts agreed to in the partnership agreement, or in equal proportions in the absence of a partnership agreement. This process is illustrated in Figure 18-1 (on the following page).

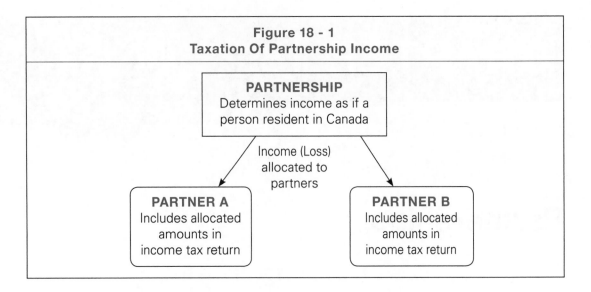

Figure 18 - 1
Taxation Of Partnership Income

PARTNERSHIP
Determines income as if a person resident in Canada

Income (Loss) allocated to partners

PARTNER A
Includes allocated amounts in income tax return

PARTNER B
Includes allocated amounts in income tax return

18-5.   We would note that, while partnerships are not taxable entities under the *Income Tax Act,* they are considered taxable entities for GST purposes (see Chapter 21). This means that, in contrast with the income tax situation, a partnership must file a GST return, pay any GST owing, or is entitled to receive any GST refund.

Chapter Coverage

18-6.   In this Chapter we will examine the income taxation rules that are applicable to partnerships. We will begin by defining partnerships. This will be followed by an examination of the various types of partnerships, as well as other arrangements that resemble partnerships. These other arrangements include co-ownerships, joint ventures, and syndicates. Our focus will then shift to looking at the rules for calculating income for a partnership and the process of allocating this income and other amounts to partners.

18-7.   Other issues that will be covered include:

- the determination of the adjusted cost base of a partnership interest;
- admitting and retiring partners;
- limited partnerships, limited partnership losses, and the at-risk rules;
- the transfer of property between the partners and the partnership; and
- reorganizing a partnership as a new partnership, as a corporation, and as a sole proprietorship.

Partnerships Defined

The Importance Of Defining A Partnership

18-8.   The general rules for determining the income tax consequences for partnerships and their members are found in Subdivision j of Division B of Part I of the *Income Tax Act,* ITA 96 through 103. However, since these rules apply specifically to partnerships, we must first determine if we are, in fact, looking at a partnership. To do this requires a definition of a partnership.

18-9.   The importance of this definition is that it allows us to distinguish a partnership from other similar types of organizations such as syndicates, joint ventures, and co-ownership arrangements. This is necessary in that, unlike the situation for these other types of organizations, there is a separate calculation of the income of a partnership.

18-10.   As we have noted, this calculation must be carried out using the assumption that the partnership is a separate person resident in Canada. Further, as the calculation must be used for allocating income to all of the members of the partnership, partners have no flexibility with respect to the amounts to be included in their required tax returns. For example, a partner does not have the discretion to take an alternative amount of CCA on property owned by the partnership. Note, however, they do have discretion with respect to CCA on property that is used by the partnership but owned by the partner (e.g., partial use of a personally owned automobile for partnership business).

18-11.   In contrast, if the organization is considered to be a co-ownership, syndicate, or joint venture (see Paragraph 18-24), there is no requirement for a separate calculation of income. This provides the participants with much greater flexibility in determining the tax procedures to be used.

Basic Partnership Elements

18-12.   Unfortunately, there is no specific definition of a "partnership" in the *Income Tax Act*. There are several definitions of certain types of partnerships. For example, ITA 102(1) defines a "Canadian Partnership" and ITA 197(1) defines a "SIFT Partnership". However, all of these specialized definitions presume that a partnership already exists. This leaves the question of defining a partnership unanswered.

18-13.   Guidance on defining a partnership is provided in IT Folio S4-F16-C1, *What Is A Partnership?* This Folio notes that "whether a partnership exists is a matter of fact and law". It then proceeds to discuss provincial law dealing with this issue, as well as several court cases that have bearing on this issue. What we would gather from reading through this material is that there are three basic elements that are required for an organization to be considered a partnership:

1.   There must be two or more persons (individuals, corporations, or trusts) involved.
2.   These persons must be carrying on a business in common.
3.   It must be the intent of the partners to carry on a business with a view to making a profit.

18-14.   Also helpful in this area, IT Folio S4-F16-C1 quotes a Supreme Court Case (*Backman v. Canada*, 2001 DTC 5149), which lists factors that would be viewed as providing evidence of the existence of a partnership:

- the contribution by the parties of money, property, effort, knowledge, skill, or other assets to a common undertaking;
- a joint property interest in the subject matter of the adventure;
- the sharing of profits and losses;
- a mutual right of control or management of the enterprise;
- financial statements prepared as a partnership;
- bank accounts in the name of the partnership; and
- correspondence with third parties as a partnership.

18-15.   The presence of a valid partnership agreement would serve to support the view that a partnership exists. Such agreements will usually include provisions that deal with many issues, including the following:

- the initial and ongoing partner contributions and ownership percentage of each partner,
- the responsibilities of each partner and the division of work between the partners,
- how income and drawings will be allocated and how much compensation is to be paid,
- signing authority on the partnership bank accounts and required approval for purchases,
- procedures for bringing in new partners, and
- procedures to deal with the withdrawal or death of a partner or the sale of the business.

Types Of Partnerships

General Partnerships

18-16.   A general partnership is one in which all of the partners are general partners. As defined in the *Guide For The T5013 Partnership Information Return* (T4068):

A **general partner** is a partner whose personal liability for the debts and obligations of the partnership are not limited.

18-17.   Provincial partnership law provides additional guidance on the rights, duties, and obligations of general partners. These include:

- Each partner is considered to act on behalf of the partnership, which means that the actions of each partner are generally binding on the other partners.
- Partners are jointly and severally liable for partnership debt and wrongful acts of other partners. This means that a partner can be liable, together with all other partners, for unpaid partnership debt and wrongful acts of other partners.
- Property contributed to the partnership or acquired with partnership funds is considered partnership property and is to be held exclusively for partnership use.
- Partners are entitled to share equally in profits and losses, unless there is an agreement to the contrary.
- Partners are not entitled to remuneration (salary or wages) or to interest on capital contributions. As is explained later in this Chapter, any remuneration or interest on capital is treated as an income allocation and is not deductible to the partnership.

18-18.   When the term partnership is used without a qualifying adjective, the reference is normally to a general partnership.

Limited Partnerships

18-19.   A limited partnership is a partnership with at least one general partner (i.e., a partner whose liability is unrestricted) and one or more limited partners. To be considered a limited partnership, the partnership has to be registered as such under the appropriate provincial registry. In the absence of such registration, the partnership will be considered a general partnership.

18-20.   A limited partner has the same rights, duties, and obligations as a general partner with one important difference: a limited partner is only liable for partnership debt and wrongful or negligent actions of other partners to the extent of the partner's actual and promised contributions to the partnership.

> **EXAMPLE**   A limited partner contributes $1,000 and agrees to contribute a further $2,000 within a certain period of time. That partner will be potentially liable for up to $3,000 of claims against the partnership.

18-21.   It should be noted, however, that a limited partner will lose his or her limited liability protection, and therefore become a general partner, if he or she participates in the management of the partnership.

Limited Liability Partnerships (LLP)

18-22.   This form of partnership is only available to certain types of professionals as specified in provincial legislation. For example, in Ontario, only lawyers and chartered professional accountants are currently permitted to form such partnerships. In contrast, Alberta extends this legislation to include several other professional groups.

18-23.   Unlike members of limited partnerships, members of limited liability partnerships are personally liable for most types of partnership debt. There is, however, an important exception. Members of limited liability partnerships are not personally liable for obligations arising from the wrongful or negligent action of:

- their professional partners; or
- the employees, agents, or representatives of the partnership who are conducting partnership business.

We suggest you work Self Study Problem Eighteen-1 at this point.

Co-Ownership, Joint Ventures, And Syndicates

Introduction

18-24.   Our major concern in this Chapter is the taxation of partnerships. However, as we have noted, there are other types of organizations that have structures similar to partnership arrangements. Co-ownership, joint ventures, and syndicates are specific types of arrangements that contain features common to partnerships. For example, each of these organizational structures requires two or more persons. This common feature is but one of several that may make it difficult to determine whether a specific arrangement is, in fact, a partnership or, alternatively, a different type of arrangement.

18-25.   As was discussed in the preceding material, the ability to distinguish these arrangements from partnerships is a critical factor in determining how a given organization will be taxed. To facilitate this process, the following material will provide additional clarification as to the nature of these other types of organizations.

Co-Ownership

18-26.   Two or more persons co-own property when they share a right of ownership in the property. For income tax purposes, the most important consideration is that profits and losses are shared in partnerships, but are typically accounted for individually by joint or co-owners.

18-27.   Two common forms of co-ownership are joint tenancy and tenancy in common. A joint tenancy is a form of property ownership where two or more joint tenants have ownership and possession of the same property. Individual interests are identical and the property cannot be sold or mortgaged without the consent of the other joint tenant(s). Spouses commonly own their principal residence and other properties in joint tenancy.

18-28.   In a tenancy in common arrangement, tenants can sell or mortgage their interests without the consent of other tenants in common. An example of a situation where a tenancy in common might be used would be the ownership of a vacation property by three brothers.

Joint Ventures

Defined

18-29.   Those of you familiar with financial reporting will recognize that some corporations are referred to as joint ventures. They are distinguished by the fact that control of the corporation is shared by two or more of the shareholders. This type of joint venture does not present any special problems in terms of tax procedures. They are subject to the same rules that are applicable to other corporate taxpayers.

18-30.   Our concern here is with unincorporated joint ventures. Like partnerships, joint ventures are not defined taxable entities under the *Income Tax Act*. Further, such arrangements are not governed by provincial legislation. However, both the *Income Tax Act* and the *Excise Tax Act* refer to joint ventures, implicitly giving recognition to this form of organization.

18-31.   The similarity of partnerships and joint ventures led the CRA to make the following statement in 1988:

> Unlike partnerships, the concept of joint venture is not recognized by statute (i.e., provincial legislation). Although the Canadian courts have, in certain cases, recognized joint venture as being a business relationship that is distinct from partnership, in our experience, many so-called joint ventures are in fact partnerships ... The CRA would rely on provincial partnership law in making such a determination.

18-32.   This would suggest that, even if participants in a joint venture call the arrangement a joint venture, if it contains the three basic partnership elements it will be considered a partnership for tax purposes and treated accordingly.

18-33.   Despite this lack of clarity, joint ventures do appear to exist for tax purposes. Factors that have been used to distinguish this type of organization include:

- co-venturers contractually do not have the power to bind other co-venturers;
- co-venturers retain ownership of property contributed to the undertaking;
- co-venturers are not jointly and severally liable for debt of the undertaking;
- co-venturers share gross revenues, not profits; and
- while partnerships may be formed for the same purpose as a joint venture, they are usually of longer duration and involve more than a single undertaking.

Tax Procedures

18-34.   If an arrangement is considered to be a joint venture rather than a partnership, there will be no separate calculation of income at the organization level. The participants will be subject to the usual rules applicable to individuals or corporations. As we have noted, this will provide these taxable entities with greater flexibility on such issues as how much CCA can be taken for the current year. You should note, however, since unincorporated joint ventures are not a recognized entity for tax purposes, they cannot have their own fiscal period.

Syndicates

18-35.   A syndicate is generally defined as a group of persons who have agreed to pool their money or assets for some common purpose. Because a syndicate is not a legal entity, a reference to an interest in a syndicate usually means an interest in the combined assets of the syndicate members. The Canadian courts have traditionally reserved the name "syndicate" for specialized projects that are financial in nature. An example of a syndicate would be an association of insurance companies who combine forces to underwrite substantial high-risk insurance policies.

18-36.   There are no specific income tax rules that apply to syndicates. This means that, if there are any activities of the syndicate that result in assessable amounts of income, the relevant amounts will have to be allocated to the members of the syndicate.

We suggest you work Self Study Problem Eighteen-2 at this point.

Partnership Income, Losses, And Tax Credits

Introduction

18-37.   The goal of partnership taxation is to apply the income tax consequences of partnership income, losses, and tax credits to the persons who are its partners. To implement this, a two stage process is involved:

Stage 1 Determine, at the partnership level, the various components of partnership income. This requires separate calculations for business income, property income, taxable capital gains, and allowable capital losses. For most partnerships, the most important component will be net business income.

Stage 2 Allocate the amounts that were determined in Stage 1 to the members of the partnership on the basis of the partnership agreement, or equally in the absence of a partnership agreement.

18-38.   In determining the business income component, we generally begin with the partnership's accounting figure for business income. The normal procedure is to convert this figure to Net Business Income for tax purposes. This conversion is based on a reconciliation process that is very similar to the reconciliation process used to determine Net Business Income For Tax Purposes (see Chapter 6). There are, however, some items that are specific to the calculation of business income for partnerships.

18-39.   Following the determination of the amount of business income to be allocated to partners, separate calculations are carried out for amounts of property income, taxable capital gains, and allowable capital losses that will be allocated to the members of the partnership. It is important to note that, in this allocation process, the various types of income retain their tax characteristics. That is, a partnership capital gain is treated as a capital gain to the partner to whom it is allocated.

18-40.   While it would be possible to calculate a Net Income For Tax Purposes for the partnership, this usually is not done. Such a figure has no real meaning for a non-taxable entity such as a partnership. Further, the calculation would serve no real purpose as the allocations to the partners are on a source-by-source basis. We would also note that there is no calculation of Taxable Income for a partnership. Again, as partnerships are not taxable entities, such a figure would have no real meaning.

Applicable Concepts

Taxation Year

18-41.   ITA 96(1)(a) indicates that partnership income must be calculated as if the partnership was a separate person resident in Canada. ITA 96(1)(b) follows this by indicating that this calculation should be made as if the taxation year of the partnership were its "fiscal period". The ITA 249.1(1) definition of "fiscal period" indicates that, if any member of a partnership is an individual or a professional corporation, the partnership must have a December 31 year end. Otherwise, the only restriction is that the fiscal period cannot end more than 12 months after it begins. In effect, this means that, if all of the members of a partnership are corporations (other than professional corporations), the partnership can use any year end.

18-42.   ITA 249.1(4) provides an exception to the general taxation year end rules that are described in the preceding paragraph. If the following conditions are met, the partnership can elect to use a non-calendar year as its fiscal period:

- all of the members of the partnership are individuals; and
- an election is filed with the CRA using a prescribed form (T1139) prior to the end of the partnership's first fiscal year. The complications associated with making this election are discussed in Chapter 6 on business income.

> **EXAMPLE**   ABC Partnership has five corporate partners, two of which are professional corporations, and one partner who is an individual. The new partnership wants to choose a March 31 fiscal year end.

> **ANALYSIS**   The partnership must use a December 31 fiscal year end. The presence of both an individual and professional corporations as partners prevents the use of a non-calendar fiscal period under the ITA 249.1(1) definition. Similarly, the presence of corporations prevents the election of a non-calendar fiscal period under ITA 249.1(4).

18-43.   The CRA has been concerned with the ability of a corporate member of a partnership to defer taxes because it has a different year end from the partnership. Consider a partnership that has a fiscal year ending on January 31, 2020, and a corporate member with a December 31, 2020, year end. The corporation would not have to include the partnership income earned during the year ending January 31, 2020, until it files its return for the fiscal year ending December 31, 2020, despite the fact that most of that income was earned in the corporation's year ending December 31, 2019. In effect, this provides an 11 month deferral of income recognition.

18-44.   To deal with this problem, special rules are applicable in situations where a partnership has a fiscal period that ends after the taxation year end of a corporation that has a significant interest (more than 10 percent) in that partnership.

18-45.   The rules would require income adjustments similar to those required for "additional business income", which is covered in Chapter 6.

18-46.   In the example from Paragraph 18-42, the legislation requires the corporation to include 334/365 of the partnership income for its year ending January 31, 2020, in its corporate tax return for the year ending December 31, 2019. This accrual would be deducted in the corporate taxation return for the year ending December 31, 2020, with a new accrual added for 334/365 of the partnership income for the year ending January 31, 2021.

Partnership Property

18-47. In general, partners legally own a percentage interest in partnership property in co-ownership. The partnership cannot own property since it is not a legal entity. This creates a problem for income tax purposes because the partnership income tax rules require that the partnership determine its income or loss as if it were a separate person.

18-48. If the partnership does not own partnership property, then gains and losses from the disposition of such property would not be considered those of the partnership. In addition, the partnership would not be able to claim CCA. The *Income Tax Act* resolves this problem with an assumption that the partnership, for income tax purposes, is considered to own partnership property.

Retention Of Income Characteristics

18-49. Partnerships are treated as a conduit for transferring income from an originating source into the hands of the partners. Further, it is an unfiltered conduit in that the character of various types of income is not altered as it flows to the partners. If a partnership earns dividend income, capital gains, or realizes a business loss, these sources would be received as dividend income, capital gains, or business losses in the hands of the partners.

> **EXAMPLE**   Partnership Deux has two equal general partners. Aside from its business income, Deux earns $50,000 of interest income and realizes a $20,000 capital gain. None of this amount is withdrawn by the two partners. Corporation Dos has two equal shareholders. It also earns $50,000 of interest income and realizes a $20,000 capital gain. The corporation does not pay out any of this amount as dividends.

> **ANALYSIS - Partnership**   For Partnership Deux, each partner is considered to have received $25,000 [(1/2)($50,000)] of interest income and to have realized a $5,000 taxable capital gain [($20,000)(1/2)(1/2)]. Note that the income is subject to taxation, despite the fact that none of it has been withdrawn from the partnership (see next section on Accrual Basis).

> **ANALYSIS - Corporation**   In the case of Corporation Dos, the shareholders will not be taxed until the income is withdrawn from the corporation. The income will, however, be taxed at the corporate level on the basis of its nature (e.g., capital gains, business, or property income). When it is distributed to the shareholders, it will not retain its characteristics as capital gains, business, or property income. Rather, the entire distribution will be taxed in the hands of the shareholders as dividends.

18-50. In addition to retaining its basic character, the originating location of each source of income is retained. If, for example, a partnership earns dividends on shares of U.S. corporations, this income would be received by the partners as foreign source dividends. Not surprisingly, the related foreign tax credits would also be flowed through to the partners.

Accrual Basis

18-51. The partnership must calculate its net business income on an accrual basis unless its partners are professionals who can elect under ITA 34 to use the billed basis of income recognition (as noted in Chapter 6, the use of the billed basis of income recognition is being phased out). On its determination, this income is then allocated to the partners. The partners include their share of this income at the time of allocation, without regard to when the funds are withdrawn from the partnership. It is the allocation, not the receipt of the funds, that creates income for the partners that is subject to tax.

18-52. In effect, this places the partners on an accrual basis for the determination of their individual business income amounts. While drawings of cash from the partnership reduce the partner's adjusted cost base, they will have no impact on the partner's Taxable Income or the amount of taxes the partner will be required to pay.

Exercise Eighteen - 1

Subject: Partnership Income - Accrual Basis

During the year ending December 31, 2020, PQR Partnership has business income of $55,000, capital gains of $40,000, and receives eligible dividends of $10,000. Norm Peters has a 50 percent interest in the income of this partnership. During 2020, Norm withdraws $30,000 from the partnership. Determine the tax consequences for Mr. Peters for the 2020 taxation year.

SOLUTION available in print and online Study Guide.

Calculating The Amounts To Be Allocated

Net Business Income

18-53. For most partnerships, the major income source to be allocated is the partnership's Net Business Income. As we have noted, this is a reconciliation process that starts with accounting Net Income. Various items are then added or subtracted to arrive at the partnership's Net Business Income. A discussion of the major items in this reconciliation process follows.

Salaries Or Wages To Partners (Add Back) Partnership agreements often provide that partners be paid salaries or wages to recognize the time they devote to partnership business. Reflecting provincial partnership legislation, the CRA does not permit the deduction of such amounts in the determination of a partnership's Net Business Income.

If salaries or wages have been deducted in determining the accounting Net Income of the partnership, they must be added back in the determination of Net Business Income for tax purposes of the partnership. While this is required in determining the total Net Business Income, it does not prevent priority allocations of this total to specific partners to reflect the work they do for the partnership. If the partnership agreement calls for such salary or wages entitlements for specific partners, the specified amounts will be allocated to those partners, with only the remaining Net Business Income allocated by some formula (e.g., a 60:40 split of the residual).

A further point here relates to whether the salaries or wages are withdrawn from the partnership. The allocated amount is included in the partner's income and added to his or her adjusted cost base. If, as would be the usual situation, the amounts are withdrawn from the partnership, they reduce the partner's adjusted cost base, but do not influence the partner's Net Income For Tax Purposes.

Interest On Partner Capital Contributions (Add Back) The preceding analysis of the treatment of partner salaries is also applicable to interest on capital contributions. If the partnership agreement calls for such amounts, they cannot be deducted in the determination of the Net Business Income of the partnership.

If interest payments on partner capital contributions have been deducted in the determination of accounting Net Income, they must be added back to arrive at the partnership's total Net Business Income. If the partnership agreement indicates that such amounts be treated as a priority allocation of the partnership's total Net Business Income, they will be included in the partner's Net Income For Tax Purposes and added to his or her adjusted cost base. If the specified amounts are withdrawn, the withdrawal does not affect the partner's Net Income For Tax Purposes. The drawings would, however, be deducted from the partner's adjusted cost base.

EXAMPLE - Salaries And Interest On Capital Contributions Bob and Ray are partners who share the Net Business Income of their partnership equally after a provision has been made for their salaries and Ray's interest on his capital contributions. For the year ending December 31, 2020, the Income Statement of the partnership, prepared in accordance with GAAP, is as follows:

Revenues		$135,000
Expenses:		
Cost Of Sales	($45,000)	
Salary To Bob	(30,000)	
Salary To Ray	(10,000)	
Interest On Ray's Capital Contributions	(11,000)	
Other Expenses	(10,000)	(106,000)
Accounting Income		$ 29,000

ANALYSIS For tax purposes, the Net Business Income of the Bob And Ray Partnership would be calculated as follows:

Accounting Income	$29,000
Add:	
Salaries To Bob and Ray ($30,000 + $10,000)	40,000
Interest On Capital Contributions	11,000
Net Business Income	$80,000
Allocations For Salaries And Interest On	
Capital Contributions ($40,000 + $11,000)	(51,000)
Residual Net Business Income (To Be Shared Equally)	$29,000

This amount would be allocated to the two partners as follows:

	Bob	Ray
Priority Allocation For Salaries	$30,000	$10,000
Priority Allocation For Interest	N/A	11,000
Allocation Of Residual On Equal Basis		
[(50%)($29,000)]	14,500	14,500
Total Business Income Allocation	$44,500	$35,500

Despite the fact that the partnership agreement may refer to salaries or wages and/or for interest on capital for the partners, from a legal point of view they are allocations of Net Business Income. Given this, the usual payroll procedures (e.g., source deductions for CPP and EI) are not required on the salaries or wages.

Drawings (Add Back) Drawings by partners are not deductible expenses in the determination of any type of partnership income. As GAAP for partnerships is not clearly laid out, partnership drawings may or may not be deducted in the determination of accounting Net Income. To the extent they have been deducted in determining accounting income, they will have to be added back in the determination of the partnership's Net Business Income.

Dividend Income (Deduct) Dividends received will be included in the partnership's accounting Net Income figure. These amounts will be allocated to partners as a separate source of income. This is discussed in more detail starting at Paragraph 18-57. Given this, dividends must be deducted in converting the partnership's accounting Net Income to the partnership's Net Business Income.

Charitable Donations (Add Back) These amounts are normally deducted in the determination of a partnership's accounting Net Income. In converting this figure to Net Business Income, these amounts will have to be added back.

Donations made by a partnership that otherwise qualify as charitable donations are flowed to the partners based on their partnership agreement. Corporations are entitled to a deduction in arriving at Taxable Income, whereas individuals are entitled to a credit against Tax Payable. Donations, and the related credit or deduction, are only allocated to those partners who are partners on the last day of the partnership's year end.

Political Contributions (Add Back)   As political contributions are normally subtracted in the determination of accounting Net Income, these amounts will have to be added back to arrive at the partnership's Net Business Income.

Qualifying political contributions are allocated to each partner as per the partnership agreement. Similar to charitable donations, the allocation of the contributions and the related credit is dependent on being a partner on the last day of the partnership's year in which the political contribution was made.

Personal Expenditures (Add Back)   In some situations, a partnership may pay personal expenses of one or more partners. While these amounts may be deducted as an expense for accounting purposes, they are not deductible to the partnership in determining Net Business Income. To the extent that these amounts have been deducted in the determination of accounting Net Income, they will have to be added back in the determination of the partnership's Net Business Income.

Business Transactions With Partners (No Adjustment)   While this may not be consistent with partnership law, administrative practice of the CRA does not restrict the ability of partners to enter into legitimate business transactions with their partnerships. Examples include loans made by partners to the partnership and the renting of a partner's property to the partnership. As long as the transactions are on regular commercial terms, such transactions will be treated for tax purposes in the same manner as transactions with persons who are not partners.

In general, such transactions will not require any adjustment of the accounting Net Income to arrive at the partnership's Net Business Income.

Capital Cost Allowance   Any CCA that is deducted on partnership property must be deducted at the partnership level. As you would expect, the half year rule, the AccII provisions, the available for use rules, the rental property restrictions, and other depreciable property rules are all applicable when determining the amount of CCA that a partnership may claim.

You should note that this requirement removes the possibility of different partners taking different amounts of CCA. If maximum CCA is deducted at the partnership level, all partners must, in effect, deduct maximum CCA.

It is not uncommon in partnership financial statements for the amortization figures to be based on the CCA amounts used for tax purposes. If this is the case, no net adjustment is required in converting accounting Net Income to the partnership's Net Business Income. However, the normal procedure, even when the amounts involved are the same, would be to add back the amortization figures used in the accounting statements and deduct the appropriate CCA figure.

Amounts Related To Dispositions Of Capital Assets   Accounting Net Income will include 100 percent of the accounting gains and losses on dispositions of depreciable and non-depreciable capital assets. These amounts must be added back (losses) or deducted (gains) in the determination of the partnership's Net Business Income.

As net taxable capital gains will be allocated to the partners as a separate source of income, these amounts are not included in the calculation of the partnership's Net Business Income. This is discussed in more detail starting at Paragraph 18-55.

As you will recall from Chapter 5, a disposition of a depreciable capital asset can also result in recapture of CCA or terminal losses. If recapture occurs, it will be added to accounting Net Income in order to arrive at the partnership's Net Business Income. Similarly, terminal losses will be deducted.

Figure 18 - 2
Conversion - Partnership Accounting Income
To Partnership Net Business Income

Additions To Accounting Income:
- Specific To Partnerships
- Salaries of partners
- Interest on capital accounts
- Drawings of partners (if deducted)
- Personal expenditures of partners (if deducted)

- General Business (Additions)
- Amortization, depreciation, and depletion of tangible and intangible assets (Accounting amounts)
- Recapture of CCA
- Tax reserves deducted in the prior year
- Losses on the disposition of capital assets (Accounting amounts)
- Charitable donations
- Political contributions
- Interest and penalties on income tax assessments
- Non-deductible automobile costs
- Fifty percent of business meals and entertainment expenses
- Club dues and cost of recreational facilities
- Non-deductible reserves (Accounting amounts)
- Fines, penalties, and illegal payments

Deductions From Accounting Income:
- Specific To Partnerships
- None

- General Business (Deductions)
- Capital cost allowances (CCA)
- Terminal losses
- Tax reserves claimed for the current year
- Gains on the disposition of capital assets (Accounting amounts)
- Deductible warranty expenditures
- Landscaping costs
- Dividends included in accounting income
- Other property income included in accounting income

Reserves The use of reserves is discussed in both Chapter 6 (e.g., reserve for bad debts) and Chapter 8 (e.g., capital gains reserve). These reserves are claimed by the partnership in exactly the same manner as partners, corporations, and trusts.

In general, the amounts involved in the application of reserve procedures are the same as the related amounts for accounting purposes. For example, the amount deducted for bad debts in the accounting statements is usually the same net amount that results from the application of reserve procedures in tax returns. However, the normal procedure here in determining the partnership's Net Business Income is to remove the accounting amounts and replace these amounts with the tax figures, even when the amounts are the same.

18-54. Figure 18-2 provides a list of the more common additions and deductions that arise in the process of converting the accounting income of a partnership into Net Business Income. You will note that many of the items presented here are the same as those presented in Figure 6-3 in Chapter 6, which covers business income.

Capital Gains And Losses
18-55. In the preceding section, we noted the need to remove any accounting gains and losses on capital asset dispositions in the determination of Net Business Income. If dispositions created recapture of CCA or terminal losses, these amounts were added or deducted in the determination of Net Business Income. However, capital gains and losses were not included.

18-56.   As you would expect, capital gains and losses are allocated to the members of the partnership to be included in their tax returns. Without going into great detail, once these amounts are allocated they are subject to the same rules that would apply if the gains and losses had resulted from dispositions by the partners themselves. One-half of the net gains will be included in Net Income For Tax Purposes. On some gains the lifetime capital gains deduction may be available and some losses may qualify as Business Investment Losses. If the partner is a private corporation, there will be an addition to the capital dividend account.

Exercise Eighteen - 2

Subject: Partnership Net Business Income

The JL Partnership has two partners. Partner J, because he is actively managing the partnership, receives an annual salary of $45,000. Because Partner L has contributed most of the capital for the business, he receives an interest allocation of $22,000. The partnership agreement calls for the remaining profits, and all other allocations, to be split 60 percent to J and 40 percent to L. The salary and interest amounts are deducted in the determination of accounting Net Income and withdrawn by the partners during the year.

During the taxation year ending December 31, 2020, the partnership's accounting Net Income is $262,000. Other relevant information is as follows:

- The accountant deducted amortization charges of $26,000. Maximum CCA is $42,000.
- Accounting Net Income includes a deduction for charitable donations of $2,500.
- Accounting Net Income includes a gain on the sale of land of $24,000.

Determine the amounts of Net Business Income that will be allocated to Partner J and Partner L for the year ending December 31, 2020.

SOLUTION available in print and online Study Guide.

Dividend Income
18-57.   As we have noted in the preceding section, dividends received by a partnership are removed in the determination of the partnership's Net Business Income. When they are allocated to the members of the partnership to be included in their tax returns, they retain their character as eligible, non-eligible, or capital dividends. Their treatment subsequent to allocation will depend on the type of taxpayer involved and/or the type of dividend received:

- Partners who are individuals must gross up the dividends by either 38 percent (for eligible dividends) or 15 percent (for non-eligible dividends). The dividends are then eligible for the usual dividend tax credits.
- Dividends allocated to corporate partners will not be grossed up. One hundred percent of the amount allocated will be included in Net Income For Tax Purposes. To the extent the dividends are from taxable Canadian corporations, they can be deducted in the determination of the corporation's Taxable Income.
- Capital dividends received by the partnership are allocated as capital dividends to both individual and corporate partners, generally retaining their tax-free nature.

Foreign Source Income
18-58.   Foreign source income received by a partnership will be allocated to the partners as either business or property income. As you would expect, the amounts that will be allocated to the partners will be the pre-withholding amounts that accrued to the partnership. That is, to the extent that foreign taxes were withheld, they will be added to the amount received for purposes of allocating this income to the members of the partnership. As the pre-withholding amounts are allocated to the partners, the *Income Tax Act* allows these partners to make use of any available foreign tax credits and/or foreign tax deductions (calculation of these credits and deductions is covered in Chapters 7 and 11).

Exercise Eighteen - 3

Subject: Partnership Income Allocations

The ST Partnership has two partners who share all types of income on an equal basis. Partner S and T are both individuals. The partnership's accounting Net Income for the year ending December 31, 2020, is $146,000. No salaries or interest payments to partners have been included in this calculation. However, the $146,000 includes $12,000 in eligible dividends, as well as a $31,000 gain on the sale of unused land. Amortization Expense deducted is equal to maximum CCA. Determine the amounts that will be included in the Net Income For Tax Purposes of Partner S and Partner T for the year ending December 31, 2020.

SOLUTION available in print and online Study Guide.

Allocations Of Related Tax Credits

18-59.   In the preceding sections, we have covered the various types of income that will be allocated to partners and the related tax credits. The type of income and expenditures that could give rise to tax credits can be summarized as follows:

- Dividend Income - tax credit is available if the partner is an individual.
- Charitable Donations - tax credit is available if the partner is an individual.
- Foreign Source Income - tax credit is available to all partners if foreign tax is withheld.
- Political Contributions - tax credit is available to all partners, but as covered in Chapter 4, the *Canada Elections Act* bans political contributions by corporations.

Exercise Eighteen - 4

Subject: Allocations To Partners - Related Tax Credits

For the year ending December 31, 2020, the MN Partnership has correctly computed its Net Business Income to be $141,000. The partnership agreement calls for all allocations to Partner M and Partner N to be on a 50:50 basis. Partner M and N are both individuals and neither partner has Taxable Income that will be taxed federally at 33 percent. In determining the Net Business Income amount, the partnership's accountant added back $3,500 in charitable donations and $1,200 in contributions to a registered political party. In addition, $4,200 in eligible dividends received were deducted. The partners have made no charitable donations or political contributions as individuals. Determine the amount of any tax credits that the partnership will allocate to Partner M and Partner N for the year ending December 31, 2020.

SOLUTION available in print and online Study Guide.

Methods Of Allocation

18-60.   As we have seen in the preceding sections, income amounts must be allocated on a source-by-source basis. While a partnership agreement might simply state that all types of income will be allocated on the same basis, there is nothing to prevent different allocations for different sources. For example, business income could be allocated on an equal basis, with capital gains being allocated to one specific partner.

18-61.   There are many ways in which the members of a partnership may agree to allocate income or losses. These allocations may be fixed, variable, or a combination of fixed and variable elements. Factors such as the value of services provided to the partnership (a salary component), capital contributions (an interest component), and amounts of risk assumed (personal assets at risk) may be taken into consideration. Alternatively, allocations may be based upon fixed ratios determined by the partners or, in the absence of some other agreement, the equal fixed ratios that automatically apply under partnership law.

18-62.   In general, the CRA will accept any income allocation agreement that is reasonable. It is possible, however, that the agreement could be constructed in a manner that would reduce or postpone taxes (e.g., an example of this would be the allocation of all partnership losses to partners with high levels of current income). In addition, an allocation could be used for income splitting purposes (e.g., allocation of large amounts of partnership income to a low-income spouse on a basis that is not consistent with his or her contribution of services or capital). In either of these circumstances, the CRA can apply ITA 103(1) or (1.1) to re-allocate the income on the basis that is reasonable in the circumstances.

> **We suggest you work Self Study Problems Eighteen-3 and 4 at this point.**

The Partnership Interest

The Concept

18-63.   A person who is a member of a partnership has the right to participate in profits and losses of the partnership and the right to an interest in partnership property, usually on the dissolution of the partnership. Such rights, collectively referred to as a partnership interest, constitute property for income tax purposes much in the same manner as a share of capital stock of a corporation.

18-64.   A partnership interest is generally considered a non-depreciable capital property that is held for the purpose of earning business or property income and, as a consequence, a disposition of a partnership interest will usually result in a capital gain or loss.

18-65.   In many cases, a partnership interest is acquired when a partnership is formed. Each member of the new organization will acquire an interest, usually through the contribution of an amount of capital that is specified in the partnership agreement.

18-66.   Alternatively, a partnership interest can be acquired from an existing partnership. This type of transaction can take two forms:

- The interest can be acquired directly from a current partner or partners by purchasing their interest.

- The interest can be acquired directly from the partnership by transferring assets to this organization.

Acquiring A Partnership Interest

New Partnership
18-67.   For founding members of a new partnership, establishment of the adjusted cost base (ACB) of the partnership interest is very straightforward. For each of the partners, the ACB of their interest will simply be the fair value of the assets contributed to the partnership. If the contributions involve non-monetary assets, appraisals may be required. This, however, is a practical complication that does not alter the basic concept that is involved.

Admission To Existing Partnership
18-68.   From a technical point of view, ITA 98(1) provides that a partnership terminates on a change in the composition of the members. This would include both the admission of a partner and the withdrawal of a partner. However, in these situations, ITA 98(6) deems the partnership to have continued unchanged. Based on the availability of this provision, in the discussion that follows we will assume that a partnership is not resolved when there is a change in membership.

18-69.   In those cases where a partnership interest is purchased directly from an existing partner, the procedures are very straightforward. If a person becomes a partner by acquiring another partner's interest, then cost will equal the purchase price. For example, if Mr. Davis acquires the one-third interest of Mr. Allan for $90,000, then both the cost to Mr. Davis and the proceeds of disposition to Mr. Allan would be $90,000.

18-70.   The situation becomes more complex when the partnership interest is acquired through direct payments to more than one partner.

EXAMPLE   An existing partnership has three equal partners, each of whom has made a capital contribution of $16,000. They would like to bring in a new equal partner, with each partner then having a 25 percent interest in the organization. The new partner, Mr. Zheng, agrees to pay $30,000 to each of the existing partners for one-quarter of their one-third interest. Note that by selling one-quarter of their one-third interest, each partner retains a 25 percent interest [(75%)(1/3) = 25%].

ANALYSIS   Mr. Zheng would have an ACB of $90,000, the consideration given up for the 25 percent interest.

Each of the original partners would have a capital gain calculated as follows:

Proceeds Of Disposition To Each Partner	$30,000
ACB of Part Interest [(25%)($16,000)]	(4,000)
Capital Gain For Each Partner	$26,000

18-71.   The capital accounts in the accounting records of the partnership and the partners' ACB will be as follows:

	Partner 1	Partner 2	Partner 3	Mr. Zheng
Capital Before Admitting Zheng	$16,000	$16,000	$16,000	Nil
Adjustment For Admission Of Zheng	(4,000)	(4,000)	(4,000)	$12,000
Ending Capital Accounts	$12,000	$12,000	$12,000	$12,000
ACB Of Partnership Interest	$12,000	$12,000	$12,000	$90,000

18-72.   Note that, while the accounting values for the interests of the original three partners are equal to their ACBs, this is not the case for Mr. Zheng. In contrast to his accounting value of $12,000, his ACB would be his cost of $90,000 [(3)($30,000)].

18-73.   To this point, we have only considered situations where assets were given to specific partners in return for the new partner's acquired interest. There are also situations in which the new partner makes a payment directly to the partnership in return for his or her interest.

18-74.   Returning to the example in Paragraph 18-70, if Mr. Zheng had paid the $90,000 directly to the partnership, there would be no tax consequences for the existing partners. No disposition of any part of their interest would have occurred and, as a consequence, no capital gain would be recorded and the ACBs of their interests would remain at $16,000. Mr. Zheng's interest would be recorded at $90,000 for both tax and accounting purposes.

Exercise Eighteen - 5

Subject: Admission Of A Partner

Alan and Balan are equal partners in the Alban Partnership. On September 1, 2020, Alan and Balan's partnership capital account balances are $48,000 each. This is also equal to the adjusted cost base of their interests. As the result of paying $40,000 to each of Alan and Balan, Caitlan is admitted as an equal partner (1/3 interest) on September 1, 2020.

Calculate the tax effects of the partner admission for Alan and Balan. In addition, determine the accounting balances for each of the partner's capital accounts after the admission of Caitlan, as well as the adjusted cost base for each partner after the admission of Caitlan.

SOLUTION available in print and online Study Guide.

Adjusted Cost Base Of The Partnership Interest

Basic Concept

18-75.   As we have noted, a partnership interest is viewed in tax legislation as a non-depreciable capital asset. A discussed in Chapter 8, the adjusted cost base (ACB) of a capital property is defined in ITA 54 as its cost plus or minus the adjustments in ITA 53.

18-76.   In the preceding section, we illustrated how the ACB of a partnership interest would be determined at the time a partnership interest is acquired.

18-77.   Subsequent to its acquisition, the partnership interest is determined by starting with the ACB of the preceding year and adjusting it for various items. The most common adjustments are for:

- current year income allocations;
- current year drawings; and
- current year capital contributions.

18-78.   There are, however, many other possible adjustments, and most of these will be covered in this section. It is important to note the importance of making these adjustments. If these adjustments were not required, any gain or loss on a subsequent sale of the partnership interest would result in these amounts becoming part of the gain or loss on the sale.

EXAMPLE   John Port acquires his partnership interest for $100,000. At a later point in time, he makes an additional capital contribution of $20,000. Subsequent to making this additional contribution, he sells his interest for $150,000.

ANALYSIS   As we shall note in the material that follows, John will add the $20,000 capital contribution to his adjusted cost base, resulting in a new value of $120,000 ($100,000 + $20,000). Given this, the capital gain on the disposition of the interest will be $30,000 ($150,000 - $120,000). If he had not made the required adjustment, the gain would have been $50,000 ($150,000 - $100,000).

Timing Of Adjustments

18-79.   Before proceeding to a discussion of the more common adjustments to the cost base of a partnership interest, some attention must be given to the timing of these adjustments. With respect to capital contributions and drawings, the timing is very straightforward. These adjustments are made at the time of the contribution or drawing.

18-80.   In contrast, those adjustments related to allocations of income or tax credits are not made during the period in which the income or tax credit arises. Rather, these adjustments to the ACB of a partnership interest are made on the first day of the following fiscal period. These procedures will be illustrated in the material that follows.

Adjustments For Partnership Income Components

18-81.   It would be unusual, in any given year, for the adjusted cost base of a partnership interest not to be adjusted for partnership income allocations. As this must be added on a source-by-source basis, specific sources are given separate consideration here:

Net Business Income   As discussed in our section on partnership income determination, accounting Net Income must be converted to the partnership's Net Business Income. This amount is allocated to each partner on the basis of the partnership agreement. The amounts so determined will be added (Net Business Income) or subtracted (Net Business Loss) to the adjusted cost base of each partner. As noted, this increase or decrease does not occur until the first day of the following fiscal period.

EXAMPLE   Tom and Theresa begin the Double T partnership in January 2020 and select December 31 as their year end. They each contribute $1,000 to Double T. During 2020, the partnership earns $21,000 in gross service revenue. The only expenses incurred are $6,000 in business meals and entertainment.

ANALYSIS   Accounting Net Income for the partnership would be $15,000 ($21,000 - $6,000). However, Net Business Income would be $18,000, the $15,000 of accounting Net Income plus $3,000, the non-deductible one-half of the expenses for business meals and entertainment. This means that each partner would be allocated $9,000 [(1/2)($18,000)] in business income, and each partnership interest would be increased by the same amount. While the income amounts would be included in the partners' 2020 tax return, the addition to the adjusted cost base would not be made until January 1, 2021.

Capital Gains And Losses   As discussed previously, these amounts will be allocated to the partners on the basis of the partnership agreement. Once these amounts are allocated, the taxable or allowable amounts (one-half) will be included in the partner's tax returns.

Despite the fact that only one-half of these amounts will be taxable or deductible, the adjustment to the ACB of the partnership interest is for the full amount and occurs on the first day of the following fiscal period. This inclusion of the full amount provides for the non-taxable one-half of the gain to be recovered on a tax free basis if the partnership interest is sold.

EXAMPLE   Weekday Partnership has four equal partners and a December 31 year end. Each partner contributed $1,950 when the partnership began on May 1, 2020. Weekday used the initial contributions of $7,800 to acquire two parcels of land. Both parcels were capital property and were sold in December, 2020. The sale of parcel A resulted in a capital gain of $5,300 and the sale of parcel B resulted in a capital loss of $700. There were no other transactions during the fiscal year.

ANALYSIS   The total capital gain for each partner is $1,150 [(1/4)($5,300 − $700)]. The allocation to each partner's Net Income For Tax Purposes will be the taxable amount of $575 [(1/2)($1,150)]. However, the allocation to the partnership interest will be, as shown in the following table, the full amount of the partner's share of the capital gain.

The ACB of each partnership interest is calculated as follows:

ACB - May 1, 2020, to December 31, 2020		$1,950
Net Capital Gain Allocated:		
Capital Gain [(1/4)($5,300)]	$1,325	
Capital Loss [(1/4)($700)]	(175)	1,150
ACB Of Partnership Interest - January 1, 2021		$3,100

Dividends   As previously discussed, taxable dividends earned by a partnership retain their character (i.e., eligible, non-eligible, or capital) when they are allocated to the partners. In calculating the ACB of a partnership interest, a partner's share of both capital and taxable dividends is added to the ACB of his partnership interest on the first day of the following fiscal period.

EXAMPLE   Fred and Barney are equal partners in Stone-Works Partnership that began operations January 1, 2020. A December 31 year end was selected. Each partner initially contributed $5,000. The only income received by the partnership was $13,000 of eligible dividends and $4,200 of capital dividends. No amounts were withdrawn from the partnership in 2020.

ANALYSIS Each partner is required to include one-half of the taxable dividends of $13,000 plus an additional 38 percent gross up in his 2020 Net Income For Tax Purposes. This amounts to income of $8,970 [(50%)($13,000)(138%)]. In conjunction with this allocation, each partner would be eligible for a federal dividend tax credit of $1,347 [(50%)($13,000)(38%)(6/11)]. The capital dividends are not included in each partner's income as they are tax free. The ACB of Fred and Barney's interest would be as follows:

ACB - January 1, 2020, to December 31, 2020	$ 5,000
Allocation Of Dividends Subject To Tax [(50%)($13,000)]	6,500
Allocation Of Capital Dividends [(50%)($4,200)]	2,100
ACB Of Partnership Interest - January 1, 2021	$13,600

Two things should be noted in this calculation. First, for purposes of calculating the ACB of the partnership interests, no gross up is added to the dividends subject to tax. Second, the dividends are not added to the ACB until the first day of the year following their allocation to the partners.

Adjustments For Capital Contributions And Drawings

18-82. These adjustments require little in the way of explanation:

- Net capital contributions are added to the adjusted cost base of the partner's interest.
- Drawings reduce the adjusted cost base of the partnership interest.

Note that bona fide loans by a partner to the partnership are not considered capital contributions. Similarly, loans from the partnership to a partner are not considered to be drawings.

EXAMPLE The ACB of Mr. Allan's partnership interest is $20,450 at January 1, 2020. In March 2020, he contributes $8,200 to the partnership as a capital contribution and makes withdrawals of $2,000 in each of May, August, and November, 2020.

ANALYSIS The ACB of Mr. Allan's partnership interest is calculated as follows:

ACB – January 1, 2020	$20,450
Capital Contributions – March 2020	8,200
Drawings – May, August, And November 2020 [($2,000)(3)]	(6,000)
ACB – December 31, 2020	$22,650

Charitable Donations and Political Contributions

18-83. Amounts donated or political contributions made by a partnership in a particular year are considered donated or contributed by each partner in proportion to that partner's profit sharing ratio. As it is the partners who enjoy the benefits of making the contributions (i.e., the deductions or tax credits), such amounts reduce the ACB of a partnership interest. Note, however, this adjustment does not occur until the first day of the following fiscal period.

EXAMPLE During the taxation year ending December 31, 2020, a partnership donated $7,500 to charitable organizations. The three partners, who are all individuals, each have a one-third interest in profits. All donations are eligible for the charitable donations tax credit.

ANALYSIS Each of the three partners would be entitled to allocations of $2,500 toward the calculation of their individual charitable donations tax credit for 2020. As a consequence of this allocation, the ACB of each of their partnership interests would be reduced by $2,500. As we have noted, this reduction does not occur until January 1, 2021.

Negative ACB

18-84.   In general, if negative adjustments to the ACB of a capital asset exceed its cost plus any positive adjustments to the ACB, the excess must be taken into income under ITA 40(3) as a capital gain. While technically an ACB can only be positive or nil, it is common to refer to assets that have experienced such adjustments as having a negative adjusted cost base.

18-85.   This creates a problem for partnership interests in that withdrawals are deducted from the ACB of the partnership interest in the year they occur, while income allocations are only recorded on the first day of the following year. As partners usually withdraw their anticipated income allocations during the year in which they accrue, negative ACBs for partnership interests would not be unusual.

18-86.   Because of this problem, the *Income Tax Act* allows general partners to carry forward a negative ACB without taking the capital gain into income. This deferral is applicable until the partner disposes of his or her interest, either through a sale or as the result of a deemed disposition at death.

> **EXAMPLE**   During 2020, in anticipation of the 2020 allocation of partnership income, a partner draws $42,000 from the partnership. For 2020, his share of partnership income is $45,000. On January 1, 2020, his partnership interest has an ACB of $25,000.
>
> **ANALYSIS**   On December 31, 2020, the ACB of this partnership interest would be nil and there would be an excess of drawings over the January 1, 2020, ACB of $17,000 ($25,000 - $42,000). In the absence of a special provision for partnership interests, $8,500 [(1/2)($17,000)] would have to be taken into the partner's income as a taxable capital gain. However, because of the special provision applicable to partnership interests, this will not be the case. Note that, on January 1, 2021, the ACB of this interest would be $28,000 ($25,000 - $42,000 + $45,000).

18-87.   When the disposition results from a deemed disposition at death, there are rollover provisions that allow a continued carry forward of the negative ACB when the partnership interest is bequeathed to a spouse or common-law partner or a trust in favour of a spouse or common-law partner.

18-88.   Note that the preceding rules only apply to active general partners. In the case of limited partners (see Paragraph 18-91) or general partners who are not active in the partnership, the deferral of the gain that is implicit in carrying forward a negative ACB is not available. Such amounts must be taken into income in the year in which they occur.

Exercise Eighteen - 6

Subject: ACB Of Partnership Interest

On January 1, 2020, Raymond and Robert form the RR Partnership. The partnership has a December 31 year end. The partnership agreement provides Robert with a 40 percent share of profits and losses. Robert initially contributes $12,500 and makes a further contribution of $7,200 on June 10, 2020. He withdraws $4,000 on October 31, 2020. RR Partnership has the following sources of income for 2020:

Capital Gain On Corporate Shares	$11,600
Eligible Dividends Received From Canadian Corporations	3,100
Net Business Income	46,700

Determine the ACB of Robert's partnership interest on December 31, 2020, and at January 1, 2021. In addition, determine the amount that would be included in Robert's 2020 Net Income For Tax Purposes as a consequence of his interest in the RR Partnership.

SOLUTION available in print and online Study Guide.

Disposition Of A Partnership Interest

Sale To An Arm's Length Party

18-89.   If a partnership interest is sold to an arm's length party, the tax effects are very straight-forward. The adjusted cost base of the partnership interest is subtracted from the proceeds resulting from its sale. If the result is positive, it is a capital gain, one-half of which will be taxed in the hands of the partner. Alternatively, if the result is negative, one-half of this amount will be an allowable capital loss, which can be deducted by the partner to the extent of his or her current year taxable capital gains. Any unused amount can be carried over to previous and subsequent years.

Withdrawal From Partnership

18-90.   When a partner withdraws from a partnership, he or she is essentially disposing of his or her interest in that partnership. While this could involve using partnership assets to buy out the partner, the more normal procedure is to have one or more of the other partners purchase the interest of the withdrawing partner.

> **EXAMPLE** The QST Partnership has three partners who share all income amounts on an equal basis. The ACB of their partnership interests are as follows:
>
> | | |
> |---|---|
> | Partner Q | $250,000 |
> | Partner S | 250,000 |
> | Partner T | 250,000 |
>
> Partner T has decided to retire and will withdraw from the partnership. In return for his interest, each of the remaining partners will pay him $175,000.
>
> **ANALYSIS** Partner T will have a taxable capital gain of $50,000 [(1/2)($175,000 + $175,000 - $250,000)]. There will no immediate tax consequences to partners Q and S. However, the ACB of each of their interests will be increased to $425,000, the original $250,000 plus the additional investment of $175,000.
>
> You might wish to note that, assuming the assets of the partnership are not revalued, the accounting values for the interests of each of the remaining partners will be $375,000 [$250,000 + (1/2)($250,000)].

We suggest you work Self Study Problems Eighteen-5 and 6 at this point.

Limited Partnerships And Limited Partners

Definitions

Limited Partner

18-91.   A limited partnership is one that has at least one limited partner and one general partner. As defined in most provincial legislation, a limited partner is one whose liability for the debts of the partnership is limited to the amount of his or her contribution to the partnership and who is not permitted to participate in the management of the partnership. A partner whose liability is limited under partnership law is considered a limited partner for income tax purposes.

18-92.   While the term "limited partner" generally refers to a partner who is relieved of general responsibility for amounts in excess of his or her capital contribution, the definition also includes partners whose liability is limited by the presence of specific contractual arrangements. Examples of this type of situation include:

- guarantees that someone will acquire their partnership interest regardless of its value;
- provisions indicating that amounts a partner has agreed to contribute to the partnership may never have to be paid; and
- provisions that guarantee the partner that he or she will be reimbursed for any partnership losses, usually by the general partner.

18-93. Note that members of a limited liability partnership (see Paragraph 18-22) do not fall within the definition of a limited partner. They have limited responsibility for certain types of liabilities (e.g., liabilities arising as the result of negligent action by their professional partners). However, they continue to have unlimited liability for other partnership obligations.

At-Risk Rules

Basic Concept

18-94. Historically, limited partnership structures have been used to fund high-risk ventures that benefit from generous income tax incentives. These structures have been used with Canadian films, Canadian mining and exploration operations, scientific research and experimental development, real estate, and construction.

18-95. General partners entice investors with limited liability protection, combined with the advantages of significant flow through of deductible losses and other tax incentives. The general partners usually do not share in the deductions, receiving their compensation through fees that are charged to the limited partners for managing the partnership.

18-96. The at-risk rules were introduced in order to restrict the ability of certain investors in partnerships, typically limited partners, to receive tax deductions or tax credits in excess of the amount that they stand to lose on their investment. In simplified terms, the at-risk rules work to ensure that $30,000 of tax deductions are not available to a limited partner who has less than $30,000 at risk.

The At-Risk Amount

18-97. The at-risk amount sets the annual limit on the amount of tax preferences and incentives that may flow through to limited partners. Specifically, the *Income Tax Act* provides restrictions on the allocation to limited partners of scientific research and experimental development credits, resource expenditures, investment tax credits, non-farming business losses, and property losses. Under ITA 96(2.2), the at-risk amount is calculated at the end of a partnership's fiscal period as follows:

ACB Of The Partnership Interest		$xxx
Share Of Partnership Income (But Not Losses) For The Current Period		
(Current Year Income Allocation For ACB Purposes - See Paragraph 18-98)		xxx
Subtotal		$xxx
Less:		
Amounts Owed To The Partnership	($xxx)	
Other Amounts Intended To Reduce The Investment Risk	(xxx)	(xxx)
At-Risk Amount		$xxx

18-98. The addition of the share of partnership income (not losses) is intended to ensure that current year income allocations, which will not be added to the ACB of the partnership interest until the following fiscal year, are taken into consideration at the end of the current year. The amount that is added here is the same income allocation that will be added to the ACB. That is, it does not include the dividend gross up, nor is it adjusted downward for the non-taxable portion of capital gains.

18-99. The at-risk amount is reduced by two amounts. The first represents the outstanding balance of any amount owing by the partner to the partnership for the acquisition of the partnership interest. This amount is subtracted as it is included in the partnership interest but, prior to its actual payment, it is not really at risk.

18-100. The second amount relates to financial incentives designed to reduce the investment risk or exposure to the limited partner. An example of this would be a promise by the general partner to acquire the partnership interest at an amount in excess of the value of the partnership interest at the option of the limited partner.

Limited Partnership Losses

18-101.   The at-risk rules limit the ability of a limited partner to utilize certain types of losses. The rules do not directly affect farm losses and capital losses since these losses carry their own restrictions. Farm losses during the current year may be limited by the restricted farm loss rules and, in addition, any carry over of such restricted farm losses can only be applied against farming income (see Chapter 6). Similarly, current year allowable capital losses are only deductible to the extent of current year taxable capital gains.

18-102.   ITA 96(2.1) indicates that a partner's share of losses, other than those associated with farming or the disposition of capital assets, can be deducted to the extent of the at-risk amount. The excess is referred to as the "limited partnership loss". It is a carry forward balance that can be carried forward indefinitely and can only be claimed against future income from the partnership or increases of the at-risk amount from that same partnership. There is no carry back of limited partnership losses.

EXAMPLE   On January 1, 2020, Jenny Johnson acquires a 10 percent limited partnership interest in Tax-Time, a partnership that provides tax preparation services. This interest cost her $15,000, with $6,000 paid in cash and the balance of $9,000 payable in 36 months, without interest. At December 31, 2020, Tax-Time determines that it has a $22,000 capital gain and an $111,000 business loss. Jenny is allocated 10 percent of these amounts.

ANALYSIS   As a 10 percent limited partner, Jenny is allocated a portion of the business loss equal to $11,100. However, her at-risk amount restricts the business loss that Jenny may be able to use. The at-risk amount is calculated as follows:

ACB Of The Partnership Interest		$15,000
Share Of Partnership Income [(10%)($22,000 Capital Gain)]		2,200
Subtotal		$17,200
Less:		
Amounts Owed To The Partnership	($9,000)	
Other Amounts Intended To Reduce		
The Investment Risk	Nil	(9,000)
At-Risk Amount – December 31, 2020		$ 8,200

For 2020, Jenny will be able to deduct her share of the total partnership loss to the extent of her $8,200 at-risk amount. This will leave a non-deductible limited partnership loss for 2020 of $2,900 ($11,100 - $8,200). In general, Jenny will be able to use the limited partnership loss in 2021 or subsequent years if her at-risk amount increases. This may occur if she makes additional contributions, is allocated additional income from the partnership in 2021, or pays the amount owed to the partnership. It should also be noted that there are special adjustments to the ACB of a limited partner's partnership interest that are beyond the scope of this material.

Exercise Eighteen - 7

Subject: Limited Partnership Loss

During 2020, Stuart Jones acquires an interest in a limited partnership for $200,000. An initial $50,000 is paid immediately, with the $150,000 balance payable in eight years. The general partner has agreed to acquire Stuart's interest at any subsequent date, returning his $50,000 payment and assuming responsibility for the $150,000 payable. For 2020, the limited partnership has allocated losses of $75,000 to Stuart. How much of this loss is Stuart entitled to claim as a deduction on his 2020 tax return? Indicate the amount of his limited partnership loss at the end of 2020.

SOLUTION available in print and online Study Guide.

We suggest you work Self Study Problem Eighteen-7 at this point.

Transfer Of Property To And From A Partnership

Definition Of Canadian Partnership

18-103.   Since the ITA treats partners as distinct from the partnership, transferring property between the partners and the partnership may have income tax consequences. Such consequences are generally dependent on the purpose of the property transfer and whether the underlying partnership meets the ITA 102 definition of a "Canadian partnership":

> **ITA 102**   In this subdivision, "Canadian partnership" means a partnership all of the members of which were, at any time in respect of which the expression is relevant, resident in Canada.

18-104.   Whether the partnership is a general, limited, or limited liability partnership is irrelevant to the determination of its status as a Canadian partnership. In addition, the definition does not require that the partnership be formed in Canada. For example, a U.S. based partnership with all Canadian resident members would qualify.

18-105.   If the required conditions are met, the *Income Tax Act* contains rollover provisions that provide for tax deferral on such transactions. However, where the conditions are not met, the transfers will be taxed as a disposition/acquisition at fair market value.

18-106.   In covering this material on property transfers, we will first look at the rules applicable to transfers of property to and from a partnership when a rollover provision is not used. This will be followed by a discussion of some of the more commonly used partnership rollover provisions.

Transfers With No Rollover Provision

Transfers From Partners To The Partnership

18-107.   If a person transfers property to a partnership of which he or she is member, or to a partnership of which he or she becomes a member as a result of the transfer, ITA 97(1) deems the person to have disposed of the property at fair market value and the partnership to have acquired the property at the same amount.

18-108.   In general, the fair market value of the transferred asset is added to the ACB of the transferor's partnership interest. However, this addition would be reduced by any consideration given to the contributor because of his or her contribution. This rule is applicable without regard to whether the partnership qualifies as a Canadian partnership.

> **EXAMPLE**   Diane Jefferson is a member of CG Partnership. She is required to make an additional 2020 capital contribution to the partnership and decides to make the contribution by transferring investments that she had purchased for $10,000. At the time of the transfer, they have a fair market value of $24,000.

> **ANALYSIS**   Diane will be considered to have disposed of the investments for $24,000. This will result in a $7,000 [(1/2)($24,000 - $10,000)] taxable capital gain for 2020. Diane will also be considered to have made a $24,000 capital contribution that will increase the ACB of her partnership interest by the same amount. The partnership will be considered to have acquired the investments from Diane for $24,000.

Exercise Eighteen - 8

Subject: Transfers From Partner To Partnership (No Rollover)

Charles Woodward is one of four equal partners in LIU Partnership (LIU). During the current year, Charles contributes a tract of land to the partnership. Charles does not use a rollover provision to make the transfer. Charles acquired the land for $33,000 and, at the time of transfer, it is valued at $100,000. Describe the tax consequences to Charles and LIU in the following three situations:

A. No consideration is received from LIU.
B. Charles receives $25,000 in cash from LIU on the transfer.
C. Charles receives $112,000 in cash from LIU on the transfer.

SOLUTION available in print and online Study Guide.

Transfers From The Partnership To Partners

18-109.   If a partnership transfers property to a partner, ITA 98(2) deems the partnership to have disposed of the property at fair market value and the partner to have acquired the property at the same amount. There is no requirement that the partner remains a partner after the transfer and the rule is applicable without regard to whether the partnership qualifies as a Canadian partnership. This provision is typically used when a partnership is dissolved or when partial distributions of partnership property are made in an ongoing partnership.

> **EXAMPLE**   Bill Davis is a 40 percent partner in the FV Partnership. The partnership owns a piece of land that has an ACB of $2,900 and transfers it to Bill in June 2020 for no consideration. The land has a fair market value of $10,000 at this time.

> **ANALYSIS**   The partnership is considered to have disposed of the land for its fair market value of $10,000, resulting in a capital gain of $7,100 ($10,000 - $2,900). Bill's share of this gain is $2,840 [(40%)($7,100)]. This amount will be allocated to Bill and, as a consequence, he will report a taxable capital gain of $1,420 [(1/2)($2,840)] in his 2020 tax return. Bill will also be considered to have acquired the land for $10,000 and to have made a withdrawal from the partnership of $10,000. The ACB of his partnership interest will be reduced by the $10,000 withdrawal and increased by the $2,840 allocation of the capital gain.

Exercise Eighteen - 9

Subject: Transfers From Partnership To Partners

Darlene is one of five equal partners in the DG Partnership. During the taxation year ending December 31, 2020, DG distributes some of its investments to each of the partners. The distributed investments have an adjusted cost base of $39,000 and, at the time of transfer, they have a fair market value of $94,000. Darlene receives one-fifth of these investments. At the time of this transfer, the adjusted cost base of Darlene's partnership interest is $30,000. What are the tax consequences to DG and Darlene with respect to this distribution? Your answer should include Darlene's adjusted cost base for the investments and the amount of her partnership interest on both December 31, 2020, and on January 1, 2021.

SOLUTION available in print and online Study Guide.

Common Partnership Rollovers

Transfers From Partners To The Partnership

18-110.   If a person transfers property to a Canadian partnership and all members of that partnership jointly elect, then property transferred to the partnership may be transferred on a rollover basis. This means that the property can be transferred at elected values (usually tax values), rather than at the fair market values that must be used in the absence of a rollover provision. This rule applies both to persons who are existing partners as well as to persons who become partners by contributing property to the partnership.

18-111.   ITA 97(2) indicates that, for this type of transfer, the ITA 85(1) rules apply. The ITA 85(1) rules are generally applicable to transfers of property to a corporation and are discussed in detail in Chapter 16. There are, however, some differences in the application of these rules when the transfer is to a partnership. The more notable of these differences are as follows:

- Real property inventory can be transferred to a partnership, but not to a corporation.

- When a transferor takes back consideration with a value less than that of the property transferred to a corporation, it may involve a gift to a related party. In the case of transfers to a partnership, the gift portion is added to the ACB of the partnership interest. As discussed in Chapter 16, if such a transfer were made to a corporation, it would usually result in double taxation of the gifted amount.

- When a transferor receives consideration in excess of the value of the property transferred to a corporation, the excess is subject to taxation. When this happens in conjunction with a transfer of property to a partnership, the excess is generally viewed as a drawing and is not subject to taxation.

18-112.   Differences between the elected amounts and consideration other than a partnership interest affect the ACB of the partnership interest.

> **EXAMPLE**   Janice Donovan will join the On-Off Partnership that provides interior lighting products. She plans to make an initial capital contribution of a parcel of land with an ACB of $100,000 and a fair market value of $250,000. She wishes to transfer the land at an elected value of $160,000. The existing members agree and file a joint election authorizing the transaction for $160,000. Janice has a choice between three different packages of consideration:
>
> A.   No cash.
> B.   Cash of $100,000.
> C.   Cash of $160,000.
>
> **ANALYSIS**   ITA 97(2) uses the transfer limits described within ITA 85. The basic acceptable transfer range is from the land's ACB of $100,000 to its fair market value of $250,000. While not applicable in this case, the elected value is also limited to the amount of non-partnership interest consideration received. The relevant values for the three cases are as follows:

Case	ACB Of Partnership Interest	Capital Gain
No Cash	$160,000	$60,000
Cash Of $100,000	$ 60,000	60,000
Cash Of $160,000	Nil	60,000

Exercise Eighteen - 10

Subject: Transfers From Partner To Partnership (With Rollover)

Samantha Floren is one of three equal partners in the SFL Partnership. During the current year, Samantha transfers land to the partnership as a capital contribution. She had acquired the land several years ago for $156,000. At the time of transfer, it is valued at $263,000. She would like to use any available rollover provision in order to minimize her current taxes. Assuming the appropriate rollover provision is used, what are the tax consequences of this transfer?

SOLUTION available in print and online Study Guide.

Partnership Property Transferred To A New Partnership

18-113.   A partnership may be dissolved in a number of situations. Included would be the addition or retirement of partners in cases where the partnership agreement does not provide for the continuation of the partnership. The dissolution of a partnership is considered to be a disposition of partnership property and, in the absence of a rollover provision, would result in tax consequences to the partners. However, this treatment can be avoided if the partnership property is transferred to a new partnership.

18-114.   ITA 98(6) provides automatic (i.e., no election is required) rollover treatment where all of the property of a Canadian partnership that has ceased to exist is transferred to a new Canadian partnership. A further condition is that all of the members of the new partnership must have been members of the old partnership.

18-115.   While many rollover provisions provide tax free treatment by providing for a deemed disposition at the tax cost of the property, ITA 98(6) takes a different approach. This Subsection deems the old and new partnerships to be the same entity, with the result being that there is no disposition of the property and no tax consequences to the transferor. This means that the ITA 98(6) rollover involves fewer complications than would be found in most rollover applications.

18-116.   It is important to note that, while all of the members of the new partnership have to have been members of the old partnership, not all of the members of the old partnership have to become members of the new partnership. This rollover is typically used when a partner retires.

18-117.   The retirement of a partner usually involves distributing some of the partnership property to the retiring partner. This makes it impossible to fully comply with the requirement of ITA 98(6) that all of the property of the old partnership be transferred. This problem was resolved by IT-338R2, "Partnership Interests - Effects On Adjusted Cost Base Resulting From The Admission Or Retirement Of A Partner," which states that all of the property of the old partnership is considered to mean all the property after the settlement of a retired partner's interest. While IT-338R2 has been cancelled, it appears that the CRA continues to maintain this position.

Partnership Property Transferred To A Sole Proprietorship

18-118.   This rollover, provided for in ITA 98(5), applies automatically where a Canadian partnership ceases to exist and, within three months of the cessation date, one of the partners continues to carry on the partnership business as a sole proprietor. This rollover treatment is provided for partnership property distributed to the proprietor and, in general, ensures that there are no tax consequences associated with the disposition of that proprietor's partnership interest.

18-119.   There is an exception in situations where the tax cost of partnership property received by the proprietor exceeds the ACB of his or her partnership interest. In this case, there will be a capital gain. Alternatively, if the ACB of the proprietor's partnership interest exceeds the tax cost of partnership property received by the proprietor, the rules allow the tax cost of non-depreciable capital property to be increased to reflect this difference. You might wish to note that this is similar to the bump that is available in amalgamations and subsidiary wind-ups (see Chapter 17)

18-120. This rollover typically applies where one of the partners in a two-person partnership retires or dies, leaving the remaining person to continue the business. As a partnership must have at least two partners, there is no possibility of the partnership continuing. Note, however, that the rollover only applies to the partner who continues the business. A retiring partner will have a disposition at fair market value with the usual tax consequences associated with such a disposition.

Partnership Property Transferred To A Corporation

18-121. The decision to convert a partnership to a corporation, or to incorporate a partnership, generally arises when a partnership that has realized losses in its initial years becomes profitable. Prior to that time, the partnership form is useful as it allows the partners to use the partnership losses to offset their income from other sources. Once the partnership has become profitable, corporate status may be preferred because of the availability of the small business deduction, the possibility of deferring taxes on income retained within the corporation, or the desire to split income with other related persons.

18-122. The process of incorporating a partnership on a tax deferred basis generally requires two rollovers, ITA 85(2) and ITA 85(3). Under ITA 85(2), eligible partnership property is transferred to a taxable Canadian corporation for either shares or a combination of shares and other consideration. The transfer takes place at elected values, which can include the tax cost of the property, thereby avoiding tax consequences to the partnership. This rollover treatment is only available if the corporation and all the partners jointly elect rollover treatment.

18-123. At this point, the partnership is holding shares in the corporation and the partners are continuing to hold their partnership interests. ITA 85(3) then provides for a transfer at tax values of the partnership's holding of the corporation's shares to the partners in return for their partnership interests. This is accompanied by a wind-up of the partnership.

18-124. If the following conditions are met, the ITA 85(3) rollover treatment is automatic, with no election required:

- The partnership must have disposed of property to a taxable Canadian corporation under ITA 85(2).

- The partnership must be wound up within 60 days of the disposition of its property to the corporation.

- Immediately before the partnership is wound up, the only property it holds is money or property received from the corporation as a result of the application of ITA 85(2).

18-125. The winding-up of a partnership usually requires the distribution of all partnership property, the settlement of partnership obligations, as well as certain provincial formalities such as de-registration.

18-126. These rules are designed to provide a tax free means of incorporating a partnership. However, tax consequences may arise in two particular instances. First, ITA 85(2) only applies to "eligible property" as defined in ITA 85(1.1). The major item that would not be included in this definition would be an inventory of real property (i.e., real property held for sale rather than use). If such non-eligible property is transferred from a partnership to a corporation, the transfer will be at fair market value, resulting in the usual tax consequences.

18-127. A second situation in which the incorporation of a partnership may result in tax consequences would arise when a partner receives consideration in excess of the ACB of his or her partnership interest. While this may result in a capital gain, it can be avoided with the proper use of the ITA 85(3) rollover provision.

EXAMPLE   Danielle and Christine are equal partners in Flag Partnership. The recent success of the business has led to a decision to incorporate. The only asset Flag owns is an inventory of flags that cost $50,000 but is currently worth $200,000. The ACB of each partner's partnership interest is $34,000. The corporation will issue only common shares as consideration for the acquisition of the flag inventory.

ANALYSIS   Danielle, Christine, and the corporation will jointly elect to transfer the inventory from Flag Partnership at its tax cost of $50,000. Flag will be deemed to have disposed of the inventory for $50,000 and the corporation will be considered to have acquired the inventory for $50,000. No tax consequences will arise on the disposition. Flag Partnership will receive common shares of the corporation that will have an ACB and PUC of $50,000. At this point, Flag Partnership owns shares of the corporation and the corporation owns the inventory.

When Flag Partnership distributes the shares to Danielle and Christine, the following tax consequences will arise:

- Flag Partnership will be considered to have disposed of the shares for their tax cost of $50,000, resulting in no tax consequences.

- Each partner will be considered to have acquired the shares for an amount equal to the ACB of her partnership interest ($34,000).

- Each partner will be considered to have disposed of her partnership interest for the cost of the shares acquired from the partnership ($34,000). As a result, there is no capital gain or loss.

We suggest you work Self Study Problem Eighteen-8 at this point.

Specified Investment Flow Through Partnerships

18-128.   Because partnerships are not taxable entities, income is flowed through such structures without income taxes being assessed at the partnership level. As we shall see in Chapter 19, trusts are also "flow through" entities. That is, even though trusts are taxable entities for income tax purposes, if all of their income is distributed to beneficiaries, no taxes will be paid at the trust level.

18-129.   At one point in time, this flow through feature of partnerships and trusts resulted in the conversion of a large number of business entities into publicly traded partnerships and trusts. As the government viewed this development as a significant form of tax avoidance, legislation was put in place that designated most of these publicly traded entities as specified investment flow through partnerships and trusts (SIFTs). The legislation was such that it made SIFTs sufficiently unattractive that, with the exception of real estate investment trusts, they have largely disappeared. Given this, we do not provide coverage of this subject in *Canadian Tax Principles*, except in Chapter 7, "Income from Property", where we have limited coverage of real estate income trusts (REITs).

Additional Supplementary Self Study Problems Are Available Online.

Key Terms Used In This Chapter

18-130.   The following is a list of the key terms used in this Chapter. These terms, and their meanings, are compiled in the Glossary located at the back of the Study Guide.

At-Risk Amount	Limited Liability Partnership
At-Risk Rules	Limited Partner
Canadian Partnership	Limited Partnership
Co-Ownership	Limited Partnership Loss
Deeming Rule	"Negative" Adjusted Cost Base
General Partner	Partner
General Partnership	Partnership
Joint Tenancy	Partnership Interest
Joint Venture	Syndicates
Limited Liability	Tenancy In Common

References

18-131.   For more detailed study of the material in this Chapter, we refer you to the following:

ITA 40(3)	Negative ACB
ITA 53(1)(e)	Addition To Cost Base Of An Interest In A Partnership
ITA 53(2)(c)	Deduction From Cost Base Of An Interest In A Partnership
ITA 85(2)	Transfer Of Property To Corporation From Partnership
ITA 85(3)	Where Partnership Wound Up
ITA 96	General Rules (Partnerships And Their Members)
ITA 97	Contribution Of Property To Partnership
ITA 98	Disposition Of Partnership Property
ITA 99	Fiscal Period Of Terminated Partnership
ITA 100	Disposition Of An Interest in a Partnership
ITA 102	Definition Of "Canadian Partnership"
ITA 103	Agreement To Share Income
S4-F16-C1	What Is A Partnership?
IT-81R	Partnerships - Income Of Non-Resident Partners
IT-231R2	Partnerships - Partners Not Dealing At Arm's Length
IT-242R	Retired Partners
IT-278R2	Death Of A Partner Or Of A Retired Partner
IT-378R	Winding Up Of A Partnership
IT-413R	Election By Members Of A Partnership Under Subsection 97(2)
IT-457R	Election By Professionals To Exclude Work In Progress From Income
IT-471R	Merger Of Partnerships
T4068	Guide for the T5013 Partnership Information Return

Problems For Self Study (Online)

To provide practice in problem solving, there are Self Study and Supplementary Self Study problems available on MyLab Accounting.

Within the text we have provided an indication of when it would be appropriate to work each Self Study problem. The detailed solutions for Self Study problems can be found in the print and online Study Guide.

We provide the Supplementary Self Study problems for those who would like additional practice in problem solving. The detailed solutions for the Supplementary Self Study problems are available online, not in the Study Guide.

The .PDF file "Self Study Problems for Volume 2" on MyLab contains the following for Chapter 18:

- 8 Self Study problems,
- 4 Supplementary Self Study problems, and
- detailed solutions for the Supplementary Self Study problems.

Assignment Problems

(The solutions for these problems are only available in
the solutions manual that has been provided to your instructor.)

Assignment Problem Eighteen - 1
(Existence of a Partnership)

Sam and Sarah Block are spouses residing east of Ottawa, Ontario. They have been married for 15 years and have three children ages 6, 8, and 11. Sarah was an elementary school teacher before she met Sam and decided just before the birth of their first child that she would leave her teaching position, become a stay-at-home mom, and devote herself full time to the care of her children.

Sam has been a police officer with the Ottawa Police Service for the last 17 years and recently passed all of the tests to become a detective – a lifelong ambition. Unfortunately his role as a detective often results in irregular hours. With Sam being away on assignments and the children all in school, Sarah has found herself with a lot of time on her hands. To occupy her time she enrolled in pottery classes and discovered a creative side that she believed she could turn into a profitable business. Upon graduation Sarah spoke with Sam about converting a small building behind their home into a pottery shop. A contractor was hired in May 2019 and three weeks later the conversion was complete.

Sarah purchased the necessary equipment and materials necessary to begin creating her specialized pieces of vases, planters, bowls, and so on. Sarah hired a specialty firm to help develop a website and obtained an agreement from Pottery-is-us Inc., a national retailer, to display her pieces for sale. While sales were initially slow an interview with a national magazine and a local news network in August 2020 have resulted in an increased demand for her pieces from both inside and outside of the country. The increased demand has resulted in Sarah having to hire two graduates from the local pottery trade school. Sarah personally interviewed over 20 candidates for the positions before carefully making her decision.

Sarah was conversant in using accounting software to create books and records but did not possess the skills necessary to deal with the preparation of financial statements and the filing of tax returns, so she hired a local accountant.

Using a December 31 fiscal year end for the business the accountant determined that the business suffered a loss for income tax purposes of $87,300 for 2019 and another loss of $126,100 in 2020. The accountant explained that the losses were not unexpected given the accelerated CCA incentives and the fact that such businesses usually did not begin to make profits until the third or fourth year. The accountant added that projections indicated that there would be a profit in excess of $60,000 in 2021.

In early 2020, on learning that Sarah's business had generated losses in 2019 and, at that time, anticipated losses for 2020, Sam had asked whether he could use some of the losses against his own income to obtain an income tax refund. The accountant explained that it would only be possible if the business were considered a partnership with Sam being considered a partner, and then a portion of the losses could be allocated to him to use against his employment income. The accountant explained that as a sole proprietorship Sarah would be unable to use of the losses in 2019 or 2020, since she had no other income to apply it against.

In support of an argument that there was a partnership of which Sam was a member they told the accountant that they had registered the business in Ontario under the name "Sarah and Sam's Pottery" and that Sam had provided financing for the business plus by co-signing lines of credit. Sam added that their home and the building used for the business was jointly owned by the two of them, and that he participated in the business on occasion. The accountant agreed to file Sam and Sarah's income tax return on the basis that the business was a partnership and that Sam was a partner. After discussions with the accountant it was agreed that Sam would be entitled to an 80 percent interest and Sarah 20 percent.

Additional Information:

- Sam and Sarah have always had one joint bank account in which Sam's salary and Sarah's monthly child benefits have been deposited. The joint account is used for all family expenditures. Sarah deposited all pottery sales in this same account in 2019 and 2020, but on the advice of her accountant she plans to open a separate bank account for the business in 2021.

- All payments to the business are only made out to Sarah, although invoices are in the same of "Sarah and Sam's Pottery".

- Sarah obtained a credit card in her own name that she uses exclusively for the pottery business. Monthly payments are made from the family joint bank account.

- When the business began in 2019 Sam loaned Sarah $40,000 interest free from funds he had received as an inheritance when his mother passed away. Sam had deposited his inheritance in an investment account under his name. These funds were used to convert their backyard building. There is no written loan agreement between them. Sarah has been making monthly payments to Sam from the business sales, which Sam has been re-depositing to his investment account.

- When the business began, Sarah needed additional financing for working capital to acquire the necessary equipment and materials and pay ongoing expenses. Sarah obtained a commercial bank loan and a line of credit with a local bank. The bank, however, was unwilling to authorize the financing without Sam's signature since Sarah did not have any income of her own at the time. Sam co-signed the bank documents.

- Sarah communicates directly with suppliers, retailers, and makes all decisions concerning the development of new products and obtaining new customers, although she asks Sam for his advice on occasion.

- When at home Sam assists Sarah by answering the odd phone call and relaying messages to her. He also picks up supplies for her when she is too busy to do it herself and has taken on a bigger responsibility of watching the children when his schedule permits. Sam recently convinced Sarah to donate some of her pieces for a charitable auction for the Ottawa Police Foundation.

- Sarah and her employees signed up for advanced pottery classes in December 2020 that involve woodworking and ceramics. She was able to finance this education without anyone's involvement (including Sam) given increased sales.

- There is no written partnership agreement.

Required:

A. Do you agree with the decision to file Sam and Sarah's income tax returns on the basis that the pottery business is a partnership? Explain your reasons.

B. Assuming that a partnership does exist, do you believe that the 80/20 split is justified? Could the CRA challenge the 80/20 split between Sam and Sarah? Explain your reasons.

C. Had there been a written partnership agreement, would it have supported the existence of a partnership?

Assignment Problem Eighteen - 2
(Existence Of Partnership)

Mr. Poliacik joined Mr. Ewing's practice by entering into a business association with Mr. Ewing. They operated under the name "Ewing/Poliacik". Mr. Poliacik made no capital contribution on joining.

Both individuals were lawyers. Mr. Poliacik's specialty was litigation. Mr. Ewing was involved in non-litigation matters.

An agreement was signed, but it never referred to the individuals as partners or the association as a partnership. When asked why they did not refer to themselves as partners, Mr. Poliacik stated that they did not know each other well enough to accept the risks of partnership. The agreement stated that all fees billed by each individual belonged to that individual.

Both parties agreed to open a combined general and trust bank account. Both parties had signing authority on the general account, although Mr. Poliacik's authority was limited to client disbursements only. Mr. Ewing had sole signing authority on the trust account. The accounts did not indicate that they were registered to a partnership.

Mr. Poliacik's fees were to be split based on a graduated scale. The first $100,000 was to be split 50:50, then 60:40 on the next $25,000, 80:20 on the next $25,000, and 90:10 thereafter. The larger percentage went to Mr. Poliacik. In addition, Mr. Poliacik was entitled to 10 percent of fees billed by Mr. Ewing to clients introduced by Mr. Poliacik.

Mr. Ewing agreed to be 100 percent liable for office expenses and bookkeeping services. Mr. Poliacik's share of the office operating expenses was $62,500 in the first year. This amount would be adjusted in the future as the expenses increased. Mr. Poliacik was not entitled to the 10 percent finder's fee from Mr. Ewing until his share of the annual expenses had been paid.

Mr. Poliacik was responsible for making his own CPP contributions and maintaining professional insurance. He will register for GST as an individual, and his personal income tax return will not include a separate calculation of partnership income.

The combined business was not registered for GST purposes. There were no filings with the law society indicating that Mr. Poliacik and Mr. Ewing were partners.

Required: Determine whether the business association is a partnership.

Assignment Problem Eighteen - 3
(Partnership Vs. Joint Venture)

Chantale Bergeron is a real estate agent who had dreamed of becoming a real estate developer for a long time. In 2017, she received a substantial inheritance and purchased a tract of land with the intention of developing a group of residential lots. She paid $1,200,000 for the land, which she had secretly learned from contacts would soon be adjacent to a new highway exit.

As Chantale had spent her inheritance purchasing the land and had no track record in the development business, she had difficulty finding financing for the required $700,000 in site servicing costs. She finally located a developer, Elise Ltd., who was willing to provide the required $700,000 on an interest free basis in return for 40 percent of the profit resulting from the sale of the lots.

By December 31, 2020, it was estimated that the land's fair market value had increased to $2,000,000 because of the opening of the highway exit. During 2021, the sites are developed, with the servicing costs coming in at the estimated $700,000. All of the lots are sold prior to December 31, 2021, for total proceeds of $3,700,000.

Case A   On December 31, 2020, Chantale and Elise Ltd. enter into a joint venture agreement. Chantale transfers the land to Elise Ltd. At the end of 2021, Elise Ltd. provides Chantale with 60 percent of the profits resulting from the development and sale of the lots.

Case B   On December 31, 2020, Chantale and Elise Ltd. form a partnership to develop the lots. Chantale transfers the land to the partnership using the ITA 97(2) rollover provision to defer the gain on the transfer. The partnership agreement specifies that Chantale is entitled to all of the deferred gain on the land transfer at December 31, 2020, as well as 60 percent of the profits resulting from the sale of the lots.

Required:

A.   Calculate the amount that will be added to Chantale's Net Income For Tax Purposes in 2020 and 2021 for Case A and Case B and compare the results.

B.   Assume that the Case B approach is used. Calculate the adjusted cost base of the partnership interest for both Chantale and Elise Ltd. on December 31, 2021, and January 1, 2022.

Assignment Problem Eighteen - 4
(Partnership Income Allocation)

Saul and Samuel Brock are brothers and Chartered Public Accountants with significant experience in tax work. Until 2020, they have worked separately. However, they have decided that working together would produce synergies that would increase their aggregate income. Given this, as of January 1, 2020, they initiate the Brock and Brock Partnership.

Saul will be entitled to a salary of $72,000 per year, while Samuel's salary will be $48,000. In addition, Samuel will receive interest at 6 percent on his average capital balance for the year. All of these amounts were withdrawn from the partnership prior to December 31, 2020. Neither brother has Taxable Income that will be taxed federally at 33 percent in 2020.

The components of their partnership agreement dealing with income allocation are as follows:

Business Income   After the allocation of priority amounts for salaries and interest on capital contributions, any remaining business income will be allocated 60 percent to Saul and 40 percent to Samuel.

Capital Gains   As Samuel has contributed the majority of capital to the partnership, he will be entitled to all capital gains that are recognized by the partnership.

Dividends   Any dividends received by the partnership will be split equally between the two partners.

For the year ending December 31, 2020, their GAAP based financial statements indicate that they had net business income of $649,522. Other information related to this result is as follows:

- Salaries to Saul and Samuel of $120,000 ($72,000 + $48,000) were deducted.

- Interest on Samuel's capital contribution of $4,800 was deducted.

- Business meals of $18,976 were deducted.

- Amortization expense of $31,632 was deducted.

- Charitable contributions of $4,520 were deducted.

Other Information

1. For tax purposes, the brothers intend to deduct maximum CCA for 2020. This amount has been calculated to be $38,597.

2. The partnership has 2020 gains on the sale of shares held as temporary investments in the amount of $16,164.

3. The partnership receives $10,462 in eligible dividends during 2020.

4. The charitable contributions will be allocated equally between the two brothers.

Required:

A. Calculate the amounts of income from the partnership that would be included in the Net Income For Tax Purposes of each of the two brothers.

B. Indicate the amount of any federal tax credits that each of the two brothers would be entitled to as a result of allocations made by the partnership at December 31, 2020.

Assignment Problem Eighteen - 5
(Partnership Income And ACB)
On January 1, 2020, a partnership is formed between two divorce lawyers who have, for a number of years, practised individually. Each partner contributes $70,000.

During 2020, each partner is allocated a salary of $125,000, as well as interest on their beginning of the year capital balances at an annual rate of 5 percent. These amounts are withdrawn during the year. Any Net Business Income that remains after the priority allocations for salaries and interest will be split 50-50 by the two partners.

For the year ending December 31, 2020, their bookkeeper has prepared the following financial statements for the partnership. No amortization was deducted in preparing these statements.

Settlements Unlimited
Balance Sheet
As At December 31, 2020

Cash	$ 45,189
Accounts Receivable	186,485
Work In Progress	232,814
Furniture And Fixtures	56,581
Computer Hardware (At Cost)	17,608
Computer Applications Software (At Cost)	13,440
Total Assets	$ 552,117

Accounts Payable	$ 109,872
Initial Partner Capital	140,000
Income For The Period	302,245
Total Equities	$ 552,117

Settlements Unlimited
Income Statement
For The Year Ending December 31, 2020

Revenues	$682,946
Meals And Entertainment	$ 23,334
Office Supplies	12,382
Partners' Salaries	250,000
Interest On Capital Contributions	7,000
Rent	46,440
Salaries	41,545
Total Expenses	$380,701
Income For The Period (Accounting Values)	$302,245

The work in progress represents work done by the lawyers at their standard charge rate that has not been billed to clients at the year end.

Required:

A. The lawyers have come to you to determine the minimum amount that they must include in their 2020 tax returns as business income from the partnership.

B. Compute the ACB of each partner's partnership interest at December 31, 2020, and January 1, 2021.

Your answers should ignore GST and PST considerations.

Assignment Problem Eighteen - 6
(Partnership Income and Sale of a Partnership Interest)

Michael Masterson and Martin Minton were competitors providing heating and cooling products and services within the same geographical region near Edmonton, Alberta. An influx of workers to the nearby oil fields brought in increased competition, causing Michael and Martin to agree to join forces by forming a general partnership registered as the Double M Partnership. They have both contributed all of their business assets, including vehicles, tools, and equipment, which have become partnership property. In addition capital cash contributions were required to provide the partnership with much needed working capital.

The general partnership was established November 12, 2019, upon the signing of a formalized written partnership agreement. The agreement required an initial cash contribution from each partner of $125,000, which was made in December 2019. The agreement further provides that each partner can draw up to a maximum of $10,000 per month to meet personal needs and expenditures beginning January 1, 2020. Profit and loss allocations will be determined at the end of each year based upon a formula that considers the number of hours worked and fees invoiced. Any capital gains or capital losses realized will be allocated on a 50:50 basis unless the gain or loss is connected to a contribution of property to the partnership by a specific partner, in which case all of the gain or loss will be allocated to that partner. In addition any investment income or capital gains/losses realized on investments acquired by the partnership with surplus cash will be allocated equally. Finally, any charitable donations made by the partnership will also be allocated equally.

The partnership operates through leased business premises where the employees and partners carry out the day to day management and administration of the business. The partnership fiscal period year end is December 31.

The partnership's 2020 Income Statement, prepared in accordance with generally accepted accounting principles, is as follows:

Income Statement
Double M Partnership Year
Ending December 31, 2020

Revenues		$991,600
Operating Expenses:		
Lease Of Business Premises	($84,000)	
Inventory And Supplies	(275,000)	
Amortization Expense (Note 1)	(31,300)	
General Office Costs	(27,000)	
Meals And Entertainment	(19,100)	
Charitable Donations	(10,000)	
Interest On Partner Loan	(7,000)	
Vehicle Operating Costs	(41,000)	
Partner Home Office Costs	(30,000)	
Office Salaries	(88,600)	(613,000)
Operating Income		$378,600
Other Income:		
Capital Gains (Note 2)	$22,200	
Non-Eligible Dividends Received From		
Private Company investment	13,000	35,200
Net Income		$413,800

Note 1 Maximum CCA for 2020 is $17,400.

Note 2 In 2020 the partnership realized a capital gain of $13,300 from partnership property contributed by Martin and a second capital gain of $8,900 from the sale of some of the share investment. None of the capital gains are eligible for the capital gains deduction.

During 2020, Michael's only income was from the partnership and his only federal tax credit, other than those allocated from or attributable to the partnership, is the basic personal credit.

On January 1, 2021, Michael sells his interest in the partnership to an arm's length individual for $875,000. Selling costs related to the sale are $7,400. Assume that the ACB of his partnership interest on January 1, 2020, is $222,160.

Additional Information:

A. At December 31, 2020, the partnership accountant determines that Michael worked more hours and invoiced more than Martin. The result is that Michael will be allocated 58.7 percent of any business income or loss while Martin will be allocated the remaining 41.3 percent.

B. In February 2020 the partnership used some surplus cash to acquire share investments in a large private corporation that manufactures the type of furnaces that the partnership installs and services. The partnership received $13,000 in non-eligible dividends and $4,200 in capital dividends from that investment in December 2020.

C. Both Martin and Michael have offices in their homes to prepare and accumulate monthly paperwork before bringing the documents and summaries to their business premises. The partnership pays them each $1,250 per month for the use of that office space and those amounts are deducted by the partnership in determining its business income.

D. In late December 2019 Michael and Martin met with their accountant to discuss working capital requirements. The accountant advised that they could use an additional $200,000. Michael agreed to loan that amount to the partnership at 3.5 percent interest, which is paid monthly. There is a written loan agreement that only requires the monthly payment of interest with no principal payments until January 2022.

E. Neither Michael nor Martin made any capital contributions to the partnership in 2020.

F. Each of Michael and Martin withdrew the maximum monthly amount of $10,000 in every month of 2020.

G. The partnership made a donation of $10,000 to the local food bank in May 2020. The food bank is a registered charitable organization for federal income tax purposes.

Required:

1. Determine Michael's Net Income, Taxable Income and federal Tax Payable for 2020. You will have to reconcile the accounting based income to Income for tax purposes and then allocate each source of partnership income for tax purposes to him.

2. Determine the tax consequences of the sale of Michael's partnership interest in 2021. You will have to provide a detailed breakdown of the ACB of his partnership interest beginning with the January 1, 2020, balance of $222,160. Show all supporting calculations.

Assignment Problem Eighteen - 7
(Withdrawal Of A Partner)

Tammy, Loretta, and Crystal formed a partnership on January 1, 2018. The partnership is organized to provide a variety of consulting services to a broad range of clients. Each partner makes an initial capital contribution of $270,000. The partners agree to use a December 31 year end.

The partnership agreement contains the following provisions with respect to the allocation of items to individual partners:

1. Both net business income and charitable contributions will be shared equally by the three partners.

2. Any capital gains realized by the partnership will be allocated on a 50-50 basis to Crystal and Loretta.

3. All of the eligible dividends received by the partnership will be allocated to Tammy.

During the period January 1, 2018, through December 31, 2020, the partnership operates successfully. The following information relates to that period:

*   The partnership earned net business income of $315,000.

*   Amounts not included in the net business income figure were as follows:

    *   The partnership received eligible dividends totaling $6,300.
    *   The partnership realized a $24,800 capital gain.
    *   The partnership made charitable donations only in 2020. The total amount involved was $9,900.

*   Withdrawals from the partnership were as follows:

    *   Tammy - $149,000
    *   Crystal - $306,000
    *   Loretta - $72,000

*   Additional capital was required to expand the operations of the office and, as a consequence, each partner contributed an additional $104,000 in cash.

Near the end of 2020, after a number of heated arguments between Tammy and Crystal regarding the types of clients the partnership was servicing, Loretta decides to withdraw from the partnership effective January 1, 2021. After some negotiations, each of the other partners agree to pay her $210,000 in cash for one-half of her interest in the partnership, a total of $420,000. The payments are made on February 1, 2021. The partnership has net business income of $27,600 during January 2021.

Loretta incurred legal and accounting fees in conjunction with this withdrawal transaction totaling $2,300.

Required:

A. Calculate the adjusted cost base of Loretta's partnership interest as of January 1, 2021.

B. Determine the amount of Loretta's gain or loss on the disposition of her partnership interest. Explain how this amount, and any other amounts related to the partnership, will be taxed in her hands during 2021.

C. Indicate how the adjusted cost base of each partner's interest will be affected by the withdrawal of Loretta from the partnership.

Assignment Problem Eighteen - 8
(Limited Partnerships – ACB, The At-Risk Amount, And Limited Partnership Losses)
In mid-December 2019 Rebecca Richardson is approached by her investment advisor with an opportunity to invest in a lucrative limited partnership that will be created in early January 2020. Rebecca has always been willing to invest in somewhat riskier ventures, and she is intrigued by this particular opportunity. After a careful review and discussions with her advisors she agrees to participate and acquires 12.0 limited partnership units of the Junction Enterprises LP that will be created under the *Limited Partnership Act* of Manitoba. The limited partnership fiscal year end will be December 31, and only 400 units will be issued and sold. Each unit will entitle the limited partner unitholder to one quarter of 1 percent of any income or loss of the limited partnership.

The terms of the limited partnership offer and agreement require a minimum purchase of two units with a maximum of twelve units for newly admitted limited partners. The per unit purchase price will be $24,000 and will require a cash down payment of 10 percent by each unitholder with the remaining amount financed by the general partner at 6.75 percent annual interest. On the last business day of December 2020, 2021, and 2022, one-third of the principal amount of the financing must be repaid. Finally, each unitholder is personally responsible to pay an annual administration fee to the general partner based on the number of units held.

In addition, to encourage unitholders to remain with the limited partnership for at least three years, the general partner agrees to repurchase all of a limited partners' units at 8 percent of the purchase price if this option is chosen within the 2020 calendar year; 16 percent for 2021; and 24 percent for 2022 and subsequent years.

Rebecca purchases the maximum 12 limited partnership units on January 18, 2020, at $24,000 each for a total price of $288,000. This number of units entitles her to 3.0 percent [(12 units) (.0025)] of any income or losses of Junction Enterprises LP. She pays 10 percent of the purchase price of $28,800 and finances the remaining amount of $259,200 through the required financing provided by the general partner.

Junction Enterprises LP earns the following income and realizes the following losses:

- 2020 business loss of $2,000,000 and eligible dividends of $118,000

- 2021 business loss of $4,400,000 and eligible dividends of $104,000

- 2022 business loss of $1,700,000 and eligible dividends of $129,000

Assume that Rebecca will remain a limited partner until 2024. Also assume that she has sufficient other sources of income to fully utilize any deductible losses allocated to her by the limited partnership including any deductible limited partnership loss carryovers.

Required: For each of 2020, 2021, and 2022, calculate the following amounts related to Rebecca's limited partnership interest in Junction Enterprises LP:

- The adjusted cost base at the beginning of each year.

- The at-risk amount at the end of each year.

- The limited partnership income or loss for each year.

- The deductible annual partnership loss and limited partnership loss for each year.

- The limited partnership loss carry forward balance at the end of each year.

In addition, calculate the ACB of the partnership interest for January 1, 2023.

Assignment Problem Eighteen - 9
(Partnership Winding-Up And Transfer To Corporation)

The Jones, Haggard, and Twitty Partnership was formed several years ago by Conway Jones, George Haggard, and Merle Twitty. To establish the partnership, each of the individuals invested $450,000 in cash. They prepared a standard partnership agreement which indicated that all income and losses would be shared on an equal basis. The partnership has a December 31 taxation year.

On January 1, 2020, the adjusted cost base of the three partnership interests are as follows:

Conway Jones	$ 880,000
George Haggard	698,000
Merle Twitty	567,000
Total	$ 2,145,000

The total tax cost of the partnership assets is $2,145,000, the same amount as the adjusted cost base of the partnership interests. On January 2, 2020, the net assets of the partnership are transferred to a corporation using the provisions of ITA 85(2). The elected values are equal to the tax costs of the individual assets and liabilities.

Through the use of an appraiser, it has been established that the fair market value of the partnership is $2,925,000. Using this value, the corporation provides the following consideration to the partnership:

Cash	$ 900,000
Preferred Shares (At Fair Market Value)	675,000
Common Shares (At Fair Market Value)	1,350,000
Total Consideration	$ 2,925,000

The partnership will be liquidated within 60 days of the ITA 85(2) rollover, and property received from the corporation by the partnership will be transferred to the three partners in accordance with ITA 85(3). Under the terms of the partnership agreement, they receive the following amounts:

	Jones	Haggard	Twitty	Total
Cash	$ 465,000	$283,000	$152,000	$ 900,000
Preferred Shares	225,000	225,000	225,000	675,000
Common Shares	450,000	450,000	450,000	1,350,000
Total	$1,140,000	$958,000	$827,000	$2,925,000

Required:

A. Determine the adjusted cost base of each of the assets received by the partners as a result of the transfer of partnership assets to the corporation.

B. Calculate the capital gain or loss for each partner resulting from the transfer of the consideration received by the partnership to the partners in return for the partnership interest.

Assignment Problem Eighteen - 10
(Additional Business Income)

Note This problem involves knowledge of "additional business income" when the election of a non-calendar fiscal period is made. This material is covered in Chapter 6 of the text.

On April 1, 2017, Craig Cardinal and Don Kvill formed a partnership to teach small craft flying lessons. They elected to use a March 31 fiscal year end, to coincide with the end of the winter aircraft maintenance program and the beginning of the summer training schedule. The two partners share equally in the profits of the partnership.

In the partnership income calculation for their 2018 tax returns, the "additional business income" was calculated to be $42,200. During the year ending March 31, 2019, the partnership earned Taxable Income of $64,000 and the partners withdrew $26,000 each.

From April 1, 2019, to March 31, 2020, the partnership earned Taxable Income of $58,000 and the partners withdrew $20,000 each.

Required: Determine the minimum amount of partnership income that Craig Cardinal and Don Kvill will have to include in their personal tax returns for the years 2019 and 2020.

CHAPTER 19

Trusts And Estate Planning

Introduction

19-1.   As is noted in Chapter 1, the *Income Tax Act* recognizes three groups of taxpayers: individuals, corporations, and trusts. In previous Chapters we have given detailed consideration to the determination of Taxable Income and Tax Payable for both individuals and corporations. In this Chapter, we will turn our attention to how this process works in the case of trusts.

19-2.   Also in Chapter 1, we provide a brief introduction to tax planning, providing general descriptions of tax avoidance, tax deferral, and income splitting. In this Chapter we will find that trusts are one of the most powerful weapons in the tax planner's arsenal. They can provide a convenient and cost effective mechanism for splitting large amounts of property income among family members. Trusts can also be used to access the deferral and income splitting opportunities that are present in estate freeze transactions. In addition, they can play a significant role in many other tax and business planning arrangements.

19-3.   While trusts remain a very powerful tax planning tool, changes in 2016 greatly reduced their effectiveness in estate planning when they eliminated graduated rates for most testamentary trusts.

19-4.   A further problem is that dealing with trusts requires an understanding of many legal issues that cannot be handled effectively by tax advisors alone. Further, legal advice in the area of trusts can be very expensive, with charges of $500 per hour or more being common for expert advice. When combined with an accountant's fees (which can vary greatly depending on the accountant), the costs to create and maintain a trust can be prohibitive. Since normally the settlor (creator) of a trust doesn't personally benefit financially from creating a trust, this makes the high cost of a trust even less acceptable to the settlor.

19-5.   We have previously encountered trusts in this text. In Chapter 7, which deals with property income, we indicated that most mutual funds are organized as trusts. Also in that Chapter, we noted the use of real estate investment trusts (REITs). In Chapter 10, when we considered various types of retirement savings arrangements, we noted that most of these arrangements involve the use of trusts. Registered Pension Plans, Registered Retirement Savings Plans, Registered Retirement Income Funds, and Deferred Profit Sharing Plans, all involve assets being contributed to a trust.

Figure 19 - 1   Personal Trust Participants

Settlor →(Property)→ Trustee(s) →(Benefits)→ Beneficiaries

19-6.   In this Chapter, we will not revisit the types of trusts that were considered in earlier Chapters. Rather, our focus in this Chapter will be on personal trusts that have been established by individuals as a part of a tax or estate planning scenario. This will include both trusts established during the lifetime of an individual, as well as trusts that arise as a consequence of the death of an individual. While trusts can be very important in tax planning arrangements that involve private corporations, we will not deal with this subject. The complexities involved in such arrangements go beyond the scope of this text.

19-7.   In our material in this Chapter on estate planning we will give specific attention to the use of trusts. In addition, due to the importance of this subject, we will expand our coverage of estate planning to issues that go beyond the use of trusts. Particular attention will be given to general coverage of estate freeze transactions.

Basic Concepts

What Is A Trust?

Legal Perspective

19-8.   From a legal perspective, a personal trust is a relationship that arises when a settlor transfers property to a trustee to hold and administer for the exclusive benefit of the beneficiaries. This relationship is depicted in Figure 19-1.

19-9.   The settlor is the person who sets up the trust and makes the initial transfer of property to the trustee. The trustee is the individual or institution that holds formal legal title to that property, while the beneficiaries are persons who will benefit from the property that is held by the trustee. The beneficiaries can have an interest in the income from the property, the capital value of the property, or both.

19-10.   While each of these roles is separate in terms of its function in the trust arrangement, it is possible for more than one of the roles to be played by a single individual. A common example of this would be a father who is the settlor of a trust in favour of his children, but also serves as one of the trustees who holds the trust assets.

19-11.   A basic feature of trust arrangements is the separation of the legal and beneficial ownership of the transferred property. Outside of trust arrangements, the legal owner of a property is normally entitled to any benefits associated with owning the property. This is not the case here. While the trustee holds legal title to the property, all of the benefits will accrue to the persons who are specified as the beneficiaries of the trust.

19-12.   A trust is not, from a legal perspective, a separate entity. A trust cannot own property, cannot enter into contracts, and cannot be a defendant or plaintiff in a legal action. With respect to the transferred property, these rights and obligations belong to the trustee(s). We would note that you should not confuse trusts with a "trust company". Trust companies are, in fact, separate legal entities that are involved in the management of trusts.

19-13.   Trusts are subject to provincial legislation and, as a consequence, the detailed rules will vary from province to province. One point to note, however, is that it is generally difficult to vary or revoke a trust. This is of particular importance in the case of deceased individuals. While the content of a will can be challenged by a disgruntled beneficiary and its intentions altered by a surviving spouse, this is a much more difficult process when assets are placed in a trust.

Tax Perspective

19-14.   Consistent with the legal perspective of trusts, the T4013 *Trust Guide* defines a trust as a binding obligation enforceable by law when undertaken. This definition also notes that it may be created by a person (either verbally or in writing), a court order, or by a statute.

19-15.   While trusts do not exist as a legal entity separate from the trustees, income tax legislation does, in fact, treat trusts as a separate taxable entity, resulting in the need to file a separate tax return (T3) for each trust. This is established in the *Income Tax Act* as follows:

> **ITA 104(2)**   A trust shall, for the purposes of this Act, and without affecting the liability of the trustee or legal representative for that person's own income tax, be deemed to be in respect of the trust property an individual, ...

19-16.   This provision means that, in general, a trust will be taxed in a similar manner as individuals. However, there are numerous special rules applicable to these entities. For example, most trusts cannot use the graduated rates (15 percent to 33 percent) that are available to individuals. However, each trust will have to determine a Net Income For Tax Purposes, a Taxable Income, and calculate a separate Tax Payable.

Trusts And Estates

19-17.   When an individual dies, there is a deemed disposition of all of his or her capital property. Property will be deemed to have been acquired at its fair market value on the date of death by various entities as per his or her will or, if there is no will, under the terms of provincial interstate succession legislation. As discussed in Chapter 9, this deemed disposition will often have significant consequences on the calculation of Tax Payable in the final tax return of the decedent (i.e., deceased individual).

19-18.   In this context, dictionaries define the term "estate" as the property of a deceased individual. This meaning is very clearly a reference to all of the property of the deceased individual and this, in effect, means that an individual can only have one estate.

19-19.   In the great majority of cases, the estate property will pass to a beneficiary or beneficiaries immediately and will not require much attention from either tax advisors or lawyers. For example, Mom dies, leaving all of her property, which consists of a savings account and a principal residence, both of which are jointly held with Dad, to Dad. We do not need to give any attention to this type of situation.

19-20.   However, some estates, particularly those of wealthier Canadians, can have many different types of property. This can include publicly traded securities, shares of private companies, rental properties, business assets, and foreign investments. In such cases, there may be a considerable period of time between the date on which the individual dies and the date on which all the assets, or the proceeds from the disposition from the assets, is transferred to his or her beneficiaries. During this period, the estate assets, which are being administered by an executor, can produce income. When this happens, the executor of the estate will have to file a T3 return that includes this income.

19-21.   As reflected in the following provision, the *Income Tax Act* has traditionally viewed the terms estate and trust as pretty much interchangeable:

> **ITA 104(1)**   In this Act, a reference to a trust or estate (in this subdivision referred to as a "trust") shall, ...

19-22.   As long as testamentary trusts were able to use graduated rates in determining their Tax Payable, using the two terms interchangeably did not present a problem. While deciding to tax the income of testamentary trusts in general at the maximum rate, the government also concluded that it would be appropriate to continue the use of graduated rates for income that accrues during the period of time that the estate assets have not yet been distributed.

19-23.   To implement this latter goal, the government introduced the concept of a graduated rate estate (GRE). While we will give more attention to this concept at a later point in this Chapter, you should be aware that GREs can only be used for assets that are still held in the estate and administered by an executor prior to their distribution to beneficiaries.

Establishing A Trust

Three Certainties

19-24.   The trusts that we are dealing with in this Chapter are established by words that are set out in a trust agreement. While some provinces allow, under limited circumstances, the use of oral trust agreements, this is rarely a wise course of action. Even if such agreements are accepted for legal purposes, the CRA tends to be skeptical of such agreements and may take the position that no trust exists.

19-25.   In deciding whether or not a trust has, in fact, been created, it is important to look at what the courts have referred to as the three certainties. These can be described as follows:

Certainty Of Intention   The person creating the trust must intend to create the trust and that intention must be clear to outside observers. This is usually accomplished by preparing a written document establishing the trust.

Certainty Of Property   The property that is to be held in the trust must be known with certainty at the time the trust is created. This is usually accomplished by specifying the property in the trust document.

Certainty Of Beneficiaries   The persons who will benefit from the trust property must be known with certainty at the time the trust is created. This is usually accomplished by specifying these persons in the trust document. Note that these persons must either be named as persons (e.g., Ms. Sally Phar) or be part of an identifiable class (e.g., my children). When a class designation is used, it must refer to a clearly identifiable group of persons. For example, designating "friends" as beneficiaries would not create an identifiable group.

19-26.   In addition to establishing the facts required by the three certainties criteria, there must be an actual transfer of the trust property to the trustee. Until this transfer is completed, the trust does not exist.

Importance Of Proper Documentation

19-27.   Care must be taken to ensure that all of the necessary actions to create a trust have been carried out effectively. If one or more of the required elements is missing, the tax consequences can be significant. For example, if an individual attempted to establish a trust to split income with his adult children, a failure to complete all of the requirements necessary to that process could result in his being taxed on the income, rather than having it taxed in the hands of his adult children. This could result in the payment of a significant amount of additional tax.

Exercise Nineteen - 1

Subject: Establishing A Trust

In each of the following Cases, an individual is attempting to establish a trust. For each of these Cases, indicate whether the attempt has been successful. Explain your conclusion.

Case A   Jack Black sends a cheque to his sister to be used for the education of her two children.

Case B   Jane Folsem transfers property to a trustee, specifying that the income from the property should be distributed to her friends.

Case C   Robert Jones transfers property to a trustee, specifying that the income from the property should be distributed to his children.

Case D   Suzanne Bush has signed an agreement that specifies that she will transfer her securities portfolio to a trustee, with the income to be distributed to her spouse.

SOLUTION available in print and online Study Guide.

Returns And Payments - Trusts

19-28.   Because they are considered by the government to be taxable entities, trusts must file tax returns. As discussed in Chapter 2, "Procedures and Administration", the trust tax return (T3 return) must be filed within 90 days of a trust's year end. With respect to the payment of taxes, the Tax Payable on trust income is due no later than 90 days after a trust's year end. We also noted in Chapter 2 that, while there is a legislative requirement that most trusts make instalment payments, administratively, the CRA does not assess interest or penalties on later payments.

19-29.   With respect to penalties and interest related to late filing or late payment of taxes, the rules for trusts are the same as those that are applicable to individuals.

Non-Tax Reasons For Using Trusts

19-30.   In this Chapter we are largely concerned with the tax planning uses of trusts. However, it is important to note that trusts have non-tax uses that, in some situations, may be more important than the tax features of the particular arrangement. Some of these non-tax uses are as follows:

Administration Of Assets   A trust can be used to separate the administration of assets from the receipt of benefits. For example, an individual with extensive investment knowledge might have assets transferred to a trust for his spouse at the time of his death. The goal here could be to provide professional management of the assets for the benefit of a spouse with only limited knowledge of investments.

Protection From Creditors   An individual proprietor of a business might place some of her personal assets in a trust in order to protect them from claims by the creditors of the business. However, if this transfer is made when the individual is experiencing financial difficulties with her business, there are provisions in bankruptcy and other legislation that may undo the transfer.

Privacy   If assets are bequeathed in a will, they will be subject to probate, the results of which are available to the public. This is not the case with assets that are in a trust when an individual dies.

Avoiding Changes In Beneficiaries   If a father places assets in a trust for the benefit of his minor children, it ensures that these children will be the ultimate beneficiaries of the property. In contrast, if, as is common, his will bequeaths his assets to his wife with the intention that his children will be the ultimate beneficiaries of his property, his wife has no legal obligation to carry out this intention. This can be a particularly important issue if the surviving spouse remarries and other children become part of her family.

19-31.   While there are additional examples of non-tax uses of trusts, the preceding should serve to give you some idea of the versatility of trust arrangements.

Classification Of Trusts

Introduction

19-32.   The CRA's *Trust Guide* lists 32 different types of trusts, largely based on definitions that are included in the *Income Tax Act*. Understanding the meaning of the terms on this CRA list is complicated by the fact that some of the listed items are, in fact, a subclassification of other items included on the list (e.g., an alter ego trust is a type of personal trust). A further roadblock to understanding the classification of trusts is that trusts are also classified in popular usage in terms of their goals or objectives. Such terms as "family trusts" and "spendthrift trusts" are commonly used, despite the fact that they have no real meaning in terms of tax legislation.

19-33.   In this material, we will not provide a comprehensive classification of trusts, nor will we attempt to provide definitions for all of the terms that are applied to trusts in tax legislation and general practice. As indicated in the introduction to this Chapter, our coverage is limited to trusts that have been established by individuals as part of a tax or estate planning scenario. As all of these trusts fall within the classification of personal trusts, we will begin by considering this category.

Personal Trusts

General Definition

19-34.   The *Income Tax Act* contains the following definition of a personal trust:

> **ITA 248(1)   Personal Trust** means
>
> (a) a graduated rate estate, or
>
> (b) a trust in which no beneficial interest was acquired for consideration payable directly or indirectly to
>
> > (i) the trust, or
> > (ii) any person or partnership that has made a contribution to the trust by way of transfer, assignment or other disposition of property;

19-35.   The basic idea here is that a personal trust is one that was not acquired for consideration paid to the trust or to any person that has contributed to the trust. An exception is made for graduated rate estates. Prior to 2016, this exception applied to all testamentary trusts.

19-36.   The importance of this inclusion for graduated rate estates is that personal trusts can pay taxes on income amounts received by the trust at the trust level. The after tax amounts can then be distributed on a tax free basis to the beneficiaries of the trust.

Testamentary Vs. Inter Vivos Trusts

19-37.   All personal trusts can be classified as either testamentary or inter vivos. With respect to testamentary trusts, they are defined as follows:

> **ITA 108(1)   Testamentary Trust** in a taxation year means a trust that arose on and as a consequence of the death of an individual, other than ...

19-38.   This same Subsection of the *Income Tax Act* provides a related definition of an inter vivos trust:

> **ITA 108(1)   Inter Vivos Trust** means a trust other than a testamentary trust.

19-39.   Within each of these classifications, there are various subclassifications. In this Chapter, we will deal with three types of testamentary trusts and four types of inter vivos trusts. The types that we will cover are outlined in Figure 19-2.

Figure 19 - 2 Classification Of Personal Trusts	
Testamentary	**Inter Vivos**
Graduated Rate Estate	Spousal Or Common-Law Partner
Spousal Or Common-Law Partner	Alter Ego
Other Beneficiaries Joint	Joint Spousal Or Common-Law Partner
	Family

Testamentary Trusts

Graduated Rate Estate

19-40.   Prior to 2016, testamentary trusts enjoyed a number of special rules that were not available to inter vivos trusts, such as:

- The ability to calculate Tax Payable using the graduated rate schedule that is available to individuals, rather than having Tax Payable calculated using the maximum rate on all income.
- The ability to use a non-calendar fiscal period.
- Classification as a personal trust without regard to the circumstances in which the beneficial interest was acquired.
- Exemption from the requirement to make instalment payments.
- Use of the $40,000 exemption in calculating alternative minimum tax.
- Extended periods for refunds, reassessment, and filing of objections.
- The ability to make investment tax credits available to their beneficiaries for computing their Tax Payable.

19-41.   The government concluded that these provisions were, in many situations, overly generous. Reflecting this view, as of January 1, 2016, these special rules are no longer generally available for testamentary trusts.

19-42.   An exception to this is the graduated rate estate (GRE). These are defined in ITA 248(1) as follows:

> **ITA 248(1)   graduated rate estate,** of an individual at any time, means the estate that arose on and as a consequence of the individual's death if
>
> (a)   that time is no more than 36 months after the death,
> (b)   the estate is at that time a testamentary trust,
> (c)   the individual's Social Insurance Number (or if the individual had not, before the death, been assigned a Social Insurance Number, such other information as is acceptable to the Minister) is provided in the estate's return of income under Part I for the taxation year that includes that time and for each of its earlier taxation years that ended after 2015,
> (d)   the estate designates itself as the graduated rate estate of the individual in its return of income under Part I for its first taxation year that ends after 2015, and
> (e)   no other estate designates itself as the graduated rate estate of the individual in a return of income under Part I for a taxation year that ends after 2015;

19-43.   While it is not perfectly clear from this definition, a GRE is only applicable to estate assets that have not been transferred to a beneficiary, either individual beneficiaries or testamentary trust beneficiaries. Stated alternatively, only if the estate has assets that are still under the administration of an executor can it be designated as a GRE.

> **EXAMPLE 1**   Gary Crotty dies on November 1, 2020. His estate (all of his property at death) consists entirely of publicly traded securities that are, under the terms of his will, immediately transferred to a spousal trust.

> **ANALYSIS - Example 1**   No GRE can be designated in this case because none of the decedent's assets remain under the administration of his executor.

> **EXAMPLE 2**   Lizabeth Jerrard dies on November 1, 2020. Her will requires that all of her estate be transferred to a spousal trust. Her estate consists of a large number of investments in real estate and CCPC shares, some of which will take considerable time to dispose of or transfer. As of December 31, 2023, some of the estate assets are still under the administration of the executor.

> **ANALYSIS - Example 2**   The executor will be required to file a T3 for the income accruing on these assets. In the first return, which can have a year end no later than October 31, 2021, the estate can be designated a GRE. As long as the estate assets remain under the administration of the executor, this designation can be used in the T3s filed within 36 months of her death.

> On December 31, 2023, even if there are still undistributed estate assets, there will be a deemed year end. In that return and any subsequent to that date, the estate will be taxed as an ordinary testamentary trust, with all of its income subject to the maximum 33 percent

rate. Note that, if the required transfer of all assets to the spousal trust had occurred prior to November 1, 2023, the estate would have lost its GRE status at that date.

19-44.   Two points are relevant here:

- Because GREs are included in the definition of a personal trust, its income can be taxed in the trust. The GRE can then distribute the after tax amounts to income beneficiaries on a tax free basis.

- If some of an estate's assets are distributed to beneficiaries, the portion that remains under the administration of an executor can be designated as a GRE.

Spousal Or Common-Law Partner Trust

19-45.   This category of trust is not defined in the *Income Tax Act*. Rather, it is a term that is used when a trust is established for a spouse or common-law partner. As shown in Figure 19-2, such trusts can either be an inter vivos trust established by a living person or, alternatively, a testamentary trust that is established when an individual dies. A spousal or common-law partner testamentary trust can never be designated a graduated rate estate.

19-46.   As will be discussed when we present material on the taxation of trusts, if a trust meets certain conditions, the *Income Tax Act* allows a settlor to transfer property into a trust without incurring any taxation on the property dispositions. The relevant rollover provisions are found in ITA 73(1.01) for inter vivos trusts and in ITA 70(6) for testamentary trusts. When these provisions are used, the resulting trust is usually referred to as a qualifying spousal or qualifying common-law partner trust.

Other Beneficiaries

19-47.   Although listed in Figure 19-2 as a type of trust, it represents a testamentary trust that is not a spousal or common-law partner trust. Common other beneficiaries would be the decedent's children or other close relatives of the decedent. Such trusts can never be designated a graduated rate estate.

Inter Vivos Trusts

Spousal Or Common-Law Partner Trust

19-48.   As noted in Paragraph 19-45, spousal or common-law partner trusts can be established as testamentary trusts on the death of the settlor or, alternatively, as inter vivos trusts by a living individual.

Alter Ego Trust

19-49.   An alter ego trust is an inter vivos trust created by an individual who is 65 years of age or older with him or herself as the sole beneficiary during his or her lifetime. As was the case with spousal or common-law partner trusts, if certain conditions are met, the *Income Tax Act* contains a rollover provision that allows property to be transferred into or out of the trust on a tax free basis.

Joint Spousal Or Common-Law Partner Trust

19-50.   A joint spousal or joint common-law partner trust is an inter vivos trust created by an individual who is 65 years of age or older. Similar to the alter ego trust, this type of trust is created with the individual and his or her spouse or common-law partner as the sole beneficiaries during their lifetimes. Also similar to the alter ego trust scenario, if certain conditions are met, there is a rollover provision in the *Income Tax Act* that allows property to be transferred into the trust on a tax free basis.

Family Trust

19-51.   While the term family trust is not always used in a consistent manner, it generally refers to a trust that has been established by an individual for the benefit of family members. While a family trust could be a testamentary trust, the term is usually used in reference to an inter vivos trust. The most common goal of this type of trust is income splitting. We would note that the extension of the TOSI to related adults has placed significant constraints on using trusts for this purpose.

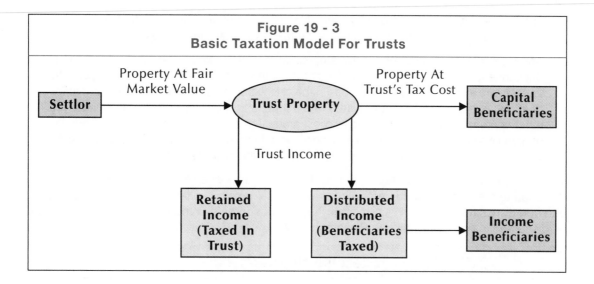

Figure 19 - 3
Basic Taxation Model For Trusts

Taxation Of Trusts

Taxation Year

19-52.   Inter vivos trusts have always been required to use the calendar year as their taxation year. In contrast, prior to 2016, testamentary trusts were allowed to use a non-calendar fiscal year. As of 2016, testamentary trusts have, in general, lost this right.

19-53.   The exception to this is graduated rate estates (GREs). As long as estate assets are under the administration of an executor and have not been distributed to beneficiaries, GREs can use a non-calendar fiscal period for up to 36 months subsequent to the decedent's date of death.

The Basic Taxation Model

19-54.   While there are many variations that depend on the particular type of trust we are dealing with, as well as complications associated with the measurement of trust Taxable Income and Tax Payable, the basic model for the taxation of trusts is as shown in Figure 19-3. There are three features of this basic model that should be noted:

Settlor's Transfer Of Property To The Trust   When property is transferred to a trust by a settlor, it generally results in a disposition for tax purposes. In the usual situation, these dispositions are deemed to occur at fair market value, triggering various tax consequences (e.g., capital gains, recapture, or terminal losses). There are, however, some important rollover provisions for property transferred into a trust. These are discussed beginning in Paragraph 19-56.

Transfers Of Trust Property To Beneficiaries   If trust property is transferred to a capital beneficiary, ITA 107(2) provides a rollover provision that allows the property to be transferred at the tax cost to the trust. The proceeds of disposition to the trust and the cost to the beneficiary will be equal to the tax cost that is recorded in the trust. For exceptions to this general provision, see Rollovers To Beneficiaries beginning in Paragraph 19-69.

Income From The Trust Property   Once property has been transferred to the trust, income will begin to accrue to the trust. It is fundamental to most of the tax planning uses of trusts that income earned in the trust can be deducted by the trust from Net Income For Tax Purposes of the trust to the extent that it is either distributed to beneficiaries or they are entitled to enforce payment. We will find that in many situations trusts will distribute all of their income, resulting in no Tax Payable at the trust level.

Any income that a trust does not distribute to beneficiaries will be taxed in the trust. Subsequent distribution of this income is on a tax free basis. At this point you should note that there is a very important difference in the calculation of Tax Payable for a testamentary trust that is designated as a graduated rate estate, and the calculation of Tax Payable for other personal trusts. As the name implies, graduated rate estates can use the schedule of graduated rates that is applicable to individuals. In contrast, most other personal trusts will have all of their income taxed at the maximum rate of 33 percent.

19-55. While it is not illustrated in Figure 19-3, there is a special anti-avoidance rule that is designed to prevent extended deferral of the potential tax on capital gains. This rule requires a deemed disposition of capital assets after they have been held in the trust for 21 years and will be discussed in detail beginning in Paragraph 19-75.

Exercise Nineteen - 2

Subject: Basic Taxation Of Trusts

On January 1, 2020, Joanne March transfers debt securities with a fair market value of $220,000 to a newly established inter vivos trust for which her 28 year old daughter, Jocelyn, is the only beneficiary. The cost of these securities to Joanne March was $200,000. During 2020, the securities earn and receive interest of $15,000, all of which is distributed to Jocelyn. On January 1, 2021, the securities are transferred to Jocelyn in satisfaction of her capital interest in the trust. At this time, the fair market value of the securities has increased to $230,000. Jocelyn sells all of the securities for $230,000 on January 5, 2021. Joanne is not a trustee of the inter vivos trust.

Indicate the tax consequences for Joanne, Jocelyn, and the trust in each of the years 2020 and 2021.

SOLUTION available in print and online Study Guide.

Rollovers To A Trust

Introduction

19-56. The general taxation model for trusts requires that contributions to the trust be recorded at fair market value, often resulting in a significant tax cost for the contributor. However, as we noted in our material on the classification of trusts, spousal or common-law partner trusts, alter ego trusts, and joint spousal or common-law partner trusts can receive such transfers on a rollover basis, provided certain specific conditions are met.

19-57. In this section we are concerned with the conditions that qualify these three special types of trusts for the tax free rollover of contributions. When the trust qualifies, the rollover is accomplished by deeming the property to have been disposed of by the settlor at either its adjusted cost base (non-depreciable capital property) or its UCC (depreciable capital property), resulting in no tax consequences for the settlor at the time of transfer. The trust is deemed to have acquired the property at a value equal to the proceeds of disposition to the settlor. In the case of depreciable property, the trust retains the settlor's original capital cost for purposes of determining recapture of CCA.

19-58. We will revisit these three types of trusts in our later section on tax planning. At that point we will discuss how these trusts can be used to reduce or defer taxes.

Qualifying Spousal Or Qualifying Common-Law Partner Trust

19-59. You may recall from Chapter 9 that ITA 73(1.01) contains a rollover provision that allows a living individual to transfer capital property to a spouse or common-law partner without tax consequences. ITA 70(6) provides for a similar rollover for the capital property of a deceased individual.

19-60.   While we did not discuss this in Chapter 9, these rollovers apply whether the transfer is directly to the spouse or common-law partner or, alternatively, to a trust in favour of a spouse or common-law partner. However, in the case of a transfer to a trust, the trust arrangement must meet certain conditions in order to qualify for the rollover. When it meets these conditions, it is commonly referred to as a qualifying spousal or common-law partner trust.

19-61.   With respect to inter vivos spousal or common-law partner trusts, the conditions for qualifying for the rollover are as follows:

ITA 73(1.01)(c)(i)   The individual's spouse or common-law partner is entitled to receive all of the income of the trust that arises before the spouse's or common-law partner's death and no person except the spouse or common-law partner may, before the spouse's or common-law partner's death, receive or otherwise obtain the use of any of the income or capital of the trust.

19-62.   A similar provision provides the rollover conditions for testamentary spousal or common-law partner trusts:

ITA 70(6)(b)   A trust, created by the taxpayer's will, that was resident in Canada immediately after the time the property vested indefeasibly in the trust and under which

(i)   the taxpayer's spouse or common-law partner is entitled to receive all of the income of the trust that arises before the spouse's or common-law partner's death, and

(ii)   no person except the spouse or common-law partner may, before the spouse's or common-law partner's death, receive or otherwise obtain the use of any of the income or capital of the trust.

19-63.   When these conditions are met, any property that is contributed to the trust, either by a living spouse or common-law partner, or as the result of the spouse or common-law partner's death, will be transferred at tax cost. For non-depreciable capital property, this value is the transferor's adjusted cost base. For depreciable property, the transfer is at the transferor's UCC amount. However, for purposes of determining recaptured CCA, the transferor's original capital cost is deemed to be the transferee's capital cost.

19-64.   While these rollover provisions are, in general, a desirable way to avoid paying taxes on transfers to a spousal or common-law partner trust, there may be circumstances where the taxpayer would prefer a transfer at fair market value. For example, if the settlor of the trust has unused capital loss carry forwards or property that is eligible for the lifetime capital gains deduction, he or she might wish to trigger capital gains in order to absorb these amounts. Fortunately, the settlor has the choice of electing out of the rollover provisions. For inter vivos transfers, the election is under ITA 73(1). For testamentary transfers the election that can be made by the settlor's legal representative is under ITA 70(6.2).

Exercise Nineteen - 3

Subject: Transfer To Spousal Trust

Louise died late this year and bequeathed a group of common shares to a qualifying spousal trust created in her will. Louise is survived by her husband who is to receive the shares from the trust three years after her death if they have not been sold. The shares have an adjusted cost base of $60,000 and were valued at $90,000 on the date of her death. Determine the tax consequences of the transfer, including the adjusted cost base for the shares in the trust and in her husband's hands if they are transferred.

SOLUTION available in print and online Study Guide.

Alter Ego Trust

19-65.   An alter ego trust is an inter vivos trust established by a settlor who is 65 years of age or older at the time the trust is settled. To qualify for a tax free rollover of assets to the trust, the *Income Tax Act* specifies the following conditions:

ITA 73(1.01)(c)(ii)   The individual is entitled to receive all of the income of the trust that arises before the individual's death and no person except the individual may, before the individual's death, receive or otherwise obtain the use of any of the income or capital of the trust.

19-66.   As was the case with the spousal or common-law partner trust, an individual can elect out of this rollover, choosing to have the transfer to the trust take place at fair market value. However, if the election is made the trust will not qualify as an alter ego trust.

Joint Spousal Or Joint Common-Law Partner Trust

19-67.   Like an alter ego trust, a joint spousal or common-law partner trust is an inter vivos trust established by a settlor who is 65 years of age or older at the time the trust is settled. The difference in this case is that both the settlor and his spouse or common-law partner are beneficiaries of the trust. More specifically, to qualify for the tax free rollover of assets to the trust, the *Income Tax Act* specifies the following conditions:

ITA 73(1.01)(c)(iii) either

(A)   the individual or the individual's spouse is, in combination with the other, entitled to receive all of the income of the trust that arises before the later of the death of the individual and the death of the spouse and no other person may, before the later of those deaths, receive or otherwise obtain the use of any of the income or capital of the trust, or

(B)   the individual or the individual's common-law partner is, in combination with the other, entitled to receive all of the income of the trust that arises before the later of the death of the individual and the death of the common-law partner and no other person may, before the later of those deaths, receive or otherwise obtain the use of any of the income or capital of the trust.

19-68.   As was the case with the alter ego trust, an individual can elect out of this rollover, choosing to have the transfer to the trust take place at fair market value.

Exercise Nineteen - 4

Subject: Transfers To Trusts

An individual has common shares with a cost of $1,000 and a current fair market value of $1,600. Seven Scenarios are presented for the transfer of these shares by the settlor to a trust. For each Scenario, indicate the tax consequences to the settlor at the time of transfer, as well as the adjusted cost base of the property within the trust.

Scenario 1:	Transfer to inter vivos trust for adult child
Scenario 2:	Transfer to inter vivos trust for minor child
Scenario 3:	Transfer to testamentary trust for friend
Scenario 4:	Transfer to inter vivos qualifying spousal trust
Scenario 5:	Transfer to testamentary qualifying spousal trust
Scenario 6:	Transfer to joint spousal trust
Scenario 7:	Transfer to alter ego trust

SOLUTION available in print and online Study Guide.

Rollovers To Capital Beneficiaries

General Rule

19-69.   As is the case with transfers by a settlor into a trust, the transfer of assets to a capital beneficiary is a disposition. However, for many trusts ITA 107(2) provides a tax free rollover for these transfers. The rollover is accomplished by deeming the property to have been disposed of by the trust at either its adjusted cost base (non-depreciable capital property) or its UCC (depreciable property).

19-70.   The beneficiary is deemed to have acquired the property at a value equal to the cost amount to the trust, resulting in no tax consequences at the time of transfer to the beneficiary. In the case of depreciable property, the beneficiary retains the capital cost of the property to the trust for purposes of determining subsequent recapture of CCA.

Exceptions

19-71.   The logic of the preceding rule is based on the fact that the transfer of assets into the trust was, in terms of the beneficial interest in the assets, a transfer of the assets to the beneficiaries. Provided that tax was assessed on the transfer into the trust, it would not be equitable to assess tax again when the asset is legally transferred to the beneficiaries.

19-72.   We have noted, however, that with certain types of trusts, the transfer from the settlor to the trust is not a taxable transaction. Specifically, qualifying spousal or common-law partner trusts, alter ego trusts, and joint spousal or common-law partner trusts can use a rollover provision to transfer assets into a trust. Since no tax was assessed on the transfer into these trusts, it would not seem equitable to allow the assets to be transferred to all beneficiaries on a rollover basis.

19-73.   Tax legislation agrees with this view. The ITA 107(2) rollover does not apply in the following cases:

- if property is transferred out of an **alter ego** trust to anyone other than the settlor,

- if property is transferred out of a **joint spousal** or common-law partner trust to anyone other than the settlor or the spouse or common-law partner, and

- if property is transferred out of a **qualifying spousal** or common-law partner trust to anyone other than a spouse or common-law partner.

19-74.   When the ITA 107(2) rollover provision does not apply, the transfer of assets from the trust to a capital beneficiary will be recorded at the fair market value of the transferred assets. This will generally result in tax consequences for the trust.

We suggest you work Self Study Problem Nineteen-1 at this point.

---

21 Year Deemed Disposition Rule

19-75.   Trust arrangements ordinarily allow capital gains on trust assets to accumulate without tax consequences for extended periods of time. Unless the capital assets are sold or distributed by the trust, accrued gains will not attract any taxes and the assets can be left in a trust for periods that exceed the life of the individual establishing the trust.

19-76.   In order to place limits on this deferral process, ITA 104(4)(b) requires that there be a deemed disposition and re-acquisition of trust capital property every 21 years. The disposition is deemed to be at fair market value, resulting in the recognition of any accrued gains on the assets. In the case of depreciable assets, if the deemed proceeds are less than the original capital cost, the original value is retained for purposes of determining recapture.

19-77.   This rule is generally applicable only to personal trusts and does not apply to trusts such as employee benefit plans or Registered Education Savings Plans. Further, the rules are modified in the case of qualifying spousal or common-law partner trusts, alter ego trusts, and joint spousal or common-law partner trusts.

Other Deemed Dispositions

19-78.   For 2016 and subsequent years, where the primary beneficiary of an alter ego, spousal, or common-law partner trust dies, or the last surviving beneficiary of a joint spousal or common-law partner trust dies, there is a deemed year end of the trust on the date of the beneficiaries death.

Net Income For Tax Purposes Of A Trust

Basic Rules

19-79.   The overriding principle in determining the Net Income For Tax Purposes of a trust results from the statement in ITA 104(2) that a trust should be treated as an individual. This means that the general rules used by individuals, as modified by trust legislation, are applicable in computing a trust's Net Income For Tax Purposes.

19-80.   Capital gains and losses are realized on the disposition of capital assets. Also, in the calculation of Net Income For Tax Purposes, any taxable dividends that are not allocated to beneficiaries are grossed up as they would be for individuals. Finally, deductions are allowed for non-capital, net capital, and certain other types of loss carry overs.

19-81.   There are, however, additional items that must be added or deducted in calculating the Net Income For Tax Purposes of a trust. These items can be described as follows:

Amounts Paid Or Payable To Beneficiaries   As was noted in our description of the basic trust taxation model, a trust can deduct amounts that are paid or payable to one or more beneficiaries. This is usually the most important of the adjustments to the trust's income in that, in many cases, all of the trust's income will be allocated to beneficiaries. Because of the importance of this deduction, it will be the subject of a separate section of this Chapter beginning in Paragraph 19-93.

Trustee's Or Executor's Fees   Any amounts paid that are related to earning trust income, or that are paid to an executor or trustee whose principal business includes the provision of such services, are deductible to the trust.

Amounts Paid By The Trust And Allocated To The Income Of A Beneficiary   A trust can make payments to third parties to provide goods or services to beneficiaries. The CRA considers such amounts to be another way of paying income to beneficiaries and, as a consequence, such amounts are deductible to the trust and included in the income of the beneficiaries.

Income Allocated To A Preferred Beneficiary   As will be discussed beginning in Paragraph 19-83, trusts can allocate income to a preferred beneficiary while retaining the income in the trust. While such retained income would normally be taxed in the trust, because it is being taxed in the hands of a beneficiary, it can be deducted from the income of the trust.

Amounts Deemed Not Paid   A trust can designate amounts to be deemed not paid when they are, in fact, paid or payable to beneficiaries. This means that the trust will include these amounts in its own Net Income For Tax Purposes and the beneficiaries will be able to receive these amounts on a tax free basis. The reasons for doing this are discussed beginning in Paragraph 19-86.

Amounts Retained For Beneficiary Under 21 Years Of Age   Provided the eventual payment is not subject to any future condition, amounts that are held in trust for a beneficiary who is under 21 at the end of the year can be deducted by the trust and taxed in the hands of the beneficiary. (See Paragraph 19-90.)

19-82.   While positive amounts of all types of income can be allocated to beneficiaries, losses cannot be. If a trust has a disposition that results in a capital loss or other activities that result in a non-capital loss, such losses must be used within the trust, either as a carry back to a previous year or as a carry forward to a subsequent year. Note, however, that if the trust distributes capital assets with accrued losses, the fact that the transfer to a beneficiary is usually at the trust's tax cost means that such accrued losses can, in effect, be transferred to a beneficiary.

Preferred Beneficiary Election

19-83.   Normally a trust can only deduct amounts that are paid or payable to a beneficiary. An exception to this can arise if a joint election is made by a trust and a beneficiary. Under this pre-ferred beneficiary election, the beneficiary will be taxed on amounts that remain in the trust [ITA 104(14)], and the trust can deduct these amounts [ITA 104(12)].

19-84.   The preferred beneficiary election is only available if:

- the beneficiary is claiming the disability tax credit; or
- the beneficiary is 18 years of age or older, is claimed by another individual as a dependant, and does not have income that exceeds the base for the beneficiary's personal tax credit.
- In addition, the beneficiary must be the settlor of the trust, the spouse or former spouse of the settlor of the trust, or the child, grandchild, or great grandchild of the settlor of the trust, or the child, grandchild, or great grandchild of the spouse of the settlor of the trust.

19-85.   This election is normally used in situations where it is desirable to have income taxed in the hands of a low-income individual without actually giving that individual full access to the funds. An example of this would be a child with a mental disability with no other source of income but who lacks the ability to deal responsibly with financial matters.

Amounts Deemed Not Paid

19-86.   Amounts paid or payable to a beneficiary are normally deducted by the trust and included in the income of the beneficiary. However, ITA 104(13.1) permits a trust to designate all or part of its income for a year as "not to have been paid" or "not to have become payable." The amounts so designated are not included in the beneficiaries' Net Income and are not deducted in computing the Net Income of the trust. As a result, the amounts are taxed in the trust and can be distributed tax free. This designation is only available to trusts that are resident in Canada throughout the taxation year and are subject to Part I tax.

19-87.   Prior to 2016, when testamentary trusts had general access to graduated rates, this provision could be used advantageously when the trust had a lower marginal tax rate than the beneficiary. Except for graduated rate estates (GREs), this can no longer occur as other testa-mentary trusts are generally taxed at the maximum federal rate of 33 percent.

19-88.   Prior to 2016, the amount deemed not paid provision could be used to avoid the instal-ment requirements that could be applicable to beneficiaries. While administratively the CRA no longer charges interest on late or insufficient instalments, instalments are required for all trusts other than graduated rate estates.

19-89.   As previously noted, a trust cannot allocate losses to beneficiaries. This means that the only way an unused current year trust loss can be utilized is through a carry over to another year. With many trusts, this cannot happen under normal circumstances because they are legally required to distribute all of their income to beneficiaries, resulting in a nil Net Income For Tax Purposes. A solution to this problem is to designate sufficient income as having not been paid to absorb the loss carry forward. This can satisfy the legal requirement to distribute the income while simultaneously creating sufficient Net Income For Tax Purposes to absorb the loss carry forward. Although this feature is still available, the 2016 changes in trust legislation restrict the application of this provision so it can only be used to eliminate losses in the trust. It cannot be used to create a positive amount of income in the trust.

Amounts Retained For A Beneficiary Under 21 Years Of Age

19-90.   If benefits are actually paid to a minor beneficiary, the amounts can clearly be deducted by the trust. However, an adult settlor may decide that it would be better for the income to be held in trust until the beneficiary reaches some specified age. Provided the beneficiary has not reached 21 years of age prior to the end of the year and none of the income has become payable, ITA 104(18) deems amounts that are retained to have actually become payable during the year. This means that the trust will be able to deduct the amount retained and the beneficiary will be subject to taxes on it.

19-91.   To qualify for this treatment, the amounts must be vested with the beneficiary and there cannot be any future condition that would prevent payment. When these amounts are eventually distributed, they will be received by the beneficiary on a tax free basis.

Taxable Income Of A Trust

19-92.   Once the Net Income For Tax Purposes of a trust is determined, calculation of Taxable Income involves the same deductions that would be available to individuals. Provided there is a positive Net Income For Tax Purposes, the trust can deduct non-capital losses of other years, net capital losses of other years, and farming and fishing losses of other years. The carry over periods for these losses that are applicable to individuals are equally applicable to trusts. Note that the ability to deduct net capital losses and restricted farm losses is dependent on having taxable capital gains or farm income included in the trust's Net Income For Tax Purposes for the current year.

Exercise Nineteen - 5

Subject: Trust Net And Taxable Income

During the current year, the Jordan family trust, an inter vivos trust, has business income of $220,000. Of this amount, $50,000 is retained in the trust with a joint election being made to have this amount taxed in the hands of a beneficiary who qualifies for the disability tax credit. This beneficiary has no other income. The remaining $170,000 is distributed to the other beneficiaries of the trust.

At the beginning of the current year, the trust had a business loss carry forward of $35,000. In order to make use of this loss, the trust designates an amount of $35,000 under ITA 104(13.1) as not having been paid during the year.

Determine the trust's Net Income For Tax Purposes and Taxable Income for the current year. Briefly explain why the trust would make the preferred beneficiary election and designate amounts not paid that were paid.

SOLUTION available in print and online Study Guide.

Income Allocations To Beneficiaries

General Rules

19-93.   Since a trust is a separate taxable entity, any income that is earned by trust assets will initially accrue to the trust. As we have noted, however, any income that is allocated to a beneficiary can be deducted in the calculation of the trust's Net Income For Tax Purposes. Correspondingly, the amount deducted by the trust must generally be included in the Net Income For Tax Purposes of the relevant beneficiary. In effect, when trust income is allocated to a beneficiary, the obligation to pay taxes on that income is transferred from the trust to the beneficiary.

19-94.   We have also noted that a trust can make payments to third parties for goods or services that will be provided to a beneficiary. These can include such expenses as day care, tuition, and medical fees. These amounts are deductible by the trust as allocations to beneficiaries, but will be considered income paid or payable to the beneficiaries.

19-95.   For a trust to be able to deduct amounts that will be distributed to beneficiaries, the amounts must be paid or payable. While it is easy to determine whether an amount has been paid, questions often arise in determining whether or not an amount is payable to a beneficiary. ITA 104(24) provides that:

> ... an amount is deemed not to have become payable to a beneficiary in a taxation year unless it was paid in the year to the beneficiary or the beneficiary was entitled in the year to enforce payment of it.

19-96.   Issuing a promissory note or a cheque payable to the beneficiary for the share of the trust income will usually fulfill the payable requirement. The CRA expands the definition of payable in IT-286R2 by stating that an amount is not considered to be payable in any of the following circumstances:

- A beneficiary can only enforce payment of an amount of income by forcing the trustee to wind up the trust.
- The beneficiary's right to income is subject to the approval of a third party.
- Payment of income is at the trustee's discretion and this provision has not been exercised.
- The beneficiary has the power to amend the trust deed and must do so to cause the income to be payable.

Discretionary And Non-Discretionary Distributions

19-97.   Both testamentary and inter vivos trusts can be set up as either discretionary or non-discretionary trusts. A discretionary trust is one in which the trustees are given the power to decide the amounts that will be allocated to each of the beneficiaries, usually on an annual basis.

19-98.   In many cases, this discretionary power will apply only to annual income distributions. However, the trust could be structured to provide discretion on both income and capital distributions, or to capital distributions only. The trustees may also be given the power to control the timing of distributions to beneficiaries.

19-99.   When discretionary trusts are used, it is important that only the amounts allocated to beneficiaries are considered to be paid or payable. If, for example, a trustee's exercise of discretion requires the approval of a third party, IT-286R2 would indicate that the amounts are not payable. This would result in the trust not being able to deduct the allocated amounts.

19-100.   A non-discretionary trust is one in which the amounts and timing of allocations to income and capital beneficiaries are specified in the trust agreement. In some cases, the trust agreement may have a combination of discretionary and non-discretionary provisions.

Flow Through Provisions
General Applicability
19-101.   Income that is paid out to beneficiaries through a trust is deemed to be property income unless there is a rule that says otherwise. Fortunately, there is a flow through rule that allows certain types of income paid out of a trust to retain the same tax characteristics as when it was earned in the personal trust. The most significant types of income covered by this flow through rule are capital gains, taxable dividends, and capital dividends. Note that business income is not covered by the flow through rule. When business income is paid to beneficiaries, it is considered to be property income.

19-102.   These flow through rules are an important feature of personal trusts in that capital gains and dividends are taxed much more favourably than other types of income. Since property income is fully taxed at an individual's regular rates, in the absence of such a flow through rule, in many instances the use of trusts would be much less attractive.

Dividends

19-103.   If either eligible or non-eligible dividends from taxable Canadian corporations are received by a trust and distributed to beneficiaries of the trust, the beneficiaries will use the same gross up and tax credit procedures that would be applicable had they received the dividends directly. At the trust level, these amounts will not be grossed up and the amount received and distributed will be deducted in the determination of the trust's Net Income.

19-104.   In contrast, if either eligible or non-eligible dividends from taxable Canadian corporations are retained in the trust, the grossed up amount of these dividends will be included in the trust's Net Income For Tax Purposes. Consistent with this, the trust will be able to deduct the appropriate dividend tax credit when it determines its Tax Payable for the year. Since capital dividends are tax free, they would have no effect on the trust's Tax Payable.

Capital Gains

19-105.   Under trust law, capital gains that are realized in the trusts are considered to be an addition to capital and, in the absence of a special provision in the trust agreement, would not be payable to income beneficiaries. However, tax legislation views one-half of capital gains as a taxable amount. As a consequence, if this amount is not paid out to beneficiaries, it will be taxed in the hands of the trust. The remaining one-half of the capital gain will become part of the trust's capital and can be paid to beneficiaries on a tax free basis at any point in time.

19-106.   If the trust pays out the full amount of the capital gain, the flow through rule means that one-half of this amount will be included in the recipient's income as a taxable capital gain. The remaining one-half is received as a tax free distribution of capital.

19-107.   It is important to note that the capital gains that we are discussing here are those that result from dispositions of trust property within the trust. As covered in Paragraph 19-69, if the trust distributes capital assets on which there are accrued capital gains, ITA 107(2) deems the transfer to be at the trust's tax cost resulting in no tax consequences to the trust. The accrued gains will not be subject to tax until the recipient beneficiary chooses to dispose of the assets that they have received.

Tax On Split Income (TOSI)

19-108.   As discussed in Chapter 11, as of 2018, individuals of any age may receive income that is subject to the TOSI. If the TOSI is applicable, tax will be assessed at the maximum federal rate of 33 percent on all such amounts, with the only available tax credits being the dividend tax credit and credits for foreign taxes assessed on foreign source income. We will not repeat the discussion of the applicability of TOSI in this Chapter.

19-109.   However, the TOSI is very relevant in this Chapter because, if the trust earns income that would have been subject to the TOSI if it had been received directly by a beneficiary, it will also be subject to the TOSI if the trust distributes the income to that beneficiary. In other words, it will retain its character when it flows through the trust. Because of this, the income will be subject to the TOSI at 33 percent, the same rate that would be applicable to the trust.

Exercise Nineteen - 6

Subject: Flow Through To Beneficiaries

During 2020, the Ho family trust received eligible dividends from publicly traded Canadian corporations in the amount of $100,000. In addition, it received non-eligible dividends from the family owned Canadian controlled private corporation in the amount of $30,000. Its only other source of income was a capital gain of $20,000 on a disposition of investments in publicly traded equity securities.

The only beneficiary of the trust is the family's 19 year old son, Bryan Ho. Bryan is actively engaged in the private corporation on a regular and continuous basis and, as a consequence, the TOSI is not applicable to the income that he receives from the trust.

During the current year, $60,000 of the eligible dividends from public companies, all of the non-eligible dividends from the family's private company, and all of the $20,000 capital gain were paid to Bryan.

Indicate the tax effects of these transactions on the Net Income For Tax Purposes for both the trust and for Bryan.

SOLUTION available in print and online Study Guide.

Business Income, CCA, Recapture, And Terminal Losses

19-110.   Under trust law, the amount of income that may be distributed to beneficiaries should be determined after providing for amortization expense calculated using methods similar to those specified under generally accepted accounting principles. While this could create a difference between a trust's accounting Net Income and its Net Income For Tax Purposes, this problem is resolved by most trustees by setting accounting amortization expense equal to maximum CCA.

19-111.   Business income must be calculated at the trust level, prior to allocation to the beneficiaries. This calculation would include the CCA deduction, as well as any recapture or terminal losses that might arise during the year. As noted, the flow through rule for trusts does not cover business income. This means that any business income allocated to beneficiaries is distributed to them as property income. If this was not the case, business income flowed through a trust could create a liability for CPP and GST/HST, which would complicate matters for many beneficiaries.

Exercise Nineteen - 7

Subject: CCA And Recapture On Trust Assets

The Husak family trust has only one beneficiary, Martin Husak, the 32 year old son of the settlor, Dimitri Husak. It is an inter vivos trust and its only asset is a rental property with a fair market value equal to its capital cost. The trust is required to distribute all of its income to Martin. During the year ending December 31, 2020, the property will have net rental income, before the deduction of CCA of $32,000. Maximum CCA for the year will be $26,000.

Dimitri is considering having the trust sell the rental property at the end of 2020. If that is done, there will be recapture of CCA of $65,000. He has asked you to compare the tax consequences for both Martin and the trust if (1) the sale takes place in December 2020 and (2) the trust continues to hold the property.

Ignore the possibility that some of the income received might be subject to the TOSI.

SOLUTION available in print and online Study Guide.

Principal Residence Exemption

19-112.   Prior to 2017, a residence held in a trust that was ordinarily inhabited by a beneficiary of the trust, or by a spouse or common-law partner, former spouse or common-law partner, or a child of a beneficiary, was eligible for the principal residence exemption (see Chapter 8). This is no longer the case. For years ending after 2016, only alter ego trusts, joint spousal or common-law partner trusts, spousal or common-law partner trusts, qualified disability trusts, or a qualifying trust for a minor child will be able to use this exemption to eliminate or reduce any capital gain resulting from the sale of a residence held in the trust. If such gains arise in other types of trusts, they will be subject to the usual capital gains taxation.

Tax Payable Of Personal Trusts

Calculation Of Basic Amount

General Approach

19-113.   In keeping with the previously expressed idea that trusts are to be taxed in the same manner as individuals, the Tax Payable for a trust is calculated using the rates applicable to individuals. However, how these rates will be applied differs, depending on whether the trust is an inter vivos trust or a regular testamentary trust, or, alternatively, a graduated rate estate. These differences will be discussed in the material that follows.

Graduated Rate Estates

19-114.   As discussed previously, in the first T3 filed subsequent to an individual's death, trust assets that are still under the administration of an executor can be designated a graduated rate estate. You will recall that this designation can remain in effect for up to 36 months subsequent to the death of the individual.

19-115.   The major benefit resulting from this designation is that, during the period in which the designation is in effect, the trust can calculate Tax Payable using the graduated rate schedule that is applicable to individuals. As described in Chapter 4, for 2020, the federal tax rates range from 15 percent on the first $48,535 of Taxable Income to 33 percent on amounts in excess of $214,368.

Inter Vivos Trusts And Regular Testamentary Trusts

19-116.   Under ITA 122(1), with the exception of graduated rate estates, both inter vivos and testamentary trusts have all of their income taxed at the maximum federal rate. This rate is currently 33 percent.

Other Tax Payable Considerations

Availability Of Tax Credits

19-117.   While, in principle, trusts are to be taxed in the same manner as individuals, there are obvious differences between a legally constructed entity and a living, breathing human being. These differences are reflected in the fact that trusts are not eligible for many of the tax credits that are available to individuals.

19-118.   To begin, ITA 122(1.1) specifically prohibits a trust from claiming any of the credits listed under ITA 118 (personal tax credits). Further, most of the other credits listed in ITA 118.1 through 118.9 are clearly directed at individuals (e.g., a trust is not likely to have medical expenses). However, some tax credits are available to trusts, generally on the same basis as they are available to individuals. These include:

- donations and gifts (as is the case with individuals, there is a credit of 15 percent on the first $200 of donations and either 29 percent or 33 percent on additional amounts.)
- eligible and non-eligible dividend tax credits
- foreign tax credits
- investment tax credits

Alternative Minimum Tax

19-119.   As is the case with individuals, trusts are subject to the alternative minimum tax legislation. However, there is one important difference. With the exception of graduated rate estates, the exemption with respect to the first $40,000 of income is not available to trusts.

Tax Free Dividends

19-120.   Because dividends use up available tax credits at a much slower pace than other types of income, individuals can receive a substantial amount of dividends on a tax free basis.

As explained in Chapter 15, this only works when income is taxed at the two lowest federal rates of 15 percent and 20.5 percent. As we have indicated, both inter vivos and most testamentary trusts are taxed at 33 percent on all of their income. When this is the case, the trust cannot receive any dividends on a tax free basis.

19-121. However, graduated rate estates can receive tax free dividends. For example, if such a trust has no other source of income, it can receive up to $35,300 in eligible dividends without paying any taxes.

Exercise Nineteen - 8

Subject: Tax Payable On Trust Dividends

A trust receives $100,000 in eligible dividends. This is the trust's only income for the current year. The only beneficiary of the trust is the settlor's 32 year old son. The son has no income other than that provided by the trust and no tax credits other than his basic personal credit and credits related to any trust income. Ignoring any alternative minimum tax implications, determine the Taxable Income and federal Tax Payable for both the trust and beneficiary under the following alternative assumptions:

A. The trust is a graduated rate estate and it distributes all of the dividends to the beneficiary. Assume that the TOSI would not be applicable to the dividends received by the settlor's son.

B. The trust is a graduated rate estate and it does not distribute any of the dividends to the beneficiary.

C. The trust is an inter vivos trust and does not distribute any of the dividends to the beneficiary.

SOLUTION available in print and online Study Guide.

We suggest you work Self Study Problems Nineteen-2, 3, and 4 at this point.

Income Attribution - Trusts

General Rules

19-122. We introduced the income attribution rules for individuals in Chapter 9. Briefly summarized, they are as follows:

Transfer To A Spouse Or Common-Law Partner   Under ITA 74.1(1), if an asset is transferred to a spouse or common-law partner for consideration that is less than fair market value, any property income earned by the asset while it is held by that person, as well as any capital gain resulting from a disposition of the asset by the transferee, will be attributed back to the transferor. These rules also apply, without regard to the value of the consideration, when the transferor does not elect out of the ITA 73 rollover provision.

Transfer To A Related Minor   Under ITA 74.1(2), if an asset is transferred to a related individual under the age of 18 for consideration that is less than fair market value, property income earned by the asset while it is held by the minor will be attributed back to the transferor until the year the individual is 18 or older. Capital gains on a subsequent sale of the asset will not be attributed back to the transferor.

We would remind you that, if the transferred property is a business, business income is not subject to the income attribution rules. Also, the rules do not apply to any income that is classified as split income.

19-123.   While we did not discuss this point in Chapter 9, these rules are equally applicable when there is a transfer to an inter vivos trust where a spouse, common-law partner, or a related minor is a beneficiary. As was the case with individuals, these rules apply to any transfer where the consideration is less than the fair market value of the asset transferred.

19-124.   You should note that attribution does not occur at the time the asset is transferred to a trust in which a spouse, common-law partner, or related minor is a beneficiary. Rather, attribution occurs when income from the asset is allocated to one of these individuals. If the trust chooses to be taxed on the income before allocation, or if the income is allocated to individuals other than a spouse, common-law partner, or related minor, income will generally not be attributed to the transferor. In addition, income attribution stops at the death of the settlor.

Exercise Nineteen - 9

Subject: Income Attribution - Trusts

Last year, Trevor Carlisle transferred to a family trust, for no consideration, bonds that pay interest of $27,000 per annum. The beneficiaries of the trust are Trevor's spouse, Carmen, and their two children, Mitch (16 years old) and Rhonda (22 years old). The beneficiaries have no income other than that from the trust. The trust income and capital gains are allocated equally and are payable to each beneficiary during the year. Total interest income earned by the trust during the year was $27,000. As well, a capital gain of $6,000 was realized on the trust's disposition of one of the bonds that Trevor transferred into the trust. Determine the Taxable Income of each beneficiary and calculate any effect the trust income will have on the Taxable Income of Trevor. How would your answer change if Trevor died on January 1 of the current year?

Ignore the possibility that some of the income received by the beneficiaries will be subject to the TOSI.

SOLUTION available in print and online Study Guide.

We suggest you work Self Study Problems Nineteen-5 and 6 at this point.

Attribution To Settlor (Reversionary Trust)

19-125.   There is a further form of income attribution that is unique to trust situations. Both income from holding the transferred property and capital gains from the disposition of the transferred property will be attributed back to the settlor if a trust meets the conditions specified in ITA 75(2).

19-126.   ITA 75(2) is applicable, without regard to the identity of the beneficiaries of the trust, if any one of the following conditions is satisfied:

1.   The transferred property can revert to the settlor at a later point in time. In this situation, the trust is commonly referred to as a reversionary trust.

2.   The transferred property will pass to persons to be determined by the settlor at a later point in time. This requirement prevents the settlor from adding additional beneficiaries, or classes of beneficiaries, subsequent to the creation of the trust.

3.   The transferred property cannot be disposed of except with the settlor's consent or in accordance with the settlor's direction.

19-127. The safest way to deal with the second condition is to not have the settlor act as a trustee. If that is not a practical alternative, it would be prudent to have at least three trustees and have majority approval of decisions. If the settlor is one of two trustees or if decisions require unanimous approval by all trustees including the settlor, ITA 75(2) may apply.

Purchase Or Sale Of An Interest In A Trust

Income Interest

19-128. An income interest in a trust is the right of a beneficiary under the trust to receive all or part of the income from the trust. The purchaser of an income interest in a trust will have a cost equal to the fair market value of the consideration given for that interest. This cost can be deducted against amounts of trust income that would otherwise be included in the individual's Taxable Income. Any portion of the cost that is not deducted against income from the trust in the current year can be carried forward for deduction against allocated trust income in subsequent years. When income allocations have reduced the cost of the interest to nil, subsequent receipts of income will be fully taxable.

19-129. From the point of view of the vendor of an income interest, the proceeds of disposition will be equal to the fair market value of the consideration received. If the cost of the income interest (often nil) is different than the proceeds received, there will be a gain or loss on the disposition. As an income interest is not a capital asset, the gain or loss on its disposition will be treated as a fully taxable or deductible property income or loss.

Capital Interest

19-130. As defined in ITA 108(1), a capital interest is all of the rights of a beneficiary of a trust, other than an income interest. As the name implies, a capital interest is a capital asset and any gain or loss on its disposition will be treated as a capital gain or loss.

19-131. When a capital interest in a trust is purchased, the adjusted cost base is equal to the fair market value of the consideration given. This amount will be reduced by future distributions of assets from the trust. As we have noted, ITA 107(2) generally provides for a tax free rollover of assets from a trust to a beneficiary.

19-132. If a beneficiary sells a capital interest in a trust, the proceeds of disposition will equal the fair market value of the consideration received. Unless the taxpayer has purchased the capital interest, its adjusted cost base will be nil. This means that the entire proceeds of disposition could be a capital gain. However, to determine the gain on a disposition of a capital interest in a trust resident in Canada, ITA 107(1)(a) defines the adjusted cost base to be the greater of:

- the adjusted cost base as usually determined, and
- the "cost amount" to the beneficiary.

19-133. ITA 108(1) defines this cost amount as the beneficiary's proportionate interest in the net assets of the trust at their carrying value to the trust. This prevents the beneficiary from being taxed on the cost amount of the trust's assets, an amount that could be received on a tax free basis as a distribution from the trust. Capital losses on capital interest dispositions are determined in the usual manner. Since the adjusted cost base is usually nil, such losses are uncommon.

Exercise Nineteen - 10

Subject: Sale Of A Capital Interest

The Jardhu family trust was established when the father transferred publicly traded securities with a cost of $120,000 and a fair market value of $250,000 into the trust. The beneficiaries of the trust are the father's two sons, Sam, aged 25, and Mehrdad, aged 27. They have an equal interest in the income and capital of the trust.

At the beginning of the current year, Mehrdad sells his capital interest in the trust to Sam. There have been no capital distributions from the trust. At the time of the sale, the fair market value of the securities in the trust is $380,000. Based on this, the transfer price for the capital interest is $190,000 [(1/2)($380,000)]. Determine the tax consequences of this transaction to each of the two brothers.

SOLUTION available in print and online Study Guide.

Tax Planning

Family Trusts

Defined

19-134.   As we have noted, the term family trust is not defined in the *Income Tax Act*. Rather, it is a term that is used in practice to refer to a personal trust that has been established with members of the settlor's family as beneficiaries. These trusts can either be inter vivos trusts established during the settlor's lifetime or, alternatively, testamentary trusts created when the settlor dies. The provisions of these trusts often contain a fixed arrangement for the payments to beneficiaries. However, in some cases they are established with the payments to the beneficiaries left to the discretion of the trustees.

19-135.   While family trusts can be used for a variety of purposes, the most common objective of these trusts is income splitting. This process was introduced in Chapter 1, with further elaboration on the role of corporate structures in income splitting discussed in Chapter 15. In this Chapter we will give attention to income splitting in the context of family trusts. As we have noted, the expansion of the TOSI to related adults makes it much more difficult to implement effective income splitting strategies.

Discretionary Trusts

19-136.   As we have noted, a family trust is usually established for income splitting purposes, typically by a wealthy individual with children or other family members who are in low tax brackets. Such individuals commonly have difficulty deciding which of their family members are, and will continue to be, the most deserving. A solution to this problem is the use of a discretionary trust.

19-137.   The provisions of discretionary trusts leave the amount and/or timing of payments to beneficiaries at the discretion of the trustees. This means that, if a particular beneficiary neglects his or her family duties on a regular basis, or appears to be profligate in his or her spending habits, his or her share of the income can be reduced, eliminated, or delayed to a later date. Tax planners like to point out that this provides the settlor with great flexibility. A less charitable view of the settlor's objectives is that this type of arrangement provides for continued control over the behaviour of family members (e.g., if a child fails to show up for family dinners, he or she can be reminded that receipts from the family trust are discretionary).

19-138.   It is important to note that the settlor of the trust cannot be in a position of unilateral control over the amount and timing of the discretionary distributions, particularly if he or she is also one of the beneficiaries. If the settlor is in a position of control, the provisions of ITA 75(2) (see Paragraph 19-126) may be applicable, resulting in all of the income being attributed back to him or her. The usual way to avoid this problem is to have at least three trustees, with the amount of the discretionary distributions determined by majority rule. The CRA has indicated that, for this approach to be effective, the settlor cannot be a required part of the majority.

Income Splitting

19-139. If a family trust is set up properly, the potential tax savings from income splitting can be significant. The following table compares the federal Tax Payable on eligible dividends of $61,534 received by:

- A father who is subject to the maximum federal tax rate of 33 percent.

- His adult daughter with no other source of income. Assume that any income distributed to the daughter will not be subject to the TOSI.

19-140. The required calculations follow. Note that, given the amounts and type of income involved in this example, the application of the alternative minimum tax (AMT) reduces the amount of the tax savings to some degree.

	Father	**Daughter**	**AMT (Daughter)**
Eligible Dividends Received	$61,534	$61,534	$61,534
Gross Up At 38 Percent	23,383	23,383	N/A For AMT
Taxable Dividends/Income	$84,917	$84,917	$61,534
Federal Tax			
[(33%)($84,917)]	$28,023		
[(15%)($48,535) + (20.5%)($36,382)]		$14,738	
[(15%)($61,534 - $40,000 Exemption)]			$3,230
Federal Dividend Tax Credit			
[(6/11)($23,383)]	(12,754)	(12,754)	N/A For AMT
Basic Personal Credit (Note)	N/A	(1,984)	(1,984)
Federal Tax Payable/AMT	$15,269	Nil	$1,246

NOTE Since the father would have other income against which he could apply his basic personal credit, it has not been taken into consideration in the preceding calculations.

19-141. This example is designed to use the maximum of tax free eligible dividends that can be paid to an individual with only the basic personal tax credit. As shown in the preceding calculations, this serves to reduce the daughter's regular Tax Payable to nil. However, AMT will be payable, resulting in a net tax savings through the use of a family trust in the amount of $14,023 ($15,269 - $1,246). The corresponding savings in provincial taxes would increase this amount significantly. Note that this tax savings would be available for each beneficiary if there were multiple beneficiaries. Of equal importance is the fact that this is not a one time event. These tax savings can be accomplished on an annual basis as long as the beneficiaries have no other source of income.

19-142. You should note that, in situations where the beneficiary will be subject to the TOSI, it would be difficult, if not impossible to achieve substantial or in fact any tax savings through the use of this tax planning vehicle.

Exercise Nineteen - 11

Subject: Family Trusts

Sarah Block is holding debt securities that produce interest income of $110,000 per year. She has other sources of income in excess of $250,000. She has two children. Her daughter, Jerri, is 22 years old and currently has no income that is subject to tax. Jerri's only tax credit is the basic personal credit. Sarah's son, Mark, is 26 years old. He is married and his wife has no income of her own. Mark has annual net rental income of $48,000.

The trust will be required to distribute all of its income on an annual basis. Determine the savings in federal taxes that could be achieved by transferring the debt securities to a family trust with her two children as equal income beneficiaries.

Assume that Mark's only tax credits are the basic personal credit and the spousal credit and that none of the income received by the beneficiaries will be subject to the TOSI.

SOLUTION available in print and online Study Guide.

Qualifying Spousal Or Common-Law Partner Trusts

19-143.   As is discussed in Chapter 9, a rollover of assets to a spouse can be accomplished without the use of a trust. In the case of a living individual, the rollover is provided for under ITA 73(1) and (1.01), while for a deceased individual, the enabling provision is ITA 70(6). This makes it clear that a trust is not required to implement a tax free transfer of property for the benefit of a spouse. Why then are we concerned with qualifying spousal or common-law partner trusts? There are essentially two important reasons:

1.   A trust can provide for the appropriate management of the transferred assets, particularly when these assets include an active business. In many cases, the spouse or common-law partner of a settlor may have no experience in the management of assets and, in such situations, the trust document can ensure that professional management is used. If the assets were simply transferred to the spouse or common-law partner, the use of such management would be left to the discretion and control of the transferee.

2.   Also of importance is that the use of a trust can ensure that the assets are distributed in the manner desired by the settlor. While qualification requires that the transferred assets must "vest indefeasibly" with the spouse or common-law partner, the trust document can specify who the assets should be distributed to after the spouse or common-law partner dies. This could ensure, for example, that the assets are ultimately distributed only to the settlor's children if the spouse or common-law partner were to remarry and have additional children.

Alter Ego Trusts

19-144.   The most commonly cited reason for using an alter ego trust is that the trust property will not be included in the settlor's estate and, as a consequence, will not be subject to probate procedures (probate is a court process that proves the authenticity and validity of a will). There are a number of advantages associated with avoiding probate:

- The probate fees can be high. In Ontario, for example, they are equal to 0.5 percent on the first $50,000 of the fair market value of the estate, plus 1.5 percent of the excess, with no upper limit. On a $10 million estate these fees would total almost $150,000, a payment that can be completely eliminated with the use of an alter ego trust.

- The probate process can be time consuming. This can create difficulties for the management of an active business, as well as liquidity problems for the estate.

- When assets such as real estate are held in more than one jurisdiction (e.g., Canada and the U.S.), the probate procedures must be undertaken in multiple jurisdictions.

- Once probated, a will is in the public domain. For a nominal fee, any interested individual can obtain a copy, with the possibility that this will invade the privacy of surviving family members.

19-145.   While this point has not been widely discussed in the literature that we have seen on this subject, an additional tax feature involved in establishing an alter ego trust is the possibility of establishing the trust in a low tax rate province. When there is a deemed disposition at death or on emigration, the taxation will occur in the province where the trust is resident. Given that, for 2020, the combined federal/provincial rate on individuals ranges from 47.5 in Saskatchewan to 54 percent in Nova Scotia, this 6.5 percentage point difference makes the province of residence of the trust a significant tax planning issue.

19-146.   We would also note that there is a significant non-tax reason for using an alter ego trust. From a legal point of view, it is much easier to challenge the validity of a will than it is to challenge the validity of a trust. Courts can be asked to consider moral obligations to family members in distributing the assets of an estate. With a trust, there is no will to challenge.

Joint Spousal Or Joint Common-Law Partner Trusts

19-147.   A joint spousal or joint common-law partner trust has the same tax characteristics as an alter ego trust. The basic difference is that these trusts are established to hold the combined assets of both an individual and his or her spouse or common-law partner. Given this, their tax planning features are largely the same as those discussed for alter ego trusts in the preceding Paragraphs.

Estate Planning

Non-Tax Considerations

19-148.   The subject of estate planning is complex and involves considerations that go well beyond the scope of this text. In fact, appropriate planning for a large estate will often involve lawyers, investment advisors, accountants, and tax advisors. Indeed, it may even be necessary to have religious advisors or psychological counsellors participate in order to deal with some of the moral or emotional issues that are involved.

19-149.   The following points are among the more important non-tax considerations in planning an estate:

Intent Of The Testator   The foremost goal of estate planning is to ensure that the wishes of the testator (a person who has died and left a will) are carried out. This will involve ensuring that the assets left by the testator are distributed at the appropriate times and to the specified beneficiaries. The primary document for ensuring that the intent of the testator is fulfilled is, of course, the will.

Preparation Of A Final Will   The major document in the estate planning process is the final will. It should be carefully prepared to provide detailed instructions for the disposition of assets, investment decisions to be made, and the extent to which trusts will be used. An executor should be named to administer the estate, and the will should be reviewed periodically to ensure that it reflects the testator's current wishes and family status.

Preparation Of A Living Will   Equally important to the preparation of a final will, a living will provides detailed instructions regarding investments and other personal decisions in the event of physical or mental incapacity at any point in a person's lifetime. A power of attorney is similar, except that it does not require the individual to be mentally or physically incapacitated in order to be used.

Ensuring Liquidity   A plan should be established to provide for liquidity at the time of death. Major expenses, often including funeral expenses and income taxes, will arise at this time. Funds needed for these payments should be available, or adequate life insurance should be arranged in advance, to avoid the need for emergency sales of capital assets to raise the necessary cash.

Simplicity   While the disposition of a large estate will rarely be simple, effective estate planning should ensure that the plan can be understood by the testator and all beneficiaries of legal age. In addition, any actions that can reduce the cost and complexity of administering the estate should be considered. This might involve disposing of investments in non-public shares or repatriating assets that are located in foreign countries that might become subject to foreign taxation.

Avoidance Of Family Disputes   Unfortunately, disputes among beneficiaries are a common part of estate settlement procedures. If equitable treatment of beneficiaries is a goal of the testator, efforts should be made to ensure that all beneficiaries believe that they have been treated in an equitable manner. If the testator wants to distribute assets in a fashion that could be viewed as inequitable by any of the interested parties, care should be taken to make this intention unequivocal.

Expediting The Transition   The procedures required in the settlement of an estate should be designed to expedite the process. A long settlement period can increase uncertainties related to the value of assets, add to the complications associated with the required distribution of the assets, and prolong the frustration of the beneficiaries.

Tax Considerations

19-150.   In addition to the preceding non-tax considerations, estate planning must also consider various tax factors. Fundamental tax planing goals for all taxpayers apply equally to estate planning. Briefly, these goals involve the legal and orderly arrangement of one's affairs, before the time of a transaction or event, to reduce and defer income taxes.

19-151.   In effective estate planning, the over-riding income tax goals are to defer and minimize tax payments. Several important issues should be considered in dealing with this objective. These can be described as follows:

Prior To Death   Planning should attempt to minimize taxes for the individual in the years prior to death. If the individual earns income that is not required in these years, attempts should be made to defer the payment of tax and transfer the before-tax income to the ultimate beneficiaries. The use of a discretionary trust can assist in achieving this goal.

Year Of Death   Planning should attempt to minimize income taxes payable in the year of death. Deemed dispositions will occur at death and, in addition, amounts in certain types of deferred income plans usually must be included in the taxpayer's final return. Relief can be achieved through tax deferred rollovers to a spouse and transfers of certain types of property (e.g., farm property) to children or grandchildren. The will can also contain instructions to ensure that the maximum RRSP contribution is made to the spouse's RRSP within the deadline.

Planning here could also involve filing multiple tax returns. For example, if the descendant owns a private corporation, declaring a dividend just prior to their death, with payment following death, could provide for the filing of a rights and things return (see Chapter 11 Appendix), a procedure that would involve significant tax savings.

Income Splitting   Effective planning should allow income splitting among family members who are in lower tax brackets. This can be accomplished by the appropriate splitting of income (e.g., paying salaries and wages for services rendered) and distributing property among beneficiaries throughout a taxpayer's lifetime, recognizing the limitations imposed by the TOSI.

Foreign Jurisdictions   Planning should normally attempt to minimize taxes that will be incurred in foreign jurisdictions. This is especially true for jurisdictions with significant estate taxes as such taxes are generally not eligible for foreign tax credits or deduction in Canada. To the extent that it is consistent with the individual's investment plans and the residence of intended beneficiaries, holdings of foreign assets at death, or distributions to beneficiaries in foreign locations, should usually be avoided by residents of Canada. Minimizing foreign investments will also simplify the administration of an estate.

Administration Period   Planning should minimize taxes payable while the estate is being administered. Discretion provided to trustees in distributing the income of an inter vivos trust may assist in achieving this goal.

19-152.   Most of the tax procedures related to these issues have already been introduced. We have discussed spouse and common-law partner rollovers in previous Chapters and the use of trusts was covered earlier in this Chapter. An important aspect of estate planning that requires additional consideration is the estate freeze. Procedures to be used in these arrangements are outlined in the material that follows.

Estate Freeze

Objectives Of An Estate Freeze

19-153.   The objective of an estate freeze is, as the name implies, to freeze the value of the estate for tax purposes at a particular point in time. Typically, arrangements are made for all future appreciation to accrue to related parties such as a spouse, children, or grandchildren.

EXAMPLE   Mr. Chisholm is a wealthy and successful entrepreneur who has a wife and two young children. He owns a variety of capital assets that are producing Taxable Income and appreciating in value. He has several objectives in creating his estate plan:

- During the remainder of his life, Mr. Chisholm would like to transfer all or part of his Taxable Income to a group of individuals and charities who will ultimately be the beneficiaries of his estate.

- Mr. Chisholm would like to freeze the tax values of his assets and allow future growth to accrue to the intended family members.

- Since the current fair market value of his assets exceeds their tax cost, Mr. Chisholm would like to avoid any immediate taxation resulting from a disposition of these assets with accrued gains.

- Mr. Chisholm would like the transfer of future growth in asset values to accrue so that his beneficiaries will not be subject to taxation in the year of the estate freeze, in any intervening years, or in the year of his death.

- Mr. Chisholm wants to retain the right to the current value of the property at the time of the estate freeze. In addition, he wishes to retain control of the use of the property until his death.

19-154.   This example will be used as a basis for discussing a variety of techniques that can be used to freeze an estate's value. Some of these techniques will achieve all of Mr. Chisholm's goals, while others will only succeed in achieving one or two of them.

Techniques Not Involving Rollovers

Gifts

19-155.   Mr. Chisholm can freeze the value of his estate without using rollover provisions. The most straightforward technique is to simply give property to his prospective beneficiaries. While this would accomplish the goal of transferring future growth in the estate to the beneficiaries, unless the transfer was to a spouse or common-law partner, this approach would have the serious drawback of attracting immediate taxation on any difference between the fair market value of the assets and Mr. Chisholm's tax cost.

19-156.   In addition, if the person receiving the gift is a spouse or minor child, income attribution rules could apply after the gift is made. Further drawbacks are the fact that Mr. Chisholm would lose control over the assets and that certain income received by related persons may be subject to the TOSI.

19-157.   While gifts result in a loss of control, Mr. Chisholm may want to accelerate his donations to registered charities. The value of the tax credit associated with such gifts can more than offset any income arising as the result of such distributions. In particular, if a gift is made of shares listed on a designated stock exchange, the capital gains inclusion rate is reduced to nil (See Chapter 11).

Instalment Sales

19-158.   Mr. Chisholm could freeze the value of the estate by selling the assets to the intended family members on an instalment basis. Capital gains could be deferred until payment is received, but the gains would need to be reported over the next five years based on the capital gains reserve calculations (10 years if a farm or fishing property is involved).

19-159.   To avoid income attribution and inadequate consideration problems, the sale should be made at fair market value. However, if the intended family members do not have sufficient assets to make the purchase, this may not be a feasible solution. A further problem is that Mr. Chisholm would lose control over the property.

Establishing A Trust

19-160.   An estate freeze can also be accomplished by setting up a trust in favour of one or more beneficiaries. Here again, this will transfer income and future growth from Mr. Chisholm's hands to the trust. The trust can be structured so that he retains some control over the assets in the trust.

19-161.   The problem with this arrangement is that, except in the case of a qualifying spouse or common-law partner trust, a joint spousal or common-law partner trust, or an alter ego trust, there is no rollover provision that provides for tax deferred transfers of assets to a trust. As a result, if the trust is set up for beneficiaries other than Mr. Chisholm or his spouse, Mr. Chisholm will incur taxation on any capital gains accrued at the time of the transfer. As well, any dividends received from a private corporation by related beneficiaries may be subject to the TOSI, whether the shares are held directly or through a trust.

Use Of A Holding Company

19-162.   Mr. Chisholm could transfer assets to a holding company in which intended family members have a substantial equity interest without using a rollover provision. This will freeze the value of his estate and, if the assets transferred have fair market values that are equal to or less than their adjusted cost base, it can be an effective vehicle for realizing losses. However, without the use of a rollover provision, such as that found in ITA 85, any capital gains or recapture amounts that have accrued to the time of the transfer will become subject to immediate taxation.

Section 86 Share Exchange

Nature Of The Exchange

19-163.   Chapter 17 provided an overview of ITA 86, which applies to the exchange of shares by a shareholder in the course of a reorganization of capital. In certain situations, a share exchange constitutes the best solution to the estate freeze problem. Specifically, this rollover is most appropriate in a situation that involves an individual who is the sole owner of a successful private corporation.

19-164.   By exchanging common shares for preferred shares that have equal value, the owner will, in effect, eliminate his participation in the future growth of the company. At the same time, common shares can be issued to intended family members or a discretionary family trust created for their benefit. These new shareholders can participate in the company's future income and any growth in the value of its assets.

Example

19-165.   While detailed consideration was given to ITA 86 rollovers in Chapter 17, the following simple example will serve to review these procedures.

> **EXAMPLE**   Over her lifetime, Mrs. Hadley has been the sole owner and driving force behind Hadley Inc., a manufacturing business located in Alberta. At the end of the current year, the condensed Balance Sheet of this company was as follows:

Hadley Inc. - Balance Sheet

Net Identifiable Assets	$ 10,000,000
Common Stock (No Par - 1,000 Shares)	$ 2,000,000
Retained Earnings	8,000,000
Total Shareholders' Equity	$10,000,000

> On the basis of an independent appraisal, the fair market value of this business was established at $15,000,000. Mrs. Hadley has a husband and three adult children and would like them to share equally in her estate. The $2,000,000 Common Stock account is both the adjusted cost base and the PUC of her shares.

19-166.   Under ITA 86, Mrs. Hadley can exchange, on a tax deferred basis, her common shares that have an adjusted cost base of $2 million (also the amount of contributed capital and PUC) for preferred shares with a redemption value of $15 million (the fair market value of the business). These preferred shares would have no participation in the future growth of the company and, as a result, Mrs. Hadley has effectively frozen the value of her estate.

19-167.   If Mrs. Hadley wishes to retain control of the company, the preferred shares can be established as the only outstanding voting shares. While this share exchange will be free of any capital gains taxation, Mrs. Hadley's adjusted cost base and PUC for the new preferred shares remains at the former common share value of $2 million. If the preferred shares are sold for their market value of $15 million, a $13 million capital gain will result ($15 million - $2 million). Alternatively, if the shares are redeemed for $15 million by the company, there will be a $13 million taxable dividend under ITA 84(3).

19-168.   The tax cost basis for the identifiable assets owned by the company has not been altered by the share exchange transaction.

19-169.   At this point, the redemption value of Mrs. Hadley's preferred shares represents the entire fair market value of the business and, as a consequence, the value of any common shares issued will not exceed the amount contributed by the investors. This means that such shares can be issued for a nominal value, without any appearance that the purchasers are indirectly receiving a gift from Mrs. Hadley. Thus, 1,000 common shares could be issued to Mrs. Hadley's intended family members at $10 per share as follows:

Spouse (250 Shares At $10)	$ 2,500
Child One (250 Shares At $10)	2,500
Child Two (250 Shares At $10)	2,500
Child Three (250 Shares At $10)	2,500
Total Common Stock Contributed	$10,000

19-170.   These common shares would benefit from the future income and growth in asset values that may be experienced by Hadley Inc.

19-171.   Prior to 2018, this Section 86 rollover would have provided an ideal solution to the estate freeze problem. It did, in fact, transfer all future growth in the estate into the hands of intended beneficiaries with no immediate tax effects on the individual making the transfer. However, there is a problem in that, with the new TOSI rules in place, income received by the family members is likely to be taxed at the maximum federal rate of 33 percent.

Rollover Provisions - Section 85 vs. Section 86

19-172.   A Section 85 rollover of property to a holding corporation can also be used to implement an estate freeze. The rollover provisions of ITA 85 were given full consideration in Chapter 16 and will not be repeated here.

19-173.   In comparing the use of ITA 85 and ITA 86, you should note that Section 85 can be used in a broader variety of circumstances than is the case with Section 86. More specifically, Section 86 deals only with exchanges of shares in the course of the reorganization of an existing corporation. This means that Section 86 can only be used in situations where the assets involved in the estate freeze are shares of a corporation. Section 85 would have to be used if the estate consists of other types of property.

19-174.   When Section 86 can be used, it is an easier procedure to implement. Unlike Section 85, which requires a formal election to be made and either an existing corporation or the formation of a new corporation, Section 86 applies automatically once the required conditions are met. By using a Section 86 reorganization, the savings in legal and accounting fees can be significant. The many complexities involved in effecting an estate freeze using rollovers make it difficult to comment on the relative desirability of Sections 85 and 86 for estate freezes in general terms.

SIFT Partnerships And Trusts

19-175.   As was noted in Chapter 18, legislation has served to largely eliminate SIFT partnerships and trusts. Given this, we do not provide coverage of this subject in *Canadian Tax Principles*, except in Chapter 7, "Income from Property," where we have limited coverage of real estate income trusts (REITs).

Additional Supplementary Self Study Problems Are Available Online.

Key Terms Used In This Chapter

19-176. The following is a list of the key terms used in this Chapter. These terms, and their meanings, are compiled in the Glossary located at the back of the Study Guide.

Alter Ego Trust
Beneficiary
Capital Interest (In A Trust)
Discretionary Trust
Estate
Estate Freeze
Executor
Family Trust
Graduated Rate Estate
Income Attribution
Income Interest (In A Trust)
Income Splitting
Inter Vivos Trust
Joint Spousal Or Common-Law
  Partner Trust
Non-Discretionary Trust
Personal Trust

Preferred Beneficiary
Preferred Beneficiary Election
Qualifying Spousal or
  Common-Law Partner Trust
Reorganization Of Capital (ITA 86)
Reversionary Trust
Rollover
Settlor
Split Income
Spousal Or Common-Law Partner Trust
Tax Planning
Testamentary Trust
Trust
Trustee
Twenty-One (21) Year
  Deemed Disposition Rule
Will

References

19-177. For more detailed study of the material in this Chapter, we would refer you to the following:

ITA 70(6)	Transfers To Spousal Trusts On Death
ITA 73(1)	Inter Vivos Transfers To Spousal Trusts
ITA 74.1 to 74.5	Attribution Rules
ITA 75(2)	Trust (Attribution To Settlor)
ITA 85(1)	Transfer Of Property To Corporation By Shareholders
ITA 86(1)	Exchange Of Shares By A Shareholder In Course Of Reorganization Of Capital
ITA 104 to 108	Trusts And Their Beneficiaries
ITA 122	Tax Payable By Inter Vivos Trust
ITA 122.1	Definitions (SIFT Trusts)
ITA 197	Tax On SIFT Partnership
IC-76-19R3	Transfer Of Property To A Corporation Under Section 85
S6-F1-C1	Residence Of A Trust Or Estate
S6-F2-C1	Disposition Of An Income Interest In A Trust
IT-209R	Inter Vivos Gifts Of Capital Property To Individuals Directly Or Through Trusts
IT-286R2	Trusts - Amount Payable
IT-291R3	Transfer Of Property To A Corporation Under Subsection 85(1)
IT-305R4	Testamentary Spouse Trusts
IT-342R	Trusts - Income Payable To Beneficiaries
IT-369R	Attribution Of Trust Income To Settlor

IT-381R3	Trusts - Capital Gains And Losses And The Flow Through Of Taxable Capital Gains To Beneficiaries
IT-394R2	Preferred Beneficiary Election
IT-406R2	Tax Payable By An Inter Vivos Trust
IT-465R	Non-Resident Beneficiaries Of Trusts
IT-510	Transfers and Loans of Property Made After May 22, 1985 to a Related Minor
IT-511R	Interspousal And Certain Other Transfers And Loans Of Property
IT-524	Trusts - Flow Through Of Taxable Dividends To A Beneficiary After 1987
T4013	Trust Guide

Problems For Self Study (Online)

To provide practice in problem solving, there are Self Study and Supplementary Self Study problems available on MyLab Accounting.

Within the text we have provided an indication of when it would be appropriate to work each Self Study problem. The detailed solutions for Self Study problems can be found in the print and online Study Guide.

We provide the Supplementary Self Study problems for those who would like additional practice in problem solving. The detailed solutions for the Supplementary Self Study problems are available online, not in the Study Guide.

The .PDF file "Self Study Problems for Volume 2" on MyLab contains the following for Chapter 19:

- 6 Self Study problems,
- 2 Supplementary Self Study problems, and
- detailed solutions for the Supplementary Self Study problems.

Assignment Problems

(The solutions for these problems are only available in
the solutions manual that has been provided to your instructor.)

Assignment Problem Nineteen - 1
(Property Transfer To And From A Trust)
Each of the following independent Cases involve transfers of property to trusts by a settlor for no consideration. Three of the Cases also involve capital distributions from trusts to capital beneficiaries.

A. A gift of non-depreciable capital property is made to a qualifying spousal inter vivos trust. The adjusted cost base of the property to the settlor was $45,700. At the time of the transfer the fair market value of the property is $51,000. At a later point in time, the property is transferred to the spouse. At this time the fair market value of the property is $49,200.

B. A gift of depreciable capital property (a rare violin) is made to an inter vivos trust in favour of the settlor's adult children. The capital cost of the violin to the settlor, a world renowned violinist, was $125,000. On the date of the gift, the UCC was $72,000 and the fair market value was $155,000.

C. A transfer of a piece of vacant land is made to a qualifying spousal testamentary trust. The cost of the land for the deceased spouse was $200,000, and the fair market value on the date of the transfer to the trust is $225,500. At the time of his death, the decedent had a large net capital loss carry forward of $78,000.

D. A depreciable property is transferred to an inter vivos trust in favour of the settlor's adult children. The capital cost of the property is $17,600 and its UCC is $9,100. It is the last asset in its class. At the time of the transfer, the fair market value of the property is $5,000.

E. A gift of non-depreciable capital property is made to an inter vivos trust in favour of the settlor's adult children. The adjusted cost base of the property to the settlor was $36,900. Its fair market value on the date of the gift is $40,200. At a later point in time, when the fair market value of the property is $51,700, the property is transferred to the children.

F. A non-depreciable capital property is transferred to an alter ego trust. The cost of the capital property to the settlor was $101,500. On the date of the transfer, the estimated fair market value is $92,300. At a later point in time, when the estimated fair market value of the property has increased to $100,000, the property is transferred back to the settlor.

Required: For each Case indicate:

1. The tax consequences to the settlor that result from the transfer of the property to the trust assuming the transfer price is chosen to optimize the tax position of the settlor.

2. The tax value(s) for the transferred property that will be recorded by the trust.

3. In those cases where property is transferred to a beneficiary, the tax consequences to the trust and the tax value(s) that will be recorded by the beneficiary.

Assignment Problem Nineteen - 2
(Inter Vivos Trusts - Income Attribution)
In the process of planning an estate freeze, Glen Marx intends to transfer a large group of publicly traded common stocks to a trust. The terms of this trust will require that, on an annual basis, 50 percent of the income of the trust be distributed to his wife, Greta Petrov, with the remaining 50 percent split equally between their son, Sergey, and daughter, Anastasia. Sergey is 23 years old and has employment income of over $35,000 per year. Anastasia is 19 years old and has employment income of over $25,000 per year.

The trust's income will consist of interest, dividends, and capital gains.

The terms of the trust require that all of the trust's assets be distributed 15 years subsequent to the date on which it was established. This distribution will use the same allocation that is used for annual distributions.

Required:

A. Identify the type of trust that is being used.

B. How should the trust's year end date be chosen?

C. Indicate the persons that will have to include the trust's income in their Net Income For Tax Purposes. Would your answer change if Anastasia were 17 years of age? If so, explain how.

D. Explain how your answer to Part C would change if Mr. Marx forms the trust by the settlement of a nominal amount of cash. Mr. Marx then lends money to the trust to purchase the portfolio investments from him at their fair market value. Assume:

1. the loan is an interest free loan;

2. the trust pays interest at the prescribed rate on the loan.

E. Would the taxation of the trust income change if Mr. Marx and Mrs. Petrov were living separately because of a marriage breakdown? Explain your conclusion.

Assignment Problem Nineteen - 3
(Trusts And Income Splitting)

Hannah Brood is an engineer with 2020 employment income of $235,000. In addition, she has holdings of debt securities that produce a total of $65,000 in interest during 2020.

She has a 19 year old son from her first marriage. The son's name is Harvey Rosen, and he is enrolled in his first year at a Canadian university. It is Harvey's life-long dream to be an accounting professor. Given this, he anticipates that he will be enrolled in university programs for at least eight more years. Hannah expects that the cost of his living expenses, tuition, and books will be about $55,000 per year during this period. Harvey's father disappeared without a trace when Harvey was born and has never paid any child support.

While she has had three other marriages, she eventually found married life very dreary and is now separated from her most recent husband. However, she still loves children. To satisfy this maternal need, she arranged to have another child with sperm donated by her gay brother-in-law. This child is now a 1 year old named Carl Brood. Currently, Carl is cared for by a nanny who is paid $17,000 per year. When Carl reaches 4 years of age, Hannah intends to send him to a private school. She anticipates that the cost of the private school will be similar to the cost of the nanny.

Hannah does not anticipate that either child will have significant income until they complete university.

Hannah would like to transfer the debt securities to a trust for her children. As her employment income is more than sufficient for her needs, she hopes to use the trust to split income both currently and in future years. She has indicated that, while she wants to support her children fully, she does not want the trust to provide them with any direct payments until they are 30 years old. Until then, she wants the trust to pay for their care, education, and other direct expenses.

Required: Outline how a trust might be used to split income with Hannah's children. Ignore the possibility that some of the trust's distributions might be subject to the TOSI.

Assignment Problem Nineteen - 4
(Graduated Rate Estates - Tax Minimization)

After a long battle with cancer, Mr. Thomas Holt died on March 3, 2019. His will specifies that all of the considerable assets in his estate are to be transferred to a testamentary trust.

Because of difficulties with locating some of Mr. Holt's assets, the transfer to a trust has not been implemented prior to December 31, 2019. Given this, the executor of his estate files a T3 tax return for the period ending December 31, 2019. This return designates Mr. Holt's estate as a graduated rate estate (GRE).

Due to administrative delays of various sorts, Mr. Holt's assets remain under the administration of the executor at December 31, 2020. Because of this, the executor files a T3 return for the GRE for the year ending December 31, 2020.

The beneficiaries of the trust are Mr. Holt's wife, Renfrew Holt. She is a very successful trial lawyer with an annual income in excess of $275,000. Their 22 year old daughter, Roxanne, has struggled for several years to have a career as a folk singer. She has not enjoyed much success and, as a consequence, she has no Taxable Income for 2020.

In his will, Mr. Holt included a provision that allowed income distributions to these beneficiaries during the period that his estate is being administered by an executor. While the provision allows for distributions to either beneficiary, the timing and amounts are at the discretion of the executor.

For the year ending on December 31, 2020, the GRE had the following income receipts:

Interest	$43,000
Eligible Dividends Received From Canadian Corporations	31,200
Total Income	$74,200

Required:

A. With a view to minimizing total Tax Payable for the GRE and the beneficiaries, determine the amounts and type of income that should be distributed to each beneficiary for 2020.

B. Using the allocations you determined in Part A, calculate the total federal Tax Payable for the GRE and Roxanne Holt for the year ending on December 31, 2020. In addition, indicate any additional taxes that would be paid by Renfrew Holt for 2020 as the result of the GRE distributions.

Ignore the possibility that some of the trust's distributions might be subject to the TOSI.

Assignment Problem Nineteen - 5
(Inter Vivos Trusts - Tax Payable)
During 2018, Valerie Larson's parents both died when their private jet was hit by a drone while circling the Toronto Island airport. As an only child, Valerie inherited a substantial estate.

Her parents had transformed the family construction business from a one man operation (her father) into a very successful online marketplace for quality construction services. Valerie and her two sons, Louis and Gabriel, had worked for the Canadian controlled private corporation, Larson Services Inc. (LS), all their working lives.

Valerie decided to transfer the investments she inherited into a trust with her two sons as beneficiaries. The fiscal year of the trust ends on December 31, and Ms. Larson has no beneficial interest in either the income or capital of the trust. As the president of LS, her compensation is more than adequate for her financial needs.

Louis is aged 30, while Gabriel is 25. The terms of the trust specify that Louis is to receive 10 percent of all of the income of the trust, while Gabriel is to receive 50 percent of this income. The reason for the difference in percentages is that Louis is addicted to opioids. After the death of his grandparents, he turned to street drugs to help cope with his grief. Louis is in a long term treatment program for his addiction and he is making impressive progress.

The undistributed income is to accumulate within the trust, to be paid out to Louis when his doctors tell Valerie his addiction is under control.

The income figures for the year ending on December 31, 2020, are as follows:

Non-Eligible Dividends Received From LS	$450,000
Interest Income On Corporate Bonds	37,000
Revenues From Rental Property	205,000
Cash Expenses On Rental Property	125,350

During 2020, the rental property was sold. The property consisted of an apartment building and the land on which it was located, all of which was transferred into the trust when Valerie inherited it. The relevant information related to the disposition is as follows:

	Building	Land
Proceeds Of Disposition	$3,200,000	$728,000
Undepreciated Capital Cost	1,881,600	N/A
Capital Cost/Adjusted Cost Base	2,000,000	500,000

This is the first disposition of capital property by the trust since its establishment.

Required:

A. Calculate the Taxable Income of the trust for the year ending December 31, 2020. In addition, calculate the increase in Taxable Income resulting from being beneficiaries of the trust for Louis and Gabriel for the same period.

B. Calculate the federal Tax Payable for the trust, for the year ending December 31, 2020.

Assignment Problem Nineteen - 6
(Graduated Rate Estates – Transfer and Tax Payable)

Sam Cook passed away on September 19, 2019. He had been a very successful entrepreneur, operating dozens of unincorporated retail outlets across the country offering vintage music, videos, and art collections. Sam had invested the profits over the previous 20 years into rental properties and investments including bonds, GICs, and shares of publicly listed corporations. In the last two years, facing declining health, Sam slowly began to sell off all of his retail outlets except for the original location in Kamloops, B.C. Sam also sold some of his rental properties and liquidated many of his investments. Sam used the proceeds to provide cash gifts to employees, friends, family members, and numerous charitable organizations.

Sam was in the process of continuing to sell off most of his assets and pay off any liabilities, including income tax, when he passed away. In anticipation of his death Sam had prepared a will that named a long-time friend as executor to administer the estate by selling off the remaining assets, paying liabilities, filing the necessary tax returns, and making distributions to his two adult daughters, Violet and Trudy.

Unfortunately, the executor was not well versed in the responsibilities, and there were considerable delays in the administration of the estate as a result. In addition both Violet and Trudy delayed the process by attempting to have the executor removed for lack of competency. A B.C. court ordered the executor to seek legal assistance to complete the estate administration. As a result the estate administration was completed in August 2021.

Sam's will contemplated delays in the administration of his estate that would likely exceed one year. As a result, Sam provided the executor with discretionary authority to allocate any income to the two beneficiaries with any remainder to be taxed within the estate. The executor designated the estate as a graduated rate estate (GRE) in the first tax return of the estate for the taxation year ending September 18, 2020.

The following sources of income were earned by the GRE for its fiscal period September 19, 2019, to September 18, 2020:

Net Business Income	$68,100
Interest	14,700
Eligible Dividends From Publicly Listed Corporations	79,500
Net Rental Income	52,500

Assume that Violet and Trudy's Taxable Income for the 2020 taxation year before any income allocations from the GRE would have been $32,000 and $98,000, respectively.

Further assume that the only personal tax credits available to both Violet and Trudy are their basic personal credit and any credits that may arise as a result of income allocations from the GRE. Ignore any potential TOSI implications except in Part D of the required.

Required:

A. Determine the Taxable Income and federal Tax Payable for 2020 for each of the GRE, Violet, and Trudy on the assumption that one-third of each source of estate income is allocated to each of Violet and Trudy with the remaining one-third taxed in the GRE.

B. Determine whether you can improve upon the result in Part A by minimizing the total combined federal income tax with a different estate income allocation. Explain the basis for the reallocations.

C. Compare the amount of federal Tax Payable determined under Part A with Part B and explain the difference.

D. Briefly describe how your answer would change if it were determined that the TOSI would have applied to any business income and rental income allocations to Violet but not to Trudy.

Assignment Problem Nineteen - 7
(Graduated Rate Estates - Transfers and Tax Payable)

Martha Dagger was killed in a paragliding accident on March 15, 2020. Her will requires that all of the property in her estate be transferred to a testamentary trust. The beneficiaries of the trust will be her 22 year old daughter, Sharon Dagger, and her 14 year old son, Morris Dagger. Because of complications related to transferring the assets to the trust, on December 31, 2020, the estate assets are still under the administration of her executor.

The executor files a T3 tax return for the fiscal period ending on December 31, 2020, designating Martha's estate as a graduated rate estate (GRE). While the executor could have chosen a non-calendar taxation year, he decided to use December 31 as the year end for the GRE.

Information on the property owned by Martha at her death is as follows:

	Tax Cost	Fair Market Value March 15, 2020
Shares In Deadly Dagger Inc. (a CCPC)	$ 897,000	$1,472,000
Corporate Debt Securities	478,000	456,000
Rental Property		
Land	562,000	864,000
Building (Cost = $1,740,000)	1,390,374	2,476,000

Deadly Dagger Inc. is a qualified small business corporation. Martha has available a lifetime capital gains deduction of $250,000 [(1/2)($500,000)] and no CNIL.

Martha's will specifies that 70 percent of any income that accrues in her estate prior to the estate assets being transferred to the testamentary trust be distributed on the basis of 40 percent to Sharon and 30 percent to Morris. The remaining 30 percent will be allowed to accumulate in the GRE.

Between March 15, 2020, and December 31, 2020, the following income and expense amounts were recorded by the GRE:

Non-Eligible Dividends Received		$124,000
Interest On Corporate Debt Securities		31,650
Net Rental Income:		
Rental Revenues	$251,600	
Rental Expenses Other Than CCA	(172,940)	
CCA Claimed	(55,615)	23,045
Total Income		$178,695

Required:

A. Determine the increase in Martha's 2020 Taxable Income that will result from her death.

B. For the fiscal period ending on December 31, 2020, determine the Taxable Income for the GRE and the total Taxable Income allocated to each beneficiary.

C. Calculate the federal Tax Payable for the GRE for the fiscal period ending on December 31, 2020.

Assignment Problem Nineteen - 8

(Business Succession)

Mr. and Mrs. Rohan are 50-50 shareholders of 987456 Ltd., a Canadian controlled private corporation (CCPC) incorporated in Manitoba in 1991. The company was formed for the purpose of manufacturing and distributing a wide variety of medical equipment to hospitals across Canada. The company has been very successful, and a recent valuation has determined that the shares of the company are worth $12,000,000. The only shares ever issued by the company were common shares issued on incorporation to each of Mr. and Mrs. Rohan for nominal consideration of $100 each. As a result, the adjusted cost base (ACB) and Paid Up Capital (PUC) of the shares are nominal.

The Rohan's have three adult children, Larissa, Kara, and Julia, all of whom are 25 years of age or older and married or living common-law. In addition they have a fourth child, Aaron, who is only 16 years old and living at home. Larissa has worked in the family business for the last 10 years along with her husband, Travis. Kara has worked in the business during summers while attending college, and Julia has never worked in the business. Aaron has shown little interest in the family business and has worked summers for a local retailer.

Mr. and Mrs. Rohan have been discussing retiring and passing the business to their children, but they anticipate at least a two year transition where they would retain some control to ensure that their children who wish to be actively involved in the business are well prepared for the road ahead. Long term, they would also like to provide future financial benefits in connection with the ongoing successful business to each of their children and indirectly their children's families, regardless of whether they intend on participating in the company business. These financial benefits would include a steady stream of dividend income from the company plus capital gain growth potential on any company shares. In addition, they want to ensure that there are some safeguards in place in case of marital, financial, or health issues among their children.

Mr. and Mrs. Rohan have taken compensation from the company since the beginning mostly in the form of salary and bonuses with the occasional non-eligible dividend. The annual corporate income has remained below the small business limit throughout as a result of annual bonuses. The company's only activity and source of income has been from an active business.

The Rohan's have told you, as their accountant, that their main objectives are to transition the business to their children with minimal cost to them while maintaining some semblance of control for a few years, to retire with sufficient assets and income, and to minimize income tax throughout the process. They have specifically asked you to provide them with an understanding and the income tax consequences of the various options to transition the company to their children, including whether they should (1) gift their shares to the children, (2) pass the shares to the children on their death through a will, or (3) undertake a standard estate freeze through ITA 86. They have also asked you to explain to them the benefits, risks, and advantages of using a family trust given their objectives.

Required: Provide Mr. and Mrs. Rohan with a brief outline of the important points that they should consider that address their objectives and that explain the income tax implications of the three methods they have identified that will result in the children becoming shareholders of the company.

In addition, provide them with the an indication of the non-tax and income tax benefits and advantages of using a family trust given their objectives.

Finally, draw a conclusion, with reasons, as to whether an estate freeze with a family trust structure is in the best interests of Mr. and Mrs. Rohan and their children given their tax and non-tax objectives.

Assignment Problem Nineteen - 9
(Estate Planning)

One of your clients, Daniel Loh, has read several articles describing the tax advantages of charitable donations. Mr. Loh is 73 years old and has had a very successful career in business in
Canada. As a consequence, he owns a wide variety of investments in publicly traded securities
and private company shares, as well as real estate in Canada and Singapore. You estimate that
his assets have a current value in excess of $15 million.

Due to a car accident in Singapore that disfigured him horribly and made him a recluse, he has
never married and has no friends or living relatives. When he dies, he intends to leave all of his
assets to a group of his favourite charities.

As he has never spent any time on estate planning, he has asked you to help him understand
the issues and give him suggestions of what he should consider.

Required: Write a brief report providing the advice requested by your client.

CHAPTER 20

International Issues In Taxation

Introduction

Subjects Covered

20-1.   This Chapter is something of a potpourri of issues that are loosely related by their association with transactions and events that extend beyond Canada's borders. In some cases, we are dealing with the application of Canadian tax law to transactions and events that occur outside of Canada. In other cases, we are concerned only with the fact that individual taxable entities are moving between Canada and other jurisdictions. Some of these transactions and events relate to taxation that is associated with the laws that exist in jurisdictions outside of Canada.

20-2.   In dealing with the diverse nature of the material covered, we have organized this Chapter as follows:

Residence   Our coverage os issues related to residence were covered in Chapter 1.

Taxation Of Canadian Source Income Earned By Non-Residents   While the basic approach to the assessment of income tax in Canada is to assess tax on Canadian residents, under certain circumstances non-residents can be required to pay Canadian income taxes. Depending on the type of income, the tax may be assessed under Part I, Part XIII, or other Parts of the *Income Tax Act*. Detailed consideration will be given to Part I and Part XIII tax as they are the most commonly applied provisions.

Immigration And Emigration   We touched on this subject in Chapter 8 when we covered the deemed disposition of most capital assets when an individual emigrates from Canada. In this Chapter, we will consider some of the other complications associated with leaving Canada, as well as tax considerations related to immigration.

Taxation Of Foreign Source Income Earned By Residents   This material begins by discussing the reporting requirements applicable to Canadian residents who have foreign investments. This is followed by material dealing with resident taxpayers who have the following types of income:

- foreign source employment income;
- foreign source income from unincorporated businesses;
- foreign source interest income; and
- capital gains resulting from the disposition of foreign assets.

The remainder of the Chapter provides limited coverage of dividend income received by Canadian residents from non-resident entities. This would include material on foreign affiliates, controlled foreign affiliates, and foreign accrual property income (FAPI). Some of this material is extremely difficult to understand and because of this, some instructors may choose not to include it in their courses.

The Role of International Tax Treaties

20-3.   Tax treaties are entered into between countries for the purpose of facilitating cross-border trade and investment by removing income tax obstacles. For example, a Canadian resident employed in the U.S. is potentially subject to Canadian tax under the residence approach. In the absence of a treaty, he or she could also be subject to U.S. tax on the same income under the source approach. This would, of course, create a significant impediment to cross-border employment.

20-4.   In addition to dealing with double taxation problems such as this, treaties also provide income tax certainty, prevent discrimination, ensure a proper division of cross-border revenues, and provide an information-sharing mechanism for the purposes of administration and enforcement of each country's tax laws.

20-5.   In cases where there are conflicts, Canada's tax treaties generally over-ride the *Income Tax Act*. This over-ride occurs through legislation that implements the tax treaty, as well as specific provisions of the *Income Tax Act* that recognize the priority given to the tax treaty. For example, ITA 2(3) requires a U.S. resident to pay Canadian tax on employment income earned in Canada. The tax treaty, on the other hand, may, in specific circumstances, state that such income is only taxable in the U.S. In such cases, the inconsistency is resolved through the application of the tax treaty with the result that no Canadian tax is payable by the U.S. resident.

Part I Tax On Non-Residents

Introduction

Applicability

20-6.   As covered in Chapter 1 in our material on residence, ITA 2(1) states that Canadian taxes are payable by residents of Canada on their worldwide Taxable Income for a taxation year. While this statement makes it clear that Canadian residents are responsible for paying Canadian income taxes, it does not address the question of whether non-residents are responsible for such taxes.

20-7.   Also as mentioned in Chapter 1, ITA 2(3) specifies that non-residents are responsible for Canadian Part I tax (tax assessed on Taxable Income) on certain types of income. As listed in that subsection, non-residents are responsible for:

- income earned while carrying on a business in Canada;
- employment income earned in Canada; and
- gains and losses resulting from dispositions of Taxable Canadian Property.

20-8.   In this Chapter we will give attention to the assessment of Canadian Part I tax on non-residents in situations where they have any of these three types of income. As part of this discussion, we will provide coverage of the provisions of the U.S./Canada tax treaty that relate to such situations. Coverage of other international tax treaties goes beyond the scope of this text.

20-9.   You will note that ITA 2(3) covers business income, employment income, and capital gains on Taxable Canadian Property, but this Subsection does not refer to property income. Further, there is no reference to pension income, management fees, or capital gains on Canadian property other than those items that are classified as Taxable Canadian Property. This means that, in general, non-residents are not responsible for paying Part I tax on these types of Canadian source income.

20-10.   However, this is not the end of the story. When these other types of income are from a Canadian source and are earned by non-residents, a separate Part XIII tax is applicable. The application of this tax will be covered beginning in Paragraph 20-31.

Filing Requirements

20-11.   In those situations where a non-resident has Tax Payable under Part I, a Canadian income tax return is required (see T4058, *Non-Residents And Income Tax*). The normal filing dates for individuals and corporations are applicable in such situations. No Canadian income tax return is required if there is no Part I Tax Payable.

Taxable Income

20-12.   As some of the items that must be included in a Canadian income tax return by non-residents are exempted by various international tax treaties, such amounts can be deducted in determining Taxable Income. In addition, under ITA 115(1), non-residents will also be able to deduct Canadian employment losses, Canadian business losses, various types of loss carry overs, Canadian stock option benefits, Canadian dividends received (corporations only), and charitable donations (corporations only).

20-13.   If 90 percent or more (substantially all) of the taxpayer's worldwide income is included in their Part I tax return, the other Taxable Income deductions that are available to residents, such as the lifetime capital gains deduction, become available to non-residents.

Tax Payable

20-14.   Unless the non-resident's Part I return includes 90 percent or more of their worldwide income, ITA 118.94 prohibits the use of the majority of non-refundable tax credits. However, the following credits will be available to non-resident filers who are individuals if they have any amount of Canadian source income included in their Part I return:

- EI and CPP tax credits
- charitable donations tax credit
- disability tax credit (for taxpayer only)
- tuition tax credit
- interest on Canadian student loans tax credit

Carrying on Business in Canada

General Rules

20-15.   As we have noted, non-residents are subject to Part I tax in Canada on income from businesses carried on in Canada. The rules for calculating business income discussed in Chapter 6 are generally applicable to non-residents. However, for non-residents, ITA 253 expands the concept of a business by deeming non-residents to be carrying on a business with respect to certain activities such as:

- Producing, growing, mining, creating, manufacturing, fabricating, improving, packing, preserving, or constructing, in whole or in part, anything in Canada.

- Soliciting orders or offering anything for sale in Canada through an agent or servant, whether the contract or transaction is to be completed inside or outside Canada.

- Disposing of certain property, such as real property inventory situated in Canada, including an interest in, or option on, such real property.

20-16.   These rules are intended to ensure that certain Canadian activities that are connected to the non-resident's foreign business are potentially taxable in Canada as business income. Without these rules, it could be questionable whether the non-resident person would be considered to be carrying on a business in Canada.

EXAMPLE A U.S. business sends sales representatives to Canada to solicit orders. If the sales contracts can only be finalized in the U.S., under the general rules applicable to business income, it could be argued that no business was carried on in Canada. However, ITA 253 makes it clear that the soliciting of orders in Canada is carrying on business in Canada, without regard to where the contracts are finalized.

Canada/U.S. Tax Treaty On Business Income

20-17. The treaty allows Canada to tax the business income of U.S. residents, provided that business is operated in Canada through what is referred to as a permanent establishment.

20-18. Article V of the Canada/U.S. tax treaty defines a "permanent establishment" as a fixed place of business through which the business of a non-resident is wholly or partly carried on. The treaty provides additional clarification by adding that fixed places of business include a place of management, a branch, an office, a factory, a workshop, a mine, an oil or gas well, a quarry, or other place of extraction of natural resources. Additional rules provide permanent establishment status only if certain conditions are met (e.g., most construction projects are only considered permanent establishments if they last for more than 12 months).

20-19. The treaty specifically excludes facilities from being considered a fixed place of business if they are used exclusively for certain activities. These activities include:

- use of facilities solely for storage, display, or delivery of goods;
- maintenance of a stock of goods or merchandise for storage, display, or delivery;
- maintenance of a fixed place of business solely for purchasing goods or merchandise or for collecting information; or
- maintenance of a fixed place of business solely for the purpose of carrying on any other activity of a preparatory or auxiliary character.

20-20. The tax treaty also deems certain persons to be permanent establishments of a non-resident. Two examples of this are as follows:

- An agent who acts on behalf of a non-resident enterprise and who is authorized to conclude contracts in the name of that enterprise is considered a permanent establishment.

- An individual who acts on behalf of a business and meets both a physical presence test (183 days or more in any 12 month period beginning or ending in the year) and a gross revenue test (that more than 50 percent of the gross active business revenues of the U.S. business are from services performed by that individual during the period the individual is in Canada) is considered a permanent establishment.

Exercise Twenty - 1

Subject: Carrying On Business In Canada

In each of the following Cases, determine whether Jazzco, a U.S. corporation, is taxable in Canada:

Case 1 Jazzco, a U.S. corporation, is the parent company of Bluesco, a company incorporated in Ontario. Jazzco produces and sells Jazz CDs, while Bluesco produces and sells Blues CDs. Jazzco sells CDs to Bluesco, who in turn sells them in Canada.

Case 2 Jazzco sets up a factory in Toronto where they produce CDs for the Canadian market. The CDs are sold exclusively to an independent Canadian franchise retail outlet at a 50 percent mark-up.

Case 3 Jazzco manufactures Jazz CDs in the U.S. Jazzco ships CDs to a warehouse located in Calgary that they have rented on a five year lease. Jazzco has employed an individual in Calgary to sell the CDs throughout western Canada. The employee, however, is not allowed to conclude contracts without approval by the U.S. office.

Case 4 Assume the same facts as in Case 3, except that the employee has the authority to conclude contracts on behalf of the employer.

Case 5 Assume the same facts as in Case 3, except that the employee has an office in the warehouse premises where he solicits orders.

SOLUTION available in print and online Study Guide.

Canadian Source Employment Income

General Rules

20-21. As noted, under ITA 2(3), non-resident individuals are subject to Part I tax on Canadian source employment income. For this purpose, net employment income is calculated using the same rules that are applicable to residents earning Canadian source employment income. These rules were covered in Chapter 3.

20-22. In addition to this provision, ITA 115(2) deems certain non-resident individuals to be employed in Canada, even when the work is not carried on in this country. Such individuals include:

- Individuals who have become residents of another country and continue to receive employment remuneration from a resident Canadian source, provided a tax treaty exempts that remuneration from taxation in the foreign country.

- Non-resident individuals who have received signing bonuses and other similar amounts that relate to services to be performed in Canada in situations where the resident Canadian employer is entitled to deduct the amounts in computing Canadian income.

20-23. The basic idea behind these provisions is that, if payments are made to a non-resident that are deductible to a Canadian resident, the payments will be taxed in Canada if they are not taxed in the other country. Note, however, that employee remuneration is generally exempted from Canadian taxation if it is subject to tax by the foreign country.

Canada/U.S. Tax Treaty On Employment Income

20-24. In general, a source country has the right to tax the employment income of non-residents when it is earned within its borders. This view is reflected in ITA 2(3), which assesses Part I tax on Canadian source employment income earned by non-residents. However, the Canada/U.S. tax treaty contains two special rules that create exceptions to this general approach:

$10,000 Rule Under this rule if, during a calendar year a U.S. resident earns employment income in Canada that is $10,000 or less in Canadian dollars, then the income is taxable only in the U.S.

183 Day Rule This rule exempts Canadian source employment income from Canadian taxation provided it is earned by a U.S. resident who was physically present in Canada for no more than 183 days during any 12 month period commencing or ending in the calendar year. This exemption is conditional on employment income not being paid by an employer with a permanent establishment in Canada who would be able to deduct the amount paid from their Canadian income. Stated alternatively, if the employment income exceeds $10,000 and is deductible in Canada, it will be taxed in Canada, even if the employee is present in Canada for less than 183 days during the year.

20-25. It is important not to confuse the 183 day period in the treaty with the 183 day sojourner rule for determining residence. (See Chapter 1.) While the treaty rule applies to any physical presence in Canada, the sojourner rule applies to temporary visits or stays. Daily commutes to Canada from the U.S. for employment purposes would count toward the 183 days in the treaty rule, but not toward the 183 days in the sojourner rule.

Exercise Twenty - 2

Subject: Non-Resident Employment In Canada

Dawn Johnson is employed by Alberta Oil Ltd. as an oil well technician in Edmonton. She has accepted a transfer to the Egyptian offices of the company for three years beginning January 1, 2020. Dawn severs her residential ties to Canada on December 31, 2019, and takes up residence in Egypt. Alberta Oil continues to pay her salary. Although the government of Egypt would normally tax such salary, the tax treaty between Canada and Egypt exempts the salary from tax in Egypt. Is Dawn required to pay Canadian tax on the salary paid to her by Alberta Oil? Justify your conclusion.

Exercise Twenty - 3

Subject: Non-Resident Employment In Canada - Canada/U.S. Tax Treaty

In each of the following Cases, determine whether the employment income is taxable in Canada:

Case 1   David resides in the state of Washington. He accepted temporary employment as a technician with a Canadian company to do service calls in the Vancouver area for four months beginning September 1, 2020. The Canadian employer agreed to pay him $2,800 Canadian per month. David remained a non-resident of Canada throughout his Canadian employment.

Case 2   Assume the same facts as in Case 1, except the employer was resident in Washington and did not have a permanent establishment in Canada.

Case 3   Sandra resides in Detroit, Michigan, and has commuted daily to a full time job in Windsor, Ontario, for the last three years. In 2020, she spent 238 days at her job in Canada. She works for the municipality of Windsor and earned C$50,000 in employment income. Sandra is a U.S. resident throughout the year.

SOLUTION available in print and online Study Guide.

Dispositions of Taxable Canadian Property

General Rules

20-26.   As we have previously noted, under ITA 2(3), non-residents are taxable on gains resulting from dispositions of Taxable Canadian Property. The general rules for dealing with capital gains and losses were covered in detail in Chapter 8. While we only considered their application to Canadian residents in that Chapter, these rules are equally applicable to non-residents.

20-27.   As defined in ITA 248(1), the main categories of Taxable Canadian Property are as follows:

- Real property situated in Canada.

- Certain capital property or inventories of a business carried on in Canada.

- A share of an unlisted corporation, an interest in a partnership, or an interest in a trust if at any time within the preceding 60 months more than 50 percent of the fair market value of the share or interest was derived from certain properties, including Canadian real property, Canadian resource properties, and timber resource properties.

- A share of a listed corporation only if at any time within the preceding 60 months at least 25 percent of the issued shares of any class were owned by the non-resident taxpayer and/or non-arm's length persons, and more than 50 percent of the shares' fair market value was derived from certain properties, including Canadian real property, Canadian resource properties, and timber resource properties.

Compliance Certificates

20-28.   There are, of course, problems related to having a non-resident comply with Canadian tax rules related to dispositions of Taxable Canadian Property. To deal with this, ITA 116 requires a non-resident who anticipates a disposal of Taxable Canadian Property to file Form T2062, "Request by a Non-Resident of Canada for a Certificate of Compliance Related to the Disposition of Taxable Canadian Property". This form, which must be filed within 10 days of the planned disposition, must be accompanied by a payment of 25 percent of the anticipated capital gain on the disposition (some types of security are acceptable). When these conditions are met, a certificate of compliance will be issued. There is a penalty for disposing of a Taxable Canadian Property without obtaining a compliance certificate.

20-29.   As Canadian tax authorities are still dealing with a non-resident, this procedure does not ensure compliance. What serves to ensure that Canadian taxes will be paid is a requirement that, if the non-resident seller does not acquire a compliance certificate, the purchaser (usually a Canadian resident) is responsible for the 25 percent payment on behalf of the non-resident. Note, however, that ITA 116(5) provides an exception to this if, after reasonable enquiry, the purchaser had no reason to believe that the seller was not resident in Canada.

Canada/U.S. Tax Treaty On Taxable Canadian Property Dispositions

20-30.   While the general rule in ITA 2(3) indicates that non-residents are taxable on gains resulting from dispositions of Taxable Canadian Property, it is necessary to examine the Canada/U.S. tax treaty to see if any of its provisions over-ride this general rule. The treaty acts to limit Canadian taxation on U.S. residents to gains arising from only the following specific types of Taxable Canadian Property:

- real property situated in Canada;
- property forming part of a permanent establishment of the non-resident in Canada; and
- investments such as shares of corporations resident in Canada and interests in partnerships and trusts where the value of those investments is primarily attributable to real property situated in Canada.

Exercise Twenty - 4

Subject: Dispositions Of Taxable Canadian Property

In each of the following Cases the individual is a U.S. resident who is disposing of a property. Determine whether any gain on the disposition is taxable under Part I in Canada.

Case 1   In 2020, Nancy Gordon disposed of shares of a widely held Canadian public company that she acquired in 2017. Nancy never owned more than one-quarter of 1 percent of the outstanding shares of this company. The company's assets consist entirely of real estate situated in Canada.

Case 2   In 2015, Joe Nesbitt acquired a condo in Whistler that he rented to Canadian residents. He sold the condo in 2020 at a considerable gain. Joe never occupied the condo.

Case 3   Assume the same facts as in Case 2, except that Joe incorporates a private corporation under British Columbia legislation solely to acquire the condo. At a later point in time, Joe sells the shares at a considerable gain.

Case 4   Assume the same facts as in Case 3, except the corporation is created under Washington state legislation.

SOLUTION available in print and online Study Guide.

We suggest you work Self Study Problem Twenty-1 at this point.

Part XIII Tax On Non-Residents

Introduction

Applicability

20-31.   In the preceding section of this Chapter, we dealt with the application of Part I tax to certain specific types of income earned by non-residents. As noted in Paragraph 20-10, this leaves many other types of Canadian source income that are not subject to Part I tax in the hands of non-residents.

20-32.   The Part XIII tax is designed to correct this situation. ITA 212 provides a long list of income types to which this tax is applicable. While most of the items on the list fall into the property income category, there are other items, such as pension benefits. Notably absent, however, are taxable capital gains on assets other than Taxable Canadian Property. Capital gains on dispositions of other Canadian assets are not taxed in the hands of non-residents, either under Part I or Part XIII.

20-33.   Three other points are relevant here:

- Part XIII tax is an alternative to Part I tax. There are no situations in which both taxes would be applied to a single income source.

- Non-residents are not required to file a Canadian tax return for income that is subject to Part XIII tax.

- In general, it is the resident payer who is responsible for withholding the Part XIII tax from payment(s) being made to the non-resident, as well as remitting the withheld amounts to the CRA. The payer is also responsible for filing an information return (NR4) indicating the amounts withheld.

20-34.   As indicated, Part XIII tax applies to a long list of income types. However, in the following material, we will limit our coverage to interest, royalties, rents, dividends, and pension benefits earned or accruing to non-residents.

The Nature Of Part XIII Tax

20-35.   This is a very different type of tax than that which is assessed under Part I. Under Part I, the relevant tax rate is applied to Taxable Income, a figure that is made up of components that are calculated on a net basis. For example, interest revenues are only included after any related expenses are deducted. In contrast, the Part XIII tax is assessed on the gross amount of income received.

> **EXAMPLE**   Ms. Johnson borrows $100,000 to invest in high yield bonds. During the current year, they produce interest income of $9,000, while the interest costs for the borrowing amount to $4,000.

> **ANALYSIS**   If Ms. Johnson were a Canadian resident being taxed under Part I of the *Income Tax Act*, the applicable tax rate would be applied to $5,000 ($9,000 - $4,000). In contrast, if Ms. Johnson were a non-resident being taxed under Part XIII, the Part XIII withholding rate would be applied to the $9,000 in interest received.

Rates

20-36.   The Part XIII rate that is specified in ITA 212(1) is 25 percent for all types of income listed in ITA 212. However, this rate is rarely applied when the recipient of the income is resident in a country with which Canada has a tax treaty. All of these treaties have provisions that, while allowing the applicability of the Part XIII tax, modify the rate. This is further complicated by the fact that the rate modifications vary between the various types of income subject to the Part XIII tax.

20-37.   Comprehensive treatment of the various rates that are applicable under Canada's many international tax treaties would not be appropriate in a general text such as this. However, because it would appear to be the most important of these treaties, attention will be given to the rates that are applicable under the Canada/U.S. tax treaty.

Interest Payments

Part XIII Rules

20-38. ITA 212(1)(b) assesses Part XIII tax on only two types of interest. These are as follows:

Participating Debt Interest Participating debt interest is defined in ITA 212(3) as interest that is dependent on the use of property (e.g., royalties) or that is calculated by reference to revenue, cash flow, or profit. What is being described here is amounts that, while they may be called interest, are more like business income. They are not based on a principal sum and the passage of time.

Interest Paid To Non-Arm's Length Non-Residents, unless the interest is **Fully Exempt Interest**. Fully exempt interest is defined in ITA 212(3) as interest paid or payable on certain types of government issued or guaranteed debt (e.g., debt issued by the Government of Canada or a province).

20-39. Another way of stating this would be to note that Part XIII tax only applies to:

- arm's length arrangements when the interest payments are related to "participating debt", and
- non-arm's length arrangements if the interest is not fully exempt.

Canada/U.S. Tax Treaty On Interest Payments

20-40. When it is established that Part XIII tax is applicable, it is then necessary to consult the relevant international tax treaty to determine whether Canada has the right to tax such amounts. For U.S. residents, the Canada/U.S. tax treaty states the following:

Article XI Interest arising in a Contracting State and beneficially owned by a resident of the other Contracting State may be taxed only in that other State.

20-41. This means that, with respect to interest paid to U.S. residents, Canada does not have the right to withhold taxes under Part XIII. Residents of the U.S. are exempt from the Part XIII tax, even in the situations described in Paragraph 20-38.

Exercise Twenty - 5

Subject: Interest Payments To Non-Residents

In each of the following Cases, determine whether the interest payments made to non-residents are subject to Part XIII withholding tax, and if so, at what rate.

Case 1 Jason, a resident of a country that does not have a tax treaty with Canada, earned $3,000 in interest from a term deposit in a Canadian bank during 2020.

Case 2 Janice, a resident of a country that does not have a tax treaty with Canada, earned interest of $1,800 on Government of Canada bonds during 2020.

Case 3 Julian, a resident of Ottawa, acquired a vacation property in a country that does not have a tax treaty with Canada. The property is mortgaged with a bank in the foreign country. Julian paid $12,000 in interest to the foreign bank in 2020.

Case 4 Jasmine, a resident of Manitoba, paid $5,000 in interest on a loan from her brother, a resident of Ohio, during 2020.

SOLUTION available in print and online Study Guide.

Dividend Payments

Part XIII Rules

20-42.   Most types of dividends are subject to the 25 percent Part XIII tax. This includes capital dividends, despite the fact that they are not subject to tax when received by Canadian residents.

Canada/U.S. Tax Treaty On Dividend Payments

20-43.   While there is nothing in the Canada/U.S. tax treaty to prevent the application of this tax to U.S. residents, the treaty serves to reduce the applicable rate. In this case, there are two different reduced rates, depending on the percentage of the dividend paying corporation that is owned by the non-resident recipient.

5 Percent Rate   If the U.S. resident recipient is a corporation and owns 10 percent or more of the voting shares of the resident Canadian company that is paying the dividend, the applicable rate is only 5 percent. This 5 percent rate for inter-corporate dividends reflects a view that dividend payments between parent companies and their subsidiaries should be less heavily taxed to encourage international trade and investment.

15 Percent Rate   Other dividends paid by resident Canadian companies to shareholders who are U.S. residents are subject to the Part XIII withholding tax at a reduced rate of 15 percent.

Royalty Payments

Part XIII Rules

20-44.   Royalties paid or credited to non-residents by a person resident in Canada are generally subject to a 25 percent Part XIII withholding tax under ITA 212(1)(d). Specifically excluded under Canadian legislation are payments for copyright use, payments made under cost-sharing arrangements where the costs are shared with non-residents, and arm's length payments made that are deductible under Part I against business income earned outside Canada.

Canada/U.S. Tax Treaty On Royalty Payments

20-45.   The Canada/U.S. tax treaty, in general, allows the imposition of Part XIII tax on royalties. However, it is at a reduced rate of 10 percent. The treaty further provides that copyright and computer software royalties are not taxable by the source country.

Rental Income

Part XIII Rules

20-46.   The situation with rent payments is more complex. While ITA 212(1)(d) lists rents as one of the items subject to Part XIII tax, the *Income Tax Act* is designed to give priority to Part I tax over Part XIII tax. However, as we have noted in our discussion of the small business deduction, a taxpayer's rental activities may be so extensive that they can be considered a business. If this is the case, the non-resident taxpayer will be earning business income, which will be subject to Part I tax in Canada. If this is the case, the taxpayer will have to file an income tax return including these amounts. However, there will then be no requirement to pay Part XIII tax on the rental revenues.

An Important Election For Rental Income Of Non-Residents

20-47.   If the non-resident is not carrying on a rental business in Canada, Part XIII tax is applicable. This creates a significant problem in that the Part XIII tax is applied to gross rental revenues, a figure that will usually be much larger than net rental income.

EXAMPLE   Marcia Dorne, a resident of a non-treaty country, owns a rental property in Canada. The gross rent on this property is $120,000 for the year and is paid monthly at a rate of $10,000. The property is so heavily financed that net rental income, as determined by the Part I rules, is $12,000 for the year before CCA of $11,000.

ANALYSIS   In the absence of an alternative approach, Marcia would be subject to Part XIII tax of $30,000 [(25%)($120,000)].

20-48.   Fortunately, there is an alternative approach. Under ITA 216, Marcia can elect to pay taxes under Part I, rather than under Part XIII. In the preceding example, this election would result in Part I taxes being paid on the net rental income of $1,000 ($12,000 - $11,000 CCA). If Marcia had no other source of Canadian income, this $1,000 would be taxed at the lowest federal rate of 15 percent and, when combined with the 48 percent federal surtax on income not earned in a province, the total Part I tax would be $222 [(15%)($1,000)(148%)]. This is well below the $30,000 that would be assessed under Part XIII.

20-49.   With respect to this election, two other points are worth noting:

- In general, this election can only be made in situations where the rental property is real property located in Canada.

- If a non-resident taxpayer makes this election, they will file a separate return including only the revenues and expenses related to their rental property. They cannot make any deductions from Net Income in the determination of Taxable Income and they cannot deduct any of the ITA 118 personal tax credits.

Solution To The Cash Flow Problem

20-50.   Unfortunately, use of the ITA 216 election to pay under Part I tax does not relieve the payer from the requirement to withhold Part XIII tax. This will, in many cases, create a significant tax flow problem for the non-resident landlord. Consider the example from Paragraph 20-47. The person paying the rent would have to withhold a total of $30,000 from the payments made to Marcia Dorne. As a result, she would have a negative cash flow of $18,000 [($120,000 - $30,000) - ($120,000 - $12,000)]. While the withheld Part XIII tax would eventually be refunded, there is a significant outflow of cash during the rental period.

20-51.   Fortunately, there is a solution to this problem. A non-resident taxpayer can file Form NR6, "Undertaking to File an Income Tax Return by a Non-Resident Receiving Rent from Real Property or Receiving a Timber Royalty". If this undertaking is filed, the payer can base the required withholding on 25 percent of the estimated net rental income before the deduction of CCA. In our Paragraph 20-47 example, the Part XIII withholding would be reduced from $2,500 per month [(25%)($10,000)] to $250 per month [(25%)(1/12)($12,000)]. Any difference between this amount and the actual net rental income, including any available deduction for CCA, would be claimed when Marcia Dorne's Part I tax return is filed.

Canada/U.S. Tax Treaty On Rental Income

20-52.   The Canada/U.S. tax treaty allows the imposition of Part XIII tax to rental income. When the rental property is real property, the statutory Part XIII rate of 25 percent is applicable. However, where the rental property is something other than real property in Canada (e.g., equipment or machinery), the Canada/U.S. tax treaty reduces the Part XIII withholding rate from 25 to 10 percent.

Exercise Twenty - 6

Subject: Rental Payments To Non-Residents

In each of the following Cases, determine how the rental payments made to non-residents will be taxed by Canada. In addition, indicate whether an election to pay Part I tax is available and whether the election would be desirable.

Case 1 Rentco is a U.S. corporation with worldwide rental facilities dedicated to various equipment rentals. Rentco has offices in Saskatchewan, where it rents out farming equipment.

Case 2 In 2017, Jack Foster, a U.S. resident, acquired a hunting and fishing lodge in northern Ontario that he rents out. In 2020, he rented the lodge to Canadian residents exclusively. Jack received $42,000 in gross rents and estimates that expenses, including CCA, totaled $14,000.

Case 3 Assume the same facts as in Case 2, with one additional consideration. Jack acquired three motor boats in 2018, which he rented to guests of the lodge. In 2020, he received $8,000 in gross boat rents and estimates boat related expenses of $7,000.

SOLUTION available in print and online Study Guide.

Pension Payments And Other Retirement Related Benefits

Part XIII Rules

20-53. Amounts received by non-residents as pension or other retirement related benefits are generally subject to tax under Part XIII. This would include OAS payments, CPP payments, death benefits, certain retiring allowances, as well as payments from RRSPs, RRIFs, and DPSPs. Payments from TFSAs are not considered pension payments, but there are special rules for individuals who own TFSAs and become non-resident.

20-54. There are some exceptions under Canadian legislation that are designed to ensure that a non-resident will only be taxed on amounts that would have been taxable had the non-resident been resident in Canada at the time the benefits were earned. For example, a non-resident may receive a pension from a former Canadian employer, most of which relates to years in which the person was non-resident and worked outside Canada. Part XIII may exempt the part of the pension that relates to employment outside Canada.

An Important Election For Pension Income Of Non-Residents

20-55. The non-resident recipient of Canadian pension income can elect under ITA 217 to be taxed under Part I of the *Income Tax Act*, rather than under Part XIII. Unlike the ITA 216 election for rental income, this alternative requires the reporting of all Canadian sourced income, not just Canadian pension income, but it allows non-residents to claim deductions and credits normally given to Canadian residents. More detailed information is available on the CRA website in T4145, "Electing Under Section 217 of the *Income Tax Act*".

20-56. For a low-income individual, choosing to use the ITA 217 election can provide a significant advantage in that it will allow the individual to make use of some of the tax credits that are available under Part I. However, for high-income individuals, the Part XIII rate is likely to be lower than the rate that would be applicable under Part I of the *Act*. In most cases, this will more than offset the loss of tax credits.

Canada/U.S. Tax Treaty On Pension Payments And Benefits

20-57. The Canada/U.S. tax treaty permits the application of Part XIII tax to pension or other retirement related benefits paid to U.S. residents. As usual, the treaty acts to reduce the applicable Part XIII rate, in this case to 15 percent. However, this rate is only available on benefits that are periodic payments. If the benefit is a lump sum payment (e.g., a retiring allowance), the statutory Part XIII rate of 25 percent must be used.

20-58.   Payments from OAS, CPP, and QPP are generally subject to Part XIII tax and eligible for the optional Part I treatment discussed in Paragraph 20-55. However, with respect to OAS and CPP payments made to a resident of the U.S., the treaty specifies that these will only be taxed in the U.S. There will be no withholding or filing requirements on these amounts.

20-59.   Two other important provisions under the U.S./Canada treaty can be described as follows:

Contributions To Local Plans By Non-Residents   The treaty allows deductions for contributions by non-residents to "qualifying retirement plans" that are located in the other country. This means that U.S. residents who contribute to a qualifying Canadian plan can deduct their contributions from Canadian income and, alternatively, Canadian residents who contribute to a U.S. plan can deduct their contributions from U.S. income. Two points are relevant here:

- For U.S. residents working in Canada, qualifying retirement plans include RPPs, DPSPs, and group RRSPs. Individual RRSPs do not qualify.

- Deductions for contributions to Canadian plans are limited by the available RRSP contribution room.

Contributions and Accruing Benefits By Residents   The second provision relates to ongoing contributions and benefits accruing under a pension plan in the country in which the individual is resident. Contributions to such plans are deductible in the other country, but benefits accruing would not be taxable. For example, if a U.S. resident employed in Canada continued to make contributions to a U.S. plan, the U.S. contributions would be deductible against Canadian employment income. However, any pension benefits that accrued would not be taxable in Canada.

Shareholder Loans To Non-Residents

20-60.   In Chapter 15, we gave attention to the rules associated with shareholder loans. It was noted that, in general, the principal of such loans had to be included in a taxpayer's Net Income For Tax Purposes. There are a number of exceptions to this rule. However, in situations where the principal is not included, there is still a taxable benefit to the shareholder if the interest rate on the loan was less than the prescribed rate.

20-61.   As non-residents are generally not required to file a Part I tax return, corporate loans to non-resident shareholders would be exempt from these rules in terms of the application of Part I tax. However, ITA 214(3)(a) indicates that if ITA 15 of the *Income Tax Act* (Benefit Conferred On Shareholder) would require an amount to be included in income, that amount will be viewed as a dividend paid to the non-resident shareholder, resulting in the application of Part XIII tax. A refund of the Part XIII tax will become available when the loan is repaid.

20-62.   Such loans to non-resident shareholders escape this treatment if they are repaid within one year of the end of the taxation year in which the loan is provided. If the principal is not included in income and the interest rate on the loan is less than the prescribed rate, a benefit will be calculated in the same manner as the interest benefit on such loans when they are made to a resident shareholder. However, when a non-resident is involved, this benefit will be treated as a dividend subject to Part XIII tax.

We suggest you work Self Study Problem Twenty-2 at this point.

Immigration And Emigration

Entering Canada - Immigration

Deemed Disposition/Reacquisition

20-63.   The rules related to entering Canada are found in ITA 128.1(1). Paragraph (b) of this Sub-section indicates that, with certain exceptions, a taxpayer is deemed to have disposed of all of their property immediately before entering Canada for proceeds equal to fair market value. Para-graph (c) calls for a deemed re-acquisition of the property at the same fair market value figure.

20-64.   This process establishes a new cost basis for the taxpayer's property as at the time of entering Canada. The goal here is to avoid having Canadian taxation apply to gains that accrued prior to the individual's immigration.

> **EXAMPLE**   An individual enters Canada with securities that cost $100,000 and have a current fair market value of $150,000.

> **ANALYSIS**   In the absence of the ITA 128.1(1)(b) and (c) deeming provisions, a subsequent sale of these securities for $150,000 would result in the $50,000 accrued gain being taxed in Canada, despite the fact that it accrued prior to the individual becoming a Canadian resident.

20-65.   The properties that are excluded from the deemed disposition/re-acquisition are listed in ITA 128.1(1)(b). In general, these are items that would already have been subject to tax in Canada if the taxpayer was a non-resident. They include:

- Taxable Canadian Property.
- Inventories and certain other capital assets of a business carried on in Canada.
- **"Excluded Right or Interest"** This concept is defined in ITA 128.1(10). The definition includes RPP balances, RRSP balances, DPSP balances, stock options, death benefits, retir-ing allowances, as well as other rights of individuals in trusts or other similar arrangements.

Departures From Canada - Emigration

Deemed Disposition On Leaving Canada

20-66.   As was noted in Chapter 8, when a taxpayer leaves Canada, ITA 128.1(4)(b) calls for a deemed disposition of all property owned at the time of departure. The disposition is deemed to occur at fair market value (see Paragraph 20-69 for treatment under the Canada/U.S. tax treaty). If the taxpayer is an individual, certain types of property are exempted from this deemed dispo-sition rule. The major categories of exempted property are:

- Real property situated in Canada, Canadian resource properties, and timber resource properties.
- Property of a business carried on in Canada through a permanent establishment. This would include capital property and inventories.
- Excluded rights or interests of the taxpayer as described in Paragraph 20-65.

Exercise Twenty - 7

Subject: Emigration

Ms. Gloria Martell owns publicly traded securities with an adjusted cost base of $28,000 and a fair market value of $49,000. During the current year, she permanently departs from Canada still owning the shares. What would be the tax consequences of her departure, if any, with respect to these securities?

SOLUTION available in print and online Study Guide.

Exercise Twenty - 8

Subject: Emigration

Mr. Harrison Chrysler owns a rental property in Nanaimo, B.C., with a capital cost of $190,000 and a fair market value of $295,000. The land values included in these figures are $45,000 and $62,000, respectively. The UCC of the building is $82,600. During the current year, Mr. Chrysler permanently departs from Canada. What are the current and possible future tax consequences of his departure with respect to this rental property?

SOLUTION available in print and online Study Guide.

Problems With The Current System

20-67.   Taxpayer emigration is a problem area for those in charge of Canadian tax policy. To begin, Canada is significantly out of line with all of its trading partners in the manner in which it deals with the accrued capital gains of emigrants.

20-68.   As an illustration of this problem, consider Mr. Poutine, who departs from Canada at a time when he owns capital assets with an adjusted cost base of $80,000 and a fair market value of $120,000. On his departure from Canada, Mr. Poutine will be deemed to have disposed of these assets at their fair market value of $120,000, resulting in an assessment for a capital gain of $40,000. In many other countries, this would not occur. Mr. Poutine would be able to remove his assets without taxation and retain an unchanged adjusted cost base.

20-69.   The deemed disposition can result in double taxation as Mr. Poutine's new country of residence may consider his adjusted cost base to be the original value of $80,000. Fortunately, the Canada/U.S. tax treaty provides a fix for this situation. Under Article XIII(7), Mr. Poutine can elect to have a deemed disposition at fair market value for U.S. tax purposes as well as for Canadian tax assessment, but this fix is not available for all countries.

20-70.   A further problem in this area is the ability of some taxpayers to avoid the Canadian emigration tax rules, resulting in large sums of money being removed from Canada on a tax free basis. Some types of assets can be removed tax free on the assumption that they will be subject to Canadian taxation at a later point in time. This might not happen if one of Canada's bilateral tax treaties prohibits Canadian taxation after an individual has been a non-resident for a specified period of time.

20-71.   Other leakages can occur when assets are bumped up in value for foreign tax purposes, with no corresponding change in the Canadian tax base. This is essentially what happened in the Bronfman trust case, in which several billion dollars in assets were removed from Canada without being subject to Canadian income taxes on accrued gains.

Elective Dispositions

20-72.   As noted in the preceding Paragraphs, certain types of property are exempted from the deemed disposition rules. There may, however, be circumstances in which an individual wishes to over-ride these exemptions and trigger capital gains at the time of departure. An important example of this would be farm property that qualifies for the lifetime capital gains deduction. (See Chapter 11 for details of this deduction.)

20-73.   An individual may wish to trigger income or losses on the exempted property at the time of departure for other reasons. An example of this would be an emigrant who wants to realize a loss on exempt property in order to offset a gain on non-exempt property.

20-74.   Such situations are provided for in ITA 128.1(4)(d), which allows an individual to elect to have a deemed disposition on certain types of properties that are exempt from the general deemed disposition rule. The properties on which the election can be made include real property situated in Canada, Canadian resource and timber resource properties, as well as property of a business carried on in Canada through a permanent establishment. Note that, if this election results in losses (capital or terminal), they can only be used to offset income resulting from other deemed dispositions. They cannot be applied against other sources of income, including capital gains from actual dispositions, for the taxation year.

Exercise Twenty - 9

Subject: Emigration

Ms. Gloria Lopez owns shares in a Canadian private company with an adjusted cost base of $120,000 and a fair market value of $235,000. In addition, she owns a rental property with a fair market value of $130,000 ($30,000 of this can be attributed to the land) and a cost of $220,000 ($60,000 of this can be attributed to the land). The UCC of the building is $142,000. During the current year, Ms. Lopez permanently departs from Canada. Calculate the minimum Net Income For Tax Purposes that will result from her departure with respect to the shares and the rental property.

SOLUTION available in print and online Study Guide.

Security For Departure Tax

20-75. The preceding deemed disposition rules can be very burdensome for an emigrating individual. If the individual has substantial amounts of property on which gains have accrued, the deemed disposition rules can result in a hefty tax bill. This is further complicated by the fact that there are no proceeds of disposition to provide funds for paying this liability.

20-76. In recognition of this problem, ITA 220(4.5) through (4.54) allow the taxpayer to provide security in lieu of paying the tax that results from the deemed dispositions. Similar provisions have been added, such as ITA 220(4.6) through (4.63) for dealing with trusts distributing Taxable Canadian Property to non-residents.

20-77. ITA 220(4.5) requires the CRA to accept "adequate security". Guidance on what constitutes adequate security is as follows:

> Bank letters of guarantee, bank letters of credit, and bonds from the Government of Canada or a province or territory of Canada are considered acceptable forms of security. Other types of security may also be acceptable, such as shares in private or publicly traded corporations, certificates in precious metals, various other marketable securities, a charge or mortgage on real property, or valuable personal property.

20-78. If the taxpayer elects under ITA 220(4.5), interest does not accrue on the tax that has been deferred until the amount becomes unsecured. This will usually be at the time when there is an actual disposition of the property that was subject to the deemed disposition.

20-79. A final point here is that ITA 220(4.51) creates deemed security on an amount that is the total amount of taxes under Part I that would be payable, at the highest tax rate that applies to individuals, on Taxable Income of $50,000. This amount is one-half of a $100,000 capital gain, and the effect of this provision is to exempt emigrants from the requirement to provide security on the first $100,000 in capital gains resulting from their departure.

We suggest you work Self Study Problem Twenty-3 at this point.

Unwinding A Deemed Disposition

The Problem

20-80.   A potential problem can arise when an individual departs from Canada and, at a later point in time, returns. A simple example will serve to illustrate this difficulty:

EXAMPLE   John Fuller emigrates from Canada on June 1, 2020. At that time, he owns shares of a private company with a fair market value of $200,000 and an adjusted cost base of $125,000. As a result of the deemed disposition/re-acquisition of these shares, he has a taxable capital gain of $37,500 [(1/2)($200,000 - $125,000)]. In 2021, he returns to Canada. At the time of immigration, he still owns the shares and their fair market value has increased to $260,000.

20-81.   In the absence of any special provision (and ignoring the deemed security rules discussed in Paragraph 20-75), Mr. Fuller's departure from Canada would cost him the taxes paid on the $37,500 taxable capital gain arising on the deemed disposition at emigration. On his return, the adjusted cost base of his property would be increased to $260,000 (deemed disposition/re-acquisition on immigration). However, the fact remains that his temporary absence has resulted in an out-of-pocket tax cost on the $37,500 taxable capital gain.

The Solution

20-82.   ITA 128.1(6) provides relief in this type of situation. With respect to Taxable Canadian Property such as Mr. Fuller's, ITA 128.1(6)(a) allows a returning individual to make an election with respect to property that was Taxable Canadian Property at the time of emigration. The effect of making this election is that the deemed disposition that was required under ITA 128.1(1)(b) at the time of departure is reversed when the individual returns to Canada. As there is no real basis for establishing whether an emigrant will eventually return as an immigrant, ITA 128.1(6) has no influence on the tax consequences arising at the time of emigration.

20-83.   Returning to our example from Paragraph 20-80, if this election is made, the addition to Taxable Income that was assessed when Mr. Fuller left Canada would be reversed through an amended return, resulting in a refund of the taxes paid.

20-84.   As the deemed disposition at departure has been reversed, there would be no need for a disposition/re-acquisition when he returns to Canada. This means that after the appropriate election and amended return are filed, Mr. Fuller would wind up in the same tax position as he was in before he departed from Canada. That is, he would own securities with an adjusted cost base of $125,000 with no net taxes paid as a result of his departure and return.

Short-Term Residents

20-85.   With the increasing presence of multinational firms in the Canadian business environment, it has become common for executives and other employees to find themselves resident in Canada for only a small portion of their total working lives. In the absence of some special provision, the deemed disposition rules could be a significant hardship to employees who are in this position.

20-86.   For example, if Ms. Eng was transferred from Hong Kong to work in Canada for three years, she could become liable on departure for capital gains taxation on all of her capital property owned at the time that she ceases to be a resident of Canada. The liability could put a severe drain on her available liquid assets and could result in taxation on personal items such as paintings and furniture (note that, in many cases, where the individual is in the country for a limited period and working for a non-resident employer, the individual would be taxed as a resident of the foreign country, and not as a resident of Canada). This would not be an equitable situation and could discourage the free movement of employees to and from Canada.

20-87.   In recognition of the preceding problem, ITA 128.1(4)(b)(iv) provides an exception to the deemed disposition rules that applies to taxpayers who, during the 10 years preceding departure, have been resident in Canada for a total of 60 months or less. For such taxpayers, the deemed disposition rules do not apply to any property that was owned immediately before the taxpayer last became resident in Canada or was acquired by inheritance or bequest during the period after he or she last became resident in Canada. However, the rules still apply to property acquired other than by inheritance or bequest during the period of residency.

Exercise Twenty - 10

Subject: Short Term Residents

During 2017, Charles Brookings moves to Canada from the U.K. He has not previously lived in Canada. At this time his capital assets consist of shares in a U.K. company and a tract of vacant land in Canada that he had inherited. The shares have a fair market value of $250,000 and an adjusted cost base of $175,000. The land had a fair market value of $95,000 when he inherited it and a fair market value of $120,000 when he moves to Canada in 2017.

During 2018, he acquires shares of a Canadian public company for $75,000. During 2020, after finding Canada a tad uncivilized for his tastes, he moves back to the U.K. At this time, the shares in the U.K. company have a fair market value of $280,000, the shares of the Canadian company have a fair market value of $92,000 and the land has a fair market value of $130,000.

What are the tax consequences of his emigration from Canada?

SOLUTION available in print and online Study Guide.

Foreign Source Income Of Canadian Residents

Introduction

20-88.   It would be a fairly easy task to write an entire book on the tax issues associated with the foreign source income of Canadian residents. One version of the draft legislation on non-resident trusts and foreign investment entities ran to nearly 900 pages in its print edition. In addition to being extensive, much of this material is extremely complex, in some cases almost beyond the understanding of mere mortals. Despite this complexity, the importance of this subject mandates that we give some attention to the issues, even in an introductory text such as this. Although some aspects of foreign source income of Canadian residents are relatively straightforward, you should be aware that this material is not an adequate resource for making important decisions in this potentially complicated area.

20-89.   We will begin this section on foreign source income of residents by discussing the reporting requirements applicable to Canadian residents who have foreign investments. This will be followed by sections dealing with resident taxpayers having the following:

- foreign source employment income;
- foreign source income from unincorporated businesses;
- foreign source interest income; and
- capital gains resulting from the disposition of foreign assets.

20-90.   The issues involved for taxpayers having these types of income sources are not overly complex. However, a completely different situation arises when Canadian resident taxpayers receive income from what tax legislation refers to as non-resident entities. These entities are defined as corporations, trusts, or any other type of entity that was formed, organized, last continued under, or governed under the laws of a country, or a political subdivision of a country, other than Canada. In order to simplify our presentation of this material, we will limit our coverage to non-resident corporations paying dividends to Canadian resident taxpayers.

Foreign Investment Reporting Requirements

20-91.   As you are aware, residents of Canada are liable for income taxes on their worldwide income. This means, for example, that if a Canadian resident has a bank account in England, any interest earned on that account should be reported in the taxpayer's Canadian tax return.

20-92.   There is little doubt that evasion of taxes on foreign income has been fairly common in the past. In an attempt to curtail tax evasion on foreign property and to amass information on foreign property owned by Canadians, the CRA requires the following:

> All Canadian resident taxpayers are required to file form T1135, *Foreign Income Verification Statement,* if at any time in the year the total cost amount (not fair market value) of all specified foreign property to the taxpayer was more than $100,000 in Canadian dollars.

20-93.   The T1135 offers a simplified reporting method to taxpayers whose specified foreign property totals more than $100,000 but less than $250,000 throughout the year. Rather than having to report the complete details on the T1135, the simplified method allows a taxpayer to report a single figure for the total income from all specified foreign property, as well as for the gain (loss) from the disposition of all specified foreign property for the year. For example, the taxpayer will be able to report a single figure for the total value of non-resident securities held, rather than having to report each individual security in this category.

20-94.   The T1135 form requires information on what is referred to as "specified foreign property". The more important types of specified foreign property are as follows:

- funds held outside Canada (e.g., funds in a foreign bank account);
- shares of a non-resident corporation (see Paragraph 20-97 for a streamlined option to these reporting requirements for foreign shares held in Canadian brokerage accounts);
- indebtedness owed by a non-resident;
- real property outside of Canada other than excluded property such as personal use or business use properties (see Paragraph 20-95); and
- an interest in a non-resident trust.

20-95.   Some of the common items excluded from the definition of specified foreign property are as follows:

- foreign securities held in Canadian mutual funds, or inside a registered account like an RRSP, RRIF, TFSA or RESP;
- a property used or held exclusively in carrying on an active business;
- a personal use property, such as a second home; and
- a share of the capital stock or indebtedness of a foreign affiliate.

20-96.   For taxpayers with less than $250,000 in specified foreign property, completing the simplified form (Part A of the T1135) is not particularly onerous. For taxpayers with specified foreign property equal to $250,000 or more, a great deal of additional information is required, such as:

- the name of the entity holding or issuing the property, or a description of the foreign property;
- the relevant country code (for the country of residence of the bank, corporation, issuer, or trust, or where the property is located);
- the maximum cost amount of the property during the year;
- the year end cost amount of the property;
- the amount of income or loss related to the property for the year; and
- any capital gain or loss realized on the disposition of the property during the year.

20-97.   Fortunately, in many if not most cases relief is available. To the extent specified foreign property is held in an account with a Canadian registered securities dealer or a Canadian trust company, the only requirements related to specified foreign property are reporting country-by-country aggregate values for maximum fair market value during the year, fair market value at the end of the year, income for the year, and gains or losses on dispositions during the year. For example, if an individual invests only in U.S. stocks and they are held with a Canadian registered securities dealer, the reporting requirements are greatly simplified. This is likely the situation for many of the individuals who are required to report their specified foreign property.

20-98.   Substantial penalties can result from failure to comply with these reporting requirements. They range from $500 per month for up to 24 months if the failure to file is done knowingly to $1,000 per month for up to 24 months if there is a failure to comply with a demand to file the T1135. After 24 months, the penalty can become more severe, i.e., 5 percent of the cost of the foreign property.

Exercise Twenty - 11

Subject: Foreign Investment Reporting

During 2020, Simon Taylor, a Canadian resident, has a bank account at the Bank of Scotland. The balance ranged from £4,000 to £52,000 during the year and has a balance of £41,000 on December 31, 2020. Interest on the account for the year totalled £1,000. In 2019, he made a two year interest free loan of £145,000 to his brother-in-law, who is a resident of Scotland. No formal loan agreement was involved. Assume 1£ = $1.70 for 2019 and 2020. Describe the foreign investment reporting obligations that Simon has for 2020 and provide the information required.

SOLUTION available in print and online Study Guide.

We suggest you work Self Study Problem Twenty-4 at this point.

Foreign Source Employment Income

The Problem

20-99.   Individuals who are residents of Canada are taxable on employment income regardless of where the employment duties are performed. This creates a potential problem in that an individual earning employment income in a foreign country could be subject to Canadian taxes because they have retained their status as a Canadian resident and, at the same time, be subject to taxes in the foreign country because it is the source of the employment income. Tax treaties would normally be used to resolve this potential conflict.

Canada/U.S. Tax Treaty - Foreign Source Employment Income

20-100.   This problem is, of course, the mirror image of the problem that arises when a U.S. resident is earning employment income while working in Canada. In our discussion of that situation (see Paragraph 20-21), we noted that, in general, the source country has the right to tax employment income. We also noted that, under the Canada/U.S. tax treaty, there were two exceptions to this rule. As applied to a situation where a Canadian resident is earning U.S. employment income, these exceptions are as follows:

$10,000 Rule   Under this rule if, during a calendar year, a Canadian resident earns employment income in the U.S. that is $10,000 or less in U.S. dollars, then the income is taxable only in Canada.

183 Day Rule   This rule exempts U.S. source employment income from U.S. taxation, provided it is earned by a Canadian resident who was physically present in the U.S. for no more than 183 days during any 12 month period commencing or ending in the calendar year. This exemption is conditional on employment income not being paid by an employer with a permanent establishment in the U.S. who would be able to deduct the amount paid from their U.S. Taxable Income. Stated alternatively, if the employment income exceeds $10,000 and is deductible in the U.S., it will be taxed in the U.S., even if the employee is present in the U.S. for less than 183 days during the year.

We suggest you work Self Study Problem Twenty-5 at this point.

Foreign Source Business Income (Unincorporated Sources)

The Problem

20-101.   The general rule that Canadian residents are taxable on their worldwide income would suggest that Canadian residents are taxable on foreign source business income. As was the case with foreign source employment income, this creates a potential problem in that a person earning business income in a foreign country could be subject to Canadian taxes because they have retained their status as a Canadian resident and, at the same time, be subject to taxes in the foreign country because it is the source of the business income.

20-102.   In many cases, the potential for double taxation is dealt with through international tax treaties. If this is not the case, a Canadian resident may have some amount of taxes withheld in the foreign jurisdiction. In these circumstances, Canada uses foreign tax credits to deal with the problem. While these credits were covered in detail in Chapter 11 for individuals and Chapter 12 for corporations, a simple example where the detailed calculations would have resulted in a foreign tax credit equal to the foreign tax withheld will serve to review the general approach used:

EXAMPLE   Ms. Johnson, a Canadian resident, is subject to a Canadian marginal tax rate of 45 percent on all of her worldwide income. During the current year, she earns foreign source business income of $1,000, from which the source country assesses and withholds taxes at a rate of 15 percent.

ANALYSIS   The pre-tax amount of foreign income would be included in Taxable Income, with the foreign taxes paid by Ms. Johnson, a Canadian resident, generating a credit against Canadian Tax Payable. Applying this to the preceding example results in the following calculations:

Foreign Business Income Received	$ 850
Foreign Tax Withheld	150
Gross Income = Taxable Income Addition	$1,000
Canadian Tax Payable [(45%)($1,000)]	$ 450
Foreign Tax Credit = Foreign Tax Withheld	(150)
Net Canadian Tax Payable	$ 300
Foreign Tax Withheld	150
Total Taxes Payable	$ 450
After Tax Retention ($1,000 - $450)	$ 550
Overall Tax Rate ($450 ÷ $1,000)	45%

As this simple example makes clear, this represents a very equitable solution to situations where foreign taxes are withheld on income that will be taxed again in Canada. The combined foreign and Canadian taxes total $450, exactly the same amount that would have been paid if Ms. Johnson had received the $1,000 in business income from a Canadian source.

Canada/U.S. Tax Treaty - Foreign Source Business Income

20-103.   As was discussed when we considered the Canadian business income of non-residents, the Canada/U.S. tax treaty indicates that business income will be taxed in the source country in those situations where the business is operated through a permanent establishment. Applying this here would mean that if a Canadian resident earns business income in the U.S. without having a permanent establishment in that country, it will be taxed in Canada rather than in the U.S. Alternatively, if the business income is earned through a permanent establishment in the U.S., it will be taxed in that country. Any taxes withheld by the U.S. would be eligible for treatment as a foreign business tax credit. (See Chapters 11 and 12 for detailed coverage of this credit.)

Exercise Twenty - 12

Subject: Foreign Tax Credits

Jason Abernathy is a Canadian resident. During 2019, he earns $18,000 of business income through a permanent establishment located in the U.S. Income taxes of $1,800 were assessed and withheld at the source on that income. In calculating his foreign tax credit, his Adjusted Division B Income is equal to $100,000 and his Tax Otherwise Payable is equal to $21,000. All amounts are in Canadian dollars. Jason's marginal combined federal/provincial tax rate is 44 percent. Determine his after tax retention and overall tax rate on his foreign source business income.

SOLUTION available in print and online Study Guide.

Foreign Source Interest Income

The Problem

20-104.   Resident Canadian taxpayers are taxable on interest income, generally without regard to the source. As was the case with employment income, this raises the possibility of double taxation. In most cases this issue will be resolved by an international tax treaty. If the issue is not resolved by treaty, the Canadian resident would have tax deductions and/or credits based on any foreign taxes withheld.

Canada/U.S. Tax Treaty - Foreign Source Interest Income

20-105.   As noted in Paragraph 20-40, Article XI of the Canada/U.S. tax treaty indicates that interest paid to the other jurisdiction will be taxed only in that jurisdiction. This means that U.S. residents receiving interest from a Canadian source are not subject to the Canadian Part XIII tax. Correspondingly, Canadian residents receiving interest income from a U.S. source will be subject to Part I taxes only in Canada.

Foreign Source Capital Gains

The Problem

20-106.   The rules of the *Income Tax Act* relating to the calculation of capital gains and losses are generally applicable to residents of Canada on dispositions of property regardless of the location of that property. As was the case with foreign source employment and business income, dispositions of foreign property may result in potential taxation in both Canada and the foreign country. Again, the tax treaties would normally offer a way to resolve any conflicts.

Canada/U.S. Tax Treaty - Foreign Source Capital Gains

20-107.   In general, the Canada/U.S. tax treaty gives priority to tax to the vendor's country of residence. However, the treaty allows the U.S. to tax gains from the disposition of real property interests situated in the U.S., as well as gains on most types of property that are used in a permanent establishment through which a Canadian resident carries on business in the U.S.

Foreign Source Dividend Income - Problems

20-108.   Most foreign source investment income is taxed under the rules that are applicable to similar sources of income earned in Canada. An exception to this is dividends received from non-resident corporations.

20-109.   As you are aware, dividends paid to Canadian residents by taxable Canadian corporations receive very favourable tax treatment. When such dividends are received by individuals, they are subject to the gross up and tax credit procedures, a process that significantly reduces the effective tax rate on this type of income. When the recipient shareholder is a corporation, the dividends generally escape all taxation in that they can be deducted under ITA 112(1) in the calculation of Taxable Income. Both of these provisions are designed to make up for the fact that the dividends represent an income stream that has already been subject to Canadian tax at the corporate level.

20-110.   The basic problem with dividends received from a non-resident corporation is that the corporation that paid the dividends has not paid taxes in Canada. In fact, in some jurisdictions (e.g., tax havens), the corporation may not have paid any taxes whatsoever. This means that the usual reason for providing favourable treatment of dividend income is not relevant when dividends are received from a non-resident corporation.

20-111.   A further problem is that the foreign source dividends do not reflect the type of income that provided for the payment of dividends by the foreign corporation. Again, as you are aware, Canadian taxes are generally assessed differently on alternative types of income. For example, a CCPC will be taxed much more heavily on property income as compared to the taxes that would be paid on active business income. To maintain fairness in the system, provisions had to be created that reflect the different sources of income that enabled the non-resident corporation to pay dividends.

20-112.   In general, foreign source dividends must be included in a resident taxpayer's Net Income For Tax Purposes under ITA 90(1). When foreign source dividends are received by individuals, they do not get the benefit of the gross up and tax credit procedures. When they are received by corporations, they are not generally deductible under ITA 112(1).

20-113.   While the elimination of favourable tax treatment for dividends from a foreign source provides a partial solution to the problem of dividends being paid out of corporate income that has not been taxed in Canada, two significant problems remain:

1.   This procedure can result in double taxation. For example, income earned by a foreign subsidiary of a Canadian corporation could be fully taxed in the foreign jurisdiction and, in the absence of the ITA 112(1) dividend deduction, it would be taxed again in Canada.

2.   Under the general rules applicable to corporations, income from a non-resident corporation will not be taxed in Canada until such time as it is distributed to Canadian residents. This means that a Canadian resident can achieve significant tax deferral by placing investments in a foreign corporation, in situations where the income from the investments is not currently needed. This is particularly attractive when the non-resident corporation is located in a jurisdiction where there is little or no taxation of investment income.

20-114.   The first of these problems has been dealt with by developing the concept of a "foreign affiliate". As will be discussed in a subsequent section of this Chapter, dividends received from this type of non-resident corporation may be deductible, in whole or in part, to a recipient Canadian corporation. A partial solution to the second problem is contained in what are referred to as the Foreign Accrual Property Income (FAPI) rules. These rules apply to a subset of foreign affiliates referred to as controlled foreign affiliates.

20-115.   In the following material, we will give consideration to dividends from foreign corporations that are received by:

- individuals resident in Canada;
- Canadian corporations that are not affiliated with the foreign corporation;
- Canadian corporations that are affiliated with the foreign corporation but do not control it; and
- Canadian corporations that control the foreign corporation.

20-116.   We would remind you that our presentation of this material is at a very basic level and should be considered only as an overview of the topic and not as a guide for making real world decisions in this complex area.

Foreign Source Dividends Received By Individuals

20-117.   If a resident Canadian individual receives a dividend from a foreign corporation and there is no withholding of tax by the foreign jurisdiction, the amount received will be converted into Canadian dollars at the time that it is received. It would then be included in that individual's Net Income For Tax Purposes. It will not be grossed up and it will not generate a dividend tax credit.

20-118.   Alternatively, if there is withholding by the foreign jurisdiction, the pre-withholding amount of the dividend will be included in the individual's Net Income For Tax Purposes. To the extent that the withholding is 15 percent or less, the individual is entitled to a foreign tax credit. Any withholding in excess of 15 percent is eligible for a deduction from Net Income For Tax Purposes.

20-119.   While it would rarely be an appropriate choice, the individual would have the alternative of deducting the entire amount withheld, rather than using the eligible portion as a tax credit.

EXAMPLE   During 2019, Martin Fingle is entitled to $25,000 in dividends from a foreign corporation in which he owns shares. The foreign jurisdiction withholds $5,000 (20 percent), providing a net receipt of $20,000. In addition to the dividend, Martin has Canadian source interest income of $22,000. Other than the foreign tax credit, he has other credits that total $2,200. He has no deductions from Net Income For Tax Purposes in determining Taxable Income.

ANALYSIS   Martin's Taxable Income would be calculated as follows:

Interest Income	$22,000
Foreign Dividends (100%)	25,000
Excess Withholding [(20% - 15%)($25,000)]	(1,250)
Net Income For Tax Purposes And Taxable Income	$45,750

His Tax Payable would be calculated as follows:

Tax Before Credits [(15%)($45,750)]	$ 6,863
Personal Tax Credits	(2,200)
Part I Tax Payable Before Foreign Tax Credit	$ 4,663
Foreign Tax Credit (See Note)	(2,548)
Federal Tax Payable	$ 2,115

Note   The foreign tax credit would be the lesser of:

- Amount Withheld (Limited To 15% Of $25,000) = $3,750

- $\left[\dfrac{\text{Foreign Non - Business Income}}{\text{Division B Income}}\right]$(Tax Payable) $= \left[\dfrac{\$25,000}{\$45,750}\right]$($4,663) = $2,548

20-120. While Martin could have deducted all of the withheld amount, his additional tax savings from this deduction would only be $382 [(15%)($2,548)]. This is clearly not as desirable as the $2,548 foreign tax credit alternative.

We suggest you work Self Study Problem Twenty-6 at this point.

Foreign Dividends Received From Non-Affiliated Corporations

20-121. The pre-withholding amount of a dividend received by a Canadian corporation from a foreign corporation is always included in the corporation's Net Income For Tax Purposes. As a foreign affiliate is not involved, there would be no deduction in the determination of the corporation's Taxable Income.

> **EXAMPLE** Martin Fingle Inc., a Canadian public corporation, is entitled to $25,000 in dividends from a foreign corporation in which it owns less than 1 percent of the shares. The foreign jurisdiction withholds $5,000 (20 percent), providing a net receipt of $20,000. The corporate tax rate on this income, after the general rate reduction, will be 25 percent (38% - 13%). Assume that Martin Fingle Inc. has no other source of income during the year.

> **ANALYSIS** The corporation's Taxable Income will be $25,000, the pre-withholding amount of the dividend. Tax Payable, before the application of the foreign tax credit, will be $6,250 [(25%)($25,000)]. As a corporation's use of foreign non-business tax credits is not limited to 15 percent, the tax credit will be $5,000, the lesser of:

> - Amount Withheld (no 15% limit) = $5,000

> - $\left[\dfrac{\text{Foreign Non - Business Income}}{\text{Division B Income}}\right]$ (Tax Payable) = $\left[\dfrac{\$25,000}{\$25,000}\right]$ ($6,250) = $6,250

Dividends Received From Non-Controlled Foreign Affiliates
Foreign Affiliate Defined
20-122. A foreign affiliate of a Canadian taxpayer is defined in ITA 95(1) as a non-resident corporation in which that taxpayer has a direct or indirect equity percentage of at least 1 percent. As well, the aggregate equity percentages of the taxpayer and each person related to the taxpayer must be at least 10 percent. The ownership percentage can be established on either a direct or indirect basis and is defined as the greatest percentage holding in any class of the non-resident corporation's capital stock.

20-123. As an example of both the direct and indirect application of this rule, consider the following example:

> **EXAMPLE** Candoo, a resident Canadian corporation, owns 70 percent of the only class of shares of Forco One, a non-resident corporation. In turn, Forco One owns 20 percent of the only class of shares of Forco Two, a second non-resident corporation.

> **ANALYSIS** Forco One is a foreign affiliate of Candoo because of Candoo's 70 percent direct ownership. Forco Two is also a foreign affiliate of Candoo because the indirect ownership percentage is 14 percent [(70%)(20%)].

20-124. We would also note that the ownership thresholds are applied on a shareholder-by-shareholder basis. A non-resident company will be a foreign affiliate of a Canadian resident only if that resident owns directly or indirectly at least 1 percent of the shares of that non-resident company and, in addition, that resident, together with related persons, owns at least 10 percent of the shares of that non-resident company.

EXAMPLE   Carson Ltd. and Dawson Inc., two resident Canadian companies, each own 8 percent of Belgique, a non-resident corporation. While Carson Ltd. is part of a related group that controls Belgique, Dawson Inc. is not related to any of the other shareholders of Belgique.

ANALYSIS   Belgique would be a foreign affiliate of Carson Ltd. as Carson Ltd. owns more than 1 percent of the shares and, in addition, is part of a related group that owns more than 10 percent of the shares. Belgique would not be a foreign affiliate of Dawson Inc.

20-125.   A foreign affiliate may or may not be a controlled foreign affiliate. In this section we are limiting our discussion to situations where control is not present. In the next section of this chapter, we will provide limited coverage of controlled foreign affiliates. Note that the rules discussed in this section apply to all foreign affiliates, whether or not control exists.

Exercise Twenty - 13

Subject   Identifying Foreign Affiliates

Canvest is a resident Canadian corporation that has three investments in the shares of non-resident corporations. For each of the investments in non-resident corporations described below, determine whether the investee is a foreign affiliate.

Forco 1   Canvest owns 3 percent of Forco 1. A wholly owned Canadian subsidiary of Canvest owns 8 percent of Forco 1.

Forco 2   Canvest owns 9 percent of Forco 2. Canvest is not related to any of the other shareholders of Forco 2.

Forco 3   Canvest owns 5 percent of Forco 3. The spouse of the shareholder who has a controlling interest in Canvest owns the other 95 percent of the shares of Forco 3.

SOLUTION available in print and online Study Guide.

Dividends Received From Foreign Affiliates - Basic Concepts

20-126.   We have previously noted that, in general, only dividends received from a taxable Canadian corporation can be deducted under ITA 112(1) in the determination of the Taxable Income of a resident Canadian corporation. However, ITA 113(1) provides a similar deduction for dividends received by a resident corporate shareholder from a foreign affiliate.

20-127.   Unlike the fairly straightforward application of ITA 112(1), the application of ITA 113(1) is very complex in that it is applied differently depending on the country where the foreign affiliate is located and income source from which the dividend is being paid. The ITA 113(1) rules are implemented by a process in which the foreign affiliate's surplus balances are tracked by type of income and source country. We would remind you that the term surplus in tax work is the equivalent of the term Retained Earnings in accounting work. We would also remind you that, while the terms are equivalent, the balances are normally different.

20-128.   While there are other types of surplus that determine the tax status of dividends from foreign affiliates, in this text we will only provide coverage of Exempt Surplus and Taxable Surplus. Coverage of other surplus balances goes beyond the scope of this introductory text.

20-129.   When a dividend is paid by a foreign affiliate it is assumed to come first from any Exempt Surplus balance that is available. If there is no Exempt Surplus balance, or if the dividend is larger than the Exempt Surplus balance, the required amount will then be removed from the Taxable Surplus balance.

Exempt Vs. Taxable Surplus

20-130.   The content of these surplus balances requires the allocation of income from four different sources. They are as follows:

- active business income
- investment income (e.g., interest and rents)
- capital gains on dispositions of assets used to produce active business income
- capital gains on dispositions of assets not used to produce active business income

20-131.   The situation is further complicated in that the classification of a particular type of income will depend on whether the foreign affiliate is located in a country with which Canada has a tax treaty or a Tax Information Exchange Agreement (TIEA). For example, active business income is allocated to Exempt Surplus in a country where a tax treaty or TIEA is in effect. Alternatively, this type of income is allocated to Taxable Surplus in other countries.

20-132.   Based on this two-way allocation, the items included in Exempt Surplus are as follows:

- For a foreign affiliate that is located in a country with which Canada has a tax treaty or a tax information exchange agreement (TIEA):
  - Active business income
  - The taxable one-half of capital gains on dispositions of property used in producing active business income.
- For all foreign affiliates, without regard to the location of the foreign affiliate:
  - The non-taxable one-half of capital gains on dispositions of all types of capital property (except shares of other foreign affiliates).

20-133.   Using a similar approach, the items included in Taxable Surplus are as follows:

- For a foreign affiliate that is located in a country with which Canada does not have a tax treaty or a TIEA:
  - Active business income
  - The taxable one-half of capital gains on dispositions of property used in producing active business income.
- For all foreign affiliates, without regard to the location of the foreign affiliate:
  - The taxable one-half of capital gains on dispositions of capital property other than that used in producing active business income.
  - Investment income, which includes income from property and from non-active businesses.

Dividends Paid From Exempt Surplus

20-134.   When a dividend is paid from a foreign affiliate's Exempt Surplus, Canadian tax legislation, in effect, cedes all of the taxation of this income stream to the foreign jurisdiction. This is without regard to the level of local taxation in the foreign jurisdiction or amounts of tax withheld by that jurisdiction.

20-135.   In order to apply this approach, ITA 113(1)(a) allows the full amount of the foreign affiliate dividend to be deducted in the determination of the resident corporation's Taxable Income.

> **EXAMPLE**   A Canadian company receives a $90,000 dividend from a foreign affiliate. The affiliate had paid a $100,000 dividend from its exempt surplus (an after foreign taxes balance), with the foreign jurisdiction withholding $10,000 from the distribution to Canada.
>
> **ANALYSIS**   The Canadian corporation will include the pre-withholding $100,000 dividend in its Net Income For Tax Purposes and will deduct the $100,000 included amount under ITA 113(1)(a) in the determination of Taxable Income under ITA 113(1)(a). No Canadian taxes will be paid on the dividend and, consistent with this result, no foreign tax credit will be available for the $10,000 that was withheld by the foreign jurisdiction.

Dividends Paid From Taxable Surplus

20-136.   With respect to foreign affiliate dividends paid from Taxable Surplus, the goal here is to apply ITA 113(1) in a manner that attempts to have the overall level of taxation, both domestic and foreign, be the equivalent of the amount of taxes that would be paid in Canada on the same stream of income. Currently this rate is equal to 25 percent.

Basic Rate (No Abatement)	38%
General Rate Reduction	(13%)
Overall Federal Rate	25%

20-137.   While this could have been accomplished using credits against Tax Payable, the government chose to do the required adjustments through deductions under ITA 113(1). Given the desire to apply an overall tax rate of 25 percent, tax amounts will have to be converted to income using a factor of 4 (1 ÷ 25%). Stated alternatively, every $1 of tax paid must be converted to Taxable Income of $4.

20-138.   To achieve the desired overall tax rate of 25 percent, two adjustments are required:

ITA 113(1)(b)   adjusts Taxable Income to reflect the income taxes paid in the foreign jurisdiction.

ITA 113(1)(c)   adjusts Taxable Income to reflect taxes withheld by the foreign jurisdiction on payments to non-residents of that jurisdiction.

20-139.   An example will serve to illustrate these provisions.

EXAMPLE   Cancor, a taxable Canadian corporation, owns 50 percent of the outstanding shares of Forco, a corporation located in a country that does not have a tax treaty or a TIEA with Canada. All of Forco's income is from active business activities. During 2020, Forco pays dividends of $90,000. Of this total, $42,750 is received by Cancor, with $2,250 being withheld by the foreign jurisdiction. Forco is subject to a tax rate of 10 percent in the foreign jurisdiction.

ANALYSIS   Dividends paid are an after tax amount. This means that the original income stream that formed the basis for the current dividend was $100,000 [$90,000 ÷ (1 - 10%)], with taxes of $10,000 being paid prior to the dividend declaration.

Given this, Cancor's share of these taxes would be $5,000 [(1/2)($10,000)]. Taking this and the $2,250 in withholding into account, to achieve an overall tax rate of 25 percent on the original $50,000 income stream would require additional Canadian taxes as follows:

Required Total Tax [(25%)($50,000)]	$12,500
Foreign Taxes Paid By Foreign Affiliate	(5,000)
Foreign Taxes Withheld From Dividend	(2,250)
Required Additional Canadian Tax	$ 5,250

As we have noted, ITA 113(1) accomplishes this result with two adjustments. The first is related to the $5,000 in foreign tax paid. The $5,000 in taxes paid reflects, at a 25 percent rate, $20,000 ($5,000 ÷ 25%) in Taxable Income. This would suggest multiplying the foreign tax paid by 4. However, this does not take into consideration the fact that income has already been reduced by $5,000, from $50,000 to $45,000 by these taxes. Given this, ITA 113(1)(b) requires that the $5,000 in foreign taxes be multiplied by a relevant factor of 3 [(1 ÷ 25%) - 1]. This deduction equals $15,000.

In applying ITA 113(1)(c), we need to adjust for the $2,250 in taxes withheld from the dividend payment. Given this, ITA 113(1)(c) requires that this amount be multiplied by 4 (1 ÷ 25%). This results in a deduction of $9,000, reflecting the amount of income that would result in the payment of $2,250 in taxes.

Putting all of this together results in the following calculation of Tax Payable:

Net Income For Tax Purposes	$45,000
ITA 113(1)(b) Deduction For Foreign Tax Paid	(15,000)
ITA 113(1)(c) Deduction For Foreign Tax Withheld	(9,000)
Taxable Income	$21,000
Required Rate	25%
Canadian Tax Payable	$ 5,250

This, as expected, is the same amount that we calculated in the preceding table using a more intuitive approach that is not based on the ITA 113 legislation.

Dividends Received From Controlled Foreign Affiliates

Controlled Foreign Affiliate Defined

20-140.   While establishing the concept of a foreign affiliate alleviated the problem of excessive taxation on dividends received by Canadian corporations from non-resident corporations, it did not deal with the problem of using a non-resident corporation to defer Canadian taxation on property income. In order to deal with this issue, the government developed the concept of a "controlled foreign affiliate".

20-141.   In somewhat simplified terms, ITA 95(1) defines a controlled foreign affiliate of a Canadian taxpayer as a foreign affiliate of that taxpayer that is:

1.   controlled by the Canadian resident on the basis of his or her own shareholdings; or

2.   controlled by the Canadian resident, together with:

   • persons (residents or non-residents) who are not at arm's length with the Canadian resident;

   • up to four Canadian residents who are not related to the taxpayer (referred to as "relevant" shareholders); and

   • any other persons (residents or non-residents) who are related to the "relevant" Canadian shareholders.

EXAMPLE   Cantext, a Canadian public company, owns 11 percent of the voting shares of Fortext, a company located in Germany. Two other resident Canadian corporations, who are not related to Cantext, each own an additional 15 percent of the voting shares of Fortext. A French subsidiary of one of these other Canadian companies owns 20 percent of the voting shares of Fortext.

ANALYSIS   Fortext is a foreign affiliate of Cantext since Cantext holds more than 10 percent of the voting shares of Fortext. It is a controlled foreign affiliate in that:

   • Cantext owns 11 percent;

   • two unrelated Canadian companies (relevant shareholders) own an additional 30 percent; and

   • a company related to one of the relevant shareholders owns another 20 percent.

This gives a total holding of 61 percent, enough to provide control of Fortext. Note that Fortext is also a controlled foreign affiliate of both the other Canadian corporations.

20-142.   The significance of the controlled foreign affiliate concept is that, if an investment in a non-resident corporation falls within this definition, the Canadian shareholder must recognize its foreign accrual property income (FAPI, hereafter) prior to its actual distribution. That is, the FAPI of controlled foreign affiliates must be recorded as it is earned, rather than when it is distributed in the form of dividends.

20-143. This provision is somewhat mitigated by the fact that Canadian residents are not required to report the FAPI of controlled foreign affiliates unless it exceeds $5,000. The $5,000 exemption figure recognizes that the calculation of FAPI is quite complex and should not be required when the amount of income is small. As FAPI income is taxed as it accrues, dividends subsequently paid out of such income are not taxable.

Foreign Accrual Property Income (FAPI)

General Rules

20-144. In simplified terms, FAPI is the passive income of a controlled foreign affiliate. FAPI includes income from property (e.g., interest, portfolio dividends), income from non-active businesses (e.g., rental income), as well as the taxable one-half of capital gains resulting from the disposition of properties that are not used in an active business. An important distinguishing feature of this type of income is that, with the exception of rental income, its source can be easily moved from one tax jurisdiction to another.

20-145. The property income definition for FAPI also includes income from a foreign investment business. This type of business is analogous to the specified investment business that is used in determining income eligible for the small business deduction (see Chapter 12).

20-146. As is the case with the specified investment business rules, a foreign affiliate would be considered to be earning active business income if it either employs more than five full time employees or the equivalent of more than five full time employees to earn income that would normally be considered property income. This "five-employee" exception is especially important in deciding whether foreign rental income is active (exempt from the FAPI rules) or passive (subject to the FAPI rules).

Taxation Of FAPI

20-147. As noted in Paragraph 20-142, if a taxpayer has an investment in a controlled foreign affiliate, FAPI must be accrued as it is earned by that affiliate. Note that this is a separate issue from the taxation of dividends from either controlled or other foreign affiliates. We will deal with this latter issue in the next section. Not surprisingly, we will find that if dividends are paid out of FAPI income that has been accrued by a taxpayer, the dividends will not be taxed a second time when received by that investor.

> **EXAMPLE**   Paul Peterson, a Canadian resident, owns 80 percent of the shares of Tabasco Ltd., a company that is incorporated in Trinidad. During 2020, the company has income of $100,000, all of which is earned by passive investments. No income taxes are paid on this income in Trinidad, and no dividends are paid out of this income to Mr. Peterson.

> **ANALYSIS**   Tabasco Ltd. is clearly a controlled foreign affiliate. Further, all of its income is from passive sources. Given this, under ITA 91(1), Mr. Peterson will have to include $80,000 [(80%)($100,000)] in his Canadian Net Income For Tax Purposes for 2020.

20-148. The preceding example was simplified by the fact that Tabasco Ltd. was not subject to taxes in the foreign country. If it had been, the income of this controlled foreign affiliate would have been subject to double taxation. Fortunately, the *Income Tax Act* provides relief in the form of a deduction under ITA 91(4) that is designed to compensate for foreign taxes that have been paid on FAPI.

20-149. Note that this is a deduction against income, rather than a tax credit. As illustrated in Paragraph 20-120, a deduction against income will reduce Tax Payable only by the amount of the deduction multiplied by the tax rate. This means that its value to the taxpayer is less than the amount of foreign taxes paid and, given this, it would not be equitable to set the deduction equal to those taxes.

20-150. The ITA 91(4) deduction recognizes this difference by multiplying the foreign taxes paid on FAPI by what is referred to as a relevant tax factor (RTF, hereafter). As defined in ITA 95(1), the RTF for individuals is different than it is for corporations.

Canadian Resident Individual   If the investor in the controlled foreign affiliate is an individual, the RTF is 1.9. This is based on the notional assumption that the Canadian tax rate on this income would have been about 52.63 percent if the individual had received it from a Canadian source (1 ÷ 52.63% = 1.9).

Canadian Resident Corporation   If the investor in the controlled foreign affiliate is a corporation, the RTF is 4. This RTF is based on 1 divided by a notional tax rate that would have applied if the income had been received from a Canadian source (1 ÷ 25% = 4). That rate of 25 percent is 38 percent less the general rate reduction of 13 percent. Note again that because foreign income is involved, the 10 percent federal tax abatement is not deducted.

20-151.   If the controlled foreign affiliate's income is taxed in the foreign jurisdiction at the notional rate applicable to the investor, the ITA 91(4) deduction will completely eliminate the FAPI. In most cases, the foreign tax rate will be below the notional rates, resulting in some FAPI being included in income. Note, however, that the ITA 91(4) deduction cannot exceed the FAPI.

EXAMPLE CONTINUED (Foreign Taxes Paid)   Paul Peterson, a Canadian resident, owns 80 percent of the shares of Tabasco Ltd., a company that is incorporated in Trinidad. During 2020, the company has income of $100,000, all of which is earned by passive investments. The company pays Trinidadian taxes at a rate of 20 percent. No dividends are paid out of this income to Mr. Peterson.

ANALYSIS   The tax consequences to Mr. Peterson would be as follows:

FAPI [(80%)($100,000)]	$80,000
Deduct Lesser Of:	
• FAPI = $80,000	
• ITA 91(4) Deduction [(1.9)(80%)(20%)($100,000)] = $30,400	(30,400)
Addition To Net Income For Tax Purposes	$49,600

Exercise Twenty - 14

Subject: FAPI

Forco is a wholly owned foreign subsidiary of Canco, a resident Canadian company. Forco earns $100,000 of investment income in 2020 and pays 18 percent in tax in the foreign jurisdiction. None of the after tax income is paid out as dividends. What is the effect of this information on Canco's 2020 Net Income For Tax Purposes?

SOLUTION available in print and online Study Guide.

Dividends From FAPI

20-152.   A final problem remains when the controlled foreign affiliate subsequently distributes the FAPI to the Canadian resident shareholders as a dividend. While these dividends must be included in income, the *Income Tax Act* provides a deduction to reflect the fact that all or a part of the dividend may have already been taxed in an earlier year as FAPI.

20-153.   The deduction is provided solely through ITA 91(5) in the case of individuals and a combination of ITA 91(5) and ITA 113(1)(b) in the case of corporations. The deductions are designed to eliminate taxation on previously taxed FAPI. It is equal to the lesser of the dividends received and the FAPI previously taxed to that shareholder after the ITA 91(4) deduction. Any withholding taxes on dividends paid to corporate shareholders of foreign affiliates are eligible for a deduction under ITA 113(1)(c). (See Paragraph 20-138.)

EXAMPLE CONTINUED (Dividend Paid)   Paul Peterson, a Canadian resident, owns 80 percent of the shares of Tabasco Ltd., a company that is incorporated in Trinidad. During 2020, the company has income of $100,000, all of which is earned by passive investments. The company pays Trinidadian taxes at a rate of 20 percent. Tabasco Ltd. declares and pays dividends of $40,000 in January 2021. There is no withholding tax on this dividend.

ANALYSIS   As shown in Paragraph 20-151, Mr. Peterson's addition to Net Income For Tax Purposes in 2020 was $49,600. The consequences of receiving the dividend in 2021 would be nil, as shown in the following calculation.

Foreign Source Dividend [(80%)($40,000)]	$32,000
Deduct Lesser Of:	
• Previous FAPI After ITA 91(4) Deduction = $49,600	
• Dividend Received = $32,000	(32,000)
Addition To Net Income For Tax Purposes	Nil

Exercise Twenty - 15

Subject: Dividends From FAPI (An Extension Of Exercise Twenty - 14)

Forco is a wholly owned foreign subsidiary of Canco, a resident Canadian company. Forco earns $100,000 of investment income in 2020 and pays 18 percent in tax in the foreign jurisdiction. In 2021, Forco distributes its net after tax FAPI of $82,000 to Canco as a dividend. Assume that there are no withholding taxes on the dividend payment. What is the effect of this information on Canco's 2021 Net Income For Tax Purposes??

SOLUTION available in print and online Study Guide.

We suggest you work Self Study Problem Twenty-7 at this point.

Additional Supplementary Self Study Problems Are Available Online.

Key Terms Used In This Chapter

20-154. The following is a list of the key terms used in this Chapter. These terms, and their meanings, are compiled in the Glossary located at the back of the Study Guide.

Business Income	International Taxation
Capital Gain	Non-Resident
Controlled Foreign Affiliate	Permanent Establishment
Dividends	Person
Double Taxation	Resident
Employment Income	Sojourner
Exempt Surplus	Tax Haven
Foreign Accrual Property Income (FAPI)	Taxable Canadian Property
Foreign Affiliate	Taxable Surplus
Interest Income	
International Tax Treaty	
(a.k.a., International Tax Convention)	

References

20-155. For more detailed study of the material in this Chapter, we would refer you to the following:

ITA 2(3)	Tax Payable By Non-Resident Persons
ITA 20(11)	Foreign Taxes On Income From Property Exceeding 15 Percent
ITA 90	Dividends Received From Non-Resident Corporation
ITA 91	Amounts To Be Included In Respect Of Share Of Foreign Affiliate
ITA 94	Application Of Certain Provisions To Trusts Not Resident In Canada
ITA 95	Definitions [Foreign Accrual Property Income]
ITA 113	Deduction In Respect Of Dividend Received From Foreign Affiliate
ITA 115	Non-Resident's Taxable Income In Canada
ITA 116	Disposition By Non-Resident Person Of Certain Property
ITA 118.94	Tax Payable By Non-Resident (Tax Credits)
ITA 126	Foreign Tax Credits
ITA 212	Tax On Income From Canada Of Non-Resident Persons (Section in ITA Part XIII that deals with Canadian property income of non-resident persons)
ITA 216	Alternatives Re Rents And Timber Royalties
ITA 217	Alternative Re Canadian Benefits
ITA 248(1)	Definitions (Taxable Canadian Property)
ITA 249	Definition Of "Taxation Year"
ITA 253	Extended Meaning Of "Carrying On Business"
IC 72-17R6	Procedures Concerning The Disposition Of Taxable Canadian Property By Non-Residents Of Canada - Section 116
IC 75-6R2	Required Withholding from Amounts Paid to Non-Resident Persons Performing Services in Canada
IC 76-12R6	Applicable Rate of Part XIII Tax on Amounts Paid or Credited to Persons in Countries With Which Canada Has a Tax Convention
IC 77-16R4	Non-Resident Income Tax

S5-F2-C1	Foreign Tax Credit
IT-137R3	Additional Tax On Certain Corporations Carrying On Business In Canada
IT-173R2	Capital Gains Derived In Canada By Residents Of The United States
IT-176R2	Taxable Canadian Property - Interests In And Options On Real Property And Shares
IT-262R2	Losses Of Non-Residents And Part-Year Residents
IT-303	Know-How And Similar Payments To Non-Residents
IT-420R3	Non-Residents - Income Earned In Canada
IT-451R	Deemed Disposition And Acquisition On Ceasing To Be Or Becoming Resident In Canada
IT-465R	Non-Resident Beneficiaries Of Trusts
IT-468R	Management Or Administration Fees Paid To Non-Residents
IT-497R4	Overseas Employment Tax Credit

Problems For Self Study (Online)

To provide practice in problem solving, there are Self Study and Supplementary Self Study problems available on MyLab Accounting.

Within the text we have provided an indication of when it would be appropriate to work each Self Study problem. The detailed solutions for Self Study problems can be found in the print and online Study Guide.

We provide the Supplementary Self Study problems for those who would like additional practice in problem solving. The detailed solutions for the Supplementary Self Study problems are available online, not in the Study Guide.

The .PDF file "Self Study Problems for Volume 2" on MyLab contains the following for Chapter 20:

- 7 Self Study problems,
- 3 Supplementary Self Study problems, and
- detailed solutions for the Supplementary Self Study problems.

Assignment Problems

(The solutions for these problems are only available in
the solutions manual that has been provided to your instructor.)

Assignment Problem Twenty - 1
(Part I Tax On Non-Residents)

The following material describes six independent Cases that involve U.S. citizens or U.S. companies that have some type of Canadian source income.

Case 1

Flager is a U.S. based manufacturing company. To facilitate Canadian sales, the company ships its product to a warehouse located in Moncton, New Brunswick. The warehouse is rented on a monthly basis, with a clause in the lease that allows cancellation on 90 days notice.

Flager has made an arrangement with Jack Martin to sell their products in the Maritime provinces. Jack works out of an office in his home. He does not have authority to conclude individual sales contracts without approval from the head office in the U.S.

Case 2

Flager is a U.S. based manufacturing company. To facilitate Canadian sales, the company ships its product to a warehouse located in Moncton, New Brunswick. The warehouse is rented on a monthly basis, with a clause in the lease that allows cancellation on 90 days notice.

Flager has made an arrangement with Jack Martin to sell their products in the Maritime provinces. Jack works out of a large office in the warehouse, which takes up a considerable portion of the total floor space. He has the authority to conclude individual sales contracts without approval from the U.S. head office.

Case 3

Genevieve Boulud is a U.S. citizen and a resident of that country. Because she speaks fluent French, her U.S. based employer transfers her to an affiliate's Montreal office for four months. She has employment income during this period of US$36,000, all of which is paid by her U.S. employer.

Case 4

Ruby Nash is a U.S. citizen and a resident of that country. During the current year she accepts an employment contract that requires her to work in Calgary for a period of three months. Her salary is C$11,000 per month. The contract is with a Canadian corporation that is responsible for paying the salary.

Case 5

Ada Taylor is a U.S. citizen and a resident of that country. She owns all of the shares in a U.S. based private company that was incorporated in the U.S. This corporation's only activity is buying and operating vacation rental properties in Canada. In order to support her increasingly decadent lifestyle, she sells all of the shares in this company during the current year. She realizes a gain on this sale of $250,000.

Case 6

Cynthia Edwards is a U.S. citizen and a resident of that country. She is a minority shareholder of a Canadian controlled private corporation. This corporation's only activity is buying and operating rental properties in major Canadian cities. Because of her concern about the inflated prices in both Toronto and Vancouver, she sells her shares in the company during the current year. The sale results in a total gain of $785,000.

Required: For each Case, indicate whether the non-resident would be subject to Part I Canadian income tax.

Assignment Problem Twenty - 2
(Permanent Establishments)

A U.S. manufacturer of furniture is considering entering the Canadian market. The company will use one of the following approaches to expand its market in Canada:

A. Direct sales to wholesalers by full time salespeople who report to a sales office in each of three Canadian provinces. The sales offices will coordinate marketing and shipping of products from two warehouses located in Canada. However, formal approval of contracts will be administered in the U.S. head office.

B. The sales offices described in Part A would be independent profit centres, with regional credit managers. The two warehouses from which orders are filled will be near the sales offices.

C. Company online sales territory would be expanded to include shipping to Canada.

D. Direct sales to wholesalers by non-exclusive agents. The agents will represent other suppliers as well.

E. Direct sales to wholesalers by full time salespeople in each of three Canadian provinces. No sales offices will be opened, and the furniture will be shipped from a warehouse in the U.S. Shipment will be made only after a customer's credit and contract are approved by the U.S. head office.

F. Selling furniture to Canadian distributors. The distributors pay the shipping costs on the furniture from the U.S. port or border crossing closest to them.

Required: For each market expansion approach, assess whether or not the U.S. manufacturer will be deemed to have a permanent establishment in Canada. Justify your conclusion and identify any other information required to support your position.

Assignment Problem Twenty - 3
(Part XIII Tax On Non-Resident Corporations And Individuals)
The following two Cases involve a non-resident corporation (Case A) and a non-resident individual (Case B) earning multiple sources of Canadian income. Assume that all amounts are in Canadian dollars and that neither of the non-residents are considered to be carrying on a business through a permanent establishment in Canada.

Case A – Non-Resident Corporation
All of the shares of Alberta Inc. are owned by its U.S. parent company, Blazes Corporation (Blazes), which is incorporated in the state of Delaware. Blazes manufactures and wholesales specialty equipment for firefighters. Its products are sold and leased in Canada through Alberta Inc. The following transactions took place between the two companies in 2020:

1. Blazes loaned Alberta Inc. $20 million at favourable interest rates in 2018, which was exclusively used in its business operations. Alberta Inc. paid Blazes interest of $310,000 for its 2020 taxation year that ended December 31. Assume that the interest is not "fully exempt interest".

2. There is a royalty agreement between Blazes and Alberta Inc. with respect to firefighting equipment made available to Alberta Inc. for lease to its customers. Blazes receives ongoing fees for such property that are calculated on the basis of the value of the property, the term of the underlying lease, and a wear and tear factor. In 2020 Alberta Inc. paid a fee of $189,000 to Blazes as a result of that agreement.

3. In December 2020 Alberta Inc. declared and paid a dividend of $600,000 to Blazes.

Case B – Non-Resident Individual
Tara Johnstone is a U.S. resident with friends and family in Canada. During relatively recent visits she learned that there are many interesting investment opportunities, particularly given the favourable currency exchange rate. As a result she made the following Canadian investments:

1. She made two loans in 2019 to businesses situated in Ontario. The first loan was made to an arm's length Canadian controlled private corporation (CCPC) for business purposes at interest rates slightly above the market rate to account for various risks. The company paid her $12,750 in interest in 2020. The second loan was made to her sister to start a clothing boutique in Toronto. The terms of the loan call for a minimal rate of interest plus an additional amount based on a percentage of gross sales. Her sister paid her $11,220 in 2020.

2. Tara owns shares in two Canadian companies. The first is a listed Canadian public company in which she owns 100 Class A common shares representing a fraction of 1 percent of all outstanding shares, and the second is an 18 percent shareholding in the CCPC in which she loaned money to as mentioned in point 1 above. In 2020 she received $7,700 in eligible dividends from the public company and $16,300 from the CCPC, $10,000 of which is a non-eligible dividend and the remaining $6,300 a capital dividend.

3. Tara also purchased two lakefront cottages – one in Alberta and one in B.C. Both properties were rented throughout 2020 to Canadian residents. The monthly rent on the Alberta property was $2,500 and total expenses totaled $36,800, excluding maximum CCA of $6,200. The monthly rent on the B.C. property was $4,250 with expenses totaling $19,000, excluding maximum CCA of $6,800.

Required:

Case A: Determine the Part XIII income tax implications of each of the three payments made by Alberta Inc. to Blazes. Include in your analysis the impact of the Canada/U.S. tax treaty. Explain how your answers would or would not have changed if Blazes had been a resident of a country that did not have a tax treaty with Canada.

Case B: Determine the Part XIII income tax implications of each of the three types of Canadian investments made by Tara. Include in your analysis the impact of the Canada/U.S. tax treaty. In addition, provide any advice with respect to the dividends and whether an election under ITA 216 for the rental properties would be recommended.

Assignment Problem Twenty - 4
(Emigration - Tax Planning)

Harlen Holt, a resident of Nova Scotia, plans to emigrate from Canada on December 31, 2020. On that date, he will own the following assets:

Automobile   Harlen owns a BMW 750 that cost $135,000. Its fair market value on December 31, 2020, is $52,000.

RRSP   The December 31 balance in Harlen's RRSP is $973,000.

Shares In Public Companies   Harlen owns a portfolio of publicly traded shares that have a total adjusted cost base of $460,000. Their fair market value on December 31, 2020, totals $535,000.

Shares In A CCPC   Harlen is a minority shareholder of a CCPC. The CCPC owns and operates five apartment buildings. More than 80 percent of the fair market value of the shares is derived from the value of these buildings. The adjusted cost base of these shares is $287,000, and they have a December 31, 2020, fair market value of $300,000.

Residence   This property was purchased for $430,000, including $150,000 for the land. Its fair market value on December 31, 2020, is $540,000, including $200,000 for the land.

Cottage   This property was purchased for $345,000, including $95,000 for the land. Because a large nearby development has flooded the market with low-price units, it has a fair market value on December 31, 2020, of $300,000, including a value for the land of $50,000. Harlen has rented out this property since its purchase and reported a small rental income every year. He has never taken CCA on the property.

Savings Account   The balance in this account is $45,600.

Required:

A.   For each of the listed assets, indicate the tax consequences, including any amounts of deferred income, that would result from Harlen's emigration from Canada. Assume that he does not make any elections at the time of his move. Ignore the lifetime capital gains deduction.

B.   Under ITA 128.1(4)(d), taxpayers can elect to have a deemed disposition on certain assets where a deemed disposition is not automatic. Determine if Harlen could use this election to minimize his tax obligation at the time of his departure. If he can, calculate the amount of the reduction in Net Income For Tax Purposes that would result from the use of this election.

Assignment Problem Twenty - 5
(Comprehensive Review Problem - Residency Of Individuals)

Note   This problem covers material from several other Chapters of the text.

Elaine Brock is a successful marketing manager for a multinational corporation based in the United States. While she has always been a Canadian resident, working out of the corporation's Toronto office, she has been offered a promotion that would require that she relocate to Tampa, Florida. As this is intended to be a permanent change, Elaine has applied for and received the documentation that will allow her to live and work in the United States. She will be moving to Tampa on July 1, 2020.

The corporation provides a $40,000 moving allowance that will be paid by the Toronto office prior to her move. While the corporation does not require documentation of this amount, Elaine estimates that she will incur $32,000 in actual moving costs.

Her common-law partner, Marion Davies, is a very popular singer and songwriter. Marion has also received documentation that will allow her to live and work in the United States. However, she is currently writing songs to complete a new album in her Toronto music studio and is not planning to join Elaine until early 2021.

The state of Florida does not assess a state income tax on its residents, largely because of the high level of tax revenues generated by Disney World. Assume that the marginal federal (U.S.) rate for Elaine would be 35 percent. This rate would only be applied to income earned in the United States.

On July 1, 2020, the date that Elaine departs for Tampa, she owns the following assets:

Description	Date Acquired	Original Cost	Fair Market Value
Registered Retirement Savings Plan	N/A	$235,000	$452,000
Canadian Paintings*	Various	125,000	232,000
Condo Residence In Toronto	2007	360,000	480,000
Huntsville Cottage	2010	225,000	175,000
Automobile	2015	85,000	62,000
Sailboat	2017	28,000	32,000
Shares In Brock Inc., A CCPC	2005	98,000	156,000
Shares In Bank Of Nova Scotia	2013	56,000	85,000

*None of the paintings had an adjusted cost base or a fair market value that was less than $1,000.

Elaine owns 100 percent of the real property. She has rented out the cottage since its purchase and reported a small rental income every year. She has never taken CCA on the property. The loss in value is related only to the land as the waterfront has been severely damaged by flooding. The value of the land has decreased from $130,000 at purchase to $80,000.

While Elaine intends to sell all of the other assets fairly soon, she plans on renting both the Toronto residence and Huntsville cottage for at least three years.

Required: Explain to Elaine the tax consequences of her move to the United States. Assume that:

- Elaine ceases to be a Canadian resident when she departs on July 1, 2020.
- Any additional income that Elaine earns in 2020 while a resident of Canada will be taxed in Canada at a combined federal/provincial rate of 47 percent.

In addition, advise Elaine as to any tax planning opportunities to minimize her Canadian Tax Payable for the current and future years. Ignore the lifetime capital gains deduction.

Assignment Problem Twenty - 6

(Foreign Investment Reporting Rules – T1135 (ITA 233.3))

Note to Instructors: We have endeavoured to include some of the more common practical situations together with frequently asked questions that have been put to and answered by the CRA concerning the T1135. We have broken down the situations into three categories: (1) shares of non-resident corporations, (2) personal-use property, and (3) miscellaneous. We suggest that you choose two from each category to illustrate the concepts.

For each of the mutually exclusive situations presented indicate whether foreign reporting is required for the 2020 taxation year and provide reasons in support of your answer. Assume that all amounts are expressed in Canadian dollars and that the persons identified do not own any other foreign property. Assume that all references to foreign reporting requirements are only to the T1135.

Shares of a Non-Resident Corporation

1. A Canadian resident individual taxpayer purchased shares in a U.S. public corporation in January 2020 for $95,000. Additional shares of the same U.S. company were purchased in late December 2020 for $10,000. No dividends were received on the shares in 2020.

2. Would your answer to #1 change if the Canadian resident individual had instead acquired shares in a non-public U.S. corporation that resulted in the individual owning a 15 percent interest in that company?

3. Would your answer to #1 change if instead of acquiring shares in a U.S. public company the Canadian resident individual acquired, for $105,000, an interest in a U.S. mutual fund that owned shares in the U.S. public company?

4. Would your answer to #1 change if instead the Canadian resident individual owned an interest in a Canadian mutual fund that owned shares in the U.S. public company?

5. Would your answer to #1 change if the shares of the U.S. public company were acquired by your self-administered RRSP?

6. A Canadian resident individual owns all of the shares of their own corporation which was incorporated in Alberta years ago. Would your answer to #1 change if the shares of the U.S. public company were acquired by the individual's Canadian corporation?

Personal-Use Property

1. A Canadian individual residing in Newfoundland acquired a vacation home in the Dominican Republic for $178,000 in March 2020. The individual plans to spend the long Canadian winters living in that home each and every year starting in September 2020. The property will remain vacant for the months it is not used.

2. A Canadian resident individual residing in Nunavut purchased a condo in the Turks and Caicos in January 2020 for $240,000. The individual plans on spending one month every year at that property. The individual has contracted with a real estate management company to oversee the property, ensuring it is well maintained and secure. To offset the management fees the individual has agreed to allow the condo to be rented for a few months every year.

3. Would your answer to #2 change if it was determined that the individual planned to use the property for one month each year during the low season and would rent the property throughout the high or busy season, making a considerable profit every year?

4. A Canadian resident individual residing in the Yukon acquired an apartment building in Hawaii for $995,000 in mid-January 2020. An additional $840,000 was spent on renovations. The apartment contains five equal-sized apartment units. The individual plans on spending a minimum of three months each year living in the apartment with the best view. When not being occupied that unit will remain empty. All of the other four units will be rented throughout the year.

5. A Canadian resident individual residing in Vancouver acquired three time shares in Las Vegas at a deep discount. The total cost was $150,000. Each of the three time share units allow the holder to spend two months each year in properties along the famous Las Vegas strip. The individual plans to use the time share units personally a few weeks each year and to rent the remaining time to arm's length persons. The individual anticipates a substantial profit that should allow recovery of the investment in as little as three years.

6. Would your answer to #5 change if it was determined that the time share units were owned 50:50 by spouses who contributed their own funds to the purchase? Both spouses are Canadian resident individuals.

Miscellaneous

1. A Canadian resident individual living in Halifax, Nova Scotia, was advised of an inheritance from a family member living in Regina, Saskatchewan, who passed away in August 2020. The individual inherited a half acre plot of land located in Tampa, Florida, that was valued at $600,000. The family member had acquired it in 1972 for $12,000.

2. A Canadian resident individual living in Saint John, New Brunswick, frequently vacations in the U.S. The individual is contemplating acquiring a U.S. currency account to avoid the fluctuations in Canadian versus U.S. currency. Assuming that the account balance will exceed $100,000 in Canadian funds, would foreign reporting be required if the individual (a) opens an account with a U.S. bank or (b) an account with a Canadian bank?

3. A U.S. resident commutes to Canada five days a week for employment purposes in 2020. The individual is a non-resident of Canada but is required to report Canadian employment income by filing an individual income tax return and paying Canadian income tax. The individual owns property in the U.S. the cost amount of which exceeds $100,000. Is the individual required to report their foreign property?

4. A Canadian resident individual residing in Ottawa, Ontario, has been asked by a sibling living in Colorado for assistance in acquiring a home near Boulder. The sibling is a non-resident of Canada. The individual agrees to help and advances the sibling an interest free loan of $200,000 in May 2020 payable over a 10 year period.

5. A Canadian resident individual living in Surrey, B.C., owns a rental property in Seattle, Washington, that was acquired 30 years ago for $75,000. No capital additions or renovations have ever been made to the property and no CCA was ever claimed for Canadian tax purposes. The property is rented throughout 2020. In October 2020 the individual opens a small store in Seattle to sell Whistler mountain souvenirs. The store, including furniture, equipment, and fixtures, are all leased. The only assets owned are the inventory. Initially the maximum cost of the inventory in 2020 is $30,000. The year end inventory value at December 31, 2020, however, is only $8,000.

6. Would your answer to #5 change if no business was established in the U.S. and the rental property was sold for $700,000 in November 2020? The proceeds net of miscellaneous legal costs were deposited in a U.S. bank account in the name of the Canadian resident individual and transferred to a Canadian bank account seven days later at which time the U.S. account was closed.

Assignment Problem Twenty - 7
(Foreign Source Investment Income And T1135)

Vickey Gateley works and resides in Niagara Falls, Ontario. A long time monarchist, she has developed a well diversified portfolio of stocks of British companies. At December 31, 2020, Ms. Gateley is holding British stocks with a cost of £800,000. She also has a British bank account with a London bank that has a balance that fluctuates between £25,000 and £50,000.

One of her boyfriends lives in Buffalo, New York. Three years ago, when she started spending many of her weekends there, she decided to purchase a condo in Buffalo. Because the building she chose had construction problems, the prices were depressed and she purchased four units for US$200,000 each. She has rented out the other three units.

During 2020, she earned the following amounts of investment income:

Dividends From British Public Corporations	
Net Of 15 Percent Withholding	£54,400
Interest On Bank Account	£ 1,300
Gross Rental Income From Rental Properties	US$86,000
Expenses Of Operating Rental Properties	US$45,000

Other Information

1. Ms. Gateley has left the interest in her British bank account and has not transferred it to Canada.

2. Ms. Gateley believes her condo units are very undervalued. Because of her concern with respect to future recapture, she does not take CCA on her rental properties.

3. The dividends from the British corporations were paid on a quarterly basis.

4. Assume that the exchange rates throughout 2020 were £1 = C$1.70 and US$1 = C$1.30.

Required:

A. Indicate the amounts of investment income that would be included in Ms. Gateley's 2020 Net Income For Tax Purposes, as well as any tax credits that would be available to Ms. Gateley to offset this income.

B. Is Ms. Gateley required to file a T1135? If yes, what assets have to be included? The detailed reporting needed on the assets is not required.

Assignment Problem Twenty - 8
(Foreign Source Dividends Received By An Individual)

Matthew Fortin is a Canadian resident who lives in London, Ontario. During the year ending December 31, 2020, he has the following sources of income:

Net Employment Income	$121,300
Taxable Capital Gains	11,400
Dividends From Canadian Public Companies	27,350
Dividends From Foreign Companies:	
Country One - Saxon Ltd. (Before Withholding Of $8,000)	40,000
Country Two - Selena Ltd. (Before Withholding Of $1,800)	18,000

His business and investment activities have been unsuccessful in previous years and, as a consequence, he has the following amounts available for reducing his 2020 Taxable Income:

Net Capital Loss Carry Forward	$16,760
Business Loss Carry Forward	13,480

His only tax credits are the basic personal credit, employment-related credits, and any credits related to the dividends received.

Required: Determine Matthew's federal Tax Payable for the year ending December 31, 2020.

Assignment Problem Twenty - 9
(Taxation of Foreign Affiliate Dividends)

CTP is a Canadian public corporation that owns 15 percent of the shares of FTP, a corporation that was created in a foreign country. During the year ending December 31, 2019, FTP earns $20,000 in investment income, $70,000 from an active business and $20,000 of capital gains from the sale of investment assets.

In early 2020, FTP distributes all of its 2019 after tax income as a dividend to all of its shareholders. FTP has no income in 2020.

In both 2019 and 2020, assume that CTP is subject to a Canadian federal tax rate of 25 percent.

In the following six Cases the information above is modified to some degree with additional or alternative assumptions that principally address the Canadian income tax impact of dividends received by residents of Canada from non-resident corporations.

Required: Provide the information that is requested in each of the following Cases.

Case 1   FTP is a foreign affiliate (FA) of CTP but not a controlled foreign affiliate (CFA). Assume that it is located in a country that does not have a tax treaty or a Tax Information Exchange Agreement (TIEA) with Canada, that this country does not assess income taxes on corporations, and does not assess withholding taxes on dividend payments to non-residents. What are the tax consequences for CTP resulting from its investment in FTP during 2019 and 2020? Include the increase in Taxable Income and the total Tax payable for both years in your solution.

Case 2   Assume the same facts as in Case 1, except that FTP is a CFA of CTP. How would the tax consequences for CTP differ from the tax consequences described in Case 1 for 2019 and 2020?

Case 3   Assume the same facts as in Case 1, except that CTP does not own sufficient shares such that FTP is not a foreign affiliate. How would the tax consequences for CTP differ from the tax consequences described in Case 1 for 2019 and 2020?

Case 4   Assume the same facts as in Case 1, except that FTP is located in a country that has a tax treaty with Canada. How would the tax consequences for CTP differ from the tax consequences described in Case 1 for 2019 and 2020?

Case 5   FTP is an FA but not a CFA of CTP. Assume that FTP is located in a country that has a tax treaty with Canada, that this country assesses income taxes on active business income at a rate of 10 percent and does not assess withholding taxes on dividend payments to non-residents. The income taxes paid by FTP in the foreign country total $7,000 [(10%)($70,000)]. What are the tax consequences for CTP resulting from its investment in FTP for its 2019 and 2020 taxation years?

Case 6   Assume the same facts as in Case 5, except that the foreign country levies the 10 percent income tax on all of FTP's 2019 income. This income tax would total $11,000 [(10%)($110,000)]. In addition, a further 8 percent withholding tax of $7,920 [(8%)($110,000-$11,000)] was assessed on the dividend paid in 2020. The resulting dividend payment was $91,080 ($110,000 - $11,000- $7,920). What are the tax consequences for CTP for its 2019 and 2020 taxation years?

Assignment Problem Twenty - 10
(Canadian Source Income - Short Cases)
Case A

Mr. Jack Holt is an employee of Stillwell Industries, an American manufacturing company. During the period June 15 through December 6 of the current year, Mr. Holt worked in Canada providing technical assistance to a Canadian subsidiary of Stillwell Industries. His salary was US$5,500 per month. During the period that Mr. Holt was in Canada, Stillwell Industries continued to deposit his salary into his normal U.S. bank account. Both his salary for this period and all of his related travelling expenses were billed to the Canadian subsidiary.

Required: Explain Mr. Holt's tax position.

Case B

Mr. John McQueen was for many years a resident of Ontario. On his retirement 10 years ago, he returned to his native Scotland and has not since returned to Canada. However, he has retained considerable investments in Canada, as follows:

- **Common Stocks**   He has a large portfolio of common stocks that are registered in the name of his Toronto broker. The broker receives all dividends and periodically sends a cheque to Mr. McQueen in Scotland.

- **Mortgage Portfolio**   He has a large portfolio of second mortgages. All collections on these mortgages are made by a Toronto law firm and are deposited into a Toronto bank account in the name of Mr. McQueen.

Required: Who is responsible for tax withholdings under Part XIII of the *Income Tax Act*, and on which amounts must withholdings be made?

Case C

Hotels International is a U.S. corporation with hotel properties throughout the world. It has recently developed a property in Nova Scotia that will open during the current year. A long term management lease has been signed with Hotel Operators Ltd., a Canadian company specializing in the management of hotels. Under the terms of the lease, Hotel Operators Ltd. will pay all of the operating expenses of the hotel and, in addition, make an annual lease payment of $1,250,000 to the American owners of the new hotel.

Required: Will the U.S. corporation, Hotels International, be subject to Canadian income taxes on the annual lease payment, and if so to what extent?

Case D

The Maple Company, a public company resident in Canada, has 2,400,000 shares of its no par common stock outstanding. Sixty percent of these shares are owned by its American parent, the Condor Company. The remaining shares are owned by Canadian residents. In addition to the common shares, the Condor Company holds all of an outstanding issue of Maple Company debenture bonds. Two of the five directors of the Maple Company are Canadian residents, while the remaining three are residents of the United States. During the current year, the Maple Company paid a dividend of $1 per share on its common stock and interest of $900,000 on its outstanding debenture bonds.

Required: Calculate the amount of Part XIII taxes to be withheld by the Maple Company with respect to the interest and dividend payments to its American parent.

CHAPTER 21

GST/HST

Introduction

Background

Introduction Of The GST

21-1.   After significant controversy, a goods and services tax (GST, hereafter) was introduced in Canada on January 1, 1991. This broadly based, multi-stage transaction tax replaced the more narrowly focused federal sales tax on manufactured goods. The GST was originally introduced at a rate of 7 percent. However, this rate was reduced to 6 percent in 2006, with a further reduction to 5 percent on January 1, 2008. There have been no other GST rate changes implemented or proposed since that date.

21-2.   The concept underlying this tax was that it would be applied in an even-handed manner to all goods and service transactions. However, tax policy is often more influenced by political considerations than it is by economic logic. As a result, by the time the tax was actually introduced, it was burdened by a complex web of exemptions and modifications that significantly increased the cost of compliance.

21-3.   The developers of this tax also hoped that the provinces would be willing to amalgamate their provincial sales taxes with the federal GST in order to provide taxpayers with a uniform national approach to the taxation of goods and service transactions. This could have resulted in very substantial savings in both compliance costs and administrative costs. This, however, did not happen.

21-4.   Only the province of Quebec showed any early signs of cooperation in this area. The provinces of Alberta, British Columbia, and Ontario initially took legal action against the federal government, claiming that the GST was unconstitutional. In 1992, Quebec introduced the Quebec Sales Tax (QST), a similar but not identical transaction tax. As part of this process, it was agreed that both the QST and all GST collected in Quebec would be administered by the province of Quebec.

Harmonized Sales Tax (HST)

21-5.   The GST situation did not change until 1997, when three of the Atlantic provinces, New Brunswick, Nova Scotia, and Newfoundland, implemented a harmonized sales tax (HST, hereafter) that contained both a federal and a provincial tax component. In the harmonization process, these provinces eliminated their separate provincial sales taxes.

21-6. The harmonized sales tax is, in effect, a combination of the 5 percent GST rate and a provincial rate that varies from 8 to 10 percent. This gives overall rates of 13 to 15 percent. Since its initial introduction in New Brunswick, Nova Scotia, and Newfoundland, both Ontario and Prince Edward have become participants in the system. British Columbia joined and then, after a bitterly fought referendum, returned to a GST/PST system.

21-7. A major advantage of the HST system is that it is administered by the federal government, eliminating the need for the dual administrative system that is required in those provinces that collect both GST and PST. This does not, however, eliminate flexibility at the provincial level. This is evidenced by the differences in the provincial tax component rate, as well as by different rebates on the provincial portion of the HST for a number of items.

The Current Situation

21-8. These developments have left Canada with a somewhat cluttered transaction tax landscape. The various arrangements are summarized in Figure 21-1.

Figure 21 - 1			
Transaction Taxes In Canada As At July 1, 2020			
Type Of Tax	**Province**	**Rates**	**Tax Administration**
GST Only	Alberta	5% + 0%	Federal
GST and PST	British Columbia	5% + 7%	Federal and Provincial
	Manitoba	5% + 7%	Federal and Provincial
	Saskatchewan	5% + 8%	Federal and Provincial
HST	New Brunswick	15%	Federal
	Newfoundland	15%	Federal
	Nova Scotia	15%	Federal
	Ontario	13%	Federal
	Prince Edward Island	15%	Federal
GST and QST	Quebec	5% + 9.975%	Provincial

NOTE: While the general British Columbia sales tax rate is 7 percent, there are several other rates that are applicable to certain specified goods and services (e.g., the rate for liquor is 10 percent).

21-9. This table illustrates some of the complexity of the current situation resulting from the use of different rates and regimes applying those rates. This is further complicated by the fact that in the HST provinces, rebates of the provincial portion of the tax are provided on some items in some provinces, but not others.

21-10. It is obvious that the transaction tax situation in Canada is extremely complex due to the use of different systems (GST only, GST plus PST, and HST), the use of different provincial rates, and the use of different provincial rebates on various classes of goods. It is not surprising that this can result in very high compliance costs for businesses.

How This Text Deals With This Complexity

21-11. It is clearly not appropriate in a general textbook on taxation to attempt detailed coverage of the GST and HST procedures applicable in each province. It is likely that an attempt to do this would require a completely separate third volume.

21-12. The GST is applicable to all provinces either as a separate tax or as a component of HST. Fortunately, many of the provisions for the HST are identical to those for the GST. This means that, in general, the concepts and procedures involved are the same for both the GST and the HST.

21-13.   Given this situation, our discussion and examples will focus on one of two scenarios:

- Situations where only the GST is applicable. Alberta is the only province where this situation applies. However, it is also applicable in the three territorial jurisdictions.

- Situations where the HST is applicable.

21-14.   We will not use examples involving those provinces where both GST and PST are in effect, nor will attention be given to the unique situation in Quebec.

21-15.   With the exceptions of a brief Chapter 3 discussion of the GST component of employee benefits and a limited presentation on the impact of the GST on business income, all of our material on GST is included in this Chapter. This includes consideration of the Employee And Partner GST Rebate, as well as the application of GST to the purchase and sale of capital assets. We have also included GST procedures and administration in this chapter, rather than in Chapter 2.

21-16.   We view this as an extremely important subject. The great majority of businesses in Canada file GST returns. In addition, many organizations, such as charities and unincorporated businesses, must file GST returns, even though they are not required to file income tax returns. Given the pervasiveness of this tax and the amounts that can be involved, it is our view that some understanding of its application is an essential component of the knowledge base of every professional accountant and businessperson.

Transaction Tax Concepts

General Description

21-17.   While taxes like the GST and HST are often referred to as commodity taxes, the title is not appropriate because the term commodity does not include services. When both goods and services are subject to a tax, what we are really concerned with is the taxation of transactions as opposed to the taxation of income.

21-18.   In both Canada and the U.S., the bulk of federal tax revenues has traditionally been generated by taxes on personal and corporate income. However, transaction taxes have been widely used in both countries at the provincial or state level. In addition, there has been a worldwide trend toward increased use of transaction taxes, with many industrialized countries now relying heavily on this type of taxation.

21-19.   Some of the factors that support the increased use of transaction taxes are as follows:

- **Simplicity**   Transaction taxes are easy to administer and collect. No forms are required from individuals paying the tax and, if the individual wishes to acquire a particular good or service, it is difficult to legally evade payment.

- **Incentives To Work**   An often cited disadvantage of income taxes is that they can discourage individual initiative to work and invest. Transaction taxes do not have this characteristic.

- **Consistency**   Transaction taxes avoid the fluctuating income and family unit problems that are associated with progressive income tax systems.

- **Keeping The Tax Revenues In Canada**   While some types of income can be moved out of Canada, resulting in the related taxes being paid in a different jurisdiction, taxes on Canadian transactions remain with Canadian taxing entities.

21-20.   Given these advantages for transaction taxes, why is income taxation still used? The answer to this question largely involves the question of fairness. In general, transaction taxes relate to consumption. When this is combined with the fact that lower income individuals usually spend a larger portion of their total income on consumption, transaction taxes are assessed at higher effective rates on individuals with lower incomes. Using more technical terminology, transaction taxes are usually regressive.

21-21.   This is in conflict with the widely held belief that fairness requires that individuals with higher incomes should have their income taxed at higher average rates. This goal is best accomplished through the continued use of a progressive income tax system.

21-22.   The Federal government has compensated for the regressive nature of the GST by providing a GST tax credit that is available to low-income individuals who file income tax returns. Similar provisions are available at the provincial level where HST is applicable.

Types Of Transaction Taxes

Alternative Methods

21-23.   There are a number of different ways in which transaction taxes can be applied. We believe that it is useful to understand how the Canadian system compares with the various alternatives that are in use in other jurisdictions. In this section, we will give consideration to the various available methods for assessing such taxes.

21-24.   In discussing the various approaches that can be used in the application of transaction taxes, a simple example is useful. Such an example is diagramed in Figure 21-2. As can be seen in Figure 21-2, our example involves a manufacturer who produces 1,000 units of product at a cost of $4 of raw materials per unit, a total cost of $4,000. All of the 1,000 units are sold to a wholesaler for $10 per unit. The wholesaler then sells 800 of the units to a retailer for $25 per unit. The retailer, in turn, sells 500 of the units to a consumer for $50 per unit.

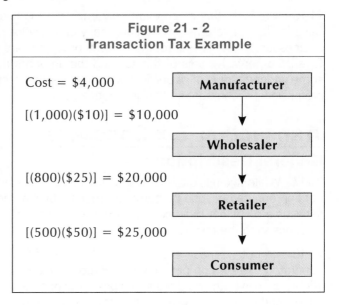

Figure 21 - 2
Transaction Tax Example

Cost = $4,000   **Manufacturer**

$[(1,000)(\$10)] = \$10,000$ **Wholesaler**

$[(800)(\$25)] = \$20,000$ **Retailer**

$[(500)(\$50)] = \$25,000$ **Consumer**

Single Stage Transaction Taxes - Retail Sales Tax

21-25.   A single stage transaction tax could be applied at any level in this example. The most common type of single stage tax is applied at the consumer level. This would be the familiar retail sales tax that is collected in several Canadian provinces. For example, if the transactions depicted in Figure 21-2 took place in Manitoba, a 7 percent retail sales tax would be assessed on the $25,000 price that the retailer charged the consumer, resulting in a provincial sales tax of $1,750 being paid by the consumer.

21-26.   The consumer level is probably the most appropriate level to apply a single stage transaction tax. The tax is visible and its incidence is relatively clear. In contrast, when a wholesale or manufacturer's tax is used, complications can arise when business relationships are formed that blur the lines between the manufacturing, wholesale, and retail levels. This can occur with vertical integration and necessitates estimates or notional values for transfers between the manufacturing, wholesale, or retail levels of an organization.

Multi-Stage Transaction Taxes - Turnover Tax

21-27.   Again referring to Figure 21-2, it would be possible to impose a multi-stage transaction tax at any combination of the various levels depicted. For example, the tax could be applied at the wholesale and retail levels, without application at the manufacturing level. Alternatively, the manufacturing and wholesale levels could be taxed without application at the retail level. An extension of this taxation to all levels is sometimes referred to as a turnover tax, with transactions being taxed at all levels in the distribution chain.

21-28.   The problem with such a turnover tax is that it involves the pyramiding of taxes when there is no credit for taxes paid earlier in the chain. For example, if there were a 5 percent turnover tax in place, the manufacturer in Figure 21-2 would charge the wholesaler $10.50 per unit. When the wholesaler applies its normal markup of 250 percent of cost ($25 ÷ $10), the price would be $26.25 per unit [($10.50)(2.5)]. Of this $26.25, $0.025 [($0.50)(5%)] would represent a tax on the tax that was charged to the wholesaler by the manufacturer. If the 5 percent tax were also applied to the transfers to the retailer and to the ultimate consumer, there would be further applications of tax on previously assessed amounts of tax. Given this pyramiding problem, turnover taxes are not widely used.

Value Added Tax (VAT) - Types

21-29.   VATs are multi-stage transaction taxes that can be assessed in two basic ways:

Accounts-Based Method   In this approach, the tax is assessed on the basis of the value added at each level of the business process. It is usually based on some type of accounting-based determination of income (e.g., value added).

Invoice-Credit Method   In this approach, tax is assessed on gross sales. The taxpayer is then provided with a credit based on purchases made. No accounting-based determination of income is required.

21-30.   These two approaches will be illustrated using our basic example from Paragraph 21-24.

Accounts-Based VAT

21-31.   Internationally, the most common type of VAT uses the accounts-based method. Using this method, transactions are taxed at each level in the distribution chain. Using whatever rate is established, the VAT is applied to the value added by the business to goods and services, rather than to the gross sales of the business.

21-32.   If we assume a 5 percent rate of tax in the example presented in Figure 21-2, this method would require the raw materials supplier to charge tax on his or her sale price of $4 per unit. The manufacturer would then charge tax on the difference between the sales price of $10 per unit sold and the related input costs of $4 per unit sold. In corresponding fashion, the wholesaler would charge the 5 percent on the difference between the manufacturer's invoice of $10 per unit sold and the wholesale price of $25 per unit sold (i.e., the value added by the wholesaler). Finally, the retailer would charge the VAT on the difference between the retail price of $50 per unit sold and the wholesaler's price of $25 per unit sold. The total tax calculation is as follows:

Raw Materials [(5%)(1,000)($4)]	$ 200
Manufacturer To Wholesaler [(5%)(1,000)($10 - $4)]	300
Wholesaler To Retailer [(5%)(800)($25 - $10)]	600
Retailer To Consumer [(5%)(500)($50 - $25)]	625
Total Value Added Tax	$1,725

Invoice-Credit VAT

21-33.   This is the approach that is used in Canada for GST/HST calculations. Under this approach, each vendor charges tax on the full selling price. This tax is then offset by a credit for the tax that was paid on the costs incurred by the business (these are referred to as input tax credits).

21-34.   Continuing to assume a 5 percent rate of tax is applied to our basic example from Figure 21-2, the invoice-credit VAT calculations would be as follows:

Raw Materials Supplier

GST Collected [(5%)(1,000)($4)] (No Input Tax Credits)	$200
Net GST Payable	$200

Manufacturer

GST Collected [(5%)(1,000)($10)]	$500
GST Paid On Costs = Input Tax Credits [(5%)(1,000)($4)]	(200)
Net GST Payable	$300

Wholesaler

GST Collected [(5%)(800)($25)]	$1,000
GST Paid On Costs = Input Tax Credits [(5%)(1,000)($10)]	(500)
Net GST Payable	$ 500

Retailer

GST Collected [(5%)(500)($50)]	$1,250
GST Paid On Costs = Input Tax Credits [(5%)(800)($25)]	(1,000)
Net GST Payable	$ 250

Net Tax - Raw Materials Supplier	$ 200
Net Tax - Manufacturer	300
Net Tax - Wholesaler	500
Net Tax - Retailer	250
Total Net Tax - All Levels	$1,250

Comparison

21-35.   The overall results for the two approaches are as follows:

Total Tax - Accounts-Based VAT	$1,725
Total Net Tax - Invoice-Credit VAT	(1,250)
Difference	$ 475

21-36.   In this example, using the invoice-credit approach results in less tax being paid. The reason for this is that, when the invoice-credit approach is used, the enterprise receives tax credits for all purchases, without regard to whether or not the goods are sold. In this example, at both the wholesale and retail levels, purchases exceed sales. The tax credits are claimed from the government on units purchased, while the taxes collected are paid to the government on units sold. This means that enterprises benefit from having their purchases exceed their sales. In contrast, under an accounts-based VAT system, the tax to be paid is based on units sold and no benefit is received for taxes paid on units that are still on hand.

21-37.   In general, if purchases and sales are equal, the tax that is assessed under an invoice-credit VAT system is similar to that assessed under an accounts-based VAT system. This can be seen at the manufacturer level in our example. In the case of the manufacturer, the units purchased and sold were equal. For this enterprise, the two VAT approaches resulted in exactly the same net tax ($300).

21-38.   Given that the accounts-based VAT approach is more commonly used on a worldwide basis, there is some question as to why Canada chose to use the alternative invoice-credit approach. While background documents on the GST legislation do not provide a direct answer to this question, it would appear that the major advantage of the invoice-credit approach is that it does not rely on an accounting determination of value added. The tax is charged on all taxable goods sold, with input tax credits available for taxes paid on all expenditures for inputs used in commercial activities. The fact that there is no matching requirement avoids the controversies that can arise when various types of cost matching and allocation procedures are required.

21-39.   It can also be argued that the invoice-credit approach is more equitable as it is more closely associated with actual cash flows than would be the case with an accounts-based system. The cash required to pay transaction taxes is based on purchases, without regard to when these inputs result in sales. As the invoice-credit approach provides for credits based on purchases, it can be argued that this approach is fairer to the enterprises that are involved in the production/distribution chain.

21-40.   There is a further question of why the government chose to use a multi-stage tax, rather than implementing a less complex, single stage, federal sales tax at the retail level. An often cited reason is related to tighter administration and control. With the multi-stage approach, a vendor does not have to determine whether or not customers of particular goods and services are exempt because they are one or more steps away from the retail or final consumption level.

21-41.   An additional reason for using a multi-stage tax is that it is applied further up the distribution chain. This, of course, means that the tax revenues accrue to the government at an earlier point in time.

Exercise Twenty-One - 1

Subject: Alternative VAT Approaches

During a taxation period, Darvin Wholesalers purchased merchandise for $233,000. Merchandise sales during this period totalled $416,000, and the cost of the merchandise sold was $264,000. Ignoring all other costs incurred by Darvin and assuming a rate of 5 percent, how much tax would be paid by Darvin under an accounts-based VAT system and, alternatively, under an invoice-credit VAT system?

SOLUTION available in print and online Study Guide.

We suggest you work Self Study Problem Twenty-One-1 at this point.

Liability For GST/HST

Basic Charging Provision

21-42.   The basic charging provision for GST is found in the *Excise Tax Act* (ETA). It is as follows:

ETA 165(1)   Imposition of goods and services tax — Subject to this Part, every recipient of a taxable supply made in Canada shall pay to Her Majesty in right of Canada tax in respect of the supply calculated at the rate of 5% on the value of the consideration for the supply. [**Byrd/Chen Note** Additional legislation changes this rate to the appropriate rate in those provinces where the HST has been adopted.]

21-43.   In order to understand this charging provision, it will be necessary to give attention to the concept of supply. We will cover this in the next section of this Chapter.

21-44.   Note that the tax is assessed on the recipient of, rather than the provider of, taxable supplies. As we shall find in a later section of this Chapter, responsibility for collection of the tax is with the provider of the taxable supplies (the GST registrant).

The Concept Of Supply

21-45.   The term "goods and services tax" implies that it is a tax that is applied to goods and services or, more specifically, transactions that involve the provision of goods and services.

The term that is used by the *Excise Tax Act* in referring to such transactions is "supply". This term is defined in the *Act* as follows:

> **ETA 123(1)** **Supply** means the provision of property or a service in any manner, including sale, transfer, barter, exchange, licence, rental, lease, gift or disposition.

21-46.   While this definition includes most of the items that we would consider to be revenues under GAAP, it is actually a much broader term. It would include all of the following:

- the sale, rental, or transfer of goods,
- the rendering of services,
- licensing arrangements for copyrights or patents,
- the lease, sale, or other transfer of real property, and
- barter transactions or gifts.

Supply Categories

> **NOTE ON GST/HST DIFFERENCES**   While the HST provinces use the same categories of supply that are used in the federal GST legislation, some fully taxable items are given point-of-sale rebates for the provincial component of the HST (e.g., Ontario provides an 8 percent point-of-sale HST rebate for children's clothing). In effect, purchasers pay only the federal GST rate of 5 percent on these items.
>
> A full description of these differences for all of the HST provinces goes beyond the scope of this text. Given this, the examples that are described in the following discussion include items that fall into the fully taxable category under the federal GST legislation. Because of provincial rebates in the HST provinces, purchasers of some of these items will not pay the full HST rate.

Taxable Supplies

General Rules

21-47.   The *Excise Tax Act* defines taxable supplies as follows:

> **ETA 123(1)** **Taxable supply** means a supply that is made in the course of a commercial activity.

21-48.   Expanding on this definition, commercial activity is defined in the *Excise Tax Act* as follows:

> **ETA 123(1)** *Commercial Activity* of a person means
>
> (a) a business carried on by the person (other than a business carried on without a reasonable expectation of profit by an individual, a personal trust or a partnership, all of the members of which are individuals), except to the extent to which the business involves the making of exempt supplies by the person,
>
> (b) an adventure or concern of the person in the nature of trade (other than an adventure or concern engaged in without a reasonable expectation of profit by an individual, a personal trust or a partnership, all of the members of which are individuals), except to the extent to which the adventure or concern involves the making of exempt supplies by the person, [**Byrd/Chen Note** In somewhat simplified terms, an adventure or concern in the nature of trade is a one-shot business venture, as opposed to an ongoing activity], and
>
> (c) the making of a supply (other than an exempt supply) by the person of real property of the person, including anything done by the person in the course of or in connection with the making of the supply.

21-49. As used here, the term business has the following meaning:

ETA 123(1) Business includes a profession, calling, trade, manufacture or undertaking of any kind whatever, whether the activity or undertaking is engaged in for profit, and any activity engaged in on a regular or continuous basis that involves the supply of property by way of lease, licence or similar arrangement, but does not include an office or employment.

21-50. Stated in practical, everyday language, this says that if you are providing goods or services in the course of business activity, or if you selling or leasing real property, you are providing taxable supplies unless:

- the business does not have a reasonable expectation of profit (this criterion only applies to businesses run by individuals, certain partnerships, or certain trusts);
- the supplies are exempt supplies; or
- the services are employment services.

21-51. Taxable supplies fall into two categories. The first category is supplies that we will refer to as fully taxable supplies. The second category is supplies that are zero-rated.

Fully Taxable Supplies

21-52. Fully taxable supplies are those that are taxed at the 5 percent federal GST rate or the appropriate HST rate (13 or 15 percent). Examples of fully taxable supplies include:

- transportation in Canada,
- restaurant meals and beverages,
- clothing and footwear,
- furniture,
- admissions to concerts, athletic, and other events
- contractors' services,
- legal and accounting fees,
- haircuts, and
- cleaning services.

Zero-Rated Supplies

21-53. The *Excise Tax Act* provides a list of taxable supplies that are designated as zero-rated. While these supplies are said to be taxable, they are taxed at zero percent rather than the regular GST or HST rate.

21-54. At first glance, this concept seems a bit senseless in that there is no tax charged on either zero-rated supplies or exempt supplies. However, an important difference exists. Because zero-rated supplies are considered to be taxable supplies, the providers of such supplies can recover the GST/HST paid on business purchases as input tax credits. In contrast, providers of exempt supplies are not eligible for input tax credits (see Paragraph 21-103).

21-55. In addition, as zero-rated supplies are considered taxable at a rate of zero percent, they are included in the threshold amounts for determining the filing frequency of a registrant's GST or HST returns. This is covered beginning in Paragraph 21-134.

21-56. Common items included in the category of zero-rated supplies are as follows:

- prescription drugs,
- medical devices such as wheelchairs, eye glasses, canes, hospital beds, and artificial limbs,
- basic groceries,
- most agricultural and fishing products,
- goods and services exported from Canada, and
- foreign travel and transportation services (see following Paragraph).

21-57. Some elaboration is required for the meaning of foreign travel. Surface travel by ship, bus, or train is zero-rated when the origin or termination point is outside Canada (e.g., a train trip to the U.S. is zero-rated). Domestic surface travel is fully taxable.

21-58.   In the case of air travel, the GST/HST rules can be complicated. International air travel is zero-rated only when flights are deemed to be outside of continental North America, not just outside of Canada. As an example of the possible complications, this broader definition can make Canadian air travel to and from the United States fully taxable.

Exempt Supplies

21-59.   As was the case with zero-rated supplies, the *Excise Tax Act* provides a list of supplies that are exempt from GST. Persons providing exempt supplies do not collect GST/HST and are not eligible for input tax credits for GST/HST paid on the related purchases. As we shall see when we discuss input tax credits, this means that suppliers of exempt supplies pay GST/HST that is not refundable to them on the fully taxable goods and services required to operate their business. As a consequence, the non-recoverable GST/HST paid is a cost of doing business that is likely to be passed on to customers in the form of higher prices.

21-60.   Some common items that are included in the category of exempt supplies are as follows:

- basic health care and dental services (which does not include cosmetic surgery),
- financial services provided to Canadian residents,
- sales of used residential housing and long term residential rents (e.g., rentals for more than 30 days),
- most land sold by individuals where the land was not used in a business,
- educational courses leading to certificates or diplomas, tutoring for credit courses, and music lessons,
- child or personal care services, and
- a wide variety of services provided by charities, not-for-profit, and government organizations (see discussion under Specific Applications at Paragraph 21-188).

Applying The GST/HST Rate

Place Of Supply

The Problem

21-61.   The rate at which GST or HST will be applied varies from a low of 5 percent in a province where only the GST is applicable (e.g., Alberta), to a high of 15 percent under the HST regime (e.g., Nova Scotia). The size of this range makes the question of which rate should be applied to a particular supply of goods and services a significant issue.

21-62.   A further question relates to whether the tax should be assessed on the basis of the location of the registrant providing the supply or, alternatively, the location of the recipient of the supply. Prior to 2010, the place of supply rules were mostly based on the location of the supplier. The current rules rely more heavily on where the recipient is located. This means that a supplier must be able to deal with the transaction taxes in any province his or her goods and services are delivered to, as well as the transaction taxes in the province where he or she is located.

21-63.   There are, of course, many complications in the application of these rules. What follows provides only a basic overview of how these rules work.

Tangible Goods

21-64.   The rules for tangible goods are relatively straightforward. A GST registrant will calculate taxes on the basis of the rules that are in effect in the province where the goods are delivered. The following example illustrates the application of this approach.

EXAMPLE   An Ontario HST registrant sells shirts online and ships them to purchasers in Ontario, Prince Edward Island, Alberta, and Quebec.

ANALYSIS   The GST/HST rate charged on the sales will vary as follows:

- Ontario recipient - HST will be charged at 13 percent.
- Prince Edward Island recipient - HST will be charged at 15 percent.

- Alberta recipient - only GST at 5 percent will be charged.

- Quebec recipient - only GST at 5 percent will be charged. This example makes the point that Quebec is using a separate transaction tax (QST), rather than harmonizing with the federal GST. If the Ontario registrant was a QST registrant as well, QST would also be charged on this sale. Note that Quebec consumers are required to voluntarily pay the relevant QST to Revenu Quebec on purchases shipped from outside Quebec that do not have QST charged. It is likely that this liability frequently remains unpaid as many Quebec consumers are either unaware of this requirement or, alternatively, deliberately choose to ignore it.

Real Property

21-65.   As real property cannot be moved across provincial boundaries, there are few complications in this area. The GST or HST will be assessed on the basis of the rules in effect in the province where the real property is located. For example, on a taxable sale of real property in Ontario, HST is applicable at 13 percent regardless of where the vendor resides.

Services

21-66.   This area has the most complications in terms of the place of supply rules. The basic idea is that the place of supply is the province where the services are used.

> **EXAMPLE**   A professor at a Manitoba university is also a freelance editor of a widely used accounting text. He does his editing in his office in Winnipeg. His editing fees are consistently in excess of $50,000 per year. Because of this, he is a GST registrant (Manitoba does not participate in the HST program). His work is sent to the Toronto office of the publisher and cheques for his fees are issued from that office.

> **ANALYSIS**   As the services are "used" in Ontario, the editor would bill HST at 13 percent.

Applying The Rate

Consideration Received

21-67.   To determine the amount of GST or HST to be charged, the appropriate rate is applied to the amount of consideration received in return for the delivery of taxable supplies. In most cases, the consideration will be monetary and the amount to be recorded is obvious. If the consideration is non-monetary (e.g., a barter transaction), GST/HST is still applicable. In this case, however, an estimate will have to be made of the fair market value of the consideration received.

21-68.   The amount of consideration to be used for purposes of calculating the GST/HST includes all non-refundable federal taxes, provincial taxes other than retail sales taxes, and duties and fees that are imposed on either the supplier or recipient in respect of the property or services supplied.

Effect Of Trade-Ins

21-69.   Where a good owned by an entity that is not registered for GST/HST is traded in toward the supply of a new good, GST/HST is only required to be levied on the net amount after the trade-in. These types of transactions are most often seen in the automotive business, where used cars are traded in when purchasing a newer automobile.

> **EXAMPLE**   John Bailey, a resident of Alberta, is acquiring a new Volvo at a cost of $52,000. He is given a trade-in allowance of $21,000 on his old vehicle.

> **ANALYSIS**   The applicable GST would be $1,550 [(5%)($52,000 - $21,000)].

Collection And Remittance Of GST/HST

21-70.   As you are aware, income taxes are collected from the same person on whom the tax is assessed. An individual will calculate his or her Tax Payable by applying the appropriate rates to his or her Taxable Income. This same individual is also responsible for the payment of this tax.

21-71. The situation is different with GST/HST. We noted previously that the basic GST/HST charging provision assesses the tax on the recipient of the taxable supply. However, the basic responsibility for the collection and remittance of the GST/HST falls on the provider of the taxable supply. This approach is implemented by requiring providers of taxable supplies to become GST registrants. Registration requirements are discussed in the section that follows.

21-72. As an example of this process, consider a situation where a retailer is featuring a GST holiday.

> **EXAMPLE** An Alberta store advertises a GST holiday, indicating that merchandise can be purchased without paying the GST. A customer pays the marked price of $2,500 for a new freezer and no additional amount is added for GST.

> **ANALYSIS** From the customer's point of view, he has not paid the GST. However, the store will have to treat the $2,500 as a GST inclusive amount. For GST purposes, the $2,500 received was made up of $2,380.95 ($2,500 ÷ 105%) for the freezer and GST of $119.05 [(5%)($2,380.95)]. The store must include the GST received of $119.05 in its GST return.

21-73. You should note that, while the vendor is responsible for the collection of GST/HST, this does not relieve the purchaser of the responsibility for payment. If a vendor fails to collect the tax, the CRA can assess the purchaser for the unremitted amount. This, however, would be a fairly rare procedure.

Registration

Meaning Of Person For GST/HST

21-74. For GST/HST purposes, the *Excise Tax Act* defines a person as follows:

> **ETA 123(1) Person** means an individual, a partnership, a corporation, the estate of a deceased individual, a trust, or a body that is a society, union, club, association, commission or other organization of any kind.

21-75. Note that this definition is broader than the one that is included in the *Income Tax Act*. For income tax purposes, the term "person" includes only individuals, corporations, and trusts. Of importance here is the fact that the GST definition includes unincorporated businesses, partnerships, and not-for profit organizations.

Who Must Register

Basic Requirement

21-76. As we have previously indicated, the collection of GST/HST is administered through a registration requirement for providers of taxable supplies. This requirement is as follows:

> **ETA 240(1)** Every person who makes a taxable supply in Canada in the course of a commercial activity engaged in by the person in Canada is required to be registered for the purposes of this Part, except where

> (a) the person is a small supplier;
> (b) the only commercial activity of the person is the making of supplies of real property by way of sale otherwise than in the course of a business; or
> (c) the person is a non-resident person who does not carry on any business in Canada.

21-77. This requirement contains several terms and concepts that require further elaboration. We will deal with these items in the section that follows.

Commercial Activity - Inclusions

21-78. ETA 240(1) requires registration only when "taxable supplies" are delivered in the course of "commercial activity". We have previously covered both of these definitions in our discussion of taxable supplies beginning in Paragraph 21-47.

21-79.   In simple terms, any person who provides non-exempt goods or services in the course of a business activity is required to register for the GST/HST unless that person is covered by one of the exceptions listed in ETA 240(1).

Commercial Activity - Exclusions

21-80.   There are several activities that might be considered commercial activity in a non-GST context that are excluded in the preceding definitions. For example, the following are not considered commercial activities for GST purposes:

- business activity that is carried on by an individual without a reasonable expectation of profit
- the provision of exempt supplies (e.g., child care services)
- the provision of employment services

21-81.   Registration for GST/HST is not required or permitted if a person is involved solely in an excluded activity.

Exemption For Non-Residents

21-82.   The ETA 240(1) requirement to register, in general, excludes non-residents. The major exception to this would be when a non-resident person carries on business in Canada. This exception would apply, without regard to whether the business is carried on through a permanent establishment. An additional exception could arise in situations where a non-resident has registered for GST/HST on a voluntary basis.

21-83.   In general, resident is defined for GST/HST purposes in the same manner that it is defined for income tax purposes. We would refer you to Chapters 1 and 20 for a discussion of the issues associated with residence determination.

Exemption For Small Suppliers

Last Four Calendar Quarters Test (Cumulative)

21-84.   The ETA 240(1) registration requirement indicates that it is not applicable to "small suppliers". The idea here is that a small supplier is a person whose delivery of taxable supplies, including those of associated businesses, is less than $30,000 per year. This provision is intended to provide compliance relief for the operators of very small businesses.

21-85.   The basic test for qualification as a small supplier is based on calendar year quarters (i.e., January to March, April to June, July to September, and October to December). Under this test, an entity qualifies as a small supplier in the current quarter and the month following the current quarter if the entity and its associated entities did not have cumulative taxable supplies exceeding $30,000 during the four calendar quarters preceding the current quarter.

21-86.   If taxable supplies accumulate to $30,000 in any period consisting of two to four quarters (they do not have to be in the same calendar year), the entity ceases to be a small supplier at the end of the month following the quarter in which the $30,000 limit was exceeded. The deemed date of registration would be the day the first supply (sale) was made after ceasing to be a small supplier. The supplier must formally register within 29 days from the deemed registration day.

> **EXAMPLE**   Supplier A opened for business on January 1, 2020, and earned the following revenues from taxable supplies during the year:

Quarter	Months	Taxable Supplies
One	January to March	$ 7,000
Two	April to June	8,000
Three	July to September	20,000
Four	October to December	9,000
Total		$44,000

ANALYSIS   Supplier A's revenues accumulate to more than $30,000 in the third quarter of 2020 ($7,000 + $8,000 + $20,000 = $35,000). This means that Supplier A is required to collect GST/HST starting on November 1, 2020, which is one month after the end of the July to September quarter. The deemed registration day is the day of the first sale on or after November 1, 2020. Formal registration is required within 29 days of the deemed registration day.

Calendar Quarter Test (> $30,000 In Single Quarter)

21-87.   An alternative to the "last four calendar quarters" test is the "calendar quarter test", where the $30,000 threshold is exceeded in a single calendar quarter. When a sale results in the $30,000 threshold being exceeded in a single quarter, the person is immediately deemed a registrant and must collect GST/HST on the supply (sale) that caused the limit to be exceeded, even though they are not yet registered. The supplier must formally register within 29 days from the deemed registration day.

EXAMPLE   Supplier B started in business on January 1, 2020. The business is an art gallery and Supplier B had only two sales in 2020, one for $39,000 on May 15 and the other for $5,000 on August 28.

Quarter	Months	Taxable Supplies
One	January to March	Nil
Two	April to June (May 15)	$39,000
Three	July to September (August 28)	5,000
Four	October to December	Nil
Total		$44,000

ANALYSIS   Supplier B would be deemed a registrant as of the May 15 sale, reflecting the fact that this single sale pushes the sales for that quarter past the $30,000 threshold amount. Starting with that sale, GST/HST should be collected on all taxable supplies made. While Supplier B does not have to register until 29 days after the May 15 sale, the collection of GST/HST is required starting with that sale.

21-88.   In reviewing the two preceding examples, note that Supplier A and Supplier B each earned taxable revenue of $44,000 in the four calendar quarters for 2020. Supplier B, however, exceeded the $30,000 threshold in Quarter Two. This results in Supplier B being deemed to be registered starting with the May 15 transaction. In contrast, Supplier A will not have to start collecting GST/HST until November 1, 2020, using the last four calendar quarters test.

Exercise Twenty-One - 2

Subject: Requirement To Register

Ms. Sharon Salome and Mr. Rock Laughton begin separate businesses on April 1, 2020. The quarterly sales of taxable items for both businesses are as follows:

Calendar Quarter	Sharon Salome	Rock Laughton
April To June 2020	$10,000	$ 8,000
July To September 2020	4,000	13,000
October To December 2020	35,000	4,000
January To March 2021	40,000	17,000

At what point in time will Ms. Salome and Mr. Laughton have to begin collecting GST? At what point will they be required to register?

SOLUTION available in print and online Study Guide.

Voluntary Registration

21-89.   The small supplier exemption can represent an advantage to persons with limited commercial activity whose clients are consumers who cannot claim input tax credits. If the vendor is not registered, the goods or services can legally be sold without charging GST/HST, which would result in savings for consumers that could be substantial.

21-90.   There is, however, a disadvantage to this exemption. If a person does not register, they cannot receive input tax credits for GST/HST paid. They are effectively treated as the final consumer. This means that the business must either absorb the GST/HST paid on its costs or, alternatively, pass the GST/HST paid on purchases and expenses on to its customers in the form of higher prices.

21-91.   Given this problem, voluntary registration is an alternative. Any person engaged in commercial activity in Canada can apply to be registered, even if taxable sales are less than the $30,000 small supplier threshold. In making a decision as to whether to use this option, the person must consider the value of the input tax credits that will be available. However, the person must also consider whether charging GST/HST will reduce the demand for his or her product or service, especially if some of the competition doesn't charge GST/HST.

Registrants Ineligible For The Small Supplier Exemption

21-92.   ETA 240 contains two other subsections that effectively prohibit the use of the small supplier exemption for certain types of suppliers. In addition, ETA 240(1.1) indicates that suppliers of taxi services must register, even if their revenues are less than $30,000 per year. By deeming the provision of commercial ride-sharing services (e.g., Uber) a taxi business, all of those drivers are required to register as well. ETA 240(2) requires registration of any nonresident who enters Canada for the purpose of making taxable supplies of admissions in respect of a place of amusement, a seminar, an activity or an event.

We suggest you work Self Study Problem Twenty-One-2 at this point.

Input Tax Credits

Vendors Of Fully Taxable And Zero-Rated Supplies

General Rules

21-93.   A GST registrant must collect and remit GST/HST on sales of fully taxable supplies. In the process of supplying these goods and services, the registrant will incur costs, some of which are likely to include GST/HST. To the extent that these costs have been incurred in commercial activity (i.e., supplying either fully taxable or zero-rated goods and services), the registrant can claim a refund of the GST/HST that has been included in these costs.

21-94.   The refunds that are available to the registrant are referred to as input tax credits. As was the case with some credits against income tax payable, input tax credits can be thought of as refundable. That is, if the available input tax credits for the period exceed the GST/HST collections for the period, the registrant can claim a GST/HST refund.

21-95.   As will be discussed in the sections that follow, the rules for claiming input tax credits vary depending on whether the GST/HST was paid on current expenditures (e.g., purchases of merchandise inventories) or, alternatively, capital expenditures (e.g., buildings or equipment). In addition, the rules also vary with the type of capital expenditure on which the GST/HST was paid.

21-96.   It is important to note that, in claiming input tax credits, there is no matching of costs and revenues. Input tax credits on inventory purchases become available at the time of purchase, not when the goods are sold and charged to income for accounting purposes. Input tax credits on capital expenditures become available when the asset is acquired, not over the useful life of the asset.

Current Expenditures

21-97.   With respect to current expenditures, if all or substantially all (generally understood in tax work to mean 90 percent or more) of a current expenditure is related to commercial activity, then all of the GST/HST that was paid can be claimed as an input tax credit. In contrast, if 10 percent or less of an expenditure is related to commercial activity, no input tax credit can be claimed. If the percentage of the current expenditure used for commercial activity is between 10 and 90 percent, the input tax credit available is calculated by multiplying the total GST/HST paid by the percentage of commercial activity usage.

Capital Expenditures

21-98.   In line with the basic idea that input tax credits are not matched against amounts of GST/HST collected on sales, the GST/HST paid on purchases of capital assets used in commercial activities is eligible for treatment as an input tax credit at the time of purchase, regardless of when the purchases are paid for or how they are amortized.

21-99.   In general, capital property for GST/HST purposes has the same meaning that is used for income tax purposes. However, for GST/HST purposes it can either be capital real property or capital personal property. In situations where a capital asset is used only partially for commercial activity, the approach used to calculate the available input tax credits will depend on the type of capital asset involved:

Capital Real Property (Land And Buildings)   For this type of property, the input tax credit available is in proportion to the extent to which the property is used in commercial activities. That is, if the building is used 35 percent for commercial activities, the input tax credit will be equal to 35 percent of the GST/HST paid on its acquisition. In other words, input tax credits on real property are available on a pro rata basis, with the available portion based on usage in commercial activities.

As is the case with current expenditures, if commercial usage is 10 percent or less, the purchaser cannot claim any input tax credit. Alternatively, if the usage is 90 percent or more, 100 percent of the GST/HST paid can be claimed as an input tax credit.

Capital Personal Property (Capital Property Other Than Real Property)   In order for the input tax credits to be available on capital personal property, the assets must be used "primarily" in commercial activities. In tax work, "primarily" is generally understood to be more than 50 percent. If commercial usage is 50 percent or less, none of the GST/HST paid on the capital personal property's acquisition can be claimed as an input tax credit. If commercial usage is more than 50 percent, the registrant is eligible for an input tax credit equal to 100 percent of the GST/HST paid.

Restrictions On Claiming Input Tax Credits

21-100.   As noted in previous Chapters of this text, income tax legislation restricts the deductibility of certain types of business costs. For many of these items, there is a corresponding restriction on the ability of the business to claim input tax credits for GST/HST purposes. Some of the more common restrictions are as follows:

Passenger Vehicles   No input tax credits are available for GST/HST paid on the portion of the cost or lease payment of a passenger vehicle that is in excess of the prescribed amounts (see Chapter 3). Also, if the vehicle is owned by a registrant who is an individual or a partnership and the vehicle is used partly for business (less than 90 percent) and partly for personal use, the input tax credit is pro-rated based on the annual CCA claimed.

Club Memberships   No input tax credit is allowed for GST/HST paid on membership fees or dues in any club whose main purpose is to provide dining, recreational, or sporting facilities.

Provision Of Recreational Facilities   No input tax credits are available for the GST/HST costs of providing certain types of recreational facilities to employees, owners, or related parties.

Figure 21 - 3 Maximum Input Tax Credits		
Taxable Purchase	**Percentage Used In Commercial Activities = X%**	**Input Tax Credit**
Current Expenditures* and Capital Real Property	X% ≤ 10%	Nil
	10% < X% < 90%	X%
	X% ≥ 90%	100%
Capital Personal Property (Excluding Passenger Vehicles*)	X% ≤ 50%	Nil
	X% > 50%	100%
*Special rules apply to certain items. See Paragraph 21-100.		

Business Meals And Entertainment   The recovery of GST/HST on deductible meals and entertainment expenses is limited to 50 percent of the amounts paid.

Personal Or Living Expenses   Input tax credits cannot be claimed on costs associated with the personal or living expenses of any employee, owner, or related individual. An exception is available when GST/HST is collected on the provision of the item to the employee, owner, or related individual.

Reasonableness   Both the nature and value of a purchase must be reasonable in relation to the commercial activities of the registrant before an input tax credit can be claimed. This is similar to the reasonableness test that is found in the *Income Tax Act*.

21-101.   Restrictions also apply to the time allowed for claiming input tax credits. For large businesses, whose sales are less than 90 percent taxable but in excess of $6 million, and listed financial institutions, the time limit is generally two years from the date the input tax credit was first available. For all other registrants the time limit is four years.

Summary Of Rules
21-102.   The rules for apportioning the maximum available input tax credits on purchases are summarized in Figure 21-3.

Vendors Of Exempt Supplies
21-103.   Vendors of exempt supplies cannot claim any GST/HST paid on purchases that relate to exempt supplies. In some situations, vendors are involved in making fully taxable or zero-rated supplies as well as exempt supplies. Since these businesses can only recover GST/HST paid on their fully taxable or zero-rated activities, they must apportion their input tax credits on a "reasonable" basis. This applies to both current and capital expenditures that cannot be directly identified with particular exempt or taxable activities.

Accounting vs. Income Tax vs. GST/HST
Differences
21-104.   The concept of matching is integral to the determination of business income for both accounting and income tax purposes. For GST/HST purposes, the matching concept is not relevant. GST/HST is collected when taxable supplies are provided and input tax credits are refunded when the inputs for taxable supplies are purchased. No attempt is made to match the input tax credits claimed with sales of the related taxable supplies.

21-105.   Other significant differences between accounting, income tax, and GST/HST procedures are as follows:

- Most accounting and income tax allocations, for example amortization or CCA, are irrelevant for GST/HST purposes. GST/HST paid on capital expenditures that are eligible for input tax credits can generally be claimed in the period in which the expenditure is made. (Differences between accounting income and income for tax purposes were discussed in Chapter 6 and would also be applicable here.)

- Many deductible expenses for income tax purposes do not affect the GST/HST payable or receivable. For example, GST/HST does not apply to employee wages, interest, property taxes, or educational services. While such costs are usually fully deductible in the calculation of Net Income For Tax Purposes, they do not require the payment of GST/HST and, as a consequence, do not generate input tax credits.

Similarities

21-106.   In contrast to these differences, there are some features that are common to GST/HST and income tax calculations. For example, GST/HST is normally collected and revenue is recognized for income tax purposes when an invoice is issued for the provision of goods or services. When the invoice is paid is not a relevant consideration for either income tax or GST/HST purposes.

21-107.   Similarly, if an account receivable becomes uncollectible, an adjustment is required for both income tax and GST/HST purposes. Also, as we have noted, some of the restrictions that apply in the deductibility of certain expenses for income tax purposes (e.g., 50 percent of business meals and entertainment and certain costs of owning or leasing automobiles) are also contained in the GST/HST legislation.

Financial Statement Presentation

21-108.   This issue is covered in IAS No. 18, *Revenue*. This international accounting standard indicates that taxes that are to be refunded should not be included in reported revenues. There is no corresponding statement with respect to expenses. However, it would be logical to assume that any GST/HST paid that is eligible for an input tax credit would not be included in the reported expense. Note, however, that even though the revenues and expenses are reported net of GST/HST, the amounts due to and recoverable from the government must be included in the receivables and payables of the enterprise.

Example One - Fully Taxable And Zero-Rated Supplies

21-109.   In this example, we will assume that the company sells only fully taxable and zero-rated supplies.

EXAMPLE   Marson Ltd. is located in the province of Alberta, which does not have a provincial sales tax and does not participate in the HST system. In the following Income Statement of Marson Ltd. for the year ending December 31, 2020, all of the items are recorded net of any GST collected or paid.

Sales	$9,500,000
Expenses:	
Cost Of Goods Sold	($6,500,000)
Amortization Expense	(900,000)
Salaries And Wages	(1,500,000)
Other Expenses	(200,000)
Total Expenses Excluding GST And Income Taxes	($9,100,000)
Net Income Before GST And Income Taxes	$ 400,000

Other Information:

1.   Of the total Sales, $6,800,000 were fully taxable supplies. The remaining $2,700,000 ($9,500,000 - $6,800,000) were zero-rated.

2.   Purchases of merchandise exceeded the Cost Of Goods Sold by $2,200,000, net of GST. All of the merchandise sold and purchased involved fully taxable supplies.

3. Of the Other Expenses, 80 percent related to fully taxable supplies, while the remaining 20 percent related to zero-rated supplies.

4. During 2020, capital expenditures totaled $7,500,000, net of GST, and the amounts have not been paid. These consisted of $5,000,000 for an office building and $2,500,000 for furniture and fixtures. The office building was used 60 percent for fully taxable supplies and 40 percent for zero-rated supplies. The furniture and fixtures were used 55 percent for fully taxable supplies and 45 percent for zero-rated supplies.

ANALYSIS   Based on this information Marson Ltd. is eligible for a GST refund calculated as follows:

GST Collected [(5%)($6,800,000)]	$340,000
Input Tax Credits:	
Purchases [(5%)($6,500,000 + $2,200,000)]	(435,000)
Amortization Expense	Nil
Salaries And Wages	Nil
Other Expenses [(5%)(80% + 20%)($200,000)]	(10,000)
Building [(5%)(60% + 40%)($5,000,000)]	(250,000)
Furniture And Fixtures [(5%)(55% + 45%)($2,500,000)]	(125,000)
GST Payable (Refund) - With Zero-Rated Supplies	($480,000)

21-110.   You will note that, while Marson Ltd. is showing a positive Net Income for accounting purposes, the company is eligible for a GST refund. This example clearly illustrates the fact that GST reporting is not based on the matching principle. The input tax credits are available on the entire amount of capital expenditures, without regard to whether they have been paid for or amortized for accounting purposes. In addition, input tax credits are available on all of the inventory purchases, without regard to whether the merchandise has been sold.

Example Two - Fully Taxable And GST Exempt Supplies

21-111.   In this example, we have revised the Marson Ltd. example so that the company sells fully taxable and GST exempt supplies. The revised information is repeated here for your convenience.

EXAMPLE   Marson Ltd. is located in the province of Alberta, which does not have a provincial sales tax and does not participate in the HST system. In the following Income Statement of Marson Ltd. for the year ending December 31, 2020, all of the items are recorded net of any GST collected or paid.

Sales	$9,500,000
Expenses:	
Cost Of Goods Sold	($6,500,000)
Amortization Expense	(900,000)
Salaries And Wages	(1,500,000)
Other Expenses	(200,000)
Total Expenses Excluding GST And Income Taxes	($9,100,000)
Net Income Before GST And Income Taxes	$ 400,000

Other Information:

1. Of the total Sales, $6,800,000 were fully taxable supplies. The remaining $2,700,000 ($9,500,000 - $6,800,000) were GST exempt supplies.

2. Purchases of merchandise exceeded the Cost Of Goods Sold by $2,200,000, net of GST. All of the merchandise sold and purchased involved fully taxable supplies.

3. Of the Other Expenses, 80 percent related to fully taxable supplies, while the remaining 20 percent related to GST exempt supplies.

4. During 2020, capital expenditures totaled $7,500,000, net of GST, and the amounts have not been paid. These consisted of $5,000,000 for an office building and $2,500,000 for furniture and fixtures. The office building was used 60 percent for fully taxable supplies and 40 percent for GST exempt supplies. The furniture and fixtures were used 55 percent for fully taxable supplies and 45 percent for GST exempt supplies.

ANALYSIS   Based on this revised information, the GST refund for Marson Ltd. would be calculated as follows:

GST Collected [(5%)($6,800,000)]	$340,000
Input Tax Credits:	
Purchases [(5%)($6,500,000 + $2,200,000)]	(435,000)
Amortization Expense	Nil
Salaries And Wages	Nil
Other Expenses [(5%)(80% + 0%)($200,000)]	(8,000)
Building [(5%)(60% + 0%)($5,000,000)]	(150,000)
Furniture And Fixtures [(5%)(100%)($2,500,000)]	(125,000)
GST Payable (Refund) - With GST Exempt Supplies	($378,000)

21-112.   In this example, where some of the costs relate to the provision of exempt supplies, only 80 percent of the GST on Other Expenses is eligible for an input tax credit. Similarly, only 60 percent of the GST paid on the Building is eligible. However, because the Furniture And Fixtures were capital personal property and used primarily (more than 50 percent) for commercial activity, the full amount of the GST paid is eligible for an input tax credit, even though 45 percent of their usage was for the provision of GST exempt supplies.

Exercise Twenty-One - 3

Subject: HST Calculation

All of the operations of March Ltd. are located in Ontario, where the relevant HST rate is 13 percent. During the current quarter, March Ltd. has taxable sales of $1,223,000 before HST. Its cost of sales for the period was $843,000 before HST and its merchandise inventories increased by $126,000, again before HST. Salaries and wages for the period totaled $87,000, interest expense was $16,000, and amortization expense was $93,000. No capital expenditures were made during the period. Determine the net HST payable or refund for the quarter.

SOLUTION available in print and online Study Guide.

Exercise Twenty-One - 4

Subject: HST Calculation

Ms. Marsha Stone lives and works in Nova Scotia, where the relevant HST rate is 15 percent. During the current year, she records headhunting service revenue of $224,000.

Rent for this period on her office premises totals $25,800, and she pays a clerical assistant an annual salary of $18,500. Her capital expenditures during the period are for new office furniture with a cost of $36,000 and computer hardware and software for $20,000.

All amounts are before the addition of HST and the assets are used 100 percent for the provision of taxable supplies. She files her HST return on an annual basis.

Determine the net HST payable or refund for the year.

Exercise Twenty-One - 5

Subject: Input Tax Credits On Capital Expenditures

Modam Ltd. is located in Alberta, a province that does not participate in the HST program and has no provincial sales tax. All of its operations are in that province. During its current quarter, Modam Ltd. purchases an office building and land for a total of $1,200,000 before GST. The company spends an additional $226,000 (before GST) on office equipment. The building will be used 40 percent for taxable supplies and 60 percent for exempt supplies. The office equipment is to be allocated in the same ratio. For accounting purposes, the building will be amortized over 40 years, while the office equipment will be written off over 4 years.

Determine the input tax credits that Modam Ltd. can claim as a result of these capital expenditures.

SOLUTIONS available in print and online Study Guide.

We suggest you work Self Study Problems Twenty-One-3 and 4 at this point.

Relief For Small Businesses

Quick Method Of Accounting

General Rules
21-113. Eligible businesses, defined as businesses with annual GST/HST included taxable sales, including those of associated businesses, of $400,000 or less during the year, can elect to use the Quick Method of determining the net GST/HST remittance. Both fully taxable and zero-rated supplies are included in calculating the $400,000 threshold, while exempt supplies, supplies made outside of Canada, sales of capital real and personal property, and provincial sales taxes are excluded. In addition, businesses involved in legal, accounting, and financial consulting services are not eligible for the Quick Method.

21-114. If the Quick Method election is filed, the registrant charges GST or HST at the normal rate on taxable sales. The major advantage of this method is that the business is not required to keep detailed records of current expenditures that are eligible for input tax credits. Note, however, that when this method is used for current expenditures, the registrant can still claim input tax credits on capital expenditures. This means that there will continue to be a need to track the input tax credits on specific capital expenditures.

21-115. In the absence of detailed records on current expenditures eligible for input tax credits, a specified percentage, the remittance rate, is applied to the GST/HST inclusive total of fully taxable sales to determine the amount of GST/HST to be remitted.

21-116. Note that the remittance rate is not an alternative GST/HST rate. It is based on an assumed relationship between revenues subject to GST/HST and costs on which input tax credits are available. For example, the Quick Method remittance rate for service providers in Alberta is 3.6 percent. The following example illustrates (without going into the algebra that is involved) that this rate is based on the assumption that, for service providers subject only to GST, eligible costs are equal to 24.4 percent of fully taxable sales.

EXAMPLE An Alberta GST registrant who is providing fully taxable services has taxable revenues of $50,000 in its second, third, and fourth quarters. Its eligible current expenditures for these quarters are $5,000 (less than 24.4 percent of revenues) for Quarter 2, $12,200 (equal to 24.4 percent of revenues) for Quarter 3, and $30,000 (more than 24.4 percent of revenues) for Quarter 4.

ANALYSIS The GST Payable calculated under the Quick Method is $1,890 [(3.6%) (105%)($50,000)]. The Quick Method results are the same for each quarter as the calculation is based on revenues and is not affected by the amount of current expenditures. GST Payable under the regular and Quick Method would be as follows:

	Quarter 2	**Quarter 3**	**Quarter 4**
GST On Revenues [(5%)($50,000)]	$2,500	$2,500	$2,500
Input Tax Credits On Costs At 5%			
[(5%)($5,000)]	(250)		
[(5%)($12,200)]		(610)	
[(5%)($30,000)]			(1,500)
GST Payable - Regular Method	$2,250	$1,890	$1,000
GST Payable - Quick Method (Note)	(1,890)	(1,890)	(1,890)
Advantage (Disadvantage) Quick Method	$ 360	Nil	($ 890)

Note The 1 percent credit described in Paragraph 21-121 would be claimed in the first quarter. Note that, in Quarter 3, when current expenditures are equal to the assumed 24.4 percent of fully taxable sales, the regular method and the Quick Method produce identical results. In Quarter 2, when current expenditures are below 24.4 percent, the Quick Method results in a lower amount payable. In contrast, in Quarter 4, when current expenditures exceed 24.4 percent, the Quick Method results in a higher amount payable.

More generally, when current expenditures, as a percent of fully taxable sales, are normally less than the percentage assumed in the Quick Method rate, use of the Quick Method is a desirable alternative. In contrast, when such expenditures normally exceed the assumed rate, the use of the Quick Method is not advantageous as it will result in a higher amount payable.

Quick Method Categories

21-117. Conceptually, an equitable application of the Quick Method would require a large number of different rates in order to reflect the various cost structures that are present in different lines of business. However, this was clearly not a practical alternative, particularly since the goal of the Quick Method was simplification. Given this, the government decided to have rates for only two broad categories.

21-118. The categories to which the two rates are applied can be described as follows:

Businesses That Resell Goods These businesses have a lower remittance rate to reflect a higher percentage of eligible costs. In order to use these rates, the cost of goods purchased for resale (GST/HST inclusive) in the previous year must be equal to 40 percent or more of the revenue from sales of taxable supplies for that year (GST/HST inclusive). Examples of types of businesses eligible for this low rate include grocery and convenience stores, hardware stores, gas service stations, antique dealers, and clothing stores.

Service Providers These higher rates (double the resellers') apply to service businesses such as consultants (other than financial), hair salons, restaurants, dry cleaners, travel agents, and taxi drivers. Since legal, accounting, and financial consulting businesses are not eligible for the Quick Method, they cannot use these rates.

Specific Quick Method Remittance Rates

21-119. As noted in the introduction to this Chapter, in addition to the GST rate of 5 percent that is used in provinces that do not participate in the HST program, there are two different HST rates as of January 1, 2019:

- 13 percent in Ontario
- 15 percent in New Brunswick, Newfoundland, Nova Scotia, and Prince Edward Island

21-120. As the Quick Method is designed to approximate the results under the regular method of calculating GST or HST, different Quick Method remittance rates are required in each of these situations. The relevant rates are as shown in Figure 21-4.

Figure 21 - 4		
Quick Method Remittance Rates As At January 1, 2019 (Excluding Quebec)		
GST/HST Rate	**Businesses That Purchase Goods For Resale**	**Service Providers**
GST Only At 5% (B.C., Alberta, Manitoba, and Saskatchewan)	1.8%	3.6%
HST At 13% (Ontario)	4.4%	8.8%
HST At 15% (Newfoundland, Nova Scotia, New Brunswick and Prince Edward Island)	5.0%	10.0%

21-121. Two things should be noted about these rates:

1. In the application of all of the rates in Figure 21-4, there is a credit equal to 1 percent of the first $30,000 of GST/HST inclusive sales in the year ($300 maximum).

2. These are the rates that are used by a business in the specified province that has all of its activities in that province. For businesses that deliver supplies in provinces other than their province of residence, calculations can be quite a bit more complicated. The CRA provides detailed information in its guide, "Quick Method Of Accounting For GST/HST" (RC4058).

Example Of Quick Method

21-122. As an example of the Quick Method, consider a quarterly filing office supply store, located and operating only in Alberta, with annual taxable sales of less than $400,000. Its first quarter taxable sales were $40,000, resulting in GST included sales of $42,000 [(105%)($40,000)]. Purchases of inventory totaled $26,600 before GST. Qualifying capital expenditures during the first quarter were $3,000 before GST. Under the regular method, the first quarter GST payable would be calculated as follows:

Sales [(5%)($40,000)]	$2,000
Purchases [(5%)($26,600)]	(1,330)
Capital Expenditures [(5%)($3,000)]	(150)
First Quarter GST Payable - Regular Method	$ 520

21-123. Alternatively, the first quarter GST payable, as determined by the Quick Method, is calculated as follows:

Basic Tax [(1.8%)(105%)($40,000)]	$756
Credit On First $30,000 [(1%)($30,000)]	(300)
Subtotal	$456
Input Tax Credit On Current Expenditures	Nil
Input Tax Credits On Capital Expenditures [(5%)($3,000)]	(150)
First Quarter GST Payable - Quick Method	$306

21-124.   The Quick Method can be preferable, even if adequate data are available to make the calculations under the regular method. For example, a freelance writer, operating out of his principal residence, is not likely to have significant expenditures that qualify for input tax credits. In this case, the Quick Method may result in a smaller net GST payment than the regular calculation of actual GST collected, less input tax credits. It will certainly be less time consuming to file his GST return since input tax credit information on non-capital expenditures will not be needed.

Exercise Twenty-One - 6

Subject: Quick Method

Robbins Hardware sells only fully taxable supplies to customers in Alberta, which does not participate in the HST program and has no provincial sales tax. During the first quarter of the year, the business has sales of $42,500, before the inclusion of GST. They have taxable purchases totaling $21,000 before GST. They do not make any capital expenditures during the quarter. Using the Quick Method, determine the GST that is payable for the quarter.

Exercise Twenty-One - 7

Subject: Quick Method

Guy's Boots sells only fully taxable shoes and boots to customers in Ontario where the HST rate is 13 percent. During the first quarter of the year, Guy's Boots has sales of $56,100, before HST. Current expenses, all of which were subject to HST, total $23,400 (before HST). Due to a major renovation of the store, Guy's Boots has capital expenditures of $42,000 (before HST). Compare the use of the Quick Method and the regular method for this quarter.

SOLUTIONS available in print and online Study Guide.

We suggest you work Self Study Problems Twenty-One-5 and 6 at this point.

Small Suppliers Exemption

21-125.   This is covered beginning at Paragraph 21-84 and will not be repeated here.

Simplified Input Tax Credit Method

21-126.   A method for claiming input tax credits and rebates is available to registrants with annual GST/HST taxable sales, including those of associated businesses, of $1,000,000 or less in the preceding year. An additional requirement is that annual GST/HST taxable purchases total no more than $4,000,000.

21-127.   Rather than tracking GST/HST paid on each purchase, the simplified method bases input tax credits on the total GST/HST inclusive amounts of fully taxable purchases. This amount would also include any non-refundable provincial sales taxes paid on taxable supplies. Once this total is established, it is multiplied by the following factor:

Factor Applicable GST/HST Rate ÷ (100 Plus The Applicable GST/HST Rate)

Examples The factor in Alberta would be 5/105. The factor in Ontario would be 13/113.

21-128. The following items are excluded from the base to which the factor is applied:

- Capital expenditures for real property (these are tracked separately for input tax credit purposes).
- Purchases of zero-rated supplies, such as groceries and prescription drugs.
- Purchases of exempt supplies, such as interest payments.
- Purchases made outside Canada, which are not subject to GST/HST.
- Purchases from non-registrants.
- Refundable provincial sales taxes (only in Quebec).
- Expenses not eligible for input tax credits (e.g., 50 percent of the cost of meals and entertainment).

21-129. There is no election required to use this method and it does not affect the calculation of the GST/HST on sales that must be remitted. The following example illustrates this method as applied in the province of New Brunswick.

EXAMPLE Garth Steel Ltd. operates solely in New Brunswick and Nova Scotia. Its only activities involve the provision of fully taxable supplies. During the current year, it has current expenditures of $75,000, real property expenditures of $145,000, and expenditures for capital property other than real property of $25,000. All of these figures are before HST, which was charged on all of these expenditures. In addition, the company paid salaries of $200,000.

ANALYSIS The company's input tax credit for the current year would be as follows:

HST Included Amounts For Taxable Expenditures Other Than	
Real Property [(115%)($75,000 + $25,000 + Nil)]	$115,000
Factor (For New Brunswick and Nova Scotia)	15/115
Input Tax Credit On Taxable Expenditures	$ 15,000
Input Tax Credit On Real Property Expenditure	
[(15%)($145,000)]	21,750
Input Tax Credit For The Current Year	$ 36,750

21-130. As noted, the simplified method base only includes purchases of fully taxable goods. A further restriction on the amounts claimed is that credits can be claimed only to the extent that the purchases included in the simplified method base are used to provide fully taxable or zero-rated goods and services. Where a supply is used to provide both taxable and exempt goods and services, the input tax credit claim must be pro-rated so that only the portion that applies to taxable goods and services is claimed.

Exercise Twenty-One - 8

Subject: Simplified Input Tax Credit Method

Simplicity Inc. operates in Alberta where there is no provincial sales tax and no participation in the HST program. For the current year, the company has GST inclusive sales of $315,000. It has GST inclusive purchases of merchandise and other current expenditures of $189,000. Capital expenditures consist of real property (land and a building) costing $150,000 and capital personal property totaling $50,000. These capital expenditure amounts are before the inclusion of GST. Using the simplified method of accounting for input tax credits, determine Simplicity's GST payable or refund for the current year.

SOLUTION available in print and online Study Guide.

GST/HST Procedures And Administration

GST/HST Returns And Payments

Timing Of Liability

21-131. In general, the supplier becomes responsible for the tax at the earliest of when the invoice for goods or services is issued, when payment is received, and when payment is due under a written agreement. Following this rule, a registrant usually becomes responsible for remitting GST/HST in the reporting period in which a customer is invoiced, even if this is not the same period in which the cash is actually received.

21-132. Similarly, input tax credits for GST/HST payable to suppliers can be claimed in the reporting period invoices are issued, even if the supplier is paid in a later period.

Taxation Year For GST/HST Registrants

21-133. Every registrant is required to have a "fiscal year" for GST/HST purposes. Normally, this fiscal year corresponds to the taxation year for income tax purposes. However, if registrants are using a non-calendar year for income tax purposes they have the option of using the calendar year or, alternatively, using their fiscal year for income tax purposes. For example, a company with a fiscal year ending on January 31, 2019, and with a quarterly filing requirement could choose a three month reporting period ending on January 31, 2019, or a three month reporting period ending on March 31, 2019. The GST/HST fiscal year determines the reporting periods and filing deadlines for GST/HST returns.

Filing Due Date

21-134. All businesses and organizations that are registered to collect GST/HST are required to file a GST/HST return on a periodic basis, even if there is no activity during the relevant period. The CRA's My Business Account service can be used to file GST/HST returns online. Filing frequencies for the remittance of GST/HST are determined by the total annual taxable supplies made by the registrant and its associated entities. The normal periods, along with the options that are available on an elective basis, are shown in Figure 21-5.

21-135. A registrant may elect to have a shorter filing period than the one that is assigned for their amount of taxable supplies. This may be advantageous for registrants who normally receive a GST/HST refund, such as businesses with significant exports or zero-rated sales (e.g., pharmacies and grocery stores). On a practical note, it may be advantageous for some annual filers to choose to file quarterly as it would force the registrant to keep their records more up-to-date. This could help decrease the work and stress that some proprietors and small businesses face when they deal with their year end accounting. As discussed in the next Section, filing quarterly would also eliminate the need to calculate and pay GST instalments.

21-136. For monthly and quarterly filers, GST/HST returns are due one month after the end of the reporting period. In general, for annual filers, GST/HST returns are due three months after the year end. There is an extension to June 15 for annual filers who are individuals with business income and a December 31 fiscal year end. This is the same filing due date applicable to income tax returns for these individuals.

Figure 21 - 5 Assigned And Optional Reporting Periods		
Threshold Amount Of Annual Taxable Supplies	**Assigned Reporting Period**	**Optional Reporting Period**
$1,500,000 Or Less	Annual	Monthly Or Quarterly
More Than $1,500,000 Up To $6,000,000	Quarterly	Monthly
More Than $6,000,000	Monthly	None

Payments And Instalments

21-137.   In general, payment of amounts owing are due when the GST/HST returns are due. This is one month after the end of the reporting period for monthly and quarterly filers, and three months after the year end for annual filers. For annual filers who are individuals with a June 15 filing due date, the payment due date is April 30. This means the filing due date and payment due date are the same as is applicable to income tax payable for these individuals.

21-138.   Instalment payments are not required for monthly or quarterly filers. However, annual filers are required to make quarterly instalments if the GST/HST remitted for the previous fiscal year was $3,000 or more. Each instalment will be one-quarter of the net tax owing from the previous year. These instalments are due one month after the end of each quarter. For example, calendar year filers are required to make instalments by April 30, July 31, October 31, and January 31. For annual filers below the $3,000 threshold, the net tax is due on the GST/HST return filing due date.

Interest

21-139.   If the GST/HST return shows an amount owing and it is not paid by the due date, interest is assessed. Interest is also assessed on late or deficient instalments. The applicable rates are the same as those used for income tax purposes:

- on taxes owed to the government, the rate is the prescribed rate plus 4 percent; and
- on amounts owed to the taxpayer, the rate is the prescribed rate plus 2 percent.

21-140.   As is the case with interest on late income tax instalments, interest paid on late GST/HST payments is not deductible.

Late Filing Penalty

21-141.   The GST/HST late filing penalty is equal to 1 percent of the unpaid amount, plus one-quarter of 1 percent per month for a maximum of 12 months. Unlike the income tax situation, there is no doubling of this penalty for a second offence.

Associated Persons

21-142.   You may have noticed that there are a number of GST/HST rules that are related to the amount of supplies delivered during the period. In order to prevent the avoidance of these rules (e.g., splitting a business into two parts so that each would qualify for the Quick Method), GST/HST legislation has rules for associated persons.

21-143.   Two or more persons are associated for GST/HST purposes where there is substantial common ownership. For example, if one corporation controls another, the two corporations are associated. An association can exist between two or more corporations, between an individual and a corporation, and among an individual, partnership, trust, and corporation.

21-144.   While associated persons file separate GST/HST returns, they must combine their total taxable sales of goods and services in certain situations, such as when determining:

- whether they qualify for the small supplier's exemption,
- whether they are eligible for the Quick Method of accounting,
- whether they are eligible for the simplified method of calculating input tax credits,
- the required filing frequency of their returns (i.e., monthly, quarterly, or annual).

Refunds And Rebates

21-145.   In a period during which input tax credits exceed GST/HST collections, a refund may be claimed in the GST/HST return for that period. Provided all required returns have been filed and are up to date, interest on unpaid refunds starts accruing 30 days after the later of the last day of the reporting period and the day after the registrant's return is filed.

21-146.   The *Excise Tax Act* also provides for a number of rebates of the GST/HST paid by consumers under certain circumstances. For example, if a GST/HST amount is paid in error, or by a foreign diplomat, a rebate of the GST/HST may be claimed on a General Rebate Application Form. Our coverage of the GST/HST rebate for new housing begins in Paragraph 21-167.

Books And Records

21-147.   For GST/HST purposes, every registrant must keep adequate books and records. This requirement is found in ETA 286(1). Such records must be maintained at the registrant's place of business or at the individual's residence in Canada.

21-148.   All books and records, along with the accounts and vouchers necessary to verify them, must be kept for a period of six years from the end of the last taxation year to which they relate. This is the same record retention limit that is applicable for income tax purposes.

Appeals

Informal Procedures

21-149.   As is the case with income tax disputes, the usual first step in disputing an assessment or reassessment is to contact the CRA. In many cases the proposed change or error can be corrected or resolved through telephone contact or by letter. In order to authorize a person or firm to represent a GST registrant in such disputes, a consent form must be signed and filed with the CRA.

Notice Of Objection

21-150.   If the informal contact with the CRA does not resolve the issue in question, the taxpayer should file a notice of objection. For GST/HST purposes, a formal notice of objection procedure is required.

21-151.   In GST/HST disputes, the notice of objection must be filed within 90 days of the date on the notice of assessment. A request for an extension is permitted as long as it is made within one year of the expiration of the 90 day period and it is justifiable and equitable given the facts.

21-152.   On receiving the notice of objection, the Minister is required to reply to the GST registrant:

- vacating the assessment;
- confirming the assessment (refusing to change);
- varying the amount of the assessment; or
- reassessing.

21-153.   Unresolved objections will be subject to review by the Assistant Director of Appeals in each Tax Services Office. These reviewers are instructed to operate independently of the assessing divisions and should provide an unbiased second opinion. If the matter remains unresolved after this review, the taxpayer must either accept the Minister's assessment or, alternatively, continue to pursue the matter to a higher level of appeal. The taxpayer has the right to bypass this notice of objection procedure and appeal directly to a higher level.

21-154.   As noted in Chapter 2, in income tax disputes, the Minister cannot institute collection procedures until after the notice of objection period has expired. When dealing with GST/HST disputes, collection procedures are not delayed by the objection process. This more aggressive approach is allowed by GST/HST legislation and probably reflects the fact that the government considers GST/HST balances assessed as amounts collected in trust by the registrant on behalf of the government.

Tax Court Of Canada, Federal Court Of Appeal, And The Supreme Court Of Canada

21-155.   Procedures for handling GST/HST disputes in these courts are basically the same as the procedures for handling income tax disputes. These procedures are described in Chapter 2 and the description will not be repeated here.

General Anti-Avoidance Rule

21-156.   The GST/HST legislation includes a general anti-avoidance rule (GAAR). This rule is found under Section 274 of the *Excise Tax Act* and is very similar to the GAAR found in the *Income Tax Act*.

21-157.   While the GST/HST GAAR is intended to prevent abusive tax avoidance transactions, it is not intended to interfere with legitimate commercial transactions. If a transaction is considered by the CRA to be an avoidance transaction, the tax consequences of the transaction may be adjusted. This could involve denying an input tax credit, allocating an input tax credit to another person, or recharacterizing a payment. But, as with the application of the income tax GAAR, it does not apply if a transaction is undertaken primarily for bona fide purposes other than to obtain a GST/HST benefit.

Employee And Partner GST/HST Rebate

General Concept

21-158.   Many of the expenses employees can deduct against employment income include a GST/HST component. If the individual was a GST registrant earning business income, these GST/HST payments would generate input tax credits. However, employment is not considered to be a commercial activity and, as a consequence, employees who have no separate commercial activity cannot be registrants. This means that they will not be able to use the usual input tax credit procedure to obtain a refund of GST/HST amounts paid with respect to their employment expenses. A similar analysis applies to partners who have partnership related expenses that are not included in partnership net income or loss.

21-159.   The Employee and Partner GST/HST Rebate allows employees and partners to recover the GST/HST paid on their employment or partnership related expenditures, including vehicles and musical instruments, in a way that is similar to the input tax credits that they could have claimed if they were GST registrants. Form GST370 is used to claim the GST/HST rebate and is filed with the employee or partner's income tax return.

21-160.   To qualify for this rebate, the individual must be either an employee of a GST registrant or a member of a partnership that is a GST registrant. Employees of financial institutions are not eligible for the rebate. However, employees of charities, not-for-profit organizations, universities, school boards, and municipalities are eligible as long as the organizations that they work for are registered. In addition, employees of provincial governments, Crown corporations, and the federal government qualify for the rebate. To claim the rebate, the individual must have unreimbursed expenses on which GST/HST was paid that are deductible against employment or partnership income.

Calculating The GST/HST Rebate Amount

21-161.   The GST/HST rebate is based on the GST/HST amounts included in those costs that can be deducted in the determination of employment income. In terms of calculations, this is accomplished by multiplying the GST/HST and non-refundable PST included in the cost by a fraction in which the GST/HST rate is the numerator and 100 plus the GST/HST rate is the denominator.

> **EXAMPLE**   Marcia Valentino is employed in British Columbia. She has deductible cell phone expenses of $2,000. She paid $100 in GST (5 percent) and $140 in non-refundable PST (7 percent). She deducted $2,240 in her calculation of employment income.

> **ANALYSIS**   Ms. Valentino's rebate would be $107 [($2,240)(5/105)]. This is more than the $100 in GST she paid as the rebate base includes the non-refundable PST.

21-162.   Eligible expenses exclude expenses for which a non-taxable allowance was received, zero-rated and exempt supplies, supplies acquired outside of Canada, supplies acquired from non-registrants, and expenses incurred when the employer was a non-registrant.

Example

21-163.   The following simple example illustrates the calculation of the GST/HST rebate for an employee:

> **EXAMPLE**   Tanya Kucharik is a very successful sales manager employed in Ontario. She used her car 93 percent and her cell phone 80 percent for employment-related purposes during 2020. She claimed the following expenses on Form T777, Statement of Employment Expenses, for 2020 (all HST taxable amounts include applicable HST at 13 percent):
>
> | | |
> |---|---:|
> | Cell phone charges (80%) | $ 1,200 |
> | Gas, maintenance, and car repairs (93%) | 17,500 |
> | Insurance on car (93%) | 1,023 |
> | Capital cost allowance (CCA) on car (93%) | 3,100 |
>
> The car on which the CCA was deducted was purchased during 2020. She did not own a car prior to this purchase. Note that car insurance is a financial service on which no HST is charged as it is an exempt supply.
>
> **ANALYSIS**   On Form GST370, her GST/HST rebate would be as follows:
>
> | | Eligible Expenses | HST Rebate (13/113) |
> |---|---:|---:|
> | Eligible Expenses Other Than CCA | | |
> | ($1,200 + $17,500) | $18,700 | $2,151 |
> | Eligible CCA On Which HST Was Paid | 3,100 | 357 |
> | Totals | $21,800 | $2,508 |

21-164.   The employment-related expenses that are listed in this calculation will be deducted in Ms. Kucharik's income tax return for 2020. Under normal circumstances, the HST rebate for 2020 expenses will be claimed in Ms. Kucharik's 2020 tax return. As a result, this amount will be received in 2021, either as part of the 2020 refund or as a decrease in the amount owed for 2020.

21-165.   As the rebate constitutes a reduction in the incurred costs that were deducted by the employee, an adjustment of the deduction is required for amounts that are received. This is accomplished by including the $2,151 HST rebate on expenses other than CCA in Net Income For Tax Purposes in the year in which it is received (2021 in Ms. Kucharik's case). In similar fashion, the amount of any rebates received that related to CCA ($357) will be deducted from the capital cost of the relevant asset in the year in which it is received (again 2021, in the case of Ms. Kucharik). The GST/HST rebate she received in 2020 that was related to her 2019 income tax return would be added to her 2020 Net Income For Tax Purposes.

21-166.   While the rebate is normally claimed in the return in which the expenses are deducted, it can be claimed in any income tax return submitted within four years of the year in which the expenses are claimed.

We suggest you work Self Study Problem Twenty-One-7 at this point.

Residential Property And New Housing Rebate

General Rules For Residential Property

21-167.   Residential real estate is an area of considerable importance to most Canadians. Given this, it is not surprising that residential real estate is provided special treatment under the GST/HST legislation.

21-168.   In somewhat simplified terms, GST/HST applies to residential property only on the first sale of a new home. If a new home is resold in substantially unaltered condition, no GST/HST will apply on this later transaction. If the homeowner undertakes renovations, such as a kitchen, GST/HST will be charged on the materials and other costs going into the renovation. By contrast, if a used home is acquired and substantially renovated before the home is lived in by the purchaser, the acquisition will be treated as a new home purchase and the transaction will be taxable for GST/HST purposes. The CRA defines a substantial renovation as one in which 90 percent or more of the interior of an existing house is removed or replaced.

New Housing Rebate

Calculating The Rebate

21-169.   While sales of new homes attract both GST and HST at the applicable rates, rebates of the amount paid are available. In provinces that do not participate in the HST program, the rebate is equal to 36 percent of the GST paid. However, the situation with participating HST provinces is much more complex, including provincial variations in the HST rebate percentage, as well as the price thresholds. Because of this additional complexity, we will deal only with non-participating provinces in this section. The CRA has a detailed guide covering the many complexities in this area, "GST/HST New Housing Rebate" (RC4028).

21-170.   With its traditional aversion to providing tax incentives related to luxury expenditures, the government has limited this rebate to a maximum value of $6,300, the amount of the GST rebate on a $350,000 home [(36%)(5%)($350,000) = $6,300]. In addition, the rebate is phased out for houses costing more than $350,000 and completely eliminated for homes costing more than $450,000. All of these amounts are before the inclusion of GST.

21-171.   The government's policy goals are accomplished by calculating the rebate as follows:

$$[A][(\$450,000 - B) \div \$100,000], \text{ where}$$

A = The lesser of 36 percent of the GST paid and $6,300; and
B = The greater of $350,000 and the cost of the home.

21-172.   A simple example will illustrate the application of this formula.

> **EXAMPLE**   Gilles and Marie Gagnon acquire a new home with a cost of $420,000, paying an additional amount of $21,000 [(5%)($420,000)] in GST.
>
> **ANALYSIS**   As 36 percent of the GST paid is $7,560, an amount in excess of the limit of $6,300, the rebate available to Gilles and Marie will be $1,890 {[$6,300][($450,000 - $420,000) ÷ $100,000]}.

Implementing The Rebate

21-173.   While the GST could be included in the price paid by the home purchaser, with that individual claiming the rebate, this is not the usual industry practice. The usual practice is for the builder to charge the purchaser an amount that is net of the rebate, with the purchaser assigning rights to the GST rebate to the builder. In the case of our example, the builder would charge Gilles and Marie $439,110 ($420,000 + $21,000 - $1,890). From the point of view of convenience for the purchaser, this appears to be an appropriate practice.

We suggest you work Self Study Problems Twenty-One-8 and 9 at this point.

Sale Of A Business

Sale Of Assets

21-174.   The sale of the assets of a business is a taxable supply for GST purposes. This applies regardless of the legal form in which the business is carried on. However, where "all or substantially all" of the assets that the purchaser needs to carry on a business are being acquired by the purchaser, the GST/HST legislation allows the vendor and purchaser to elect to treat the supply as if it were zero-rated.

21-175.   This applies to businesses that provide exempt supplies, as well as to businesses that provide fully taxable or zero-rated supplies. The use of the election is not permitted when the vendor is a registrant and the purchaser is a non-registrant. However, without regard to the type of business, the election can be used when both the vendor and the purchaser are not GST registrants.

21-176.   If the election is made, the vendor does not collect GST/HST on the sale of taxable supplies, and the purchaser cannot claim an input tax credit. As a result, a transfer of the assets of a business can be made without payment of GST/HST. If the election is not made, GST/HST will be collected on the sale. Offsetting input tax credits may be available to the purchaser through the normal input tax credit procedures.

21-177.   In determining whether "all or substantially all" of the assets necessary to carry on the business are transferred, the CRA relies on a 90 percent or more test. The CRA has several policy papers on this election in order to provide registrants with guidance in determining compliance with the 90 percent or more test.

Sale Of Shares

21-178.   As a general rule, the sale of shares in a corporation is not a taxable supply because, under the GST/HST legislation, the sale of a financial instrument such as a share is an exempt supply. As a result, share for share exchanges are not taxable for GST/HST purposes.

Other Situations

Section 85 Rollovers

21-179.   When property used in a commercial activity is rolled into a corporation under Section 85 of the *Income Tax Act*, the rollover is a taxable transaction for GST/HST purposes. For example, if a sole proprietorship or partnership transfers property when a business is incorporated, the rollover of property will be deemed to be a taxable supply for consideration equal to the fair market value of the property. This amount will then be subject to GST/HST.

21-180.   A joint election may be available to avoid any related GST/HST liability, providing the vendor sells or transfers all, or substantially all (i.e., 90 percent or more) of the assets that can reasonably be regarded as being necessary for the purchaser to carry on the business. A further requirement is that, if the vendor is a GST registrant, the purchaser must also be a GST registrant.

21-181.   If the transfer of property is a taxable supply, GST/HST will be payable on the total fair market value of the share and non-share consideration exchanged for the property, with the elected amount under Section 85 of the *Income Tax Act* being irrelevant. If the transferred property is subsequently used in commercial activities, an input tax credit may be claimed by the transferee for any GST/HST paid on the transfer of the property.

Amalgamations, Mergers, Winding-Up Of A Business

21-182.   Where two corporations are merged or amalgamated into a single corporation, or the activities of one corporation are wound up through a merger with another corporation, the new corporation is generally treated for GST/HST purposes as a person separate from each of the predecessor corporations.

21-183.   If the transfer of assets involves an amalgamation under ITA 87 or a winding-up under ITA 88(1), the transfer of assets is deemed not to be a taxable supply for GST/HST purposes and no election is required. The asset or property transferred on the merger or amalgamation is not a taxable supply under the legislation. As a result, there are no GST/HST consequences.

Transfers Within Corporate Groups

21-184.   Transfers of goods and services between members of corporate groups will normally attract GST/HST. However, an election can be made to have such transfers deemed to be made for nil consideration (only for GST/HST purposes), resulting in no required payment of GST/HST.

21-185.   The conditions for this election are quite strict and require either the ownership of at least 90 percent of the voting shares of one corporation by the other, or that the companies be sister corporations owned by a parent corporation. In addition, the electing corporations must be Canadian residents and the supplies involved must be used exclusively (more than 90 percent) in a commercial activity.

Holding Companies

21-186.   Although many holding companies only hold shares or debt and do not carry on a "commercial activity" in the usual sense, GST/HST legislation allows holding companies to register for the GST/HST and claim input tax credits if they hold shares or debt in another company that owns property that is used at least 90 percent for commercial activities. These provisions allow holding companies to obtain refunds of GST/HST paid on the purchase of property or services solely related to the holding of the shares or debt.

Ceasing To Carry On Business

21-187.   When a person ceases to carry on a commercial activity, or becomes a small supplier and, as a result, ceases to be a registrant, the person is deemed to have sold all assets at fair market value upon deregistration. If the assets were used for commercial purposes, GST/HST will be payable on the deemed dispositions.

Specific Applications

21-188.   There are many GST/HST procedures that are specific to certain types of transactions or organizations (e.g., import transactions or charitable organizations). Detailed coverage of such procedures clearly goes beyond the scope of a text that focuses on income taxation. However, we do believe that it is useful to provide you with some general information on some of these specific areas:

- **Imports**   In general, imports are subject to GST/HST.

- **Exports**   In general, exports of goods and services from Canada are zero-rated. This means that while no GST/HST is charged on exports, input tax credits can be claimed by the exporter.

- **Charities**   In general, the revenues of registered charities are exempt from GST/HST. However, revenues from commercial activities (e.g., museum gift shop revenues) are fully taxable subject to the small supplier threshold of $50,000 (a special rule for charities expands the small supplier threshold from $30,000 to $50,000). A special provision provides for a 50 percent rebate of the federal GST paid on purchases related to exempt activities. In the HST provinces, there is a 50 percent rebate of the federal portion of the HST on such purchases, as well as an additional rebate of the provincial portion of the HST. The provincial rebate varies from province to province.

- **Not-For-Profit Organizations**   In general, the revenues of not-for-profit organizations are fully taxable (in contrast to the situation with registered charities). However, exemptions are provided for such services as subsidized home care and meals on wheels. As was the case with registered charities, qualifying not-for-profit organizations receive a 50 percent rebate of the federal GST paid on purchases related to exempt activities. In the HST provinces, there is a 50 percent rebate of the federal portion of the HST on such purchases, as well as an additional rebate of the provincial portion of the HST. The provincial rebate varies from province to province.

  To be classified as a qualifying not-for-profit organization, the organization must receive significant government funding. Such funding is regarded as significant when at least 40 percent of total revenues come from this source.

- **Government Bodies**   All federal government departments receive a full rebate of the GST/HST paid on purchases by means of a tax remission order. Each provincial and territorial government is registered as a separate entity for the GST/HST and uses "certificates" to receive point of purchase relief from the GST/HST.

- **Crown Corporations**   Crown corporations are not GST/HST exempt and are registered as separate persons for purposes of the GST/HST.

- **Municipalities, Universities, Schools, And Hospitals (MUSH)**   These organizations are classified as "Public Institutions" in the GST/HST legislation and, except where there are specific exemptions, their revenues are fully taxable. Examples of exemptions include property taxes for municipalities, course fees for universities, and medical services for hospitals. Rebates for the federal GST paid on purchases related to exempt activities are available, with the rates varying from 67 percent for universities to 83 percent for hospitals to 100 percent for municipalities. In the HST provinces, the same rebates are available for the federal portion of the HST, as well as an additional rebate of the provincial portion of the HST. The provincial rebate varies from province to province.

- **Financial Institutions**   The GST/HST legislation defines financial institutions to include "listed" financial institutions, such as banks and insurance companies, as well as deemed financial institutions (e.g., businesses with financial revenues exceeding specified threshold levels). Revenues from providing financial services are designated as exempt. This means that, for an institution where the bulk of its revenues is from the provision of financial services, only limited input tax credits will be available.

21-189.   These brief comments serve only to give a very general view of the approach taken to these specific types of transactions and organizations. If you are dealing with any of these applications you will, of course, have to consult a more specialized source of information.

Partnerships And GST/HST

General Rules

21-190.   The ITA treats a partnership as a person only for the purpose of computing income or loss to its partners. The *Excise Tax Act* considers partnerships to be persons that are generally required to register for the GST/HST with respect to commercial activities. In addition, anything a partner does with respect to partnership activities is considered done by the partnership and not by the partners themselves.

21-191.   The result is that it is the partnership, and not the partners, who is required to register for the GST/HST with respect to partnership business. Given this, partnerships are required to collect and remit GST/HST on taxable supplies and are eligible for input tax credits. Partners are jointly and severally liable, however, with respect to GST/HST that relates to the partnership business.

Partner Expenses

21-192.   Non-reimbursed expenditures for property or services incurred personally by individual partners, which relate to the partnership business and that are deductible for income tax purposes by the partners, are generally eligible for the Employee And Partner GST/HST Rebate. Such property and services include office expenses, travel expenses, meals and entertainment, parking, lodging, and CCA on certain capital assets such as motor vehicles. This rebate was discussed beginning in Paragraph 21-158.

21-193.   A partner can only claim a rebate to the extent that the partnership could have otherwise claimed an ITC if it had incurred the expense directly. This means that, if a partnership provides only exempt goods or services, the partners would not be eligible to claim a GST/HST partner rebate for expenses that they deduct from their share of partnership income.

Disposition Of A Partnership Interest

21-194.   A partnership interest may be disposed of or acquired in many situations. These include the admission of a new partner or retirement of an existing partner. A partnership interest is considered a "financial instrument" and is exempt from the GST/HST. In addition, any legal and accounting fees related to the acquisition or disposition of a partnership interest are not eligible for an input tax credit since they relate to a financial instrument and not to the partnership's business. Finally, drawings and capital contributions that specifically relate to a partnership interest are considered "financial services" and are also exempt from the GST/HST.

Transfers Between Partners And Partnerships

21-195.   In general, there is no GST/HST counterpart to the rollover rule that allows property to be transferred by a partner to a partnership on a tax deferred basis. An exception to this is the case where a business is being transferred and 90 percent or more of the property that is necessary to carry on that business is also transferred. In such cases, the transfer is not subject to GST/HST as long as both transferor and transferee are registrants.

21-196.   Transfers of property between partnerships and partners may be subject to GST/HST, generally depending on the status of the transferor and transferee as registrants and whether they are engaged in commercial activities. GST/HST is not applicable to transfers of cash, accounts receivable, or debt, however, since these are either not considered property for GST/HST purposes or are considered exempt financial services.

Reorganization Of The Partnership

21-197.   The admission of new partners or retirement of existing partners that terminate the old partnership and result in the creation of a new partnership will not cause the new partnership to register for GST/HST as a new person. As a result, there are no GST/HST implications on the transfer of the old partnership property to the new partnership.

21-198.   There are no GST/HST implications to the new partnership where a partnership has ceased to exist, more than half of its members form a new partnership, and transfer 90 percent or more of the property they receive on the cessation of the old partnership to the new partnership. The new partnership is considered to be a continuation of the old partnership for GST/HST purposes.

Trusts And GST/HST

21-199.   A trust is included in the definition of person under the *Excise Tax Act* and, as a consequence, a trust that is engaged in commercial activities is required to register and collect GST/HST on taxable supplies. However, an interest in a trust is considered to be a financial instrument, so the sale of an interest in a trust is an exempt financial service and is not subject to GST/HST.

21-200.   A distribution of trust property by a trustee to a beneficiary of a trust is treated as a supply by the trust. The consideration is the same as proceeds of disposition for purposes of the *Income Tax Act*. Distributions of non-commercial property by a trust in the process of the settlement of an estate are generally not considered to be in the course of commercial activities of the trust and are GST/HST exempt. Similarly, a distribution of financial securities is GST/HST exempt as a financial service. The GST/HST only applies to properties acquired by the trust that are used in a commercial activity.

21-201.   Where property is settled through the use of an inter vivos trust, including an alter ego or joint spousal or common-law partner trust, the consideration for the property transferred is deemed to equal the amount determined under the *Income Tax Act*. The supply is considered to be made at fair market value and GST/HST is payable on all taxable supplies. However, when an estate is settled, an election can be filed to distribute any property of a deceased registrant without the payment of GST/HST. In this situation, the beneficiary of the deceased's estate must be a registrant, and the beneficiary is deemed to have acquired the property for use exclusively in a commercial activity.

Additional Supplementary Self Study Problems Are Available Online.

Key Terms Used In This Chapter

21-202. The following is a list of the key terms used in this Chapter. These terms, and their meanings, are compiled in the Glossary located at the back of the Study Guide.

Capital Personal Property	New Housing GST/HST Rebate
Commercial Activity	Partner And Employee GST/HST Rebate
Commodity Tax	Quick Method
Employee And Partner GST/HST Rebate	Registrant
Exempt Goods And Services	Simplified ITC Accounting
Fully Taxable Goods And Services	Small Suppliers Exemption
Goods And Services Tax (GST/HST)	Supply
Harmonized Sales Tax (HST)	Transaction Tax
Input Tax Credit (ITC)	Value Added Tax (VAT)
MUSH	Zero-Rated Goods And Services

Problems For Self Study (Online)

To provide practice in problem solving, there are Self Study and Supplementary Self Study problems available on MyLab Accounting.

Within the text we have provided an indication of when it would be appropriate to work each Self Study problem. The detailed solutions for Self Study problems can be found in the print and online Study Guide.

We provide the Supplementary Self Study problems for those who would like additional practice in problem solving. The detailed solutions for the Supplementary Self Study problems are available online, not in the Study Guide.

The .PDF file "Self Study Problems for Volume 2" on MyLab contains the following for Chapter 21:

- 9 Self Study problems,
- 6 Supplementary Self Study problems, and
- detailed solutions for the Supplementary Self Study problems.

Assignment Problems

(The solutions for these problems are only available in
the solutions manual that has been provided to your instructor.)

Assignment Problem Twenty-One - 1
(Turnover Tax vs. GST)

You have been appointed tax policy advisor to a country that has never used taxes on goods or services. Because of the increasing need for revenues, the Finance Minister, Maximus Surplus, is committed to introducing a sales tax. He is considering two alternatives:

- A 5 percent value added tax using the same invoice-credit approach that has been incorporated into Canada's GST system.

- A turnover tax that is applied as goods move from the raw materials supplier, to the manufacturer, to the wholesaler, to the distributor, to the retailer, and finally to the consumer. Minister Surplus would like you to calculate the turnover tax rate that would produce the same amount of revenue as the alternative 5 percent GST.

  In illustrating this to Minister Surplus, he would like you to assume a sale price of $250, plus tax, by the raw materials supplier to the manufacturer. At this and subsequent turnover points, he would like you to assume a markup by each seller equal to 40 percent of their before tax cost.

Required: Provide the requested information with an explanation of your calculations.

Assignment Problem Twenty-One - 2
(Registration Requirements – Small Supplier Exemption)

Clarisa Cole began operating a storefront business making specialty sandwiches plus offering catering services. The business opened February 4, 2020, and is operated as a sole proprietorship. Clarisa decided not to voluntarily register for the GST. She operates in a province that is not harmonized with the HST.

Calendar quarterly sales of taxable supplies from her business since the business began up to and including June 30, 2021, are as follows:

January 1 to March 31, 2020	$ 6,200
April 1 to June 30, 2020	9,000
July 1 to September 30, 2020	10,200
October 1 to December 31, 2020	27,500
January 1 to March 31, 2021	42,300
April 1 to June 30, 2021	31,700

Required: Clarisa wants to delay registering for the GST as long as possible. As her accountant, based on the following assumptions, let her know (1) when she has lost small supplier status, (2) when she is required to begin charging and collecting GST, and (3) when she is officially required to register for the GST with the CRA.

Situation 1: Assume that all sales occur evenly throughout each calendar quarter and that the first sale in February 2021 occurs February 3.

Situation 2: Assume that Clarisa catered a New Years' Eve event on January 1, 2021, billing $32,000 without GST. The remaining $10,300 of sales in the first calendar quarter of 2021 was earned evenly throughout February and March 2021 after Clarisa returned from a January winter vacation.

Situation 3: Assume that the sales in the fourth calendar quarter of 2020 (October 1 to December 31) were $37,500 instead of $27,500 and that the sale that exceeded the $30,000 small business limit took place December 14.

Assignment Problem Twenty-One - 3
(Registration Requirements And GST Collectible)

After years of study, Martin believes that he has developed a process for making perfect macaroons. He also believes that there is significant demand for these tasty treats. Based on this, on March 1, 2020, he opens a retail operation in an Edmonton mall.

His new business will have a December 31 year end. All of his sales will be in Alberta, a province that has no provincial sales tax. Martin wants to delay collecting GST for as long as legally possible.

Martin's Macaroons had monthly sales for 2020 as follows:

Month	Sales
March	$ 2,420
April	4,650
May	13,780
June	13,240
July	13,780
August	15,760
September	16,480
October	16,670
November	18,490
December	21,750

Required:

A. Indicate the date on which Martin's Macaroons will be required to start collecting GST and the date by which Martin will be required to register.

B. Assume that Martin's Macaroons has elected to file GST on a quarterly basis . Calculate the GST collectible for each quarter of 2020 and specify the due date of each GST return and payment.

C. Assume that Martin's Macaroons files GST on an annual basis. Calculate the GST collectible for 2020 and specify the due date of the GST return and payment.

D. Assume that in January 2020, Martin comes to you for advice on when he should register for the GST. What factors should he consider?

Assignment Problem Twenty-One - 4
(Regular GST Return)

Lotor Inc. (Lotor) is a Canadian controlled private corporation (CCPC) that was incorporated in Alberta in 2012. Lotor operates exclusively within the province and is registered for GST purposes as an annual filer. Since Alberta does not have a provincial sales tax nor does it participate in the HST, the only sales tax obligations to Lotor are the 5 percent GST.

The Income Statement for the current year without the inclusion of any amounts for GST is as follows:

Sales		$2,980,000
Less Expenses:		
Cost Of Fully Taxable Goods Sold	($471,200)	
Cost Of Zero-Rated Goods Sold	(288,500)	
Amortization Expense	(350,000)	
Salaries And Wages	(232,000)	
Interest Expense	(142,000)	
Other Operating Expenses	(427,000)	
Income Taxes	(223,000)	(2,133,700)
Net Accounting Income		$ 846,300

Other Information:

1. Reported sales for the year are broken down as 12.5 percent exempt supplies, 20.5 percent for zero-rated supplies, and 67 percent for taxable supplies.

2. All of the cost of goods sold represents either taxable or zero-rated supplies. During the year, inventories of taxable goods declined by $52,100 while inventories of zero-rated goods increased by $7,900.

3. Lotor purchased a new office building in the year for $2,075,000 plus GST of $103,750 [(5%)($2,075,000)]. The company estimated that the office building will be used 53 percent for the provision of fully taxable supplies and 29 percent for the provision of zero-rated supplies.

4. The company also purchased furniture, fixtures, and office equipment for the new office building totaling $1,145,000 plus GST of $57,250 [(5%)($1,145,000)]. The company estimated that these capital expenditures will be used 64 percent for the provision of fully taxable supplies and 32 percent for the provision of zero-rated supplies.

5. Other Operating Expenses includes $28,000 for a corporate golf club membership, $41,000 for life insurance premiums on the lives of company executives, and $63,000 for meals and entertainment. Assume that all of the remaining expenses are business related and that the company

has estimated that all of the expenses in this category can be broken down as 68 percent for the provision of fully taxable supplies and 17 percent for the provision of zero-rated supplies.

6. The company also estimated that 93 percent of the Salaries And Wages are either for the provision of fully taxable or zero-rated supplies.

7. All of the interest expense represents mortgage interest on the purchase of the new office building.

Required: Calculate the net GST payable or refund that Lotor will remit or receive for the current year. Show all supporting calculations and, where you excluded a particular item, provide the reason for the exclusion.

Assignment Problem Twenty-One - 5
(Regular HST Return)

Conan's Comics is an unincorporated business owned by Conan Barbarian. All of its operations are located in Newfoundland. The HST rate in that province is 15 percent.

The business is an HST registrant that sells both fully taxable and zero-rated goods. In addition, Conan's Comics provides exempt services. The business is an annual filer for HST purposes.

The Income Statement for the current year is as follows. All amounts are before the addition of applicable HST.

Revenues:		
Fully Taxable Goods	$643,431	
Zero-Rated Goods	311,412	
Exempt Services	416,253	$1,371,096
Less Expenses:		
Cost Of Fully Taxable Goods Sold	($489,567)	
Cost Of Zero-Rated Goods Sold	(203,642)	
Amortization	(106,911)	
Salaries And Wages	(62,435)	
Interest Expense	(16,243)	
Other Operating Expenses	(28,968)	(907,766)
Income Before Taxes		$ 463,330
Less: Federal And Provincial Income Taxes		(157,243)
Net Income		$ 306,087

Other Information:

1. Inventories of fully taxable goods decreased by $24,650 during this period, while inventories of zero-rated goods increased by $19,243. The zero-rated sales were generated by purchasing and selling zero-rated supplies.

2. Capital expenditures for this period amounted to $1,950,000, with HST being paid on all amounts. Of this total, $1,260,000 was for a building that will be used 35 percent for the provision of fully taxable supplies and 25 percent for the provision of zero-rated supplies. The remaining $690,000 was for equipment that will be used 38 percent in the provision of fully taxable supplies and 27 percent for the provision of zero-rated supplies. HST was paid on the acquisition of all assets on which amortization is being taken during this period.

3. Of the Other Operating Expenses, 62 percent were related to the provision of fully taxable supplies and 24 percent to the provision of zero-rated supplies.

4. Of the Salaries And Wages, 65 percent were paid to employees involved in providing exempt supplies.

Required: Calculate the net HST payable or refund that Conan's Comics will remit or receive for the current year.

Assignment Problem Twenty-One - 6
(Quick Method)

John, Alice, Alex, and Jerry Rangi are quadruplets. Their father financed an unincorporated business for each of them three years ago. They were each allowed to select their own line of business. As an incentive, their father has indicated that the child who owns the business that generates the most income in the first five years will receive a gift of $1,000,000 in cash.

All of the businesses are located in Ontario, with all of the revenues being generated in that province. As all of the business were expected to have taxable supplies well in excess of $30,000, each business was registered for the Ontario HST at its inception.

The siblings provide you with the following annual information for their businesses. All amounts are reported inclusive of HST. None of the sales or purchases were zero-rated or exempt, and none of the businesses made any capital expenditures during the year.

	Type Of Business	Sales	Purchases
John	Computer Sales, Repairs, And Tutoring	$ 103,960	$ 26,160
Alice	Bicycle Sales And Service	194,360	159,330
Alex	Menswear Sales And Custom Tailoring	126,560	47,460
Jerry	Tarot Card Reading And Cell Phone Sales	84,750	41,810

The HST rate in Ontario is 13 percent. The Quick Method remittance rates are 4.4 percent for resellers and 8.8 percent for service providers. When calculating the applicable remittance rate, assume the sales and purchases of the previous year were equal to those of the current year.

Required: Recommend whether any of the businesses should use the Quick Method to calculate net HST remittances. Show all of your calculations.

Assignment Problem Twenty-One - 7
(Regular And Quick Method GST Returns)

Johnny Dangerous has successfully engaged in criminal activity since he was 12 years old. Financially, he has been very successful and, to date, he has no criminal record. All of his activity is carried out in Ontario. The HST rate for Ontario is 13 percent. The Ontario Quick Method rates are 4.4 percent for businesses that purchase goods for resale and 8.8 percent for service providers.

Early in his career, his father taught him that the notorious Chicago gangster Al Capone was sent to jail not for his many murders and other illegal acts, but for tax evasion. Taking this lesson to heart, Johnny has been very diligent about filing both income tax returns and GST returns on time. For the 2020 taxation year, his activities fall into three categories:

Contract Assassinations   Johnny accepts contracts for assassinations at a base rate of $15,000. He offers volume discounts and charges higher fees for particularly difficult cases. As he enjoys the work, Johnny handles all of this activity personally.

During 2020, his revenues from this work totaled $323,000. While he does not specifically advise his clients that they are paying HST, he files his GST return on the basis that the amounts collected are HST included.

Export Of Illegal Drugs   A growing part of Johnny's activities involve exporting heroin and other illegal drugs to the U.S. market. His 2020 revenues from this activity totaled $113,000.

Loan Sharking   As a service to his clients, he offers extremely high interest rate loans to individuals who cannot find other sources of financing. Revenue from this source totaled $87,000 for 2020.

Johnny has an assistant, Cruella Ratched, who works on a full time basis for his business. Since he lost his driver's licence two years ago, her duties include driving him to his jobs using her car. Her salary for 2020 is $85,000, which includes a $12,000 car allowance.

Johnny maintains an office that he rents for $4,000 per month, plus HST. During the year, miscellaneous office costs total $6,900 plus applicable HST. This includes $400 for business insurance. The furniture, fixtures, and art in the office are leased at a cost of $2,000 per month, plus HST. Telephone and internet cost $125 per month, plus HST.

Johnny has calculated that these costs should be allocated to his three business activities as follows:

Contract Assassinations	65%
Export Of Illegal Drugs	20%
Loan Sharking	15%

Expenditures specific to his various activities are as follows:

Contract Assassinations   Johnny uses a Glock 9mm for this activity. He disposes of each gun after a single use, making this a significant cost of doing business. On January 1, 2020, he had five of these guns on hand. Their total capital cost was $3,101, plus HST, and they had been allocated to class 8. They were the only assets in this class and on January 1, 2020, the UCC for this class was $2,792. During 2020, Johnny acquires an additional 19 guns at $549 each, plus HST. After using each weapon once, he disposes of 20 of his guns. There were no proceeds associated with the disposals.

His only other costs associated with this activity were for travel. Airline, hotel, and taxis totaled $12,000 plus HST. Meals while travelling totaled $7,492 plus HST.

Export Of Illegal Drugs   Costs associated with this activity are as follows:

Purchases Of Processing Equipment (Including HST)	$11,300
Security Service For Lab (Including HST)	5,650
Shipping Costs (No HST- Using Illegal Immigrants)	3,000
Bribes To Customs Officials (No HST)	4,500
Cost Of Materials Exported (No HST)	21,700

Loan Sharking   Johnny used bank loans to finance these loans. Interest on these loans for 2020 was $12,600. When he experienced difficulties with collections he used a former World Wrestling Entertainment champion to enforce the payment of the loans. Costs for this service for 2020 were $4,800 (no HST- small supplier).

Required:

A. Determine Johnny's HST payable (refund) for the year ending December 31, 2020, using the regular method of determination.

B. Determine whether Johnny can use the Quick Method for determining his HST payment or refund for 2020.

C. Without regard to your conclusion in Part B, determine Johnny's HST payable (refund) for the year ending December 31, 2020, using the Quick Method.

Assignment Problem Twenty-One - 8
(Regular And Quick Method HST Returns)
For the year ending December 31, 2020, the Income Statement of Sloan Inc. is as follows (all amounts are without the inclusion of applicable HST):

Revenues:		
Sales of Fully Taxable Goods	$291,600	
Provision of Exempt Services	105,300	$396,900
Less Expenses:		
Cost Of Goods Sold	($166,050)	
Amortization Expense	(75,600)	
Salaries And Wages	(16,200)	
Rent	(56,700)	
Interest Expense	(12,150)	
Other Operating Expenses	(36,450)	(363,150)
Income Before Taxes		$ 33,750
Less: Federal And Provincial Income Taxes		(10,800)
Net Income		$ 22,950

Other Information:

1. Sloan Inc. is a retail business located in Ontario where all of the company's revenues and expenses are incurred. The HST rate in Ontario is 13 percent. The Quick Method rates applicable to the province are 4.4 percent for businesses that purchase goods for resale, and 8.8 percent for service providers.

2. For the previous year ending December 31, 2019, Sloan's cost of goods purchased for resale totaled $148,500 and the revenue from sales of taxable supplies totaled $407,700. Both amounts are before HST.

3. Inventories of taxable goods decreased by $10,800 during the year.

4. All of the Other Operating Expenses involved the acquisition of fully taxable supplies and were acquired to assist in the provision of fully taxable supplies.

5. Of the Salaries And Wages, 52 percent were paid to employees involved in providing exempt services.

6. A capital expenditure was made during the year at an HST inclusive cost of $83,620. The expenditure was for furniture and fixtures that will be used 60 percent for the provision of fully taxable goods. HST was paid on the acquisition of all assets on which amortization is being taken during this period.

Required: For the year ending December 31, 2020:

A. Determine if Sloan is eligible to use the Quick Method and the Quick Method remittance rate that would be applicable.

B. Calculate the net HST payable or refund that Sloan Inc. will remit or receive using regular HST calculations.

C. Assume that Sloan is eligible to use the Quick Method. Calculate the net HST payable or refund that Sloan Inc. will remit or receive using the Quick Method.

Assignment Problem Twenty-One - 9
(Employee HST Rebate Including CCA)

Sarah Martin is a resident of Ontario, a participating province that assesses HST at a 13 percent rate. Her employer is a large public company with all of its operations in that province.

Sarah's work requires extensive travel on behalf of her employer. For this travel, she uses her own car. The car was purchased in 2019 at a price before HST of $27,500. HST raised the total cost to $31,075 [(113%)($27,500)]. In 2019 she claimed maximum CCA of $13,984 [(1.5)(30%)

($31,075)]. The portion of her HST rebate related to her car's CCA equaled $1,609 [(13/113) ($13,984]. Sarah indicates that she plans to claim maximum CCA in 2020.

The family uses her husband's car for all personal purposes so that Sarah's car is used 100 percent for employment-related activities. Sarah does not receive any reimbursement or allowance from her employer for her travel or car expenses.

In her 2020 tax return, Sarah deducts the following amounts in the calculation of her net employment income:

Accommodation (Includes HST Of $1,560)	$13,560
Business Meals And Entertainment - Deductible Amount	
(Includes HST of $1,170)	10,170
Automobile Costs:	
Gas And Maintenance (Includes HST Of $1,430)	12,430
Interest On Automobile Loan	1,805
Insurance	1,460
Total Deductions Excluding CCA	$39,425

Required: Calculate the maximum CCA that Sarah can claim on her car for 2020. In addition, calculate the 2020 HST rebate that Sarah will claim as a result of her deductible expenses.

Assignment Problem Twenty-One - 10
(Regular And Simplified HST Returns)

Adeedas Sports is a retail business located in Nova Scotia. All of its revenues occur and expenses are incurred in that province. It has no associated business and files its GST return on an annual basis. Nova Scotia has a 15 percent HST rate.

Adeedas's Income Statement for the current year is as follows. All amounts are shown without the relevant HST.

Revenues:		
Fully Taxable Goods	$397,523	
Exempt Services	109,564	$507,087
Less Expenses:		
Cost Of Goods Sold (All Taxable)	($201,372)	
Amortization Expense	(34,784)	
Salaries And Wages	(25,679)	
Rent	(27,841)	
Interest Expense	(75,964)	
Other Operating Expenses	(31,478)	(397,118)
Income Before Taxes		$109,969
Less: Federal And Provincial Income Taxes		(21,489)
Net Income		$ 88,480

Other Information:

1. Inventories of taxable goods decreased by $19,561 during the year.

2. A capital expenditure was made during the year at an HST inclusive cost of $105,294. The expenditure was for equipment that will be used 60 percent for the provision of fully taxable goods. HST was paid on the acquisition of all assets on which amortization is being taken during this period.

3. All of the Other Operating Expenses involved the acquisition of fully taxable supplies and were acquired to assist in the provision of fully taxable supplies.

4. The rent was not subject to HST as it was paid to a non-registrant. The proportion of the leased property that is used for the provision of exempt services is 20 percent.

5. Of the Salaries And Wages, 40 percent were paid to employees involved in providing exempt services.

Required:

A. Calculate the net HST payable or refund that Adeedas Sports will remit or receive for the current year using regular GST calculations.

B. Calculate the net HST payable or refund that Adeedas Sports will remit or receive for the current year using the Simplified Input Tax Credit Method.

Assignment Problem Twenty-One - 11
(New Housing GST Rebate)

An individual residing in Alberta purchases a newly constructed home from a builder. GST is charged on the sale price at 5 percent. Since Alberta does not have a provincial sales tax nor does it participate in the HST, the only sales tax obligations to the individual is the 5 percent GST.

Required: Calculate the GST New Housing Rebate and the percentage of GST paid that is rebated in each of the three following situations:

Case A The sales price is $200,000.

Case B The sales price is $300,000.

Case C The sales price is $400,000.

INDEX

This index includes the entries for both Volume I and II. Volume II begins on page 505.

This index includes the entries for both Volume I and II. Volume II begins on page 505.

This index includes the entries for both Volume I and II. Volume II begins on page 505.

This index includes the entries for both Volume I and II. Volume II begins on page 505.

This index includes the entries for both Volume I and II. Volume II begins on page 505.

This index includes the entries for both Volume I and II. Volume II begins on page 505.

This index includes the entries for both Volume I and II. Volume II begins on page 505.

Medical Expenses

This index includes the entries for both Volume I and II. Volume II begins on page 505.

This index includes the entries for both Volume I and II. Volume II begins on page 505.

This index includes the entries for both Volume I and II. Volume II begins on page 505.

Tax Credits, continued

This index includes the entries for both Volume I and II. Volume II begins on page 505.

NOTES

NOTES